International Organization

INTERNATIONAL ORGANIZATION

by

NORMAN HILL

PROFESSOR OF INTERNATIONAL LAW AND RELATIONS
UNIVERSITY OF NEBRASKA

 HARPER & BROTHERS PUBLISHERS NEW YORK

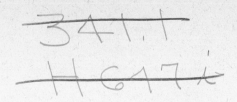

To the Memory of

LIEUTENANT ROWLAND G. HILL, JR.

Contents

Preface

At no time has an understanding of international organization, its methods and problems, seemed more imperative than today. Twice in less than four decades there have been world wars, each succeeded by an effort to organize the states of the world into an effective system of security and coöperation. The League of Nations was a disappointment to those who hoped it would maintain peace, and now the United Nations is the butt of widespread criticism on the ground that it, too, is lacking in the power needed to prevent war. World federation, in the opinion of some people, is the urgent need of our times. Certainly the untoward events of the postwar years have focused attention more than ever upon the problem of world organization.

As this book has been getting closer to completion, all signs have pointed to the imminence of another world war; indeed, the fighting in Korea has been looked upon by a number of people as the opening phase of such a war. As ever, the future is closed to us. If we should be spared a general war, in all probability the United Nations will continue at work and will eventually develop into something stronger. Should World War III come, whether now or later, the United Nations may be expected to go the way of the League of Nations, to be followed no doubt by a new organization, perhaps a better one. In either case, the future must start from the present; whatever may be ahead in the way of world organization, to be practicable, must have some relation to our experience with the League of Nations and the United Nations.

The assumption underlying this volume is that the student of

international affairs should be conversant with the machinery and
processes by which the nations promote their common interests and
try to adjust their differences. I have tried, therefore, not only to
describe existing machinery and processes but also to bring out their
points of strength, their limitations, and the problems which have
attended their establishment and functioning. This undertaking has
required an analysis and discussion at many points of the work of
international agencies—the issues brought before them, the points of
view expressed, and the solutions or deadlocks that have been
reached. No effort has been made to deal with the broad field of
international politics, however, except at those points where it
touches international organization. In the last two chapters there
is a departure from the usual practice of describing existing organization; both of these chapters relate to projects for the future.

Following most of the chapters are appendixes, mainly documents
which students should be able to use to advantage. No introductions
to them or explanatory notes have seemed necessary, for their relation to the respective chapters will be apparent.

This book deals almost exclusively with public international organization; only occasional references are made to private agencies operating among the peoples of different states. The objectives, methods,
and problems of the private agencies are so different from those of
the public that it has seemed best to deal with the former only at
those points where they come into direct contact with the latter.

Acknowledgment is hereby made of the courtesy of the Appleton-
Century-Crofts Co. in permitting me to incorporate into the last
chapter of this volume material which I wrote for *The Study of
Comparative Government,* by Professor J. B. Shannon and others,
published in 1949.

NORMAN HILL

*Lincoln, Nebraska
December 1, 1951*

Part One: General Aspects

I The Nature and Functions of International Organization

AㅤNALYZING PRESENT-DAY INTERNATIONAL ORGANIZATION for the first time, a person will be struck by the fact that it is built along very different lines from the national governments with which he is familiar. This will seem even more surprising when the point is made that, viewed in the large, the purposes and objectives of international organization are not greatly at variance with those of the United States Government or those of any other national system; it works for peace, justice, and the wholesome development of the economic, social, cultural, and intellectual life of mankind. With the usual objectives of government, how can it be that international organization is so essentially different in structure and methods?

Political institutions are conditioned, and should be conditioned, by the societies which they serve. This is true for nations; the American Constitution, for instance, is quite satisfactory for the American people, but in China, Russia, or Siam it would probably be a complete misfit. The international society which is served by international organization is radically different from those of the separate nations and it requires a constitutional system of an entirely different type. It is made up of states, sovereign states, rather than of human beings as in the case of national societies. There are some seventy-five such units within the international community, as contrasted with the millions of human beings ordinarily residing within a national community. Among the states of the world there is a di-

3

versity in language, culture, religion, and history much more extreme than that existent within any one state. To these characteristic features of the society of nations international organization must be properly adjusted if it is to be effective.

Internationalism—Its Adjustment to World Conditions

Conceivably, there are three ways in which the world might be organized for political purposes. The first, and the one now employed, is that of international organization. This assumes the existence of nation states, by whom agencies are set up for the attainment of their common purposes, for the solution of their disputes, and for the maintenance of peace among themselves. Internationalism is, of course, the only type of world organization that is suited to powerful nation states; anything stronger in the way of union would put an end to the sovereign status which the modern state claims to have, and would take from the state rights and powers which for centuries have been cherished.

There is a flexibility in internationalism which has kept it fairly well adjusted to the changing conditions of the last few centuries in the fact that it can be employed in varying degrees. There can be only a few or a large number of international agencies, and there can be little or much in the way of coöperation between nations. In the early years of the nation state's career, bilateral diplomacy was practically all there was to international organization and consequently internationalism was at a minimum. Now there are many organizations, and coöperation between nations has reached an all-time high. The feeling is widespread, however, that still more is needed in the way of world government nowadays than can be provided by international action, that internationalism has outlived its usefulness and should be supplanted by something stronger.

Federalism presents a second possible solution to the problem of world government. The advocate of world federalism wants to retain the existing states of the world, but he would diminish their vitality and importance, giving them about the same position in world affairs that the forty-eight states of the United States now occupy in our own government. The transfer of authority from the states to a central regime would create a world government of strength. Proponents of world federation argue that this strength is needed today to cope successfully with the multiplicity of complex problems that face the nations. International organization, they maintain, is now inadequate.

A third possible method of organizing the world would be to establish a world government that is unitary rather than federal in form. This would involve a complete annihilation of the present nation state except, perhaps, that it might be retained for administrative purposes. The closest the world has ever come to this type of government was in the days of the Roman Empire, when practically all of the civilized world was incorporated into the one existing state and governed from Rome.

A strong world government, whether federal or unitary, has been impossible in modern times because of the entrenched position of the nation state. This nation state has dominated the political scene so long that it has made a firm place for itself in the realm of political action. There is strong popular attachment to it everywhere, and people are in the habit of looking to it for the performance of countless services—the provision of good roads, economic opportunity, educational facilities, social security, and every available means to a good life. To abolish it completely or even to push it into the background runs counter to political thinking of recent centuries. Certainly a unitary world government would be a complete misfit; only by world conquest on the part of some new Rome could it be achieved. That Germany under Hitler had such aspirations and that communist Russia now has them is the opinion of many persons.

Perhaps federation, at least for a limited portion of the world, will be attainable in the not too distant future; this is the view of the proponents of federalism. Internationalism is still, however, the accepted thing, functioning chiefly through the United Nations at the present time. Since World War II, as the nations have moved rapidly in the direction of World War III, dissatisfaction with the United Nations and internationalism has mounted. What the future will hold is not foreseeable, but that it will bring a change in world organization first or last is inevitable.

Sovereignty

On the theoretical side the nation state, which is the basis for the international organization of today, is said to be "sovereign." The precise meaning of that term, however, has always been in doubt. Historically, the concept of sovereignty originated in the late Middle Ages as the new nation state was emerging from feudalism, when theorists, bent on finding a logical basis for the absolute monarchs who had come into power, first propounded it. Chief among those writers was the Frenchman Jean Bodin, who in the sixteenth century sought to bring order out of the medieval anarchy of rival authorities by recognizing in the monarch final authority to define and pronounce the law within each nation, and to settle disputes and allot jurisdictions among minor law-enforcing officials.

Volumes have been written by careful students on the subject of sovereignty, and many points of view have been advanced regarding it. Among them are several which bear directly upon the external relations of state and consequently upon the nature of world organization. The acceptance of some of these doctrines would permit a world organization with power, whereas adoption of others would require a weak organization with little or no authority.

A rather extreme point of view in opposition to sovereignty is taken by the pluralists, who look upon the state as only one of many groups to which an individual may belong and who consequently deny that he has any unified allegiance. This view of the state necessarily leads to a repudiation of sovereignty in the conventional sense of supreme authority. As Professor Laski, one of their ablest spokesmen, stated, to a pluralist "sovereignty means no more than ability to secure assent"; and, continuing his attack on the concept, "There is no sanction for law other than the consent of the human mind." Turning from the concept of sovereignty as applied internally within the state to one referring to the position of the state in its external relations, Professor Laski argued, "The notion of an independent sovereign state is, on the international side, fatal to the well-being of humanity." The pluralist view has at least the virtue that it would remove sovereignty as an obstacle to world organization with power.

A second point of view, and one with much in its favor, is that sovereignty applies only in the internal affairs of states, and not in their external relations. Professor Garner has written an excellent account of this doctrine.[1] In his own words, ". . . sovereignty is a term of constitutional law and political science and not of international law, and it implies nothing more than the legal right of the state to determine its own internal life, regulate its own purely domestic affairs and make law for its own subjects within its own territory." Essentially, this was the original meaning of sovereignty back in the time of Bodin. Accepted as theoretically sound, this view too would clear the way for effective international law and organization. Professor Garner brought out this fact when he said, "When the manifestation of the will of the state takes effect *a l'exterieur* it is limited by the rights of other states and of their nationals to say nothing of the rights of the society of states as a whole." He goes on to point out that this doctrine conforms to the teaching of many eminent writers on international law such as Vattel, who in the eighteenth century asserted that a nation is master of its own actions only when those actions do not affect the rights of others.

If it be agreed that sovereignty is a matter of constitutional law rather than international law, and that in fact it has no bearing upon the external relations of states, then the conclusion obviously follows that there is no theoretical obstacle to any form of world organization. Whether it be a United Nations or a world federation, states which are sovereign only internally would be free to join without giving up their essential characteristics; such states could submit to a superior law and could be governed by a supreme authority. Convincing as the doctrine may appear from the point of view of both history and logic, and convenient as it might be in managing world affairs, it does not have the benefit of a widespread support in popular thinking. Consequently, the doctrine is not and cannot be made at the present time a basis for world organization.

---

[1] J. W. Garner "Limitations on National Sovereignty in International Relations," *American Political Science Review*, 1925, vol. 19, pp. 1–24.

A third point of view is that sovereignty can not be understood as implying complete freedom of action but, like the "liberty" of the individual in internal affairs, is subject to reasonable limitations. This doctrine has been well presented by Miss Margaret Spahr[2] who, after raising the question, "Does the concept of sovereignty under law necessarily involve a self-contradiction?" goes on to answer that question in the negative. Substantially, her argument is that as the liberty of the individual is not absolute but subject to limitations in the interest of the community as a whole, so the sovereignty of the state is subject to reasonable restrictions set up for the benefit of the general community of states. She quotes and applies the following passage from John Locke's "Second Treatise on Civil Government," as follows:

If man in a state of nature be so free as has been said, if he be absolute lord of his own person and possessions, equal to the greatest and subject to nobody, why will he give up his empire, and subject himself to the dominion and control of any other power? To which it is obvious to answer, that though in the state of nature he hath such a right yet the enjoyment of it is very uncertain and constantly exposed to the invasion of others. . . . It is not without reason that he is willing to join in society with others who are already united or have a mind to unite for the mutual preservation of their lives, liberties and estates, which I call by the general name "property."

An acceptance of the analogy between individual liberty and national sovereignty would, like the first two doctrines examined, open the road to strong world organization. Whatever its form, effective world organization would impose restrictions upon the national freedom of action in the interests of all. If the conception of sovereignty that is held permits such a limitation, then world organization is possible, even though that organization involves coercion against states. In substance this is what Professor P. B. Potter, in his volume entitled *An Introduction to the Study of International Organization*, meant by the phrase "self-imposed limitation upon sovereignty" in attempting to reconcile sovereignty with international law and or-

---

[2] Margaret Spahr, "Sovereignty under Law: A Possible Redefinition of Sovereignty in the Light of Locke's Theory of Liberty," *American Political Science Review*, 1945, vol. 39, pp. 350–355.

ganization.[3] He also uses the term "doctrine of original agreement," by which he means that whatever restrictions may be placed by international organization on the freedom of action of a state may be traced in its origin to the consent of that state in becoming a party to the agreement or constitution by which the organization was created. Although this view has the support of a number of writers, it cannot be said to have been widely adopted by the people.

A somewhat unusual view which has been expounded by Mr. Robert Lansing, one-time Secretary of State, holds that sovereignty in the best sense of the word resides in the world community. Mr. Lansing criticized the sovereignty of the separate states on the ground that "sovereignty in every modern state lacks the essential of real sovereignty, namely independence."[4] Explaining this further, he said, "When two or more states, each with an independent sovereign come into opposition so that the wills of their sovereigns do not harmonize, and each sovereign attempts to be independent and to exercise exclusive sovereignty, the state of affairs resulting is paradoxical, for manifestly two supreme authorities cannot exist within the same sphere"; in other words, national sovereignty can have no application in the external relations of states. His statement of world sovereignty follows:

Since it is possible to conceive of the human race as one body composed of a large number of political groups, including millions of individuals, or as one body with these individuals as units, and, in either case as a community, it follows from the very nature of things that in this unorganized mass of humanity, there *must* be a certain body of individuals possessing a physical might sufficient to compel obedience by every member of the human race throughout the world. Such superior physical might constitutes sovereignty, and since its only limit is the earth, it may properly be termed "World Sovereignty."

Mr. Lansing conceded that such world sovereignty "has not yet developed into the positive type that is manifest in a political state," that it "is still unformed and necessarily a theoretical conception," but he believed that "powerful political and moral influences are at

---

[3] P. B. Potter, *An Introduction to the Study of International Organization*, 5th ed., New York, 1948, p. 185.
[4] Robert Lansing, *Notes on Sovereignty*, Washington, 1931, p. 61.

work in the world to change the theory into practice." The best expression of world sovereignty will, so he believed, "be the organization of a world state."

It may seem that this doctrine of ultimate world sovereignty is a belabored effort to pave the way for a world state. Certainly in practical affairs it is still without any evidence of existence, still a "theoretical conception," as Mr. Lansing called it thirty years ago. The admission must, however, be made that in time there may be a world state, and if such a development should take place, then Mr. Lansing's theory would become a fact.

All of the above doctrines of sovereignty admit international law and international organization with coercive power. In this respect they are at variance with the more conventional point of view that the sovereignty of the state is absolute, not susceptible of limitation imposed from without. According to this point of view, as the Commission to Study the Organization of Peace phrased it some years ago, "A sovereign state, at the present time, claims the power to judge its own controversies, to enforce its own conception of its rights, to increase its armaments without limit, to treat its own nationals as it sees fit, and to regulate its economic life without regard to the effect of such regulation upon its neighbors."[5]

Although the masses of the people are not worried about sovereignty, and certainly they have not grappled with the problem in any serious way, no doubt the conception most commonly held by them is that sovereignty is illimitable and that a nation may do anything that it can in the realm of foreign policy. Evidence of the prevalence of this attitude is provided in words and actions of politicians who, believing that they represent the public, always take great pains to show their determination to protect the nation's sovereignty. American senators in 1919, debating the League of Nations, and Stalin bitterly opposing the Marshall Plan are both examples of appeals to the popular belief in the absolute sovereignty of nations.

In the construction of world organization the view that states are sovereign both in foreign and domestic affairs operates in three ways

---

[5] Commission to Study the Organization of Peace, *Preliminary Report*, November, 1940, p. 11.

to determine machinery and processes. First, it furnishes a theoretical justification or argument which governments eager to be free of restrictions on their actions may use. Second, the vitality of sovereignty as a prejudice held by the masses can never be ignored. No doubt it is true that the people have only very vague ideas as to what sovereignty is. As some one has said, about all that most people know about sovereignty is that they would fight for it. It is a sacred cow, and woe be unto the politician who would defame it by proposing a world organization in which the separate states could be commanded by a superior authority. The third effect of sovereignty on the construction of world organization is the result of the first two—it requires that international organization be weak in comparison with government as found within nations.

Some years ago Mr. Wendell Willkie, attempting to get rid of the obstruction which sovereignty has commonly set up against effective world organization, recommended that we cease looking upon it as a negative concept, something to be safeguarded at the expense of world peace and order, and regard it rather as an instrumentality for the United States to use "in partnership with the sovereign power of other peace-loving nations, to create and operate a world organization which will give better protection to the rights of all nations, on a wider political, economic and social basis, than has ever been attempted in history."[6] He went on to attack the prevailing tendency to apply sovereignty in the field of international relations, stating that "The idea of the absolute sovereignty of any nation in international relationships is as impractical in operation as the idea of the absolute separateness of any nation." Elaborating his views from the angle of a practical man of affairs, he continued as follows:

To the extent that the term sovereignty is taken to mean that we have the right to do exactly as we please in dealings with other nations, and that what we choose to do is not properly of concern to any other nation, it is out of date. During roughly 125 years of our national existence we assumed that this conception of sovereignty was valid. We even got into the habit of believing that it was an essential part of national freedom. Its

[6] W. L. Willkie, "Our Sovereignty: Shall We Use It?" *Foreign Affairs*, 1944, vol. 22, pp. 347–354.

invalidity was brought home to us only with the development of modern communications. To try to defend it against the facts of modern life would be unrealistic and dangerous. Nor would we thereby be preserving freedom.

Many of us remember when there were so few motorcars that each driver was left free to make his own rules of the road. It was generally understood that a good citizen behind the wheel of a two-cylinder runabout would slow down on corners and either stop or make as little noise as possible when he encountered a horse. Beyond that, if he didn't deliberately run into people, "reckless driving" meant only that he would break a spring or his own neck. But as the roads became filled with powerful automobiles there had to be traffic lights and motor cops. A man could no longer make his own rules of the road. Today if there were no traffic laws no one of us would dare take his car out of the garage. The red and green lights give us freedom to use our automobiles.

Let us face the analogous situation in the relationships of nations. The highways of the world now are crowded. From Hong Kong to Narvik, and from the North Pole to the South, there are no empty seas, no air spaces which are not traversed, no land where rights and interests of many peoples do not meet and may not conflict. The United States or any other nation cannot make the rules of the road all by itself.

International Organization as a Means to Coöperation

Presumably, international organization as we now know it is founded upon the assumption that states are sovereign. The Charter of the United Nations, for instance, specifically asserts that "The Organization is based on the principle of the sovereign equality of all its Members." The preamble of the Charter of the Organization of the American States makes reference to "respect for the sovereignty of each one" of its participating states. Starting with this assumption that states are sovereign, international organization cannot be government of the type to be found within states, by which a supreme authority is able to enunciate rules of conduct and compel obedience thereto on the part of the individual.

There are international organs with authority over states and even over individuals in some few instances, but when it comes to working out programs of action, formulating new rules of law for nations, and taking other measures which impose new obligations upon states, international agencies are essentially means to coöperation.

This fact is made clear in Article 1 of the Charter of the United Nations, which asserts that the purposes of the organization are "to take collective measures for the prevention and removal of threats to peace . . . ," "to develop friendly relations among nations . . ." and "to achieve international coöperation in solving international problems of an economic, social, cultural, or humanitarian character. . . ." Similarly, the Charter of the Organization of American States asserts that the purposes of that Organization are: "to provide for common action on the part of those States in the event of aggression," "to seek the solution of political, juridical, and economic problems . . . ," and "to promote, by coöperative action, their economic, social and cultural development." Generally, then, the diplomatic side of international organization is essentially coöperative in nature.

Sometimes where there appears to be an element of coercion in international organization, upon closer analysis the action to be taken may turn out in fact to be a matter of coöperation. Chapter VII of the Charter of the United Nations provides for coercion against a disturber of the peace, but to undertake such a venture the Security Council must rely upon the forces of the individual states coöperating together, for it possesses no army, navy, or air force of its own. In a sense it is true that the members of the United Nations obligated themselves to coöperate for the preservation of peace when they accepted the Charter, but their freedom of action is nevertheless protected by the following devices: (1) the "special agreements" to be made under Article 43 in which members of the United Nations specify the nature of the coöperation which they will provide to the Security Council; (2) the veto, under which any of the five permanent members of the Security Council may block any effort for collective coercion; and (3) the need for the Security Council in any emergency to "call upon" members to act, which in fact, if not in law, leaves those members free to do as they please.[7]

Thousands of treaties, informal agreements, and resolutions testify to the great utility of present-day international coöperation. By voluntary coöperation nations have done much to improve their condition and that of their citizens in matters of health, labor relations,

---

[7] For further discussion of this subject, see Chapter X.

economic status, education, and even in the avoidance of war. To draw up a list of the accomplishments made possible by coöperation would be a stupendous undertaking. That international organization promotes coöperation within the United Nations, the specialized agencies (such as the United Nations Educational, Scientific, Cultural Organization and the Food and Agriculture Organization), the Organization of American States, the Council of Europe, and many other agencies is undeniably constructive.

The Limitations of Coöperation

Despite its imposing accomplishments, coöperation as a method of getting things done is not without its limitations. When, for some reason, nations prefer not to work together, the result is inaction, and if the matter be one involving vital interests this inaction can bring about a serious deterioration in the welfare of the nations and in the whole field of international relations. Often, too, it is the most vital interests that are the most difficult to deal with by coöperation.

Both the League of Nations and the United Nations have tried through the instrumentality of coöperation to find ways to minimize the passport regulations imposed by the sovereign states upon travelers. Today, travel across boundaries for purposes of residence, business and pleasure is common; it is an inevitable consequence of the technological developments—the railroad, the steamship, and the airplane—which have made transportation so easy, quick, and cheap. Yet the voluminous passport regulations enacted during the last three or four decades have set up artificial barriers to travel and have necessitated a great deal of delay and inconvenience to people wishing to go abroad. Back in the nineteenth century before these regulations became so general and so complicated, a person needed only a day or two to make arrangements for a trip requiring several weeks of travel; now several weeks of preparation are necessary for the same trip which by modern methods of transportation takes only a day or two. International action designed to minimize passport regulations is needed, and consequently the League of Nations and the United Nations have both directed their efforts toward a solution of the problem. To date it has been too much for the sovereign states to solve by the methods of international coöperation.

Out of the modern migration of people has also arisen an international problem of health. Travelers may carry germs, or germs may infest articles of commerce, so that, unless measures of a preventive nature are undertaken, diseases are freely transported from one country to another. National action can go only so far, for the problem is genuinely worldwide in scope. In other ways too, health is an international problem. Since modern facilities for trade have enabled people to purchase medicine in other countries, the need has developed for a standardization of medical products such as sera and vitamins. Scientific progress in the treatment of disease has created the problem of finding a means of disseminating newly acquired knowledge, in order that mankind in every part of the world may have the best possible advantages in the common fight against illness. Much has been accomplished by the coöperative efforts of the sovereign states in this field, but the world as a whole is still much less of a unit for health purposes than is an individual state.

The technological progress of the past century has multiplied the contacts of nations to the point that almost all economic and social problems have taken on an international character. Railways and buses, particularly in crowded areas in which there are many adjoining sovereign states, have posed the problem of traffic across boundaries. To be most useful, the airplane should be given permission to traverse the air freely without regard to national boundary lines. The radio has placed before governments the need for international action allocating wave lengths if disastrous competition is to be avoided, and it has raised an issue as to the desirability and possibility of regulating propaganda activities. By no means least among the problems imposed upon the world by technology is the need for freeing the arteries of trade from national restrictions, for modern industrial production is a process requiring trade on a large scale, both import and export, if raw materials and finished products are to be kept moving. These problems have all been taken up in international agencies with a view to working out solutions coöperatively, but frequently without success. Arrangements have been made to facilitate railway and bus transportation and to allocate wave lengths, but to date little more than a beginning has been made in the establishment of free trade among nations, in the provision of freedom of the air for planes, and in the control of propaganda.

In recent years there has been great disappointment over the fact that atomic energy has not been placed under international control by the processes of coöperation. Every effort was made in the Atomic Energy Commission of the United Nations to do so but it was impossible to reconcile the American and Russian points of view, and inaction resulted. Russia was unwilling to agree to the American plan for a foolproof system of international inspection of raw-material sources, plants and other facilities within nations; she advocated the outlawry of atomic bombs, leaving the bulk of the enforcement to the individual nations and limiting international inspection in such a manner as to permit evasions of the law.

The prevention of war has always been too much of a task for the processes of international coöperation. There have been alliances to prevent war, agreements to limit armaments, nonaggression pacts, treaties by which the parties agreed not to resort to "war as an instrument of national policy" (notably the Pact of Paris, 1928), arbitration treaties, and efforts to set up sanctions to be used against aggressors. These efforts, however, have not provided security against war. Now that modern technology has made war so much more destructive than it used to be, the inability to prevent it seems infinitely more serious a matter than ever before.

Authority in International Organs

In a number of instances international organs have been clothed with authority; where this is true they resemble agencies of national government, possessing as they do the right of action in designated situations. Generally, the authority which these organs exercise is in the settlement of disputes or in the field of administration, although the point should be made clear that most of the agencies operating within those fields do not have authority over nations. The tendency during recent decades has been toward the creation of a greater number of agencies with authority, although even yet there are not a large number of them. A few illustrations of such agencies will show the nature of their work.

(Arbitral and judicial bodies dealing with international disputes possess the authority to make awards or judgments) Whether the proceedings in those bodies are instituted by the application of one party under a system of compulsory jurisdiction or by means of an agreement between the parties, the right exists and an arbitral award or a judgment of a court of justice is binding upon the disputants. (The present International Court of Justice,) for instance, had the right in the Corfu Channel case between Great Britain and Albania to settle the dispute, and in 1948–1949 it did so by means of three binding judgments. This kind of action is clearly quite similar to that taken by national courts. (The authority of national courts is, however, much more extensive for the reason that they have a right to deal with a much larger number of disputes than nations have thus far been willing to give to international tribunals.[8]

In the field of international administration, control is exercised by the Joint Commission for the United States and Canada over the use of boundary waters for commercial purposes by individuals and corporations. The Central Rhine Commission possesses authority over states in matters relating to developmental projects for the Rhine River. Other agencies of a similar nature could be mentioned.[9] While the powers of such organs are rarely extensive and almost never relate to vital matters, they furnish ample evidence of the fact that international organization is, in isolated instances at least, something more than coöperation.

Some Facts and Forces Determining the Nature of International Organization

Like all political structures, modern international organization embodies compromises resulting from divergent points of view and interests. Three facts and forces are fundamental to those compromises: (1) theory relating to the state, (2) national power, and

---

[8] For further discussion of this subject see Chapters VI and VII.
[9] Administrative agencies are discussed in Chapter XV.

(3) considerations of efficiency. Whether one or another of them dominates in the construction of agencies and processes depends upon the relative strength with which they are presented, the nature of the subject to be placed under international control (whether or not it touches vital national interests), and the attitude of public opinion.

Of the three basic factors that have been mentioned, theory as to the nature of the state is probably talked about as much as any, although in fact it may be less important than it seems or a cover for a deeper purpose. Certainly theory is not appealed to because nations are greatly concerned lest organization fail to square with some abstraction, but rather because the theory itself squares with some vital national interest. For instance, when a government insists that some international agency in process of construction shall do full and proper honor to the prevailing theory of sovereignty, it is safe to say that the concern expressed is much less for the preservation of a doctrine than for the preservation of the right of the nation to act freely and independently without interference by any outside authority.

Besides sovereignty, the theory most frequently appealed to is the closely related doctrine of state equality. It is an old doctrine, one of its earliest exponents being Emerich de Vattel in *The Law of Nations* (1758). It was Vattel's contention that "Since men are by nature equal, and their individual rights and obligations the same, as coming equally from nature, nations, which are composed of men and may be regarded as so many free persons living together in a state of nature, are by nature equal and hold from nature the same obligations and rights." The close relation between the idea of sovereignty and that of equality is well brought out in the term "sovereign equality" already mentioned as one of the principles stated in the Charter to be basic to the organization of the United Nations. The logic of the term is that if all states are sovereign in the sense of being absolute and unlimited, then it would follow that they are equal as well.

The doctrine of state equality has been iterated and reiterated in many places and by many authorities. Said Chief Justice Marshall in *The Antelope* (1825), "No principle of international law is more uni-

versally acknowledged than the perfect equality of states." In like manner, the Inter-American Convention on the Rights and Duties of States (1933) recognized the "juridical equality" of states.

While there is general admission that states are equal, there is little agreement as to the implications of the doctrine. It is clear that the concept of equality is essentially a legal one, for in matters of size and power states are obviously unequal. This was brought out in Vattel's statement that "A dwarf is as much a man as a giant is; a small Republic is no less a sovereign State than the most powerful Kingdom."

For international organization the principal question is whether all states, large and small, being equal, are entitled to equal representation and equal voting power. Professor E. D. Dickinson, in a well-known volume on the subject of equality, denies that the doctrine "is inconsistent with inequalities of representation, voting power and contribution in international organization"; not an equality of rights but "an equal capacity for rights" is, in his opinion, the essential.[10] Many of the small states would be loath to accept Professor Dickinson's interpretation of the doctrine. Certainly the doctrine is a hazy one, hard to pin down to an exact meaning. The important fact is that nations appeal to it when international organizations are under construction and that they are sometimes given full satisfaction or a form of compromise. In the United Nations, members are equal in the General Assembly, but notwithstanding the Charter statement of the principle of sovereign equality, the members are far from equal in the Security Council. For the maintenance of the United Nations, financial contributions are made by members on an unequal basis which contrasts strikingly with the equal voting power in the General Assembly and even with the unequal voting rights within the Security Council.

It is national power that most frequently opposes the doctrine of equality, and compromises in international organization are common between large states with power and small states advocating equal-

---

[10] E. D. Dickinson, *The Equality of States in International Law,* Cambridge, 1920, pp. 334–335.

ity. Large nations with great power like to say that power brings responsibility, which in turn justifies more than the average amount of representation and voting strength. However much the fact may be deplored, power stands out everywhere in international affairs, and it would be strange, even lacking in realism, to expect to ignore that power in the field of organization. Mr. Bertrand Russell's statement that "Every man would like to be God, if it were possible" applies equally to states, for all strive for the utmost in power. In any case there is the bald fact that without superior rights powerful states would often be unwilling to join international organizations. Whether it be right or wrong to give the large powers advantages in representation or voting, or both, in international bodies, it is usually necessary to do so where those bodies deal with vital interests.

Although international organization must give wide recognition to national power, equality, and sovereignty, to some degree it embodies principles of efficiency. To the extent that it is feasible to do so, nations strive to construct agencies that will be expeditious, fair, and inexpensive. That they succeed to a high degree is attested by the many accomplishments of international organs. That they fail sometimes and especially in matters relating to the maintenance of peace is due to the fact that here efficiency is not given priority.

Behind the facts and forces that have been described is, of course, public thinking. It is because people throughout the world believe in sovereignty, equality, national power, and efficiency that international organization must be a compromise between those ideas. William Penn's statement that "governments, like clocks, go from the motion that men give them" applies to political institutions on both the national and international level. Were international organization to lag far behind prevailing popular attitudes in the nations which are its sponsors, its inadequacy would be a subject of general complaint; were it to advance far ahead of public thinking, it would become an unworkable abstraction.

Functions of International Agencies

Within national governments there are three types of functions that are commonly undertaken: legislative, executive, and judicial. Because international organization is founded upon sovereign states, the functions undertaken through its agencies cannot be classified under those headings. Generally speaking, however, the functions of international organization correspond roughly to the legislative, executive, and judicial work of national governments but, giving recognition to sovereignty, they are more confined in scope and subject in their exercise to restrictions safeguarding the position of the participating states.

Corresponding to the legislative function within states, there is the diplomatic function of international organization. Among the tasks of diplomacy is the determination of the courses of action, or policies, that are to be followed by coöperating nations. In this function of policy-determination, diplomatic bodies are trying to do on an international scale what legislatures (and executive officials) do within states. For instance, the conference of the International Labor Organization deliberates on programs for the improvement of the conditions of labor, and the conference of UNESCO discusses methods of promoting the cause of education in the world. The types of diplomatic bodies which function in this manner are two: special diplomatic conferences set up by the participating states on an *ad hoc* basis; and the conferences of permanent international agencies, such as the International Labor Organization, UNESCO, and the United Nations.

Where diplomatic bodies, such as the above, differ from legislatures is in procedure and in the nature of the ultimate products of their work. International conferences do not enact; they negotiate. Both of these procedures involve deliberation, debate, compromise, and very likely the use of committees, but in very dissimilar settings. In legislative bodies, the participants are the representatives of districts or occupational groups free to vote as they please although subject to political pressure from the special interests; in international diplomatic bodies, the participants are the delegates of sovereign states acting under instructions. In legislation, voting is by individuals and, as a rule, the majority win; in international conferences, voting is ordinarily by states and, unless there is a special arrangement to the contrary, no decision can be taken except by unanimous vote.

The product of the deliberation of a legislature is law, and the statute books provide ample evidence that legislative bodies are highly prolific. On the other hand, international conferences do not and cannot enact law; they are able only to formulate treaties which may become law after ratification by the coöperating states, or to adopt recommendations to states which can have no legal force unless and until the states involved have enacted them as national statutes.) For instance, the conferences of the International Labor Organization produce draft treaties subject to subsequent ratification and recommendations which the states agree to submit to their respective legislatures for adoption in the form of statutes. Where agreeable to all of the participating states, a course of action adopted within an international conference may be in the form of an executive agreement, requiring no ratification or consideration of suggested legislation. Some conferences confine themselves to consultation and put out little or nothing in the way of official documents; these bodies bear the least resemblance of all international conferences to legislatures.

An international conference may assume the role of a national constitutional convention as well as that of a legislature. When there is a new international agency to be set up, the usual method is to arrange a conference to draft a constitution for it. The Charter of the United Nations was drafted at conferences held at Dumbarton Oaks and at San Francisco. Similarly, the Constitution of UNESCO was the product of a series of conferences begun in 1942 and continued on into 1945. The constitutions drafted by such bodies are always subject to ratification, whereas those adopted by national constitutional conventions may or may not require popular ratification, depending on the precise powers granted to those bodies in each case.

The second function of international organization is administration. There is no international executive function in the proper sense, no international chief executive with force at his disposal for the execution of the laws. The only provision for coercion is in the sanctions of the United Nations, and they are intended only for the maintenance of the peace against aggression, not for the enforcement of law generally.

Most programs collectively sponsored by nations are carried into effect by the separate action of national governments. A treaty of commerce, for instance, is made effective by national laws and orders, and a disarmament treaty is put into force by orders scrapping excess military or naval equipment. Occasionally, however, an international program is carried into force by an international administrative agency—a commission, board, bureau, or secretariat—set up for that particular purpose. The Inter-American Coffee Board, by way of illustration, had the authority to give effect to specified provisions of the Inter-American Coffee Convention of 1940; the Board went out of existence in 1948.

Finally, international organization has the function of dealing with disputes between nations, corresponding only in a general way to the judicial function within national governments. Among the differences between these national and international systems is the distinction in the former between civil and criminal cases, whereas in the latter there can be no criminal prosecution. There is no international criminal law applying to the actions of states, no prosecuting officials, and no courts with criminal jurisdiction. The Charter for the Trial of War Criminals adopted in 1945 does not apply to the actions of states but rather to the actions of state officials.

In national governments the courts have a wide range of compulsory jurisdiction; they are able to deal with criminal cases without the consent of the defendants when these cases are begun by the appropriate prosecuting authority, and in civil cases the right of suit enables one individual to bring another into court without the latter's consent. In international organization, however, states cannot be brought before tribunals except by previous consent. In a later chapter it will be shown that by signing the optional clause a considerable number of the members of the International Court of Justice have agreed to allow themselves to be sued in disputes of a legal character, although in some instances they have stipulated certain reservations to this procedure.[11]

The most vital distinction between national and international methods of dealing with disputes is in the matter of procedure. In national governments, controversies are usually resolved by adjudi-

[11] See Chapter VII.

cation when they have passed the point where the disputants can settle them. International organization provides a variety of procedures, most of which are not in the nature of adjudication; some of them clearly recognize the sovereignty of states. When bilateral diplomacy has failed to settle a dispute, a third state may use its good offices or offer mediation, multilateral diplomacy may be resorted to, the parties may employ commissions of inquiry and conciliation, or they may submit to arbitration or to a more strictly judicial procedure in a court of justice.

All in all, the pattern of international organization bears only a surface resemblance to that of national governments. The similarities are bound to remain nebulous so long as national sovereignty remanis a fetish to be preserved at all costs. So striking are the differences between national and international agencies that the term "international government," sometimes employed in place of "international organization," may be looked upon as a misnomer.[12] International agencies "govern" very little because their powers are so slight; they are, with some exceptions, conveniences made available to sovereign states, for their use when they are in a mood to take advantage of them. While it may seem a mere quibble over words as to whether this machinery of internationalism should be designated "international organization" or "international government," the former term is usually preferred for the reason that it is less misleading than the latter, avoiding implications which rightly or wrongly the word "government" is likely to convey.

Types of International Organization

International organizations are of several types. From the point of view of membership they are (1) bilateral, (2) regional, or (3) universal. Bilateral organization is represented by ordinary diplomacy and by such organizations as the International Joint Commission for the United States and Canada and the Anglo-Egyptian Condominium for the Sudan.[13] Regional organization is typified by the Organi-

---

[12] See W. E. Rappard, "The Beginnings of International Government," *American Political Science Review*, 1930, vol. 24, pp. 1001–1016.

[13] Both of these are administrative agencies. For further information on them see Chapter XV.

zation of American States.[14] Universalism was the objective of the League of Nations, and today it is the ultimate logic of the United Nations, thus far not achieved in practice, for its list of members does not yet include all of the nations and peoples of the world.

From the point of view of activities, international organizations are either (1) general in nature or (2) functional. The United Nations and the Organization of American States are both general, the range of their activities extending to practically every subject of international concern—economic, social, legal, and political. A functional agency is constructed to deal with some one problem; the International Cotton Advisory Committee and the Rubber Study Group are both functional.[15]

The suggestion has been made that international organization should give more room to functional agencies, either within or without a universal organization like the United Nations. In 1943 Professor Mitrany, in a pamphlet which was given wide attention, suggested that the postwar organization then under consideration be formed along functional lines. According to him, "The essential principle is that activities would be selected specifically and organized separately, each according to its nature, to the conditions under which it has to operate and to the needs of the moment."[16] He believed that functional agencies would be highly practicable and that they could be readily adjusted in membership to the needs and interests of nations. Later chapters of this volume will refer to a number of functional organizations now operating either independently or as specialized agencies of the United Nations.

---

[14] See Chapter IV.
[15] See Chapter XIII.
[16] D. Mitrany, *A Working Peace System*, London, 1943, p. 33.

II Development of Organization—The League of Nations

T**O A PERSON LIVING A FEW CENTURIES AGO THE MULTITUDE** of international agencies now in existence would be incomprehensible. In a publication issued by the Department of State in 1949 there were listed sixty-six organizations of which the United States government is a member or in whose work it participates.[1] When William Penn advocated a European diet in 1694, it was not surprising that his project was completely ignored, for there was nothing in the way of permanent international organization at that time except bilateral diplomacy, and the proposal to go from nothing at all to a considerable degree of European unity seemed utterly Utopian. Even in 1900 there was no intimation in the community of nations that so many coöperative agencies would be at work a half-century later. A great deal of the international organization of today has been constructed during the past three or four decades.

How Organization Has Developed

A prerequisite to the development of international organization was the establishment of the modern state system. Although the nation state is now assumed to be the basic unit of international relations, it is in fact a phenomenon of modern history. There had been city-states as in ancient Greece, empire as in the time of Rome, and the feudalism of the Middle Ages; but states based upon the ethnic concept of a nation were not firmly established until the Peace of West-

---

[1] See Appendix I to this chapter.

phalia (1648), and even then there were only a few of them, all located in western Europe, where they had been gradually taking shape as a result of the wars and politics of the preceding centuries.

Once the modern state had made its advent, international organization on a large scale became possible but by no means inevitable. In the beginning the contacts of nations were almost entirely bilateral, with only two states coöperating toward a common end—simplicity itself as compared with the vast multinational operations of today. The principal bilateral organization was diplomacy, involving among governments a mutual exchange of permanent diplomatic representatives. No one thought of this as international organization; rather, it was considered an extension of national organization into the realm of international relations.

One early exception to bilateral organization, even as far back as 1648, was the peace conference, where all of the belligerents worked together for the formulation of a peace settlement following a war. In 1648 the Congress of Westphalia was such an organization, coming at the end of the Thirty Years War and setting up in Europe a new foundation of peace. Later there were others, such as the Congress of Utrecht (1713) and the Congress of Vienna (1815). The importance of such assemblies as multilateral international organizations appears slight, however, when the simplicity of their methods, at least until the nineteenth century, is understood. At the Congress of Westphalia, for instance, there were no general discussions; in effect it was only a gathering together of diplomats for the facilitation of bilateral diplomacy.

The first departure from bilateralism in the treatment of international disputes, which at first were handled only by diplomacy, came with the practice of arbitration. Introduced to the modern state system by the Jay Treaty of 1794, arbitration became a common resort of nations in dispute throughout the nineteenth century. Because arbitral tribunals ordinarily included, in addition to a judge appointed by each party, an "umpire" from some third state, there was an obvious departure from bilateralism and a corresponding recognition of community interest and responsibility in the solution of international controversies.

The creation of the Rhine River Commission in 1804 also broadened the basis of international organization, this time in the administrative field, involving as it did some control over the navigation of that river. Here was an agency supported by several states of western Europe, designed to accomplish a specific task of interest to all of them. Under this arrangement a group of uniform regulations and tolls were adopted, and a committee with a Director General of tolls was established to assist in the execution of the document.

The next move toward multilateralism was in the realm of diplomacy and took the form of conferences in time of peace for the promotion of common interests. Between 1815 and 1822, the members of the quadruple alliance—Great Britain, Prussia, Russia, and Austria—held four meetings at convenient European cities for the purpose of developing common policies; France was allowed to attend some of these meetings. A few years later, in 1826, the first conference of American states, attended, however, by a relatively small number of them, was held at Panama City.

The alliance represents the first effort of nations to place security upon a multinational basis. Viewed in the large, the alliance is an ancient institution, predating the nation state by many centuries. Throughout history it has been a convenient mechanism by which several states have bound themselves together for protection against a common enemy. Even yet, the alliance is relied upon very widely as a method of providing security; the North Atlantic Pact is evidence of that fact.

Whenever it passed beyond the bilateral stage, international organization tended at first to be regional or limited before it became universal in character. The Rhine River Commission of 1804, for instance, was a regional project pure and simple. The Panama Conference, twenty-two years later, was also an effort at regional cooperation. Alliances have always been based on a limited membership, often on a regional basis. The first effort toward universalism was made in 1865, when the International Telegraphic Union was set up; it was limited to the regulation of only one subject. It was followed in 1875 by the Universal Postal Union, also functional in nature. The first international organization concerned with a large number of subjects was the Inter-American Organization, a regional organization set up on a permanent basis in 1889, three decades before the establishment of the League of Nations, the first organization with an inclusive program of action that aimed at universalism.

Why International Organization Developed

The steady and sometimes rapid expansion of international organization during recent decades has been in answer to the growing need of nations for machinery and processes with which to accomplish tasks essential to their welfare and security. Back in 1648, international relations were very simple because contacts between nations were few and far between. Devastating as they were, the wars of that period could not begin to match those of today in the havoc and ruin which they brought; the Thirty Years War caused widespread suffering, especially in Germany, but today a war could probably inflict a like amount of suffering in a matter of hours.

The changes in world society which have brought nations together in close contact at so many points are the work of modern technology. The industrial revolution, with new methods of travel, communication, production, and trade, has revolutionized the life of the community of nations fully as much as it has that of individual nations. Today there are hundreds of contacts between states for every one back in 1648. Reference has already been made to the large volume of travel and trade that goes on between nations at the present time, and to some of the resulting international problems. New methods of production have had much the same complicating effect. Because the new technology enables nations to make more goods and to make them faster, the necessity arises for export markets to take the surpluses. At the same time, the new production has created a need for import markets, because the complex products of modern industry require a variety of raw materials which no one nation can hope to provide for itself. To make a telephone, according to a Western Electric Company publication, thirty-six basic materials are needed and of these several must be imported, such as nickel from Canada, tungsten from China, cobalt from the Belgian Congo, and tin from Bolivia or Malaya.[2] The manufacturer of automobiles is even more dependent on imports—cork from Algeria or Portugal, tin from Bolivia or Malaya, chrome from Rhodesia, shellac from India, and so on.

In effect, modern technology has produced a world community of highly interdependent parts out of the isolated nations of a few centuries back. For this reason, problems that were once local or national are now world-wide in scope: health, poverty, nutrition, unemployment, and many others. For the same reason, wars, which were once of an essentially local nature, are now of general concern, for, like diseases, they spread rapidly.

To deal with the multitude of problems which modern technology has introduced, the world-community must be organized. There are programs of common action to adopt and put into force; there are disputes to be settled, disturbers of the peace to be reckoned with, and countless tasks of all kinds to be performed. So prodigious is the work to be done that most critics agree that international organization has lagged behind the needs, and despite the multitude of agencies—conferences, courts, councils, assemblies, and commissions—it remains quite inadequate to the requirements placed upon it.

In addition to the Industrial Revolution, there have been other changes in world society which have pointed to a need for organization. There are now seventy-five or eighty states as compared with some eight or ten in 1648. This means more boundaries, more trade restrictions, and a long list of possible disputants to come before international tribunals. Today there are more than two billion people in the world, about four times as many as in 1800. From this fact there have developed population pressures in wide areas. There are more hungry mouths to feed, more minds to harbor national prejudices, and more hands to manufacture and to engage in trade. The nations have been pushed closer together by demographic forces just as they have by technology and the expansion of the state system.

As a result of these pressures there has been a continual transfer

---

[2] *The Far Corners of the Earth*, Western Electric Co., 4th ed., 1939.

of subjects from domestic to international control. In the process, described by Professor Potter some years ago, the first step was protest against an action taken by one nation, the protest coming from other states adversely affected.[3] This led to negotiation and to bilateral agreement, by which the international character of the subject in question became firmly established. It was in this way that the treatment of fugitives from justice became a matter of international concern. During the major part of the eighteenth century, nations regarded the action to be taken against fugitive criminals as a matter for local national concern. When such action incited protest, bilateral treaties came into being, and consequently extradition had become a matter of international regulation.

After a subject had been transferred from national to bilateral international control, it might later be moved on to multilateral treatment if perchance it lent itself to that method. This was true of international postal communication, which was first under national control, then bilateral international action, and still later was placed under multilateral management (1875). Even when multilateral control by treaty had been established, international machinery and processes would not be created unless there were some continuing functions to be performed. Such functions clearly existed in the case of postal communication, and for that reason the convention of 1875 established the Universal Postal Union, which is now one of the specialized agencies of the United Nations.

Development of Diplomacy

The word "diplomacy" is used with several meanings. At times it is a synonym for "foreign policy" or for "negotiation"; in its worst connotation it represents, as Mr. Harold Nicolson has said, "the more guileful aspects of tact."[4] In its most precise sense, according to the Oxford dictionary, "diplomacy is the management of international relations by negotiation; the method by which these relations are adjusted and managed by ambassadors and envoys; the business or art of the diplomats."

---

[3] P. B. Potter, "The Expansion of International Jurisdiction," *Political Science Quarterly*, 1926, vol. 41, pp. 548–549.

[4] Harold Nicolson, *Diplomacy*, 2nd ed., New York, 1950, p. 14.

Whenever there have been independent political communities living side by side and obliged to get along together, there has been something in the nature of diplomacy. Again quoting Mr. Nicolson, "The theorist of the sixteenth century contended that the first diplomats were angels and that they served as 'angeloi' or messengers between heaven and earth." In the time of the Greek city-states, diplomacy was a well-established practice. The ambassadors of that era were selected for their ability as orators and were sent to plead for their respective cities in the assemblies of other cities.

Modern diplomacy is an outgrowth of the diplomatic system of the city-states of northern Italy, which flourished in the late Middle Ages and in the early modern period of history. The original practice of those city-states was to dispatch to each other temporary diplomatic officials whenever there were problems to be solved; noted among the Florentine diplomats were Dante, Petrarch, Boccaccio, and later on Machiavelli. At that time, only the Church maintained permanent representation anywhere and it had but one such mission, established in Constantinople in A.D. 450.

The first permanent mission among the city-states themselves was that established at Genoa in 1455 by Francesco Sforza, Duke of Milan. A few years later, the Duke of Savoy set up permanent representation in Rome. Venice was the first to send a permanent mission outside of Italy, when in 1496 two *sub-ambasciatores* were established at London. It was not long until permanent ambassadors of the Italian cities were located in Paris, London, and a number of other capitals. Introduced to a system of permanent diplomatic representation by the city-states of Italy, the new nation states of western Europe continued to use it, so that today it is a fixture in the relations of nations. Now it is understood that every government will maintain a permanent embassy or legation at the capital of every country that it recognizes.

From this bilateral basis diplomacy gradually moved on to a multilateral basis. As has already been pointed out, peace conferences were the first agencies of a multilateral nature to be used in international organization. Beginning in the first quarter of the nineteenth century, conferences in time of peace became more and more frequent, so that by the last quarter of the century there were an imposing number of them, including the St. Petersburg Conference (1868), the Brussels Conference (1874), the Conference of Berlin (1884–1885), and the Hague Conferences of 1899 and 1907. After World War I, the conference method was greatly expanded, a fact which may be explained by the multitude of pressing postwar problems, the ease of communication and travel, and, most important of all, the widespread popularity of the conference idea. Conference followed conference in rapid succession. There was a conference in Washington in 1921–1922 on disarmament and Far Eastern problems. An economic conference met at Genoa in 1922 for the purpose of stimulating trade. There was another disarmament conference at Geneva in 1927, and still another at London in 1930. In the same year a meeting occurred at the Hague to deal with nationality problems—and so it went. The term "diplomacy by conference" came to be used to describe the frequent recourse to this method of doing business.

The development of diplomacy was carried one step further when permanent international organizations were set up in which recurring, as well as specially arranged, conferences became the order of the day. First among these international organizations were the public unions created during the late decades of the nineteenth century: the Telegraphic Union of 1865, the Universal Postal Union of 1875, and the Railway Freight Transportation Union for Europe of 1893. On a somewhat larger scale the Pan-American system was established in 1889, incorporating as a part of its mechanism the practice of holding general conferences every five years and special conferences as needed. Still more pretentious was the League of Nations system of 1919, in which the sessions of the Assembly and Council, as well as the meetings of the technical committees and organizations, were actually conferences, although somewhat different in nature and organization from the usual run. Special conferences, too, were arranged under the auspices of the League of Nations to deal with traffic in opium, communication and transit, and many other problems. Now the United Nations has a complicated conference system, modeled in some respects after that of the

League, and some of the most important work of diplomacy is now taken care of by the meetings which are part of the United Nations.

Development of Organization for the Treatment of Disputes

Aside from diplomacy, which has always been the first method of dealing with disputes, arbitration is the oldest of all. The ancient Greeks were familiar with arbitration and practiced it among themselves. It was used, too, by some of the city-states of medieval Europe. Then for centuries it was abandoned.

Reference has already been made to the revival of arbitration in 1794, when Great Britain and the United States made provision in the Jay Treaty for the arbitration of several outstanding controversies. This experience gave the procedure a new lease on life, and in the nineteenth century scores of cases were submitted to arbitral tribunals. Great Britain set the pace in the number of cases submitted, and the United States followed closely. Some of the most notable cases of the nineteenth century were those between the United States and Great Britain; the Alabama Claims case of 1872, the Bering Sea arbitration of 1892, and the North Atlantic Fisheries of 1910 are well-known cases settled by this procedure. To facilitate recourse to arbitration, the Permanent Court of Arbitration was set up in 1899; in 1907 the constitution of that Court was revised to its present form. Finally, to carry the process of arbitration still further, nations began making general arbitration treaties calling for the submission of specified types of dispute to the procedure, were they to arise. The first effort to make such a treaty was in 1895 between the United States and Great Britain—an effort which failed, but was renewed several years later, with the result that a new period of treaty-making in the settlement of disputes was begun. During the last few decades there has been an extensive network of treaties of arbitration, involving most of the states of the world.

At about the turn of the century, new processes of settling international disputes were advocated and adopted. Inquiry to discover the facts of disputes was first provided in 1899 by the same document that set up the Permanent Court of Arbitration, known as the International Convention for the Pacific Settlement of International Disputes. There were also provisions for the use of good offices and mediation (both old procedures) in the same convention, which were intended to stimulate the intercession of third parties in disputes, with a view to bringing about a peaceful settlement. Conciliation as a method of handling controversies came to the front only a few years later; it was employed frequently in the League of Nations. In the 1920's and 1930's a long list of bilateral and multilateral treaties was concluded by the nations in which inquiry or conciliation or both were made available; very little use, however, was made of these treaties.

The first international court of justice was set up by the Central American states in 1907, and it lasted for approximately a decade. In answer to a persistent demand made during World War I for a world court of justice, the Permanent Court of International Justice was created in 1921 and remained active until World War II. In its place today is the International Court of Justice, which, for the most part, is a continuation of the old Permanent Court.

Added to these complicated organizations and procedures for the settlement of disputes were those of the League of Nations, and now those of the United Nations. Viewed in the large, the methods of these two organizations have been adaptations of earlier ones with certain modifications and improvements.

Development of International Administration

One of the earliest recorded instances of anything in the nature of international administration was that in the Amphictyonic League of ancient Greece, an organization concerned primarily with religious interests and only incidentally with political. There was no general executive office within the League and its principal organ was a representative council; a small number of administrative agents were designated to manage the common purse, to provide a common coinage, and to have charge of the temple.

In modern international organization, the administrative side was slowest to develop. Reference has already been made to the Rhine River Commission of 1804 as the first important agency. A few decades later, to prevent the spread of epidemics which were ravaging certain areas of trade, Sanitary Councils were set up at Constantinople (1838) and Tangier (1840). Nearly all of the administrative agencies now in existence, however, were set up after 1850. They have dealt with rivers of international concern, the control of undeveloped areas, postal communication, opium control, and a long list of other interests and activities. Here again as in the other branches of international organization, the League of Nations and the United Nations have expanded the field. The mandate system of the former and the trusteeship system of the latter rank high among the systems of administration now at work. Both the League and the United Nations have maintained large secretariats whose work in administration has been vital, although it has involved little in the way of discretionary power.

The Idea of Uniting into a League

The idea of uniting states into a league of nations is an old one. The city-states of ancient Greece were thoroughly familiar with it, and from the seventh to the fourth centuries B.C. they formed among themselves amphictyonic leagues and other confederations. Most prominent among them were the Achaean League of twelve cities and the Delphic Amphictyony which, with the inspiration of a common religion, brought together almost all of the Greek people.

For centuries there have been men of vision in Europe who have advocated unions of states although, as a rule, they have stood alone without much support from their contemporaries. For the most part, their plans were looked upon as idealistic and unworkable, and little attention was given to them by hard-headed men of affairs. One of the first of the plans was that of Pierre Dubois, a French scholar, who in 1305 proposed that the Christian powers unite to maintain peace among themselves, working through a common council and a court of arbitration; he believed that the Christian world would have to become a unit before it could achieve any measure of success against the heathen. At about the same time Dante advocated a world government based upon law. In 1461 King Podiebrad of Bohemia worked out a plan for a federal union of all Christian states with a permanent council, to be located at Basle, as its supreme authority; the members of the union would be obliged to arbitrate their differences and to assist each other in case of attack.

One of the most interesting of all the early projects was the "Grand Dessein" submitted by Henry IV of France and his minister, Sully, to other European governments in 1603. It proposed a European federation of fifteen states, and in order to make them physically equal, it suggested a redistribution of territory. The organization of this *république universelle* was to be made up of a Senate of sixty delegates and six local councils. Disputes were to be settled by arbitration, and a joint military force was to be on hand to keep the peace.

In 1623 Emeric Crucé in *Le Nonveau Cynée* proposed a world union of states. He was in favor of including in his organization both the Christian and the non-Christian states. The general council which was to be in charge of the union was to be located at Venice.

From this point on, projects followed each other in increasing numbers. Most prominent among their authors were the following: Leibnitz (a German philosopher, 1676); Charles (Duke of Lorraine, 1688); William Penn (American Quaker, 1694); John Bellers (English Quaker, 1710); Abbé de Saint-Pierre (French churchman, 1712); Jeremy Bentham (English philosopher, 1789); and Emanuel Kant (German philosopher, 1795).

During the nineteenth century, peace societies were formed in a number of countries, and among their activities was often the advocacy of some kind of league or union of states. The American Peace Society, under the leadership of Mr. William Ladd, published in 1840 a collection of essays on a Congress of Nations. In France the *Ligue de la Paix et de la Liberté* raised the issue of a United States of Europe.

Interesting and deserving as many of these plans for some kind of a league of nations were, they did not have any serious official discussion. They were far ahead of their times. It was not until the twentieth century that any considerable interest, popular or governmental, was displayed toward the idea of union on a wide basis.

Universal International Organization—the League of Nations

International organization with aspirations for universal membership and with activities embracing diplomacy, administration, the settlement of disputes, and the prevention of aggression was first widely advocated during World War I. Although President Woodrow Wilson of the United States was its principal proponent, and a most eloquent advocate, there were people all over the world committed to the project, all bent upon the establishment of an organization able to knit the world more closely together in economic and social matters, and empowered to deal effectively with the problem of war. Consequently, the delegates of the war-weary nations which met at Paris in 1919 made the establishment of a League of Nations a primary aim of the peace settlement. By this time a large number of plans, official and unofficial, were available to provide ideas, and from them the Paris Peace Conference drew heavily in drafting the Covenant. When the first draft was completed, President Wilson returned to the United States, where several suggested changes were offered by Republican leaders, including the recognition in the Covenant of the right of withdrawal, periodic reëxamination of armaments-limitation agreements by the Council, the adoption of the unanimity rule in the Council and Assembly, recognition of the Monroe Doctrine, and the exclusion of domestic questions from League's jurisdiction. All of these suggestions were incorporated into the final draft of the Covenant. In its completed form the Covenant was embodied in the treaties of peace, and thus for better or worse the fortunes of the League and the peace settlement were inextricably tied together.[5]

In the American Senate the Covenant, and the treaties of which it was a part, ran into irreconcilable opposition. Several groups of amendments were offered but to no avail and in the end the Senate rejected both the League and the proposed peace settlement. Despite this rejection the Covenant was adopted by enough nations so that on January 10, 1920, it went into force.

The membership of the League of Nations was a shifting matter, as new members were admitted from time to time and old ones withdrew. During most of the League's history, the total membership was somewhere in the middle fifties; as of December 31, 1938, there were fifty-eight states in the organization. Among the great

---

[5] For the text of the Covenant see Appendix II to this chapter.

powers, Germany was admitted in 1926 and in 1933 she gave notice of her intention to withdraw; Russia was admitted in 1934 and in 1940 the Council voted to expel her. A large number of withdrawals in 1938 and 1939, and the extinction of other members by conquest (Austria and Ethiopia) reduced the membership to forty-nine by the time World War II broke out.

The organization of the League included a Council, an Assembly, a Secretariat, and a number of auxiliary organizations of a technical nature (such as the Health Organization, the Permanent Mandates Commission, and the Intellectual Coöperation Organization). The International Labor Organization and the Permanent Court of International Justice were not parts of the League of Nations, but there were several points of contact between the three organizations, as for instance in financial matters where all were taken care of by the same budget.

As originally provided in the Covenant, the Council was to be composed of nine states, of which five—the United States, the United Kingdom, France, Italy, and Japan—were to be permanent members, with the other four nonpermanent members selected by the Assembly. The rejection of the Covenant by the United States left the organ with only four permanent seats. Under the authority of Article 4 of the Covenant, which provided that "With the approval of the majority of the Assembly, the Council may appoint additional members of the League whose representatives shall always be members of the Council," Germany and Russia were given permanent seats during the periods when they were in the League. Using a similar procedure, as authorized by the Covenant, the number of nonpermanent members of the Council was increased to six in 1922, to nine in 1926, to ten in 1933, and to eleven in 1936. By 1939, therefore, there were a total of fifteen states in the Council. At all times there was a lively competition for the nonpermanent seats in the Council, and during the League's history several states —Brazil, Spain, and Poland—were miffed that they were not given permanent seats.

The Council was obliged to meet at least four times a year, and in fact it met much oftener than that; in 1920 it met eleven times, in

1928 five times, in 1933 eight times, and in 1936 seven times. Its decisions were taken by a unanimous vote except where otherwise provided in the Covenant and in the treaties of peace; the most important exception was in voting on questions of procedure. The presidency of the Council rotated in the alphabetical order of the names in French of the countries represented.

Most significant of the many duties of the Council was that of dealing with disputes and trying to maintain the peace. The competence of the organ was very broadly defined in Article 4 of the Covenant which permitted it to "deal at its meetings with any matter within the sphere of action of the League or affecting the peace of the world." The Council was also authorized to approve appointments to the staff of the Secretariat made by the Secretary-General, formulate plans for disarmament, elect judges of the Permanent Court of International Justice (with the Assembly), act as the final authority in the mandate system, nominate a Secretary-General, and deal with petitions from minority peoples.

The Assembly of the League was the representative organ to which all members sent delegations, with each entitled to one vote. It met for its regular session at Geneva in September of every year, and it met occasionally in extraordinary sessions. The president of the Assembly was elected by that body at the beginning of each regular session. There were six principal committees through which much of the work of the organ was done: (1) legal and constitutional questions; (2) technical organizations; (3) reduction of armaments; (4) budgetary questions; (5) social and general questions; (6) political questions.

Like the Council, the Assembly was authorized "to deal at its meetings with any matter within the sphere of action of the League or affecting the peace of the world." It exercised electoral functions in several instances: approving the appointment of a Secretary-General; electing judges to the Permanent Court of International Justice (with the Council); and electing nonpermanent members of the Council. One of the most far-reaching duties of the Assembly was that of formulating and approving the budget, an activity which provided an opportunity to give some direction to the work of the

League and its affiliated bodies. Still another function of the Assembly was that of admitting new members. Perhaps one of the most useful contributions of the Assembly to the day and age which it served was simply its provision of a forum for the discussion of international problems on the basis of free speech; many indeed were the international problems debated from its rostrum.

Like the Council, the Assembly took its decisions by a unanimous vote, except in procedural questions and in a few special matters such as the admission of new members to the League. In both the Council and the Assembly it was understood that absence or abstention from voting would not be considered as an obstacle to unanimity.

The Secretariat, headed by a Secretary-General, was the chief administrative organ of the League. The international civil service which its staff constituted was made up of some 650 staff members. The complaint was common for a long time that there were too many British, French, and Italian nationals within the Secretariat, and consequently in 1932 the Assembly inaugurated reform measures which prevented too many nationals of any one state from holding posts at the same time. There were in the Secretariat fifteen sections (political, legal, information, minorities, mandates, economic relations, etc.), eight administrative services (personnel office, publications service, internal services, registry, direction of personnel and internal administration, documents service, stenographic service, and secretariat of the staff pension fund), and a library, all located at Geneva. Several auxiliary offices were maintained in other cities.

The duties of the Secretariat were many and varied. Among them were the following: registering and publishing treaties; assisting in the drafting of the agenda of the Council, Assembly, and other organs; providing secretarial services in those bodies; exercising custody over the records of the various meetings within the League; and publishing documents and other materials. These were not spectacular activities but they were most vital to a proper functioning of the organization.

The auxiliary agencies of the League—various "organizations," "commissions," and "institutes"—were to assist and advise the Council, Assembly, and member states in the performance of their duties in relation to economic, social, and political problems. Generally speaking, they were looked upon as experts of the League, helping it in its treatment of the highly complex problems that came before it.[6]

The League of Nations was equipped to engage in all of the principal types of activity known to international organization. Consultation on all kinds of international problems was constantly in progress in the Council, Assembly, and technical organizations. Treaties and agreements were negotiated in the special conferences set up from time to time.[7] International disputes were treated, sometimes successfully and sometimes not, in the Council and occasionally in the Assembly.[8] Machinery was at hand for the prevention of aggression, although the admission must be made that it was not effectively used.[9] Administrative activities could be and were carried on by the Secretariat and by a number of special agencies.[10] In these fields the League was most active.

The greatest successes of the League were in the furtherance of coöperation in economic and social matters. Its work in relation to health, traffic in opium, communication and transit, economic and financial problems, slavery, the protection of refugees, intellectual coöperation, and traffic in women and children was so substantial that the United States, a nonmember, became an active participant in many of the meetings and conferences in which they were taken up.

The first decade of the League's career appeared in every way to be quite promising. Not only was there general recognition that its work in promoting coöperation in economic, social, and cultural matters was constructive, but a widespread feeling developed among the laity, if not among statesmen, that its peace machinery could be made to work. As a matter of fact, several disputes were effectively handled by the League before it ran head-on into the knotty problem

---

[6] For further discussion of these bodies see Chapter XIV.
[7] See Chapter XIV.
[8] See Chapter IX for frequent references to the League's work in the treatment of disputes.
[9] Some discussion of this subject is provided in Chapter X.
[10] See Chapter XVI.

of Japanese aggression in Manchuria in 1931. Fired with the doctrines of expansionism, the Japanese war machine in 1931–1932
conquered Manchuria and set up the puppet state of Manchukuo
despite all efforts of the League to prevent a forceful disruption of
the *status quo*. This was a serious blow to the League of Nations, to
the organization's prestige and future usefulness, for Japan had
demonstrated to the world that a powerful nation could defy the
authority of the organization and get away with it, even if smaller
nations might be reluctant to undertake such action.

Four years later, in 1935, Italy followed the example of Japan and
challenged the League's machinery of peace by invading Ethiopia.
This was blow number two to the organization's standing in the
world, for although economic sanctions were undertaken, they were
not enough to prevent the success of the Italian campaign, and Ethiopia was annexed to the Italian Empire. Clearly the League could
not stay the hand of a powerful aggressor. The road had been paved
for the German aggressions of 1938 and 1939 in Austria, Czechoslovakia, and Poland.

The failure of the League of Nations was the result of many facts
and forces. Soon after World War II broke out in 1939, the International Consultative Group of Geneva published a careful analysis
of the conditions that had led to the League's downfall.[11] The Group
expressed the opinion that "The failure of the United States to ratify
(and thereby become a member) was certainly the hardest blow to
the new institution." It mentioned also the split which developed
between France and Great Britain, the tendency of the latter "to
pull away from Europe," the lack of farsighted leadership in the
nations, the problem of Germany, social discontent, and "spiritual
anarchy." This stress by the Group upon adverse attitudes and conditions within the states rather than upon organizational inadequacies
appeared quite convincing in view of the fact that the League had,
and could have, little life other than that imparted to it by the nations which were its members.

Among the adverse conditions in which the League had func-

---

[11] International Consultative Group of Geneva, "Causes of the Peace Failure, 1919–
1939," *International Conciliation*, no. 363, October, 1940.

tioned, the Group asserted that the political and psychological were the most significant and that "the role of economic factors in the peace failure of 1919–39 was not of first importance." Economic problems relating to markets, tariffs, and raw materials had often been on the surface of international relations, but beneath them, so the Group believed, were political motives, the desire for national power, and the fear of war.

The Group asserted that the usual criticism made of the Geneva institutions was that they were founded upon and recognized national sovereignty. This, in their opinion, was to mistake cause for effect. "A juridicial doctrine," so they said, "is seldom more than a decent theoretical garment to cloak current political thought and action." They went on to say that "The doctrine serves to justify the essential amorality of states."

The Group gave considerable attention to what they called the "spiritual factors in the peace failure." They laid great stress upon the "beliefs, ideologies, and fundamental values actuating peoples in the last twenty years." Nationalism and "destructive ideologies" were singled out as particularly to blame for the world's plight. All systems of peace depend, so the Group said, upon "a willingness to live together in harmony, which itself depends upon some underlying unity of spirit." World War II was called "an expression of European disintegration rather than its cause." After quoting Sir Alfred Zimmern's statement that the Covenant assumed "a new spirit in the whole field of international politics," and that "it presupposes a transformation of power politics into responsibility politics," the Group stated that these presuppositions had not been fulfilled.

The machinery of the League of Nations could be criticized at many points—its voting methods, its lack of effective sanctions, the right of members to withdraw, and so on. Whether these weaknesses could have been eliminated by members devoted to power politics and often seething with economic and political unrest is doubtful; and even had the defects been eliminated on paper, it is not certain that the nations could have fitted themselves into the more powerful world organization that would have resulted. In his last days President Wilson expressed the view that "perhaps it was just as well" that the League had failed in the Senate because "the American people were not ready for it." As the United States contributed to the downfall of the League from the outside, so did many of its members from the inside. The world as a whole did not appear ready for it.

The Establishment of the United Nations

The term "United Nations" originated on January 1st, 1942, with the signing of the official Declaration of the United Nations. So used, it was the name of the wartime coalition committed to support the Atlantic Charter of August 14, 1941, and to continue to fight until the Axis was defeated. Throughout the war there were announcements of peace aims, and instrumentalities of coöperation were created, most of which had to do with coöperation in war. The first permanent organization set up as a part of the United Nations to operate in peace was the Food and Agriculture Organization (1943), whose Constitution was written by the representatives of forty-four nations, meeting at Hot Springs, Virginia. In July, 1944, a United Nations Monetary and Financial Conference met in Bretton Woods, New Hampshire, at the invitation of President Roosevelt, and set up the International Bank and the International Fund, thereby adding to the permanent peacetime organization of the United Nations.

Except for the utterances of individual statesmen in the nations at war with the Axis, no official announcement of the intention to found a new world-wide organization to keep the peace and to promote coöperation was made until the Moscow Conference of October, 1943. At the end of that meeting, the representatives of the four nations in attendance—China, Russia, the United Kingdom, and the United States—issued a statement urging the "necessity of establishing at the earliest practicable date a general international organization, based on the principle of the sovereign equality of all peace-loving members, and open to membership by all such states, large and small, for the maintenance of international peace and security."

The first important step in the creation of the United Nations as a general postwar organization was taken at Dumbarton Oaks in Washington, D.C., where a conference of the representatives of China, Russia, the United Kingdom, and the United States met for exploratory conversations. These discussions were in two phases. The first part of the conference (August 21 to September 28, 1944) involved the representatives of only Russia, the United Kingdom, and the United States; later (from September 29 to October 7) the representatives of China, the United Kingdom, and the United States continued the conversations. The result of these deliberations was the so-called Dumbarton Oaks Proposals, setting forth some of the major provisions of the new world organization.[12] These were given wide publicity in the hope that constructive criticism and wide popular support would result.

The Charter of the United Nations in its present form was written at the San Francisco Conference, which opened its sessions on April 25, 1945. The avowed purpose of the Conference was "to prepare the charter of such an organization along the lines proposed in the informal conversations at Dumbarton Oaks." Invitations were issued to forty-two nations by the four sponsoring governments—the United States, the United Kingdom, Russia, and China. When the Conference opened, all of the sponsoring and invited governments were represented. Before the Conference had got under way, it was decided, after a heated debate, to invite four additional countries: Argentina, Byelorussia, Ukrainia, and Denmark, bringing the total number of participating governments up to fifty. Although the delegations from all the nations were active in framing the Charter, throughout the Conference the representatives of the four sponsoring governments were especially influential.

The San Francisco Conference met in an atmosphere of bright optimism. The new world organization which it would fashion had been a lively topic of discussion in churches, schools, newspapers, and other forums both in the United States and abroad. There was a widespread feeling that, with the war ending victoriously, a splendid opportunity presented itself to set up a system of enduring peace. In large part it was this popular enthusiasm that was responsible for the decision to open meetings to an unusual degree to the public. Representatives of more than forty business, professional, agricultural, and religious groups were present, and 2600 press and radio men were on hand. In his transmittal of the Charter to the Sen-

---

[12] The proposals were based in large part upon a project worked out in the Department of State.

ate for approval, President Truman stated that "No international document has been drawn up in a greater glare of publicity."

Hardly had the conference got under way, however, before disturbing differences of opinions became apparent. These had been foreshadowed by the gaps left in the Dumbarton Oaks proposals some months before. The differences related to projects of conference organization and procedure as well as to the provisions of the Charter.[13] Although these differences were discussed in a fine spirit, at least most of the time, they portended (1) that the Charter would not measure up to the high expectation of many people, in large part because of the veto, and (2) that Russia held points of view on international affairs which might prove to be troublesome in the years to come.

The Charter was signed on June 26, 1945. It came into force on October 24, 1945, by which time China, France, Russia, the United Kingdom, the United States, and a majority of the other signatories had ratified the document. The inclusive nature of its purposes was expressed in Article 1, which states that

The Purposes of the United Nations are:

1. To maintain international peace and security, and to that end: to take effective collective measures for the prevention and removal of threats to the peace, and for the suppression of acts of aggression or other breaches of the peace, and to bring about by peaceful means, and in conformity with the principles of justice and international law, adjustment or settlement of international disputes or situations which might lead to a breach of the peace;
2. To develop friendly relations among nations based on respect for the principle of equal rights and self-determination of peoples, and to take other appropriate measures to strengthen universal peace;
3. To achieve international cooperation in solving international problems of an economic, social, cultural, or humanitarian character, and in promoting and encouraging respect for human rights and for fundamental freedoms for all without distinction as to race, sex, language or religion; and
4. To be a center for harmonizing the actions of nations in the attainment of these common ends.

---

[13] The organization and work of the conference is further discussed in Chapter XII.

▲

APPENDIX TO CHAPTER II

I

List of International Organizations in Which the United States Participates (1949)*

General:
  United Nations
  Organization of American States
  Inter-American Defense Board

Agriculture and Fisheries:
  Food and Agriculture Organization of the United Nations
  Inter-American Institute of Agricultural Sciences
  International Seed-Testing Association
  International Whaling Commission

Commodity:
  Combined Tin Committee
  International Cotton Advisory Committee
  International Sugar Council
  International Tin Study Group
  International Wheat Council
  International Wool Study Group
  Rubber Study Group

Economic and Financial:
  Interim Commission for the International Trade Organization
  International Bank for Reconstruction and Development
  International Monetary Fund
  International Union for the Protection of Industrial Property
  International Union for the Publication of Customs Tariffs
  Organization for European Economic Coöperation

* From *International Organizations in which the United States Participates,* 1949,
Department of State Publication 3655, February, 1950.

Educational, Scientific, and Cultural:
    Central Bureau of the International Map of the World on the Millionth Scale
    Inter-American Statistical Institute
    International Bureau of Weights and Measures
    International Council of Scientific Unions and Associated Unions
    International Hydrographic Bureau
    International Meteorological Organization
    Pan American Institute of Geography and History
    United Nations Educational, Scientific and Cultural Organization

Occupation and Peacemaking:
    Allied Commission for Austria
    Allied Control Council for Germany
    Allied Council for Japan
    Council of Foreign Ministers
    Far Eastern Commission
    Inter-Allied Reparation Agency
    International Authority for the Ruhr
    Tripartite Boards of the Western Zones of Germany
    Tripartite Commission for the Restitution of Monetary Gold

Political and Legal:
    Committee of Control of the International Zone of Tangier
    Interparliamentary Union for the Promotion of International Arbitration
    Permanent Court of Arbitration

Regional:
    Caribbean Commission
    South Pacific Commission

Social and Health:
    American International Institute for the Protection of Childhood
    Central International Office for the Control of the Liquor Traffic in Africa

Inter-American Commission of Women
Inter-American Conference on Social Security
Inter-American Indian Institute
√ International Bodies for Narcotic Control
√International Criminal Police Commission
International Labor Organization
√ International Penal and Penitentiary Commission
International Refugee Organization
√Pan American Sanitary Organization
United Nations International Children's Emergency Fund
World Health Organization

Transport and Communications:
Central Commission for Navigation of the Rhine
Inter-American Radio Office
International Civil Aviation Organization
ᐱ International Commission of the Cape Spartel Light
√ International Telecommunication Union
(International Union of Official Travel Organizations
Pan American Railway Congress Association
Permanent International Association of Navigation Congresses
Postal Union of the Americas and Spain
Provisional Maritime Consultative Council
Universal Postal Union

▲

II

Covenant of the League of Nations*

THE HIGH CONTRACTING PARTIES,

In order to promote international coöperation and to achieve international peace and security.

by the acceptance of obligations not to resort to war,

---

* The Covenant is given with annotations as found in *Ten Years of World Coöperation.* Amendments are included in the text in italics.

by the prescription of open, just and honourable relations between nations,

by the firm establishment of the understandings of international law as the actual rule of conduct among Governments, and

by the maintenance of justice and a scrupulous respect for all treaty obligations in the dealings of organised peoples with one another,

Agree to this Covenant of the League of Nations.

ARTICLE 1

1. The original Members of the League of Nations shall be those of the Signatories which are named in the Annex to this Covenant and also such of those other States named in the Annex as shall accede without reservation to this Covenant. Such accession shall be effected by a Declaration deposited with the Secretariat within two months of the coming into force of the Covenant. Notice thereof shall be sent to all other Members of the League.

2. Any fully self-governing State, Dominion or Colony not named in the Annex may become a Member of the League if its admission is agreed to by two-thirds of the Assembly, provided that it shall give effective guarantees of its sincere intention to observe its international obligations, and shall accept such regulations as may be prescribed by the League in regard to its military, naval and air forces and armaments.

3. Any Member of the League may, after two years' notice of its intention so to do, withdraw from the League, provided that all its international obligations and all its obligations under this Covenant shall have been fulfilled at the time of its withdrawal.

ARTICLE 2

The action of the League under this Covenant shall be effected through the instrumentality of an Assembly and of a Council, with a permanent Secretariat.

ARTICLE 3

1. The Assembly shall consist of Representatives of the Members of the League.

2. The Assembly shall meet at stated intervals and from time to time as occasion may require at the Seat of the League, or at such other place as may be decided upon.

3. The Assembly may deal at its meetings with any matter within the sphere of action of the League or affecting the peace of the world.

4. At meetings of the Assembly, each Member of the League shall have one vote, and may have not more than three Representatives.

ARTICLE 4

1. The Council shall consist of Representatives of the Principal Allied and Associated Powers, together with Representatives of four other Members of the League. These four Members of the League shall be selected by the Assembly from time to time in its discretion. Until the appointment of the Representatives of the four Members of the League first selected by the Assembly, Representatives of Belgium, Brazil, Spain and Greece shall be Members of the Council.

2. With the approval of the majority of the Assembly, the Council may name additional Members of the League, whose Representatives shall always be Members of the Council; the Council with like approval may increase the number of Members of the League to be selected by the Assembly for representation on the Council.

2 bis. The Assembly shall fix by a two-thirds majority the rules dealing with the election of the non-permanent Members of the Council, and particularly such regulations as relate to their term of office and the conditions of re-eligibility.

3. The Council shall meet from time to time as occasion may require, and at least once a year, at the Seat of the League, or at such other place as may be decided upon.

4. The Council may deal at its meetings with any matter within the sphere of action of the League or affecting the peace of the world.

5. Any Member of the League not represented on the Council shall be invited to send a Representative to sit as a member at any meeting of the Council during the consideration of matters specially affecting the interests of that Member of the League.

6. At meetings of the Council, each Member of the League represented on the Council shall have one vote, and may have not more than one Representative.

ARTICLE 5

1. Except where otherwise expressly provided in this Covenant or by the terms of the present Treaty, decisions at any meeting of the Assembly or of the Council shall require the agreement of all the Members of the League represented at the meeting.

2. All matters of procedure at meetings of the Assembly or of the Council, including the appointment of Committees to investigate particular matters, shall be regulated by the Assembly or by the Council and may be decided by a majority of the Members of the League represented at the meeting.

3. The first meeting of the Assembly and the first meeting of the Council shall be summoned by the President of the United States of America.

ARTICLE 6

1. The permanent Secretariat shall be established at the Seat of the League. The Secretariat shall comprise a Secretary-General and such secretaries and staff as may be required.

2. The first Secretary-General shall be the person named in the Annex; thereafter the Secretary-General shall be appointed by the Council with the approval of the majority of the Assembly.

3. The secretaries and staff of the Secretariat shall be appointed by the Secretary-General with the approval of the Council.

4. The Secretary-General shall act in that capacity at all meetings of the Assembly and of the Council.

5. *The expenses of the League shall be borne by the Members of the League in the proportion decided by the Assembly.**

ARTICLE 7

1. The Seat of the League is established at Geneva.

2. The Council may at any time decide that the Seat of the League shall be established elsewhere.

---

* This paragraph came into force August 13, 1924.

3. All positions under or in connection with the League, including the Secretariat, shall be open equally to men and women.

4. Representatives of the Members of the League and officials of the League when engaged on the business of the League shall enjoy diplomatic privileges and immunities.

5. The buildings and other property occupied by the League or its officials or by Representatives attending its meetings shall be inviolable.

ARTICLE 8

1. The Members of the League recognise that the maintenance of peace requires the reduction of national armaments to the lowest point consistent with national safety and the enforcement by common action of international obligations.

2. The Council, taking account of the geographical situation and circumstances of each State, shall formulate plans for such reduction for the consideration and action of the several Governments.

3. Such plans shall be subject to reconsideration and revision at least every ten years.

4. After these plans shall have been adopted by the several Governments, the limits of armaments therein fixed shall not be exceeded without the concurrence of the Council.

5. The Members of the League agree that the manufacture by private enterprise of munitions and implements of war is open to grave objections. The Council shall advise how the evil effects attendant upon such manufacture can be prevented, due regard being had to the necessities of those Members of the League which are not able to manufacture the munitions and implements of war necessary for their safety.

6. The Members of the League undertake to interchange full and frank information as to the scale of their armaments, their military, naval and air programmes, and the condition of such of their industries as are adaptable to warlike purposes.

ARTICLE 9

A permanent Commission shall be constituted to advise the Council on the execution of the provisions of Article 1 and 8 and on military, naval and air questions generally.

ARTICLE 10

The Members of the League undertake to respect and preserve as against external aggression the territorial integrity and existing political independence of all Members of the League. In case of any such aggression or in case of any threat or danger of such aggression the Council shall advise upon the means by which this obligation shall be fulfilled.

ARTICLE 11

1. Any war or threat of war, whether immediately affecting any of the Members of the League or not, is hereby declared a matter of concern to the whole League, and the League shall take any action that may be deemed wise and effectual to safeguard the peace of nations. In case any such emergency should arise the Secretary-General shall on the request of any Member of the League forthwith summon a meeting of the Council.

2. It is also declared to be the friendly right of each Member of the League to bring to the attention of the Assembly or of the Council any circumstance whatever affecting international relations which threatens to disturb international peace or the good understanding between nations upon which peace depends.

ARTICLE 12*

1. The Members of the League agree that if there should arise between them any dispute likely to lead to a rupture they will submit the matter either to arbitration *or judicial settlement* or to enquiry by the Council and they agree in no case to resort to war until three months after the award by the arbitrators *or the judicial decision* or the report by the Council.

2. In any case under this Article, the award of the arbitrators *or the judicial decision* shall be made within a reasonable time, and the report of the Council shall be made within six months after the submission of the dispute.

ARTICLE 13**

1. The Members of the League agree that whenever any dispute shall arise between them which they recognise to be suitable for sub-

* The amendments printed in italics relating to these articles came into force on September 26, 1924.
** See preceding footnote.

mission to arbitration *or judicial settlement,* and which cannot be satisfactorily settled by diplomacy, they will submit the whole sub-ject-matter to arbitration *or judicial settlement.*

2. Disputes as to the interpretation of a treaty, as to any question of international law, as to the existence of any fact which, if estab-lished, would constitute a breach of any international obligation, or as to the extent and nature of the reparation to be made for any such breach, are declared to be among those which are generally suitable for submission to arbitration *or judicial settlement.*

3. *For the consideration of any such dispute, the court to which the case is referred shall be the Permanent Court of International Justice, established in accordance with Article 14, or any tribunal agreed on by the parties to the dispute or stipulated in any conven-tion existing between them.*

4. The Members of the League agree that they will carry out in full good faith any award *or decision* that may be rendered, and that they will not resort to war against a Member of the League which complies therewith. In the event of any failure to carry out such an award *or decision,* the Council shall propose what steps should be taken to give effect thereto.

ARTICLE 14

The Council shall formulate and submit to the Members of the League for adoption plans for the establishment of a Permanent Court of International Justice. The Court shall be competent to hear and determine any dispute of an international character which the parties thereto submit to it. The Court may also give an advisory opinion upon any dispute or question referred to it by the Council or by the Assembly.

ARTICLE 15*

1. If there should arise between Members of the League any dis-pute likely to lead to a rupture, which is not submitted to arbitration *or judicial settlement* in accordance with Article 13, the Members of

---

* The amendment to the first paragraph of this article came into force on September 26, 1924.

the League agree that they will submit the matter to the Council. Any party to the dispute may effect such submission by giving notice of the existence of the dispute to the Secretary-General, who will make all necessary arrangements for a full investigation and consideration thereof.

2. For this purpose the parties to the dispute will communicate to the Secretary-General, as promptly as possible, statements of their case with all the relevant facts and papers, and the Council may forthwith direct the publication thereof.

3. The Council shall endeavour to effect a settlement of the dispute and, if such efforts are successful, a statement shall be made public giving such facts and explanations regarding the dispute and the terms of settlement thereof as the Council may deem appropriate.

4. If the dispute is not thus settled, the Council either unanimously or by a majority vote shall make and publish a report containing a statement of the facts of the dispute and the recommendations which are deemed just and proper in regard thereto.

5. Any Member of the League represented on the Council may make public a statement of the facts of the dispute and of its conclusions regarding the same.

6. If a report by the Council is unanimously agreed to by the Members thereof other than the Representatives of one or more of the parties to the dispute, the Members of the League agree that they will not go to war with any party to the dispute which complies with the recommendations of the report.

7. If the Council fails to reach a report which is unanimously agreed to by the members thereof, other than the Representatives of one or more of the parties to the dispute, the Members of the League reserve to themselves the right to take such action as they shall consider necessary for the maintenance of right and justice.

8. If the dispute between the parties is claimed by one of them, and is found by the Council, to arise out of a matter which by international law is solely within the domestic jurisdiction of that party, the Council shall so report, and shall make no recommendation as to its settlement.

9. The Council may in any case under this Article refer the dispute to the Assembly. The dispute shall be so referred at the request of either party to the dispute provided that such request be made within fourteen days after the submission of the dispute to the Council.

10. In any case referred to the Assembly, all the provisions of this Article and of Article 12 relating to the action and powers of the Council shall apply to the action and powers of the Assembly, provided that a report made by the Assembly, if concurred in by the Representatives of those Members of the League represented on the Council and of a majority of the other Members of the League, exclusive in each case of the Representatives of the parties to the dispute, shall have the same force as a report by the Council concurred in by all the members thereof other than the Representatives of one or more of the parties to the dispute.

ARTICLE 16

1. Should any Member of the League resort to war in disregard of its covenants under Articles 12, 13 or 15, it shall *ipso facto* be deemed to have committed an act of war against all other Members of the League, which hereby undertake immediately to subject it to the severance of all trade or financial relations, the prohibition of all intercourse between their nationals and the nationals of the covenant-breaking State, and the prevention of all financial, commercial or personal intercourse between the nationals of the covenant-breaking State and the nationals of any other State, whether a Member of the League or not.

2. It shall be the duty of the Council in such case to recommend to the several Governments concerned what effective military, naval or air force the Members of the League shall severally contribute to the armed forces to be used to protect the covenants of the League.

3. The Members of the League agree, further, that they will mutually support one another in the financial and economic measures which are taken under this Article, in order to minimise the loss and inconvenience resulting from the above measures, and that they will mutually support one another in resisting any special measures

aimed at one of their number by the covenant-breaking State, and that they will take the necessary steps to afford passage through their territory to the forces of any of the Members of the League which are co-operating to protect the covenants of the League.

4. Any Member of the League which has violated any covenant of the League may be declared to be no longer a Member of the League by a vote of the Council concurred in by the Representatives of all the other Members of the League represented thereon.

ARTICLE 17

1. In the event of a dispute between a Member of the League and a State which is not a Member of the League, or between States not Members of the League, the State or States not Members of the League shall be invited to accept the obligations of membership in the League for the purposes of such dispute, upon such conditions as the Council may deem just. If such invitation is accepted, the provisions of Articles 12 to 16 inclusive shall be applied with such modifications as may be deemed necessary by the Council.

2. Upon such invitation being given the Council shall immediately institute an enquiry into the circumstances of the dispute and recommend such action as may seem best and most effectual in the circumstances.

3. If a State so invited shall refuse to accept the obligations of membership in the League for the purposes of such dispute, and shall resort to war against a Member of the League, the provisions of Article 16 shall be applicable as against the State taking such action.

4. If both parties to the dispute when so invited refuse to accept the obligations of membership in the League for the purposes of such dispute, the Council may take such measures and make such recommendations as will prevent hostilities and will result in the settlement of the dispute.

ARTICLE 18

Every treaty or international engagement entered into hereafter by any Member of the League shall be forthwith registered with the Secretariat and shall as soon as possible be published by it. No such

treaty or international engagement shall be binding until so regis-
istered.

ARTICLE 19

The Assembly may from time to time advise the reconsideration
by Members of the League of treaties which have become inappli-
cable and the consideration of international conditions whose continuance might endanger the peace of the world.

ARTICLE 20

1. The Members of the League severally agree that this Covenant
is accepted as abrogating all obligations or understandings *inter se*
which are inconsistent with the terms thereof, and solemnly undertake that they will not hereafter enter into any agreements inconsistent with the terms thereof.

2. In case any Member of the League shall, before becoming a
Member of the League, have undertaken any obligation inconsistent
with the terms of this Covenant, it shall be the duty of such Member
to take immediate steps to procure its release from such obligations.

ARTICLE 21

Nothing in this Covenant shall be deemed to affect the validity of
international engagements, such as treaties of arbitration or regional
understandings like the Monroe doctrine, for securing the maintenance of peace.

ARTICLE 22

1. To those colonies and territories which as a consequence of the
late war have ceased to be under the sovereignty of the States which
formerly governed them and which are inhabited by peoples not yet
able to stand by themselves under the strenuous conditions of the
modern world, there should be applied the principle that the well-
being and development of such peoples form a sacred trust of civilisation and that securities for the performance of this trust should be
embodied in this Covenant.

2. The best method of giving practical effect to this principle is

that the tutelage of such peoples should be intrusted to advanced nations who, by reason of their resources, their experience or their geographical position, can best undertake this responsibility, and who are willing to accept it, and that this tutelage should be exercised by them as Mandatories on behalf of the League.

3. The character of the mandate must differ according to the stage of the development of the people, the geographical situation of the territory, its economic conditions and other similar circumstances.

4. Certain communities formerly belonging to the Turkish Empire have reached a stage of development where their existence as independent nations can be provisionally recognised subject to the rendering of administrative advice and assistance by a Mandatory until such time as they are able to stand alone. The wishes of these communities must be a principal consideration in the selection of the Mandatory.

5. Other peoples, especially those of Central Africa, are at such a stage that the Mandatory must be responsible for the administration of the territory under conditions which will guarantee freedom of conscience and religion, subject only to the maintenance of public order and morals, the prohibition of abuses such as the slave trade, the arms traffic and the liquor traffic, and the prevention of the establishment of fortifications or military and naval bases and of military training of the natives for other than police purposes and the defence of territory, and will also secure equal opportunities for the trade and commerce of other Members of the League.

6. There are territories, such as Southwest Africa and certain of the South Pacific islands, which, owing to the sparseness of their population, or their small size, or their remoteness from the centres of civilisation, or their geographical contiguity to the territory of the Mandatory, and other circumstances, can best be administered under the laws of the Mandatory as integral portions of its territory, subject to the safeguards above mentioned in the interests of the indigenous population.

7. In every case of mandate, the Mandatory shall render to the Council an annual report in reference to the territory committed to its charge.

8. The degree of authority, control or administration to be exercised by the Mandatory shall, if not previously agreed upon by the Members of the League, be explicitly defined in each case by the Council.

9. A permanent Commission shall be constituted to receive and examine the annual reports of the Mandatories, and to advise the Council on all matters relating to the observance of the mandates.

ARTICLE 23

Subject to and in accordance with the provisions of international conventions existing or hereafter to be agreed upon, the Members of the League:

a. will endeavour to secure and maintain fair and humane conditions of labor for men, women, and children, both in their own countries and in all countries to which their commercial and industrial relations extend, and for that purpose will establish and maintain the necessary international organisations;

b. undertake to secure just treatment of the native inhabitants of territories under their control;

c. will entrust the League with the general supervision over the execution of agreements with regard to the traffic in women and children and the traffic in opium and other dangerous drugs;

d. will entrust the League with the general supervision of the trade in arms and ammunition with the countries in which the control of this traffic is necessary in the common interest;

e. will make provision to secure and maintain freedom of communications and of transit and equitable treatment for the commerce of all Members of the League. In this connection, the special necessities of the regions devastated during the war of 1914–1918 shall be borne in mind;

f. will endeavour to take steps in matters of international concern for the prevention and control of disease.

ARTICLE 24

1. There shall be placed under the direction of the League all international bureaux already established by general treaties if the

parties to such treaties consent. All such international bureaux and all commissions for the regulation of matters of international interest hereafter constituted shall be placed under the direction of the League.

2. In all matters of international interest which are regulated by general conventions but which are not placed under the control of international bureaux or commissions, the Secretariat of the League shall, subject to the consent of the Council and if desired by the parties, collect and distribute all relevant information and shall render any other assistance which may be necessary or desirable.

3. The Council may include as part of the expenses of the Secretariat the expenses of any bureau or commission which is placed under the direction of the League.

ARTICLE 25

The Members of the League agree to encourage and promote the establishment and co-operation of duly authorised voluntary national Red Cross organisations having as purposes the improvement of health, the prevention of disease and the mitigation of suffering throughout the world.

ARTICLE 26

1. Amendments to this Covenant will take effect when ratified by the Members of the League whose Representatives compose the Council and by a majority of the Members of the League whose Representatives compose the Assembly.

2. No such amendment shall bind any Member of the League which signifies its dissent therefrom, but in that case it shall cease to be a Member of the League.

ANNEX

I. ORIGINAL MEMBERS OF THE LEAGUE OF NATIONS, SIGNATORIES OF THE TREATY OF PEACE

United States of America	Brazil
Belgium	British Empire
Bolivia	Canada

ANNEX—(Continued)

I. ORIGINAL MEMBERS OF THE LEAGUE OF NATIONS, SIGNATORIES OF
THE TREATY OF PEACE—(*Continued*)

British Empire—(*Continued*)

Australia	Italy
South Africa	Japan
New Zealand	Liberia
India	Nicaragua
China	Panama
Cuba	Peru
Ecuador	Poland
France	Portugal
Greece	Roumania
Guatemala	Serb-Croat-Slovene State
Haiti	Siam
Hedjaz	Czechoslovakia
Honduras	Uruguay

STATES INVITED TO ACCEDE TO THE COVENANT

Argentine Republic	Persia
Chile	Salvador
Colombia	Spain
Denmark	Sweden
Netherlands	Switzerland
Norway	Venezuela
Paraguay	

II. FIRST SECRETARY-GENERAL OF THE LEAGUE OF NATIONS

The Honorable Sir James Eric Drummond, K.C.M.G., C.B.

III Participation in International Organization

INTERNATIONAL ORGANIZATION IS MERELY A GROUP OF agencies—courts, assemblies, councils, conferences, commissions, bureaus, secretariats, and committees—provided with procedures for accomplishing objectives. Like the factory that produces automobiles, or like the automobile itself, it is an aggregation of machinery, and like them it does not get into motion except from the impetus of an external force. This impetus in the case of international organization is furnished by the participating states and individuals. Because members of organizations are states, most of the activities are state-sponsored, but occasionally individuals and private groups in their own name have the right of participation. The precise rules governing membership and participation are invariably stipulated in the fundamental law of an organization—its constitution, charter, covenant, or statute.

States as Participants

The list of states eligible to become members and to participate in international organizations is constantly changing. At the present time there are close to eighty, more than at any time since the unification of Germany and Italy (both consummated in 1871) but many less than before that date, when there were several hundred independent states in the German area alone. Oldest among the group are the states of western Europe which broke away from feudalism during the late Middle Ages: England (now the United Kingdom), France, Spain, Portugal, Denmark, Sweden, and Norway. Since that

time, many others have appeared and disappeared on the map—
products of the inexorable forces set loose by war, revolution, and
diplomacy. Twenty-one were added when the states of the New
World achieved independence from their European masters; first the
United States of America, which declared its independence in 1776,
and then those of Central and South America, most of which became
free from Spain and Portugal in the early decades of the nineteenth
century. China, oldest of all but long in seclusion, was opened to the
West by the Opium War of 1840–1842; Japan was brought into the
world community by Commodore Perry in 1854; and Korea was
forced in by Japan in 1876, only to lose her independence in 1905,
when she became a Japanese protectorate. The revolt of the Balkan
peoples from Turkey in the nineteenth and early twentieth centuries
added Greece, Roumania, Serbia, Bulgaria, Albania, and Montenegro (now a part of Yugoslavia). At the end of World War I, Austria-Hungary vanished and a group of new or revived states came
into being in Europe: Austria, Hungary, Poland, Czechoslovakia, and
Yugoslavia (an enlargement of Serbia). Esthonia, Latvia, and Lithu-
ania became independent of Russia during World War I but in 1940
were swallowed up again by the expanding communist colossus of
eastern Europe. Austria was absorbed by Germany in 1938 but re-
gained her independence after World War II; the active participation of Germany and Austria (and Japan and Korea) was, however,
held in abeyance after World War II during the period of military
occupation. Recently, several dependencies of the British Empire
have been transformed into states: Burma, India, Pakistan, and Ceylon. And in the Near East, Lebanon, Syria, and the new Jewish state
of Israel have appeared on the scene. The ups and downs of world
politics are constantly at work, adding to or subtracting from the list
that make up the community of nations.

What is this entity the "state" which, with others of its kind, creates and maintains international organization? A great deal has been
said and written on this subject, most of which deals with the state as
a philosophic abstraction and does not help appreciably in coming to
an understanding of the state as a unit of international organization.
Looking at the matter from a practical rather than a philosophic or

theoretical point of view, and employing the language of the Inter-
American Convention on the Rights and Duties of States (1933),
"A state as a person of international law should possess the following
qualifications: (a) a permanent population; (b) a defined territory;
(c) government; and (d) capacity to enter into relations with other
states." While this statement may seem somewhat stilted and even
ambiguous—i.e., how permanent must the population be, and how
much capacity for international relations must be present?—still the
fact remains that in the practice of nations these four qualifications
are vital in the identification of a state.

From a strictly legal point of view the existence of a state is admitted by the process of recognition. When political independence
has been gained by a people, existing states may if they wish recognize *de jure* the achievement of statehood by that people. When this
is done, diplomatic representatives are exchanged and formal diplomatic relationships are begun. For instance, Israel's successful war
against the Arabs was followed by the widespread recognition of
Israel as a state, and by the commencement of full diplomatic relationships. Although this is the normal procedure when a new political community has come into being, it is quite possible to withhold
recognition even though all of the four qualifications listed in the
Inter-American Convention on the Rights and Duties of States have
been met. The United States and a number of other governments
withheld recognition from Manchukuo after 1931, when Japan set
up what was claimed to be a new state in Manchuria.

Among the seventy-five or eighty states of today the dominions of
the British Commonwealth of Nations are properly included. While
Canada, Australia, New Zealand, South Africa, India, Pakistan,
Burma, and Ceylon are parts of the British Commonwealth, their autonomous and independent character is incontestable. They are tied
to the United Kingdom only by formal bonds, and the British Government has no control over them. The dominions are constitutionally free to engage in diplomacy, to make treaties, to declare war,
and to enter into international organizations.

Modern states are commonly referred to as "nation states." Generally speaking, they are indeed both nations and states, or to be

more explicit, they are at once ethnical units and political units. France is a nation in the sense that it is composed of people with a similar ethnic background, speaking the same language and possessing the same cultural and historical heritage. Italy represents this same coincidence of ethnic and political unity.

Useful as the term "nation state" may be, it should be understood as representing only an approximation of existing conditions, for there is no state which is composed of all of the people belonging to its ethnic group and which includes no minority group. Even France does not include all Frenchmen, and within France there live some Germans, some Italians, and small numbers of other peoples. In the United Kingdom where the English, Scotch, Welsh, and northern Irish live under one flag, there is still less ethnic unity. There are Germans, French, and Italians living side by side in Switzerland. The United States, traditionally a "melting pot," is completely lacking in ethnical unity. Despite these and other exceptions, it is nevertheless true that the political state of our day is founded upon the nation. In this respect the modern state contrasts strikingly with the city-states of ancient Greece and of sections of Europe in the late Middle Ages, and with the empire of Rome, which embraced many peoples.

A most significant aspect of the nation state, and one closely related to the functioning of international organization, is the nationalism of its people. The facts of history have brought it about that the inhabitants of the nation states are intensely, often fanatically, loyal. During the fifteenth, sixteenth, and seventeenth centuries there had been some stimulation of national consciousness, but it was not until the French Revolution with its stress on self-determination that those early sparks of nationalism were fanned to a flame. The nineteenth century was a century of nationalism. It witnessed the unification of the peoples of Germany and Italy, and the ousting of Turkey from the Balkan Peninsula to make way for the new nation states of Greece, Bulgaria, Roumania, Montenegro, and Serbia. The fervor of nationalism has increased as the twentieth century has unfolded, with the break-up of Austria-Hungary in 1918 to give way to several new or revived nation states, and the development in the 1930's of extreme nationalism in nazi Germany and fascist Italy, the former basing itself "scientifically" on the Aryan doctrine of superiority. Even yet, the nationalist movement has not spent itself but is growing apace in China, India, Burma, Indo-China, the East Indies, the Arab countries, and elsewhere in the Far and Middle East.

In two conspicuous ways, today's nationalism retards the progress of international organization. First, it complicates the problem of war, the most baffling of all the problems which international organization endeavors to solve, to the point that at the present time no effective system of prevention or control appears within reach. This it does by the prejudices and hatreds, as well as the superiority complexes, which it stimulates, for, as Mr. Hans Kohn has so aptly said, "Nationalism is first and foremost a state of mind." Because the attitudes which it instills incline one to hate rather than to love his neighbors, and because the loyalty of nationalism induces individual sacrifices in behalf of the group, governments encourage it, regarding it as a source of national power.

The second significant effect of nationalism on international organization is that it diminishes the willingness of peoples to coöperate with each other, setting up the suspicions, fears, and hatreds that make joint enterprises difficult. Moreover, it is a natural result of nationalism that a people should seek economic independence to match their political independence and therefore strive for self-sufficiency; this tendency is enhanced by the fear of war which usually accompanies the hatreds and prejudices that are an adjunct of nationalism. If there has been increased international coöperation during recent decades, it is because the need for coöperation is immeasurably greater than ever before and the possibility of isolation in economic, social, and political matters has well-nigh vanished. Generally speaking, strong nationalism and strong world organization cannot both inhabit the same world.

Another characteristic of the modern state affecting its conduct as a participant in international organization is its jealously guarded possession of power. There is, of course, an obvious inequality in the power positions of the seventy-five or eighty nations of the world, ranging from the United States, Russia, and the United Kingdom on down to nations with almost negligible strength, like Luxembourg,

Panama, and Cuba. The power which they possess takes the form not only of armies, navies, and air forces, but also of industrial productivity, natural resources, population, national unity, and morale. However logical it might be for nations to disarm as international organization is developed and put to work, in fact they have not done so, and of course there is no reasonable way in which they can rid themselves of the economic strength and the man power which today play so vital a role when a nation is fighting. Consequently, it has been the lot of both the League of Nations and the United Nations to carry on in the atmosphere of power politics. As nations have discussed their problems in the forums of those organizations, they have kept their swords sharp so that if reason should fail, power could be relied upon. That international organization has been handicapped by the power which has been kept available can scarcely be doubted. If, as the German historian von Treitschke and others would have us believe, the essence of the state is power, then international organization must inevitably continue under this handicap, unless perchance by a major operation the state were to be shorn of its power. Said von Treitschke, "The right of arms distinguishes the state from all other forms of corporate life."[1] Certainly states without power would be an innovation in international life, although the forty-eight states of the United States provide a model which might be followed. This, of course, is a part of the argument of the world federalist, whose aim is avowedly to reduce the states of the world to the position occupied by the states of the United States.

The obstacles to effective international organization presented by the characteristics of sovereignty and equality claimed for the state have already been outlined. Fully as obstructive as either is the actual inequality of states from a physical point of view and the dissimilarities among them in matters of wealth, religion, law, and government. China has a population of 450,000,000 people; France has 41,000,000 inhabitants; and Vatican City 1000. Italy is Roman Catholic, Greece has the Orthodox Catholic Church, Sweden is Protestant, the United States has both Roman Catholics and Protestants, Eng-

---

[1] H. von Treitschke, *Politics*, vol. 1, p. 305.

land is Anglican, the Arab States are Mohammedan, and the USSR pretends to be both atheistic and tolerant. The United States is wealthy, with thriving industrial and agricultural communities; Great Britain is industrial and by no means wealthy; Italy is definitely poor, with inadequate industry and agriculture; and the United States of Indonesia is still essentially primitive in its economy. In types of government there are fascist Spain, democratic United States, and communist Russia.

Is it possible to construct an effective system of international organization in which states with such extreme physical inequalities and dissimilarities can and will coöperate side by side? Recently, the governmental or ideological differences between nations led by communist Russia and democratic United States have split the United Nations wide open. For dissimilar states to work together requires a modicum of tolerance, and whereas tolerance is more or less attainable where differences in wealth, economy, and even religion are concerned, it is far more difficult in the ideological controversy going on between Russia and the West, for the world revolution advocated by the communist calls for interference in the affairs of other states. In the midst of a conflict of this magnitude, international organization must be at a standstill.

Participation by Individuals and Private Groups

Although participation in international organization is normally by states, there are a few special exceptions to this rule. Indeed, the exceptions are bound to be rare and relatively unimportant, for sovereign states cannot turn over to individuals power and rights without losing some of their hold upon world affairs. Were international agencies allowed direct contact with individuals on a large scale, national sovereignty would be seriously impaired, and in place of the present system of international organization a world federation would have emerged, for one of the characteristics of federation is the ability of the central government to regulate the individual directly and the right of the individual to direct participation in the organs of the central government.

Examining that branch of international organization which handles disputes, one observes immediately that whether the agency be judicial, arbitral, fact-finding, conciliatory, or diplomatic, the parties are nearly always states. Furthermore, only states were allowed to be parties to the cases that came within the jurisdiction of the Permanent Court of International Justice; and at the present time, as Article 34 of the Statute of the International Court of Justice states, "Only states may be parties in cases before the Court." Even where the basis for the case has been a claim or grievance of an individual or a private group, only states have been able to come into Court; in cases of this nature, the state of which the claimant is a citizen must be willing to support him and plead his cause if he is to place it before the tribunal. Take, for instance, the case of the Mavrommatis Palestine concessions placed before the Permanent Court of International Justice by the Greek Government in 1924; here the claim of a Greek subject, Mavrommatis, to £234,000 as damages for an alleged injury arising out of a concession was sponsored by his government against Great Britain. Similarly, in a case brought to the Court by agreement between France and Brazil in 1927 the former sought to protect the interests of French holders of Brazilian bonds, demanding payment in gold rather than in paper money.

In arbitration as in adjudication, only states are allowed to act as parties, even though the interests or claims are those of individuals. In the Pious Fund Case, arbitrated in 1902 by the United States and Mexico, the claim presented by the former was in behalf of the Catholic Church of California to an amount of money in the form of accrued interest from a fund known as the Pious Fund of California. Also in claims commissions set up to deal with private claims, the participants are states. In 1926 the General Claims Commission for Mexico and the United States dealt, *inter alia,* with a claim by Salomé de Galvan against the government of the United States for an alleged denial of justice arising out of a delay in prosecuting the murderer of the claimant's son.

When disputes are handled by commissions of inquiry, by conciliation commissions, or by diplomatic agencies, states are usually involved. The Greek Border Commission, set up in 1946 by the Security Council of the United Nations, was composed of one representative each from Australia, Belgium, Brazil, China, Colombia, France, Poland, Syria, Russia, the United Kingdom, and the United States; it was authorized to report upon alleged border violations along the frontier between Greece on the one hand and Albania, Bulgaria, and Yugoslavia on the other. Similarly, the commission created by the General Assembly of the United Nations in 1947 to study and make recommendations on the Palestine problem was composed of representatives of states, numbering in this instance eleven.

Among the exceptions which permit the direct participation of individuals in the treatment of disputes, mention may first be made of those agencies whose personnel is not selected on a representative basis but rather on the basis of personal qualifications. Outstanding in this group of agencies is the International Court of Justice, where, according to Article 2 of the Statute, "The Court shall be composed of a body of independent judges, elected regardless of their nationality from among persons of high moral character, who possess the qualifications required in their respective countries for appointment to the highest judicial offices, . . ." The force of this provision is slightly diminished by the statement in Article 3 that "The Court shall consist of fifteen members, no two of whom may be nationals of the same state." It is further diminished by the practice followed by the Security Council and the General Assembly in the election of judges of making certain that some are chosen from the great powers; this unwritten rule ensures the selection of judges from the United States, Great Britain, France, Russia, and China. Some of the commissions authorized to investigate disputes or to conciliate have also been composed without regard to the idea of state representation but altogether on the basis of personal qualifications. For instance, the members of the so-called Lytton Commission, nominated by the president of the Council of the League of Nations under the Council resolution of December 10, 1931, were named as individuals, not as representatives of states.

The Central American Court of Justice, active from 1907 to 1917, provided a unique exception to the rule that litigants in international courts must be states, for it permitted individuals to bring cases against foreign nations of the Central American group before the Tribunal. Several such cases were heard by the Court.

In the war-crimes trials after World War II, individuals were made defendants in the international tribunal at Nuremberg set up to try nazi leaders. Prior to that time, it had been the custom to hold defeated states responsible for acts of an irregular nature committed during war, but under the Charter of the International Military Tribunal (1945), individuals were compelled to appear before the Tribunal and answer charges. The Charter specified three types of acts as "crimes coming within the jurisdiction of the Tribunal for which there shall be individual responsibility": crimes against peace, war crimes, and crimes against humanity. Following the program set forth in the Charter of the International Military Tribunal, high officials in the German Government were tried, and many were found guilty and punished.

An instance of some interest in which individuals rather than states are actors in international organization is provided by the Joint Commission for the United States and Canada, set up in 1909. Here an individual or firm desiring to use the boundary waters between the two countries for commercial purposes must go before the Commission and obtain permission.

A consultative status has been given to private groups in the work of the Economic and Social Council under Article 71 of the Charter of the United Nations, which says that "The Economic and Social Council may make suitable arrangements for consultation with non-governmental organizations which are concerned with matters within its competence." Under the authority of this article, between seventy-five and one hundred private organizations have been listed as available for consultation.

The Basis of Membership in International Organization

Whether membership in international organization be looked upon as an obligation or merely as a privilege to be accepted or rejected depends fundamentally upon the prevailing views as to the nature of the international community. The position has been taken that the international community is to be regarded as analogous to communities of individuals within a city, village, or state. Actually residing within a state, an individual becomes automatically a part of its political structure; he is normally a citizen and as such he may vote, hold office, and become an active supporter of a political party. As a member of the community, he is obliged to obey the law and he is the recipient of the benefits of political organization—good roads, education, protection against crime, and so on. By analogy, so the theory goes, states are members of the world community by the mere fact that they exist and live side by side, and therefore it should be assumed that they will take on the benefits and duties of membership without any necessity of joining the community; as residents in the world community they should not be expected to take any special action to become members any more than do the individuals who reside in a state.

This theory of automatic membership was advocated during and after World War II when projects for a new world organization were under discussion. A declaration made by the Inter-American Committee of Jurists insisted that "The international community must be organized on the basis of the cooperation of all nations," and that "no nation is privileged to remain aloof from the organizations thus established." Proponents of the doctrine are careful to point out that they are thinking only of general international organization—a world-wide league of nations or perhaps a world federation—not of regional and special organizations. They would not object to an organization such as the Organization of American States of the British Commonwealth of Nations operating on the basis of limited membership.

Were it to be conceded that the states of the world do in fact constitute a community in substantially the same sense that the inhabitants of a city or state do, then several conclusions regarding participation would follow. First, there would indeed seem to be little need for provisions regarding membership in the constitution setting up the political structure of the world; states would be assumed to be members, and they would have no option of joining or not joining. Second, there would be no way of expelling members from the world organization, and it would be impossible for them to withdraw. No doubt a state might refuse to take an active part as a member, and it might even act as though it were not a member, but in that event, so runs the theory, it would be deprived of the benefits which the rest of the community enjoy, such as a universal mail service, opportunities for trade, health protection, and protection against attack.

While the analogy between a national or local community and the world of states is striking, it is by no means exact. National and local communities are composed of individuals, thousands or millions of them, whereas the world community is made up of seventy-five to eighty states. The individual has accustomed himself from infancy to working with his fellows in matters of common interest and he readily submits to the regulations which the community has drafted; in short, he has a highly developed community spirit built upon a recognition of the fact that he and his fellows are better off when they work together in a system of law and order than when each does as he pleases without regard to the rights of others. The states which make up the world community do not have this point of view so highly developed and are still for the most part convinced that their own sovereign wills are supreme, that they will be better off doing as they please than in submitting to the dictates of society. The sovereign quality so commonly ascribed to the state represents the antithesis of community life, perpetuating in the state a freedom of action and a right of aloofness not at all characteristic of the gregarious individuals who live within the boundaries of cities and states.

Should the idea of sovereignty be abandoned in some future era in favor of the concept of a world community, then the doctrine of automatic membership would no doubt become applicable. Along with this innovation, other startling changes might be expected to take place. No doubt the states would lose their position of primacy in the business of governing mankind, and the world organization, in its new strength and vigor, would become a federation, with the states taking on the subordinate character of the forty-eight states of the United States.

Certainly in the present-day practice of international organization, membership is in no sense automatic. States are not assumed to be members and are free to remain aloof if they so desire. The United States preferred in 1919 to remain outside the League of Nations, but in 1945 decided to join the United Nations. Russia joined the United Nations, but she has not become a member of most of the specialized agencies of the United Nations. As a general rule, international organizations are founded upon "constitutions," "charters," "covenants," or "statutes"—all these documents being in the nature of treaties; to become a member of an organization it may therefore be necessary for a state to become a party to the treaty, doing so by its own constitutionally provided processes. In the United States, treaty-making is by the president with the advice and consent of two-thirds of the Senate, and consequently we normally join international organizations by action of those authorities. A notable exception occurred in 1934, when Congress by joint resolution authorized the president to accept an invitation to join the International Labor Organization, constituting in effect an executive agreement made under the authority of Congress.

In the actual practice of international organization it may be impossible for a nation to become a member of an organization, even if it wishes to do so. This is because the constitutions of international organizations commonly set up conditions to be met by new members and procedures to be followed for their admission. Whereas "original members" of an organization join by becoming parties to the treaty or constitution by which it is established, the "admitted members" are usually obliged to meet stipulated conditions and to have their applications passed upon by authorized bodies. This distinction between original and admitted members is a common one, made by the Covenant of the old League of Nations and now widely recognized in international organizations. Original members of the League were "those of the signatories [of the Covenant] which are named in the Annex to this Covenant and also such of those other signatories named in the Annex as shall accede without reservation to this Covenant." Any "fully self-governing State, Dominion or Colony not named in the Annex" could become a member if admitted by a two-thirds vote of the Assembly, provided it would give "effective guarantees of its sincere intention to observe its international obligations" and agree to accept such regulations with regard to its military forces as might be prescribed by the League. Germany was anxious to become a member but was not admitted until 1926.

Representation

In all three of the main types of international organizations—diplomatic, administrative, and those dealing with disputes—the method of representation has been a perennial subject of controversy. In agencies for the treatment of international disputes, the issue has boiled particularly hot in connection with the bench of a court of justice, where for many years the failure to find a solution prevented the creation of a court. In 1907, when the establishment of such a court was proposed for the first time, the large states wanted permanent representation on the bench and were willing to give the smaller states only occasional representation. The small states strongly opposed this plan, maintaining that the doctrine of state equality entitled them to as much representation as the large states. The issue came up again in 1920, when the Permanent Court of International Justice was in process of creation, and it was settled by a compromise according to which judges would be selected by the Council of the League of Nations, where large states were dominant, and the Assembly, the vast majority of whose members were small. This plan was also applied to the present International Court of Justice. Theoretically the issue of representation appears out of place in the composition of judicial bodies, for the ideal in a court is an impartial bench, not a representative one. That it has been crucial and that a compromise even now is the only practical way to handle the matter arises out of the fact that in the competition of international politics, practical consideration of national power, as much as theory, dictate the course of events.[2]

The issue of equality of representation versus inequality has also been troublesome in diplomatic and administrative bodies, and al-

---

[2] This too is the reason why a state party to a dispute in the International Court of Justice is allowed to have a temporary "national judge" on the bench if it does not already have a regular judge on the bench. This will be discussed in the chapter on the International Court of Justice.

ways it has been a case of small states citing theory against the large nations with power. For years the tendency has been toward acceptable compromises by which theory is applied in one place but thrown to the winds elsewhere, with a frank recognition that the influence possessed by large and powerful states in world affairs entitled them to a privileged position. Examples of such compromises are not uncommon and as a rule they are patterned after that adopted for the International Court of Justice. Within the United Nations there is an arrangement whereby the five great powers are allowed the special position of possessing permanent seats in the Security Council, while in the General Assembly all members are equal in representation and voting strength.

In some organizations the members are, on paper at least, treated as equals, although in practice ways are found to give large powers a representational advantage over small ones. The Economic and Social Council of the United Nations consists of eighteen member states elected by the General Assembly for three-year terms; legally those eighteen may be any member states, but the practice has developed of reëlecting the five permanent members of the Security Council—the United States, Russia, the United Kingdom, France, and China—whenever their terms run out. The provision of the Charter making retiring members of the Council eligible for reëlection is understood to have been adopted in order to make the development of this practice possible.

Most of the specialized agencies of the United Nations adhere to the principle of equal representation in their deliberative bodies and each nation has one vote; this is true in the UNESCO Conference, the FAO Conference, and the Assembly of ICAO, to mention only a few. The executive committees of the agencies, however, are restricted in membership, each containing as a rule less than twenty states selected by the deliberative body; here, too, the practice is prevalent of retaining the great powers as members, just on the practical ground that the presence of those powers is vital to a proper conduct of business.

Probably no international organs are more frankly indifferent to equality of representation, and for that matter to the idea of representation itself, than are some of the administrative bodies. The officials of the United Nations Secretariat, for instance, are not representative and are not permitted to "seek or receive instructions from any authority external to the organization"; they must, however, be recruited on "as wide a geographical basis as possible."

Voting Rights

Like representation, voting arrangements in international agencies have been the result of three forces: (1) the principle of the sovereign equality of states; (2) the factual preponderance of a few great powers; and (3) the pressure for efficiency. Accordingly, as one or another of these pressures has been given priority, voting has been either under the rule of unanimity, unequal, or by majority action; various combinations of these arrangements have also been adopted. Considered generally, the tendency has been away from unanimity and toward the majority principle, and away from equality toward inequality; in other words, the doctrine of the sovereign equality of states, even though frequently recognized in principle (as in the Charter of the United Nations), has been giving way to the hard incontrovertible fact that some states are stronger and more influential in world affairs than others, and to the urge to have international machinery that will function smoothly and efficiently.

Before the time of the League of Nations, unanimity in voting was the general rule, with the exceptions few and inconsequential. As M. Nelidov, President of the Second Hague Conference of 1907, put it, "No delegation has the right to accept a decision of the majority which would be contrary to the will of its government," and "The first principle of every conference is that of unanimity. . . ." The most notable exceptions to this rule were in nonpolitical organizations; the Cape Spartel Lighthouse Commission, by way of illustration, was obliged to vote unanimously when changing the convention under which it operated, but acted under the majority rule in the exercise of its supervisory duties.

It was also in nonpolitical organizations that equality in voting was first discarded and a system of weighted votes introduced. In the General Assembly and the Permanent Committee of the International Institute of Agriculture, organized in 1905, states were divided into several groups both for voting purposes and for financial contributions. In some organizations (e.g., the Universal Postal Union) the allotment of votes to colonial possessions provided a means of inequality.

The general rule in the Council and Assembly of the League of Nations was equality of votes to represented states and unanimity. There were, however, important exceptions to the rule of unanimity provided in the Covenant, as in the admission of new members by a two-thirds vote of the Assembly, the appointment of a Secretary-General by simple majority, and the decision of all matters of procedure by both the Council and Assembly. According to the rules of the Assembly, delegates abstaining from voting were counted as absent. Although proposals were defeated by the rule of unanimity in the Assembly, more often they were withdrawn or watered down when it became clear that there was opposition.

In the United Nations equal voting rights to represented states is the common practice, but there are a few conspicuous exceptions. In the International Fund and International Bank, votes are apportioned unequally according to quotas and subscriptions. A very different type of inequality is provided for in the Security Council, where only the five permanent members have the right of veto. The rule of unanimity does not operate in any of the organs of the United Nations.[3]

---

[3] Voting methods in the United Nations are taken up in Chapter V.

Part Two: Regional and Universal Organization

IV Regional International Organization

HE TERM "REGIONALISM" IS A RELATIVELY NEW ONE, BOTH
in international organization and in political science generally. According to Mr. Hedwig Hintze, it was first used in 1874, in the works
of the Provencal poet de Berluc-Pérussis; it did not, however, come
into wide circulation until the 1890's.[1] The original application of
the term was to areas within a nation having an inclination toward
particularism, as in French Brittany or Corsica. More recently, it
has been applied on a world-wide basis to a group of nations, usually
neighboring nations, with strong tendencies toward coöperation,
such as the twenty-one American republics. So applied, the regions
are subdivisions of the world itself. International coöperation on a
regional basis is something more than bilateralism, but more confined in its scope than universalism or what passes as universalism
in the form of the United Nations.

Although regional organization is now an accepted fact, just what
constitutes a geographic "region" capable of furnishing a basis for
such organization is a moot question. Professor Wirth uses the term
as applying within a nation to an area in which there exists "a high
degree of conformity between the geographic, economic and cultural
contour lines," but this definition is none too helpful in the actual
practice of regionalism, for the phrase "high degree" leaves uncertain just how much conformity is required.[2] Professor Hertzler points

---

[1] Hedwig Hintze, "Regionalism," *Encyclopaedia of Social Sciences*, vol. 7, pp. 208–218.

[2] L. Wirth, "The Prospects of Regional Research in Relation to Social Planning," *Publications of the American Sociological Society*, vol. 29, pp. 107–114.

out that, whereas in most regions within nations there exists "a certain geographical compactness," such as a great plains area or a river valley, there is nothing analogous to serve as bases of regions within the world as a whole.[3] If, therefore, international organization were to be promoted on a regional plan, there would be no obvious geographic regions to be taken as a starting point. As Professor Hertzler argues, even continents or combinations of continents are not natural areas in any sense except that they are "separated from the other land parts of the earth by oceans"; for example, within South America, there are mountain ranges, impenetrable tropical jungles, sparsely settled savannahs, and semidesert areas which break the continent into parts inaccessible to each other. Were an effort made to follow the diverse physiographic and cultural conditions to be found within a continent in the construction of regional organization, the result would be a very large number of regions, perhaps as many or more than the present number of states.

Still another concept of a geographic "region," at least as a foundation for international organization, bases itself upon the fact that the states involved are neighboring states. This is the view of Ambassador Van Kleffens, who has explained his position as follows:

. . . it is submitted that the term "regional" may be thus defined: "limited to sovereign states within a certain area or having common interests in that area." A regional arrangement or pact is a voluntary association of sovereign states within a certain area or having common interests in that area for a joint purpose, which should not be of an offensive nature, in relation to that area. No association may have for its object the territory of a sovereign state without the participation or consent of that state.[4]

To Ambassador Van Kleffens a regional organization must (1) be based upon an area, (2) be based upon common interests which are not offensive in nature, and (3) be a voluntary association of sovereign states.

Probably no exact definition is available for a geographic area capable of being organized regionally. Judge Alejandro Alvarez of

---

[3] J. O. Hertzler, "Some Basic Queries Respecting World Regionalism," *Social Forces*, vol. 22, pp. 371–387.

[4] E. N. Van Kleffens, "Regionalism and Political Pacts," *American Journal of International Law*, 1949, vol. 43, no. 4, p. 669.

Chile, now a judge of the International Court of Justice, has stated this fact and given his own conception of the term as follows: "There is no rule to determine regions. Their existence must be shown by circumstances, and, in particular, by the agreements made by the states who constitute them. . . . Regions are constituted by certain countries having affinities of race, institutions, or, above all, political interests."[5] This concept omits all reference to geographical facts and stresses the affinities of the coöperating group, particularly in political interests. Clearly it is broad enough so that the British Commonwealth of Nations—Great Britain, Canada, Australia, the Union of South Africa, New Zealand, Pakistan, India, Burma, and Ceylon—would qualify as a region.

Some authorities place more emphasis upon the geographical proximity of the participating states in their definitions. A spokesman of the French delegation in the Assembly of the League of Nations in 1936 referred to a region as containing "states linked together by reason of their geographic situation or their community of interests."[6] While geographic proximity may be an element of regionalism by this definition, it is not a requisite element but only an alternative to a "community of interests"; an organization like the British Commonwealth of Nations must be looked upon as a region by this definition, as by that of Judge Alvarez.

Although the Organization of American States is commonly regarded as a regional organization, the question may very well be raised as to whether South America, Central America, and North America up to the Canadian boundary constitute a "region" in any other sense than that they are presumed to have common interests; certainly they are not a region in any other geographic sense than that they form contiguous territory. Were Canada a member, then all of the Western Hemisphere would be included, and in a sense, though in no very meaningful sense, there would seem to be a geographic region. Insofar as the proximity of the twenty-one members

[5] A. Alvarez, "La Reforme du Pacte de la Société des Nations sur des bases continental et régionales," a report to the fifth session of the *Union Juridique Internationale,* 1926, p. 99.

[6] Quoted by E. N. Van Kleffens, "Regionalism and Political Pacts," *American Journal of International Law,* 1949, vol. 43, no. 4, p. 667.

to each other is concerned, it may be pointed out that parts of South America are closer to Africa than to the United States. When the Inter-American Organization was set up in 1889, the economic ties of the Latin-American community were stronger with Europe than with the United States.

In practice it appears that a "region" in the field of international organization is more a matter of assumed interests than geography. Even when the geographic element is present it is only in the sense that the participants are neighbors, not in the sense that in some scientific way they constitute a geographic region. "When I use a word," said Humpty Dumpty in *Through the Looking Glass,* "it means just what I choose it to mean." Apparently it is much like this when men and nations use the term "regional organization." For this reason the term "limited international organization" instead of "regional international organization" might be more precise and less confusing.

The Pros and Cons

What are the merits of so-called regional organization when compared with universal organization? Debate on this question has been frequent and sometimes rather furious. The regionalist contends, on his side, that universalism is, as Professor P. B. Potter has expressed it, "a result of hasty, superficial and, to some extent, sentimental reactions."[7] The regionalist pictures himself as a realist concerned with hard facts and practical situations. He argues that states living in close proximity to each other have interests in common, as a community of people have common interests. Living side by side, they will probably have intimate trade relationships, as in the case of the United States and Canada. It is quite possible that they will face similar health and social problems, as in 1949 Mexico and the United States were together involved in an effort to stamp out the hoof-and-mouth disease among cattle. In some instances, though by no means everywhere, it can be pointed out that neighboring states have much the same cultural backgrounds; this is true among the Latin-Ameri-

---

[7] P. B. Potter, "Universalism vs. Regionalism in International Organization," *American Political Science Review,* vol. 37, p. 851.

can states, and for the United States and Canada, but it does not hold for the United States and Mexico. The Locarno Pact of 1926, whereby the boundary between Germany on the one hand and France and Belgium on the other was guaranteed by Great Britain, France, Germany, Belgium, and Italy, used to be cited by regionalists as more realistic than the world-wide sanctions of the League of Nations; when tested by Hitler's Germany, however, neither was able to stand up.

Universalism, to the regionalist, is impracticable. The extreme differences which exist among the seventy-five or more nations of the world, so he argues, is an insuperable obstacle to effective world-wide union of any kind and even to effective coöperation. To include diminutive Vatican City, or even some of the Central American states, in the same organization with Russia and the United States, seems to him fanciful. To fit states that are poor, like Italy or Japan, in with the wealthy, like the United States, and to bring together nations of diverse religions, language, and culture, the regionalist contends, is equally impossible. If a unity is forged out of such dissimilar nations, then it must, as the regionalist sizes up the situation, be frail and unstable. He believes that it is possible to form an organization of restricted membership which is strong, and that such a union is preferable to a universal organization which is weak.

The universalist answers the arguments of the regionalist by stating that all subjects of contemporary international action are of world-wide concern and denying that anything of significance can be limited in its interest to a particular area or region. Peace, so he argues, is indivisible, in the sense that war in one part of the world tends to spread until all nations are affected. Trade, he points out, is sometimes greater between nations thousands of miles apart than between neighbors and, as proof of this, he mentions the trade between the United States and Great Britain, the largest in volume of that of any two nations. The platitude is cited that economic depression in one part of the world tends to be contagious and soon permeates other parts. Health, too, is mentioned as an international problem of universal concern for the reason that germs are no respecters of boundary lines and are carried indiscriminately from

place to place. As the universalist looks at the subject, he is the one
with his feet on the ground and the regionalist is not alive to the
fact that the world is one community. To these proponents of world
unity, regionalism appears as isolationism badly disguised in a new
garb; it is failure to see the full implications of the technical developments of the modern world—the airplane, the radio, and atomic
energy.

There is some appeal in the logic of both sides. It is difficult to
contradict the statement of the universalist that practically all international problems, at least those which do not yield to bilateral treatment, are of world-wide concern; to insulate a "region" against the
rest of the world is about as impossible as to insulate a state. The
fact is significant that practically every problem—security, trade,
health, intellectual coöperation, agriculture, and others—dealt with
by the Organization of American States occupies also a conspicuous
spot on the agenda of United Nations organs.

Where "regional" organization is best justified is where a limited
group of nations have an awareness of a problem which others do
not have. In this case, action by the few is unquestionably to be
preferred over inaction by the many. Perhaps the North Atlantic
Pact could best be justified on this ground, including as it does nations keenly alive to the danger of communist aggression. The
proposal for a union of the democracies made some years ago by Mr.
Clarence Streit could be supported, in part at least, by the similar
attitudes toward international problems found within democratic
nations.

Instead of considering regional organization and universal organization as antagonistic concepts, it is possible to look upon them as
complementary. With international coöperation so desperately
needed, is it not the better course of wisdom to take it in whatever
form it can be obtained? If nations are willing to do through a limited organization something constructive which they refuse to do
in a universal organization, or vice versa, there is nothing to be
gained and much to be lost by quibbling over the nature of the
union through which they operate. The two types of organization
can exist, and in fact do exist, side by side.

The United Nations and Regionalism

The practice of regionalism was given the formal sanction of the Covenant of the League of Nations in Article 21, which stated that "Nothing in this Covenant shall be deemed to affect the validity of international engagements such as treaties of arbitration or regional understandings like the Monroe doctrine for securing the maintenance of peace." Whether this article was inserted as a sop to the United States, as some believe, or for its intrinsic merits, it enabled the Organization of American States and other groups of nations to flourish unmolested by the League's universalism. Between the two wars several important regional groups came into existence. The Little Entente, composed of Czechoslovakia, Roumania, and Yugoslavia, was established shortly after World War I, and in 1933 it drew closer together by setting up new agencies of coöperation. The Balkan Alliance was created in 1934, inspired by a common fear of the new nazi government in Germany. Both of these vanished from the scene when in 1938–1939 nazi Germany became aggressive and too strong to be defied. Between the two wars, the Scandinavian powers in the North of Europe met from time to time in conference and worked out programs of coöperation.

At the San Francisco Conference of 1945, much discussion was given to the problem of regional organization in relation to world organization.[8] The subject was one of special interest to the United States because of our alignment with the Latin-American states in the Organization of American States, and for that reason we bent our efforts toward securing a full recognition of regional arrangements. In the end the Charter committed itself strongly to regionalist ventures. By Article 52 it is declared that "nothing in the present Charter precludes the existence of regional arrangements or agencies for dealing with such matters relating to the maintenance of international peace and security as are appropriate for regional action provided that such arrangements or agencies and their activities are consistent with the Purposes and Principles of the United Nations."

---

[8] See *Documents of the United Nations Conference on International Organization*, vol. 11, pp. 556–558.

Chapter VIII of the Charter goes on to encourage the settlement of international disputes by regional agencies before Security Council action. It further makes possible the use of regional arrangements for enforcement action, but in this event the authorization of the Security Council is ordinarily required. The Charter specified in Article 54 that the Security Council be kept informed of "activities undertaken or in contemplation under regional arrangements or by regional agencies for the maintenance of international peace and security." Together these articles give regionalism a firm place within the universalism of the United Nations, treating the two concepts as complementary rather than as incompatible.

Although the Charter permits "regional arrangements or agencies," it does not define them. The Egyptian delegation at the San Francisco Conference proposed the following definition, to be incorporated in the Charter:

> There shall be considered as regional arrangements organizations of a permanent nature grouping in a given geographical area several countries which, by reason of their proximity, community of interests or cultural, linguistic, historical or spiritual affinities, make themselves jointly responsible for the peaceful settlement of any disputes which may arise between them and for the maintenance of peace and security in their region, as well as for the safeguarding of their interests and the development of their economic and cultural relations.

The proposal was rejected on the ground that as a definition it was too narrow; it placed more emphasis on geography than some national delegates could accept.

In fact, it was understood, at least by some of the delegates at San Francisco, that limited organizations in operation at the time or in the process of being formed would certainly qualify under the Charter; these included the Organization of American States, the League of Arab States, and probably the British Commonwealth of Nations.[9] These organizations were not, however, given individual approval. Referring in Article 53 to "regional arrangements directed against renewal of aggressive policy on the part of any such [enemy]

---

[9] L. M. Goodrich and E. Hambro, *Charter of the United Nations, Commentary and Documents*, rev. ed., Boston, 1949, pp. 311–312.

state," the Charter was also understood to sanction a number of bilateral alliances then in effect against any new acts of aggression by Germany or Japan. Included among such alliances were those of Russia and the United Kingdom (1942), Russia and Czechoslovakia (1943), Russia and France (1944), and Russia and China (1945). In addition to these regional arrangements others might be formed, but there was no standard set up whereby an organization proposed in the future could be accurately classified as regional or not. Since the war, the classification of "regional arrangement" has been claimed by the western European states in their movement for union, and by the supporters of the North Atlantic Pact, as has already been stated. The term has also been applied to Russia and the "satellites" in eastern Europe and in the Far East.

In 1950, the status of the Arab League was raised in the Legal Committee of the General Assembly. At that time it was decided to extend an invitation to the Secretary-General of the Arab League to attend future sessions of the Assembly as an observer, as in 1948 the Organization of American States had been given the same privilege. The delegate from Israel voted against the proposal on the ground that to extend the invitation would imply that the Arab League is a regional organization under the Charter, comparable to the Organization of American States. He maintained that the League is not a regional arrangement in the proper sense but rather an "ethnical" organization. Although the decision to extend the invitation has been regarded by some as a recognition of the regional character of the organization, by others it has not been so regarded.

Much controversy has been waged over the issue of whether or not the North Atlantic Treaty is a "regional arrangement" under the Charter. This question will be discussed later in this chapter.

The Organization of American States

The movement for organized Pan-Americanism was launched in 1826 at the Panama Conference, called by Simón Bolívar. For more than half a century thereafter the movement was under Latin-American leadership and was largely confined to the Latin-American states of this hemisphere. In 1889, leadership passed to the United

States, which at that time convened a conference of the American
states in Washington; this was the first "Pan American Conference"
as we now understand that term. Since 1889, a permanent organization has existed and Inter-American coöperation has been carried
into many fields of interest; the organization is the most active and
highly organized system of regional coöperation now at work.

Until 1948, the Inter-American system had no formal constitutional basis and its organization was carried on by resolutions from
conference to conference. An attempt was made in 1928 to supply
such a basis when a treaty of organization was framed at Havana,
but at the same conference a resolution was also adopted continuing
the whole organization in its then existing form; because the resolution seemed adequate, the treaty was never ratified and therefore
never went into effect. At the Ninth International Conference of
American States held at Bogotá, Colombia, in 1948, a "Charter of
Organization" was negotiated and given the form of a treaty. Although, like all treaties, this Charter required ratification, it was
given immediate effect by a resolution of the conference, a most
unusual procedure in international relations.

An affirmation of the regional character of the Organization of
American States and of its compatibility with the United Nations is
made in Article 1 of its Charter: "Within the United Nations, the
Organization of the American States is a regional agency."[10] The preamble makes statements in which the nature of the interests that are
presumed to hold the region together and justify collective action is
to some extent clarified. First mentioned is the "historic mission of
America to offer man a land of liberty, and a favorable environment
for the development of his personality and the realization of his just
aspirations"; this is an announcement of ideological unity and is no
doubt intended to set the American republics off against the tyrannical systems which in late decades have infested Europe. References to "American solidarity," to "good neighborliness," and to the

---

[10] Article 102 of the Charter makes a specific statement of the compatibility of
the Organization of American States and the United Nations in the assertion that
"None of the provisions of this Charter shall be construed as impairing the rights
and obligations of the member states under the charter of the United Nations."

need for "intensive continental coöperation" are all in accord with the ideals and aspirations of regionalism.

Membership in the Organization of American States is limited to "all American states that ratify the present Charter," as Article 2 expresses it. This limitation of membership on a geographical basis was, of course, a continuation of the practice of the past. There have been suggestions that Canada should become a member, and Article 2 would appear to make that possible, but as an active member of the British Commonwealth of Nations, it is not probable that she will do so. For a long time the Organization has included twenty-one American republics, and so it is likely to remain.

In its major outlines the organization of the Inter-American system under its Charter is much the same as before 1948, when it rested solely on resolutions. There have been some slight changes in nomenclature and in details, but these do not materially affect the organization or its operation in practice. Because its functions are much the same as those of the United Nations, so, too, is the general framework of its organs and agencies. Founded and operated by sovereign states, like the United Nations, the Inter-American Organization is also without powers of control over states; it makes coöperation possible and convenient but beyond that point it does not go.

The organs of Inter-American coöperation listed by the Charter are as follows:

1. The Inter-American Conference
2. The Meeting of Consultation of Ministers of Foreign Affairs
3. The Council
4. The Pan American Union
5. The Specialized Conference
6. The Specialized Organizations

The supreme organ, according to Article 33, is the Inter-American Conference, which normally meets once every five years and "decides the general action and policy of the organization." Each of the twenty-one republics is entitled to be represented at the conferences, and each has the right to one vote. Like most international deliberative bodies, the conference's work is put out in two forms: (1)

treaties requiring ratification and (2) resolutions, frequently recommending some kind of national action.

The Meeting of Consultation of Ministers of Foreign Affairs is to deal with "problems of an urgent nature and of common interest to the American States." If one of the foreign ministers is, for some reason, unable to attend a meeting, he may appoint a special delegate to serve in his place.

The Council is composed of one delegate from each member state of the Organization especially appointed for the purpose and holding the rank of ambassador. It is in substance the same agency formerly called the "Governing Body." Chief among its duties are the following: (1) to draft proposals for the creation of new specialized organizations for submission to the Inter-American Conference; (2) to formulate the program and regulations of the Inter-American Conference; (3) to make agreements with the specialized organizations for the purpose of determining their relationship to the Inter-American system as a whole; (4) to promote coöperation between the Organization of American States and the United Nations; and (5) to perform other duties mainly of a minor character assigned to it by the Charter.

The Pan American Union is the permanent organ of the Organization of American States. It is in the nature of a general secretariat and as such it performs many of the duties which are under the control of the Secretariat of the United Nations. At the head of the Pan American Union is the Secretary-General, selected by the Council for a ten-year term.

The specialized conferences and agencies deal with technical matters or special aspects of Inter-American coöperation when so decided by the Inter-American Conference, the Meeting of Consultation of Ministers of Foreign Affairs, or the Council. Among the specialized agencies there are at present the Inter-American Institute of Agricultural Sciences, the American International Institute for the Protection of Childhood, the Pan-American Institute of Geography and History, and others which perhaps are less well known.

The activities performed in the Organization of American States range into all of the principal types of functions carried on by international organization—diplomacy, administration, the settlement of disputes, and the prevention of aggression. The diplomatic function operates in the various conferences held from time to time; it will be discussed in a later chapter. Although the administrative activities are centered in the Pan American Union, they are also undertaken by a few other agencies. The work of dealing with disputes is taken care of by several agencies, of which only the Council among the six permanent parts of the Organization mentioned in Article 32 of the Charter is included. The Meeting of Consultation of the Ministers of Foreign Affairs has most of the responsibility for action against aggressors.

The peaceful settlement of international disputes has long been one of the main interests of the Organization of American States, and treaties have been promoted for inquiry, conciliation, and arbitration. All of the major conferences since 1933 have had the subject on their agendas. The Charter of 1948 lays down the general principle that "All international disputes that may arise between American States shall be submitted to the peaceful procedures set forth in this Charter, before being referred to the Security Council of the United Nations." It then goes on to name "direct negotiations, good offices, mediation, investigation and conciliation, judicial settlement and arbitration" as peaceful procedures. The detailed procedures of peaceful settlement are left by the Charter to a special treaty.

The special treaty governing peaceful settlement, like the Charter itself, was concluded at Bogotá in 1946; it is known as the Pact of Bogotá. Only three types of disputes are excluded from the procedures set up: (1) those within the domestic jurisdiction of one of the parties;[11] (2) those already settled by arrangement between the parties, by arbitral award, by an international court, or covered by treaties in force at the time of the conclusion of the Pact of Bogotá; and (3) those involving questions of diplomatic protection. The Pact makes provision for good offices and mediation in disputes, to be undertaken by a third state or by a citizen of a third state.[12] In the event that these efforts at a settlement fail, the disputants agree to have recourse to some other procedure named in the Pact.

[11] These disputes may at the request of any of the parties be referred to the International Court of Justice.

[12] The provision allowing citizens of third states to act is an innovation originally placed in the Buenos Aires Treaty of Good Offices and Mediation (1936).

Among the other procedures described by the Pact of Bogotá are investigation and conciliation. The Council of the Organization of American States is authorized to assist disputants in setting up commissions to perform the duties of investigation and conciliation. Should conciliation fail, either party may refer the dispute to the International Court of Justice, except that on agreement of both parties it may instead be arbitrated.

In disputes of a juridical nature the signatories to the Pact of Bogotá recognize the jurisdiction of the International Court of Justice as compulsory. By agreement of the parties, however, such disputes may instead be referred to arbitration. In fact arbitration is, on agreement of the parties, always a substitute for any of the procedures of the Pact. If one of the parties fails to carry into effect a judicial decision or an arbitral award, the other party may request a Meeting of Consultation of the Ministers of Foreign Affairs to agree upon measures of enforcement before appealing to the Security Council of the United Nations.

Several disputes have recently been treated by the Organization of American States: Costa Rica vs. Nicaragua (1948); Haiti vs. the Dominican Republic (1949); and the Caribbean conspiracies (1950). All involved charges of negligence in failing to prevent revolutionary conspiracies directed at neighboring governments. In every case the Council, acting as the organ of consultation, appointed a commission of inquiry to find the facts. On the basis of the reports of the commissions the Council found negligence of some type or degree in each case and recommended adjustments.

The prevention of aggression against the American states is handled in the Inter-American Defense Treaty of 1947, concluded at Rio de Janeiro. By the Treaty all of the American republics agree to assist any state in meeting an attack upon it. The Charter of 1948 makes it the duty of the Meeting of Consultation of Foreign Ministers to meet "without delay" to deal with the matter. It has the assistance of an Advisory Defense Committee which corresponds to the Military Staff Committee of the United Nations.[13]

---

[13] For current information on the activities of the Organization of American States and other regional organizations, see the issues of *International Organization,* published by the World Peace Foundation.

The Integration of Western Europe

The movement for European integration is an old one. At the opening of the fourteenth century the poet Dante, in his *De Monarchia*, advocated in vain a supreme ruler for all Christendom. Many other plans were propounded during succeeding centuries—among them *Eternal Peace* (1795) by Immanuel Kant, and "A Plan Towards the Present and Future Peace of Europe by the Establishment of a European Diet, Parliament or Estates" (1694) by William Penn. These, and all others like them, were doomed to failure because they lacked the support of governments and people alike. They were regarded as the visions of dreamers, hardly worth the attention of realists. The cynicism of a contemporary of Kant who said that the title of the philosopher's project reminded him of inscriptions found on tombstones suggested a view often held both then and now—that peace is not a part of this existence.

In 1930, the movement for European integration for the first time had government support when M. Briand, Foreign Minister of France, proposed a "United States of Europe." His plan stressed political union over economic union and was no doubt based in part on the French fear of aggression from Germany. The governments of Europe took it under consideration and submitted replies disclosing a wide interest in the project, but also an extreme caution which insisted upon qualifications and reservations. Some apprehension was expressed lest the proposed organization undermine the League of Nations. Study of the project continued for several years but achieved no lasting results.

In recent years the movement for the unity of Europe, or, to be more precise, western Europe, has become a down-to-earth program of hard-headed statesmen, men of the stamp of Winston Churchill. What is more, an impressive beginning has already been made in the actual establishment of western European organization. No one has been so sanguine as to expect that the communist part of Europe will become a part of this structure.

The beginning in western European unity dates from September, 1944, when Belgium, The Netherlands, and Luxembourg created a customs union known as "Benelux," a name formed out of the first letters of the names of those three countries. In June, 1948, this project was enlarged, with complete economic union its goal. Under the pressure of economic distress, France and Italy made a somewhat similar move in 1948 by an agreement to set up a customs union. The Scandinavian countries have discussed a similar union, but to date no agreement has been reached.

The economic side of the movement for western European integration was carried further by the organization set up under the Marshall Plan, which itself was the outgrowth of a speech made by Secretary of State Marshall at Harvard University on June 5, 1947. To promote European economic coöperation, the OEEC (Organization for European Economic Cooperation) was established, with representatives from all sixteen of the Marshall Plan countries participating. The principal objectives of the OEEC were to remove barriers to trade among the sixteen nations, to promote economic and financial stability, and to hasten by all possible measures the recovery of the nations of western Europe, so that American aid in balancing their trade accounts would become less and less needed. Like the OEEC, the so-called Schuman Plan, as adopted in 1951, will tend to knit western Europe closer together. By this arrangement the coal and steel resources of the principal nations of the area will be pooled and placed under international authority.

Although these economic measures are piecemeal and fall far short of complete economic union, they are indicative of strong forces at work. The admission must be made, however, that neither the OEEC nor the Schuman Plan has had clear sailing. The United States has expressed regret that under the former the nations of western Europe have not accomplished more in eliminating obstacles to trade. The Schuman Plan has not had the coöperation from the British which had been anticipated.

On the military side, the nucleus for western European unity was the Brussels Five-Power Pact of 1948; this agreement set up among the three Benelux countries, together with France and Great Britain, a fifty-year mutual defense system. In 1949 this alliance was expanded in the North Atlantic Treaty to include, in addition to the signatories of the Brussels Pact, Iceland, Denmark, Norway, Portugal, Italy, and three non-European countries—the United States, Canada, and Iceland. Concluded for a period of twenty years, this

Treaty stipulated that "An armed attack against one or more of them in Europe or North America shall be considered as an attack against them all," and each signatory agreed either "individually or in concert with the other parties" to take "such action as it deems necessary, including the use of armed force, to restore and maintain the security of the North Atlantic Area." The stimulus behind the nations in the formation of this Pact was the danger of Russian aggression. That the Pact has played an important role in the movement for western European integration is clear. Including as it does non-European states, it also supports a union movement of a broader nature and at least suggests the possibility of a North Atlantic region.

The movement toward western European integration has also made substantial progress in the political field. The Council of Europe, whose Statute was signed on May 5, 1949, is ample evidence of this fact.[14] The original signatories numbered ten, all western European nations, and other nations might be invited to join; western Germany has since become a member. The provision for "associate membership" is one of the novel features of the organization, and whereas an associate member may take part in the Consultative Assembly, it may not take part in the Committee of Ministers. Any member may withdraw on simple notification to the Secretary-General of its intention to do so.

The seat of the Council of Europe is at Strasbourg, Germany. Its principal organs are (1) the Committee of Ministers, and (2) the Consultative Assembly; both are assisted by a Secretariat. The former is ordinarily composed of the ministers of foreign affairs of the member states; but a substitute may be appointed in place of a foreign minister, and when this is done it is expected that he will be a member of the government. This Committee of Ministers, either on its own initiative or at the suggestion of the Consultative Assembly, may "consider the action required to further the aim of the Council of Europe, including the conclusion of conventions or agreements and the adoption by Governments of a common policy with regard to particular matters." When the effort is to promote a common policy, the Committee's action may take the form of a recom-

---

[14] See G. L. Powell, "The Council of Europe," *International Law Quarterly*, vol. 3, no. 2, pp. 164–196.

mendation to the member governments, and it may request that the members keep it informed of whatever effect may be given to the suggestion. Resolutions relating to important matters must be adopted by unanimous vote of the Committee, although other resolutions may be adopted by two-thirds vote and procedural questions may be disposed of by a simple majority.

The Consultative Assembly is referred to as the "deliberative organ of the Council of Europe." The principal job of the Assembly is to "debate matters within its competence" and "present the conclusions, in the form of recommendations, to the Committee of Ministers." In its discussions it confines itself to matters referred to it by the Committee or approved by that body. As fixed by the Statute of the Council of Europe, the composition of the Consultative Assembly is as follows: Belgium, 6; Denmark, 4; France, 18; the Irish Republic, 4; Italy, 18; Luxembourg, 3; The Netherlands, 6; Norway, 4; Sweden, 6; and the United Kingdom, 18. Whereas the doctrine of equality is admitted in the structure of the Committee of Ministers, it is completely repudiated in the Assembly.

On August 18, 1950, the Consultative Assembly of the Council of Europe adopted by an overwhelming majority a series of resolutions for the purpose of strengthening the organization. They provided as follows:

1. A request that each member state appoint a special minister to handle affairs relating to the Council of Europe;
2. Modification of the present veto power in the Committee of Ministers by allowing a minister to approve a project on general principles without being obliged to apply it in his own country;
3. A provision for Assembly resolutions for the consideration of the parliaments of the member states;
4. Election of all members of the Consultative Assembly by national parliaments (some members were already using that method of selection);
5. A closer relationship between the Council of Europe and other intergovernmental organizations, such as the Brussels Pact Secretariat and the Marshall Plan Organization for European Economic Cooperation;
6. A closer relationship between the Council of Europe and the "North American nations" (the United States and Canada).

Despite the innovations adopted by the Consultative Assembly in 1950, the Council of Europe is still limited in its activities to cooperation and coördination. No coercive authority over members is provided, and where programs of action are agreed upon, each government, under rule 2 above, is as free as ever to apply or not to apply them at home. This lack of power has been a source of disappointment to exponents of closer European unity such as Mr. Winston Churchill.

This drawing together of the states of western Europe, and their association on some points with the United States, is a striking new tendency within the realm of limited international organization that is commonly referred to as regionalism. Adding up the coöperation in military, economic, and political matters arranged by the different agreements, the sum total is astounding. The precise groups of states participating in the separate ventures are not identical, it is true, but within the three groups is a common nucleus, as can be seen in the following lists:

OEEC	North Atlantic Treaty	Council of Europe
France	France	France
Great Britain	Great Britain	Great Britain
Belgium	Belgium	Belgium
Netherlands	Netherlands	Netherlands
Luxembourg	Luxembourg	Luxembourg
Denmark	Denmark	Denmark
Norway	Norway	Norway
Italy	Italy	Italy
Sweden		Sweden
Portugal	Portugal	
Iceland	Iceland	
Ireland		Ireland
Switzerland	United States	Western Germany
Austria	Canada	
Greece		
Turkey		

The future of the movement is of course uncertain, but it is already a momentous factor in world affairs. It is evidence of the power of a common fear to bind nations together. The motives and pressures behind the development of international organizations are many and diverse.

The North Atlantic Area

The point has already been made that the North Atlantic Pact, while supporting western European integration, involves several non-European states as well—the United States, Canada, and Iceland. To implement the Pact, a number of agencies were set up, most important of which is the North Atlantic Council, composed of the foreign ministers of the coöperating countries. A Defense Committee, made up of the chiefs of staff of the coöperating countries, was also created; this Committee has been in session and has agreed upon measures of common defense. Within the Defense Committee is a "Steering Group," made up of chiefs of staff of the United States, Great Britain, and France. Evidence of the high degree of unity in military matters which has come out of the North Atlantic Pact is provided by the agreement of the North Atlantic Council in 1950 to set up a system of "balanced collective defense," as Secretary of State Acheson has referred to it. Under this system each of the coöperating governments is expected to contribute toward the common defense in whatever way it is best qualified to do so without maintaining a balanced national defense system of its own. This would substitute international for national planning in matters of defense, and it was not surprising that fears were expressed that the plan would impinge upon the sovereignty of the members. Certainly, as a permanent arrangement, this project gives the North Atlantic Pact great practical significance in the realm of world politics.

Is the North Atlantic Pact a "regional arrangement" within the meaning of Article 52 of the Charter? Secretary of State Acheson, arguing for the North Atlantic Pact in a speech given on March 18, 1949, several times referred to a "North Atlantic community" and to a "North Atlantic area." The following statements are taken from his address:

It is important to keep in mind that the really successful national and international institutions are those that recognize and express underlying realities. The North Atlantic community of nations is such a reality. It is based on the affinity and natural identity of interests of the North Atlantic powers.

The North Atlantic Treaty, which now formally unites them, is the product of at least three hundred and fifty years of history, perhaps more. There developed on our Atlantic coast a community, which has spread across the continent, connected with Western Europe by common institutions and moral and ethical beliefs. Similarities of this kind are not superficial, but fundamental. They are the strongest kind of ties, because they are based on moral conviction, on acceptance of the same values in life.

The very basis of western civilization, which we share with the other nations bordering the North Atlantic, and which all of us share with many other nations, is the ingrained spirit of restraint and tolerance. This is the opposite of the Communist belief that coercion by force is a proper method of hastening the inevitable. Western civilization has lived by mutual restraint and tolerance. This civilization permits and stimulates free inquiry and bold experimentation. It creates the environment of freedom, from which flows the greatest amount of ingenuity, enterprise, and accomplishment.

These principles of democracy, individual liberty, and the rule of law have flourished in this Atlantic community. . . .[15]

In a speech against the Treaty, Mr. Gromyko of the USSR advanced the following argument: "The character and text of the Pact show that this is not a regional arrangement of the kind permissible under the United Nations Charter. It comprises states located in two different continents. Its signatories have not set themselves the task of settling any regional questions. Members of even a truly regional arrangement made in accordance with the Charter have no right to take military action without an authorization from the Security Council. . . ."[16] M. Mayer of France retorted, "The Charter does not provide for any construction to be placed upon the word 'regional.' "[17] For the first time the definition of the word "regional" had become a matter of great importance from a practical, if not from a legal, point of view.

Sir W. Eric Beckett, Legal Adviser to the British Foreign Office, has taken the attitude that the North Atlantic Treaty is not in the proper sense a regional arrangement. His contention is (1) that collective self-defense, the principal purpose of the Treaty, is not men-

---

[15] *Department of State Bulletin*, vol. 20, no. 508 (1949), p. 385.

[16] The text of the speech may be found in "The North Atlantic Treaty," *United Nations Bulletin*, vol. 6, no. 9 (1949), p. 410.

[17] Ibid., p. 414.

tioned in the provisions of the Charter which deal with regional arrangements, and (2) that in a genuine regional arrangement, enforcement action may be applied "in case of a conflict between any two or more members of this union."[18] He does not pass judgment upon whether or not the area covered by the Treaty is in any sense a region.

In a recent issue of the *American Journal of International Law,* Professor Hans Kelsen has taken issue with Sir W. Eric Beckett.[19] Admitting that "the Charter allows contradictory interpretations," he takes the point of view that "the most plausible," although "not the only possible interpretation" of Chapter 8 of the Charter is that the North Atlantic Treaty is a regional arrangement within the provisions of that document. Enforcement action in the nature of collective self-defense he believes to be possible in a regional arrangement. Analyzing carefully the articles of the Charter, Professor Kelsen also contends that in a regional arrangement there is no requirement that enforcement action be applicable against a member committing aggression. He does not deal with the nature of a region from a geographic point of view except to say that ". . . it is not required that the parties to the regional agreement be geographically neighbors."

The admission must be made that the characteristics of a regional arrangement within the provisions of the Charter of the United Nations cannot be stated with finality. Had the collective security system of the United Nations taken shape as intended in the Charter and proved itself workable, the North Atlantic Treaty, in all probability, would never have been concluded. In other words, the present need for a definition is the result of a condition not foreseeable when the Charter was written.

A project has been formulated for a closer and more comprehensive union among the twelve signatories of the Treaty. There is an assumption in the proposal that there is indeed a North Atlantic community, one of sufficient vitality to furnish the basis for a federal union.

---

[18] Sir W. Eric Beckett, *The North Atlantic Treaty, the Brussels Treaty, and the Charter of the United Nations,* London, 1950, p. 34.

[19] Hans Kelsen, "Is the North Atlantic Treaty a Regional Arrangement?" *American Journal of International Law,* vol. 45 (1951), pp. 162–166.

A resolution was introduced in the United States Senate in 1950 requesting the President to invite the signatories to the North Atlantic Treaty to a convention at which the project for federal union of the Atlantic states might be taken up.[20] In spite of Secretary Acheson's statement that an Atlantic community exists, the Department of State did not see fit to support the resolution. The proposal was not favorably recommended to the Senate by the Foreign Relations Committee. Nevertheless, a private organization under the leadership of Mr. Clarence Streit has continued to advocate a federal union of the North Atlantic nations.

Whether the twelve states party to the North Atlantic Pact do in fact constitute a region which might properly be organized into a federal union is a moot question. Mr. Gromyko's contention that the twelve states do not even constitute a region within the meaning of that term as it is used in the Charter has already been quoted. In any case, there is no present evidence that a federal union will be formed in the near future.

The Arab League

Another regional organization is the Arab League, organized in 1945. The area of the organization takes in parts of North Africa and the Near East, with a total population of approximately forty million people. The member states include Egypt, Syria, Lebanon, Trans-Jordan, Iraq, Saudi Arabia, and Yemen. While the program of the organization envisages educational and economic development, there is no doubt that the principal cementing force of the organization, at the outset at least, was the Palestine question; by 1945 it was clear that the future status of Palestine would be a perplexing postwar problem. England had had difficulties as mandatory for the territory, and it was doubtful that she would continue in that role. The refugees from Europe seeking a home in Palestine also posed acute problems. It was clear too that Arab opposition to the establishment of a new state in Palestine would be stronger if based upon unity.

The formal organization of the Arab League consists of a Council, six committees, and a General Secretariat. It is a coöperative organi-

---

[20] See Chapter XVIII.

zation pure and simple, lacking actual authority over its members. Within its constitutional framework is a significant provision for common action against aggression.

The Arab League faced a severe test when its war with the Jews began. With the Arab defeat in that war, the League and its organization seemed near the point of dissolving. This appeared all the more possible with the development of critical differences among its members and with Iraq and Syria drawing closer together in their policies to the exclusion of other members. In 1949, a conference was held at Cairo at which the future of the League was discussed. The decision was made to attempt to restore the organization to its former position.

The British Commonwealth of Nations

Although there is no official declaration to the effect that the British Commonwealth of Nations is a "regional organization," the defeat of the Egyptian proposal to define the term was accomplished, in part at least, in order that no question might be raised as to the compatibility of the Commonwealth with the United Nations. The fact that its members, the British Dominions, are scattered about as widely as could be possible makes it a very dubious "region" in any geographic sense; but then, although some of the signatories of the North Atlantic Pact are separated by the Atlantic Ocean, they have claimed their organization to be regional. In any case, the Commonwealth is a limited international organization, and it bears much the same relationship to the United Nations as does the Organization of American States.

The Dominions which, with the United Kingdom, make up the Commonwealth are Canada, Australia, New Zealand, the Union of South Africa, Eire, India, Pakistan, and Ceylon.[21] Dominion status, a matter of slow evolution during the late nineteenth and early twentieth centuries, carries with it full independence. As the Balfour Report of the Imperial Conference of 1926 asserted, the United King-

---

[21] Eire is regarded by the British as a member of the Commonwealth but, under an Irish law passed in 1936 it claims to be in "external relation" with the organization.

dom and the Dominions are "autonomous communities within the British Empire, equal in status, in no way subordinate one to another in any aspect of their domestic or external affairs, though united by a common allegiance to the Crown, and freely associated as members of the British Commonwealth of Nations."[22]

Like the Organization of the American States, the Commonwealth is a means of coöperation. Its members meet in common and agree to common action; there is no authority to compel or coerce. The organization of the Commonwealth, which has been kept at a minimum, is therefore adapted to consultation. By all odds, the most important part of the organization is the Conference of the Prime Ministers, once called the "Imperial Conference," which meets, as a rule, every four years. It adopts resolutions, but those resolutions can have no legal effect until they are later accepted by the individual governments. For the most part, the rest of the organization of the Commonwealth is *ad hoc*, as, for example, the Imperial War Graves Commission. The organization has no written constitution and no executive. Proposals have been made for a permanent secretariat, but none has been established.

The Status of the Alignment of Russia and Her Satellites

The question has been raised as to whether the treaties of alliance among the nations constituting the Soviet bloc are in the nature of regional agreements. In that they are between neighboring states assumed to have common interests, they would appear to qualify. In one respect, however, they are different from other so-called regional arrangements; the element of compulsion by Russia is so clear that the grouping of the states parties to the treaties is basically different from those organizations which are usually looked upon as regional, such as the Organization of American States and the League of Arab States. It does not appear to be a voluntary association of states. The element of compulsion amounts in fact to Russian domination of a type characteristic of imperialism. Russia with her "satellites"

---

[22] There is no longer common allegiance to the crown; India and Eire have both broken that relationship.

forms a unit which is more in the nature of a communist empire than a regional organization of the type envisaged in the Charter of the United Nations.

Regional Commissions

Operating on a more modest basis than the regional organizations already examined in this chapter are a number of regional commissions, three of which are subsidiary bodies to the Economic and Social Council of the United Nations. Two of the three were set up by the Economic and Social Council on March 28, 1947—the Economic Commission for Europe (ECE), and the Economic Commission for Asia and the Far East (ECAFE). Both have been concerned primarily with problems of reconstruction in their respective areas.

The ECE is composed of European members of the United Nations. It has maintained a group of committees to assist it in its work: Industry and Materials Committee, Manpower Committee, Steel Committee, Timber Committee, Electric Power Committee, Inland Transport Committee, Coal Committee, and an *ad hoc* Committee on Agricultural Problems. In a number of ways the ECE has tried to improve Europe's economy. For instance, early in 1948 its Inland Transport Committee drafted an agreement supported by a number of European countries for a resumption of the prewar practice of exchanging railway cars in international traffic. This same committee has also helped to facilitate, in coöperation with the Food and Agriculture Organization, the movement in trade of perishable goods.[23] The path of the ECE, despite these and other accomplishments, has not always been smooth, for like many international organs it has been in the way of the East-West controversy. Charges have been made in the Economic and Social Council by representatives of communist nations that its work has been hampered by the policies of the United States, particularly by the Marshall Plan.[24] That the ECE has constructive achievements to its credit is, however, indisputable; and it would be the claim of the United States that the

---

[23] For the activities of the ECE and other regional commissions see current issues of *International Organization*.

[24] See "Economic and Social Council Achievements," *United Nations Bulletin*, vol. 6, no. 7 (1949), pp. 304–305.

Marshall Plan and the ECE have been complementary, rather than conflicting.

The ECAFE is made up of representatives of Australia, Burma, China, France, India, The Netherlands, New Zealand, Pakistan, the Philippine Republic, Siam, the United States, Russia, and the United Kingdom. Any other state in the area, on becoming a member of the United Nations, may become a member of the Commission. Food supplies, agricultural equipment, industrial development, trade, and flood control have been prominent among the subjects taken up by the organization. Coöperation with the FAO has been undertaken by the ECAFE, as by the ECE. The future status of both bodies will be considered by the Economic and Social Council in 1952, for both have been regarded primarily as postwar agencies devoted to reconstruction work.

The Economic Commission for Latin America (ECLA) was created in 1948 to deal with economic problems arising out of the war and to stimulate economic activities within the Latin-American countries; after it had operated for three years, its future was to be taken up. At the opening meeting of the ECLA on May 29, 1949, Secretary-General Lie asserted that "Powerful influences can be mobilized by the smaller and medium-sized countries in the United Nations for economic and social progress," adding a little later that "One of the most important ways this can be done is through regional coöperation within the framework of the United Nations."[25]

For some time a project has been pending for the establishment of an Economic Commission for the Middle East. An *ad hoc* committee set up by the Economic and Social Council in 1948 to examine the need for such a commission recommended that one be created. This recommendation has been on the agenda of the Economic and Social Council several times, but to date an Economic Commission for the Middle East has not been established. To an extent, the need for such an agency is being met by the Economic Committee of the Arab League. The International Islamic Economic Organization, which held its first session in 1949, covers an even wider area and its

[25] "Opening the Havana Session," *United Nations Bulletin,* vol. 6, no. 12 (1949), p. 616.

activities have diminished the pressure for a United Nations economic commission. The need for an improvement of the economy of the Middle East was brought out by a survey of the economic conditions of the area by the Secretariat, recently reported to the Economic and Social Council.[26]

Two other regional commissions have been playing important roles in international affairs: the Caribbean Commission and the South Pacific Commission. Both are consultative in nature. They are described in Chapter XIII of this volume.

▲

APPENDIX TO CHAPTER IV

I

*Charter of the Organization of American States (1948)**

ARTICLE 1

The American States established by this Charter the international organization that they have developed to achieve an order of peace and justice, to promote their solidarity, to strengthen their collaboration, and to defend their sovereignty, their territorial integrity and their independence. Within the United Nations, the Organization of American States is a regional agency.

ARTICLE 2

All American States that ratify the present Charter are Members of the Organization.

ARTICLE 3

Any new political entity that arises from the union of several Member States and that, as such, ratifies the present Charter, shall become a Member of the Organization. The entry of the new politi-

---

[26] "Middle East Economy Surveyed," *ibid.*, vol. 10, no. 6 (1951), pp. 276–281.
* *Department of State Bulletin,* 1948, vol. 28, no. 464, pp. 465–473.

cal entity into the Organization shall result in the loss of membership of each one of the States which constitute it.

ARTICLE 4

The Organization of American States, in order to put into practice the principles on which it is founded and to fulfill its regional obligations under the Charter of the United Nations, proclaims the following essential purposes:

a. To strengthen the peace and security of the continent;

b. To prevent possible causes of difficulties and to ensure the pacific settlement of disputes that may arise among the Member States;

c. To provide for common action on the part of those States in the event of aggression;

d. To seek the solution of political, juridical and economic problems that may arise among them; and

e. To promote by coöperative action their economic, social and cultural development.

.   .   .   .   .

IV. Pacific Settlement of Disputes
ARTICLE 20

All international disputes that may arise between American States shall be submitted to the peaceful procedures set forth in this Charter, before being referred to the Security Council of the United Nations.

ARTICLE 21

The following are peaceful procedures: direct negotiation, good offices, mediation, investigation and conciliation, judicial settlement, arbitration, and those which the parties to the dispute may especially agree upon at any time.

ARTICLE 22

In the event that a dispute arises between two or more American States which, in the opinion of one of them, cannot be settled through the usual diplomatic channels, the Parties shall agree on some other peaceful procedure that will enable them to reach a solution.

ARTICLE 23

A special treaty will establish adequate procedures for the pacific settlement of disputes and will determine the appropriate means for their application, so that no dispute between American States shall fail of definitive settlement within a reasonable period.

V. Collective Security
ARTICLE 24

Every act of aggression by a State against the territorial integrity or inviolability of the territory or against the sovereignty or political independence of an American State shall be considered an act of aggression against the other American States.

ARTICLE 25

If the inviolability or the integrity of the territory or the sovereignty or political independence of any American State should be affected by an armed attack or by an act of aggression that is not an armed attack, or by an extra-continental conflict, or by a conflict between two or more American States, or by any other fact or situation that might endanger the peace of America, the American States, in furtherance of the principles of continental solidarity or collective self-defense, shall apply the measures and procedures established in the special treaties on the subject.

VI. Economic Standards
ARTICLE 26

The Member States agree to coöperate with one another, as far as their resources may permit and their laws may provide, in the broadest spirit of good neighborliness, in order to strengthen their economic structure, develop their agriculture and mining, promote their industry and increase their trade.

.   .   .   .   .   .

IX. The Organs
ARTICLE 32

The Organization of American States accomplishes its purposes by means of:

a. The Inter-American Conference;
b. The Meeting of Consultation of Ministers of Foreign Affairs;
c. The Council;
d. The Pan American Union;
e. The Specialized Conference; and
f. The Specialized Organizations.

X. The Inter-American Conference
ARTICLE 33

The Inter-American Conference is the supreme organ of the Organization of American States. It decides the general action and policy of the Organization and determines the structure and functions of its Organs, and has the authority to consider any matter relating to friendly relations among the American States. These functions shall be carried out in accordance with the provisions of this Charter and of other Inter-American treaties.

ARTICLE 34

All Member States have the right to be represented at the Inter-American Conference. Each State has the right to one vote.

ARTICLE 35

The Conference shall convene every five years at the time fixed by the Council of the Organization, after consultation with the government of the country where the Conference is to be held.

ARTICLE 36

In special circumstances and with the approval of two-thirds of the American Governments, a special Inter-American Conference may be held, or the date of the next regular Conference may be changed.

ARTICLE 37

Each Inter-American Conference shall designate the place of meeting of the next Conference. If for any unforeseen reason the Conference cannot be held at the place designated, the Council of the Organization shall designate a new place.

ARTICLE 38

The program and regulations of the Inter-American Conference shall be prepared by the Council of the Organization and submitted to the Member State for consideration.

XI. The Meeting of Consultation of Ministers of Foreign Affairs
ARTICLE 39

The Meeting of Consultation of Ministers of Foreign Affairs shall be held in order to consider problems of an urgent nature and of common interest to the American States, and to serve as the Organ of Consultation.

ARTICLE 40

Any Member State may request that a Meeting of Consultation be called. The request shall be addressed to the Council of the Organization, which shall decide by an absolute majority whether a meeting should be held.

ARTICLE 41

The program and regulations of the Meeting of Consultation shall be prepared by the Council of the Organization and submitted to the Member State for consideration.

ARTICLE 42

If a Minister of Foreign Affairs, for exceptional reasons, is unable to attend the Meeting, he shall be represented by a special delegate.

ARTICLE 43

In case of an armed attack within the territory of an American State or within the region of security delimited by treaties in force, a Meeting of Consultation shall be held without delay. Such Meeting shall be called immediately by the Chairman of the Council of the Organization, who shall at the same time call a meeting of the Council itself.

ARTICLE 44

An Advisory Defense Committee shall be established to advise the Organ of Consultation on problems of military coöperation that may arise in connection with the application of existing special treaties on collective security.

ARTICLE 45

The Advisory Defense Committee shall be composed of the highest military authorities of the American States participating in the Meeting of Consultation. Under exceptional circumstances the Governments may appoint substitutes. Each state shall be entitled to one vote.

ARTICLE 46

The Advisory Defense Committee shall be convoked under the same conditions as the Organ of Consultation, when the latter deals with matters relating to defense against aggression.

ARTICLE 47

The Committee shall also meet when the Conference or the Meeting of Consultation or the Governments, by a two-thirds majority of the Member States, assign to it technical studies or reports on specific subjects.

XII. The Council
ARTICLE 48

The Council of the Organization of American States is composed of one Representative for each Member State of the Organization, especially appointed by the respective Government, with the rank of Ambassador. The appointment may be given to the diplomatic representative accredited to the government of the country in which the

Council has its seat. During the absence of the titular Representative, the Government may appoint an interim Representative.

ARTICLE 49

The Council shall elect a Chairman and a Vice Chairman, who shall serve for one year and shall not be eligible for reelection to either of those positions for the term immediately following.

ARTICLE 50

The Council takes cognizance, within the limits of the present Charter and of inter-American treaties and agreements, of any matter referred to it by the Inter-American Conference or the Meeting of Consultation of Ministers of Foreign Affairs.

ARTICLE 51

The Council shall be responsible for the proper discharge by the Pan American Union of the duties assigned to it.

ARTICLE 52

The Council shall serve provisionally as the Organ of Consultation when the circumstances contemplated in Article 43 of this Charter arise.

ARTICLE 53

It is also the duty of the Council:

a. To draft and submit to the Governments and to the Inter-American Conference proposals for the creation of new Specialized Organizations or for the combination, adaptation or elimination of existing ones, including matters relating to the financing and support thereof;

b. To draft recommendations to the Governments, the Inter-American Conference, the Specialized Conferences or the Specialized Organizations, for the coordination of the activities and programs of such organizations, after consultation with them;

c. To conclude agreements with the Inter-American Specialized Organizations to determine the relations that shall exist between the respective agency and the Organization;

d. To conclude agreements or special arrangements for coöperation with other American organizations of recognized international standing;

e. To promote and facilitate collaboration between the Organization of American States and the United Nations, as well as between Inter-American Specialized Organizations and similar international agencies;

f. To adopt resolutions that will enable the Secretary General to perform the duties envisaged in Article 84.

g. To perform the other duties assigned to it by the present Charter.

ARTICLE 54

The Council shall establish the bases for fixing the quota that each Government is to contribute to the maintenance of the Pan American Union, taking into account the ability to pay of the respective countries and their determination to contribute in an equitable manner. The budget, after approval by the Council, shall be transmitted to the Governments at least six months before the first day of the fiscal year, with a statement of the annual quota of each country. Decisions on budgetary matters require the approval of two-thirds of the members of the Council.

ARTICLE 55

The Council shall formulate its own regulations.

ARTICLE 56

The Council shall function at the seat of the Pan American Union.

ARTICLE 57

The following are organs of the Council of the Organization of American States:

a. The Inter-American Economic and Social Council;

b. The Inter-American Council of Jurists; and

c. The Inter-American Cultural Council.

A. The Inter-American Economic and Social Council
ARTICLE 63

The Inter-American Economic and Social Council has for its principal purpose the promotion of the economic and social welfare of the American nations through effective coöperation for the better utilization of their natural resources, the development of their agriculture and industry and the raising of the standards of living of their peoples.

ARTICLE 64

To accomplish this purpose the Council shall:

a. Propose the means by which the American nations may give each other technical assistance in making studies and formulating and executing plans to carry out the purposes referred to in Article 26 and to develop and improve their social services;

b. Act as coördinating agency for all official inter-American activities of an economic and social nature;

.   .   .   .   .

B. The Inter-American Council of Jurists
ARTICLE 67

The purpose of the Inter-American Council of Jurists is to serve as an advisory body on juridical matters; to promote the development and codification of public and private international law; and to study the possibility of attaining uniformity in the legislation of the various American countries, insofar as it may appear desirable.

ARTICLE 68

The Inter-American Juridical Committee of Rio de Janeiro shall be the permanent committee of the Inter-American Council of Jurists.

ARTICLE 69

The Juridical Committee shall be composed of Jurists of the nine countries selected by the Inter-American Conference. The selection of the jurists shall be made by the Inter-American Council of Jurists from a panel submitted by each country chosen by the Conference. The members of the Juridical Committee represent all Member States of the Organization. The Council of the Organization is empowered to fill any vacancies that occur during the intervals between Inter-American Conferences and between meetings of the Inter-American Council of Jurists.

ARTICLE 70

The Juridical Committee shall undertake such studies and preparatory work as are assigned to it by the Inter-American Council of Jurists, the Inter-American Conference, the meeting of Consultation of Ministers of Foreign Affairs, or the Council of the Organization. It may also undertake those studies and projects which on its own initiative it considers advisable.

. . . . .

C. The Inter-American Cultural Council
ARTICLE 73

The purpose of the Inter-American Cultural Council is to promote friendly relations and mutual understanding among the American peoples, in order to strengthen the peaceful sentiments that have characterized the evolution of America, through the promotion of educational, scientific and cultural exchange.

. . . . .

XIII. The Pan American Union
ARTICLE 78

The Pan American Union is the central and permanent organ of the Organization of American States and the General Secretariat of the Organization. It shall perform the duties assigned to it in this Charter and such other duties as may be assigned to it in other Inter-American treaties and agreements.

ARTICLE 79

There shall be a Secretary General of the Organization, who shall be elected by the Council for a ten-year term and who may not be reelected or be succeeded by a person of the same nationality. In the event of a vacancy in the office of Secretary General, the Council shall, within the next ninety days, elect a successor to fill the office for the remainder of the term, who may be reelected if the vacancy occurs during the second half of the term.

ARTICLE 80

The Secretary General shall direct the Pan American Union and be the legal representative thereof.

ARTICLE 81

The Secretary General shall participate with voice, but without vote, in the deliberations of the Inter-American Conference, the Meeting of Consultation of Ministers of Foreign Affairs, the Specialized Conferences, and the Council and its organs.

ARTICLE 82

The Pan American Union, through its technical and information offices, shall, under the direction of the Council, promote economic, social, juridical and cultural relations among all the Member States of the Organization.

ARTICLE 83

The Pan American Union shall also perform the following functions:

a. Transmit *ex officio* to Member States the convocation to the Inter-American Conference, the Meeting of Consultation of Ministers of Foreign Affairs, and the Specialized Conferences;

b. Advise the Council and its organs in the preparation of programs and regulations of the Inter-American Conference, the Meeting of Consultation of Ministers of Foreign Affairs, and the Specialized Conferences;

c. Place, to the extent of its ability, at the disposal of the Government of the Country where a conference is to be held the technical aid and personnel which such government may request;

d. Serve as custodian of the documents and archives of the Inter-American Conferences, of the Meetings of Consultation of Ministers of Foreign Affairs and, insofar as possible, of the Specialized Conferences;

e. Serve as depository of the instruments of ratification of Inter-American agreements;

f. Perform the functions entrusted to it by the Inter-American Conference, and the Meeting of Consultation of Ministers of Foreign Affairs;

. . . . . .

XIV. The Specialized Conferences
ARTICLE 93

The Specialized Conferences shall meet to deal with special technical matters or to develop specific aspects of inter-American coöperation, when it is so decided by the Inter-American Conference or the Meeting of Consultation of Ministers of Foreign Affairs; when inter-American Agreements so provide; or when the Council of the Organization considers it necessary, either on its own initiative or at the request of one of its organs or of one of the Specialized Organizations.

ARTICLE 94

The program and regulations of the Specialized Conferences shall be prepared by the organs of the Council of the Organization or by the Specialized Organizations concerned; they shall be submitted to the Member Governments for consideration and transmitted to the Council for its information.

XV. The Specialized Organizations
ARTICLE 95

For the purposes of the present Charter, Inter-American Specialized Organizations are the inter-governmental organizations established by multilateral agreements and having specific functions with respect to technical matters of common interest to the American States.

ARTICLE 96

The Council shall, for the purposes stated in Article 53, maintain a register of the Organizations that fulfill the conditions set forth in the foregoing Article.

ARTICLE 97

The Specialized Organizations shall enjoy the fullest technical autonomy and shall take into account the recommendations of the Council, in conformity with the provisions of the present Charter.

ARTICLE 98

The Specialized Organizations shall submit to the Council periodic reports on the progress of their work and on their annual budgets and expenses.

ARTICLE 99

Agreements between the Council and the Specialized Organizations contemplated in paragraph c of Article 53 may provide that such organizations transmit their budgets to the Council for approval. Arrangements may also be made for the Pan American Union to receive the quotas of the contributing countries and distribute them in accordance with the said agreements.

ARTICLE 100

The Specialized Organizations shall establish coöperative relations with world agencies of the same character in order to coördinate their activities. In concluding agreements with international agencies of a world-wide character, the Inter-American Specialized Organizations shall preserve their identity and their status as integral parts of the Organization of American States, even when they perform regional functions of international agencies.

ARTICLE 101

In determining the geographic location of the Specialized Organizations the interests of all the American States shall be taken into account.

Chart of the Organization of American States

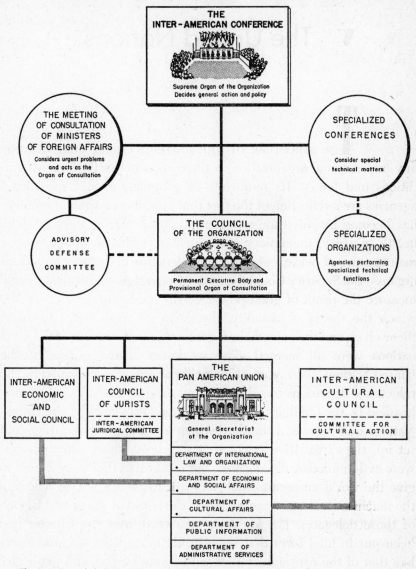

· The Directors of these Departments are the Executive Secretaries of the respective Councils.

The International Organization of the 21 American Republics established by the Charter signed at the Ninth International Conference of American States, Bogotá, Colombia, 1948. (From *A Decade of American Foreign Policy, Basic Documents, 1941–1949,* 81 Congress, 1 Session, Doc. No. 123, p. 446.)

V The United Nations

THE STRUCTURE OF THE UNITED NATIONS, LIKE THAT OF any international organization, is the composite result of many conditions and forces. Its multitude of commissions and specialized agencies are a reflection of the fact that almost every public problem has become by this time an international problem, whether it be health, poverty, unemployment, nutrition, traffic in opium, or the maintenance of peace and order. The structure of its more important organs—the Security Council and the General Assembly—is in large measure the result of great-power versus small-power dickering, by which the theory of equality, the desire of small states to assert themselves, and the overwhelming influence and strength of the great nations were all merged. The weakness of the organs of the United Nations, their most striking characteristic, is explained by the reluctance of nations to submit to any exterior authority, a position justified by the familiar term "sovereignty." If in any way the United Nations falls short of a standard which a self-appointed critic might set up, the explanation is not that the delegates at San Francisco were evil-minded or ill-informed, but rather that they were bound to give the world an organization for which it was fitted, to reflect in the machinery and processes created the world of states as it is. One of those delegates, Jan Masaryk, remarked after the Charter had been put in final form that his attitude toward the document was like that of the expectant father who wanted a boy and got a girl, "but that he loved it just the same."

To understand the United Nations one must understand that in the usual sense of the word it is not a "government," and that for the most part it is an instrument of coöperation; in its principal activities it is diplomacy grown up to maturity. What the United Nations is not was well brought out by Mr. Herbert V. Evatt, Australian delegate at San Francisco in 1945 and President of the third regular session of the General Assembly, in the following words: "We often speak of the United Nations as though it were responsible for every ill of an international character that exists in the world today, and also for the absence of freedom that exists in many parts of the world. The United Nations is not an executive body. It cannot legislate, it cannot say what is to be done. It cannot issue an order to governments or to parliaments. It has got to proceed upon that footing."[1]

The Organization of the United Nations[2]

The six "principal organs" of the United Nations are the General Assembly, the Security Council, the Economic and Social Council, the Trusteeship Council, the Secretariat, and the International Court of Justice. Together they are able to deal with all types of international problems—economic, social, undeveloped areas, disputes between nations, aggression, and breaches of the peace. The facilities which they offer can be used for conference, for the negotiation of programs of action, for the application of sanctions against an aggressor, for the settlement of international controversies, for research, for investigation, for publicity, and for purposes of international administration.

An overall view of the United Nations discloses that, in addition to the six principal agencies, there are many of a subsidiary nature. The Charter specifies in Article 7, paragraph 2, that "such subsidiary organs as may be found necessary may be established in accordance with the present Charter." The majority of the subsidiary organs thus far set up are those of the Economic and Social Council, which embrace a long list of "commissions" (the Commission on Human Rights, the Commission on Narcotic Drugs, the Economic and Employment Commission, the Statistical Commission, and many others)

---

[1] Spoken in an address in Paris. See *International Conciliation*, November, 1948, no. 445, "Three Years of the United Nations."

[2] See Appendix 1 to ths chapter for the Charter of the United Nations.

and in addition the "specialized agencies" (the International Labor Organization, the Food and Agriculture Organization, the International Bank, the International Fund, etc.).[3] The Security Council numbers among its subsidiary agencies the important Atomic Energy Commission and the Commission for Conventional Armaments; the Military Staff Committee, required by the Charter, is also responsible to the Security Council. The General Assembly, too, has its subordinate committees and commissions, among which the "Little Assembly," or Interim Committee as it is properly called, is particularly important; when the Interim Committee was created by the Assembly, Russia vehemently protested that it was not a "subsidiary organ," as the phrase is used in the Charter.

Comparison of the United Nations Organization with the League

A striking similarity it discernible in the organization and processes of the present United Nations and those of the old League of Nations, which for a period of two decades struggled with world problems. To be sure, there are plenty of differences of detail and a few in matters of importance; but both organizations have left the position of the sovereign state virtually undisturbed, both have relied on diplomacy and agreement to achieve their ends, and both have utilized much the same type of organs and agencies. Corresponding to the Security Council of the United Nations, there was the Council of the League, composed of permanent and nonpermanent members whose precise number fluctuated during the League's history; although the Council was originally expected to have eleven members, of whom five were to be permanent, in fact it varied from eight (1920–1922) to sixteen (for six months after September, 1934). The League also had its Assembly, composed of delegates from all of the member states, and a Secretariat, headed by a Secretary-General, to do much the same type of work now performed by the United Nations Secretariat. Analogous to the commissions and specialized agencies of the United Nations were the "technical organizations" of the League (Health Organization, Economic and Financial Organization, and Communication and Transit Organization) and the

---

[3] See Chapter XIV for a description of the commissions and specialized agencies.

"technical commissions" dealing with such matters as intellectual coöperation, mandates, armament, traffic in dangerous drugs, and so on; the International Labor Organization, like the old Permanent Court of International Justice, was a separate body but closely related organically to the League.

The principal differences between the League of Nations and the United Nations in matters of organization and procedure are as follows:

1. The organs of the League adhered more closely to the rule of unanimity in voting than do those of the United Nations. Unanimity in the League Council meant that every member had a veto, not just the great powers, as at present. Unanimity in the old Assembly, insofar as it was used, implied the availability of the veto to all members there, in contrast to the present General Assembly where there is none at all. These voting methods will be discussed in greater detail later in this chapter.

2. The present Economic and Social Council, with its many commissions and specialized agencies, represents an even more ambitious effort to deal with problems of peacetime coöperation than that put forth by the technical organizations and advisory committees of the League. The organization of the former is larger and its objectives are more inclusive than were those of the latter. Then, too, the present specialized agencies have an autonomous status not matched by the agencies of the League dealing with the same subjects. Whereas it was possible under the League system for older international agencies, such as the Universal Postal Union, to become affiliated with the main organization, as a matter of fact they were not brought so generally into a working relationship with the League as has been true of them under the United Nations. In other words, the United Nations embraces an even larger percentage of the total existing international organization than did the old League.

3. The United Nations system of sanctions is more elaborate, involving as it does an obligation on the part of states to make agreements with the Security Council defining their respective contri-

butions to the prevention of aggression, and supported as it is by a Military Staff Committee, an organ for which there was no counterpart in the League. In 1950 the system was expanded further by an arrangement giving the General Assembly the right to employ military sanctions when the Security Council is deadlocked by a veto.

4. The Trusteeship Council and the International Court of Justice are given the status of "principal organs" of the United Nations along with the other four (General Assembly, Security Council, Secretariat, and the Economic and Social Council), unlike the Mandates Commission and the Permanent Court of International Justice of the old system.

The General Assembly

A unique feature of the Assembly is that it is the only one of the principal organs of the United Nations in which all of the members of the United Nations are represented. Although each member may send as many as five delegates to a meeting, it may cast only one vote. In practice, states usually send with their delegates an equal number of alternates to serve in case one of the regular delegates is incapacitated, and a group of experts for advisory purposes. The regular sessions of the Assembly begin every year on the third Tuesday in September, and a special session may occur whenever the Secretary-General, at the request of the Security Council or of a majority of the members of the United Nations, shall convoke it. A session may be divided into parts held at different times; the first part of the first session of 1946, for instance, met in London from January 10 to February 14, and the second part met in New York from October 23 to December 15. Several special sessions have been held; the first from April 28 to May 15, 1947, dealt with the Palestine problem and was called at the instigation of Great Britain, which had had enough of the affair and was eager to turn it over to the United Nations.

Although the Assembly is a deliberative body, able to deal with all types of international problems, it is in no sense a legislature; in this respect its name could be misleading, for the word "assembly" is often applied to a legislature, as in France today, where the "National Assembly" is in every way a parliamentary body. It has been referred to as a "debating society," and indeed much in the way of debate goes on within its walls. It would be a mistake, however, to conclude that the debates which occur in the Assembly are so completely futile as the term "debating society" might seem to indicate. Much of the debate is pointed toward action of some kind, although not toward the enactment of statutes as in a national legislature. Even when no particular action is contemplated, a free discussion of international problems and disputes can be quite constructive. As someone has said, it is a forum, a "soapbox" on the village green where nations through their delegates may speak their minds. Senator Vandenberg called it the "town meeting of the world." A vehicle of free speech, it is a place where the Arabs have been able to criticize British policy in the Near East, and where the policy of the Union of South Africa toward Southwest Africa has been under heavy fire. There is a wholesomeness in this kind of debate, not only as a safety valve for explosive ideas which men and nations may harbor, but also as a means of bringing out in the open a festering problem requiring public attention. Like free speech everywhere, it is subject to abuse and may lead to such reprehensible demeanor as name-calling and slanderous propaganda; that Russia has used the forum of the Assembly for propaganda purposes is generally admitted, at least outside of Russia, and that the denunciation by Vishinsky of American political leaders as "warmongers" led to bitter feeling and complicated still further the relations of the USSR and the United States is undeniable. Secretary-General Lie is responsible for the statement that a nation using the rostrum of the Assembly for propaganda purposes "is submitting itself to the judgment of mankind." This freedom to talk is based upon John Milton's well-known statement: "Let truth and falsehood grapple. Whoever knew the truth to be put to the worse in a free and open encounter?"

When the debate of the Assembly is directed toward action, which, according to Secretary-General Lie, is most of the time, that action usually takes the form of a recommendation. The organ is amply authorized by the Charter "to initiate studies and make recommendations" in the promotion of coöperation in political matters, in the development of international law, in "economic, social, cultural, educational and health fields," in the promotion of human rights, and in its duties relating to the specialized agencies and the Economic and Social Council. Scores of resolutions have already been adopted by the Assembly recommending to governments action which was deemed beneficial to somebody somewhere. On December 14, 1946, a recommendation was made to members that they adopt at the earliest possible moment the Constitution of the World Health Organization. On November 17, 1947, a resolution was approved recommending that member states encourage instruction in their schools in subjects relating to the United Nations. Several times, to the chagrin of the Union of South Africa, the Assembly has recommended that Southwest Africa be placed under a trusteeship rather than be incorporated as a part of the Union itself, a step which was eventually taken. Recommendations have been made for a more restrained use of the veto in the Security Council, for the condemnation of war propaganda, and for the submission of more disputes to the International Court. That these and the other Assembly recommendations are often ignored must be conceded, but it would be unfair to denounce them for this reason as useless. Frequently there has been some measure of compliance, as with the Assembly recommendation of December 12, 1946, to the effect that member states should withdraw their heads of diplomatic missions to Spain as an expression of disapproval of the Franco regime. Even when complete indifference is shown by members to the various recommendations, the publicity given to a cause or attitude may be well worth gaining; certainly this was true of the recommendation on Southwest Africa when the Union of South Africa was placed on the defensive before the world for her policy of assimilating her former mandate.

This power of making recommendations extends into the realm of international disputes. The Charter, in Article 11, paragraph 2, makes this clear in the statement that "The General Assembly may discuss any questions relating to the maintenance of international peace and security brought before it by any member of the United Nations, or by the Security Council, or by a state which is not a member of the United Nations . . . and, except as provided in Ar-

ticle 12 may make recommendations. . . ." The exception provided
by Article 12 is that the Assembly may not make a recommendation
on a dispute which is at that time before the Security Council unless
so requested by the Council. As a matter of practice, the Assembly
has in a number of disputes made recommendations. In the Palestine
and Greek disputes, for instance, resolutions were adopted asking
the disputants to comply with conditions or suggestions formulated
by the Assembly; the well-known partition plan for Palestine was a
recommendation. How far this right of recommending may be carried is shown by the plan of sanctions adopted in 1950, according to
which the Assembly may, when the use of military coercion has been
vetoed in the Security Council, recommend to states that they dispatch forces to put down aggression; this will be described in a later
chapter.

Another function of the General Assembly is to review and criticize the work of other United Nations organs. In this role it serves
as a general overseer to keep the organization working at top efficiency. It resembles in this respect the legislative bodies of most national governments, which spend much of their time examining and
criticizing the work of the executive departments; in Great Britain
the "question hour," when the ministers are required to answer questions submitted by members of the House of Commons, and in the
United States the investigating committees of Congress, which pry
into the doings of the departments—the investigation of communism
in the Department of State, for instance—are examples of this function. To be sure, this activity of the General Assembly is less highly
developed than in national legislatures, and nothing like the idea of
responsibility as it operates in the British cabinet system has been
developed.

The Assembly's work of review and criticism is based on the annual and special reports submitted to it by other agencies. The Security Council reports to the Assembly on the efforts which have been
made to keep the peace, and the Secretary-General gives the Assembly an annual report on the work of the United Nations as a whole.
The agenda of the General Assembly at its regular sessions makes
room for these reports and for those from the Economic and Social

Council, the Trusteeship Council, the International Court of Justice, the subsidiary agencies of the Assembly, and from the specialized agencies. The submission of these reports may occasion debate from which criticism, commendation, or suggestions will emerge. On October 8, 1948, the Assembly commended the Secretary-General for the progress which he had made toward a better geographical distribution of his staff and suggested that he continue this undertaking. As a matter of fact, the Assembly may at any time, wholly apart from the discussion of annual reports, make suggestions to the Economic and Social Council, as Chapter X of the Charter makes clear. For instance, on October 31, 1947, the Assembly suggested that the Economic and Social Council make a survey annually of world economic conditions and trends. Certainly this work of overseeing the operations of the other organs can exert a wholesome effect on their standards of achievement.

In the field of peace and security the General Assembly's activities extend not only to the handling of specific disputes, as already noted, but also to the consideration of "general principles of coöperation in the maintenance of international peace and security, including the principles governing disarmament and the regulation of armaments. . . ." In another article of the Charter the Assembly is charged with the "progressive development of international law and its codification." In fact, the Assembly has been actively endeavoring to discharge these duties. It has turned over to its Interim Committee, or the "Little Assembly" as it is popularly known, the job of promoting principles of coöperation in the maintenance of peace, and that Committee has studied and reported upon the subject. To develop international law the Assembly created an International Law Commission which has been hard at work on the subject.

Not least among the duties of the General Assembly is the formulation and adoption of an annual budget. Every year to date, the budget has been increased in size—from $27,740,000 for 1947 to $43,487,128 for 1949. If this seems large, in comparison with national budgets the sum is quite inconsequential; the United States budget, for instance, has been more than a thousand times as large as the United Nations budget for 1949, and since the rearmament program was begun in 1950 the comparison has been even more striking.

The United Nations budget is raised by contributions from the member states. It is the duty of the General Assembly to determine the percentage of the total amount which each state shall contribute. To the United States is assigned the highest percentage (39.89 percent) and there are eight states paying the smallest percentage allotted (0.04 percent)—Costa Rica, Haiti, Honduras, Iceland, Liberia, Nicaragua, Paraguay, and Yemen. The Russian assignment is 6.34 percent, and that of the United Kingdom 11.8 percent. While the financial obligations of no nation may seem large in comparison with the figures usually to be found in national budgets, in fact many of the members of the United Nations have been hard-pressed to make their payments because of their poverty, their lack of dollars, or both.

The General Assembly also has a number of other duties relating to the functioning of the United Nations as a whole. It elects the six nonpermanent members of the Security Council, the eighteen members of the Economic and Social Council, and the elective members of the Trusteeship Council. With the Security Council it participates in the election of the judges of the International Court of Justice. And on the recommendation of the Security Council, the Assembly appoints a Secretary-General. At the recommendation of the Security Council it may admit, suspend, or expel a member. Finally, it is the right of the Assembly to participate in the process of amending the Charter. In summary form, the General Assembly deals with the following matters:

the admission, suspension, and expulsion of members of the United Nations (on recommendation of the Security Council);

any question or matter within the scope of the Charter or relating to the powers or functions of any United Nations organ;

general principles of coöperation in the maintenance of peace, including principles governing disarmament and the regulation of armaments;

any question relating to the maintenance of peace, including disputes between nations;

the promotion of coöperation in the political field and in economic, social, cultural, educational, and health matters, as well as in the field of human rights;

the development of international law;

reports submitted by the Secretary-General, the Security Council, and
other organs;

the trusteeship system;

the budget of the United Nations and the apportionment of contributions;

the election of nonpermanent members of the Security Council, the
Secretary-General (on recommendation of the Security Council), a
portion of the members of the Trusteeship Council, the judges of the
International Court of Justice (with the Security Council), members
of the Economic and Social Council;

the determination of conditions on which nations not members of the
United Nations may become members of the International Court of
Justice;

the determination of regulations governing the appointment of the staff
of the Secretariat appointed by the Secretary-General;

the authorization of United Nations agencies to request advisory opinions from the International Court of Justice;

the diplomatic privileges and immunities of representatives of states to
the United Nations and to officials of the United Nations;

amendments to the Charter (action not final).

A body as large as the General Assembly requires a well-con-
structed organization if it is to proceed with efficiency and dispatch
to the conclusion of its work. This is apparent from the congested
agenda which the Assembly, like the Economic and Social Council
and some of the other organs of the United Nations, invariably faces.
There were seventy-five items on the agenda of the third session of
the General Assembly, which met on September 21, 1948, at Paris.
Despite eighteen hundred hours of plenary and committee meetings,
the Assembly did not have its work completed when it adjourned on
December 12. Consequently, it met again for the second part of the
third session at Flushing Meadow on April 5, 1949, with several
items on the agenda carried over and a number of new items added.
There were seventy-three items of the agenda at the session which
began on September 17, 1950; this session was not divided into two
parts but continued on into March, 1951.

Under the Charter, the General Assembly is free to adopt its own
rules of procedure for dealing with its large volume of business and
to use whatever subsidiary agencies it may need. Presiding at its sessions is a president or one of its seven vice-presidents; the holders of

these offices are elected from among the delegates at the beginning of each session. At the opening of a session the chairman of the delegation from which the president of the preceding session was chosen presides until the new president is selected. To date, the Assembly has been disposed to pick its president from the delegation of one of the smaller countries; for the regular session of 1949, Mr. Romulo of the Philippine delegation was elected and his work as a presiding officer was marked by high distinction, and in 1950 Mr. Entezam of Iran was chosen.

The major portion of the work of the General Assembly is done in committee, following in this respect the practice of national legislatures. There are four types of committees maintained by the Assembly, as follows:

1. The Main Committees.

   These are the most important of all, for to them are referred agenda items and it is the business of these committees to draft resolutions for presentation to the main body. Every state is entitled to representation on every one of these committees. There are six main committees: First Committee (Political and Security), Second Committee (Economic and Financial), Third Committee (Social, Humanitarian, and Cultural), Fourth Committee (Trusteeship), Fifth Committee (Administrative and Budgetary), and the Sixth Committee (Legal).

2. Procedural Committees.

   The two procedural committees deal with the organization and conduct of the Assembly's work. One, the General Committee, is composed of the president, the seven vice-presidents, and the chairmen of the six main committees. The second is the Credentials Committee (nine members) to pass upon the credentials of delegates.

3. Standing Committees.

   There are two standing committees set up under the Assembly's rules of procedure to deal with continuing problems: The Advisory Committee on Administrative and Budgetary Problems; and the Committee on Contributions. In addition a Board of Auditors has been created and an International Law Commission to work on the progressive development of international law.

4. *Ad hoc* Committees.

The Assembly or any of its committees may provide for *ad hoc* or temporary bodies to perform assigned duties whenever they may be needed. In practice a considerable number have been set up, as the Temporary Commission on Korea, the Special Committee on the Balkans, and the Headquarters Advisory Committee.

Reference has been made to the Interim Committee or "Little Assembly." It was created by a resolution of the General Assembly adopted on November 13, 1947, at the suggestion of the delegation of the United States, speaking through its chairman, Secretary of State Marshall. It is composed of one representative from each member of the United Nations, and was detailed to take up matters referred to it by the General Assembly. The following subjects were specifically assigned to it: the consideration of methods of implementing the responsibility of the Assembly for taking up general principles of coöperation in the maintenance of peace (Article 11, paragraph 1); a study of the veto; consideration of disputes proposed for inclusion on the agenda under Articles 11 (2), 14, or 35; and the recommendation, if it saw fit, of a special session of the Assembly.[4] No doubt a principal motive of the United States in proposing the creation of the Interim Committee was to find a way of limiting the frustrating veto in the Security Council. It was set up first for a period of one year, but later it was made a permanent body. It immediately created the following subcommittees at the beginning of its work: (1) Sub-Committee One on rules of procedure; (2) Sub-Committee Two on promotion of coöperation in the political field; (3) Sub-Committee Three on voting in the Security Council; (4) Sub-Committee Four on making the Interim Committee permanent.[5]

---

[4] See Appendix II to this chapter for the original terms of reference for the Interim Committee.

[5] Although the Interim Committee has been less active than was expected, it has proved itself useful. It made a report on the veto which was in large part embodied in a resolution of the General Assembly, it contributed to the decision of the United Nations for the disposition of Eritrea, and it authorized an election in South Korea. The communist members of the United Nations have refused to take any part in its work.

Further information on the Interim Committee may be obtained in Yuen-li Liang, "Some Aspects of the Work of the Interim Committee," *American Journal of International Law*, 1948, vol. 42, no. 4, pp. 887–900.

In the General Assembly and within the United Nations generally, there has been a striking tendency for members to group themselves into blocs. Most clearly discernible among them is the communist bloc, composed of Russia and her satellites; with few exceptions this group of nations—Russia, Poland, Czechoslovakia, the Byelorussian SSR, and the Ukrainian SSR—vote together.[6] The western bloc has been larger, including within its ranks the United States, western Europe, Latin America, the Philippines, Greece, Turkey, and Nationalist China; this group, however, has displayed much less cohesion than the communist bloc, often voting on opposite sides of a question, especially when the issue is not closely tied to the power relationships of nations. India and the Asian countries have often held together, attempting to follow a middle-of-the-road policy between the communist nations on the one hand and the western countries on the other, but leaning at times toward the western bloc. The Arab nations have often associated themselves with the Asian group, and indeed some of them are Asian, but they too have at times shown favoritism toward the West. These groupings correspond to the realities of world politics outside the United Nations. Except for the communist bloc, they have, however, represented tendencies rather than rigid cleavages.

In the development of the United Nations the growing importance and prestige of the General Assembly has been the subject of frequent comment. In his report for the year 1948–1949, Secretary-General Lie referred to the evolution of the organ into "one of the strongest forces for peace that the world has ever known." He gave three explanations for this evolution. First he mentioned the "moderating" influence of the many small nations of the Assembly on great-power conflicts and he was thinking primarily, of course, of the rivalry between the USSR and the Anglo-American bloc. His second explanation was that "the attention of the world is focused on the General Assembly as on no other international body"; there "as nowhere else," so he said, are "policies subjected to the searching scru-

---

[6] Yugoslavia, another communist nation, frequently voted with the communist bloc when she was under the domination of Moscow, but she has generally been more independent than the present satellite nations.

tiny and judgment of world public opinion." His third reason was that the Assembly had demonstrated its ability to work effectively in the treatment of international disputes, and had thus proved itself "a powerful complement to the work of the Security Council."

The Security Council[7]

The Security Council is the United Nations' special watchdog of peace, or as the Charter puts it, the members of the United Nations "confer on the Security Council primary responsibility for the maintenance of international peace and security." This means, first, that, although disputes may go before the General Assembly, as a rule they will be taken to the Council, and second, that the sanctions of the United Nations available against aggressors and peace-breakers are under the control of this same organ. This job of keeping the world at peace is the principal concern of the Council and it has been a man-sized task in the unstable world of recent years.

In addition to its principal duty, there are a number of less spectacular and less vital functions which the Security Council must perform. It recommends to the General Assembly new members for admission to the United Nations, and when necessary under Articles 5 and 6 of the Charter, it recommends the suspension or expulsion of members; it recommends to the same organ a candidate for appointment as Secretary-General. Like the Assembly, it takes part in the election of judges of the International Court of Justice. Two other duties relating to the Court are (1) recommending to the Assembly the conditions on which states not members of the United Nations may adhere to the Statute, and (2) determining the conditions under which a state not a member of the Court may bring a case before that tribunal. Finally, the Council exercises trusteeship functions for those trust areas which are classified as "strategic areas," and its approval of the terms of the trusteeship agreements for those territories is required.

The composition and the general role of the Security Council in

---

[7] For further information on the Security Council, see Hans Kelsen, "The Organization and Procedure of the Security Council," *Harvard Law Review,* vol. 59, pp. 1087–1121.

the United Nations were determined in large part at the Dumbarton Oaks Conference in 1944. It was agreed at that meeting that the large powers should have permanent seats on the Council, but it was expected at that time that only Russia, the United States, China, and the United Kingdom would immediately qualify; France "in due course" was to become the fifth permanent member. The San Francisco Conference of 1945 changed this plan by giving France the privilege of permanent membership from the beginning.

One of the problems which was not foreseen when the composition of the Security Council was finally determined at San Francisco was the possibility of civil war within the territory of one of the permanent members, the outcome of which would be the establishment of a new government of such nature that many members of the United Nations would not see fit to accord it recognition. When the communists won over all of China except Formosa in 1949, a serious issue was raised concerning their claim to take over the Chinese seat in the Security Council, and in the other organs of the United Nations as well. Because a considerable group of members, led by the United States, refused to seat the Chinese communists, Russia took the position that she would not take part in meetings of the Council and in other United Nations organs in which the old Nationalist Government of China continued to be represented. Because there was no procedure to resolve the deadlock, it continued. Russia withdrew her boycott of the Council, however, on August 1, 1950, when it came her turn to take over the presidency of the body.

In addition to the five permanent members, there are six nonpermanent members of the Security Council elected by the General Assembly for two-year terms; three of these are selected each year at the Assembly's annual session. On December 31, 1950, Cuba, Egypt, and Norway gave way to Brazil, Turkey, and The Netherlands, and one year later new members elected in the session of 1951 took the place of Ecuador, India, and Yugoslavia. In making its selection the Assembly is expected to take into account "the contribution of Members of the United Nations to the maintenance of peace and security" and "equitable geographical distribution" (Article 23 of the Charter). The geographical balance at present maintained rests upon the selection of two from the Latin-American countries, one from the British Commonwealth of Nations, one from the Middle East, one from western Europe, and one from eastern Europe.

In the election of the nonpermanent members of the Security Council which took place in 1949, a lively contest developed over the selection of the eastern European member. There was no difficulty over the selection of the other two members, Ecuador and India obtaining the requisite two-thirds vote on the first ballot, but neither Yugoslavia nor Czechoslovakia, the two candidates for the eastern European seat, could muster the support needed. The United States and the nations of the West were pulling for the election of Yugoslavia, then in a state of tension with Russia and therefore more likely than Czechoslovakia to be independent of control by the eastern communist bloc; for the same reason, Russia was anxious to have Czechoslovakia chosen. On the second ballot Yugoslavia won by a vote of 39 to 19. Angered, Soviet delegate Andrei Vishinsky raised his hand, marched to the rostrum, shouted over the hammering of the gavel that the election was illegal, that it violated a "gentlemen's agreement" to the effect that support would be given to the eastern European candidate selected by the nations of that region. Secretary of State Acheson admitted that by tradition and perhaps by agreement eastern Europe is entitled to a nonpermanent seat, but he denied the existence of any agreement by which his government was bound to support the eastern European candidate nominated by Russia. The outbursts by Mr. Vishinsky proved to be futile, and Yugoslavia was seated in the Security Council.

An advantage of the Security Council in its work of maintaining the peace is the fact that it functions continuously; it meets either at the seat of the United Nations or elsewhere and is always ready for business. With members maintaining permanent representation to the United Nations in New York, it is a very simple matter to call the Council into session on short notice. This was brought out when, on June 25, 1950, communist-controlled Northern Korea invaded United Nations-sponsored Southern Korea; at 3 A.M. the United States Government asked Secretary-General Lie for an emergency meeting of the Security Council, and by 1 P.M. of the same day the Council was ready to take up the problem.

The presidency of the Security Council rotates among the members according to the English alphabetical order of their names, and the incumbent holds office for one month at a time. There had been little significance attached to the office until the August meetings of 1950, when the presidency went to Russia, who instantly terminated her wrathful boycott of the Council and sent Mr. Jacob A. Malik to preside. During the month, Mr. Malik used his office to obstruct further action by the Council on the Korean problem and to try to place the United States in the light of an aggressor in Korea. The organization became tied up in knots over procedural problems; as someone put it, they were forever debating what they would debate. Or as the Chinese Nationalist delegate to the Security Council summarized the situation:

. . . we have been taken by the president for a ride in a merry-go-round, or rather in a misery-go-round. He has, in the words of my distinguished colleague of Ecuador, vetoed our rules of procedure. By an arbitrary dictatorial fiat, he has pronounced our decisions in the latter part of June illegal. In fact he has treated the Security Council as if it were the Politbureau of the Bolshevik party of Russia with himself playing the role of Generalissimo Stalin.

Widespread criticism of these tactics led to unofficial suggestions that the Council's rules be altered to substitute for the system of rotation in the presidency a process by which the office would be filled by election. It was argued that election by the Council of a president would ensure that the will of the majority could not be blocked by an unfriendly presiding officer. No official action on the matter has been taken.

The Security Council is free to fix its own rules of procedure and to establish whatever subsidiary organs it may need. Two standing committees, each consisting of representatives from all of the eleven members of the Council, have been set up: the Committee of Experts (to deal with rules of procedure) and the Committee on the Admission of New Members. Other subsidiary bodies reporting to the Council are the following: (1) the Military Staff Committee, required by the Charter, to advise the Council on military matters relating to the maintenance of peace; (2) the Commission for Conventional Armaments, to assist in the formulation of plans for the reduction of armaments; and (3) the Atomic Energy Commission, set up by the General Assembly in 1946 to draft a plan for the international control of atomic energy.

The Secretariat

If less spectacular than the General Assembly and Security Council, rarely making the headlines except for some occasional statement or project of the Secretary-General, the Secretariat of the United Nations is, nevertheless, a vital part of the United Nations, thoroughly deserving its rating as one of the "principal organs." Generally speaking, it is to the United Nations what the administrative departments and civil service are to national governments, but this analogy could not be pushed too far, for the Secretariat lacks the extensive powers of national administrative bodies to give effect to statutes. As an administrative agency it is but a faint shadow of national agencies, much as in legislative and judicial matters international organization lags far behind the standards of national governments.

The Secretary-General, the head of the organ, is responsible for the staff and for the organization of the Secretariat. He acts as the chief secretary in all meetings of the General Assembly, the Security Council, the Economic and Social Council, and the Trusteeship Council. In addition, he has numerous duties described in the Charter, such as submitting annual reports to the General Assembly on the work of the United Nations, bringing to the attention of the Security Council "any matter which in his opinion may threaten the maintenance of international peace and security," and convoking special sessions of the General Assembly when properly requested. Under the Statute of the International Court of Justice he has several duties, including the submission of requests for the nominations of judges to states members of the organization. Some of the most important assignments of duties to the Secretary-General and his staff are made in the resolutions of the General Assembly, requiring him to communicate with members for one purpose or another, or to undertake a special task which the Assembly wants done. In 1947 he was asked to facilitate consultations between members on relief plans; he has been asked to prepare draft conventions, such as the convention on genocide; he was given the job of organizing the United Nations Appeal for Children; and he was authorized to enter into a Headquarters Agreement with the United States.

One of the outstanding duties of the Secretary-General and his subordinates is the preparation of meetings of the various organs, committees, and conferences which are a part of the United Nations. There is work to be done in the formulation of agenda, the preparation of documents, the convocation of sessions, and the provision of necessary staffs. Closely related to this work is that of preparing studies and reports to be used by organs of the United Nations in reaching decisions on problems before them. In view of the fact that the success of meetings is dependent to a very considerable degree upon the preparations which have been made for them, this work is of a nature to affect the activities of the United Nations in all their aspects.

The Secretary-General has the responsibility of preparing the budget of the United Nations for submission to the General Assembly; he allocates and collects the annual contributions of members and acts as guardian for those funds. In the field of financial administration, as in other matters, he is subject to the control of the General Assembly, whose Provisional Financial Regulations detail the manner in which he shall act.[8]

When the United Nations was in the process of being set up, there were two schools of thought as to the proper way to organize the Secretariat, the majority view being that it should be constituted on a functional basis, each unit relating to some particular activity and available to organs of the United Nations dealing with that type of work, whereas the minority maintained that each of the principal organs should have its own office in the Secretariat. Following the majority point of view, the Assembly decided that the Secretariat should be made up of the following eight units: Department of Secu-

---

[8] For further discussion of the activities of the Secretariat see Chapter XVI.

rity Council Affairs, Department of Economic Affairs, Department of Social Affairs, Department of Trusteeship and Information from Non-Self-Governing Territories, Department of Public Information, Legal Department, Conference and General Services, and Administrative and Financial Services.

The Secretary-General is appointed by the General Assembly upon the recommendation of the Security Council. In accordance with this stipulation of the Charter, Mr. Trygve Lie, former Foreign Minister of Norway, was appointed on February 1, 1946, for a term of five years. In October, 1950, when that term was running out, the Security Council took up the question of selecting a successor for Mr. Lie, but after an extended discussion found itself unable to agree. Russia was opposed to the reappointment of Mr. Lie, contending that he had shown favoritism toward the Western powers and that in the Korean affair he had accused North Korea of aggression before the Security Council had done so. The United States, along with the other Security Council members, supported Mr. Lie; the American delegate warned that, if necessary, he would cast the first American veto in opposition to any alternative candidate. Confronted with this deadlock in the Council, the General Assembly took up the problem and voted to extend Mr. Lie's term for three more years. This was legally possible because the Charter does not specify a term of office for the Secretary-General and the original designation of five years had been by action of the Assembly itself.

The staff of the Secretariat is appointed by the Secretary-General in accordance with regulations adopted by the General Assembly. In his selection he must take into account personal qualifications and an equitable geographic distribution of the appointees. Written tests are given to applicants for positions as typists, linguists, officials of the junior professional and junior administrative types, and for other such positions. Appointments are either "indeterminate" (indefinite tenure) or "temporary." The three thousand and more members of the Secretariat are divided into nineteen grades for salary purposes, with grade one ranging from $1580 to $2130 per year and those of grade nineteen from $10,000 to $11,000; excluded from these grades are certain top-ranking officials such as the Assistant Secretaries-General with a salary of $13,500. The Secretary-General himself, Mr. Trygve Lie of Norway, receives an annual salary of $20,000, together with a representation allowance of $20,000 a year.

The intention of the United Nations and its founders in creating the Secretariat was to make it genuinely international in character, with its members devoted to the service of the community as a whole and as free from national control as possible. The Charter stipulates in Article 100 that its officials, including the Secretary-General, "shall not seek or receive instructions from any government . . . ," and that member states agree "to respect the exclusively international character of the responsibilities of the Secretary-General and the staff and not to seek to influence them in the discharge of their responsibilities." Each staff member on entering office takes an oath "in all loyalty, discretion and conscience to work as an international civil servant in the interests of the United Nations." This, too, was the theory of the League of Nations Secretariat, but in practice it was found most difficult to establish, and complaints were made that the staff did not measure up to the high standard of impartiality expected of it. In this day of strong national attachments it would be expecting too much of employees to ask them to give up the loyalties and hatreds of their national groups; at most, they can be required only to act without bias regardless of their feelings, and this too is difficult, for it is the way of human beings to base their actions upon their feelings.

On November 15, 1947, the General Assembly adopted a resolution affirming the need for efficiency and integrity as qualifications of staff members and approving the principle of recruiting on a wide geographical basis; and then the resolution went on to request the Secretary-General to examine the existing geographical basis with a view to improving the geographical distribution. In particular he was asked to make whatever arrangements he could to take on staff members from countries not then represented in the Secretariat, and to examine the competence of the staff at that time with a view to the replacement of some of the least qualified. A year later, the Assembly noted with approval the progress made by the Secretary-General toward a better geographical distribution of his staff. The competence of the Secretariat is still a subject of criticism.[9]

The Economic and Social Council

The Economic and Social Council is the dynamo which keeps in action the work of the United Nations for the improvement of the economic and social status of mankind. It is founded upon the sound doctrine that no peace can be stable unless it rests upon nations whose peoples are living in decent surroundings with good health and an adequate supply of the necessities of life. An impoverished people living in degradation are easy prey to false "isms" and to agitators in behalf of aggression and expansion. To improve the lot of mankind, the Economic and Social Council is authorized by the Charter to "make or initiate studies and reports with respect to international economic, social, cultural, educational, health and related matters" and to make recommendations on these subjects to the General Assembly, to members of the United Nations, and to the specialized agencies; the promotion of human rights is also within the competence of the agency.

The eighteen members of the Economic and Social Council are elected by the General Assembly, one-third (six) of them every year for three-year terms. Although there is no requirement to that effect, to date it has been the custom to keep all of the five permanent members of the Security Council on the Economic and Social Council. This is entirely possible from the point of view of the Charter for the reason that reëlection indefinitely is allowed. From a practical point of view the custom is sound, because plans for economic and social progress would be quite meaningless were they to be made without taking into account at least three of the Big Five—Russia, the United States, and the United Kingdom.

In order to accomplish the tasks assigned to it, and Economic and Social Council makes use of a variety of subsidiary and related agen-

---

[9] See W. R. Crocker, "Some Notes on the United Nations Secretariat," *International Organization*, 1950, vol. 4, no. 4, pp. 598–613. Mr. Crocker criticizes the staff for "the average quality of its chiefs and the average quality of its personnel."

cies. In addition to *ad hoc* committees which it may create as needed, there are nine "functional commissions" to deal respectively with economic and employment problems, transport and communication, statistics, human rights, social problems, the status of women, narcotic drugs, fiscal problems, and population. There are three "regional commissions," one for Europe, one for Latin America, and one for Asia and the Far East. The "standing committees" of the Council include one on negotiations with intergovernmental agencies, a second on arrangements for consultation with nongovernmental organizations, a third on the Council's agenda, and a fourth on programs of meetings.

In its work the Economic and Social Council may consult with nongovernmental organizations, and in fact finds it advantageous to do so. Three categories of such organizations are recognized: (1) those which have a basic interest in most of the Council's work and are closely related to the economic or the social life of the areas they represent (e.g., American Federation of Labor, International Chamber of Commerce, World Federation of Trade Unions, International Cooperative Alliance); (2) organizations concerned primarily with only a few of the Council's fields of activity (e.g., Commission of the Churches on International Affairs, International Bar Association, International Council of Women); and (3) organizations primarily concerned with public opinion (e.g., Rotary International, International Association of Lions Clubs).[10]

The Specialized Agencies

Operating under the Economic and Social Council are a group of "specialized agencies," as they are denoted by the Charter. In the sense that each has its own constitution, organization, and methods, they are autonomous bodies. In harmony with the common practice in international organization, their constitutions are in the nature of intergovernmental agreements, and as the Charter phrases it, they have "wide international responsibilities, as defined in their basic instruments, in economic, social, cultural, educational, health and related fields." In fact, they are highly active agencies providing to

---

[10] These nongovernmental organizations are further discussed in Chapter XIV.

nations and individuals many services of a constructive nature without which this world would be in a much more lamentable state than it is. Without the work of the Universal Postal Union and the facility of international postal communication which it provides, individuals and business would find in national boundaries almost impenetrable barriers to normal and profitable intercourse abroad. It is not too much to say that many thousands of people are alive and many thousands of others are in good health because of the work of the World Health Organization.

Among the specialized agencies are several which were in existence before the Charter of the United Nations was written. The oldest of the group is the Universal Postal Union, whose convention was written in 1874 and went into force approximately one year later. The International Labor Organization was set up in 1919 as an autonomous institution for the purpose of improving the conditions of labor, with its original constitution incorporated into the peace treaties following World War I. The International Telecommunication Union came into being in 1931, although its predecessor, the International Telegraph Union, was founded in 1865. The constitutions of three of the specialized agencies—the Food and Agriculture Organization, the International Bank, and the International Fund—were negotiated during World War II, but none of them began functioning until the war was over, except that the Food and Agriculture Organization from July, 1943, until October, 1945, operated through an Interim Commission.

The specialized agencies are related to the United Nations proper through detailed agreements which they have made with the Economic and Social Council. It is the duty of the Economic and Social Council to "coordinate the activities of the specialized agencies through consultation with and recommendations to such agencies and through recommendations to the General Assembly and to the members of the United Nations," as stipulated by the Charter (Article 63). The Council receives reports from the agencies and therefore is in a position to know what they are doing and to be able to coördinate their activities.

The usual practice within the specialized agencies of the United Nations is to allow for both "original" and "admitted" members, but the precise provisions do not follow any uniform pattern. The Monetary Fund, for instance, has as its original members those states which attended the Bretton Woods Conference and which at a later date accepted membership; other states may be admitted "at such times and in accordance with such terms as may be prescribed by the Fund." To give one other illustration: UNESCO's original members were those members of the United Nations which at the time indicated a desire to join; other states are admitted by a two-thirds vote of the General Conference.

The Trusteeship Council

After World War I, the former colonies of Germany and the dependent peoples of the Near East who had been under Turkish domination were made into mandates under the League of Nations. This meant that they were governed by designated nations—Great Britain, France, Belgium, Australia, the Union of South Africa, and New Zealand—acting separately as mandatories for them, and these mandatory nations were responsible to the League of Nations for their actions. This arrangement was based upon the theory that the areas were the collective responsibility of the community of nations. In this mandate system the authority of the League was ultimately in the Council, but immediately in the Mandates Commission set up by the Council to be in direct contact with the mandatory powers.

At the end of World War II, it was decided that the system should be retained with some modifications of detail, and no doubt this decision was a wise one, for, with all its faults, the mandate system was the first substantial alternative to old-style imperialism ever devised. The new successor to the "mandate system" within the United Nations was called the "trusteeship system." The detailed organization and operation of the system will be discussed in a later chapter dealing with international administration, but at this point it is appropriate to point out that from a structural point of view trusteeship within the United Nations is somewhat different from the mandatory arrangements within the League of Nations. Instead of the Security Council, the General Assembly, under the trusteeship system, has the final responsible authority except for areas designated as "strategic," where the Security Council is in general charge;

the trust areas of the United States in the Far Pacific—the island groups which formerly were mandates of Japan—are the only strategic areas at the present time. A second major change from the mandate system is the creation of the Trusteeship Council to take the place of the old Mandates Commission and the granting to this Council of the rating of one of the six "principal organs" of the United Nations; in its operations the Trusteeship Council is accountable to the General Assembly.

The Trusteeship Council is made up of three groups of members. First, nations administering trust territories are *ipso facto* represented on the Council; this group includes Australia, Belgium, France, New Zealand, the United Kingdom, the United States, and Italy. Second, any nation which is a permanent member of the Security Council is a member of the Trusteeship Council even though it does not have a trust area under it, and in this category are China and Russia. Finally, there are a group of elected members, as many as may be needed to ensure that the number of states not administering trust areas is equal to those who do; these members are elected by the General Assembly for three-year terms and at present there are five of them.[11]

The International Court of Justice

Status as one of the "principal organs" of the United Nations is also accorded to the International Court of Justice. The Charter in Chapter XIV describes a few of the characteristics of the Court, but the tribunal has a constitution of its own known as its "Statute," which deals in detail with its organization, jurisdiction, and procedure. As stated in Article 92 of the Charter, this Statute "forms an integral part of the present Charter."[12]

Membership in the United Nations[13]

Following the practice of the old League of Nations, the Charter of the United Nations distinguishes between original and admitted

---

[11] The trusteeship system is discussed in Chapter XVI.

[12] See Chapter VII for a full discussion of the International Court of Justice.

[13] For a list of members of the United Nations and the specialized agencies, see Appendix III to this chapter.

members. In committee sessions at San Francisco in 1945, Uruguay proposed that participation in the new organization be obligatory and that membership be universal, but the proposal failed to secure support and was dropped in favor of the older practices of leaving membership optional and prescribing conditions to be met for admitted members. Consequently, it was provided that original members would be those nations which took part in the San Francisco Conference of 1945 or signed the wartime Declaration of January 1, 1942, provided in every case that such nations signed and ratified the Charter. Some fifty nations were eligible for original membership under these provisions. Other "peace-loving" nations might be voted into membership by the General Assembly on recommendation of the Security Council provided they were both able and willing to meet their international obligations.

As a matter of fact, there has been a great deal of friction and bitterness in deliberations over the admission of new members. During the first eight months of 1946 there were eight states which applied for admission. After the rejection by the USSR of the American proposal to admit *en bloc*, it was decided in the Security Council to deal with them one by one. Only three of the eight applicants—Afghanistan, Iceland, and Siam—were recommended for admission by the Security Council. The other five failed to obtain the required majority of seven including the votes of all the permanent members; in some instances there was a majority of seven but not all the permanent members voted affirmatively. It was the veto of the USSR that kept several applicants from membership. Russia explained her negative vote in some cases on the ground that diplomatic relations had not been established by the USSR with the applicants, and in other cases by the unfriendly behavior of applicants in World War II. The United States at a later date voted against Hungary, but announced that she would not employ the veto to keep a nation out. In this deadlock Albania, Mongolia, Trans-Jordan, Ireland, and Portugal were prevented from joining the United Nations. Sometime later there were new applicants, among which Sweden, Yemen, and Pakistan were given the nod of approval, while Italy, Hungary, Austria, Roumania and Bulgaria were blackballed. In 1950 the United States of Indonesia applied and was accepted as the sixtieth member of the United Nations.

The General Assembly, incensed that so many applicants were rejected simply because they were caught in the ever-widening web of Russo-American animosity, took up the problem of membership in November, 1947. It adopted eight resolutions, some expressing the Assembly's favorable stand toward a number of the applicants, one asking the Security Council to try to resolve the deadlock, and the last submitting to the International Court of Justice a question for an advisory opinion. Russia had taken the position that she would vote for certain nations on condition that certain others were admitted. The General Assembly asked the Court whether such a condition could legally be attached to a vote. In answer to this question the International Court of Justice on May 28, 1948, handed down an advisory opinion against the attachment of such conditions to the vote of members of the Security Council.

A second request for an advisory opinion on a question of membership was made by the General Assembly in 1949. This time the International Court of Justice was asked to say whether the Assembly could admit a state to the United Nations when the Security Council had made no recommendation for admission. The opinion of the Court, delivered on March 3, 1950, was in the negative.[14]

Withdrawal

In conformity with the ideas of sovereignty then current and in answer to a widespread feeling in the United States that such a provision was desirable, the Covenant of the League of Nations allowed members to withdraw. It was required, however, that a member should give two years' notice of the intention to withdraw and that actual withdrawal should not become definitive unless the state had met "all its international obligations and all its obligations under this Covenant." Well-intentioned as these conditions were, they availed little in actual practice. After giving notice of withdrawal, states ceased participating in the work of the League and to all intents and purposes acted as though they were not members, although legally

---

[14] These advisory opinions are taken up in Chapter VII.

they were of course still bound by the provisions of the Covenant. No procedure was ever devised to ascertain whether withdrawing states had met their obligations, obviously a most difficult fact to establish although always a fertile field for suspicions.

There were a considerable number of withdrawals from the League, some of which were occasioned by the daring of the organization in calling members on the carpet for their aggressive activities. In 1933 Japan gave notice of withdrawal after the Council and Assembly had tried persistently, though without success, to restrain Japanese aggression in Manchuria; her government stated that the measures taken by the League left "no further room for cooperation." After the Assembly, in the conflict between Bolivia and Paraguay over the Gran Chaco, lifted the embargo on arms for the former but retained it for the latter, the Government of Paraguay in 1935, indignant, gave notice. The League's restraining efforts against Italy in 1935 when the fascists took Ethiopia led to a withdrawal announcement from Mussolini's Government.

The Charter of the United Nations contains no provisions for withdrawal. Discussions of the matter took place at San Francisco in 1945, and a variety of opinions were brought forward. Many of the delegates felt that an express statement permitting withdrawal might have the undesired effect of encouraging the withdrawal of states offended by some course of action taken by the organization, following the practice within the League of Nations. Although some delegations were in favor of a withdrawal provision for one reason or another, the majority opposed it and advocated instead an interpretative declaration making clear that members might withdraw but without the benefit of an express Charter statement to that effect. The interpretation, incorporated into a committee report and subsequently approved by the Conference in plenary session, contained the following statement:

The Committee adopts the view that the Charter should not make express provision either to permit or to prohibit withdrawal from the Organization. The Committee deems that the highest duty of the nations which will become members is to continue their cooperation within the Organization for the preservation of international peace and security. If, however, a Member because of exceptional circumstances feels constained to withdraw, and leave the burden of maintaining international peace and security on the other Members, it is not the purpose of the Organization to compel that Member to continue its cooperation in the Organization.

To date there have been no withdrawals; rumors have circulated, however, from time to time that Russia has considered getting out of the organization.

Suspension and Expulsion

The Covenant of the League of Nations authorized the expulsion of a member, but made no provision for suspensions. The authorization was in Article 16, the sanction article, and it would appear therefore that an expulsion would be in the nature of a punitive measure. Only once in the two decades of the League's existence was expulsion undertaken, and that was in 1940 when the Council voted to expel Russia for her attack on Finland.

By Article 5 of the Charter, the General Assembly of the United Nations, on the recommendation of the Security Council, may suspend "from the exercise of the rights and privileges of membership" a member against whom preventive or enforcement action has been taken. By a similar procedure, Article 6 permits the expulsion of a member "which has persistently violated the Principles contained in the present Charter." To date, no action has been taken under either article. Whether resort to expulsion against a member violating the Charter would in any way contribute to the peace of the world is highly debatable.

Voting in the United Nations

The United Nations has departed from the principle of unanimity in voting much more than did the League of Nations. Indeed, none of its organs is obliged to achieve unanimity in taking decisions and the only place where the doctrine has been applied in any form is within the Security Council, where the veto power implies, as the phrase has it, "great power unanimity." Although the majority principle is general throughout the United Nations, there are frequent qualifications as to the size of the majority necessary for decisions.

The General Assembly in all of its work takes decisions by vote of a majority of those members present and voting. Important decisions require a two-thirds majority, but others are by simple majority; the Charter in Article 18 gives the following list of "important questions" to which the two-thirds rule must be applied:

recommendations with respect to the maintenance of international peace and security, the election of the non-permanent members of the Security Council, the election of the members of the Economic and Social Council, the election of members of the Trusteeship Council in accordance with paragraph 1 (c) of Article 86, the admission of new Members to the United Nations, the suspension of the rights and privileges of membership, the expulsion of Members, questions relating to the operation of the trusteeship system, and budgetary questions.

By simple majority the Assembly may add other questions to the above list.

The phrase "present and voting" has occasioned some misunderstanding in the General Assembly. At the first session, a ruling was made by the chairman that sixteen of the members present but not voting should be regarded as having participated in the vote, but this ruling was voted down by the Assembly. The question was raised again by the USSR at a special session, and again it was held that only the votes of those for and those opposed to a motion should be counted and that an abstention is not a vote.

The voting methods of the Security Council are notorious for the heated controversies which have centered about them. The veto—the requirement that among the seven votes required on substantive questions, those of all five of the permanent members shall be included—has been an effective instrument of obstruction in the United Nations and has given rise to much dismay on the part of supporters of the organization. At least two arguments in its favor may, however, be mentioned. In the first place, it is an advance over the voting methods of the Council of the League of Nations, where complete unanimity was the rule. Second, however reluctantly the admission must be made, the veto does conform to the realities of world politics and particularly to the fact that the United States and Russia would have rejected membership in an organization empowered to act against their respective wills on vital matters. Smaller nations denounced the veto at San Francisco, and they have since taken every opportunity to speak their minds. Sir Carl Berendsen of New Zealand, a prominent spokesman of the group, referred to the veto in 1946 as a "part of the price that the smaller Powers were called upon by the Great Powers to pay for the very existence of the United Nations."[15]

The frequent use of the veto by Russia has caused much concern within the United Nations and has led to a movement for some modification of the practice.[16] Russia on her part has remained adamant in her will to retain it in its present form. At the General Assembly meeting in 1946, Russian delegate Molotov said that the abolition of the veto "would mean in practice the liquidation of the United Nations organization."[17] The United States has advocated a modification of the veto, retaining it for major decisions relating to the maintenance of peace but discarding it in thirty-one types of votes which were listed and submitted to the Interim Committee of the General Assembly for consideration.

On November 21, 1947, the General Assembly requested its Interim Commission to examine the problem of the veto. On the basis of its findings, a draft resolution setting forth thirty-five types of decisions of the Security Council which might be treated as procedural and therefore not subject to veto was formulated and placed before the *ad hoc* Political Committee of the Assembly.[18] Adopted with little change by the *ad hoc* Political Committee, the resolution became a portion of a group of recommendations adopted by the General Assembly on April 14, 1949, after what President H. V. Evatt called a "very long" and a "very important" debate. The recommendations listed thirty-four decisions which the Assembly suggested be regarded as procedural, one of which has had the effect of practically eliminating the "double veto" (a veto on the question of whether a vote to be taken was procedural or substantive, fol-

[15] Statement to the General Assembly. See *Journal of the United Nations,* October 29, 1946.
[16] See Appendix IV to this chapter for some of the uses of the veto.
[17] Statement to the General Assembly, October 29, 1946. Text in the New York *Times,* November 30, 1946.
[18] "Record of the General Assembly at Paris," *United Nations Bulletin,* vol. 6, no. 1 (1949), p. 15.

lowed by an opportunity for a second veto in votes decided to be substantive). It was also suggested that the Big Five try to reduce the use of the veto by consultation among themselves. Members of the United Nations were urged that, when they confer special duties on the Security Council by treaties and agreements, they exclude the application of the veto from decisions to be taken under those agreements.

The recommendations of the General Assembly have had little, if any, effect. They have for the most part gone unheeded. Doubtless, a change in the law of the Charter would be necessary to effect any modification of existing practice, and that is out of the question for the reason that proposed Charter amendments themselves require great-power unanimity.

Special mention should be made of the fact that abstention from voting or absence from the Security Council is not regarded as a negative vote.[19] Russian objection to this rule has been unavailing. Although Russia protested the decisions of the Security Council taken in her absence in 1950 as illegal, those decisions have been regarded as binding and have been made the basis of action.

The Economic and Social Council and the Trusteeship Council both vote by simple majority of those present and voting. The adoption of this principle in the Economic and Social Council may be explained by the fact that, unlike the Security Council, it makes no pretense of exercising coercive authority. As stated in the Stettinius Report to the President of the United States on the San Francisco Conference, it "could aid in the solution of economic and social problems, but could not interfere with the functions and powers of sovereign states"; its tools are "study, discussion, report and recommendation." In the Trusteeship Council the interests of the great powers are somewhat protected by their right to seats, and even more by the fact that this Council, too, is unable to coerce; its findings can be made highly embarrassing to administering authorities, three of whom are great powers, but they have been willing to run this risk in order to have the advantages of majority action.

---

[19] See Yuen-li Liang, "Abstention and Absence of a Permanent Member in Relation to Voting in the Security Council," *American Journal of International Law,* vol. 44, no. 4 (1950), pp. 694–708.

Majority action, sometimes qualified, is the general rule within the specialized agencies. Most decisions taken by the Conference of FAO are by simple majority, but some few require a two-thirds vote. To give another example, voting in the General Conference of UNESCO is by simple majority except where the two-thirds rule is expressly required by the Constitution.

After examining voting methods now in vogue and comparing them with those of the past, most observers would venture the ready opinion that there has been a steady improvement in the course of the years. We may picture the nineteenth-century diplomat returned to view his craft as it is now practiced on this strife-torn planet as quite awe-struck by the scarcity of the old rule of unanimity which he knew so well, much as we like to imagine Benjamin Franklin speechless in the presence of electric lights, the radio, and atomic power. If, however, that diplomat were as canny as the members of his craft are generally reputed to be, he could point out that much of the change does not represent improvement, that the majority rule obtains principally where the decisions taken do not affect state authority and national policy, and that where it really matters, decisions cannot even yet be imposed on a state, at least not upon a strong state entitled by the fact of its strength to a permanent seat in the Security Council. International organization may recommend, advise, investigate, and call attention to something by majority action; but it cannot compel or command unless the state involved is a nonpermanent member of the Security Council, and not even then if one of the great powers will come to its support by use of the veto.

▲

APPENDIX TO CHAPTER V

I

Charter of the United Nations

WE THE PEOPLES OF THE UNITED NATIONS DETERMINED

to save succeeding generations from the scourge of war, which twice in our lifetime has brought untold sorrow to mankind, and to reaffirm faith in fundamental human rights, in the dignity and worth of the human person, in the equal rights of men and women and of nations large and small, and

to establish conditions under which justice and respect for the obligations arising from treaties and other sources of international law can be maintained, and

to promote social progress and better standards of life in larger freedom,

AND FOR THESE ENDS

to practice tolerance and live together in peace with one another as good neighbors, and

to unite our strength to maintain international peace and security, and

to ensure, by the acceptance of principles and the institution of methods, that armed force shall not be used, save in the common interest, and

to employ international machinery for the promotion of the economic and social advancement of all peoples,

HAVE RESOLVED TO COMBINE OUR EFFORTS TO ACCOMPLISH THESE AIMS

Accordingly, our respective Governments, through representatives assembled in the city of San Francisco, who have exhibited their full powers found to be in good and due form, have agreed to the present Charter of the United Nations and do hereby establish an international organization to be known as the United Nations.

I. Purposes and Principles
ARTICLE 1

The Purposes of the United Nations are:

1. To maintain international peace and security, and to that end: to take effective collective measures for the prevention and removal of threats to the peace, and for the suppression of acts of aggression or other breaches of the peace, and to bring about by peaceful means, and in conformity with the principles of justice and international law, adjustment or settlement of international disputes or situations which might lead to a breach of the peace;

2. To develop friendly relations among nations based on respect for the principle of equal rights and self-determination of peoples, and to take other appropriate measures to strengthen universal peace;

3. To achieve international cooperation in solving international problems of an economic, social, cultural, or humanitarian character, and in promoting and encouraging respect for human rights and for fundamental freedoms for all without distinction as to race, sex, language, or religion; and

4. To be a center for harmonizing the actions of nations in the attainment of these common ends.

ARTICLE 2

The Organization and its Members, in pursuit of the Purposes stated in Article 1, shall act in accordance with the following Principles.

1. The Organization is based on the principle of the sovereign equality of all its Members.

2. All Members, in order to ensure to all of them the rights and benefits resulting from membership, shall fulfil in good faith the obligations assumed by them in accordance with the present Charter.

3. All Members shall settle their international disputes by peaceful means in such a manner that international peace and security, and justice, are not endangered.

4. All Members shall refrain in their international relations from the threat or use of force against the territorial integrity or political independence of any state, or in any other manner inconsistent with the Purposes of the United Nations.

5. All Members shall give the United Nations every assistance in any action it takes in accordance with the present Charter, and shall refrain from giving assistance to any state against which the United Nations is taking preventive or enforcement action.

6. The Organization shall ensure that states which are not Members of the United Nations act in accordance with the Principles so far as may be necessary for the maintenance of international peace and security.

7. Nothing contained in the present Charter shall authorize the United Nations to intervene in matters which are essentially within the domestic jurisdiction of any state or shall require the Members to submit such matters to settlement under the present Charter; but this principle shall not prejudice the application of enforcement measures under Chapter VII.

II. Membership
ARTICLE 3

The original Members of the United Nations shall be the states which, having participated in the United Nations Conference on International Organization at San Francisco, or having previously signed the Declaration by United Nations of January 1, 1942, sign the present Charter and ratify it in accordance with Article 110.

ARTICLE 4

1. Membership in the United Nations is open to all other peace-loving states which accept the obligations contained in the present Charter and, in the judgment of the Organization, are able and willing to carry out these obligations.

2. The admission of any such state to membership in the United Nations will be effected by a decision of the General Assembly upon the recommendation of the Security Council.

ARTICLE 5

A Member of the United Nations against which preventive or enforcement action has been taken by the Security Council may be suspended from the exercise of the rights and privileges of membership by the General Assembly upon the recommendation of the Security Council. The exercise of these rights and privileges may be restored by the Security Council.

ARTICLE 6

A Member of the United Nations which has persistently violated the Principles contained in the present Charter may be expelled from the Organization by the General Assembly upon the recommendation of the Security Council.

III. Organs
ARTICLE 7

1. There are established as the principal organs of the United Nations: a General Assembly, a Security Council, an Economic and Social Council, a Trusteeship Council, an International Court of Justice, and a Secretariat.

2. Such subsidiary organs as may be found necessary may be established in accordance with the present Charter.

ARTICLE 8

The United Nations shall place no restrictions on the eligibility of men and women to participate in any capacity and under conditions of equality in its principal and subsidiary organs.

IV. The General Assembly

Composition

ARTICLE 9

1. The General Assembly shall consist of all the Members of the United Nations.

2. Each Member shall have not more than five representatives in the General Assembly.

Functions and Powers

ARTICLE 10

The General Assembly may discuss any questions or any matters within the scope of the present Charter or relating to the powers and functions of any organs provided for in the present Charter, and, except as provided in Article 12, may make recommendations to the Members of the United Nations or to the Security Council or to both on any such questions or matters.

ARTICLE 11

1. The General Assembly may consider the general principles of cooperation in the maintenance of international peace and security, including the principles governing disarmament and the regulation

of armaments, and may make recommendations with regard to such principles to the Members or to the Security Council or to both.

2. The General Assembly may discuss any questions relating to the maintenance of international peace and security brought before it by any Member of the United Nations, or by the Security Council, or by a state which is not a Member of the United Nations in accordance with Article 35, paragraph 2, and, except as provided in Article 12, may make recommendations with regard to any such questions to the state or states concerned or to the Security Council or to both. Any such question on which action is necessary shall be referred to the Security Council by the General Assembly either before or after discussion.

3. The General Assembly may call the attention of the Security Council to situations which are likely to endanger international peace and security.

4. The powers of the General Assembly set forth in this Article shall not limit the general scope of Article 10.

ARTICLE 12

1. While the Security Council is exercising in respect to any dispute or situation the functions assigned to it in the present Charter, the General Assembly shall not make any recommendation with regard to that dispute or situation unless the Security Council so requests.

2. The Secretary-General, with the consent of the Security Council, shall notify the General Assembly at each session of any matters relative to the maintenance of international peace and security which are being dealt with by the Security Council and shall similarly notify the General Assembly, or the Members of the United Nations if the General Assembly is not in session, immediately the Security Council ceases to deal with such matters.

ARTICLE 13

1. The General Assembly shall initiate studies and make recommendations for the purpose of:

a. promoting international cooperation in the political field and encouraging the progressive development of international law and its codification;

b. promoting international cooperation in the economic, social, cultural, educational, and health fields, and assisting in the realization of human rights and fundamental freedoms for all without distinction as to race, sex, language, or religion.

2. The further responsibilities, functions, and powers of the General Assembly with respect to matters mentioned in paragraph 1 (b) above are set forth in Chapters IX and X.

ARTICLE 14

Subject to the provisions of Article 12, the General Assembly may recommend measures for the peaceful adjustment of any situation, regardless of origin, which it deems likely to impair the general welfare or friendly relations among nations, including situations resulting from a violation of the provisions of the present Charter setting forth the Purposes and Principles of the United Nations.

ARTICLE 15

1. The General Assembly shall receive and consider annual and special reports from the Security Council; these reports shall include an account of the measures that the Security Council has decided upon or taken to maintain international peace and security.

2. The General Assembly shall receive and consider reports from the other organs of the United Nations.

ARTICLE 16

The General Assembly shall perform such functions with respect to the international trusteeship system as are assigned to it under Chapters XII and XIII, including the approval of the trusteeship agreements for areas not designated as strategic.

ARTICLE 17

1. The General Assembly shall consider and approve the budget of the Organization.

2. The expenses of the Organization shall be borne by the Members as apportioned by the General Assembly.

3. The General Assembly shall consider and approve any financial and budgetary arrangements with specialized agencies referred to in Article 57 and shall examine the administrative budgets of such specialized agencies with a view to making recommendations to the agencies concerned.

Voting

ARTICLE 18

1. Each member of the General Assembly shall have one vote.

2. Decisions of the General Assembly on important questions shall be made by a two-thirds majority of the members present and voting. These questions shall include: recommendations with respect to the maintenance of international peace and security, the election of the non-permanent members of the Security Council, the election of the members of the Economic and Social Council, the election of members of the Trusteeship Council in accordance with paragraph 1 (c) of Article 86, the admission of new Members to the United Nations, the suspension of the rights and privileges of membership, the expulsion of Members, questions relating to the operation of the trusteeship system, and budgetary questions.

3. Decisions on other questions, including the determination of additional categories of questions to be decided by a two-thirds majority, shall be made by a majority of the members present and voting.

ARTICLE 19

A Member of the United Nations which is in arrears in the payment of its financial contributions to the Organization shall have no vote in the General Assembly if the amount of its arrears equals or exceeds the amount of the contributions due from it for the preceding two full years. The General Assembly may, nevertheless, permit such a Member to vote if it is satisfied that the failure to pay is due to conditions beyond the control of the Member.

Procedure

ARTICLE 20

The General Assembly shall meet in regular annual sessions and in such special sessions as occasion may require. Special sessions shall be convoked by the Secretary-General at the request of the Security Council or of a majority of the Members of the United Nations.

ARTICLE 21

The General Assembly shall adopt its own rules of procedure. It shall elect its President for each session.

ARTICLE 22

The General Assembly may establish such subsidiary organs as it deems necessary for the performance of its functions.

V. The Security Council

Composition

ARTICLE 23

1. The Security Council shall consist of eleven Members of the United Nations. The Republic of China, France, the Union of Soviet Socialist Republics, the United Kingdom of Great Britain and Northern Ireland, and the United States of America shall be permanent members of the Security Council. The General Assembly shall elect six other Members of the United Nations to be non-permanent members of the Security Council, due regard being specially paid, in the first instance to the contribution of Members of the United Nations to the maintenance of international peace and security and to the other purposes of the Organization, and also to equitable geographical distribution.

2. The non-permanent members of the Security Council shall be elected for a term of two years. In the first election of the non-permanent members, however, three shall be chosen for a term of one year. A retiring member shall not be eligible for immediate reelection.

3. Each member of the Security Council shall have one representative.

Functions and Powers

ARTICLE 24

1. In order to ensure prompt and effective action by the United Nations, its Members confer on the Security Council primary responsibility for the maintenance of international peace and security, and agree that in carrying out its duties under this responsibility the Security Council acts on their behalf.

2. In discharging these duties the Security Council shall act in accordance with the Purposes and Principles of the United Nations. The specific powers granted to the Security Council for the discharge of these duties are laid down in Chapters VI, VII, VIII, and XII.

3. The Security Council shall submit annual and, when necessary, special reports to the General Assembly for its consideration.

ARTICLE 25

The Members of the United Nations agree to accept and carry out the decisions of the Security Council in accordance with the present Charter.

ARTICLE 26

In order to promote the establishment and maintenance of international peace and security with the least diversion for armaments of the world's human and economic resources, the Security Council shall be responsible for formulating, with the assistance of the Military Staff Committee referred to in Article 47, plans to be submitted to the Members of the United Nations for the establishment of a system for the regulation of armaments.

Voting

ARTICLE 27

1. Each member of the Security Council shall have one vote.

2. Decisions of the Security Council on procedural matters shall be made by an affirmative vote of seven members.

3. Decisions of the Security Council on all other matters shall be made by an affirmative vote of seven members including the concurring votes of the permanent members; provided that, in decisions under Chapter VI, and under paragraph 3 of Article 52, a party to a dispute shall abstain from voting.

Procedure

ARTICLE 28

1. The Security Council shall be so organized as to be able to function continuously. Each member of the Security Council shall for this purpose be represented at all times at the seat of the Organization.

2. The Security Council shall hold periodic meetings at which each of its members may, if it so desires, be represented by a member of the government or by some other specially designated representative.

3. The Security Council may hold meetings at such places other than the seat of the Organization as in its judgment will best facilitate its work.

ARTICLE 29

The Security Council may establish such subsidiary organs as it deems necessary for the performance of its functions.

ARTICLE 30

The Security Council shall adopt its own rules of procedure, including the method of selecting its President.

ARTICLE 31

Any Member of the United Nations which is not a member of the Security Council may participate, without vote, in the discussion of any question brought before the Security Council whenever the latter considers that the interests of that Member are specially affected.

ARTICLE 32

Any Member of the United Nations which is not a member of the Security Council or any state which is not a Member of the United

Nations, if it is a party to a dispute under consideration by the Security Council, shall be invited to participate, without vote, in the discussion relating to the dispute. The Security Council shall lay down such conditions as it deems just for the participation of a state which is not a Member of the United Nations.

VI. Pacific Settlement of Disputes

ARTICLE 33

1. The parties to any dispute, the continuance of which is likely to endanger the maintenance of international peace and security, shall, first of all, seek a solution by negotiation, enquiry, mediation, conciliation, arbitration, judicial settlement, resort to regional agencies or arrangements, or other peaceful means of their own choice.

2. The Security Council shall, when it deems necessary, call upon the parties to settle their dispute by such means.

ARTICLE 34

The Security Council may investigate any dispute, or any situation which might lead to international friction or give rise to a dispute, in order to determine whether the continuance of the dispute or situation is likely to endanger the maintenance of international peace and security.

ARTICLE 35

1. Any Member of the United Nations may bring any dispute, or any situation of the nature referred to in Article 34, to the attention of the Security Council or of the General Assembly.

2. A state which is not a Member of the United Nations may bring to the attention of the Security Council or of the General Assembly any dispute to which it is a party if it accepts in advance, for the purposes of the dispute, the obligations of pacific settlement provided in the present Charter.

3. The proceedings of the General Assembly in respect of matters brought to its attention under this Article will be subject to the provisions of Articles 11 and 12.

Article 36

1. The Security Council may, at any stage of a dispute of the nature referred to in Article 33 or of a situation of like nature, recommend appropriate procedures or methods of adjustment.

2. The Security Council should take into consideration any procedures for the settlement of the dispute which have already been adopted by the parties.

3. In making recommendations under this Article the Security Council should also take into consideration that legal disputes should as a general rule be referred by the parties to the International Court of Justice in accordance with the provisions of the Statute of the Court.

Article 37

1. Should the parties to a dispute of the nature referred to in Article 33 fail to settle it by the means indicated in that Article, they shall refer it to the Security Council.

2. If the Security Council deems that the continuance of the dispute is in fact likely to endanger the maintenance of international peace and security, it shall decide whether to take action under Article 36 or to recommend such terms of settlement as it may consider appropriate.

Article 38

Without prejudice to the provisions of Articles 33 to 37, the Security Council may, if all the parties to any dispute so request, make recommendations to the parties with a view to a pacific settlement of the dispute.

VII. Action with Respect to Threats to the Peace, Breaches of the Peace, and Acts of Aggression

Article 39

The Security Council shall determine the existence of any threat to the peace, breach of the peace, or act of aggression and shall make recommendations, or decide what measures shall be taken in accordance with Articles 41 and 42, to maintain or restore international peace and security.

ARTICLE 40

In order to prevent an aggravation of the situation, the Security Council may, before making the recommendations or deciding upon the measures provided for in Article 39, call upon the parties concerned to comply with such provisional measures as it deems necessary or desirable. Such provisional measures shall be without prejudice to the rights, claims, or position of the parties concerned. The Security Council shall duly take account of failure to comply with such provisional measures.

ARTICLE 41

The Security Council may decide what measures not involving the use of armed force are to be employed to give effect to its decisions, and it may call upon the Members of the United Nations to apply such measures. These may include complete or partial interruption of economic relations and of rail, sea, air, postal, telegraphic, radio, and other means of communication, and the severance of diplomatic relations.

ARTICLE 42

Should the Security Council consider that measures provided for in Article 41 would be inadequate or have proved to be inadequate, it may take such action by air, sea, or land forces as may be necessary to maintain or restore international peace and security. Such action may include demonstrations, blockade, and other operations by air, sea, or land forces of Members of the United Nations.

ARTICLE 43

1. All Members of the United Nations, in order to contribute to the maintenance of international peace and security, undertake to make available to the Security Council, on its call and in accordance with a special agreement or agreements, armed forces, assistance, and facilities, including rights of passage, necessary for the purpose of maintaining international peace and security.

2. Such agreement or agreements shall govern the numbers and types of forces, their degree of readiness and general location, and the nature of the facilities and assistance to be provided.

3. The agreement or agreements shall be negotiated as soon as possible on the initiative of the Security Council. They shall be concluded between the Security Council and Members or between the Security Council and groups of Members and shall be subject to ratification by the signatory states in accordance with their respective constitutional processes.

ARTICLE 44

When the Security Council has decided to use force it shall, before calling upon a Member not represented on it to provide armed forces in fulfillment of the obligations assumed under Article 43, invite that Member, if the Member so desires, to participate in the decisions of the Security Council concerning the employment of contingents of that Member's armed forces.

ARTICLE 45

In order to enable the United Nations to take urgent military measures, Members shall hold immediately available national air-force contingents for combined international enforcement action. The strength and degree of readiness of these contingents and plans for their combined action shall be determined, within the limits laid down in the special agreement or agreements referred to in Article 43, by the Security Council with the assistance of the Military Staff Committee.

ARTICLE 46

Plans for the application of armed force shall be made by the Security Council with the assistance of the Military Staff Committee.

ARTICLE 47

1. There shall be established a Military Staff Committee to advise and assist the Security Council on all questions relating to the Security Council's military requirements for the maintenance of in-

ternational peace and security, the employment and command of forces placed at its disposal, the regulation of armaments, and possible disarmament.

2. The Military Staff Committee shall consist of the Chiefs of Staff of the permanent members of the Security Council or their representatives. Any Member of the United Nations not permanently represented on the Committee shall be invited by the Committee to be associated with it when the efficient discharge of the Committee's responsibilities requires the participation of that Member in its work.

3. The Military Staff Committee shall be responsible under the Security Council for the strategic direction of any armed forces placed at the disposal of the Security Council. Questions relating to the command of such forces shall be worked out subsequently.

4. The Military Staff Committee, with the authorization of the Security Council and after consultation with appropriate regional agencies, may establish regional subcommittees.

Article 48

1. The action required to carry out the decisions of the Security Council for the maintenance of international peace and security shall be taken by all the Members of the United Nations or by some of them, as the Security Council may determine.

2. Such decisions shall be carried out by the Members of the United Nations directly and through their action in the appropriate international agencies of which they are members.

Article 49

The Members of the United Nations shall join in affording mutual assistance in carrying out the measures decided upon by the Security Council.

Article 50

If preventive or enforcement measures against any state are taken by the Security Council, any other state, whether a Member of the United Nations or not, which finds itself confronted with special economic problems arising from the carrying out of those measures shall have the right to consult the Security Council with regard to a solution of those problems.

ARTICLE 51

Nothing in the present Charter shall impair the inherent right of individual or collective self-defense if an armed attack occurs against a Member of the United Nations, until the Security Council has taken the measures necessary to maintain international peace and security. Measures taken by Members in the exercise of this right of self-defense shall be immediately reported to the Security Council and shall not in any way affect the authority and responsibility of the Security Council under the present Charter to take at any time such action as it deems necessary in order to maintain or restore international peace and security.

VIII. Regional Arrangements
ARTICLE 52

1. Nothing in the present Charter precludes the existence of regional arrangements or agencies for dealing with such matters relating to the maintenance of international peace and security as are appropriate for regional action, provided that such arrangements or agencies and their activities are consistent with the Purposes and Principles of the United Nations.

2. The Members of the United Nations entering into such arrangements or constituting such agencies shall make every effort to achieve pacific settlement of local disputes through such regional arrangements or by such regional agencies before referring them to the Security Council.

3. The Security Council shall encourage the development of pacific settlement of local disputes through such regional arrangements or by such regional agencies either on the initiative of the states concerned or by reference from the Security Council.

4. This Article in no way impairs the application of Articles 34 and 35.

ARTICLE 53

1. The Security Council shall, where appropriate, utilize such regional arrangements or agencies for enforcement action under its authority. But no enforcement action shall be taken under regional arrangements or by regional agencies without the authorization of the Security Council, with the exception of measures against any enemy state, as defined in paragraph 2 of this Article, provided for pursuant to Article 107 or in regional arrangements directed against renewal of aggressive policy on the part of any such state, until such time as the Organization may, on request of the Governments concerned, be charged with the responsibility for preventing further aggression by such a state.

2. The term enemy state as used in paragraph 1 of this Article applies to any state which during the Second World War has been an enemy of any signatory of the present Charter.

ARTICLE 54

The Security Council shall at all times be kept fully informed of activities undertaken or in contemplation under regional arrangements or by regional agencies for the maintenance of international peace and security.

IX. International Economic and Social Coöperation
ARTICLE 55

With a view to the creation of conditions of stability and well-being which are necessary for peaceful and friendly relations among nations based on respect for the principle of equal rights and self-determination of peoples, the United Nations shall promote:

a. higher standards of living, full employment, and conditions of economic and social progress and development;

b. solutions of international economic, social, health, and related problems; and international cultural and educational coöperation; and

c. universal respect for, and observance of, human rights and fundamental freedoms for all without distinction as to race, sex, language, or religion.

ARTICLE 56

All Members pledge themselves to take joint and separate action in coöperation with the Organization for the achievement of the purposes set forth in Article 55.

ARTICLE 57

1. The various specialized agencies, established by intergovernmental agreement and having wide international responsibilities, as defined in their basic instruments, in economic, social, cultural, educational, health, and related fields, shall be brought into relationship with the United Nations in accordance with the provisions of Article 63.

2. Such agencies thus brought into relationship with the United Nations are hereinafter referred to as specialized agencies.

ARTICLE 58

The Organization shall make recommendations for the coördination of the policies and activities of the specialized agencies.

ARTICLE 59

The Organization shall, where appropriate, initiate negotiations among the states concerned for the creation of any new specialized agencies required for the accomplishment of the purposes set forth in Article 55.

ARTICLE 60

Responsibility for the discharge of the functions of the Organization set forth in this Chapter shall be vested in the General Assembly and, under the authority of the General Assembly, in the Economic and Social Council, which shall have for this purpose the powers set forth in Chapter X.

X. The Economic and Social Council

Composition

ARTICLE 61

1. The Economic and Social Council shall consist of eighteen Members of the United Nations elected by the General Assembly.

2. Subject to the provisions of paragraph 3, six members of the Economic and Social Council shall be elected each year for a term of three years. A retiring member shall be eligible for immediate re-election.

3. At the first election, eighteen members of the Economic and Social Council shall be chosen. The term of office of six members so chosen shall expire at the end of one year, and of six other members at the end of two years, in accordance with arrangements made by the General Assembly.

4. Each member of the Economic and Social Council shall have one representative.

Functions and Powers

ARTICLE 62

1. The Economic and Social Council may make or initiate studies and reports with respect to international economic, social, cultural, educational, health, and related matters and may make recommendations with respect to any such matters to the General Assembly, to the Members of the United Nations, and to the specialized agencies concerned.

2. It may make recommendations for the purpose of promoting respect for, and observance of, human rights and fundamental freedoms for all.

3. It may prepare draft conventions for submission to the General Assembly, with respect to matters falling within its competence.

4. It may call, in accordance with the rules prescribed by the United Nations, international conferences on matters falling within its competence.

ARTICLE 63

1. The Economic and Social Council may enter into agreements with any of the agencies referred to in Article 57, defining the terms on which the agency concerned shall be brought into relationship with the United Nations. Such agreements shall be subject to approval by the General Assembly.

2. It may coördinate the activities of the specialized agencies through consultation with and recommendations to such agencies and through recommendations to the General Assembly and to the Members of the United Nations.

ARTICLE 64

1. The Economic and Social Council may take appropriate steps to obtain regular reports from the specialized agencies. It may make arrangements with the Members of the United Nations and with the specialized agencies to obtain reports on the steps taken to give effect to its own recommendations and to recommendations on matters falling within its competence made by the General Assembly.

2. It may communicate its observations on these reports to the General Assembly.

ARTICLE 65

The Economic and Social Council may furnish information to the Security Council and shall assist the Security Council upon its request.

ARTICLE 66

1. The Economic and Social Council shall perform such functions as fall within its competence in connection with the carrying out of the recommendations of the General Assembly.

2. It may, with the approval of the General Assembly, perform services at the request of Members of the United Nations and at the request of specialized agencies.

3. It shall perform such other functions as are specified elsewhere

in the present Charter or as may be assigned to it by the General Assembly.

Voting

ARTICLE 67

1. Each member of the Economic and Social Council shall have one vote.

2. Decisions of the Economic and Social Council shall be made by a majority of the members present and voting.

Procedure

ARTICLE 68

The Economic and Social Council shall set up commissions in economic and social fields and for the promotion of human rights, and such other commissions as may be required for the performance of its functions.

ARTICLE 69

The Economic and Social Council shall invite any Member of the United Nations to participate, without vote, in its deliberations on any matter of particular concern to that Member.

ARTICLE 70

The Economic and Social Council may make arrangements for representatives of the specialized agencies to participate, without vote, in its deliberations and in those of the commissions established by it, and for its representatives to participate in the deliberations of the specialized agencies.

ARTICLE 71

The Economic and Social Council may make suitable arrangements for consultation with non-governmental organizations which are concerned with matters within its competence. Such arrangements may be made with international organizations and, where appropriate, with national organizations after consultation with the Member of the United Nations concerned.

ARTICLE 72

1. The Economic and Social Council shall adopt its own rules of procedure, including the method of selecting its President.

2. The Economic and Social Council shall meet as required in accordance with its rules, which shall include provision for the convening of meetings on the request of a majority of its members.

XI. Declaration Regarding Non-Self-Governing Territories
ARTICLE 73

Members of the United Nations which have or assume responsibilities for the administration of territories whose peoples have not yet attained a full measure of self-government recognize the principle that the interests of the inhabitants of these territories are paramount, and accept as a sacred trust the obligation to promote to the utmost, within the system of international peace and security established by the present Charter, the well-being of the inhabitants of these territories, and, to this end:

a. to ensure, with due respect for the culture of the peoples concerned, their political, economic, social, and educational advancement, their just treatment, and their protection against abuses;

b. to develop self-government, to take due account of the political aspirations of the peoples, and to assist them in the progressive development of their free political institutions, according to the particular circumstances of each territory and its peoples and their varying stages of advancement;

c. to further international peace and security;

d. to promote constructive measures of development, to encourage research, and to coöperate with one another and, when and where appropriate, with specialized international bodies with a view to the practical achievement of the social, economic, and scientific purposes set forth in this Article; and

e. to transmit regularly to the Secretary-General for information purposes, subject to such limitation as security and constitutional considerations may require, statistical and other information of a technical nature relating to economic, social, and educational conditions in the territories for which they are respectively responsible other than those territories to which Chapters XII and XIII apply.

ARTICLE 74

Members of the United Nations also agree that their policy in respect of the territories to which this Chapter applies, no less than in respect of their metropolitan areas, must be based on the general principle of good-neighborliness, due account being taken of the interests and well-being of the rest of the world, in social, economic, and commercial matters.

XII. International Trusteeship System
ARTICLE 75

The United Nations shall establish under its authority an international trusteeship system for the administration and supervision of such territories as may be placed thereunder by subsequent individual agreements. These territories are hereinafter referred to as trust territories.

ARTICLE 76

The basic objectives of the trusteeship system, in accordance with the Purposes of the United Nations laid down in Article 1 of the present Charter, shall be:

a. to further international peace and security;

b. to promote the political, economic, social, and educational advancement of the inhabitants of the trust territories, and their progressive development towards self-government or independence as may be appropriate to the particular circumstances of each territory and its peoples and the freely expressed wishes of the peoples concerned, and as may be provided by the terms of each trusteeship agreement;

c. to encourage respect for human rights and for fundamental freedoms for all without distinction as to race, sex, language, or religion, and to encourage recognition of the interdependence of the peoples of the world; and

d. to ensure equal treatment in social, economic, and commercial matters for all Members of the United Nations and their nationals, and also equal treatment for the latter in the administration of justice, without prejudice to the attainment of the foregoing objectives and subject to the provisions of Article 80.

ARTICLE 77

1. The trusteeship system shall apply to such territories in the following categories as may be placed thereunder by means of trusteeship agreements:

a. territories now held under mandate;

b. territories which may be detached from enemy states as a result of the Second World War; and

c. territories voluntarily placed under the system by states responsible for their administration.

2. It will be a matter for subsequent agreement as to which territories in the foregoing categories will be brought under the trusteeship system and upon what terms.

ARTICLE 78

The trusteeship system shall not apply to territories which have become Members of the United Nations, relationship among which shall be based on respect for the principle of sovereign equality.

ARTICLE 79

The terms of trusteeship for each territory to be placed under the trusteeship system, including any alteration or amendment, shall be agreed upon by the states directly concerned, including the mandatory power in the case of territories held under mandate by a Member of the United Nations, and shall be approved as provided for in Articles 83 and 85.

ARTICLE 80

1. Except as may be agreed upon in individual trusteeship agreements, made under Articles 77, 79, and 81, placing each territory under the trusteeship system, and until such agreements have been concluded, nothing in this Chapter shall be construed in or of itself to alter in any manner the rights whatsoever of any states or any

peoples or the terms of existing international instruments to which Members of the United Nations may respectively be parties.

2. Paragraph 1 of this Article shall not be interpreted as giving grounds for delay or postponement of the negotiation and conclusion of agreements for placing mandated and other territories under the trusteeship system as provided for in Article 77.

ARTICLE 81

The trusteeship agreement shall in each case include the terms under which the trust territory will be administered and designate the authority which will exercise the administration of the trust territory. Such authority, hereinafter called the administering authority, may be one or more states or the Organization itself.

ARTICLE 82

There may be designated, in any trusteeship agreement, a strategic area or areas which may include part or all of the trust territory to which the agreement applies, without prejudice to any special agreement or agreements made under Article 43.

ARTICLE 83

1. All functions of the United Nations relating to strategic areas, including the approval of the terms of the trusteeship agreements and of their alteration or amendment, shall be exercised by the Security Council.

2. The basic objectives set forth in Article 76 shall be applicable to the people of each strategic area.

3. The Security Council shall, subject to the provisions of the trusteeship agreements and without prejudice to security considerations, avail itself of the assistance of the Trusteeship Council to perform those functions of the United Nations under the trusteeship system relating to political, economic, social, and educational matters in the strategic areas.

ARTICLE 84

It shall be the duty of the administering authority to ensure that the trust territory shall play its part in the maintenance of international peace and security. To this end the administering authority may make use of volunteer forces, facilities, and assistance from the trust territory in carrying out the obligations towards the Security Council undertaken in this regard by the administering authority, as well as for local defense and the maintenance of law and order within the trust territory.

ARTICLE 85

1. The functions of the United Nations with regard to trusteeship agreements for all areas not designated as strategic, including the approval of the terms of the trusteeship agreements and of their alteration or amendment, shall be exercised by the General Assembly.

2. The Trusteeship Council, operating under the authority of the General Assembly, shall assist the General Assembly in carrying out these functions.

XIII. The Trusteeship Council

Composition

ARTICLE 86

1. The Trusteeship Council shall consist of the following Members of the United Nations:

a. those Members administering trust territories;

b. such of those Members mentioned by name in Article 23 as are not administering trust territories; and

c. as many other Members elected for three-year terms by the General Assembly as may be necessary to ensure that the total number of members of the Trusteeship Council is equally divided between those Members of the United Nations which administer trust territories and those which do not.

2. Each member of the Trusteeship Council shall designate one specially qualified person to represent it therein.

Functions and Powers

ARTICLE 87

The General Assembly and, under its authority, the Trusteeship Council, in carrying out their functions, may:

a. consider reports submitted by the administering authority;

b. accept petitions and examine them in consultation with the administering authority;

c. provide for periodic visits to the respective trust territories at times agreed upon with the administering authority; and

d. take these and other actions in conformity with the terms of the trusteeship agreements.

ARTICLE 88

The Trusteeship Council shall formulate a questionnaire on the political, economic, social, and educational advancement of the inhabitants of each trust territory, and the administering authority for each trust territory within the competence of the General Assembly shall make an annual report to the General Assembly upon the basis of such questionnaire.

Voting

ARTICLE 89

1. Each member of the Trusteeship Council shall have one vote.

2. Decisions of the Trusteeship Council shall be made by a majority of the members present and voting.

Procedure

ARTICLE 90

1. The Trusteeship Council shall adopt its own rules of procedure, including the method of selecting its President.

2. The Trusteeship Council shall meet as required in accordance with its rules, which shall include provision for the convening of meetings on the request of a majority of its members.

ARTICLE 91

The Trusteeship Council shall, when appropriate, avail itself of the assistance of the Economic and Social Council and of the specialized agencies in regard to matters with which they are respectively concerned.

XIV. The International Court of Justice
ARTICLE 92

The International Court of Justice shall be the principal judicial organ of the United Nations. It shall function in accordance with the annexed Statute, which is based upon the Statute of the Permanent Court of International Justice and forms an integral part of the present Charter.

ARTICLE 93

1. All Members of the United Nations are *ipso facto* parties to the Statute of the International Court of Justice.

2. A state which is not a Member of the United Nations may become a party to the Statute of the International Court of Justice on conditions to be determined in each case by the General Assembly upon the recommendation of the Security Council.

ARTICLE 94

1. Each Member of the United Nations undertakes to comply with the decision of the International Court of Justice in any case to which it is a party.

2. If any party to a case fails to perform the obligation incumbent upon it under a judgment rendered by the Court, the other party may have recourse to the Security Council, which may, if it deems necessary, make recommendations or decide upon measures to be taken to give effect to the judgment.

ARTICLE 95

Nothing in the present Charter shall prevent Members of the United Nations from entrusting the solution of their differences to other tribunals by virtue of agreements already in existence or which may be concluded in the future.

ARTICLE 96

1. The General Assembly or the Security Council may request the International Court of Justice to give an advisory opinion on any legal question.

2. Other organs of the United Nations and specialized agencies, which may at any time be so authorized by the General Assembly, may also request advisory opinions of the Court on legal questions arising within the scope of their activities.

XV. The Secretariat
ARTICLE 97

The Secretariat shall comprise a Secretary-General and such staff as the Organization may require. The Secretary-General shall be appointed by the General Assembly upon the recommendation of the Security Council. He shall be the chief administrative officer of the Organization.

ARTICLE 98

The Secretary-General shall act in that capacity in all meetings of the General Assembly, of the Security Council, of the Economic and Social Council, and of the Trusteeship Council, and shall perform such other functions as are entrusted to him by these organs. The Secretary-General shall make an annual report to the General Assembly on the work of the Organization.

ARTICLE 99

The Secretary-General may bring to the attention of the Security Council any matter which in his opinion may threaten the maintenance of international peace and security.

ARTICLE 100

1. In the performance of their duties the Secretary-General and the staff shall not seek or receive instructions from any government or from any other authority external to the Organization. They shall refrain from any action which might reflect on their position as international officials responsible only to the Organization.

2. Each Member of the United Nations undertakes to respect the exclusively international character of the responsibilities of the Secretary-General and the staff and not to seek to influence them in the discharge of their responsibilities.

ARTICLE 101

1. The staff shall be appointed by the Secretary-General under regulations established by the General Assembly.

2. Appropriate staffs shall be permanently assigned to the Economic and Social Council, the Trusteeship Council, and, as required, to other organs of the United Nations. These staffs shall form a part of the Secretariat.

3. The paramount consideration in the employment of the staff and in the determination of the conditions of service shall be the necessity of securing the highest standards of efficiency, competence, and integrity. Due regard shall be paid to the importance of recruiting the staff on as wide a geographical basis as possible.

XVI. Miscellaneous Provisions

ARTICLE 102

1. Every treaty and every international agreement entered into by any Member of the United Nations after the present Charter comes into force shall as soon as possible be registered with the Secretariat and published by it.

2. No party to any such treaty or international agreement which has not been registered in accordance with the provisions of paragraph 1 of this Article may invoke that treaty or agreement before any organ of the United Nations.

ARTICLE 103

In the event of a conflict between the obligations of the Members of the United Nations under the present Charter and their obligations under any other international agreement, their obligations under the present Charter shall prevail.

ARTICLE 104

The Organization shall enjoy in the territory of each of its Members such legal capacity as may be necessary for the exercise of its functions and the fulfillment of its purposes.

ARTICLE 105

1. The Organization shall enjoy in the territory of each of its Members such privileges and immunities as are necessary for the fulfillment of its purposes.

2. Representatives of the Members of the United Nations and officials of the Organization shall similarly enjoy such privileges and immunities as are necessary for the independent exercise of their functions in connection with the Organization.

3. The General Assembly may make recommendations with a view to determining the details of the application of paragraphs 1 and 2 of this Article or may propose conventions to the Members of the United Nations for this purpose.

XVII. Transitional Security Arrangements
ARTICLE 106

Pending the coming into force of such special agreements referred to in Article 43 as in the opinion of the Security Council enable it to begin the exercise of its responsibilities under Article 42, the parties to the Four-Nation Declaration, signed at Moscow, October 30, 1943, and France, shall, in accordance with the provisions of paragraph 5 of that Declaration, consult with one another and as occasion requires with other Members of the United Nations with a view to such joint action on behalf of the Organization as may be necessary for the purpose of maintaining international peace and security.

ARTICLE 107

Nothing in the present Charter shall invalidate or preclude action, in relation to any state which during the Second World War has been an enemy of any signatory to the present Charter, taken or authorized as a result of that war by the Governments having responsibility for such action.

XVIII. Amendments
ARTICLE 108

Amendments to the present Charter shall come into force for all Members of the United Nations when they have been adopted by a vote of two-thirds of the members of the General Assembly and ratified in accordance with their respective constitutional processes by two-thirds of the Members of the United Nations, including all the permanent members of the Security Council.

ARTICLE 109

1. A General Conference of the Members of the United Nations for the purpose of reviewing the present Charter may be held at a date and place to be fixed by a two-thirds vote of the members of the General Assembly and by a vote of any seven members of the Security Council. Each Member of the United Nations shall have one vote in the conference.

2. Any alteration of the present Charter recommended by a two-thirds vote of the conference shall take effect when ratified in accordance with their respective constitutional processes by two-thirds of the Members of the United Nations including all the permanent members of the Security Council.

3. If such a conference has not been held before the tenth annual session of the General Assembly following the coming into force of the present Charter, the proposal to call such a conference shall be placed on the agenda of that session of the General Assembly, and the conference shall be held if so decided by a majority vote of the members of the General Assembly and by a vote of any seven members of the Security Council.

XIX. Ratification and Signature
ARTICLE 110

1. The present Charter shall be ratified by the signatory states in accordance with their respective constitutional processes.

2. The ratifications shall be deposited with the Government of the United States of America, which shall notify all the signatory states of each deposit as well as the Secretary-General of the Organization when he has been appointed.

3. The present Charter shall come into force upon the deposit of ratifications by the Republic of China, France, the Union of Soviet Socialist Republics, the United Kingdom of Great Britain and

Northern Ireland, and the United States of America, and by a majority of the other signatory states. A protocol of the ratifications deposited shall thereupon be drawn up by the Government of the United States of America which shall communicate copies thereof to all the signatory states.

4. The states signatory to the present Charter which ratify it after it has come into force will become original Members of the United Nations on the date of the deposit of their respective ratifications.

ARTICLE 111

The present Charter, of which the Chinese, French, Russian, English, and Spanish texts are equally authentic, shall remain deposited in the archives of the Government of the United States of America. Duly certified copies thereof shall be transmitted by that Government to the Governments of the other signatory states.

IN FAITH WHEREOF the representatives of the Governments of the United Nations have signed the present Charter.

DONE at the city of San Francisco the twenty-sixth day of June, one thousand nine hundred and forty-five.

II

Interim Committee of the General Assembly*

2. The Interim Committee, as a subsidiary organ of the General Assembly established in accordance with Article 22 of the Charter, shall assist the General Assembly in the performance of its functions by discharging the following duties:

> a. To consider and report, with its conclusions, to the General Assembly on such matters as have been referred to it by the General Assembly;
>
> b. To consider and report with its conclusions to the General Assembly on any dispute or any situation which, in virtue of Articles 11 (paragraph 2), 14 or 35 of the Charter, has been

---

* From the Resolution of the General Assembly Establishing the Committee, November 13, 1947.

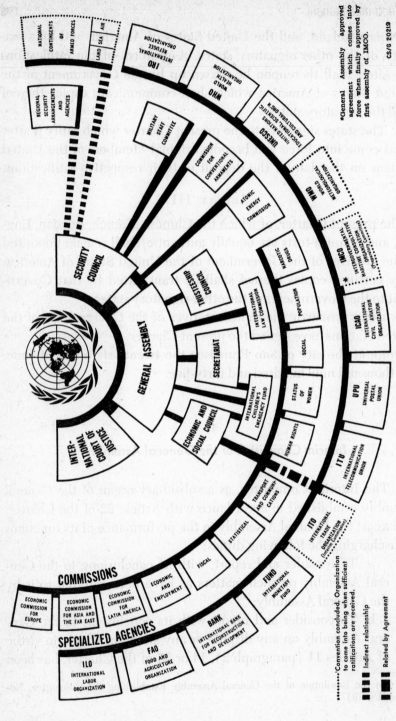

Organization of the United Nations

NATIONAL CONTINGENTS OF ARMED FORCES
LAND SEA AIR

IRO
INTERNATIONAL REFUGEE ORGANIZATION

WHO
WORLD HEALTH ORGANIZATION

UNESCO
UNITED NATIONS EDUCATIONAL, SCIENTIFIC AND CULTURAL ORGANIZATION

WHO
WORLD METEOROLOGICAL ORGANIZATION

IMCO
INTERGOVERNMENTAL MARITIME CONSULTATIVE ORGANIZATION (Preparatory Committee)

ICAO
INTERNATIONAL CIVIL AVIATION ORGANIZATION

UPU
UNIVERSAL POSTAL UNION

ITU
INTERNATIONAL TELECOMMUNICATION UNION

ITO
INTERNATIONAL TRADE ORGANIZATION (Interim Commission)

FUND
INTERNATIONAL MONETARY FUND

BANK
INTERNATIONAL BANK FOR RECONSTRUCTION AND DEVELOPMENT

FAO
FOOD AND AGRICULTURE ORGANIZATION

ILO
INTERNATIONAL LABOR ORGANIZATION

SPECIALIZED AGENCIES

COMMISSIONS

ECONOMIC COMMISSION FOR EUROPE

ECONOMIC COMMISSION FOR ASIA AND THE FAR EAST

ECONOMIC COMMISSION FOR LATIN AMERICA

ECONOMIC AND EMPLOYMENT

FISCAL

STATISTICAL

TRANSPORT AND COMMUNICATIONS

HUMAN RIGHTS

STATUS OF WOMEN

SOCIAL

POPULATION

NARCOTIC DRUGS

ATOMIC ENERGY COMMISSION

COMMISSION FOR CONVENTIONAL ARMAMENTS

MILITARY STAFF COMMITTEE

REGIONAL SECURITY ARRANGEMENTS AND AGENCIES

SECURITY COUNCIL

TRUSTEESHIP COUNCIL

GENERAL ASSEMBLY

SECRETARIAT

INTERNATIONAL LAW COMMISSION

INTERNATIONAL CHILDREN'S EMERGENCY FUND

ECONOMIC AND SOCIAL COUNCIL

INTERNATIONAL COURT OF JUSTICE

*General Assembly approved agreement which comes into force when finally approved by first assembly of IMCO.

•••••• Convention concluded. Organization to come into being when sufficient ratifications are received.

▪▪▪ Indirect relationship

▬▬ Related by Agreement

CS/G 20219

proposed for inclusion in the agenda of the General Assembly by any Member of the United Nations or brought before the General Assembly by the Security Council, provided the Committee previously determines the matter to be both important and requiring preliminary study. Such determination shall be made by a majority of two-thirds of the members present and voting, unless the matter is one referred by the Security Council under Article 11 (paragraph 2), in which case a simple majority will suffice;

c. To consider, as it deems useful and advisable, and report with its conclusions to the General Assembly on methods to be adopted to give effect to that part of Article 11 (paragraph 1), which deals with the general principles of coöperation in the maintenance of international peace and security, and to that part of Article 13 (paragraph 1a), which deals with the promotion of international coöperation in the political field;

d. To consider, in connexion with any matter under discussion by the Interim Committee, whether occasion may require the summoning of a special session of the General Assembly and, if it deems that such session is required, so to advise the Secretary-General in order that he may obtain the views of the Members of the United Nations thereon;

e. To conduct investigations and appoint commissions of enquiry within the scope of its duties, as it may deem useful and necessary, provided that decisions to conduct such investigations or enquiries shall be made by a two-thirds majority of the members present and voting. An investigation or enquiry elsewhere than at the headquarters of the United Nations shall not be conducted without the consent of the State or States in whose territory it is to take place;

f. To report to the next regular session of the General Assembly on the advisability of establishing a permanent committee of the General Assembly to perform the duties of the Interim Committee as stated above with any changes considered desirable in the light of experience;

3. In discharging its duties the Interim Committee shall at all

times take into account the responsibilities of the Security Council under the Charter for the maintenance of international peace and security as well as the duties assigned by the Charter or by the General Assembly or by the Security Council to other Councils or to any committee or commission. The Interim Committee shall not consider any matter of which the Security Council is seized;

III

Members of the United Nations and the Specialized Agencies

The following data is as of September 15, 1949. Since that time the United States of Indonesia have become the sixtieth member of the United Nations. (From *International Organizations in Which the United States Participates,* Department of State Publications 3655, released February, pp. 327–329.)

Members	United Nations	ILO	UNESCO	FAO	ICAO[b]	Fund	Bank	WHO	IRO	ITU[c]	UPU[d]
Afghanistan	▲	▲	▲	....	▲	....	....	▲	....	▲	▲
Albania	......	▲	....		....	....	....	▲	....	▲	▲
Argentina	▲	▲	▲	....	▲	....	....	▲	....	▲	▲
Australia	▲	▲	▲	▲	▲	▲	▲	▲	▲	▲	▲
Austria	......	▲.	▲	▲	▲	▲	▲	▲	....	▲	▲
Belgium	▲	▲	▲	▲	▲	▲	▲	▲	▲	▲	▲
Bolivia	▲	▲	▲	▲	▲	▲	▲	....	....	▲	▲
Brazil	▲	▲	▲	▲	▲	▲	▲	▲	....	▲	▲
Bulgaria	......	▲						▲	....	▲	▲
Burma	▲	▲	▲	▲	▲			▲	....	▲	......
Byelorussian SSR	▲	....						▲[e]	....	▲	▲
Canada	▲	▲	▲	▲	▲	▲	▲	▲	▲	▲	▲
Ceylon	......	▲	....	▲	▲			▲	....	▲	......
Chile	▲	▲	....	▲	▲	▲	▲	▲	....	▲	▲
China	▲	▲	▲	▲	▲	▲	▲	▲	▲	▲	▲
Colombia	▲	▲	▲	▲	▲	▲	▲	....	....	▲	▲
Costa Rica	▲	▲	....	▲		▲	▲	▲	....	▲	▲
Cuba	▲	▲	▲	▲	▲	▲	▲	....	....	▲	▲
Czechoslovakia	▲	▲	▲	▲	▲	▲	▲	▲	....	▲	▲
Denmark	▲	▲	▲	▲	▲	▲	▲	▲	▲	▲	▲
Dominican Republic	▲	▲	▲	▲	▲	▲	▲	▲	▲	▲	▲
Ecuador	▲	▲	▲	▲	......	▲	▲	▲	▲	▲	▲
Egypt	▲	▲	▲	▲	▲	▲	▲	▲	....	▲	▲

Members	United Nations	ILO	UNESCO	FAO	ICAO[b]	Fund	Bank	WHO	IRO	ITU[c]	UPU[d]
El Salvador	▲	▲	▲	▲	▲	▲	▲	▲		▲	▲
Ethiopia	▲	▲		▲	▲	▲	▲	▲		▲	▲
Finland		▲		▲	▲	▲	▲	▲		▲	▲
France	▲	▲	▲	▲	▲	▲	▲	▲	▲	▲	▲
Greece	▲	▲	▲	▲	▲	▲	▲	▲		▲	▲
Guatemala	▲	▲		▲	▲	▲	▲	▲	▲	▲	▲
Haiti	▲	▲	▲	▲	▲			▲		▲	▲
Honduras	▲		▲	▲	▲		▲	▲		▲	▲
Hungary		▲	▲	▲				▲		▲	▲
Iceland	▲	▲		▲	▲	▲	▲	▲	▲	▲	▲
India	▲	▲	▲	▲	▲	▲	▲	▲		▲	▲
Iran	▲	▲	▲			▲	▲	▲		▲	▲
Iraq	▲	▲	▲	▲	▲	▲	▲	▲		▲	▲
Ireland		▲		▲	▲			▲		▲	▲
Israel	▲	▲						▲		▲	
Italy		▲	▲	▲	▲	▲	▲	▲	▲	▲	▲
Japan										▲	▲
Korea								▲			▲
Lebanon	▲	▲	▲	▲		▲	▲	▲		▲	▲
Liberia	▲	▲		▲	▲			▲		▲	▲
Luxembourg	▲	▲	▲	▲	▲	▲	▲	▲	▲	▲	▲
Mexico	▲	▲	▲	▲	▲	▲	▲	▲		▲	▲
Monaco			▲					▲		▲	
Netherlands	▲	▲	▲	▲	▲	▲	▲	▲	▲	▲	▲
New Zealand	▲	▲	▲	▲	▲			▲	▲	▲	▲
Nicaragua	▲			▲	▲	▲	▲			▲	▲
Norway	▲	▲	▲	▲	▲	▲	▲	▲	▲	▲	▲
Pakistan	▲	▲		▲	▲			▲		▲	▲
Panama	▲	▲		▲		▲	▲	▲		▲	▲
Paraguay	▲			▲	▲	▲	▲	▲		▲	▲
Peru	▲	▲	▲	▲	▲	▲	▲	▲		▲	▲
Philippines	▲	▲	▲	▲	▲	▲	▲	▲		▲	▲
Poland	▲	▲	▲	▲	▲	▲	▲	▲		▲	▲
Portugal		▲		▲	▲					▲	▲
Rumania								▲			▲
San Marino											▲
Saudi Arabia	▲		▲	▲				▲		▲	▲
Southern Rhodesia										▲	
Sweden	▲	▲			▲			▲		▲	▲
Switzerland		▲	▲	▲	▲			▲	▲	▲	▲
Syria	▲	▲	▲	▲		▲	▲	▲		▲	▲
Thailand	▲	▲	▲	▲	▲	▲	▲	▲		▲	▲
Jordan, Hashemite Kingdom of the					▲			▲			▲
Turkey	▲	▲	▲	▲	▲	▲	▲	▲		▲	▲
Ukrainian SSR	▲							▲[e]		▲	▲
U. of South Africa	▲	▲	▲	▲	▲	▲	▲	▲		▲	▲
USSR	▲							▲[e]		▲	▲
United Kingdom	▲	▲	▲	▲	▲	▲	▲	▲	▲	▲	▲

Members	United Na- tions	ILO	UNESCO	FAO	ICAO[b]	Fund	Bank	WHO	IRO	ITU[c]	UPU[d]
United States	▲	▲	▲	▲	▲	▲	▲	▲	▲	▲	▲
Uruguay	▲	▲	▲	▲	.....	▲	▲	▲	....	▲	▲
Vatican City	.....			.....						▲	▲
Venezuela	▲	▲	▲	▲	▲	▲	▲	▲	▲	▲	▲
Yemen	▲									▲	▲
Yugoslavia	▲	.....	.....	▲		▲	▲	▲		▲	▲
Total of members	59	[a]60	[a]48	58	[b]54	48	48	[a]66	18	[b]81	[c]83

ABBREVIATIONS

ILO — International Labor Organization

UNESCO — United Nations Educational, Scientific and Cultural Organization

FAO — Food and Agriculture Organization of the United Nations

ICAO — International Civil Aviation Organization

Fund — International Monetary Fund

Bank — International Bank for Reconstruction and Development

WHO — World Health Organization

IRO — International Refugee Organization

ITU — International Telecommunication Union

UPU — Universal Postal Union

[a] A specialized agency is an intergovernmental organization which, in the terms of article 57 of the United Nations Charter, has "wide international responsibilities in economic, social, cultural, educational, health and related fields" and which has entered into a formal agreement with the United Nations. These agreements cover coördination of programs, the establishment of budgetary and financial relationships, coöperation in the development of personnel and statistical services, and the avoidance of competitive or overlapping administrative and technical services. Each specialized agency has its own constitution and receives its basic legal power not from the United Nations but from the governments which accept its constitution.

[b] Spain is not participating in the ICAO although legal debarment from membership will not become effective until 28 States have ratified the amendment to the ICAO Convention debarring Spain.

[c] In addition to the 74 members shown on this chart, ITU's total membership of 81 includes the following:

Indonesia
U.S. Territories
U.K. Colonies
Belgian Congo and Ruanda-Urundi
French Colonies and Protectorates
French Morocco and Tunisia
Portuguese Colonies
(Curaçao and Surinam included with Netherlands)
(Southwest Africa included with Union of South Africa)

A protocol to the 1947 ITU Convention provides for German accession to the Convention "at such time as the responsible authorities consider such accession appropriate" and for the accession of Spain, the Spanish Zone of Morocco and the totality of the Spanish possessions when the provisions of the United Nations General Assembly resolution of Dec. 12, 1946, barring them from membership in the specialized agencies, "shall be abrogated or cease to be applicable."

IV

Some Uses of the Veto*

The Syria-Lebanon Case

The United States proposed a resolution under which the Security Council would have expressed confidence that foreign troops in Syria and Lebanon would be withdrawn as soon as practicable and that negotiations to that end would be undertaken without delay, and would have requested that it be informed of the results of the negotiations (Journal, p. 337). The following vote occurred on this resolution—for: Australia, Brazil, China, Egypt, Mexico, Netherlands, and United States; against: Union of Soviet Socialist Republics; abstentions: Poland, France, United Kingdom. After indicating approval of the resolution during the discussion, France and the United Kingdom abstained, but did not say they were parties to the dispute (Journal, pp. 346–7, 339, 343)† (February 16, 1946).

---

^d In addition to the 72 members shown on this chart, UPU's total membership of 83 includes those listed below:

Algeria
Belgian Congo
Indochina
The whole of the British Overseas Territories, including the Colonies, the Protectorates, and the Territories under Mandate or under Trusteeship exercised by the United Kingdom
French Morocco
Indonesia
Curaçao and Surinam
Portuguese Colonies in West Africa
Portuguese Colonies in East Africa, in Asia, and Oceania
Tunisia
The whole of the possessions of the United States

The final protocol of the UPU Convention, signed in July, 1947, provides for German adherence to the Convention "when the responsible authorities consider it opportune," and for the adherence of Spain, the Spanish Zone of Morocco and the Whole of the Spanish Colonies when the provisions of the United Nations General Assembly Resolution of December 12, 1946, barring them from membership, "shall be repealed or become inoperative."

^e Byelorussia, Ukraine, and the USSR announced their resignations from the WHO. However, inasmuch as the WHO Constitution does not provide for withdrawal, the WHO Assembly on June 25, 1949, adopted a resolution designed to obtain the reconsideration of these countries.

* From *Background Information on the Soviet Union,* Report of the Committee on Foreign Affairs Pursuant to H. Resol. 206, 81st Congress, 2nd Session, House Report No. 3135, 1950, pp. 33–37.

† References are to United Nations documents.

Even though France and the United Kingdom did not specifically concede that they were parties to a dispute, it seems clear that their abstention was not intended to be the equivalent of a negative vote, especially since after the resolution failed of adoption both the United Kingdom and France indicated their intention to abide by its terms. *The President of the Council, after discussion, specifically ruled that the resolution failed to carry because of the negative vote of the U.S.S.R.*

The Spanish Case

A resolution was proposed to adopt the amended recommendations which the Subcommittee on Spain made after its study of the Spanish question (June 13, 1946) (Journal, pp. 742–743). Nine votes were cast in favor of the adoption of the resolution, with the U.S.S.R. against and the Netherlands abstaining (Journal, p. 795) (June 25, 1946).

The Spanish Case

Australia and the United Kingdom proposed a resolution to keep the Spanish case on the list of matters of which the Security Council is seized without prejudice to the rights of the General Assembly (Journal, p. 822). All members voted in favor except the Soviet and Polish representatives, who voted in the negative, as they objected to the final "without prejudice" clause (Journal, p. 834) (June 26, 1946).

The President of the Council ruled that the Australian–United Kingdom resolution (Journal, p. 822; see above, pt. III, par. 1) was a question of procedure. This ruling was put to a vote (Journal, p. 841). Eight members voted that the matter was procedural; France and the Union of Soviet Socialist Republics voted that it was not; Poland abstained (Journal, p. 841) (June 26, 1946).

(NOTE.—*This is the first example of a "double veto." It could properly be counted as two vetoes.*)

The Third Greek Case

The resolution proposed by the United States to adopt the proposals for the maintenance of international peace made by the majority of the members of the Committee of Investigation established by the Security Council received nine supporting votes, with Poland and the U.S.S.R. voting in the negative.

The resolution failed to carry because of the negative vote of the U.S.S.R. (S/P.V./170, p. 41) (July 29, 1947).

Membership of Trans-Jordan

The application of Trans-Jordan for membership in the United Nations, upon submission for the second time to the Security Council on August 18, 1947, received nine affirmative votes, one negative, with Poland abstaining.

The negative vote of the U.S.S.R. prevented the proposal from being carried (S/P.V./186, pp. 83–85.)

Membership of Ireland

The application of Ireland for membership in the United Nations, upon submission for the second time to the Security Council on August 18, 1947, received nine affirmative votes, one negative with Poland abstaining.

The negative vote of the U.S.S.R. prevented the proposal from being carried (S/P.V./186, p. 87) (August 18, 1947).

The Czechoslovakian Case

Before a vote was taken on the Chilean draft resolution to establish a subcommittee to hear evidence and testimony in regard to the coup in Czechoslovakia, the President asked for a preliminary vote on whether the vote on the resolution would be considered one of procedure. Eight members voted in the affirmative, two members voted in the negative (U.S.S.R., Ukraine) and one member abstained (France). The President ruled that since a permanent member had voted in the negative, the vote on the resolution would be a substantive vote (S/P.V./303, pp. 66–70). (May 24, 1948.)

Second Indonesian Case

The final paragraph of the resolution concerning the Indonesian question which requested the United Nations Commission for Indonesia to continue to discharge the responsibilities entrusted to it by the Security Council and in particular to observe and assist in the implementation of the agreements reached at the round table conference and to report thereon to the Security Council received eight affirmative votes with U.S.S.R. and the Ukraine voting in the negative.

The resolution failed to carry because of the negative vote of the U.S.S.R. (S/P.V. 456, pp. 81–85). (December 13, 1949.)

Part Three: Disputes and the Maintenance of Peace

VI Methods of Treating Disposes

THE MAINTENANCE OF PEACE, ALWAYS CITED AS THE principal business of international organization, is a continuing process, not one which can be accomplished by a single act and then forgotten. The Commission to Study the Organization of Peace, a private study group in the United States, emphasized this fact several years ago in one of its reports, by the following assertion: "Peace under modern conditions cannot be a static condition of life achieved by the renunciation of war, nor a mere pious desire to live at peace. Peace must be a dynamic and continuous process for the achievement of freedom, justice, progress, and security on a world-wide scale. Many problems can never be finally solved. They recur in different forms as eternally as life itself."[1] The processes of adjustment which this conception of peace necessitates must be equipped to settle disputes between nations, to develop international law, and to effect modifications in the treaty relations of states.

It may be doubted whether any conceivable structure of world society could prevent the recurrence of disputes between nations; no national society has thus far been able to eliminate them between individuals, and even within the federal system of the United States the forty-eight states, though shorn of their sovereign powers, become involved in controversies.

Disputes between nations do not just happen, nor are they always

---

[1] Commission to Study the Organization of Peace, *Preliminary Report and Monographs,* published originally in *International Conciliation,* no. 369, April, 1941.

205

the result of the perversities of mankind; they are the result of contacts between states, for in the world of states as in the mechanical world, contacts cause friction. These contacts are sometimes between governments pursuing conflicting policies or asserting conflicting rights, sometimes between governments and aliens, and at other times between individuals of different nationalities in the course of trade or travel. The range of subject matter involved in the disputes to which such contacts give rise is as wide as the field of international relations itself; there are disputes over boundaries, trade, the protection of aliens, the interpretation of treaties, the provisions of international law, citizenship, propaganda, armament, loans, immigration laws, concessions, and so on.

It is true that in their relations nations often appear more disputatious than necessary, even cantankerous. Sir Benegal N. Rau, Indian delegate to the Security Council, early in September, 1950, lightened the heavy atmosphere of that body, then in the process of dealing with the Korean problem, by telling the experience of one of his fellow countrymen with the American football. After watching the twenty-two football players scrapping it out for sixty minutes, the Indian suggested to Sir Benegal that perhaps such a struggle might be avoided if each of the twenty-two men were given a football of his own. Sir Benegal apparently thought that the Security Council's rabid dissension on the Korean affair was about as senseless as his friend's conception of a football game.

Whether great or small, the controversies of nations are of vital concern to the international community. Even a minor dispute, if allowed to drag on for years, may become an obstacle to coöperation and perhaps a contributing cause of war, whereas a dispute successfully settled tends to stabilize the peace. It is not surprising that the branch of international organization which deals with disputes is commonly regarded as the most critically placed of all.

That international disputes are more numerous and probably more complicated nowadays than ever before is understandable. There are more states to be at odds with each other than there were fifty years ago. Furthermore, the states of today are in more frequent contact now than at any time in the past, and they are obliged to deal with each other diplomatically on nearly every subject of human endeavor.

Types of Issues

Several procedures are now available for the treatment of disputes between nations, and the one that will be used in a particular situation will depend primarily upon the nature of the controversy and the preference of the parties. Insofar as possible the remedy must be suited to the disease, and for the multitude of disputes which arise between nations there is no cure-all. A certain controversy may yield to one procedure and be impervious to another. Or, what is still more probable, disputants may be willing to submit their differences to one procedure or tribunal, whereas they would not to another. In the present condition of world affairs, states are not obliged to submit disputes to an international tribunal unless, either at the time or at some earlier date, they have agreed to do so. Always alert to their own interests and wary lest they get the worst of a decision, states are indeed cautious, and there is therefore wisdom in maintaining a variety of procedures.

An international dispute is rarely so simple as it may appear to the layman, who often feels himself competent to propose a ready solution. It may have been cumulative over a period of many years, with each party guilty of delinquencies and blunders. If the affair has reached the public ear, the chances are that points of view have hardened and sensibilities have sharpened to the point that diplomats cannot proceed to a solution without the necessity of justifying their actions to millions of onlookers as well as to their respective governments. As a rule, the issues involved are many and complex, so that an analysis of them must be made before constructive measures can be taken. Any one or more of three types of issues are likely to be found in an international dispute of much consequence.

Among the types of issues involved in international controversies there is first the factual, wherein the parties are in disagreement over facts, usually facts relating to incidents or events. It is an occurrence on a large scale of the "you did"—"I didn't" brand of dispute that so often arises among human beings. Still another analogy

is the issue so frequently before criminal courts of guilt or inno-
cence, whether the defendant did or did not commit certain acts.

Many illustrations can be given of factual issues. In 1904, during
the Russo-Japanese War, a dispute arose between Russia and Great
Britain when the former sank some British fishing vessels in the
North Sea, mistaking them for Japanese torpedo boats. The main
issue involved was essentially factual—were the conditions of
weather and visibility such as to explain and justify such a mistake?
In 1934, when King Alexander of Yugoslavia and Louis Barthou,
French Foreign Minister, were assassinated at Marseilles, Yugoslavia alleged that the Hungarian Government was implicated in
this and in other terroristic activities against subjects of Yugoslavia;
Hungary's denial of any implication raised a question of fact. One
of the justifications used by Hitler in 1938 when he took the Sude-
tenland from Czechoslovakia was an alleged maltreatment of Germans by the Czechs in that area, an allegation which was promptly
denied by the Government of Czechoslovakia.

A second type of issue frequently presented in international disputes is the legal, where charges of violations of international law
or treaties are made. This type of issue requires for its treatment a
statement of what the law is and a decision on the question of
whether or not an infraction has in fact occurred. This is a task commonly performed by the courts in national government when they
interpret statutes and the constitution so that litigants may have
final rulings on the law.

Among the countless legal issues involved in international disputes, special reference may be made to a few. In the early 1920's
the United States Government attempted to enforce against foreign
ships as far as twelve miles off the coast liquor prohibition under the
eighteenth amendment. The British Government protested that this
was a violation of the three-mile limit, and thus a controversy ensued as to whether international law might be so construed as to
permit an exception to the usual three-mile rule for such a purpose.
More recently, legal issues were raised when on January 10, 1947,
the British Government placed before the Security Council its
charge against Albania of illegal conduct in the use of mines in

Corfu Channel against British ships, and on her side Albania contended that Britain had violated the law by sweeping the Channel. Frequently questions of law are raised in the interpretation of treaties, as shown in many of the judgments and advisory opinions of the Permanent Court of International Justice before World War II; the advisory opinion in *The Exchange of Greek and Turkish Populations* dispute (1927), in which the meaning of certain clauses of the treaty of 1923 on the exchange of minorities was raised, and the judgment of 1924 interpreting the Treaty of Neuilly are examples.

Finally, there are political issues in international disputes—issues which arise out of conflicting national policies. In such controversies the arguments of the disputants do not relate to legal rights and duties but to national needs and interests. It is a case of two or more nations with ambitions or aspirations that are at variance and require harmonization. They seek the same territory, trade, or some other advantage, and either there is no law applicable or if there is law, one or both of the disputants are not satisfied with the solution which the law would provide to the dispute. A rough analogy would be a contest or controversy between two firms for the same business where no charges of illegal conduct are made.

The political issue in international controversies is by all odds the most troublesome. Because vital interests are likely to be at stake, the disputants usually assume an adamant position and resist any and every form of international settlement unless perchance they believe that they will be favored in a decision. Moreover, the political issue may at times be difficult to identify, for the arguments of the disputants are often framed for popular consumption and therefore are related to ethical principles, abstract justice, or even historical facts.

In the past, it has nearly always been the political issue that has caused war, whatever may have been the reasons offered by belligerents to justify their military action. In 1898 the sinking of the *Maine* was used by the United States Government as an occasion for pressing demands upon Spain in regard to the status of Cuba, but behind all the statements of public officials was the urgent policy of the Washington government to improve the nation's security by ousting Spain as a neighbor; opposed to this American objective was the strong desire of Spain to retain her colonial possessions in the Caribbean. World War I ostensibly was caused by the assassination of the Archduke of Austria-Hungary, but actually it was the result of a German policy of expansion running head-on into the determination of Great Britain and France to maintain the *status quo* and the policy of Russia to resist all expansion but her own in the Balkans. In World War II, the basic issue again was the expansionist aspirations of the Axis nations versus the *status quo* policies of the opposition. More recently, the cold war between Russia and the West has been in substance a rivalry of two ideologies or ways of living; the specific subjects of controversy—the control of Berlin, Korea, the regulation of atomic energy, and the like—are merely manifestations of the life-and-death struggle for survival and dominance which those two ideologies have been waging. Factual and legal issues arose, to be sure, in the controversies over Berlin and Korea, but the overall issue between Russia and the West has to do with interests and ambitions.

Diplomacy in the Treatment of Disputes

Invariably the problems of international relations are taken up in the ordinary channels of diplomacy. If the controversy is one between the United States and Russia, the usual practice is for the American ambassador in Moscow, or the Russian ambassador in Washington, or both, to discuss it and try to reach an agreement. Most of the problems between nations are successfully disposed of by this procedure, and consequently to the world at large they do not appear as disputes. When this procedure fails to produce an accord of some nature, the issue takes on the character of a "dispute."

To deal with a dispute which has come to a deadlock in the negotiations of two states, diplomacy offers two special procedures—good offices and mediation. Both are provided by a third party, preferably a disinterested party, anxious to reconcile the disputants and preserve peace. The essential difference between good offices and mediation is that in the former the third party attempts only to bring the disputants together so that negotiations will be continued or renewed, whereas in the latter the neutral concerns himself more with the substance of the dispute and tries to help the parties reach a solution; in mediation, the third party may even go so far as to sign the treaty in which the final settlement is embodied. A procedure begun in the nature of good offices may easily develop into mediation. This was true when in 1905 President Theodore Roosevelt brought Russia and Japan together at Portsmouth by his good offices to end the war at that time in progress; later he took an active part in drafting the terms of the settlement. Obviously the usefulness of a third party in bringing disputants together or in mediating a dispute depends in large measure upon the degree of confidence which the disputants are able to repose in that third party. When President Franklin Roosevelt in 1939 offered to mediate for the prevention of the war then imminent, he had the confidence of only one side; but in view of the critical nature of the situation it is doubtful that any third party, even if accepted, could have prevented the holocaust that followed.

To encourage resort to good offices and mediation, the nations wrote into the Convention for the Pacific Settlement of International Disputes in 1899 (revised in 1907) several significant provisions.[2] The signatories agreed that they would use the procedures whenever possible, and that as parties to disputes they might even request third parties to make their services available. To dispel the suspicion which in the past had often been directed toward third parties offering their services, the convention stated that such an offer should never be regarded as an unfriendly overture. The role of the third party, according to the convention, never goes beyond that of advising; there is never a right of making an award or any form of binding decision. The procedures were recognized as available both in time of peace to prevent a dispute from getting out of hand, and in time of war to bring belligerents together around a table and thus to reëstablish a condition of peace.

The ready availability of the procedures of good offices and mediation ensures their continued usefulness for a long time to come. "Negotiation" and "mediation" are significantly among the proce-

---

[2] See Appendix I to this chapter for the text of the Convention.

dures which disputants agree in Article 33 of the Charter of the United Nations to use in seeking solutions, and which the Security Council "shall, when it deems necessary, call upon the parties" to use. Also included in the list are "enquiry," "conciliation," "arbitration," and "judicial settlement"—procedures which will be taken up in the remainder of this chapter.

Commissions of Inquiry and Conciliation

While inquiry and conciliation are separate and different processes, it is not uncommon to combine them and place them together in the hands of a single commission. In other situations they have been kept separate, with a commission designated either to conduct an inquiry or to conciliate, but not to do both. The process of inquiry is based upon the assumption that the solution of a controversy will be promoted or even accomplished by a convenient access to facts and information. As stated by the Interim Committee of the General Assembly, inquiry is for "the establishment of the facts involved in a dispute and a clarification of the issues in order that their elucidation may contribute to the settlement of the dispute."[3] For this reason it is well adapted to those disputes in which the parties are at odds over their allegations of what did or did not happen in any situation. Even if the dispute involves vital interests or law, there is often a great advantage in having an accurate account of a series of events or a factual analysis of a complicated situation. In a dispute over territory, for instance, there is little likelihood of a settlement so long as each side claims to have the most people in the contested area with no means of proof. There are few international controversies where all of the statements of fact by the two disputants are in complete harmony. To make a fair decision even in arbitration and judicial settlement, international tribunals are usually obliged to obtain in some way certain data or information which they need to clarify a situation that has been obscured by the conflicting statements of the parties concerned.

Because a commission has conducted an inquiry and thus in-

---

[3] *Reports of the Interim Committee of the General Assembly,* January 5–August 5, 1948, Paris, 1948, p. 25.

formed itself of the details of an international dispute, it is well equipped to attempt to find a solution. For this reason it is common practice to place upon a commission of inquiry the task of recommending in its report some solution to the controversy in question. For instance, the League of Nations commission of inquiry for Manchuria, set up in 1931, included in its report a number of recommendations which it hoped would be adopted as a means of terminating the dispute between China and Japan over the control of the Manchurian area.

Frequently commissions of inquiry have also been authorized to conciliate, as has already been said, although in other instances special commissions of conciliation have been set up to which no special investigatory function has been assigned. As it is possible to have inquiry without conciliation, so it may be arranged that a commission may conciliate without being expected to conduct an extensive inquiry. It is the nature of conciliation that an effort is made to reconcile the parties and to bring them around to an agreement. Consultation, discussion, argument, and compromise are characteristic of the process.

Only a minor distinction can be made between conciliation and mediation. Their substantial identity was brought out in a statement by Professor P. B. Potter some years ago that "When regarded from without, as a form of action for the settlement of disputes, often performed by an international commission or organ such as the League Council, rather than from within, as an action of a mediatory state, mediation is referred to as conciliation."[4] The terms "conciliation" and "mediation" are frequently used as synonyms. When a distinction is attempted, it has referred only to the method of instituting proceedings, and not to the nature of the action undertaken, for in both cases the effort is to get the two parties around to a common point of view. In the Chino-American proposals to the Interim Committee of the General Assembly on the peaceful settlement of disputes, the statement was made that "Mediation, unlike other methods of pacific settlement mentioned in Article 33 [which included conciliation] of the Charter, can commence upon the ini-

---

[4] P. B. Potter, "Mediation," *Encyclopedia of Social Sciences*, vol. 5, p. 272.

tiative either of an individual or of a state not a party to the dispute."[5] This is the only distinction made in the proposals, and clearly it does not relate to the nature of the procedure itself but rather to the manner in which the procedure is begun. The usual, but by no means universal, practice is for conciliation to be accomplished either by a commission or by some international body like the Security Council, whereas mediation is usually undertaken by a state or an individual who may or may not be appointed by an international organization. Thus, in its treatment of the Palestine dispute, the General Assembly of the United Nations named a committee of five to appoint a "mediator" to use his good offices to get the Arabs and Jews together; the appointee, Count Bernadotte of Sweden, served until his assassination, when Mr. Ralph Bunche of the United States took his place.

Commissions of inquiry were first given prominence by the Hague Conference of 1899, which inserted in the famous Convention for the Pacific Settlement of International Disputes (revised in 1907) a number of provisions designed to make such agencies available to nations. By Article 9 it was agreed that "In disputes of an international nature involving neither honor nor vital interests, and arising from a difference of opinion on points of fact . . . the parties who have not been able to come to an agreement by means of diplomacy, should as far as circumstances allow, institute an international commission of inquiry, to facilitate a solution of these differences by elucidating the facts by means of impartial and conscientious investigation." Under the convention the procedure of inquiry would be set up by special agreement between the disputants which would define the points to be elucidated, the mode and time for the commission to be formed, and provide other detailed regulations. Ordinarily, Hague Commissions of Inquiry are composed of five members selected by the parties in such manner that one is completely neutral. The nature of their role in the treatment of disputes is well brought out by Article 35 of the convention,

---

[5] The Chino-American proposal may be found in *International Conciliation*, no. 444, October, 1948, p. 567.

which states that "the report of the commission is limited to a statement of facts, and has in no way the character of an award," and goes on to say that the parties have complete "freedom as to the effect to be given to the statement."

Several disputes have been treated by the Hague Commissions of Inquiry. The North Sea Incident of 1904 between Russia and Great Britain, mentioned earlier in this chapter, was the first case. At the suggestion of France, a commission of admirals from the British, Russian, French, American, and Austrian navies was set to work to investigate the sinking of the British fishing vessels by the Russian navy and to fix responsibility. The commission found that there were no Japanese torpedo boats anywhere near the scene of the affair to justify the Russian identification of the British fishing vessels as enemy torpedo boats, but it agreed that circumstances were such as to cast no discredit upon the Russian squadron or its commander. The report was accepted and Russia paid damages to the extent of $300,000. Later on, two more cases were treated by Hague Commissions: (1) in 1912 the *Tavignano* dispute, which involved a French mail steamer seized by an Italian torpedo boat off the coast of Tunisia; and (2) in 1922 the *Tubantia,* in which an inquiry was made into the involvement of German submarines in the sinking of a Dutch ship during World War I.

Mr. William Jennings Bryan was an enthusiastic proponent of inquiry as a method of dealing with international disputes. Through editorials published in the *Commoner* in 1905, and in speeches made during the course of a trip around the world in 1905–1906, Mr. Bryan gave wide publicity to the idea. Because the process of inquiry implies no obligation to accept a report and carries with it no right of making a decision, Mr. Bryan advocated the compulsory submission of disputes to the procedure. When he became Secretary of State in 1913, he proceeded to negotiate a long list of bilateral treaties providing for the investigation of disputes. In all, twenty-two such treaties were concluded, with provisions that "when ordinary diplomatic proceedings have failed and the High Contracting Parties do not have recourse to arbitration," disputes would be submitted for "investigation and report" to permanent international commissions of five members each, constituted in accordance with the terms of the agreements. While these treaties represented commendable progress for the principle of inquiry, as a matter of fact none was ever used in the settlement of a dispute.

After World War I, a large number of treaties, bilateral and multilateral, were concluded, establishing inquiry or conciliation or both. Among the multilateral were the Central American Treaty (1923), the Baltic Treaty (1925), the General Act of Geneva (1928), and several Inter-American treaties. Here again the procedures set up by treaty were rarely put into service. Indeed, as far as actual practice is concerned, it was in the League of Nations that inquiry and conciliation first came into their own as dispute after dispute was submitted to special commissions set up by the Council. The procedures have been given further testing in the United Nations, and on the whole they have proved to be very practicable. Not only has the United Nations used the procedures extensively, but under Article 33 of the Charter, as already explained, they are listed among the methods of settling disputes which members of the organization agree to use in seeking solutions to controversies by "peaceful means of their own choice."

Arbitration

The word "arbitration" is ineptly used to cover the peaceful settlement of disputes generally. Strictly speaking, it is only one of the methods of peaceful settlement, and as a method it is applicable not only in international disputes but also in controversies of all kinds, whether between business groups, management and labor, or individuals.

As defined in the Hague Convention on the Pacific Settlement of International Disputes (1899, and revised in 1907), international arbitration "has for its object the settlement of disputes between states by judges of their own choice and on the basis of respect for law." The most characteristic features of the process are (1) that the disputants select the judges, (2) that the judges have the right to make a binding decision, or "award" as it is properly called, and

(3) that international law is used and usually, although not always, is basic to the award made.

Arbitration is an ancient procedure for the treatment of international disputes. It was used among the city-states of ancient Greece and among the city-states of Europe in the Middle Ages. For several centuries it then went into desuetude, until in 1794 it was revived in the Jay Treaty between Great Britain and the United States for the solution of several disputes outstanding between the two countries. During the nineteenth century, arbitration was used frequently, and it still remains one of the more common methods for the solution of international controversies.

Ad hoc (or temporary) arbitration tribunals may be composed in any manner satisfactory to the disputants, but as a matter of fact they normally follow one of three patterns. Most common of all is the practice of setting up a tribunal of five members of which there are two chosen directly by each disputant in such manner that only one of the two is a national of the disputing state, and a fifth member, the "umpire," selected by common agreement. Inevitably when this is the method of choosing the tribunal, each disputant will have among the judges one of its own nationals and one national of a friendly state who can be counted upon to vote in favor of that disputant's cause; the vote of the umpire, therefore, decides the case, in effect breaking the tie of two versus two which would otherwise result. A second method of selecting a tribunal is to limit its membership to three judges: one representing each disputant, and the third a neutral umpire selected by agreement between the two disputants. The third method is to allow each disputant two judges, only one of whom may be a national, and to do without the umpire unless the four are deadlocked.

Submission of a dispute to arbitration is effected by means of a special agreement known as a *compromis*. This prescribes the composition of the tribunal, defines the issue or issues to be settled, and lays down whatever rules the disputants may agree upon as to procedure, evidence, filing cases and countercases, dates for hearings, place of hearings, and rules to be followed by the judges in making their decision. Because the disputants are able in the *compromis* to control tribunals and their methods so completely, arbitration as a procedure for settling disputes has a particular appeal to sovereign states, ever fearful lest in some way or another they may be obliged to submit to something against their liking. From a strictly judicial point of view this extensive control is criticized on the ground that "what is good for the goose should be good for the gander," and that all disputants in every dispute should expect and be willing to use whatever tribunal and procedures the community may see fit to prescribe as just and fair. If, however, the parties to a dispute wish to settle it in some special manner, is it not possible that the community's interests are best served by permitting them to do so rather than by requiring some prescribed procedure which to the detached observer may seem more strictly judicial? It is the practical appeal of arbitration, not abstract logic, that has led nations to resort to the procedure so frequently and so successfully.

The control which disputants may exercise over arbitration may and occasionally does reach the point where the parties may prescribe in place of international law some other standard of justice to be followed by the tribunal in reaching an award. Usually, however, in order to base the award upon a "respect for international law," as the Hague Convention phrases it, the *compromis* for the submission of a dispute will specify that the judges must follow the rules of international law. Special rules were set up in the *compromis* for the arbitration of the Alabama Claims case between the United States and Great Britain, decided in 1872. The case had to do with claims made by the United States Government for acts done by several vessels, including the *Alabama,* during the Civil War. Our government maintained that Great Britain was responsible for those acts because she had allowed the vessels to be fitted out in her ports for hostilities against the North. The *compromis* submitting the case to a tribunal of five arbitrators listed three rules governing the duty of a neutral nation respecting the use of its waters and ports by belligerents in war.

Although arbitration is best suited to the solution of disputes involving questions of law, it is not necessarily limited to such controversies. Arbitral tribunals are often called upon to determine the facts of a dispute—to find out precisely what has happened in order to know how to apply the law. Disputes involving basic national policies are rarely submitted to arbitration; frequently, treaties of arbitration exclude them from the procedure under the heading of "vital interests."

For some years it has been the practice of nations to conclude among themselves so-called "general treaties of arbitration." These treaties do not submit particular disputes, as do the *compromis*, but rather they impose upon the parties the obligation to resort to arbitration in the event that stated types of disputes arise in the future. These treaties have varied widely in the types of disputes regarded as arbitrable. Some have been "all out," as the British designate them, in the sense that they embrace all disputes wherein diplomacy has failed. More often, arbitration is limited to disputes of a legal nature.

General treaties of arbitration made by the United States have been highly cautious. Both the treaties negotiated by Mr. Elihu Root during the administration of President Theodore Roosevelt and those made by Mr. Frank Kellogg in 1928 specified disputes of a legal nature. The former named as exceptions controversies affecting "the vital interests, the independence, or the honor of the two Contracting States," and those which "concern the interests of third parties." The Kellogg treaties would not require the submission of questions within "the domestic jurisdiction" of either party, those involving the "interests of third parties," and those relating to the Monroe Doctrine. By means of Senate reservations in consenting to the ratification of both the Root and the Kellogg treaties it was stipulated that a *compromis* submitting a particular dispute must be, insofar as the United States is concerned, a treaty, not an executive agreement, as for other countries. The total effect of this precaution was to vitiate the force of the general treaties to the point where their worth is questionable; as someone has said, the treaties provided for arbitration only until an actual dispute arose, and then the many loopholes left the disputants free to do as they pleased.

In fact, arbitration has, during the past century and a half, been a frequent resort of nations, and, despite American caution in making general treaties of arbitration, our government has referred many cases to the procedure—probably more than any other country except Great Britain. Financial claims and boundary problems have been the most common subjects of reference to arbitral tribunals. The admission must be made that of the questions submitted, both by the United States and by other nations, few have involved matters of great moment or situations in which public opinion has been violently aroused; probably no other case to which the United States has been a party has aroused so much public feeling as the *Alabama* case. It is highly improbable that arbitration has in any instance been an alternative to war. But the solution of any international misunderstanding, whether of major or minor importance, always promotes friendly relationships between nations. Add to this the fact that only very rarely has an arbitral award been rejected, and it becomes apparent that the practice of arbitration has been one of the constructive aspects of international organization.

The Permanent Court of Arbitration

Because so many disputes were arbitrated during the nineteenth century and it seemed desirable to encourage an even greater use of the procedure, the Permanent Court of Arbitration was set up in 1899 at The Hague. Its constitution is a portion of the Convention for the Pacific Settlement of International Disputes, and like the entire Convention, it underwent some slight modifications in 1907. There is an International Bureau attached to the Court to serve as a registry, to communicate with individual states, and to have charge over the archives.

Each state which is a member of the Court names four persons to a panel from which arbitrators are selected for specific disputes. Each disputant is entitled to select two persons from the panel, of whom only one can be its own national or chosen from among the persons named by it to the panel. These four arbitrators so selected together choose an umpire; if the votes are equally divided, the umpire is named by a complicated process defined in Article 45 of the Convention.

When the Permanent Court of Arbitration was set up, the expectation was that the nations would bring many cases before it. As a matter of fact, there were a fair number referred to the Court during the first fifteen years of its existence; seventeen awards were handed down prior to the opening of World War I. Since 1920 it has handled only two cases, owing no doubt to the availability of a court of justice, first the Permanent Court of International Justice and now the International Court of Justice of the United Nations.[6]

One of the most important cases that has been before the Permanent Court of Arbitration was the North Atlantic Fisheries case, decided in 1910. It dealt with the age-old problem of the fishing rights of Americans in Canadian waters under the treaty of 1818. Seven questions relating to those rights were submitted to the Court, and were answered, some in favor of the British contention and others for the United States. The award of the Court brought to an end a controversy which had recurred frequently for nearly a century, and it thus contributed notably to a better relationship between the United States and its neighbor to the north.

In 1928 the Court heard the last case to be referred to it—the Palmas Island case between the United States and The Netherlands. The dispute in the case arose out of the fact that the Palmas Island, located near the Philippines, was found by the United States to be under the Dutch flag although it had been ceded by Spain to this country after the Spanish-American War. The Dutch maintained that they had been in occupation for many years, while the United States argued that the island had been discovered by Spain and ceded to us. The award of the court supported the Dutch claim, giving force to international law in its stress upon effective occupation as a legal claim to territory.

Courts of Justice

Because arbitration was criticized as lacking some of the judicial qualities characteristic of courts within nations, a movement was

---

[6] The two cases were (1) the Norwegian claims against the United States (1922), and (2) the Palmas Island case between the United States and The Netherlands (1928).

launched early in the present century to set up for the world a court of justice whose bench would be fixed, permanent, beyond the control of litigants, and strictly bound in its decisions by international law. The Permanent Court of Arbitration, so it was commonly said, was neither "permanent" nor, in the proper sense, a "court." The only permanent thing about it was the lengthy panel of names; each case was heard by a different tribunal, which, composed of arbitrators rather than judges, did not have the essential detachment of a genuine court.

The first court of justice to be set up for disputes between nations was the Central American Court of Justice (1907). The seat of the Court was first placed at Cartago, Costa Rica, but later it was moved to San José, where it was provided with a building by Mr. Andrew Carnegie, the donor of the Peace Palace at The Hague, which has housed the Permanent Court of Arbitration, the Permanent Court of International Justice, and the International Court of Justice. The building at San José, however, was not completed until 1917, so that the Court was able to occupy it only a few months before it went out of existence in March, 1918.

The Central American Court of Justice was a novel, and in some ways a remarkable, experiment in international organization. Certainly it represented a conception of justice in the affairs of nations several steps ahead of anything that the great powers of the world were able to achieve at that time. The Court was composed of five regular judges, one appointed by each of the five Central American states party to the convention of December 20, 1907, by which it was set up. Each state also appointed two substitute judges. All of the judges, regular and substitute, served for five-year terms, and each was paid a salary of $8000 per year. To hear a case, all five judges or their substitutes had to be in attendance; a judge was not disqualified by the fact that the state of which he was a national was a party in court.

The jurisdiction of the Central American Court was more extensive than that of any international tribunal before or since. It included "all controversies or questions which may arise among them, of whatsoever nature and no matter what their origin may be, in case the respective Departments of Foreign Affairs should not have been able to reach an understanding." The Court's jurisdiction was broad enough to cover cases filed by a national of one country against the government of another country. By special agreement the Court could hear cases between one of the Central American states and a state in some other part of the world, but, in fact, no such case was ever submitted. Under an "optional clause" which was signed by all the members except Costa Rica, the Court could deal with conflicts between the legislative, executive, and judicial branches of a government, but in such cases "the public law of the respective state" was to be followed. The wide area of compulsory jurisdiction in disputes between states and in controversies involving states and the citizens of other states, combined with optional jurisdiction in other types, marked the court as an agency destined to play a role of importance within the region which it served.

During its lifetime of approximately ten years, the Central American Court of Justice dealt with ten cases. Five of the cases were brought by individuals against a state, and all of them were decided against the individuals concerned. The initiative in three of the cases was taken by the Court itself, a procedure which was regarded as legal under the Constitution of the Court.

In 1916 the Central American Court heard two cases involving the Bryan-Chamorro Treaty, signed in 1914 by the representatives of the United States and Nicaragua, by which the United States was given canal rights, a naval base in the Gulf of Fonseca, and a 99-year lease of Corn Islands. The cases were brought by Costa Rica and El Salvador against Nicaragua. The decisions of the Court were regarded as unsatisfactory both by the United States and Nicaragua. Consequently, Nicaragua gave notice in 1917 of her intention to terminate the convention of 1907 by which the Court had been set up; on March 12, 1918, the Court ceased to exist. To take its place, the Central American states established in 1923 a new International Central American Tribunal, an arbitration tribunal, whose jurisdiction was quite limited.

In 1907, the same year in which the Central American Court was set up, the Government of the United States proposed to the conference then in session at The Hague that an international court of justice be established. The project had general support, but inability to agree on the method of choosing judges finally led to its abandonment. In the years which followed, there was growing agitation in favor of such a court, but nothing much was accomplished toward its creation until the Covenant of the League of Nations was written in 1919. Article 14 of that document placed upon the Council the duty of working out the details of a plan. As a consequence, the Permanent Court of International Justice came into existence in 1921. It was superseded after World War II by the International Court of Justice, to be discussed in a later chapter.

▲

APPENDIX TO CHAPTER VI

I

Convention for the Pacific Settlement of International Disputes, 1907*

Part I. The Maintenance of General Peace
ARTICLE 1

With a view to obviating as far as possible recourse to force in the relations between States, the *contracting* Powers agree to use their best efforts to insure the pacific settlement of international differences.

Part II. Good Offices and Mediation
ARTICLE 2

In case of serious disagreement or dispute, before an appeal to arms, the *contracting* Powers agree to have recourse, as far as circumstances allow, to the good offices or mediation of one or more friendly Powers.

ARTICLE 3

Independently of this recourse, the *contracting* Powers deem it expedient *and desirable* that one or more Powers, strangers to the

---

* U.S. Statutes at Large, XXXVI, 2199. Italics indicate changes in the Convention as drawn in 1907.

dispute, should, on their own initiative and as far as circumstances may allow, offer their good offices or mediation to the States at variance.

Powers strangers to the dispute have the right to offer good offices or mediation even during the course of hostilities.

The exercise of this right can never be regarded by either of the parties in dispute as an unfriendly act.

ARTICLE 4

The part of the mediator consists in reconciling the opposing claims and appeasing the feelings of resentment which may have arisen between the States at variance.

ARTICLE 5

The functions of the mediator are at an end when once it is declared, either by one of the parties to the dispute or by the mediator himself, that the means of reconciliation proposed by him are not accepted.

ARTICLE 6

Good offices and mediation undertaken either at the request of the parties in dispute or on the initiative of Powers strangers to the dispute have exclusively the character of advice, and never have binding force.

ARTICLE 7

The acceptance of mediation can not, unless there be an agreement to the contrary, have the effect of interrupting, delaying, or hindering mobilization or other measures of preparation for war.

If it takes place after the commencement of hostilities, the military operations in progress are not interrupted in the absence of an agreement to the contrary.

ARTICLE 8

The *contracting* Powers are agreed in recommending the application, when circumstances allow, of special mediation in the following form:

In case of a serious difference endangering peace, the States at variance choose respectively a Power, to which they intrust the mission of entering into direct communication with the Power chosen on the other side, with the object of preventing the rupture of pacific relations.

For the period of this mandate, the term of which, unless otherwise stipulated, can not exceed thirty days, the States in dispute cease from all direct communication on the subject of the dispute, which is regarded as referred exclusively to the mediating Powers, which must use their best efforts to settle it.

In case of a definite rupture of pacific relations, these Powers are charged with the joint task of taking advantage of any opportunity to restore peace.

Part III. International Commissions of Inquiry
Article 9

In disputes of an international nature involving neither honor nor vital interests, and arising from a difference of opinion on points of fact, the *contracting* Powers deem it expedient *and desirable* that the parties who have not been able to come to an agreement by means of diplomacy, should, as far as circumstances allow, institute an international commission of inquiry, to facilitate a solution of these disputes by elucidating the facts by means of an impartial and conscientious investigation.

Article 10

International commissions of inquiry are constituted by special agreement between the parties in dispute.

The inquiry convention defines the facts to be examined; *it determines the mode and time in which the commission is to be formed* and the extent of the powers of the commissioners.

It also determines, if there is need, where the commission is to sit, and whether it may remove to another place, the language the commission shall use and the languages the use of which shall be authorized before it, as well as the date on which each party must deposit its statement of facts, and, generally speaking, all the conditions upon which the parties have agreed.

If the parties consider it necessary to appoint assessors, the convention of inquiry shall determine the mode of their selection and the extent of their powers.

ARTICLE 11

If the inquiry convention has not determined where the commission is to sit, it will sit at The Hague.

The place of meeting, once fixed, can not be altered by the commission except with the assent of the parties.

If the inquiry convention has not determined what languages are to be employed, the question shall be decided by the commission.

ARTICLE 12

Unless an undertaking is made to the contrary, commissions of inquiry shall be formed in the manner determined by Articles 45 and 57 of the present Convention.

ARTICLE 13

Should one of the commissioners or one of the assessors, should there be any, either die, or resign, or be unable for any reason whatever to discharge his functions, the same procedure is followed for filling the vacancy as was followed for appointing him.

ARTICLE 14

The parties are entitled to appoint special agents to attend the commission of inquiry, whose duty it is to represent them and to act as intermediaries between them and the commission.

They are further authorized to engage counsel or advocates, appointed by themselves, to state their case and uphold their interests before the commission.

ARTICLE 15

The International Bureau of the Permanent Court of Arbitration acts as registry for the commissions which sit at The Hague, and

*shall place its offices and staff at the disposal of the contracting
Powers for the use of the commission of inquiry.*

ARTICLE 16

*If the commission meets elsewhere than at The Hague, it ap-
points a secretary general, whose office serves as registry.*

*It is the function of the registry, under the control of the presi-
dent, to make the necessary arrangements for the sittings of the
commission, the preparation of the minutes, and, while the inquiry
lasts, for the charge of the archives, which shall subsequently be
transferred to the International Bureau at The Hague.*

ARTICLE 17

*In order to facilitate the constitution and working of commissions
of inquiry, the contracting Powers recommend the following rules,
which shall be applicable to the inquiry procedure in so far as the
parties do not adopt other rules.*

ARTICLE 18

*The commission shall settle the details of the procedure not cov-
ered by the special inquiry convention or the present Convention,
and shall arrange all the formalities required for dealing with the
evidence.*

ARTICLE 19

On the inquiry both sides must be heard.

*At the dates fixed, each party communicates to the commission
and to the other party the statements of facts, if any, and, in all
cases, the instruments, papers, and documents which it considers
useful for ascertaining the truth, as well as the list of witnesses and
experts whose evidence it wishes to be heard.*

ARTICLE 20

*The commission is entitled, with the assent of the Powers, to
move temporarily to any place where it considers it may be useful to
have recourse to this means of inquiry or to send one or more of its*

members. *Permission must be obtained from the State on whose territory it is proposed to hold the inquiry.*

ARTICLE 21

Every investigation, and every examination of a locality, must be made in the presence of the agents and counsel of the parties or after they have been duly summoned.

ARTICLE 22

The commission is entitled to ask from either party for such explanations and information as it considers necessary.

ARTICLE 23

The *parties* undertake to supply the commission of inquiry, as fully as they may think possible, with all means and facilities necessary to enable it to become completely acquainted with, and to accurately understand, the facts in question.

They undertake to make use of the means at their disposal, under their municipal law, to insure the appearance of the witnesses or experts who are in their territory and have been summoned before the commission.

If the witnesses or experts are unable to appear before the commission, the parties will arrange for their evidence to be taken before the qualified officials of their own country.

ARTICLE 24

For all notices to be served by the commission in the territory of a third contracting Power, the commission shall apply direct to the Government of the said Power. The same rule applies in the case of steps being taken on the spot to procure evidence.

The requests for this purpose are to be executed so far as the means at the disposal of the Power applied to under its municipal law allow. They can not be rejected unless the Power in question considers they are calculated to impair its sovereign rights or its safety.

The commission will equally be always entitled to act through the Power on whose territory it sits.

ARTICLE 25

The witnesses and experts are summoned on the request of the parties or by the commission of its own motion, and, in every case, through the Government of the State in whose territory they are.

The witnesses are heard in succession and separately, in the presence of the agents and counsel, and in the order fixed by the commission.

ARTICLE 26

The examination of witnesses is conducted by the president.

The members of the commission may, however, put to each witness questions which they consider likely to throw light on and complete his evidence, or get information on any point concerning the witness within the limits of what is necessary in order to get at the truth.

The agents and counsel of the parties may not interrupt the witness when he is making his statement, nor put any direct question to him, but they may ask the president to put such additional questions to the witness as they think expedient.

ARTICLE 27

The witness must give his evidence without being allowed to read any written draft. He may, however, be permitted by the president to consult notes or documents if the nature of the facts referred to necessitates their employment.

ARTICLE 28

A minute of the evidence of the witness is drawn up forthwith and read to the witness. The latter may make such alterations and additions as he thinks necessary, which will be recorded at the end of his statement.

When the whole of his statement has been read to the witness, he is asked to sign it.

ARTICLE 29

The agents are authorized, in the course of or at the close of the inquiry, to present in writing to the commission and to the other party such statements, requisitions, or summaries of the facts as they consider useful for ascertaining the truth.

ARTICLE 30

The commission considers its decisions in private and the proceedings are secret.

All questions are decided by a majority of the members of the commission.

If a member declines to vote, the fact must be recorded in the minutes.

ARTICLE 31

The sittings of the commission are not public, nor the minutes and documents connected with the inquiry published except in virtue of a decision of the commission taken with the consent of the parties.

ARTICLE 32

After the parties have presented all the explanations and evidence, and the witnesses have all been heard, the president declares the inquiry terminated, and the commission adjourns to deliberate and to draw up its report.

ARTICLE 33

The report is signed by all the members of the commission.

If one of the members refuses to sign, the fact is mentioned; but the validity of the report is not affected.

ARTICLE 34

The report of the commission is read at a public sitting, the agents and counsel of the parties being present or duly summoned.

A copy of the report is given to each party.

ARTICLE 35

The report of the commission is limited to a statement of facts, and has in no way the character of an award. It leaves to the parties entire freedom as to the effect to be given to the statement.

ARTICLE 36

Each party pays its own expenses and an equal share of the expenses incurred by the commission.

Part IV. International Arbitration

I. *The System of Arbitration*

ARTICLE 37

International arbitration has for its object the settlement of disputes between States by judges of their own choice and on the basis of respect for law.

Recourse to arbitration implies an engagement to submit in good faith to the award.

ARTICLE 38

In questions of a legal nature, and especially in the interpretation or application of international conventions, arbitration is recognized by the *contracting* Powers as the most effective, and, at the same time, the most equitable means of settling disputes which diplomacy has failed to settle.

Consequently, it would be desirable that, in disputes about the above-mentioned questions, the contracting Powers should, if the case arose, have recourse to arbitration, in so far as circumstances permit.

ARTICLE 39

The arbitration convention is concluded for questions already existing or for questions which may arise eventually.

It may embrace any dispute or only disputes of a certain category.

ARTICLE 40

Independently of general or private treaties expressly stipulating recourse to arbitration as obligatory on the *contracting* Powers, the said Powers reserve to themselves the right of concluding new agreements, general or particular, with a view to extending compulsory arbitration to all cases which they may consider it possible to submit to it.

II. *The Permanent Court of Arbitration*

ARTICLE 41

With the object of facilitating an immediate recourse to arbitration for international differences, which it has not been possible to settle by diplomacy, the *contracting* Powers undertake to *maintain the* Permanent Court of Arbitration, *as established by the First Peace Conference,* accessible at all times, and operating, unless otherwise stipulated by the parties, in accordance with the rules of procedure inserted in the present Convention.

ARTICLE 42

The Permanent Court *is* competent for all arbitration cases, unless the parties agree to institute a special tribunal.

ARTICLE 43

The Permanent Court sits at The Hague.

An International Bureau serves as registry for the Court. It is the channel for communications relative to the meetings of the Court; it has charge of the archives and conducts all the administrative business.

The *contracting* Powers undertake to communicate to the Bureau, *as soon as possible,* a certified copy of any conditions of arbitration arrived at between them and of any award concerning them delivered by a special tribunal.

They likewise undertake to communicate to the Bureau the laws, regulations, and documents eventually showing the execution of the awards given by the Court.

ARTICLE 44

Each *contracting* Power *selects* four persons at the most, of known competency in questions of international law, of the highest moral reputation, and disposed to accept the duties of arbitrator.

The persons thus selected *are* inscribed, as members of the Court, in a list which shall be notified to all the *contracting* Powers by the Bureau.

Any alteration in the list of arbitrators is brought by the Bureau to the knowledge of the *contracting* Powers.

Two or more Powers may agree on the selection in common of one or more members.

The same person can be selected by different Powers.

The members of the Court are appointed for a term of six years. These appointments are renewable.

Should a member of the Court die or resign, the same procedure is followed for filling the vacancy as was followed for appointing him. *In this case the appointment is made for a fresh period of six years.*

ARTICLE 45

When the *contracting* Powers wish to have recourse to the Permanent Court for the settlement of a difference which has arisen between them, the arbitrators called upon to form the tribunal with jurisdiction to decide this difference must be chosen from the general list of members of the Court.

Failing the direct agreement of the parties on the composition of the arbitration tribunal, the following course shall be pursued:

Each party appoints two arbitrators, *of whom one only can be its national or chosen from among the persons selected by it as members of the Permanent Court.* These arbitrators together choose an umpire.

If the votes are equally divided, the choice of the umpire is intrusted to a third Power, selected by the parties by common accord.

If an agreement is not arrived at on this subject each party selects a different Power, and the choice of the umpire is made in concert by the Powers thus selected.

If, within two months' time, these two Powers can not come to an agreement, each of them presents two candidates taken from the list of members of the Permanent Court, exclusive of the members se-

lected by the parties and not being nationals of either of them. Drawing lots determines which of the candidates thus presented shall be umpire.

ARTICLE 46

The tribunal being thus composed, the parties notify to the Bureau their determination to have recourse to the Court, *the text of their compromis,* and the names of the arbitrators.

The Bureau communicates without delay to each arbitrator the compromis, and the names of the other members of the tribunal.

The tribunal assembles at the date fixed by the parties. *The Bureau makes the necessary arrangements for the meeting.*

The members of the *tribunal,* in the exercise of their duties and out of their own country, enjoy diplomatic privileges and immunities.

ARTICLE 47

The Bureau is authorized to place its offices and staff at the disposal of the *contracting* Powers for the use of any special board of arbitration.

The jurisdiction of the Permanent Court may, within the conditions laid down in the regulations, be extended to disputes between *non-contracting* Powers or between *contracting* Powers and *non-contracting* Powers, if the parties are agreed on recourse to this tribunal.

ARTICLE 48

The *contracting* Powers consider it their duty, if a serious dispute threatens to break out between two or more of them, to remind these latter that the Permanent Court is open to them.

Consequently, they declare that the fact of reminding the parties at variance of the provisions of the present Convention, and the advice given to them, in the highest interests of peace, to have recourse to the Permanent Court, can only be regarded as friendly actions.

In case of dispute between two Powers, one of them can always address to the International Bureau a note containing a declaration that it would be ready to submit the dispute to arbitration.

The Bureau must at once inform the other Power of the declaration.

ARTICLE 49

The Permanent Administrative Council, composed of the diplomatic representatives of the *contracting* Powers accredited to The Hague and of the Netherland Minister for Foreign Affairs, who will act as president, is charged with the direction and control of the International Bureau.

The Council *settles* its rules of procedure and all other necessary regulations.

It *decides* all questions of administration which may arise with regard to the operations of the Court.

It *has* entire control over the appointment, suspension, or dismissal of the officials and employees of the Bureau.

It *fixes* the payments and salaries, and controls the general expenditure.

At meetings duly summoned the presence of *nine* members is sufficient to render valid the discussions of the Council. The decisions are taken by a majority of votes.

The Council communicates to the *contracting* Powers without delay the regulations adopted by it. It furnishes them with an annual report on the labors of the Court, the working of the administration, and the expenditure. *The report likewise contains a résumé of what is important in the documents communicated to the Bureau by the Powers in virtue of Article 43, paragraphs 3 and 4.*

ARTICLE 50

The expenses of the Bureau shall be borne by the *contracting* Powers in the proportion fixed for the International Bureau of the Universal Postal Union.

The expenses to be charged to the adhering Powers shall be reckoned from the date on which their adhesion comes into force.

III. *Arbitration Procedure*

ARTICLE 51

With a view to encouraging the development of arbitration, the *contracting* Powers have agreed on the following rules, which are applicable to arbitration procedure, unless other rules have been agreed on by the parties.

ARTICLE 52

The Powers which have recourse to arbitration sign a compromis, in which the subject of the dispute is clearly defined, *the time allowed for appointing arbitrators, the form, order, and time in which the communication referred to in Article 63 must be made, and the amount of the sum which each party must deposit in advance to defray the expenses.*

The compromis likewise defines, if there is occasion, the manner of appointing arbitrators, any special powers which may eventually belong to the tribunal, where it shall meet, the language it shall use, and the languages the employment of which shall be authorized before it, and, generally speaking, all the conditions on which the parties are agreed.

ARTICLE 53

The Permanent Court is competent to settle the compromis, if the parties are agreed to have recourse to it for the purpose.

It is similarly competent, even if the request is only made by one of the parties, when all attempts to reach an understanding through the diplomatic channel have failed, in the case of—

1. A dispute covered by a general treaty of arbitration concluded or renewed after the present Convention has come into force, and providing for a compromis in all disputes and not either explicitly or implicitly excluding the settlement of the compromis from the competence of the Court. Recourse can not, however, be had to the Court if the other party declares that in its opinion the dispute does not belong to the category of disputes which can be submitted to compulsory arbitration, unless the treaty of arbitration confers upon the arbitration tribunal the power of deciding this preliminary question.

2. A dispute arising from contract debts claimed from one Power by another Power as due to its nationals, and for the settlement of which the offer of arbitration has been accepted. This arrangement is not applicable if acceptance is subject to the condition that the compromis should be settled in some other way.

ARTICLE 54

In the cases contemplated in the preceding article, the compromis shall be settled by a commission consisting of five members selected in the manner arranged for in Article 45, paragraphs 3 to 6.

The fifth member is president of the commission ex officio.

ARTICLE 55

The duties of arbitrator may be conferred on one arbitrator alone or on several arbitrators selected by the parties as they please, or chosen by them from the members of the Permanent Court of Arbitration established by the present Convention.

Failing the constitution of the tribunal by direct agreement between the parties, the course *referred to in Article 45, paragraphs 3 to 6, is followed.*

ARTICLE 56

When a sovereign or the chief of a State is chosen as arbitrator, the arbitration procedure is settled by him.

ARTICLE 57

The umpire is president of the tribunal ex officio.

When the tribunal does not include an umpire, it appoints its own president.

ARTICLE 58

When the compromis is settled by a commission, as contemplated in Article 54, and in the absence of an agreement to the contrary, the commission itself shall form the arbitration tribunal.

ARTICLE 59

Should one of the arbitrators either die, retire, or be unable for any reason whatever to discharge his functions, the same procedure is followed for filling the vacancy as was followed for appointing him.

ARTICLE 60

The tribunal sits at The Hague, unless some other place is selected by the parties.

The tribunal can only sit in the territory of a third Power with the latter's consent.

The place of meeting once fixed can not be altered by the tribunal, except with the consent of the parties.

ARTICLE 61

If the question as to what languages are to be used has not been settled by the compromis, it shall be decided by the tribunal.

ARTICLE 62

The parties are entitled to appoint special agents to attend the tribunal to act as intermediaries between themselves and the tribunal.

They are further authorized to retain for the defense of their rights and interests before the tribunal counsel or advocates appointed by themselves for this purpose.

The members of the Permanent Court may not act as agents, counsel, or advocates except on behalf of the Power which appointed them members of the Court.

ARTICLE 63

As a general rule, arbitration procedure comprises two distinct phases: pleadings and oral discussions.

The pleadings consist in the communication by the respective agents to the members of the tribunal and the opposite party of *cases, counter-cases, and, if necessary, of replies; the parties annex thereto all papers* and documents called for in the case. This communication shall be made *either directly or through the intermediary of the International Bureau,* in the *order* and within the time fixed by the *compromis.*

The time fixed by the compromis may be extended by mutual agreement by the parties, or by the tribunal when the latter considers it necessary for the purpose of reaching a just decision.

The discussions consist in the oral development before the tribunal of the arguments of the parties.

ARTICLE 64

A *certified copy* of every document produced by one party must be communicated to the other party.

ARTICLE 65

Unless special circumstances arise, the tribunal does not meet until the pleadings are closed.

ARTICLE 66

The discussions are under the control of the president.

They are only public if it be so decided by the tribunal, with the assent of the parties.

They are recorded in minutes drawn up by the secretaries appointed by the president. These minutes *are signed by the president and by one of the secretaries and* alone have an authentic character.

ARTICLE 67

After the close of the pleadings, the tribunal is entitled to refuse discussion of all new papers or documents which one of the parties may wish to submit to it without the consent of the other party.

ARTICLE 68

The tribunal is free to take into consideration new papers or documents to which its attention may be drawn by the agents or counsel of the parties.

In this case, the tribunal has the right to require the production of these papers or documents, but is obliged to make them known to the opposite party.

ARTICLE 69

The tribunal can, besides, require from the agents of the parties the production of all papers, and can demand all necessary explanations. In case of refusal the tribunal takes note of it.

ARTICLE 70

The agents and the counsel of the parties are authorized to present orally to the tribunal all the arguments they may consider expedient in defense of their case.

ARTICLE 71

They are entitled to raise objections and points. The decisions of the tribunal on these points are final and can not form the subject of any subsequent discussion.

ARTICLE 72

The members of the tribunal are entitled to put questions to the agents and counsel of the parties, and to ask them for explanations on doubtful points.

Neither the questions put, nor the remarks made by members of the tribunal in the course of the discussions, can be regarded as an expression of opinion by the tribunal in general or by its members in particular.

ARTICLE 73

The tribunal is authorized to declare its competence in interpreting the compromis, as well as the other *papers and documents* which may be invoked, and in applying the principles of law.

ARTICLE 74

The tribunal is entitled to issue rules of procedure for the conduct of the case, to decide the forms, *order*, and time in which each party must conclude its arguments, and to arrange all the formalities required for dealing with the evidence.

Article 75

The parties undertake to supply the tribunal, as fully as they consider possible, with all the information required for deciding the case.

Article 76

For all notices which the tribunal has to serve in the territory of a third contracting Power, the tribunal shall apply direct to the Government of that Power. The same rule applies in the case of steps being taken to procure evidence on the spot.

The requests for this purpose are to be executed as far as the means at the disposal of the Power applied to under its municipal law allow. They can not be rejected unless the Power in question considers them calculated to impair its own sovereign rights or its safety.

The Court will equally be always entitled to act through the Power on whose territory it sits.

Article 77

When the agents and counsels of the parties have submitted all the explanations and evidence in support of their case the president shall declare the discussion closed.

Article 78

The tribunal considers its decisions in private and *the proceedings remain secret.*

All questions are decided by a majority of the members of the tribunal.

Article 79

The award must give the reasons on which it is based. *It contains the names of the arbitrators; it is signed by the president and registrar or by the secretary acting as registrar.*

Article 80

The award is read out in public sitting, the agents and counsel of the parties being present or duly summoned to attend.

ARTICLE 81

The award, duly pronounced and notified to the agents of the parties, settles the dispute definitively and without appeal.

ARTICLE 82

Any dispute arising between the parties as to the interpretation and execution of the award shall, in the absence of an agreement to the contrary, be submitted to the tribunal which pronounced it.

ARTICLE 83

The parties can reserve in the compromis the right to demand the revision of the award.

In this case and unless there be an agreement to the contrary, the demand must be addressed to the tribunal which pronounced the award. It can only be made on the ground of the discovery of some new fact calculated to exercise a decisive influence upon the award and which was unknown to the tribunal and to the party which demanded the revision at the time the discussion was closed.

Proceedings for revision can only be instituted by a decision of the tribunal expressly recording the existence of the new fact, recognizing in it the character described in the preceding paragraph, and declaring the demand admissible on this ground.

The compromis fixes the period within which the demand for revision must be made.

ARTICLE 84

The award is not binding except on the parties *in dispute*.

When it concerns the interpretation of a Convention to which Powers other than those in dispute are parties, they shall inform all the signatory Powers *in good time*. Each of these Powers is entitled to intervene in the case. If one or more avail themselves of this right, the interpretation contained in the award is equally binding on them.

ARTICLE 85

Each party pays its own expenses and an equal share of the expenses of the tribunal.

VII The International Court of Justice

IN THE WORDS OF THE CHARTER, THE INTERNATIONAL Court of Justice is "the principal judicial organ of the United Nations." Its task is to promote what Mr. Cordell Hull, as Secretary of State, called "Order under law," which, as he said, "lies at the very foundation of social institutions. . . ." Indeed, it would be difficult to imagine a stable society of nations without a law binding upon its members by which the rights and duties of states are stated.

For many centuries, international law has been in the process of development. Even in ancient Greece there were primitive rules for the regulation of relationships among the city-states, and in Rome the *Jus Gentium* was a system of law applicable to the many peoples within the Empire. Modern international law originated during the late Middle Ages as the new system of nation states was getting under way. During the late decades of the sixteenth century a number of Spanish writers—Suarez and Vitoria in particular—devoted considerable effort to the subject, but it remained for the Dutchman Hugo Grotius in 1625 to lay the foundations of the modern law in his famous work *The Law of War and Peace*. Since that time, international law has grown steadily, and it has come to be relied upon more and more as a basis for national conduct. As far back as 1864, Señor Barrenchia, a Spanish diplomat, asserted that "the principles of international law form one of the most precious conquests of modern civilization." Since that time it has been expanded into new fields and has become even more useful. Still, however, international law is imperfect, and it is far less of a force for order and stability than its exponents would like it to be. Its shortcomings must be admitted, although it is doubtful whether they are as serious as the layman, who hears about the violations but not about the accomplishments of the law, would have us believe. Mr. John Bassett Moore, eminent American jurist of a few decades ago and the first American judge in the Permanent Court of International Justice, once expressed the view that there are no more violations of international law than of national law. That governments appeal to the law frequently in their diplomatic relationships and that they do not profess indifference to it are further evidences of its utility.

The International Court of Justice may be looked upon as an agency in which international law can be ascertained and applied in international disputes; in addition, it gives opinions on legal questions that arise in the conduct of international relations and in the operation of international agencies. By its activities the Court not only adds to the usefulness of the law but also develops and stabilizes the law.

Having the status of one of the principal organs of the United Nations, the present International Court of Justice is unlike its predecessor, the Permanent Court of International Justice, which, although affiliated with the League of Nations, was not one of its organs. The practical consequences of this difference are not impressive, for in most particulars the relationship between the present Court and the other organs of the United Nations are the same as that formerly obtaining between the old Court and the League of Nations. The most significant result of the present relationship is that members of the United Nations are automatically members of the International Court. This means, among other things, that by joining the United Nations the United States automatically became a member of the Court; the type of debate that went on in the United States Senate over membership in the old Permanent Court of International Justice in the 1920's and 1930's was therefore obviated. Professor Manley Hudson has asserted that another consequence of the organic relationship between the court and the United Nations "may be that various provisions of the Charter must be taken into consideration in the interpretation of the Statute."[1] He also suggests that reference to the Court as the principal judicial organ of the United Nations "would seem to leave open the way for the creation by the United Nations of other judicial organs."

Continuity with the Permanent Court of International Justice

In a strictly technical sense it may be said that the present International Court of Justice is the second World Court, and that the first was the Permanent Court of International Justice, set up in 1921 with a Statute or constitution of its own. The Permanent Court of International Justice opened its doors at The Hague on January 30, 1922, and they remained open until the summer of 1940, when the German invasion of The Netherlands closed them; even then, the Court remained officially in existence, its final session being held from October 26 to 31, 1945, at which time arrangements were made for the transfer of its library, furniture, and archives to the new International Court of Justice. During the eighteen years of its active life seventy-nine cases were submitted to the Permanent Court of International Justice, of which fifty-one were contentious cases and twenty-eight were requests for advisory opinions. The contributions of this work to peaceful coöperation and understanding were universally acknowledged, and the prestige of the Court was high. Moreover, its activities provided a wealth of experience from which the new International Court of Justice could draw heavily as it set to work in the new postwar era.

The question was raised during and after World War II as to whether the old Court should be retained or a new one created. The Dumbarton Oaks project provided no answer to the question but merely pointed out the alternatives: to revise the old Statute or to draft a new one. No dissatisfaction with the old Court was expressed either at the Dumbarton Oaks meeting or at the San Francisco Conference. On the contrary, it was lauded on several occasions; for instance, a report by Professor Basdevant, in behalf of a Committee of Jurists working on the problem, referred to "the respect attaching

---

[1] M. O. Hudson, "The Twenty-Fourth Year of the World Court," *American Journal of International Law*, 1946, vol. 40, p. 11.

to the name of the Permanent Court of International Justice." Indeed, there was a strong current of opinion at San Francisco in favor of continuing the old Court with some few modifications.

The decision to set up a new court was dictated in the last analysis by certain practical difficulties in the way of adjusting the Permanent Court of International Justice to the new order set up at San Francisco. First was the fact that the Statute of the Permanent Court had no provision for amendment, and consequently no means were at hand for revisionary measures generally regarded as desirable. Second, sixteen members of the old Court were not present at San Francisco for the reason that they were not among the United Nations group, and therefore they could not participate in the work of revision. There was a third difficulty in the fact that the old Court was open to membership only for states in the League of Nations and for those named in the annex of the Covenant; this restriction would have ruled out a number of the states represented at San Francisco.

The point should be emphasized that, although the International Court of Justice is in a technical sense a new Court, to all intents and purposes it is a continuation of the old Permanent Court of International Justice. The new name for the tribunal has been explained by Professor Hudson on the ground that "the word 'permanent' seemed to smack of unfulfilled prophecy, and the qualification of 'Justice' as 'International' was thought to be too limitative."[2] There is a new Statute for the present Court, but in most places it reads word for word like the old Statute; there are a few differences of some significance, but most of the differences are stylistic rather than substantive in nature.

That the International Court of Justice was not to be regarded as a break with the Permanent Court of International Justice was made plain in the report of Committee 1 at San Francisco, as follows: "The creation of the new Court will not break the chain of continuity with the past, not only will the Statute of the new Court be based upon the Statute of the old Court, but this fact will be expressly set down in the Charter. In general the new Court will

_____
[2] *Ibid.*, p. 10.

have the same organization as the old, and the provisions concerning its jurisdiction will follow very closely those in the old Statute."[3] Some legal basis for the continuity is provided in Article 92 of the United Nations Charter, which asserts that the Statute of the new Court "is based upon the Statute of the Permanent Court of International Justice. . . ."

The Statute

The Charter of the United Nations (Articles 92–96) furnishes a part of the constitutional basis for the International Court, dealing as it does with membership, compliance with decisions, resort to other tribunals, and advisory opinions. Annexed to the Charter is the Statute or the organic law of the Court, according to which, as the Charter says, the tribunal "shall function." There are Chinese, English, French, Russian, and Spanish versions of the Statute as in the case of the Charter, and all are equally authentic, whereas the Statute of the old Court appeared officially only in English and French.

The striking parallelism between the old Statute and the new has already been mentioned. There were sixty-eight articles in the old as compared with seventy in the new, the two additional articles in the present document dealing with the process of amending the Statute, a subject not treated in the first Statute. The lack of a procedure for amending the Statute of the Permanent Court of International Justice had been a considerable handicap in the development of that tribunal. The Statute was in the nature of a multilateral treaty and lacking a provision for amendment, it could be altered only by the unanimous consent of all the members. This was a most cumbersome process, for there were in the neighborhood of fifty members and to obtain the approval of all was necessarily time-consuming. At a conference of members, a protocol amending the Statute was adopted and signed on September 14, 1929, but ratifications were so slow in coming in that the amendments could not become effective until February 1, 1936.

Amendments to the present Statute may be made by the same

---

[3] *Ibid.*, quoted.

procedure as that used to alter the Charter, subject to whatever provisions the General Assembly may make for the participation of
states which are members of the International Court but not of the
United Nations. This means that amendments would normally be
adopted by a two-thirds vote in the General Assembly followed by
ratification on the part of two-thirds of the members of the United
Nations, including all of the permanent members of the Security
Council; an alternative method permits the recommendation of
amendments by a general conference of United Nations members,
with similar requirements as to ratification. The Court itself is authorized by the Statute to propose amendments—a sound arrangement, for the need for changes would in all probability become evident to the tribunal before it would to any other organ of the United
Nations.

Membership in the Court

Membership in the International Court of Justice and in the specialized agencies of the United Nations is separate from membership in
the United Nations itself. According to Article 93 of the Charter,
"All members of the United Nations are *ipso facto* parties to the
Statute of the International Court of Justice," but the Article goes
on to provide that a state which is not a member of the United Nations may join the Court on such conditions as may be determined
in each case by the General Assembly on the recommendation of
the Security Council. Taking advantage of this latter provision,
Switzerland, not a member of the United Nations, applied for admission to the Court and was accepted on three conditions stipulated in a resolution adopted by the General Assembly on December
11, 1946: (1) that Switzerland agree to the provisions of the Statute, (2) that she accept the obligations of a member of the United
Nations under Article 94 of the Charter, and (3) that she undertake
to contribute to the expenses of the Court. In 1948 the government
of Hyderabad, also a nonmember of the United Nations, applied for
membership in the Court, but because of uncertain political conditions then existing in that country, the Security Council did not pass
upon the application.

The Judges

In point of size the International Court of Justice takes up where the Permanent Court of International Justice left off, with fifteen judges. Originally the Permanent Court was composed of eleven regular judges and four deputy judges; later this was changed to fifteen regular and no deputy judges. These judges of the International Court of Justice are selected for terms of nine years, but only one-third, or five, of the judges, are ordinarily selected at the same time, thus providing an element of continuity in the personnel of the Court. The nominees for judges are made "by the national groups in the Permanent Court of Arbitration"; that is to say, the four persons named by a member state of the Permanent Court of Arbitration to the panel of that court, acting together, select that state's nominees for the International Court of Justice. For instance, the four American members of the panel of the Permanent Court of Arbitration choose the American nominees for the International Court of Justice. If a state is a member of the International Court of Justice but not of the Permanent Court of Arbitration, its candidates for the former shall be named by national groups specifically appointed for this purpose. No group may nominate more than four candidates, of whom only two may be its nationals. From the list of nominees thus drawn up, the fifteen judges of the court are elected by the General Assembly and the Security Council, voting separately. If necessary, the Assembly and Council must continue balloting in order to obtain an absolute majority for the same individual candidates. If, after three ballots, they have not come to agreement, the Assembly and Council may arrange a joint conference of representatives of the two organs to assist them in filling whatever vacancies still remain. As a last resort in case the joint conference is deadlocked, the judges already selected may fill the seats still vacant from among the candidates who have obtained votes in the Security Council or General Assembly.

The men elected to the bench of the International Court of Justice, like those of the old Court, are well-known experts in international law; this is in keeping with the injunction of Article 2 of the

Statute, which requires that the Court shall be composed of persons qualified for appointment "to the highest judicial offices" in their respective countries, or of jurisconsults of recognized competence in international law." The first election was in 1945, at which time the fifteen elected judges were divided into three groups—one-third to serve until 1949, one-third to serve until 1952, and one-third to serve until 1955, as follows:

Judges elected to serve until 1949 (renewed to 1958)

A. H. Badawi Pasha	Egypt
Hsu Mo	China
J. E. Read	Canada
B. Winiarski	Poland
M. Zoricitch	Yugoslavia

Judges elected to serve until 1952

H. Klaestad	Norway
S. B. Krylov	Russia
G. H. Hackworth	United States
C. DeVisscher	Belgium
I. F. Alfara	Mexico

Judges elected to serve until 1955

J. Azevedo	Brazil
A. Alvarez	Chili
J. Basdevant	France
Sir A. McNair	United Kingdom
J. J. Guerrero	El Salvador

In 1948, the five judges whose term would have expired the following year were reëlected to serve until 1958. There were forty nominees in that election, including all of the five whose terms would otherwise have expired. Although several ballots were necessary before agreement was possible on the entire list, the deadlock was overcome without great difficulty.

An analysis of the present list of the judges of the International Court reveals several types of background experience. A considerable number of the members have served as legal advisers to foreign offices; Mr. Hackworth of the United States is such a person. Also among the list are several professors, well-known as authorities on international law, as, for example, Sir Arnold McNair of the United Kingdom and Professor Basdevant of France. A few have had experience in diplomacy, as Señor Guerrero, formerly Foreign Minister of El Salvador. Although nationals of all five of the permanent members of the Security Council are at present on the bench, the majority of the Court come from small countries. All of the judges, however, are expected to serve solely in an individual capacity, and, in theory at least, they are chosen without regard to their nationality.

The Statute admonishes in Article 2 that the Court shall be composed of "independent judges, elected regardless of their nationality. . . ." A court of fair-minded judges unbiased by national loyalties is certainly to be sought if states are to be expected to submit to its rulings, and if it is to make for itself a place in the society of nations. For the most part, the International Court measures up to this standard adequately; but in this day and age, when nationalism is rampant everywhere, it would be futile to expect that even a judge could completely divest himself of his national loyalty. This is one reason why the Statute provides that no two of the fifteen judges may be nationals of the same state, in spite of the fact that they are all supposed to be selected on their individual merits, irrespective of nationality.

When the Committee of Jurists that wrote the Statute of the Permanent Court of International Justice was at work in the summer of 1920, the question was raised as to whether a judge should be allowed to sit on a case where his own state was a party. If so, should the other disputant in Court be allowed a temporary judge for the case, if by chance it had no regular judge? The Committee of Jurists that wrote the Statute was fully convinced that there should be equality of treatment to litigants, but there was some difference of opinion as to whether equality could be attained most satisfactorily by the process of addition (allowing a disputant without a regular judge to send an *ad hoc* judge for the case) or by that of subtraction (requiring a judge whose state was in Court to remain out of Court for that case). If an *ad hoc* judge were to be allowed to one of the disputants when it had no regular judge in Court, should both disputants be allowed the privilege when neither had a regular judge?

The final answer to these questions was to allow litigants to appoint *ad hoc* judges to the bench whenever they were without regular judges, except that when there were several litigating states in the same interest they were to be reckoned as one party only and allowed but one *ad hoc* judge. The Committee of Jurists in 1920 justified their recommendation in favor of "national judges" by the following argument:

> If both parties have a judge upon the Bench, it would be logical if both of these judges abstained from sitting. But it might well happen that the number of judges would in this way be too much diminished, especially if several states had a joint interest in the same proceedings. There would be a risk that the various forms of civilization and the principal legal systems of the world, which are to give our Court its character as a World Court, would not be sufficiently represented for the satisfactory administration of justice.

> Further, it is highly desirable that the judges should be able up to the last minute during deliberations, to put forward and explain the statements and arguments of the states, and to ensure that the sentence, however painful it may be in substance, should be drawn up so as to avoid ruffling national susceptibilities in any way. . . .

The experience of the Permanent Court of International Justice with the institution of national judges was highly satisfactory, however illogical it may seem that disputants should be represented on the bench of a court authorized to decide their case. Invariably, litigating states made use of their right to appoint *ad hoc* judges when they had no regular judges in the Court. Usually the national judges voted in support of the interests and contentions of their respective states, but there were a number of exceptions, as in the Mavrommatis Jerusalem Concessions case, where both the British judge and the Greek judge supported the decision of the Court.

Because the system of national judges in the Permanent Court of International Justice had come to be looked upon with favor, it was carried over into the present International Court of Justice. By Article 31 of the Statute, each party to a case in Court is assured of the

right of having one of its own nationals present as a judge, either a
regular judge retaining the right to take part in the case or an *ad hoc*
judge; the provision still holds that "should there be several parties
in the same interest, they shall . . . be reckoned as one party only."
This system of national judges applies both in judgments and in advisory opinions.

There is another concession to nationality, or, more precisely in
this instance, to national importance. The practice was followed
throughout the history of the Permanent Court of International Justice of including on the bench judges from all the great-power members; furthermore, a national of the United States, a nonmember,
was always selected. This favoritism toward the large powers has
been carried over in the selection of judges of the present Court, so
that each of the permanent members of the Security Council has
had a national of its own on the bench. The Statute contains no provision on the subject, and the practice would be justified chiefly on
the ground that the great powers do in fact play a larger role in
world affairs than do the smaller nations, and have more extensive
interests; on the basis of abstract justice, little can be said for it.

Jurisdiction

The jurisdiction of international tribunals has always been a highly
controversial subject. Generally it is admitted that the jurisdiction
of courts of justice should extend primarily to "justiciable" disputes.
What exactly constitutes a justiciable question is, however, a matter
of difference of opinion, and the definitions of able authorities have
been in disagreement. A convincing view, and one which has been
receiving more and more support, is that in the best sense of the
term a justiciable dispute is one in which the parties direct their
arguments toward their respective rights and duties; international
law or treaties, the sources of rights and duties, will thus be involved
in these cases.

Since international courts, both the old Permanent Court of International Justice and the International Court of Justice, have been
well equipped to deal with justiciable or legal disputes, the proposi-
tion has often been advanced that they should have compulsory

jurisdiction over all controversies of that nature. By analogy it is pointed out that national courts have been granted the right of compulsory jurisdiction over individuals.

At this point the question may be raised as to what is meant by "compulsory jurisdiction" as that term is applied to the treatment of international disputes. Properly it means something more than an agreement to submit a case or a category of cases to a court. Numerous arbitration treaties have been made by nations from time to time in which it is agreed that stated categories of cases would be turned over by the parties to a designated tribunal; the so-called Root Treaties made by the United States during the presidency of Theodore Roosevelt provided for the submission of legal questions which did not involve national honor, vital interests, or the interests of third parties. The actual submission of a dispute under such a treaty could be effected, however, only by a special agreement; there was no right on the part of one nation to bring its opponent into court against its will in the manner that one person has the right to sue another in a national court. "Compulsory jurisdiction," as applied to international courts, implies an equivalent of the individual's right to sue; it means that one nation can by unilateral action force another into court to defend itself. The term "sue" is not ordinarily used between nations; when compulsory jurisdiction exists in international courts, a case is instituted "by application" on the part of one of the parties.

The problem of compulsory jurisdiction arose in the Committee of Jurists which in 1920 wrote the Statute of the Permanent Court of International Justice. After an extended debate in which the arguments for and against were all elaborated upon, a decision in favor of compulsory jurisdiction was taken. The Council of the League of Nations, reviewing the recommendations of the Committee of Jurists decided to delete the provision for compulsory jurisdiction. Finally the debate was reopened in the Assembly when that body received the proposed text of the Statute, and a strong feeling was expressed in favor of placing the provision back in the Statute. This difference between the Council and the Assembly may be explained by the fact that the former was to a large extent under the control

of the large states, which traditionally have been reluctant to accept
compulsory jurisdiction; whereas the latter was dominated by the
smaller states, always eager to be able to force the large powers into
a court where national power and prestige counts for little. Out of
the debate in the League of Nations Assembly, a compromise solution was proposed by Brazil and eventually adopted as a part of
Article 36 of the Statute; it came to be known as the "optional
clause." Under this arrangement it became a matter of choice for
the respective members of the Court to accept the jurisdiction of
that tribunal as compulsory or to continue under a system of optional jurisdiction. It was assumed that the jurisdiction of the Court
for a given member would not be obligatory unless that member
signed the optional clause. Paradoxical as it may sound, when a
member signed the optional clause, his state placed itself within
the compulsory jurisdiction of the Court. As a matter of fact, the
majority of the members signed the optional clause, generally with
stipulated conditions and reservations.

The issue of compulsory jurisdiction came up again at San Francisco in 1945. As before, most of the nations present showed a strong
preference for the adoption of compulsory jurisdiction in all legal
disputes. The Russian delegates and those of the United States,
along with some few others, took exception to this view and indicated that they would be extremely reluctant to become members
of a tribunal with such powers. New Zealand proposed that compulsory jurisdiction be extended only to certain categories of disputes. The decision of the Committee which worked on the problem was to retain the optional clause as it had operated under the
old Statute. This decision was taken by a vote of 31 to 14. Accordingly, Article 36 of the Statute of the International Court of Justice
now provides that:

2. The states parties to the present Statute may at any time declare that
   they recognize as compulsory *ipso facto* and without special agreement
   in relation to any other state accepting the same obligation, the jurisdiction of the Court in all legal cases concurring:

   a. the interpretation of a treaty;
   b. any question of international law;

   c. the existence of any fact which, if established, would constitute a breach of an international obligation;

   d. the nature or extent of the reparation to be made for the breach of an international obligation.

3. The declarations referred to above may be made unconditionally or on condition of reciprocity on the part of several or certain states, or for a certain time.

The Statute of the International Court further stipulates that signatures to the optional clause of the old Permanent Court of International Justice would be understood to carry over and to be binding on the signatory nations as members of the present Court. There are seventeen states now bound by earlier acceptances of the optional clause of the old Court.[4] In addition, eighteen other states had by the beginning of 1950 made declarations accepting the compulsory jurisdiction of the International Court, as follows:

Belgium, 1949	Netherlands, 1946
Bolivia, 1948	Norway, 1946
Brazil, 1948	Pakistan, 1948
China, 1946	Philippines, 1947
Denmark, 1946	Sweden, 1947
France, 1947	Switzerland, 1948
Guatemala, 1947	Turkey, 1947
Honduras, 1948	United Kingdom, 1946
Mexico, 1947	United States, 1946

The acceptance of the optional clause by the United States was made subject to several conditions: (1) that it would be reciprocal and therefore binding only in cases against other states which had signed the clause; (2) that it would apply only in legal disputes; (3) that it would not be operative where an agreement had been made to use some other tribunal, where the question was within the realm of domestic jurisdiction, or where multilateral treaties were involved unless all parties should acquiesce; and (4) that the signa-

---

[4] Australia, Canada, Colombia, the Dominican Republic, El Salvador, Haiti, India, Iran, Luxembourg, New Zealand, Nicaragua, Panama, Paraguay, Siam, Union of South Africa, United Kingdom, Uruguay.

ture by the United States would be binding for five years and thereafter until six months' notice should have been given.

Instruments Providing Reference to the Court

There is another area of jurisdiction for the Court, some of it compulsory, and this, too, is a continuation of an arrangement set up
for the Permanent Court of International Justice. It is described in
the first sentence of Article 36 of the Statute as follows: "The jurisdiction of the Court comprises all cases which the parties refer to it
and all matters specially provided for in the Charter of the United
Nations, or in treaties and conventions in force." The last part of
this provision enables states making treaties to specify that questions arising under them shall be referred to the Court for decision.
Hundreds of clauses of this nature have been inserted in treaties,
in the constitutions of the specialized agencies, and in trusteeship
agreements. Many of the treaties were made when the Permanent
Court of International Justice was functioning and therefore they
named that tribunal, but it is understood that for those treaties
which are still in effect, the present International Court of Justice
is substituted for the old Court.

Some of these clauses call for reference by both parties rather
than for unilateral application in the submission of disputes relating
to the treaties of which they are part. For instance, the Treaty of
Alliance between the United Kingdom and Trans-Jordan, entered
into on March 22, 1946, contained the following clause: "Should
any difference arise relative to the application or the interpretation
of the present Treaty, and should the High Contracting Parties fail
to settle such difference by direct negotiation, the difference shall
be referred to the International Court of Justice unless the parties
agree to another mode of settlement."[5]

A Treaty of Friendship, Commerce, and Economic Development
between the United States and Uruguay, signed on November 23,
1949, stated that "Any dispute between the Parties as to the interpretation or application of the present Treaty, not satisfactorily adjusted by diplomacy or other peaceful means, shall be submitted

---

[5] *British Treaty Series*, no. 32, 1946, *Cmd.* 6916.

to the International Court of Justice."[6] Although not too explicit, this clause also seems to envisage submission by agreement of the parties rather than by unilateral application.

There are other treaties, many of which do permit the unilateral submission of disputes arising under them; these agreements add substantially to the Court's compulsory jurisdiction. The first case submitted to the Permanent Court of International Justice (1922), the *S. S. Wimbledon,* was by application on the part of Great Britain, France, Italy, and Japan against Germany, made possible by a clause in the Treaty of Versailles giving the Court compulsory jurisdiction over disputes relating to the Kiel Canal. A recent treaty with a clause of that nature is the Convention for the Suppression of Traffic in Persons (December 2, 1949), which stipulated that "if any dispute shall arise between the Parties to the Present Convention relating to its interpretation or application and if such dispute cannot be settled by other means, the dispute shall, at the request of any one of the Parties to the dispute, be referred to the International Court of Justice."[7]

The Proposal for Jurisdiction in Criminal Matters

Recently there has been a development which might give the International Court of Justice a new type of jurisdiction. The United Nations General Assembly on December 9, 1948, adopted a resolution stating that in the future there will be "an increasing need of an international judicial organ for the trial of certain crimes under international law." The resolution went on to invite the International Law Commission to examine into the feasibility of establishing such a judicial organ, either as a separate tribunal or as "a criminal chamber of the International Court of Justice." This idea of an International Criminal Court has engaged the casual interest of students and statesmen for many years. Recently, the attention which has been given to war crimes and to the individual responsibility of government officials for violations of international law has

---

[6] Quoted by M. O. Hudson, in "The Twenty-Eighth Year of the World Court," *American Journal of International Law,* 1950, p. 34.

[7] *Ibid.,* p. 34, quoted.

given the subject a new and greater importance. Whether the new jurisdiction were given to the International Court of Justice or to some special tribunal, there would be many problems to solve. A public prosecutor would have to be provided, and a decision would have to be made on whether there should be one or more criminal courts.[8] In 1950 the International Law Commission unanimously agreed not to recommend the establishment of a criminal chamber within the International Court of Justice. During discussions of the project, it became clear that most of the members of the Commission believe that international criminal jurisdiction is desirable, although not feasible at the present time.[9]

Organization and Procedure

As a rule, the International Court of Justice sits in full session, with an understanding that nine of the Judges constitute a quorum. It is possible under the Statute, however, for the Court to form special chambers, each to be composed of three or more judges for the purpose of dealing with particular categories of cases; the Court is also empowered to form a special chamber for an individual case when considered desirable. One special chamber is required, known as the Chamber for Summary Procedure, to be available for the speedy dispatch of business when disputants wish to use it; the Court delegates annually five of its judges to this chamber. Thus far the Chamber for Summary Procedure has not been used for a case, although a similar chamber of the Permanent Court of International Justice was given a small amount of business.

Like the old Court, the International Court of Justice sits at The Hague in the Peace Palace, donated some years ago by Mr. Andrew Carnegie for the Permanent Court of Arbitration. The Court is in continuous session except for judicial vacations as provided whenever the tribunal sees fit to have them. The old Permanent Court of

---

[8] The project for a criminal court is taken up by V. W. Pella, in "Towards an International Criminal Court," *American Journal of International Law*, 1950, vol. 44, no. 1, pp. 37–68.

[9] "Law Commission Declares Criminal Court Desirable," *United Nations Bulletin*, vol. 9 (1950), p. 19.

International Justice started out by meeting in periodical sessions but in 1929 (effective in 1936) changed to the practice of remaining permanently in session.

The official languages of the Court are French and English. The language for any particular case shall be French, if the parties so agree, or English if the parties prefer that language. The publications of the Court are in both French and English. At the request of one of the parties the Court may authorize the use of some third language.

The parties to a dispute are represented in Court by agents, and they may have the assistance of legal counsel. The presiding officer is the President of the Court, who is one of the judges elected to serve in that capacity by the Court. The sessions of the Court are open to the public unless the Court for some reason shall decide otherwise. After a case is heard and oral and written proceedings have both been completed, several conferences of the judges take place before a final decision is made. The majority of the Court may decide a case, and their opinion, written up by one of the judges, becomes "the opinion of the Court." Dissenting and concurring opinions are allowed and in fact are frequently made. After serving as a judge in the Permanent Court of International Justice, Mr. Charles Evans Hughes expressed admiration for the thoroughness of the Court's methods, and particularly for the practice of requiring each judge to write a preliminary opinion on every case before any consultation by the full Court. This requirement, he believed, made the judges work intensively on every case, for none wanted to appear among his colleagues at a disadvantage. As he said, such a practice is possible only in a court with an abundance of time at its disposal.

Advisory Opinions

An advisory opinion is an opinion given by the court on a legal question submitted to it by a qualified authority. It is a procedure often followed in national courts, but not within the Supreme Court of the United States. In the old Permanent Court of International Justice, it was possible for either the Assembly or Council of the League of Nations to submit such questions, although the former never availed itself of this privilege. Twenty-eight questions were submitted by the Council. Once given, these opinions were treated with great respect and given the same force that was accorded to judgments. Some were questions relating to disputes before the Council, as in the Tunis-Morocco nationality case, while others related to the powers of international agencies like the International Labor Organization. Taken together, these opinions proved to be very helpful both as aids in the settlement of disputes and as contributions to the effective functioning of international organization.

The new International Court of Justice has this same duty of giving advisory opinions. The Charter specifically bestows on the General Assembly and the Security Council the right of requesting opinions, and other organs of the United Nations may be authorized by the General Assembly to do so. To date, several of the specialized agencies have been allowed to make requests for advisory opinions, including the International Labor Organization, the World Health Organization, the United Nations Educational, Scientific and Cultural Organizations, the Food and Agricultural Organization, the International Refugee Organization, the International Civic Aviation Organization, the International Bank, and the International Monetary Fund. In December, 1946, the Economic and Social Council was authorized to make requests, and about a year later the right was given to the Trusteeship Council.

One use to which advisory opinions may be put is the interpretation of the Charter and other international constitutional documents. It is the nature of written constitutions that they often give rise to differences of opinion as to their meaning in particular situations; for this reason, the functioning of international organization is promoted by the provision of a procedure for interpretation. To encourage recourse to the International Court of Justice for interpretation of the Charter and of the constitutions of the specialized agencies, the General Assembly on November 14, 1947, adopted a resolution recommending the submission to the Court of such questions for advisory opinions.

The Enforcement of Court Decisions

The judgments of the International Court of Justice are binding upon the parties. They are final and there is no possibility of appeal, but the Court is obligated to construe its judgments when one of the parties so requests. The Charter of the United Nations, after placing upon litigating states an obligation to comply with the judgments of the Court, authorizes the Security Council to "make recommendations or decide upon measures to be taken" in the event that one of the parties fails to accept a decision. Noncompliance by one of the parties with a Court decision may be brought to the attention of the Security Council by the other party.

Acceptance by disputants of the decisions of international tribunals has never been a problem of any importance. If nations are willing to go into court, almost without exception they are willing to follow a decision. In the long list of arbitration cases to which the United States has been a party, two have been denounced on the ground that the tribunals exceeded their powers, and in one of those two cases the other party, Great Britain, agreed with the American point of view; also one award (case of claims against Venezuela, 1866) was denounced by the United States on the ground that a member of the tribunal had acted fraudulently. There was strong resentment in Congress regarding the appropriation of an amount of money due to Norway as a result of an award in a claims case against the United States in 1920; but unpopular as the award was in this country, the money was forthcoming.

All of the judgments and advisory opinions of the Permanent Court of International Justice were accepted and put into effect. None of them, it is true, related to vital interests, but then very rarely does a case involving an infringement of vital interests come before an international tribunal for a decision. Probably the most criticized action of the Permanent Court of International Justice was its advisory opinion on a proposal for a customs union between Germany and Austria (1931), but no nation advocated ignoring the opinion; in fact, two days before the opinion was given by the Court, Germany and Austria announced their intention to drop the project for a

customs union. To date, every judgment and advisory opinion of the
new International Court of Justice has likewise been accepted.

The Work of the Court

For some time after the International Court of Justice opened its
doors for business, no contentious cases or requests for advisory
opinions were brought to it. The first election of judges was on February 6 and 9, 1946, and it was not until May 22, 1947, that the first
contested case, the Corfu Channel case, was submitted. A couple of
months before that case was placed before the Court, Judge Hackworth was quoted as saying that "all of the judges would be very
glad indeed to see some honest-to-goodness business."[10]

The Corfu Channel case was begun by an application against Albania, filed by the government of the United Kingdom with the
Registry of the Court. The dispute in this case had to do with an
incident of October 22, 1946, when two British destroyers passing
through the Corfu Channel struck a mine and were damaged, and
several members of the crews were killed. Following this incident,
warships of the British Navy investigated the channel for other
mines, found some, and removed them. The matter was discussed in
the Security Council, where Albania, as a nonmember of the United
Nations, was asked, under Article 32 of the Charter, to take part on
condition that she accept all of the obligations of a member for the
case. Albania accepted this invitation. After a Council resolution
unfavorable to Albania failed to receive the necessary votes in the
Security Council, another resolution was adopted on April 9, 1947,
recommending that the disputants refer the case to the International
Court of Justice. On May 22, the Government of the United Kingdom filed an application with the Registry of the Court asking for a
decision against Albania and for a statement of reparations due. A
question was raised at this point by Albania as to whether the
United Kingdom could institute proceedings by a unilateral application since Albania was not a member of the United Nations or of the
Court, but at the same time the Albania government indicated a
willingness to appear before the Court; its objection was only to the

---

[10] New York *Times*, March 24, 1947.

method used by the United Kingdom in submitting the case. The first judgment of the Court on the case, delivered on March 25, 1948, rejected the Albanian objection.

The Court then proceeded with the merits of the Corfu Channel case and on April 9, 1949, handed down its judgment. It found the Corfu Channel to "belong to a class of international highways through which passage cannot be prohibited by a coastal state in time of peace," and Albania to have acted illegally in placing mines there. The subsequent action of the British warships in sweeping the Corfu Channel of mines, however, was held to be without legal justification. A third judgment of the Court, given on December 15, 1949, fixed the amount of the compensation to be paid by Albania to the United Kingdom at £843,947.

During the year 1949, three more contested cases were instituted in the Court as follows:

1. Case begun by application (October 13) of the French government against Egypt regarding the protection of French nationals in Egypt (ordered off the docket of the Court on March 29, 1950, after France so requested);
2. Case begun by application (October 15) of the Colombian Government against Peru on a question of asylum granted by the Colombian Embassy in Peru to a Peruvian citizen;
3. Case begun by application (September 29) of the United Kingdom against Norway on the question of the limits of Norwegian territorial waters, particularly as regards fishing.[11]

On November 20, 1950, the Court handed down its judgment in the asylum case between Colombia and Peru. The case had involved Señor Haya de la Torre, leader of the powerful American People's Revolutionary Alliance (APRA), who had taken refuge in the Colombian Embassy following an uprising in Callao in 1948. Peru contended, among other things, that Señor Haya de la Torre was guilty of common-law crimes; Colombia treated him as a political criminal only. In its judgment the Court held that Colombia could not decide unilaterally to qualify a person seeking asylum as a politi-

---

[11] For recent developments in the work of the Court, see the January issues each year of the *American Journal of International Law* (articles by Professor Manley O. Hudson). Also see current issues of *International Organization*.

cal refugee. It also decided that Peru was not bound to accord him
safe conduct out of the country. Other points too were covered in
the decision. After the judgment was announced, spokesmen for
Colombia criticized it on the ground that it gave no specific ruling
on the question as to whether Señor Haya de la Torre should be
surrendered to Peruvian authorities; Peru viewed the judgment
otherwise, holding that it implied an obligation to surrender the
man. In this uncertainty the Colombian Government petitioned the
Court for an interpretation of its judgment.

Among the advisory opinions which have been issued to date was
that which grew out of the assassination of Count Bernadotte. While
stationed in Palestine as United Nations mediator, Count Bernadotte
was killed by Israeli terrorists. Could the United Nations hold the
Israeli Government responsible for such an action and institute legal
proceedings? In its opinion (April 11, 1949) the Court said that the
United Nations does in fact have the capacity to bring an international claim against either a *de jure* or *de facto* government with a
view to obtaining reparation.

Another advisory opinion of considerable interest was that relating to votes within the Security Council in the admission of new
members to the United Nations. A question had arisen out of the fact
that in considering the applications of several nations for admission
to the United Nations Russia had voted conditionally; it was the
Russian viewpoint that she would support certain applicants on condition that other applicants were approved by the Security Council.
Was it possible to cast a vote of this nature? The opinion of the International Court (May 28, 1948) was in the negative.

Three requests for advisory opinions were made in 1949, as follows:

1. By the General Assembly (October 22) on certain questions relating to
   the interpretation of peace treaties with Bulgaria, Hungary, and Roumania;
2. By the General Assembly (November 22) on the question as to
   whether the General Assembly may vote to admit a new member of
   the United Nations when the Security Council has made no recommendation for admission;

3. By the General Assembly (December 6) on questions relating to the obligations of the Union of South Africa toward Southwest Africa.

By July 11, 1950, the Court had completed its work in connection with these requests.

On March 30, 1950, the Court handed down its opinion on the interpretation of the peace treaties with Bulgaria, Hungary, and Roumania. Four questions had been submitted to the Court by the General Assembly, all arising out of the alleged mistreatment of minorities by those three countries in contravention of the peace treaties which they had made with the Allied powers after World War II. The Allied powers had called upon the three nations, in accordance with the provisions of the treaties of peace, to coöperate in the appointment of commissions for the settlement of the dispute, but in vain. Consequently, the General Assembly asked the Court for an advisory opinion on the following questions:

I. Do the diplomatic exchanges between Bulgaria, Hungary and Roumania, on the one hand, and certain Allied and Associated Powers signatories to the Treaties of Peace, on the other, concerning the implementation of Article 2 of the Treaties with Bulgaria and Hungary and Article 3 of the Treaty with Roumania, disclose disputes subject to the provisions for the settlement of disputes contained in Article 36 of the Treaty of Peace with Bulgaria, Article 40 of the Treaty of Peace with Hungary, and Article 38 of the Treaty of Peace with Roumania?

In the event of an affirmative reply to question I:

II. Are the Governments of Bulgaria, Hungary and Roumania obligated to carry out the provisions of the articles referred to in question I, including the provisions for the appointment of their representatives to the Treaty Commissions?

In the event of an affirmative reply to question II and if within thirty days from the date when the Court delivers its opinion, the Governments concerned have not notified the Secretary-General that they have appointed their representatives to the Treaty Commissions, and the Secretary-General has so advised the International Court of Justice:

III. If one party fails to appoint a representative to a Treaty Commission under the Treaties of Peace with Bulgaria, Hungary and Roumania where that party is obligated to appoint a representative to the Treaty Commission, is the Secretary-General of the United Nations authorized to appoint the third member of the Commission upon the request of the other party to a dispute according to the provisions of the respective Treaties?

In the event of an affirmative reply to question III:

IV. Would a Treaty Commission composed of a representative of one party and a third member appointed by the Secretary-General of the United Nations constitute a Commission, within the meaning of the relevant Treaty articles, competent to make a definitive and binding decision in settlement of a dispute?

The Court answered the first two of these questions in the affirmative. The third question was answered in the negative; for this reason no answer to the fourth was necessary.

On March 3, 1950, the International Court of Justice gave its opinion on the question as to whether the General Assembly may vote to admit a new member of the United Nations when the Security Council has made no recommendation for admission. The answer of the Court was in the negative.

The questions submitted to the Court in relation to Southwest Africa were as follows:

What is the international status of the Territory of Southwest Africa and what are the international obligations of the Union of South Africa arising therefrom, in particular:

1. Does the Union of South Africa continue to have international obligations under the Mandate for Southwest Africa and, if so, what are those obligations?

2. Are the provisions of Chapter XII of the Charter applicable and, if so, in what manner, to the Territory of Southwest Africa?

3. Has the Union of South Africa the competence to modify the international status of the Territory of Southwest Africa, or, in the event of a negative reply, where does competence rest to determine and modify the international status of the Territory?

They had arisen from the fact that the Union of South Africa had persisted in her refusal to place Southwest Africa under the trusteeship system of the United Nations despite repeated requests from the General Assembly that the territory be made a trust area. To question (1), the Court gave the opinion that "Southwest Africa is a territory under the international Mandate assumed by the Union of South Africa on December 17, 1920" (under the League of Nations). It held on question (2) that "the provisions of Chapter XII of the Charter are applicable to the Territory of Southwest Africa in the sense that they provide a means by which the Territory may be brought under the Trusteeship system," but that the Charter does "not impose on the Union of South Africa a legal obligation to place the Territory under the Trusteeship System." To question (3), the Court answered that the Union of South Africa alone could not change the international status of Southwest Africa, and that the power to do so "rests with the Union of South Africa acting with the consent of the United Nations."

The Place of the Court

What may reasonably be expected of such an organization as the International Court of Justice? What contribution can it be expected to make to the maintenance of order and to the prevention of war? The answer to these questions must take into account the fact that the Court is a highly specialized type of agency fitted to deal primarily with legal issues. No one would pretend that it is able to handle all types of issues, at least not with equal facility. The function of the Court as stated by Article 38 (paragraph 1) of the Statute is "to decide in accordance with international law such disputes as are submitted to it." That the Court is not prevented from dealing with nonlegal disputes is made clear by paragraph 2 of the same Article, which says, "This provision shall not prejudice the power of the Court to decide a case *ex aequo et bono,* if the parties agree thereto." Although this right to decide cases on the basis of equity enables the Court to deal with nonlegal cases, in practice it has been confined to legal disputes. It is unthinkable that the Court would be given a chance to deal with the basic issues involved in the cold war between Russia and the United States.

While the limitations of the Court may be frankly admitted, one should not underestimate its usefulness. True it is that the disputes which have come before the Court could not by any stretch of the imagination have caused war. But the settlement of any dispute is always helpful to the peaceful functioning of international relations. In the realm of international affairs, as elsewhere, great misunderstandings can grow out of small incidents. To have disposed successfully of the Corfu Channel incident before it had time to be magnified into unreasonable proportions was helpful to both Albania and Great Britain. In addition to the settlement of disputes by means of binding judgments, the Court has contributed to an orderly world society by those of its advisory opinions that have clarified the rights, duties, or methods of international agencies. It was an advantage, for instance, to be able to get an answer to the question as to whether a member of the Security Council may vote conditionally on the admission of a state to the United Nations. All told, the Court has strengthened the legal foundations of international relations at many points, and, given a fair chance, it will carry this work much further in the future.

▲

APPENDIX TO CHAPTER VII

I

Statute of the International Court of Justice

ARTICLE 1

The International Court of Justice established by the Charter of the United Nations as the principal judicial organ of the United Nations shall be constituted and shall function in accordance with the provisions of the present Statute.

I. Organization of the Court
ARTICLE 2

The Court shall be composed of a body of independent judges, elected regardless of their nationality from among persons of high moral character, who possess the qualifications required in their respective countries for appointment to the highest judicial offices, or are jurisconsults of recognized competence in international law.

ARTICLE 3

1. The Court shall consist of fifteen members, no two of whom may be nationals of the same state.

2. A person who for the purposes of membership in the Court could be regarded as a national of more than one state shall be deemed to be a national of the one in which he ordinarily exercises civil and political rights.

ARTICLE 4

1. The members of the Court shall be elected by the General Assembly and by the Security Council from a list of persons nominated by the national groups in the Permanent Court of Arbitration, in accordance with the following provisions.

2. In the case of Members of the United Nations not represented in the Permanent Court of Arbitration, candidates shall be nominated by national groups appointed for this purpose by their governments under the same conditions as those prescribed for members of the Permanent Court of Arbitration by Article 44 of the Convention of The Hague of 1907 for the pacific settlement of international disputes.

3. The conditions under which a state which is a party to the present Statute but is not a Member of the United Nations may participate in electing the members of the Court shall, in the absence of a special agreement, be laid down by the General Assembly upon recommendation of the Security Council.

ARTICLE 5

1. At least three months before the date of the election, the Secretary-General of the United Nations shall address a written request to the members of the Permanent Court of Arbitration belonging to the states which are parties to the present Statute, and to the members of the national groups appointed under Article 4, paragraph 2, inviting them to undertake, within a given time, by national groups, the nomination of persons in a position to accept the duties of a member of the Court.

2. No group may nominate more than four persons, not more than two of whom shall be of their own nationality. In no case may the number of candidates nominated by a group be more than double the number of seats to be filled.

ARTICLE 6

Before making these nominations, each national group is recommended to consult its highest court of justice, its legal faculties and schools of law, and its national academies and national sections of international academies devoted to the study of law.

ARTICLE 7

1. The Secretary-General shall prepare a list in alphabetical order of all the persons thus nominated. Save as provided in Article 12, paragraph 2, these shall be the only persons eligible.

2. The Secretary-General shall submit this list to the General Assembly and to the Security Council.

ARTICLE 8

The General Assembly and the Security Council shall proceed independently of one another to elect the members of the Court.

ARTICLE 9

At every election, the electors shall bear in mind not only that the persons to be elected should individually possess the qualifications required, but also that in the body as a whole the representation of the main forms of civilization and of the principal legal systems of the world should be assured.

ARTICLE 10

1. Those candidates who obtain an absolute majority of votes in the General Assembly and in the Security Council shall be considered as elected.

2. Any vote of the Security Council, whether for the election of judges or for the appointment of members of the conference en-

visaged in Article 12, shall be taken without any distinction between permanent and non-permanent members of the Security Council.

3. In the event of more than one national of the same state obtaining an absolute majority of the votes both of the General Assembly and of the Security Council, the eldest of these only shall be considered as elected.

ARTICLE 11

If, after the first meeting held for the purpose of the election, one or more seats remain to be filled, a second and, if necessary, a third meeting shall take place.

ARTICLE 12

1. If, after the third meeting, one or more seats still remain unfilled, a joint conference consisting of six members, three appointed by the General Assembly and three by the Security Council, may be formed at any time at the request of either the General Assembly or the Security Council, for the purpose of choosing by the vote of an absolute majority one name for each seat still vacant, to submit to the General Assembly and the Security Council for their respective acceptance.

2. If the joint conference is unanimously agreed upon any person who fulfils the required conditions, he may be included in its list, even though he was not included in the list of nominations referred to in Article 7.

3. If the joint conference is satisfied that it will not be successful in procuring an election, those members of the Court who have already been elected shall, within a period to be fixed by the Security Council, proceed to fill the vacant seats by selection from among those candidates who have obtained votes either in the General Assembly or in the Security Council.

4. In the event of an equality of votes among the judges, the eldest judge shall have a casting vote.

ARTICLE 13

1. The members of the Court shall be elected for nine years and may be re-elected; provided, however, that of the judges elected at

the first election, the terms of five judges shall expire at the end of three years and the terms of five more judges shall expire at the end of six years.

2. The judges whose terms are to expire at the end of the above-mentioned initial periods of three and six years shall be chosen by lot to be drawn by the Secretary-General immediately after the first election has been completed.

3. The members of the Court shall continue to discharge their duties until their places have been filled. Though replaced, they shall finish any cases which they may have begun.

4. In the case of the resignation of a member of the Court, the resignation shall be addressed to the President of the Court for transmission to the Secretary-General. This last notification makes the place vacant.

ARTICLE 14

Vacancies shall be filled by the same method as that laid down for the first election, subject to the following provision: the Secretary-General shall, within one month of the occurrence of the vacancy, proceed to issue the invitations provided for in Article 5, and the date of the election shall be fixed by the Security Council.

ARTICLE 15

A member of the Court elected to replace a member whose term of office has not expired shall hold office for the remainder of his predecessor's term.

ARTICLE 16

1. No member of the Court may exercise any political or administrative function, or engage in any other occupation of a professional nature.

2. Any doubt on this point shall be settled by the decision of the Court.

ARTICLE 17

1. No member of the Court may act as agent, counsel, or advocate in any case.

2. No member may participate in the decision of any case in which he has previously taken part as agent, counsel, or advocate for one of the parties, or as a member of a national or international court, or of a commission of enquiry, or in any other capacity.

3. Any doubt on this point shall be settled by the decision of the Court.

ARTICLE 18

1. No member of the Court can be dismissed unless, in the unanimous opinion of the other members, he has ceased to fulfil the required conditions.

2. Formal notification thereof shall be made to the Secretary-General by the Registrar.

3. This notification makes the place vacant.

ARTICLE 19

The members of the Court, when engaged on the business of the Court, shall enjoy diplomatic privileges and immunities.

ARTICLE 20

Every member of the Court shall, before taking up his duties, make a solemn declaration in open court that he will exercise his powers impartially and conscientiously.

ARTICLE 21

1. The Court shall elect its President and Vice-President for three years; they may be re-elected.

2. The Court shall appoint its Registrar and may provide for the appointment of such other officers as may be necessary.

ARTICLE 22

1. The seat of the Court shall be established at The Hague. This, however, shall not prevent the Court from sitting and exercising its functions elsewhere whenever the Court considers it desirable.

2. The President and the Registrar shall reside at the seat of the Court.

ARTICLE 23

1. The Court shall remain permanently in session, except during the judicial vacations, the dates and duration of which shall be fixed by the Court.

2. Members of the Court are entitled to periodic leave, the dates and duration of which shall be fixed by the Court, having in mind the distance between The Hague and the home of each judge.

3. Members of the Court shall be bound, unless they are on leave or prevented from attending by illness or other serious reasons duly explained to the President, to hold themselves permanently at the disposal of the Court.

ARTICLE 24

1. If, for some special reason, a member of the Court considers that he should not take part in the decision of a particular case, he shall so inform the President.

2. If the President considers that for some special reason one of the members of the Court should not sit in a particular case, he shall give him notice accordingly.

3. If in any such case the member of the Court and the President disagree, the matter shall be settled by the decision of the Court.

ARTICLE 25

1. The full Court shall sit except when it is expressly provided otherwise in the present Statute.

2. Subject to the condition that the number of judges available to constitute the Court is not thereby reduced below eleven, the Rules of the Court may provide for allowing one or more judges, according to circumstances and in rotation, to be dispensed from sitting.

3. A quorum of nine judges shall suffice to constitute the Court.

ARTICLE 26

1. The Court may from time to time form one or more chambers, composed of three or more judges as the Court may determine, for dealing with particular categories of cases; for example, labor cases and cases relating to transit and communications.

2. The Court may at any time form a chamber for dealing with a particular case. The number of judges to constitute such a chamber shall be determined by the Court with the approval of the parties.

3. Cases shall be heard and determined by the chambers provided for in this Article if the parties so request.

ARTICLE 27

A judgment given by any of the chambers provided for in Articles 26 and 29 shall be considered as rendered by the Court.

ARTICLE 28

The chambers provided for in Articles 26 and 29 may, with the consent of the parties, sit and exercise their functions elsewhere than at The Hague.

ARTICLE 29

With a view to the speedy despatch of business, the Court shall form annually a chamber composed of five judges which, at the request of the parties, may hear and determine cases by summary procedure. In addition, two judges shall be selected for the purpose of replacing judges who find it impossible to sit.

ARTICLE 30

1. The Court shall frame rules for carrying out its functions. In particular, it shall lay down rules of procedure.

2. The Rules of the Court may provide for assessors to sit with the Court or with any of its chambers, without the right to vote.

ARTICLE 31

1. Judges of the nationality of each of the parties shall retain their right to sit in the case before the Court.

2. If the Court includes upon the Bench a judge of the nationality of one of the parties, any other party may choose a person to sit as judge. Such person shall be chosen preferably from among those persons who have been nominated as candidates as provided in Articles 4 and 5.

3. If the Court includes upon the Bench no judge of the nationality of the parties, each of these parties may proceed to choose a judge as provided in paragraph 2 of this Article.

4. The provisions of this Article shall apply to the case of Articles 26 and 29. In such cases, the President shall request one or, if necessary, two of the members of the Court forming the chamber to give place to the members of the Court of the nationality of the parties concerned, and, failing such, or if they are unable to be present, to the judges specially chosen by the parties.

5. Should there be several parties in the same interest, they shall, for the purpose of the preceding provisions, be reckoned as one party only. Any doubt upon this point shall be settled by the decision of the Court.

6. Judges chosen as laid down in paragraphs 2, 3, and 4 of this Article shall fulfil the conditions required by Articles 2, 17 (paragraph 2), 20, and 24 of the present Statute. They shall take part in the decision on terms of complete equality with their colleagues.

ARTICLE 32

1. Each member of the Court shall receive an annual salary.

2. The President shall receive a special annual allowance.

3. The Vice-President shall receive a special allowance for every day on which he acts as President.

4. The judges chosen under Article 31, other than members of the Court, shall receive compensation for each day on which they exercise their functions.

5. These salaries, allowances, and compensation shall be fixed by the General Assembly. They may not be decreased during the term of office.

6. The salary of the Registrar shall be fixed by the General Assembly on the proposal of the Court.

7. Regulations made by the General Assembly shall fix the conditions under which retirement pensions may be given to members of the Court and to the Registrar, and the conditions under which members of the Court and the Registrar shall have their traveling expenses refunded.

8. The above salaries, allowances, and compensation shall be free of all taxation.

ARTICLE 33

The expenses of the Court shall be borne by the United Nations in such a manner as shall be decided by the General Assembly.

II. Competence of the Court
ARTICLE 34

1. Only states may be parties in cases before the Court.

2. The Court, subject to and in conformity with its Rules, may request of public international organizations information relevant to cases before it, and shall receive such information presented by such organizations on their own initiative.

3. Whenever the construction of the constituent instrument of a public international organization or of an international convention adopted thereunder is in question in a case before the Court, the Registrar shall so notify the public international organization concerned and shall communicate to it copies of all the written proceedings.

ARTICLE 35

1. The Court shall be open to the states parties to the present Statute.

2. The conditions under which the Court shall be open to other states shall, subject to the special provisions contained in treaties in force, be laid down by the Security Council, but in no case shall such conditions place the parties in a position of inequality before the Court.

3. When a state which is not a Member of the United Nations is a party to a case, the Court shall fix the amount which that party is to contribute towards the expenses of the Court. This provision shall not apply if such state is bearing a share of the expenses of the Court.

ARTICLE 36

1. The jurisdiction of the Court comprises all cases which the parties refer to it and all matters specially provided for in the Char-

ter of the United Nations or in treaties and conventions in force.

2. The states parties to the present Statute may at any time declare that they recognize as compulsory *ipso facto* and without special agreement, in relation to any other state accepting the same obligation, the jurisdiction of the Court in all legal disputes concerning:

    a. the interpretation of a treaty;

    b. any question of international law;

    c. the existence of any fact which, if established, would constitute a breach of an international obligation;

    d. the nature or extent of the reparation to be made for the breach of an international obligation.

3. The declarations referred to above may be made unconditionally or on condition of reciprocity on the part of several or certain states, or for a certain time.

4. Such declarations shall be deposited with the Secretary-General of the United Nations, who shall transmit copies thereof to the parties to the Statute and to the Registrar of the Court.

5. Declarations made under Article 36 of the Statute of the Permanent Court of International Justice and which are still in force shall be deemed, as between the parties to the present Statute, to be acceptances of the compulsory jurisdiction of the International Court of Justice for the period which they still have to run and in accordance with their terms.

6. In the event of a dispute as to whether the Court has jurisdiction, the matter shall be settled by the decision of the Court.

ARTICLE 37

Whenever a treaty or convention in force provides for reference of a matter to a tribunal to have been instituted by the League of Nations, or to the Permanent Court of International Justice, the matter shall, as between the parties to the present Statute, be referred to the International Court of Justice.

ARTICLE 38

1. The Court, whose function is to decide in accordance with international law such disputes as are submitted to it, shall apply:

a. international conventions, whether general or particular, establishing rules expressly recognized by the contesting states;

b. international custom, as evidence of a general practice accepted as law;

c. the general principles of law recognized by civilized nations;

d. subject to the provisions of Article 59, judicial decisions and the teachings of the most highly qualified publicists of the various nations, as subsidiary means for the determination of rules of law.

2. This provision shall not prejudice the power of the Court to decide a case *ex aequo et bono*, if the parties agree thereto.

III. Procedure

ARTICLE 39

1. The official languages of the Court shall be French and English. If the parties agree that the case shall be conducted in French, the judgment shall be delivered in French. If the parties agree that the case shall be conducted in English, the judgment shall be delivered in English.

2. In the absence of an agreement as to which language shall be employed, each party may, in the pleadings, use the language which it prefers; the decision of the Court shall be given in French and English. In this case the Court shall at the same time determine which of the two texts shall be considered as authoritative.

3. The Court shall, at the request of any party, authorize a language other than French or English to be used by that party.

ARTICLE 40

1. Cases are brought before the Court, as the case may be, either by the notification of the special agreement or by a written application addressed to the Registrar. In either case the subject of the dispute and the parties shall be indicated.

2. The Registrar shall forthwith communicate the application to all concerned.

3. He shall also notify the Members of the United Nations through the Secretary-General, and also any other states entitled to appear before the Court.

ARTICLE 41

1. The Court shall have the power to indicate, if it considers that circumstances so require, any provisional measures which ought to be taken to preserve the respective rights of either party.

2. Pending the final decision, notice of the measures suggested shall forthwith be given to the parties and to the Security Council.

ARTICLE 42

1. The parties shall be represented by agents.

2. They may have the assistance of counsel or advocates before the Court.

3. The agents, counsel, and advocates of parties before the Court shall enjoy the privileges and immunities necessary to the independent exercise of their duties.

ARTICLE 43

1. The procedure shall consist of two parts: written and oral.

2. The written proceedings shall consist of the communication to the Court and to the parties of memorials, countermemorials and, if necessary, replies; also all papers and documents in support.

3. These communications shall be made through the Registrar, in the order and within the time fixed by the Court.

4. A certified copy of every document produced by one party shall be communicated to the other party.

5. The oral proceedings shall consist of the hearing by the Court of witnesses, experts, agents, counsel, and advocates.

ARTICLE 44

1. For the service of all notices upon persons other than the agents, counsel, and advocates, the Court shall apply direct to the government of the state upon whose territory the notice has to be served.

2. The same provision shall apply whenever steps are to be taken to procure evidence on the spot.

ARTICLE 45

The hearing shall be under the control of the President or, if he is unable to preside, of the Vice-President; if neither is able to preside, the senior judge present shall preside.

ARTICLE 46

The hearing in Court shall be public, unless the Court shall decide otherwise, or unless the parties demand that the public be not admitted.

ARTICLE 47

1. Minutes shall be made at each hearing and signed by the Registrar and the President.

2. These minutes alone shall be authentic.

ARTICLE 48

The Court shall make orders for the conduct of the case, shall decide the form and time in which each party must conclude its arguments, and make all arrangements connected with the taking of evidence.

ARTICLE 49

The Court may, even before the hearing begins, call upon the agents to produce any document or to supply any explanations. Formal note shall be taken of any refusal.

ARTICLE 50

The Court may, at any time, entrust any individual, body, bureau, commission, or other organization that it may select, with the task of carrying out an enquiry or giving an expert opinion.

ARTICLE 51

During the hearing any relevant questions are to be put to the witnesses and experts under the conditions laid down by the Court in the rules of procedure referred to in Article 30.

ARTICLE 52

After the Court has received the proofs and evidence within the time specified for the purpose, it may refuse to accept any further oral or written evidence that one party may desire to present unless the other side consents.

ARTICLE 53

1. Whenever one of the parties does not appear before the Court, or fails to defend its case, the other party may call upon the Court to decide in favor of its claim.

2. The Court must, before doing so, satisfy itself, not only that it has jurisdiction in accordance with Articles 36 and 37, but also that the claim is well founded in fact and law.

ARTICLE 54

1. When, subject to the control of the Court, the agents, counsel, and advocates have completed their presentation of the case, the President shall declare the hearing closed.

2. The Court shall withdraw to consider the judgment.

3. The deliberations of the Court shall take place in private and remain secret.

ARTICLE 55

1. All questions shall be decided by a majority of the judges present.

2. In the events of an equality of votes, the President or the judge who acts in his place shall have a casting vote.

ARTICLE 56

1. The judgment shall state the reasons on which it is based.

2. It shall contain the names of the judges who have taken part in the decision.

ARTICLE 57

If the judgment does not represent in whole or in part the unanimous opinion of the judges, any judge shall be entitled to deliver a separate opinion.

Article 58

The judgment shall be signed by the President and by the Registrar. It shall be read in open court, due notice having been given to the agents.

Article 59

The decision of the Court has no binding force except between the parties and in respect of that particular case.

Article 60

The judgment is final and without appeal. In the event of dispute as to the meaning or scope of the judgment, the Court shall construe it upon the request of any party.

Article 61

1. An application for revision of a judgment may be made only when it is based upon the discovery of some fact of such a nature as to be a decisive factor, which fact was, when the judgment was given, unknown to the Court and also to the party claiming revision, always provided that such ignorance was not due to negligence.

2. The proceedings for revision shall be opened by a judgment of the Court expressly recording the existence of the new fact, recognizing that it has such a character as to lay the case open to revision, and declaring the application admissible on this ground.

3. The Court may require previous compliance with the terms of the judgment before it admits proceedings in revision.

4. The application for revision must be made at latest within six months of the discovery of the new fact.

5. No application for revision may be made after the lapse of ten years from the date of the judgment.

Article 62

1. Should a state consider that it has an interest of a legal nature which may be affected by the decision in the case, it may submit a request to the Court to be permitted to intervene.

2. It shall be for the Court to decide upon this request.

ARTICLE 63

1. Whenever the construction of a convention to which states other than those concerned in the case are parties is in question, the Registrar shall notify all such states forthwith.

2. Every state so notified has the right to intervene in the proceedings; but if it uses this right, the construction given by the judgment will be equally binding upon it.

ARTICLE 64

Unless otherwise decided by the Court, each party shall bear its own costs.

IV. Advisory Opinions
ARTICLE 65

1. The Court may give an advisory opinion on any legal question at the request of whatever body may be authorized by or in accordance with the Charter of the United Nations to make such a request.

2. Questions upon which the advisory opinion of the Court is asked shall be laid before the Court by means of a written request containing an exact statement of the question upon which an opinion is required, and accompanied by all documents likely to throw light upon the question.

ARTICLE 66

1. The Registrar shall forthwith give notice of the request for an advisory opinion to all states entitled to appear before the Court.

2. The Registrar shall also, by means of a special and direct communication, notify any state entitled to appear before the Court or international organization considered by the Court, or, should it not be sitting, by the President, as likely to be able to furnish information on the question, that the Court will be prepared to receive, within a time limit to be fixed by the President, written statements, or to hear, at a public sitting to be held for the purpose, oral statements relating to the question.

3. Should any such state entitled to appear before the Court have failed to receive the special communication referred to in paragraph

2 of this Article, such state may express a desire to submit a written statement or to be heard; and the Court will decide.

4. States and organizations having presented written or oral statements or both shall be permitted to comment on the statements made by other states or organizations in the form, to the extent, and within the time limits which the Court, or, should it not be sitting, the President, shall decide in each particular case. Accordingly, the Registrar shall in due time communicate any such written statements to states and organizations having submitted similar statements.

Article 67

The Court shall deliver its advisory opinions in open court, notice having been given to the Secretary-General and to the representatives of Members of the United Nations, of other states and of international organizations immediately concerned.

Article 68

In the exercise of its advisory functions the Court shall further be guided by the provisions of the present Statute which apply in contentious cases to the extent to which it recognizes them to be applicable.

V. Amendment
Article 69

Amendments to the present Statute shall be effected by the same procedure as is provided by the Charter of the United Nations for amendments to that Charter, subject however to any provisions which the General Assembly upon recommendation of the Security Council may adopt concerning the participation of states which are parties to the present Statute but are not Members of the United Nations.

Article 70

The Court shall have power to propose such amendments to the present Statute as it may deem necessary, through written communications to the Secretary-General, for consideration in conformity with the provisions of Article 69.

II

Acceptance of Compulsory Jurisdiction of the Court by the United States (1946)

(Declaration of President Truman, *Department of State Bulletin,* 8 September 1948, pp. 452–3.)

I, Harry S. Truman, President of the United States of America, declare on behalf of the United States of America, under Article 36, paragraph 2, of the Statute of the International Court of Justice, and in accordance with the Resolution of August 2, 1946, of the Senate of the United States of America (two-thirds of the Senators present concurring therein), that the United States of America recognizes as compulsory *ipso facto* and without special agreement, in relation to any other state accepting the same obligation, the jurisdiction of the International Court of Justice in all legal disputes hereafter arising concerning

1. the interpretation of a treaty;

2. any question of international law;

3. the existence of any fact which, if established, would constitute a breach of an international obligation;

4. the nature or extent of the reparation to be made for the breach of an international obligation;

Provided, that this declaration shall not apply to

1. disputes the solution of which the parties shall entrust to other tribunals by virtue of agreements already in existence or which may be concluded in the future; or

2. disputes with regard to matters which are essentially within the domestic jurisdiction of the United States of America as determined by the United States of America; or

3. disputes arising under a multilateral treaty, unless (1) all parties to the treaty affected by the decision are also parties to the case before the Court, or (2) the United States of America specially agrees to jurisdiction; and

Provided further, that this declaration still remain in force for a period of five years and thereafter until the expiration of six months after notice may be given to terminate this declaration.

Done at Washington this fourteenth day of August 1946.

HARRY S. TRUMAN

VIII   The United Nations System—Background and Authority

THAT AN INTERNATIONAL DISPUTE BETWEEN TWO OR MORE nations is a matter of concern to the entire community was a basic principle of the League of Nations. To some extent a foundation for this principle was laid in 1899 when at The Hague in The Netherlands the nations concluded the Convention for the Pacific Settlement of International Disputes. The League system was several long steps ahead of the methods of the Hague Convention: it imposed upon disputants more in the way of obligations to resort to pacific settlement; it offered them more in the way of machinery and procedures; and in practice it was much more active. On the experience gained by the League, the United Nations built its structure of peaceful settlement.

The Background Experience of the League of Nations

The League of Nations system of dealing with disputes was at work for two decades, and during that time it had before it a long list of controversies, both major and minor. The period was one of adjustment after war, in which powerful new forces were rampant, particularly those of economic depression, fascism, and communism, so that disputes were not lacking on which to turn loose the machinery of the Geneva organization.

All of the major organs of the League—the Council, the Assembly, and the Secretariat—had roles to play in the treatment of disputes, but upon the Council was placed the burden of the responsibility. The Secretariat's contributions in this field were, of course, of a perfunctory nature, involving the receipt and dispatch of communications, summoning Council meetings to deal with emergencies, and taking down the minutes of meetings.

The constitutional bases of the League of Nations' authority to deal with international disputes was provided by Articles 3, 4, 11–15 of the Covenant. The portion of Article 3 which pertained to the subject stated broadly, "The Assembly may deal at its meetings with any matter within the sphere of action of the League or affecting the peace of the world." Within Article 4 was a provision in almost identical words giving to the Council the same right. Articles 11–15 were much more detailed, and because of their concise statements of obligations, rights, and methods they are listed below:[1]

ARTICLE 11
Action in Case of War or Threat of War

1. Any war or threat of war, whether immediately affecting any of the Members of the League or not, is hereby declared a matter of concern to the whole League, and the League shall take any action that may be deemed wise and effectual to safeguard the peace of nations. In case any such emergency should arise, the Secretary-General shall, on the request of any Member of the League, forthwith summon a meeting of the Council.

2. It is also declared to be the friendly right of each Member of the League to bring to the attention of the Assembly or of the Council any circumstance whatever affecting international relations which threatens to disturb international peace or the good understanding between nations upon which peace depends.

ARTICLE 12
Disputes to Be Submitted for Settlement

1. The Members of the League agree that, if there should arise between them any dispute likely to lead to a rupture they will submit the matter either to arbitration *or judicial settlement* or to inquiry by the Council and they agree in no case to resort to war until three months after the award by the arbitrators *or the judicial decision,* or the report by the Council.

2. In any case under this Article, the award of the arbitrators *or the*

---

[1] Italicized portions of the articles are amendments.

judicial decision shall be made within a reasonable time, and the report of the Council shall be made within six months after the submission of the dispute.

Article 13
Arbitration or Judicial Settlement

1. The Members of the League agree that, whenever any dispute shall arise between them which they recognize to be suitable for submission to arbitration *or judicial settlement,* and which can not be satisfactorily settled by diplomacy, they will submit the whole subject-matter to arbitration *or judicial settlement.*

2. Disputes as to the interpretation of a treaty, as to any question of international law, as to the existence of any fact which, if established, would constitute a breach of any international obligation, or as to the extent and nature of the reparation to be made for any such breach, are declared to be among those which are generally suitable for submission to arbitration *or judicial settlement.*

3. *For the consideration of any such dispute, the court to which the case is referred shall be the Permanent Court of International Justice, established in accordance with Article 14, or any tribunal agreed on by the parties to the dispute or stipulated in any convention existing between them.*

4. The Members of the League agree that they will carry out in full good faith any award *or decision* that may be rendered, and that they will not resort to war against a Member of the League which complies therewith. In the event of any failure to carry out such an award *or decision,* the Council shall propose what steps should be taken to give effect thereto.

Article 14
Permanent Court of International Justice

The Council shall formulate and submit to the Members of the League for adoption plans for the establishment of a Permanent Court of International Justice. The Court shall be competent to hear and determine any dispute of an international character which the parties thereto submit to it. The Court may also give an advisory opinion upon any dispute or question referred to it by the Council or by the Assembly.

Article 15
Disputes Not Submitted to Arbitration or Judicial Settlement

1. If there should arise between Members of the League any dispute likely to lead to a rupture, which is not submitted to arbitration *or judicial*

settlement in accordance with Article 13, the Members of the League agree that they will submit the matter to the Council. Any party to the dispute may effect such submission by giving notice of the existence of the dispute to the Secretary-General, who will make all necessary arrangements for a full investigation and consideration thereof.

2. For this purpose the parties to the dispute will communicate to the Secretary-General, as promptly as possible, statements of their case, with all the relevant facts and papers, and the Council may forthwith direct the publication thereof.

3. The Council shall endeavor to effect a settlement of the dispute and, if such efforts are successful, a statement shall be made public giving such facts and explanations regarding the dispute and the terms of settlement thereof as the Council may deem appropriate.

4. If the dispute is not thus settled, the Council, either unanimously or by a majority vote, shall make and publish a report containing a statement of the facts of the dispute and the recommendations which are deemed just and proper in regard thereto.

5. Any Member of the League represented on the Council may make public a statement of the facts of the dispute and of its conclusions regarding the same.

6. If a report by the Council is unanimously agreed to by the Members thereof other than the Representatives of one or more of the parties to the dispute, the Members of the League agree that they will not go to war with any party to the dispute which complies with the recommendations of the report.

7. If the Council fails to reach a report which is unanimously agreed to by the members thereof, other than the Representatives of one or more of the parties to the dispute, the Members of the League reserve to themselves the right to take such action as they shall consider necessary for the maintenance of right and justice.

8. If the dispute between the parties is claimed by one of them, and is found by the Council, to arise out of a matter which by international law is solely within the domestic jurisdiction of that party, the Council shall so report, and shall make no recommendation as to its settlement.

9. The Council may in any case under this Article refer the dispute to the Assembly. The dispute shall be so referred at the request of either party to the dispute, provided that such request be made within 14 days after the submission of the dispute to the Council.

10. In any case referred to the Assembly, all the provisions of this Article and of Article 12 relating to the action and powers of the Council shall apply to the action and powers of the Assembly, provided that a report made by the Assembly, if concurred in by the Representatives of

those Members of the League represented on the Council and of a majority of the other Members of the League, exclusive in each case of the Representatives of the parties to the dispute, shall have the same force as a report by the Council concurred in by all the members thereof other than the Representatives of one or more of the parties to the dispute.

Together, these articles made it possible for the League to deal in some way with almost every type of dispute. Under Articles 3 and 4 the Assembly and Council, respectively, could take up any dispute which affected "the peace of the world." Article 11 permitted the Assembly and Council to deal with any "circumstance" threatening to disturb peace and "good understanding between nations," a formula sufficiently inclusive to embrace nearly the entire field of controversy. Article 12 used the more restrictive phrase "any dispute likely to lead to a rupture." The one type of dispute which was excluded from the Council, at least insofar as making a recommendation was concerned, was one found to be within the domestic jurisdiction of one of the disputants.

The initiative in placing controversies before the Assembly or Council rested in several places. Under Articles 3 and 4, it was possible for the two organs to act on their own initiative if they saw fit to do so. Third parties, acting under Article 11, had the "friendly right" to call the attention of the Assembly or Council to disputes; in practice they made use of this right on many occasions, so that Article 11, more than any other article, became the basis of League intervention in disputes. Aside from Articles 3, 4, and 11, the initiative was to be taken by the disputants themselves, who agreed under stated circumstances to submit their differences to peaceful settlement.

Except for Articles 14 and 15, the Covenant was lacking in directives as to how the Council should proceed in its treatment of disputes. Even Article 15 left much unsaid, requiring the Council to "endeavor to effect a settlement" without specifying the procedures to be employed; the article was specific, however, in providing that if a settlement were effected, the Council should publish the terms of agreement, whereas if no settlement could be reached, the Council should publish a report whose effect upon the disputants would depend upon whether it were adopted unanimously or by majority action. Article 14 contained a sentence enabling the Permanent Court of International Justice to give an advisory opinion upon "any dispute or question" referred to it by the Council or Assembly, thereby implying a right on the part of those two League organs to ask for advisory opinions in disputes before them.

Because the Covenant said so little about methods and procedures, the Council was obliged to hammer them out in practice as dispute after dispute was brought before it for solution. In this situation it was natural to bring into play the procedures that had been in use earlier, giving them new twists of one sort or another in order to add to their effectiveness or to adapt them to the League's methods or structure. Diplomatic intercession, mediation, inquiry, and conciliation were all given a newer and broader usefulness. Although the Council itself was not fitted to arbitrate, the Covenant recognized arbitration as a method of peaceful settlement, and at times the Council encouraged recourse to it. A new tool was placed in the hands of the Council by the creation of the Permanent Court of International Justice, for, as has already been stated, the Council could request from it advisory opinions helpful in the treatment of disputes. Another new tool which the Council devised for itself to use in emergencies when hostilities were already in progress was the "cease-fire" order, by which the parties were asked to withdraw their troops behind designated lines.

In 1927, the methods available to the Council for the treatment of disputes under Article 11 were explained in some detail by a Report approved by both the Council and Assembly. The procedures elaborated in the Report as available under paragraph 2 of Article 11 (where a dispute would be brought by a friendly third party to the Council) were listed as follows:

a. The Council will consider the question at a meeting, to be called specially if necessary, to which the contending parties would be summoned.

b. The Council can request an organization, or even a private individual appointed by it to exercise conciliatory action on the parties.

c. The Council may also suggest that the dispute be referred to arbitration or judicial settlement, in accordance with Article 13 of the Covenant.

d. If there is doubt as to the facts of the dispute, a League Commission may be sent to the *locus in quo* to ascertain what has actually happened or is likely to happen. It is understood that such a commission cannot go into territory of either party without the consent of the State to which the territory belongs.

e. If for the accomplishment of its task, the Council deems it necessary, it can, in certain appropriate cases, ask for an advisory opinion from the Permanent Court, or else, in certain special circumstances, from a Committee of Jurists appointed by it.

For emergency situations in which there was "war or threat of war," as explained in paragraph 1 of Article 11, the Report outlined the following courses of action:

a. Everything shall be done to ensure that the Council meets with the greatest promptitude. . . .

b. Even before the Council meets it is desirable that the Acting President should send telegraphic appeals to the parties to the dispute to refrain forthwith from any hostile acts. The nature of the appeal will necessarily vary with the circumstances of each case.

If, owing to exceptional circumstances, the Secretary-General considered that the Acting President was not in a position to act, he might request the ex-President most recently in the office who is available to take this step in the name of the Council.

c. As soon as the Council meets, it will no doubt verbally urge on the representatives of the nations in dispute the great importance of avoiding a breach of the peace.

d. Further, the Council may take such steps to see that the *status quo ante* is not disturbed in such manner as to aggravate or extend the dispute and thus to compromise the pacific settlement thereof. For this purpose it may indicate to the parties any movements of troops, mobilization operations, and other similar measures from which it recommends them to abstain. Similar measures of an industrial, economic, or financial nature may also be recommended. The Council may request the parties to notify their agreement on these points within the shortest possible space of time, the length of which will, if necessary, be fixed by the Council.

The details of these measures, and even their nature, obviously depend upon the whole of the circumstances of the dispute. It should be mentioned that, in certain cases with which it has had to deal, the Council fixed a neutral zone on either side, from which the parties to the dispute were called upon to withdraw their troops.

e. In order to satisfy itself on the way in which these measures have been carried out and to keep itself informed of the course of events, the

Council may think it desirable to send representatives to the locality of the dispute. The Secretary-General, duly authorized by the Council, would keep lists of experts—political, economic, military, etc.—on the basis of lists supplied by States Members of the League and of applications for employment submitted direct to him. These lists, classified according to categories, would be held by the Secretary-General at the disposal of the Council, which in case of crisis would thus have names of suitable experts before it. The Council may also have recourse in this connexion to diplomatic personages stationed in the neighborhood who belong to States not parties to the dispute.

f. Should any of the parties to the dispute disregard the advice or recommendations of the Council, the Council will consider the measures to be taken. It may manifest its formal disapproval. It may also recommend to its members to withdraw all their diplomatic representatives accredited to the State in question, or certain categories of them. It may also recommend other measures of a more serious character.

g. If the State in default still persists in its hostile preparations or action, further warning measures may be taken such as a naval demonstration. Naval demonstrations have been employed for such a purpose in the past. It is possible that air demonstrations might within reasonable limits be employed. Other measures may be found suitable according to the circumstances of the case.

Like the Council, the Assembly was free to use whatever method of adjustment seemed best suited to deal with the disputes brought before it. In only six cases was the Assembly set to work on disputes, but these six were exceptionally hot ones: the Japanese invasion of Manchuria, 1931–1932; the Paraguay-Bolivian war over the Gran Chaco, 1934; the invasion of Ethiopia by Italy, 1935; the intervention of Germany and Italy in the internal affairs of Spain, 1936; Japanese hostilities in China, 1937; and the Russian invasion of Finland, 1939. Twice (the Japanese invasion of Manchuria of 1931, and the Paraguay-Bolivian War of 1934), the Assembly issued reports under Article 15, paragraph 4, of the Covenant. Once (the Italian invasion of Ethiopia of 1935), it found a nation guilty of going to war in violation of Article 16. Once (the Russian invasion of Finland of 1940), it passed a resolution condemning a member for violating the Covenant. Several times it set up commissions or committees to accomplish assigned tasks.

More than forty disputes were considered by the Council from

1920 to 1939. It cannot be said that all were successfully handled, although in the great majority of them the work of the Council would be regarded by most critics as constructive. Certainly the Council was tenacious and always it used the means at its disposal with all the skill it could command. Some of the more prominent cases brought before both the Council and Assembly, along with the methods of settlement employed, are listed in the following chart:

The Dispute	States Involved	League Organ Acting	Principal Methods Employed
Status of the Aaland Islands, 1920	Finland Sweden	Council	Commission of Inquiry Commission of Jurists
Nationality Decrees in Tunis and Morocco, 1922	France Great Britain	Council	Advisory Opinion
Property of Hungarian Optants, 1923	Roumania Hungary	Council	Direct method (discussions with and suggestions to the parties)
Frontier Delimitation in Irak, 1924	Great Britain Turkey	Council	Commission of Inquiry Advisory Opinion
Invasion of frontiers, 1925	Greece Bulgaria	Council	Cease-fire Commission of Inquiry
Frontier, 1927	Poland Lithuania	Council	Direct Military Commission
Frontier (Chaco), 1928	Paraguay Bolivia	Council Assembly	Direct
Japanese Invasion of Manchuria, 1931–32	Japan China	Council Assembly	Direct Commission of Inquiry Report of Assembly under Art. 15
Frontier (Leticia), 1933	Peru Colombia	Council	Report under Art. 15
War-Chaco, 1933–34	Paraguay Bolivia	Council Assembly	Commission of Inquiry Armistice Assembly Committee of 22 Assembly Report under Art. 15 Embargo on arms (Settled by American States)
Invasion of Ethiopia, 1935	Italy Ethiopia	Council Assembly	Conciliation Arbitration Council Committees Council & Assembly finding that Italy violated Article 16
Japanese Invasion of China 1937	Japan China	Assembly	Advisory Committee Declaration of Japanese Violation of 9-Power Treaty & Pact of Paris Recommended Support of China

The Organization of the United Nations for Handling Disputes

That the Charter makers at San Francisco realized the need for machinery and processes to settle disputes was made clear by the fact that first among the purposes of the United Nations listed in Article 1 was the maintenance of peace and security. To accomplish this end, Article 1 went on to say that collective measures would be undertaken to suppress aggression and "to bring about by peaceful means, and in conformity with the principles of justice and international law, adjustment or settlement of international disputes or situations which might lead to a breach of the peace."

One reason why the Security Council was given the burden of responsibility for the accomplishment of this purpose was that, as a small organ functioning continuously, it would be able to act quickly and effectively. Reference has been made to the prompt meeting of the Council only a few hours after the North Korean invasion of South Korea was begun on June 25, 1950. The presence of all of the major powers in the Council was another reason for placing that body in the role of peacemaker, for no action in the treatment of a dispute could be expected to be definitive unless all of the great powers, or at least the big three among them—Russia, the United States, and Great Britain—were in agreement. Should the Council act with great-power unanimity, its will would indeed be hard to resist. If, however, the great powers should be in disagreement, then the settlement of disputes by that organ would be most difficult. When the Charter was written, no one clearly foresaw the split that was to arise between Russia and the West, and thus it was not realized that in its work the Security Council would be under this serious handicap. While a cleavage as deep and wide as that which developed between East and West would inevitably hinder any international agency at work on the job of keeping the peace, it was bound to be especially paralyzing in the Security Council because of the veto.

The General Assembly, too, is equipped by the Charter with rights and duties in the settlement of disputes. As Article 11 explains, it "may discuss any question relating to the maintenance of international peace and security brought before it by any member of the United Nations or by the Security Council or by a state which is not a member of the United Nations. . . ." In view of the difficulties faced in the Security Council by reason of the inability of Russia and the West to get along and the frequency of the vetoes, there has been a tendency to look more and more to the General Assembly for solutions to controversies.

The Secretariat of the United Nations, like that of the old League of Nations, makes itself useful to the Security Council and to the General Assembly when those organs are dealing with disputes. The most vital contribution which the Secretary-General himself may make is, under Article 99 of the Charter, to "bring to the attention of the Security Council any matter which, in his opinion, may threaten the maintenance of international peace and security." In the treatment of disputes by the Council or Assembly the Secretariat is expected to communicate with the disputants and to provide secretarial assistance of many kinds.

Placing a Dispute Before the Security Council

In the contemplation of the Charter, the first recourse of nations in dispute should be to methods of their own choice. Article 33 (1) brings this out in its statement that "the parties to any dispute, the continuance of which is likely to endanger the maintenance of international peace and security, shall first of all seek a solution by negotiation, inquiry, mediation, conciliation, arbitration, judicial settlements, resort to regional agencies or arrangements, or other peaceful means of their own choice." This would be justified, first, on the ground that it would relieve the United Nations of the burden of handling too large a number of controversies and, second, that it would minimize the interference of the United Nations in the affairs of sovereign states.

The help of the Security Council in treating disputes may be invoked in a variety of ways and by a number of different authorities. When the parties fail to use the methods of solution mentioned in Article 33 (1), the Security Council is authorized by Article 33 (2) "to call upon the parties to settle their dispute by such means."

When the parties try to resolve their difficulties peacefully but fail, they are obliged under Article 37 (1) to place the matter before the Security Council. On its own initiative the Security Council may "at any stage" of a dispute recommend "appropriate procedures or methods of adjustment." Should any member of the United Nations wish to do so, it may call the attention of the Security Council (or General Assembly) to a dispute or situation whose continuance is a danger to international peace. A nonmember, too, may place before the Council (or Assembly) a dispute to which it is a party, providing "it accepts in advance, for the purposes of the dispute, the obligations of pacific settlement provided in the present Charter." The General Assembly is also among those authorized to bring to the attention of the Security Council "situations" likely to endanger peace and security. Finally, the Secretary-General may place before the Council any "matter" which in his opinion may threaten the maintenance of international peace and security. Under varying circumstances, therefore, the Security Council's efforts may be invoked: (1) by itself and on its own initiative; (2) by any member of the United Nations; (3) by a nonmember which is a party to a dispute; (4) by the disputants; (5) by the General Assembly; and (6) by the Secretary-General. It would be difficult to add substantially to this list of nations and authorities able to set in motion the peace machinery of the United Nations.

What the Security Council May Do

The statements of the Charter on the action to be taken by the Security Council, once it is seized of a dispute or situation jeopardizing the peace, relate primarily to the authority of the organ. That its authority is not extensive is apparent from the lack of vigor in the verbs which the Charter uses in Chapter VI: "call upon," "investigate," and "recommend." Operating within the limits of these terms, the Council may suggest, argue, and persuade, and this in fact is about as far as it may go in dealing with a dispute unless under Article 39 there is a threat to the peace, a breach of the peace, or an act of aggression, in which case it "shall make recommendations, or decide what measures shall be taken in accordance with Articles

41 and 42. . . ." In no instance, however, may the Council step in and settle a dispute on its merits.

In the run-of-the-mill type of dispute, where the peace is not immediately endangered, the Security Council has several courses open to it, and the one to be used will depend upon the circumstances at the time:

1. It may call upon the parties to use peaceful means of their own choice.
2. At any stage of a dispute, it may recommend appropriate procedures, including reference to the International Court of Justice.
3. It may investigate a dispute or situation to determine whether its continuance is likely to endanger the peace.
4. If the parties to a dispute fail to settle it themselves and the Council believes that the continuance of the dispute would be a danger to the peace, it may either recommend a procedure of settlement or recommend terms of settlement.
5. When so requested by the parties to a dispute, the Council may make recommendations with a view to peaceful settlement.

Only under two conditions, therefore, may the Security Council concern itself with the subject matter of a dispute: (1) after the parties have failed to settle it, if in the view of the Council its continuance will endanger the peace; and (2) when requested by the parties. These conditions are broad enough, especially the first (under Article 37), to justify action in almost any case where the Council so desires. The stress of the Charter is certainly upon settlement by the disputants themselves, and the duty of the Security Council in the first instance is to prod them on toward success. If, viewed in the large, the authority of the Council seems inadequate, and no doubt it does fall short of an ideal arrangement, recommending and investigating are nevertheless useful processes which should not be underestimated. If disputants want a peaceful settlement, these processes stand a good chance of meeting with success; if the disputants are adamant and impervious to reason, it is probable that no procedure properly respectful of sovereignty could succeed.

In an emergency, when there is a threat to the peace, a breach of peace, or an act of aggression (under Article 39), the Security Council's authority becomes under the Charter somewhat greater, but its enlarged powers are aimed primarily at the prevention of aggression and war, if necessary by the use of the sanctions. In two respects, however, the kind of emergency referred to by the Article increases the Council's authority in dealing with disputes. First, the Council is presented with alternative courses of action under Article 39—it "shall make recommendations, or decide what measures shall be taken" in the nature of sanctions under Articles 41 and 42; were it to select the first alternative, as would be possible if the emergency were not too extreme, it could attempt to get a settlement of the issues involved, again by submitting recommendations. The second enlargement of the Security Council's powers resulting from the kind of an emergency envisaged in Article 39 follows under the provision of Article 40 that it "may, before making the recommendations or deciding upon the measures provided for in Article 39, call upon the parties concerned to comply with such provisional measures as it deems necessary or desirable." This permits the Council to suggest temporary arrangements, but the Charter makes clear the fact that they are "without prejudice to the rights, claims, or positions of the parties concerned." The principal use which has been made of provisional measures to date has been in the issuance of cease-fire orders to disputants already engaged in hostilities.

Role of the Assembly

Although the Charter is less detailed in its description of the place of the General Assembly in the treatment of disputes than in its outline of the role of the Security Council, the former is at no great disadvantage. Disputes may be referred to the Assembly by a member of the United Nations, by a state which is not a member, or by the Security Council; the Assembly, which is able to "discuss any questions or any matters within the present Charter . . . ," is also in a position to deal with a dispute on its own initiative if it wishes. When a dispute is before the Assembly, that organ may "make recommendations" for its solution to the states concerned, to the Security Council, or to both. This authority is broad enough to permit the Assembly to recommend procedures to disputants or, if it prefers, to go into the merits of a controversy and recommend terms of settlement.

One limitation has been placed on the activities of the General Assembly in the treatment of disputes to the effect that it may not make a recommendation with regard to any dispute or situation on which the Security Council is currently working. The Secretary-General is obliged to keep the Assembly informed as to the disputes before the Council. It has been pointed out by M. Alexandre Parodi that since the Security Council determines its own agenda "it becomes indirectly able to permit or to prevent the Assembly from dealing with certain questions. . . ."[2] While this seems to be a far-reaching power, the assumption that it will be reasonably exercised is a fair one, and the practice up to the present time clearly supports that assumption.

Problems

Certain vagaries and ambiguities of the Charter have been the cause of general misunderstanding and obscurity when controversies have in fact been before the United Nations.[3] While some have not been of great consequence, others have been highly obstructive in the work of maintaining peace. In several instances it has been possible to reach agreement as to the meaning of the Charter, but in others the uncertainties have remained to plague the Security Council.

A problem of no mean proportion has arisen in regard to Article 37 (1), which places on parties to disputes whose continuance is dangerous to peace, the obligation to refer their difficulty to the Security Council when, under Article 33 (1), they have themselves failed to settle the affair. Does this Article allow one party alone to take a matter to the Council, or must the parties be in agreement that their dispute shall be so referred? When this question was discussed in Committee III/2 of the San Francisco Conference, it appeared to be the sense of the group that submission could be effected by one

---

[2] M. Alexandre Parodi, "Peaceful Settlement of Disputes," *International Conciliation*, no. 445 (1948), on "Three Years of the United Nations," p. 618.

[3] For legal problems relating to the United Nations, see H. Kelsen, *Law of the United Nations*, New York, 1950.

party alone. In practice, Article 37 has several times been invoked by one disputant alone, to be followed inevitably by debates in which the propriety of such action was questioned. It was invoked by Egypt in her controversy with Great Britain, and by the United States in its proposal of June 27, 1947, for a Balkan Commission to deal with the efforts of communists in Bulgaria, Roumania, and Yugoslavia to subvert the Government of Greece. On both occasions the issue was in large measure side-stepped by using other articles as bases for action. While no authoritative pronouncement has been forthcoming on the problem, it is the contention of many people that the intention of the makers of the Charter to allow one disputant alone to submit a case should be controlling. It must be admitted, however, that a literal interpretation of Article 37 provides strong argument to those who take the contrary view, for that article states clearly that "they" shall refer the dispute to the Security Council. The work of the Security Council would be facilitated if, in some manner, this uncertainty could be dispelled.

Articles of the Charter refer to a "dispute" and to a "situation which might lead to international friction or give rise to dispute," but no definition of the two terms is given. No doubt there is a distinction between the two; Messrs. Goodrich and Hambro have attempted to make it in their statement that a dispute may be considered as "a disagreement or matter at issue between two or more states which has reached a stage at which the parties have formulated claims and counter-claims sufficiently definite to be passed upon by a court or other body set up for purposes of pacific settlement."[4] A "situation," in contrast to a "dispute," quoting the same authorities, is "a state of affairs which has not as yet assumed the nature of a conflict between parties but which may, though not necessarily, come to have that character." The Spanish problem, as it came before the Security Council in 1946, met the specifications of this definition of a "situation." This point of view seems to assume that "situation" is a broader term than "dispute." From Article 34 there would appear to be three types of "situations": (1) those which

---

[4] L. M. Goodrich and E. Hambro, *Charter of United Nations Commentary and Documents*, rev. ed., Boston, 1949, p. 249.

upon investigation do not appear likely to lead to international friction or to give rise to a dispute; (2) those which "might lead to international friction"; and (3) those which might "give rise to a dispute." In other words, a "situation" may be harmless, it may become serious without taking on the character of a "dispute" in which nations present claims and counterclaims, or it may be a "dispute" in embryo. Without an official pronouncement as to the meaning of the two terms, speculation on the matter should not be too dogmatic. What is needed is an official pronouncement by the Security Council itself or by the International Court of Justice on request of the Council for an advisory opinion.

Something rather close to an official pronouncement of the nature of a "dispute" was given by the Interim Committee of the General Assembly in a recent report dealing with the Assembly's role in treating with international controversies; no distinction between "dispute" and "situation," however, was undertaken.[5] According to this report there are three characteristics "normally possessed" by a dispute, as follows:

1. A dispute must be a disagreement; in other words, there must be a controversy between the parties. This takes the form of claims, which are met with refusals, counterclaims, denials or countercharges, accusations, etc. The fact that one or more of the parties has applied to a competent international organ to deal with the dispute with a view to obtaining a solution of the problem, requesting protection or instituting legal proceedings, is evidence of the existence of a disagreement.

2. There must be parties to a dispute and the parties must be States. . . . The parties to a dispute must be States directly concerned. . . . In exceptional cases it may be necessary for the General Assembly to treat a *de facto* government as a party to a dispute. . . .

3. Subject of dispute: it must relate to a specific question of interest or law. . . .

---

[5] *Report of the Interim Committee of the General Assembly* (3rd session: January 16–September 18, 1950), Supplement no. 14 (A/1388).

Question of interest: The interest may be material or moral and affect one or more parties.

Question of law: The dispute must concern the interpretation of a point of law, usage, prevention of usage, abuse, violation of right, etc.

A practical reason why the difference between "dispute" and "situation" needs to be clarified is that under Article 27 of the Charter the parties to a "dispute" do not vote in the Council; without a definition of a "dispute," the application of this article is impossible. In certain cases the members of the Security Council have voluntarily refrained from voting when cases affecting their interests have been under discussion. The United Kingdom and France, for instance, refrained from voting in an action taken by the Council in the Lebanon and Syria case. Similarly, the United Kingdom did not vote on the question of asking the parties to refer the Corfu Channel case to the International Court of Justice. As yet, the Security Council has not even made a general ruling on the question of whether the determination of the existence of a "dispute" is a procedural or a substantive question.

Another problem arises out of the relationship between Articles 33 (1) and 34. By the former, the parties to a dispute whose continuance "is likely to endanger the maintenance of international peace and security" agree to seek a solution, first of all, by means of their own choosing. Then by Article 34 it is made the duty of the Security Council to determine when the continuance of a dispute is likely to endanger the maintenance of international peace and security. This would seem to place upon disputants an obligation to wait until the Security Council by investigation has proved that a given controversy does in fact constitute a danger to peace before resorting to negotiation, inquiry, mediation, conciliation, arbitration, or judicial settlement, as expected of them under Article 33 (1). To be consistent, either the Charter should have specified that investigation by the Council would precede resort to negotiation, inquiry, and the other methods mentioned by Article 33, or resort to those processes by the disputants should have been freed from any qualification that the dispute in question be one the "continuance of which is likely to endanger the maintenance of international peace and security." The latter method would no doubt be better suited to the needs of international society than the former. The United Nations system of dealing with disputes would be more smooth-running and certainly more comprehensible to a nation trying to meet its requirements if the first recourse in *all* disputes—whether or not they are likely to endanger peace—were specifically stated to be negotiation, inquiry, conciliation, arbitration, judicial settlement, regional agencies, or other procedures selected by the disputants.

Another problem is to find the appropriate relationship between Articles 33 (1), 35 (1), and 37 (1). By Articles 33 (1) and 37 (1), the "parties" to disputes are expected to do certain things (settle by methods of their own choice in Article 33, and if those methods fail by reference to the Security Council under Article 37), but by Article 35 (1), "any member of the United Nations" may bring disputes dangerous to peace directly to the Security Council or the General Assembly. "Parties" to disputes are usually, although not necessarily, "members of the United Nations." Is Article 35 (1), which refers to "members of the United Nations," to be interpreted as including disputants or excluding them? In other words, may disputants which are members of the United Nations come first of all to the Security Council or General Assembly, or are they to follow 33 (1) and resort first of all to negotiation, inquiry, conciliation, and other means of their own choice? Professor Hans Kelsen has expressed the following view of this problem:

In order to reconcile the provisions of Article 35 (1) with the provisions of Article 33 (1) and Article 37 (1), it would be advisable to interpret Article 35 (1)—in conformity with the spirit of Chapter VI though not with the wording of Article 35 (1)—to mean that only members who are not parties to a dispute may bring the dispute to the attention of the Security Council whereas to the members who are parties to the dispute Article 33 (1) and Article 37 (1) apply.[6]

---

[6] On this subject see Hans Kelsen, "The Settlement of Disputes by the Security Council," *International Law Quarterly*, vol. 2, summer, 1948, p. 199.

As a matter of practice, however, parties to disputes which are members of the United Nations have appealed to the Security Council under Article 35 (1).

Domestic Questions

According to Article 2 (7) of the Charter, "Nothing contained in the present Charter shall authorize the United Nations to intervene in matters which are essentially within the domestic jurisdiction of any state, or shall require the members to submit such matters to settlement under the present Charter. . . ." This provision is obviously an effort to protect the sovereign independence of the members of the United Nations against the intrusion of any outside party into their internal affairs. But what is a "domestic question"? In the Tunis-Morocco Nationality case, the Permanent Court of International Justice in 1923 maintained that nationality questions are ordinarily within the field of domestic jurisdiction; in this particular case, however, there were applicable treaties which had removed it from the area of domestic questions to that of international. In the opinion of the Court, whether or not a given subject comes within the domestic or international area is "a relative question," depending upon the status of international relations at the time. When the Covenant of the League of Nations was before the United States Senate in 1919, that body attempted a definition of "domestic" questions, hoping by so doing to prevent the League from expanding its jurisdiction into doubtful areas of action. The Senate in a proposed reservation to the treaty of Versailles made this statement: "The United States reserves to itself exclusively the right to decide what questions are within its domestic jurisdiction and declares that all domestic and political questions relating wholly or in part to its internal affairs, including immigration, labor, coast-wise traffic, the tariff, commerce, the suppression of traffic in women and children, and in opium and other dangerous drugs, and all other domestic questions, are solely within the jurisdiction of the United States. . . ." In the last analysis, the definition of domestic questions is a legal problem. For that reason it is properly an issue for the International Court of Justice to decide when the claim is made by a nation that the United Nations is invading its field of domestic jurisdiction.

In the Security Council's treatment of the Spanish affair in 1946, the question was raised as to whether the Franco regime in that country could be regarded as an international problem. The view was expressed that the government of a nation is purely a domestic matter, outside the jurisdiction of the Council. The majority opinion, however, was to the contrary; it was admitted that ordinarily the government of a nation is a domestic affair, but in this instance the Franco regime was considered to have international implications and to be a potential cause of international discord.

When in July and August of 1947 the fighting in progress in Indonesia between the Dutch and the natives was brought to the Security Council, a discussion ensued as to whether the problem was domestic or international in nature. Mr. Van Kleffens, delegate from The Netherlands, argued that the affair was not a proper one for the Council, that there was involved no dispute or situation threatening to endanger international peace and security. The British delegate, Mr. Bevin, strongly supported the Dutch position, stating, "The question of what is done in Indonesia is a matter for the Dutch Government of its own volition." He went on to inquire, "When internal troubles arise are we always going to be sending commissions to investigate and deal with the problems arising within a sovereign power?" Other members of the Security Council maintained that the Indonesian Government had been given *de facto* recognition by a considerable number of states, including The Netherlands, and that as a consequence there was a breach of the peace under Article 39. Although the issue was not decided officially one way or the other, the Security Council continued to deal with the problem in Indonesia.

The plea that a domestic question was at stake was made in a curious way in the Hyderabad case, placed before the Security Council on August 21, 1948.[7] At that time, Hyderabad by cablegram

[7] This case is ably discussed by C. Eagleton, "The Case of Hyderabad Before the Security Council," *American Journal of International Law*, 1950, vol. 44, no. 2, pp. 277–302.

informed the Council that she "has been exposed in recent months to violent intimidation, to threats of invasion, and to crippling economic blockade" by India. One of the "princely states" during British rule in India, Hyderabad was assumed to have become independent under the Indian Independence Act, and, in fact, the Government of India had interpreted the Act as conferring independence upon the princely state. The appeal to the Security Council was made under Article 35 (2) of the Charter, which permits a nonmember of the United Nations to submit disputes to the Council "if it accepts in advance, for the purpose of the dispute, the obligations of pacific settlement provided in the present Charter." India maintained at first that Hyderabad was not competent to bring the case to the United Nations on the ground that "it is not a state," and on the correct assumption that the Council may decide its own competence. A few days later, before any action had been taken in the Council, Hyderabad was conquered by India.

At this point in the case, India shifted her argument and maintained that the matter was not an international question but a domestic question under Article 2, paragraph 7, of the Charter. This implied that Hyderabad was now a part of India, and that as a general principle a completed conquest of one nation by another is to be regarded as outside the jurisdiction of the Security Council. Sir Zaffrullah Khan, representative of Hyderabad, pointed out this fact and denied that the destruction of a nation's independence by force makes a dispute leading up to the conquest a domestic question. As he said: "If that were so, then, after every annexation by one State or territory belonging to another State, once the annexation had been completed as the result of military action—I shall describe it in no harsher terms—the State that had gained the accession might say, 'Well, this is now a domestic question. Today, it is a domestic matter. The territory is part of our territory and there is no trouble about it.'" Although there was no positive decision that the dispute was based upon a domestic question, the Security Council's subsequent inaction appeared to imply that such was the case. The matter was kept on the Council's agenda but was not discussed further.

The Security Council's treatment of the Hyderabad case has been severely criticized. Professor Eagleton has remarked, "To accept such a conquest as a domestic question under the Charter would be to negate the purposes of the Charter."[8] Certainly the inaction of the Council, whatever its reason, would be most difficult to justify.

In 1951, when the Iranian dispute with Great Britain over the nationalization of oil was before the Security Council, the government of Iran contended that the action it had taken fell clearly within the area of its domestic jurisdiction. After some discussion the Council decided to ask for an advisory opinion from the International Court of Justice on the matter.

---

[8] *Ibid.*, p. 287.

IX The United Nations in Action

In the united nations, just as in national government, processes and techniques are made available not only by the written provisions of constitutions but also as the result of practice. This is particularly evident within the field of international disputes, for the Charter of the United Nations has little to say about the methods to be employed by the Security Council and the General Assembly in the treatment of controversies. Most of the Charter provisions reviewed in the preceeding chapter relate to the authority of those organs, their right to deal with disputes, rather than to the techniques to be employed. The Security Council and the General Assembly are authorized under stated conditions to make "recommendations" in disputes before them, but the Charter does not specify how those agencies shall arrive at the recommendations which they make. No doubt the makers of the Charter were wise to leave matters of this nature to be worked out as disputes were brought in for treatment; any explicit mention of techniques might have been construed as ruling out those that were not included, and furthermore, it would have detracted from the mobility which the Council and Assembly now possess in trying to adapt methods to needs.

The actual practice of the United Nations in handling international disputes is an outgrowth of the methods developed within the League of Nations, as the latter, in turn, had been adaptations of processes that had been earlier in use within the loosely knit society of nations of pre-World War I days. Many disputes had been handled by the League, and from its experiences there emerged a number of procedures, tried and tested, which the United Nations could not afford to ignore. It follows, therefore, that although the provisions of the Charter on the treatment of disputes are somewhat at variance with those of the Covenant of the League, actual practice under the United Nations does not deviate sharply from that of the League.

The Principal Disputes and Situations Handled by the United Nations

During its brief career to date, the United Nations has had an impressive list of disputes before it, most of them quite difficult to handle. Of all the articles under which they might have been submitted, Article 35 (1) has been the one most frequently used. In some instances the nations involved were already fighting, and when this was true, the first effort would invariably be to get a cessation of hostilities before considering procedures to deal with the issues and problems that had occasioned the altercations. When disputes had not reached the fighting stage, the United Nations would proceed immediately in an effort to get the parties together in a solution. Following are the main disputes and situations brought to the United Nations and the methods used for their solution:

Nations Involved	Subject of the Dispute	Brought to UN	Treated by	Principal Methods Used
Iran and USSR	The presence of Russian troops in Iran after March 2, 1946, contrary to the Tripartite Treaty of alliance of 1942	By Iran, 1946	Security Council	Direct
The Netherlands and Indonesia	Hostilities in progress from native opposition to Dutch rule	by Australia and India, 1947 (case brought by Ukrainia in 1946 on presence of British troops in Indonesia not acted upon)	Security Council	Cease-fire order Committee of good offices Commission for Indonesia Consular (conciliation) commission

Nations Involved	Subject of the Dispute	Brought to UN	Treated by	Principal Methods Used
Syria and Lebanon, Great Britain and France	The presence of British and French troops in Syria and Lebanon	by Syria and Lebanon, 1946	Security Council	Direct
The Spanish Situation (no immediate disputants)	The charge that the Fascist Government of General Franco in Spain was a threat to peace	by Poland, 1946	Security Council General Assembly	Discussion Assembly recommendation that UN members recall ambassadors and ministers from Madrid
Great Britain and USSR	Presence of British troops in Greece	by USSR, 1946	Security Council	Direct (case concluded by statement of the president of the Council, taking note of statements made by Great Britain and Greece)
Greece and Albania, Bulgaria, and Yugoslavia (involved but not as disputants)	Frontier incidents	by Ukrainian SSR, 1946	Security Council General Assembly	Discussion Commission of Inquiry (and subsidiary) Committee (Assembly) to observe compliance with recommendations
India and South Africa	Treatment of Indians in South Africa	by India, 1946	General Assembly	Discussion Resolutions with requests to the parties
Great Britain and Albania	Corfu Channel case —Damage to British warships and injury to personnel, and British minesweeping in the channel	by Great Britain, 1947	Security Council	Direct Recommendation of reference to the International Court of Justice
Arab states and Israel	Future status of Palestine Hostilities at times during the hearing of the case	by Great Britain (former mandatory) 1947	General Assembly Security Council	Direct Commission of Inquiry Mediator Conciliation commission Cease-fire
Egypt and Great Britain	British troops in Egypt and the condominium in the Sudan	by Egypt, 1947	Security Council	Direct

Nations Involved	Subject of the Dispute	Brought to UN	Treated by	Principal Methods Used
U.S. and USSR (most concerned but not as disputants)	Future status of Korea	by United States, 1947	General Assembly	Discussion Joint Commission Temporary Commission
India and Pakistan	Invasion of Jammu and Kashmir—status of those territories	by India, 1948	Security Council	Direct Inquiry Conciliation Cease-fire
U.S., USSR, and China (most concerned but not as disputants)	Invasion of South Korea by North Korea and Chinese Communists	by United States, 1950	Security Council General Assembly	Discussion Cease-fire (by Council) Military sanctions Cease-fire committee (Assembly)

The Direct Method

After a dispute or a situation threatening to international peace and security has been placed before the Security Council, it then becomes necessary for that body to adopt a procedure of action. In form, at least, the procedure which it uses will be pointed toward the accomplishment of the Council's duties under the Charter—calling upon the parties to settle it themselves, investigating to determine whether a continuance of the controversy is a danger to peace, suggesting procedures to the disputants, and recommending terms of settlement.

One of the most commonly used procedures is called the "direct method," for it brings the Security Council into direct relationship with the disputants. This may take the form of a communication addressed to one or both of the disputants, reminding them of their obligations as members of the United Nations; several times such a communication was addressed to disputants by the Council of the League of Nations. Frequently, the Security Council places itself in direct contact with the disputants by asking them to send delegates to be present at a meeting in which the affair will be discussed. The Iranian delegate, for instance, was in attendance at several meetings of the Security Council in the spring of 1946 to discuss with that body, in which Russia was already represented, the problem of the continued presence of Russian troops in Iran. Again, after the Indian representative on January 1, 1948, complained to the Security Council that Pakistan was giving assistance to raiders into Jammu and Kashmir, the Council got in touch with the governments of India and Pakistan by dispatching to them identical telegrams asking them to refrain from any action which might aggravate the situation. A little later, representatives of India and Pakistan presented the cases of their respective governments to the Security Council in person.

At such a meeting the Security Council may bend its efforts toward getting the parties to settle the affair themselves, or it may adopt resolutions in favor of some course of action; if hostilities are in progress, it will make its first objective the reëstablishment of peaceful relationships. The methods employed are purely diplomatic; the Council has no right of taking a decision binding upon the parties. It is essentially a procedure of friendly counsel, with spokesmen for the world community trying, in concert with spokesmen of the disputants, to find a way to end the quarrel. Thus it derives such virtue as it may possess from the resourcefulness of the participating men and nations, and from the force of whatever public opinion may be aroused in the world at large by the discussions. Certainly on occasion it appears to have been highly successful, although to attempt to assess its accomplishments in any particular situation would be hazardous because of the many factors that enter into the final disposition of a dispute. The discussion of the Russo-Iranian problem in 1946 within the Security Council was followed by the withdrawal of Russian troops, but there is no way of ascertaining whether this would have happened anyway.

This direct method did not always achieve its objective when it was used by the Council of the League of Nations—as in the Chino-Japanese dispute over Manchuria in 1931. In this case there had been an explosion along the South Manchurian Railway, which the Japanese had used as an occasion to take over all of Manchuria and a part of northern China. Within a few days the League Council was in session, trying to bring an end to the violence, with particular emphasis upon the withdrawal of troops by Japan. Resolutions were adopted pledging Japanese withdrawal as soon as possible and committing the Japanese to a statement of no territorial designs; but instead of withdrawing, the troops advanced farther. In short, the direct method was ineffectual. After several months of discussion, resort was taken to another method—a commission of inquiry—and it may be pointed out that the agreement to use this kind of agency was itself a result of the direct discussions within the Council. The dispute between Bolivia and Paraguay (1928–1935) over the possession of the territory known as the Gran Chaco was discussed within the Council during portions of seventeen sessions, in conjunction with the use of other procedures.

The only method used within the Security Council for the treatment of the Syrian and Lebanese problem early in 1946 was the direct method. The problem was placed before the Security Council on February 4, 1946, by the heads of the delegations of Lebanon and Syria to the United Nations, who asserted that British and French troops still remained in their countries even though World War II was ended, and that those troops refused to leave except on conditions which were inconsistent with the Charter. The discussions within the Security Council led to the presentation of several resolutions, but all were defeated. One of the resolutions, proposed by the United States, expressed confidence that the troops would be removed soon and asked the parties to notify the Council when negotiations to that end had been completed. A veto prevented the adoption of the resolution. Although the resolution was not legally adopted, Great Britain and France agreed to comply with its provisions as representative of the views of the majority. On April 30 and May 1, the Security Council was informed that agreements for withdrawal had been completed.

In some cases the conditions are such that some or all of the nations concerned or involved in a dispute or situation before the Council cannot be approached in a direct manner or invited to appear at a meeting. This was true, for instance, in the Security Council's treatment of the Spanish problem. Under these circumstances, the Council proceeds with a discussion of the problem without attempting to use the direct method.

Commissions of Inquiry

One of the most useful procedures available to the Security Council is that of inquiry by means of a commission set up to get the facts, report its findings, and recommend a solution. This procedure was highly developed by the League of Nations, which converted it from little more than theory into a common practice. In a long list of cases the findings of commissions of inquiry were incorporated into plans of settlement, some of which were accepted and put into force. The League's experience proved that when there is sufficient time for a commission to be appointed, go to the spot and, without too much haste, collect pertinent data, its findings can be highly constructive. As a rule, the reports of the League's commissions covered many phases of the disputes investigated—the historical, economic, political, and so on—as in the dispute over the future of the Aaland Islands between Finland and Sweden in 1921.

Perhaps the most notable League of Nations case involving a commission of inquiry was the Chino-Japanese dispute of 1931, to which reference has already been made. The commission in this case, popularly called the "Lytton Commission" after its chairman, the Earl of Lytton, was composed of five members, all neutrals. It spent months in the Far East, stopping at Tokyo and at Chinese and Manchurian cities for weeks at a time, its members conferring with individuals, receiving petitions and letters, and examining documents and newspapers all along the way. Its report was a model of clarity, exactness, and fairness in which was surveyed the background history of the case, the interests of Japan and China in Manchuria, the issues involved, and such facts as it possessed on the Japanese invasion and the establishment of the new state of "Manchukuo." The commission admitted its inability to discover all the information that it had sought, but the large amount of data which it presented was evidence that it had been thorough in its work. Although blame was placed on both Japan and China for the unhappy relationship existing between the two countries, the commission was strongly of the opinion that the Japanese invasion was unwarranted. At the end of the report were specific suggestions to serve as a basis of settlement. Excellent as the report was, it came out too late to prevent a deterioration of the situation. Its findings were, however, made basic to the action of the Assembly of the League of Nations, which found Japan unjustified in its invasion of Manchuria and recommended a settlement. Japan voted against these Assembly measures and gave notice of withdrawal from the League.

It was the good fortune of the United Nations to fall heir to this experience of the League of Nations. In several cases the United Nations has put commissions of inquiry to work and, as a rule, with helpful results. The Ukrainian SSR on August 24, 1946, called the attention of the Security Council to the political situation in Greece, alleging that it constituted a threat to peace. Greece denied the charge and complained of frontier incidents supposedly provoked by Albania. At this point several resolutions were offered, one proposed by the United States which called for a commission to investigate "the border incidents along the frontier between Greece on the one hand and Albania, Bulgaria, and Yugoslavia on the other." This resolution was rejected, but when, a few weeks later, Greece herself called the attention of the Security Council to the situation along her northern border, a commission was created, composed of one representative from each state on the Council in 1947 (Australia, Belgium, Brazil, China, Colombia, France, Poland, Syria, USSR, United Kingdom, and United States). The commission was authorized to ascertain the facts relating to the border incidents and to submit proposals aimed at averting future disturbances. That commissions of this nature are quite adjustable and are not required to fit into any one pattern may be seen from the decision of the Council (April 18, 1947), taken on the suggestion of the United States, to maintain in the area a subsidiary group of the Commission, composed of a representative for each member, to fulfill whatever special functions the main commission might prescribe.

The Balkan Commission went to the spot and from January to April, 1947, investigated the alleged activities of Albania, Bulgaria, and Yugoslavia in connection with the guerrilla warfare in northern Greece. Then it drafted a report, which was made public on June 25. The majority of the commission agreed that Yugoslavia, and to a lesser extent Albania and Bulgaria, had supported the guerrillas. They found, too, that Yugoslavia and Bulgaria had been promoting the separatist movement of the Macedonian Slavs in Greece. On the other hand, the commission reported that the unstable conditions in

Greece, together with the frequent statement by Greece of territorial claims against Bulgaria and Albania, were irritants which in some measure added to the tension in the area. A minority report by the commission, handed in by the representatives of the USSR and Poland, contended that the evidence cited by the majority was inadequate and challenged statements of witnesses. According to this report, Albania, Bulgaria, and Yugoslavia were innocent of the charges made against them.

The majority report and its recommendations were the basis for the discussions of the problem which occurred within the Security Council throughout July and August of 1947. Several proposals based upon the report were formulated, but all were rejected. Finally, in order to enable the General Assembly to take it over, the Security Council on September 15 removed the problem from its agenda, having in mind Article 12 of the Charter, which forbids the General Assembly to make a recommendation on any dispute currently before the Council unless so requested.

In the Kashmir dispute between India and Pakistan, already referred to, the Security Council on January 20, 1948, provided for the creation of a commission of three authorized not only to investigate but also to mediate. Here is another indication of the adjustability of commissions in regard to function. Later, the size of the commission was increased to five, one selected by India, one by Pakistan, two by the Council, and the fifth, by agreement of the two nations, selected jointly by India and Pakistan. When a deadlock occurred in the selection of the fifth member, the Council named the United States. In this case the mediatory work of the commission overshadowed its investigatory activities. The principal recommendation coming out of the commission's labors was that a plebiscite be held to determine Kashmir's future status.

Commissions of inquiry have been used by the General Assembly in its treatment of disputes as well as by the Security Council; a description of those cases will be given elsewhere in this chapter. The combined experience of the Security Council and the General Assembly in working through such agencies gives strong support to the conclusion that inquiry has come to be one of the most useful procedures of the United Nations in handling disputes. It enables the organs of the United Nations to procure a reasonably unbiased statement of facts from which to proceed with an effort at settlement, thus clearing the atmosphere of the prejudice and recrimination likely to be engendered by the disputants. This is not to say that commissions are without imperfections and limitations. There are times when desired facts are not obtainable, and commissions have admitted as much. Some commissions have even been charged with bias, but never have such charges been substantiated; indeed, they usually have emanated from a disputant which was not treated as it would like to have been by a report.

Conciliation and Mediation

Other procedures used in the League of Nations and the United Nations have been conciliation and mediation. As has already been shown, the effort of both procedures is to get the disputants on common ground, reconciling diverse points of view and arriving at agreement by compromise or otherwise. An aspect of the "direct" method of dealing with disputes used formerly by the Council of the League of Nations and now by the Security Council of the United Nations is this conciliatory process—hearing the viewpoints of the parties and suggesting solutions or methods of arriving at solutions. Nearly all of the disputes to come before both international organizations have been subjected to this kind of treatment, and often to great advantage.

The work of conciliation, like that of inquiry, may be carried on through special commissions, formerly set up by the Council of the League of Nations and now made available by the Security Council of the United Nations. The commission of five named by the League Council in 1933 to go to South America and endeavor to get a solution of the dispute between Paraguay and Bolivia over the Gran Chaco—a large stretch of land between the two countries whose ownership had led to hostilities—was essentially an agency of conciliation. The commission labored diligently but did not succeed in establishing peace.

The United Nations, even to a greater extent than the League, has made use of agencies of conciliation. In the Indonesian dispute, brought to the attention of the Security Council by the Ukrainian SSR on January 21, 1946, several methods of settlement were employed, among which was conciliation. In this case there were hostilities between the forces of The Netherlands and those of the Republic of Indonesia, trying to establish itself as an independent nation free from Dutch control. It was a red-hot dispute, one of the most complicated to be brought to the United Nations. After several months of ineffectual efforts to end the controversy, the Security Council on August 25 set up a Committee of Good Offices, composed of one Council member selected by each of the parties and a third chosen by the two members so selected. This Committee was a medium through which the Security Council tendered its good offices to the parties, an agency available to assist in bringing them together if they wished to use it. In a later resolution (November 1, 1947) the Security Council took note of the fact that no substantial effort had been made by either party to come to an agreement with the other, and called upon the disputants "to consult with each other, either directly or through the Committee of Good Offices," as to the means to be employed to give effect to the cease-fire resolution which the Council had adopted. Still later (January 28, 1949), the name of the Committee was changed to the "United Nations Commission for Indonesia," and its duties were expanded to include consultation with Indonesian groups and submitting recommendations to the parties. Some months later, hostilities were terminated, much to the credit of the Commission, which had worked tirelessly and had made valuable contributions to the successful solution.

In the dispute between India and Pakistan over Kashmir, the commission appointed in 1948 to go to the spot was authorized both to investigate and to mediate. Its instructions were, *inter alia,* "to proceed at once to the Indian subcontinent and there place its good offices and mediation at the disposal of the Governments of India and Pakistan." The efforts of this body were in large part responsible for the subsequent agreement between the parties to hold a plebiscite.

The fact that conciliation or mediation by special agencies was used in three of the most heated disputes that have been placed before the United Nations—Indonesia, Palestine, and Kashmir—is evidence of the high esteem in which these procedures are held. That they produced positive results in each case is convincing proof that consultation, discussion, and the submission of suggestions are useful processes for settling controversies between sovereign nations ever fearful of subjecting themselves to tribunals with power.

Commissions and Agencies with Other Duties

In the fulfillment of its duties in the treatment of disputes, an agency such as the Security Council must follow up many lines of approach. It cannot be limited by any definition of processes or by stereotyped procedures, but must be able to avail itself of any and all methods which seem promising, provided, of course, that there is no contravention of the Charter. This means that there are various odd jobs to be done, some highly important, for whose accomplishment a committee or some other type of agency will be necessary.

The Council of the League of Nations made use of a variety of special agencies in its treatment of disputes. In the Aaland Islands case (1921), which came to it before the Permanent Court of International Justice was ready for business, the Council appointed a special Committee of Jurists to give a ruling on the question of whether or not the issue involved was of an international character or essentially domestic, as Finland claimed. In the Leticia dispute between Colombia and Peru (1933), the Council appointed an "Administrative Commission" to take over the temporary control of the disputed territory of Leticia, pending a final solution of the controversy. One of the agencies set up for the treatment of the Chino-Japanese dispute of 1931–1933 was a committee made up of consular representatives of certain members of the Council in China to keep the Council informed of developments. These are merely illustrations and by no means a complete list of the special agencies delegated by the League Council to expedite its work.

Within the United Nations, special agencies to assist in the settlement of disputes have been set up both by the Security Council and by the General Assembly. One commission with special functions created by the former was the Consular Commission for Indonesia, established by a resolution of August 26, 1947, to keep the Council informed of the observance of the cease-fire order which had been issued to the warring parties; certain members of the Security Council, including Russia, had desired to give the commission the power of "supervising" the observance of the order, but this project failed of adoption. The Commission was composed of the consular representatives of those members of the Council which maintained such officials in Batavia.

After the decision was made in 1948 to hold a plebiscite in Kashmir in order to determine whether that territory should go to India or Pakistan, the need arose for some authority to be in charge and to see to it that the vote would be taken fairly. For this purpose the Council provided that when the conditions within the area would permit a plebiscite, a special plebiscite administration headed by an appointee of the Secretary-General of the United Nations would be at hand to be responsible.[1]

Reference to the International Court of Justice

Legal issues involved in disputes before the Security Council may be referred to the International Court of Justice with requests for advisory opinions. This is a practice followed earlier by the Council of the League of Nations with considerable success, the tribunal to which questions were submitted at that time being the Permanent Court of International Justice. For instance, when the Council in 1924 attempted to settle the dispute between Great Britain and Turkey as to the future status of the territory of Mosul and the issue was raised as to the authority of the Council under the Treaty of Lausanne to deal with the problem, the Court was asked to give opinions (1) on the extent of the Council's jurisdiction in the case and (2) whether the parties could vote. The Court replied that the Council's authority was sufficient to deal with the dispute, and that when it did so, the parties were to refrain from voting. Once the Council's authority had been made clear, it proceeded to fix a boundary in Mosul.

Although the Security Council is able to seek the assistance of the

---

[1] At the date of this writing the plebiscite has not taken place.

International Court on legal issues involved in disputes before it, to date it has done so only once and that was in the Iranian oil case, when a request was made to the Court for an advisory opinion on whether the issues involved were international or domestic. The General Assembly, which also possesses such a right, has thus far not exercised it. The advisory opinions which have been given by the Court have had to do mainly with the powers and methods of international agencies. In the dispute brought to the General Assembly in 1946 on the charge that the Union of the South Africa was mistreating the Indian minority of that country, there was a proposal to ask the International Court for an advisory opinion, but it was turned down. The proposal arose out of the contention of the Union of South Africa that the people whom India was trying to protect were not nationals of India but of the Union, and that consequently the issue was purely domestic in character and not one suited for Assembly discussion. India maintained that the so-called Capetown Agreement of 1927 between herself and South Africa relating to the status of Indians gave the matter an international character. The Union of South Africa asked that the Court be requested to render an opinion on the question as to whether or not the issue was domestic. When the proposal was rejected, the two parties continued to negotiate over the matter.

The Security Council has the authority to recommend to nations the reference of a legal dispute to the International Court of Justice for a judgment, in addition to the right to seek advisory opinions from that tribunal on legal questions involved in controversies which it is treating. A recommendation of this nature was made in the Corfu Channel case between the United Kingdom and Albania, brought to the Council by the former in 1947. The International Court of Justice in three judgments successfully settled the dispute.[2]

Cease-Fire Orders

A dispute which has reached the point where hostilities have broken out presents a serious challenge to an organization like the League of Nations or the United Nations. Theoretically, such an occasion is one for sanctions, but in view of the general reluctance to resort to

---

[2] For the details of the case see the chapter on the International Court of Justice.

coercion, every effort is employed to get a return to peace and reason by some other means. Attempts to get a truce have been made through conciliation and mediation, and, as has already been shown, they have at times proved successful. Obviously, whatever the method used, there is a better chance of success if the disputants are small or weak nations. The League failed lamentably to halt hostilities in both the Chino-Japanese dispute of 1931–1933 over Manchuria and the Italo-Ethiopian controversy of 1935; in both instances large powers were involved.

The cease-fire order as a method of ending hostilities was first used by the Council of the League of Nations in the Greco-Bulgarian incident of 1925. On October 19, 1925, a Greek soldier crossed the Bulgarian border and fired upon a Bulgarian sentry, who, returning the fire, shot and killed the Greek. The feeling between the two countries had been so strained that this incident led to general hostilities, the Greek army advancing several miles into Bulgaria as it prepared to launch a large-scale offensive. The Bulgarian Government appealed to the Council. An extraordinary session of the Council met immediately in Paris, and, as a result, telegrams were sent to the Greek and Bulgarian governments reminding them of their obligations under the Covenant and asking them to withdraw their troops behind their respective frontiers. The two governments were asked to notify the Council within twenty-four hours that orders had been given for troop withdrawals and within sixty hours that the orders had been carried into effect. Compliance with the Council's request was given, and the Council was then in a position to appoint a commission of inquiry to look into the causes of the incident and to recommend measures which would prevent a recurrence.

The United Nations has issued cease-fire orders on several occasions. Constitutionally, they may be justified for the Security Council as coming within the provisions of Article 40 of the Charter, which states, "In order to prevent an aggravation of the situation, the Security Council may, before making the recommendations or deciding upon measures provided for in Article 39, call upon the parties concerned to comply with such provisional measures as it deems necessary or desirable." Although the reference to Article 39 appears to connect provisional measures with threats to peace, breaches of the peace, or acts of aggression, in practice the Security Council has not made formal declarations of the existence of such conditions before asking the parties to observe provisional measures. In view of the fact that Article 40 does not specify the type of provisional measures to be used, the Security Council is free to use whatever types it wishes, but presumably the most likely ones would be requests for a cessation of hostilities (or cease-fire orders), the removal of armed forces from designated areas, and, possibly, policing arrangements of some kind. Article 40 makes clear that the adoption of such measures is "without prejudice to the rights, claims, or position of the parties concerned."

The fighting between the armed forces of The Netherlands and the Republic of Indonesia was brought to the attention of the Security Council on July 30, 1947, by India and Australia. Two days later the Council called upon the parties to cease hostilities. Both the Republic of Indonesia and The Netherlands accepted the Council resolution and ordered their armies to stop fighting by August 5. Because charges were made that these orders had not been fully complied with, the Security Council on August 25–26 asked a Consular Commission of representatives of members of the Council in Batavia to report to it on the observance of the cease-fire order. Even then the hostilities continued, and the reports of the Consular Commission took note of that fact. Finally, on January 17, 1948, a truce agreement was signed on board the *U.S.S. Renville* and both parties issued cease-fire orders to their troops and got to work on the principles of a settlement; before a final settlement was reached at The Hague in 1949, however, there had been a renewal of hostilities.

In the India-Pakistan dispute over Kashmir and Jammu, brought to the Security Council in 1947, the parties were called upon to stop fighting, conclude a truce, and then set up conditions favorable to a plebiscite. The Commission sent "to place its good offices and mediation at the disposal of the Governments of India and Pakistan" was authorized to help in carry out these requests. Although the Council resolution embodying this program was adopted on April

17, 1948, it was not until January 1, 1949, that any pretense was made that the cease-fire had come into effect.

At one time, when the Palestine dispute was before the United Nations, the Security Council (May 29, 1948) called upon the governments and others concerned to order a cease-fire, to agree not to send their forces into specified areas, not to mobilize, and not to import war material. Hostilities did not cease, however, and it was some time before a truce was arranged through the mediatory efforts of Mr. Ralph Bunche.

The Security Council issued a cease-fire directly at the outset of its treatment of the hostilities in Korea on June 25, 1950. It went unheeded, however, by the North Korean Government.[3]

The basic nature of the cease-fire action of the Council is debatable. Whether the right of the Security Council "to call upon" the parties to cease hostilities is the equivalent of an order, as implied in the United States proposal of May 17, 1948, when the Palestine problem was under discussion, is not of great importance, for the inescapable truth is that the Council has had no means of getting compliance on the part of nations engaged in hostilities. Whatever it may be from a legal point of view, a cease-fire is treated as a mere request.

So far, the cease-fire requests have not been given the respect which an action of the Security Council should merit. To flout such a request is, no doubt, to lower the prestige and therefore the usefulness of the United Nations. Were the United Nations to have the armed forces at its command that are provided for in the Charter, a cease-fire might achieve more positive results.

The Assembly's Treatment of Disputes

Looking at developments from the point of view of practice during the few short years of the United Nations' existence, one is impressed by the fact that the General Assembly has been somewhat more active in the treatment of international disputes than was expected. Certainly the disputes with which it has concerned itself

---

[3] The United Nations action in the Korean case is discussed in detail in the chapter on sanctions.

have been among the most crucial and perplexing of those that have come before the United Nations. This unexpected prominence of the Assembly in the field of peaceful settlement may be attributed in part to its representative nature, including as it does all of the members of the United Nations, and in part to its function as a deliberative body; as a result of these two characteristics, its discussions reach the public ear the world over and affect public thinking. There is also the highly practical consideration that the Assembly takes its decisions by a two-thirds vote on matters of importance, unencumbered by a veto, whereas the Security Council will be deadlocked unless its permanent members are in agreement.

On several occasions the way has been opened for the General Assembly to take over a dispute by action of the Security Council in removing from its agenda the controversy in question; it will be remembered that the Assembly may not make recommendations on a dispute being dealt with by the Council unless the latter so requests. This was done on November 4, 1946, on the Spanish question, in order to enable the Assembly to make recommendations; on December 12, 1946, the Assembly recommended that Franco Spain be barred from the United Nations and its agencies, and that states withdraw their ambassadors and ministers from Madrid. On September 15, 1947, the Greek question was taken off the Security Council's agenda, and the General Assembly thereupon set to work on certain phases of that dispute.

The problem of Palestine was given to the Assembly at the outset. On April 2, 1947, Great Britain asked the Secretary-General "to place the question of Palestine on the agenda of the General Assembly at its next regular session." At the same time a request was made for a special session of the Assembly to meet as soon as could be arranged for the purpose of setting up a committee to formulate a project for consideration at the regular session. In a similar way, the dispute between India and the Union of South Africa was placed on the agenda at the second part of the first session of the Assembly at the request of the Indian Government; no special session was asked for, as in the Palestine problem.

To assist it in the treatment of disputes and in certain other duties, the General Assembly has available its First Committee on political and security problems, which can hold hearings, initiate proposals, and prepare projects for action by the full Assembly. Another mechanism which the Assembly may use is its Interim Committee, set up in 1947, whose terms of reference include disputes, along with other matters which the General Assembly may refer to it. From the very beginning the Assembly has made use, too, of a variety of *ad hoc* committees and agencies in the treatment of disputes.

Viewed in the large, the procedures which the General Assembly has used in handling the controversies which have come before it have borne a striking resemblance to those employed by the Security Council. Although there is no exact replica of the "direct" method of the latter organ, there is something quite similar in the right of Assembly delegates to debate on issues at hand. For instance, Indian and South African delegates were both present in 1946 when the controversy over the treatment of the Indians in the territory of the Union of South Africa was under debate; both were present, too, in the First Committee. In order to have a fair presentation of the divergent points of view relating to a dispute, special groups are allowed to appear before the Assembly's First Committee. Thus, in the Palestine dispute, authorization was given for the Jewish Agency for Palestine and the Arab Higher Committee to come before the Committee and present their arguments.

Like the Security Council, the Assembly has learned that the commission of inquiry is a useful mechanism; the findings of the commission appointed for the Palestine dispute were basic to subsequent Assembly discussions. Agencies of conciliation and mediation, too, have been employed to good advantage by the Assembly, as Mr. Ralph Bunche's work in the Palestine case shows. Other *ad hoc* agencies, such as the special committee of eleven appointed in 1947 to observe the compliance by the four Balkan governments—Albania, Bulgaria, Yugoslavia, and Greece—with its recommendations, have been utilized by the Assembly.

The only experience the General Assembly has had with cease-fire was in connection with the Korean affair in 1950, when the

Chinese communists entered the struggle on the side of the North
Koreans. At that time, a committee of three men was set up to arrange a cease-fire with the Communist Government of China. No
pretense was made of issuing an order to the Chinese. Whether
either the Security Council or the Assembly may issue an order requiring compliance is questionable, for Article 40 of the Charter
authorizes the Security Council only to "call upon" the parties to
comply with provisional measures, and the action of the General
Assembly in this connection is only under its general authority. That
either may request a truce or cease-fire is, however, undoubted.

The General Assembly side-stepped a difficult problem in November, 1950, when the Chinese communists invaded Tibet. Because
the United Nations was already deeply involved in the Korean
crisis, its members did not see fit to take on another case of aggression at that time. El Salvador offered a resolution in the Assembly
condemning Communist China's invasion as an act of "unprovoked
aggression," and asking that a committee study "appropriate measures" that might be taken. The resolution was dropped for lack of
support. No doubt the Assembly's inaction was due to the fact that
there appeared to be no effective course of action open to it. A
cease-fire request would certainly have been ignored, and sending
troops to the country was clearly impracticable; had troops been
available at that time, they would have been sent to Korea to
strengthen the United Nations' forces there.

The Assembly in the Palestine Dispute

One of the most complicated of the disputes that have come before
the United Nations was that over Palestine, submitted to the General Assembly on April 2, 1947. The background of the controversy
was such as to inflame violent passions and to affect basic national
interests. The origins of the affair go back into the period of World
War I, when Palestine was freed from Turkish control by the Allied
and Associated Powers. Great Britain had pledged herself to develop the territory into a national home for the Jewish people, but
she was also committed to Arab independence, and the Arab people
looked upon Palestine as a part of their national domain. The solu-

tion which was attempted to this triangular controversy involving Great Britain, with her traditional interests in the Eastern Mediterranean, the Jewish people, and the Arabs was to make Palestine a class-A mandate under the British Government. From the very beginning of this regime, however, there was discord, for by no possible combination of policies could the British satisfy both Arab and Jew at the same time. Throughout the 1920's and 1930's there were outbreaks of violence, and it was only by the heavy hand of force that a semblance of order was maintained.

During and after World War II, the Palestine dispute was aggravated by several new conditions. Because of their widespread persecution in Europe, the Jews were anxious to emigrate to Palestine. Were the British Government to countenance such an immigration, they would arouse the hostility of the Arabs, whereas to forbid it was a sure method of fanning to a flame Jewish discontent. Then, because American oil groups were flocking into Arab lands on a large scale and because Russia, always alert to spread communist doctrine, had her eye on possible victims, the Palestine issue had come to be a part of the so-called East-West struggle. Finally, the issue took on a new aspect when it became clear that Great Britain had emerged from the war too exhausted to spare the money and men required to keep the peace in the trouble-ridden country.

After trying vainly to find a solution that would permit her to remain in Palestine, Britain, on April 2, 1947, submitted the problem to the General Assembly, washing her hands of the whole mess. In answer to the British request, a special session of the Assembly met in New York City from April 28 to May 15. The only item on the agenda was the establishment of a special committee to prepare a project for the Assembly to consider at its next regular session. The representatives of the Arab states of Egypt, Iraq, Lebanon, Saudi Arabia, and Syria tried to add a second item—the termination of the mandate for Palestine and the declaration of its independence—but failed to do so. In the end, a special committee was set up by a vote of forty-five in favor and seven against, but not without a timely debate as to its composition and terms of reference. This United Nations Special Committee on Palestine (UNSCOP) was given wide authority to find and report facts, to examine all of the issues at stake, and to make recommendations. Its work could be carried on in Palestine, or wherever it chose, and it was to report not later than September 1, 1947.

UNSCOP went to work on May 26, 1947, and was ready to report by August 31. It held sixteen public and thirty-six private meetings. The majority report of the Commission recommended the permanent division of Palestine into three parts—an Arab state, a Jewish state, and the city of Jerusalem—the three to be linked together in an economic union. When it met in regular session, the Assembly appointed an *ad hoc* Committee on the Palestine Question to consider the report. After a lively debate, the partition plan of UNSCOP was adopted by the Assembly. At the same time the Assembly set up a Palestine Commission, consisting of Bolivia, Czechoslovakia, Denmark, Panama, and the Phillippines, to implement the plan, and the Security Council was asked to contribute whatever it could toward that end, even to declare the situation a threat to the peace if it should see fit to do so.

The Palestine Commission found that it was unable to discharge its duty of implementing the Assembly decision without armed forces. The situation deteriorated, as the Jews and Arabs resorted to violence on an increasingly large scale. After relieving the Palestine Commission of its responsibilities, the Assembly decided on May 14, 1948, to appoint a mediator to attempt to get the parties together. Count Bernadotte, President of the Swedish Red Cross, was selected for the post.

At this point in the controversy the Security Council became active. On April 23, 1948, it set up a Truce Commission, composed of those members of the Council which had career consuls in Jerusalem, to bring about an end to the fighting. But the situation became still more desperate, and therefore on May 22 the Security Council called upon all governments and authorities in Palestine to abstain from further hostilities and to issue a cease-fire order to become effective within thirty-six hours after midnight, May 22, 1948. At the request of the Arab states, the time limit was extended by forty-hours. When compliance was not obtained, the Security Council on

May 29 called upon the governments and authorities concerned to
order a cessation of hostilities for a period of four weeks, and Mediator Bernadotte, in concert with the Truce Commission, was instructed to supervise the observance of this Council resolution. The
Mediator's efforts were successful, and the truce became effective
on June 11. At the expiration of the truce on July 9, hostilities broke
out again. A renewal of the cease-fire order undertaken by the Security Council was unavailing, and on September 17, 1948, Mediator Bernadotte was assassinated. Dr. Ralph Bunche was named as
his successor.

During the first part of the third regular session of the General Assembly in 1948, a three-member Conciliation Commission was created, consisting of France, Turkey, and the United States, to assist
the governments and authorities to reach a final settlement. The
Commission met at Geneva, Switzerland, early in 1949. Ultimately,
the mediatory efforts of Dr. Bunche, assisted by the Conciliation
Commission, bore fruit, and general armistice agreements were concluded between the Egyptian and Israeli Governments on February
24, 1949, to be followed soon thereafter by armistices with other
Arab governments.

The Palestine dispute brought into play all of the guns in the Assembly's arsenal of peaceful settlement and some of those at the
command of the Security Council. Certainly both organs worked
hard and long to bring the situation under control. In the end they
were rewarded by success, but not, it must be admitted, until much
blood had been shed and the final victory of the Israeli forces had
seemed fairly certain. Throughout the struggle, the United Nations
had shown itself in need of a strong right arm with which to compel
obedience to its will. Within the limitations of its resources, it is
difficult to see how the United Nations could have done more.

APPENDIX TO CHAPTER IX

I

United Nations Mediator for Palestine
Resolution of the General Assembly, May 14, 1948

The General Assembly,

Taking account of the present situation in regard to Palestine,

1

Strongly affirms its support of the efforts of the Security Council to secure a truce in Palestine and calls upon all Governments, organizations and persons to coöperate in making effective such a truce;

2

1. *Empowers* a United Nations Mediator in Palestine, to be chosen by a committee of the General Assembly composed of representatives of China, France, the Union of Soviet Socialist Republics, the United Kingdom and the United States of America, to exercise the following functions:

a. To use his good offices with the local and community authorities in Palestine to:

(*i*) Arrange for the operation of common services necessary to the safety and well-being of the population of Palestine;

(*ii*) Assure the protection of the Holy Places, religious buildings and sites in Palestine;

(*iii*) Promote a peaceful adjustment of the future situation of Palestine;

b. To coöperate with the Truce Commission for Palestine appointed by the Security Council in its resolution of 23 April 1948;

c. To invite, as seems to him advisable, with a view to the promotion of the welfare of the inhabitants of Palestine, the assistance and coöperation of appropriate specialized agencies of the United Nations, such as the World Health Organization, of the International

Red Cross, and of other governmental or non-governmental organizations of a humanitarian and non-political character;

2. *Instructs* the United Nations Mediator to render progress reports monthly, or more frequently as he deems necessary, to the Security Council and to the Secretary-General for transmission to the Members of the United Nations;

3. *Directs* the United Nations Mediator to conform in his activities with the provisions of this resolution, and with such instructions as the General Assembly or the Security Council may issue;

4. *Authorizes* the Secretary-General to pay the United Nations Mediator an emolument equal to that paid to the President of the International Court of Justice, and to provide the Mediator with the necessary staff to assist in carrying out the functions assigned to the Mediator by the General Assembly;

3

Relieves the Palestine Commission from the further exercise of responsibilities under resolution 181 (II) of 29 November 1947.

II

Cease-Fire for Korea (June 25, 1950)*

The Security Council,

RECALLING the finding of the General Assembly in its resolution of 21 October 1949 that the Government of the Republic of Korea is a lawfully established government "having effective control and jurisdiction over that part of Korea where the United Nations Temporary Commission on Korea was able to observe and consult and in which the great majority of the people of Korea reside; and that this Government is based on elections which were a valid expression of the free will of the electorate of that part of Korea and which were observed by the Temporary Commission; and that this is the only such Government in Korea";

MINDFUL of the concern expressed by the General Assembly in its resolutions of 12 December 1948 and 21 October 1949 of the consequences which might follow unless Member states refrained from

---

* *Department of State Bulletin*, XXIII, no. 574, July 3, 1950, p. 4.

acts derogatory to the results sought to be achieved by the United Nations in bringing about the complete independence and unity of Korea; and the concern expressed that the situation described by the United Nations Commission on Korea in its report menaces the safety and well-being of the Republic of Korea and of the people of Korea and might lead to open military conflict there;

NOTING with grave concern the armed attack upon the Republic of Korea by forces from North Korea,

Determines that this action constitutes a breach of the peace,

I. *Calls upon* the authorities of North Korea (a) to cease hostilities forthwith; and (b) to withdraw their armed forces to the thirty-eighth parallel.

II. *Requests* the United Nations Commission on Korea (a) to observe the withdrawal of the North Korean forces to the thirty-eighth parallel; and (b) to keep the Security Council informed on the execution of this resolution.

III. *Calls upon* all Members to render avery assistance to the United Nations in the execution of this resolution and to refrain from giving assistance to the North Korean authorities.

III

Commissions Used in Disputes*

1. The General Assembly and the Security Council, as principal organs normally sitting at the Headquarters of the United Nations, often need auxiliary organs on the spot. These auxiliary organs, in the form of commissions, have played an indispensable part in the work of the United Nations. In dealing with its particular problems, each commission has developed its methods and procedures for itself. A considerable body of practical experience has thus been accumulated.

2. This study attempts to examine the machinery that has been built up in eleven cases in which the commission has been used in one form or another, and to gather together some of the resulting

---

* *Report of the Interim Committee of the General Assembly,* January 31–August 17, 1949, General Assembly Official Records: Fourth Session, Supplement no. 11 (A/966), pp. 13, 1–22.

precedents. It is a composite statement based on the eleven memoranda prepared by the Secretariat concerning the work of individual commissions. It is not confined to data drawn from these papers, but also includes tentative conclusions.

5. The following are the eleven commissions which have been the subject of memoranda by the Secretariat. They are listed in the chronological order of their creation, with short titles used in this study:

a. The United Nations Commission of Investigation concerning Greek Frontier Incidents (*Greek Frontier Incidents Commission*), established by the Security Council resolution of 19 December 1946, functioned from 30 January to 15 September 1947;

b. The Subsidiary Group of the United Nations Commission of Investigation concerning Greek Frontier Incidents (*the Subsidiary Group*), established by Security Council resolution of 18 April 1947, functioned from 19 May to 15 September 1947;

c. The United Nations Special Committee on Palestine (*UNSCOP*), established by General Assembly resolution 106 (S-1), functioned from 26 May to 31 August 1947;

d. The Security Council Consular Commission at Batavia (*Consular Commission at Batavia*), formed under Security Council resolution 25 August 1947, held its first meeting on 1 September; the Commission is still technically in existence;

e. The Security Council Committee of Good Offices on the Indonesian Question (*Indonesian Committee of Good Offices*), established by Security Council resolution of 25 August 1947, functioned from 20 October 1947 to 28 January 1949. It was replaced by the United Nations Commission for Indonesia.

f. The United Nations Special Committee on the Balkans (*UNSCOB*), established by General Assembly resolution 109 (II) of 21 October 1947, convened for the first time on 21 November 1947. . . ;

g. The United Nations Palestine Commission (*Palestine Commission*), established by General Assembly resolution 181 (II) of 29 November 1947, functioned from 9 January to 17 May 1948;

h. The United Nations Temporary Commission on Korea (*UNTCOK*), established by General Assembly resolution 112 (II) of 14 November 1947, functioned from 12 January to 13 December 1948. It was replaced by the United Nations Commission on Korea, by General Assembly resolution 195 (III) of 12 December 1948;

i. The Security Council Truce Commission for Palestine (*Palestine Truce Commission*) established under Security Council resolution of 23 April 1948;

j. The United Nations Mediator in Palestine (*Mediator or Acting Mediator*), established by General Assembly resolution 186 (S-2) of 14 May 1948, entered upon his duties on 21 May 1948; after the assassination of the Mediator on 17 September 1948, he was succeeded by the Acting Mediator, . . ;

k. The United Nations Commission for India and Pakistan (*UNCIP*), established by Security Council resolutions of 20 January and 21 April 1948.

6. Of the eleven commissions under examination, six were established by the Security Council (Greek Frontier Incidents Commission, the Subsidiary Group, Consular Commission at Batavia, Indonesian Committee of Good Offices, Palestine Truce Commission and UNCIP) and five by the General Assembly (UNSCOP, UNSCOB, Palestine Commission, UNTCOK, and Mediator).

7. The functions of commissions fall into four classes: investigation; cease-fire and truce arrangements; conciliation, good offices and mediation; and political administration. In practice, most commissions have been required to perform more than one function, and their character has at times been determined as much by evolving circumstances as by the original terms of reference. This has affected their organization, internal procedure, and methods of operation.

A. Investigation or Inquiry

93. All commissions are faced, at one time or another, with the need to ascertain or clarify the facts. However, this task is most varied, both in subject matter and in method.

94. The terms of reference of UNSCOP directed it, for the pur-

pose of preparing a report on the question of Palestine to the next
session of the General Assembly, to "conduct investigations in Palestine and wherever it may deem useful, receive and examine written or oral testimony, whichever it may consider appropriate in
each case, from the Mandatory Power, from representatives of the
population of Palestine, from Governments and from such organizations and individuals as it may deem necessary." The Commission
was given "the widest powers" to ascertain facts and record them,
and to investigate "all questions and issues relevant to the problem
of Palestine." Pursuant to these terms, UNSCOP adopted a two-fold
method of operation. It attempted in the first place to arrive at an
understanding of the issues involved in the problem by conducting
a preliminary survey of the land, its peoples and their aspirations,
and of the social, economic and religious systems. Secondly, it considered factual evidence and views presented by the parties and by
private persons on the problem (Memorandum on UNSCOP, paragraphs 52–53).

1. Area Surveys

100. The commissions have found it necessary, as part of their
task of investigation, to ascertain facts in various localities, or, in
some instances, to make comprehensive on-the-spot surveys of particular areas for particular purposes. The commissions have, in general, been authorized to use their own discretion in making such
area surveys. It is, therefore, for each commission to decide for itself what aspects of the problem under investigation require fact-
finding on the spot. . . .

2. Investigating Teams or Observation Groups

104. Investigation and observation of the facts relating to alleged
frontier violations were conducted not only directly by the Greek
Frontier Incidents Commission but also through the agency of its
special investigating teams. These teams, seven in number, enabled
the Commission to cover a wide area in its investigation and to hear
the maximum number of witnesses. UNSCOB has established observation groups with a well-defined scheme of organization and de-

tailed rules for their operations. The observer groups are under the general charge of a chief observer. The observers are provided by the States represented on UNSCOB, but are to exercise in all loyalty, discretion and conscience the functions entrusted to them, and discharge those functions and regulate their conduct with the interests of the United Nations in view, and accept instructions in regard to the performance of their duties only from UNSCOB. There are six observation groups, each being assigned a different zone of activity. The observation groups communicate with UNSCOB mainly through UNSCOB's own radio network; an air courier service has also been organized between Athens and Salonika and the bases of the observation groups. The groups make periodical and, when necessary, special reports to UNSCOB. . . .

3. Oral Hearings

106. Two main problems arise in connexion with testimony: one concerns the selection of witnesses; the other concerns the presentation of evidence. . . .

4. Written Communications

a. Unsolicited communications by the parties

113. Communications sent out by the parties at their own initiative are usually treated as official commission documents.

b. Unsolicited communications from non-official sources

114. Unsolicited communications from non-official sources—individuals as well as organizations—are normally numerous and their relevance is often questionable. It has been the accepted practice for the secretariat to draw up periodic lists of such communications, so that members of the commission or the commission as a whole may request the opportunity to examine any individual items.

c. Solicited communications from the parties

115. Some commissions (Indonesian Committee of Good Offices, Palestine Commission and UNCIP) adopted the practice of submitting written questionnaires to the parties to fill in the gaps of infor-

mation already obtained either through oral hearings or through unsolicited communications.

d. Solicited communications from organizations and individuals

116. UNSCOP, on the other hand, issued a blanket invitation to all organizations and individuals so desiring to transmit written communications to the commission.

IV

Methods Used by the General Assembly*

Section A

Precautionary Measures

95. These are appeals or recommendations by the General Assembly designed either to prevent the aggravation of a dispute or special political problem by actions of States or authorities directly concerned, or to insulate the area of dispute from political influence or military interference likely to obstruct the General Assembly's efforts at peaceful settlement. Precautionary measures have been taken before or at the same time as general measures of settlement; they may be in general terms or specific, and may be directed to all States, to all Members, to particular States including non-members, or even to the inhabitants of countries. . . .

Elucidation of Facts

98. For the elucidation of facts underlying a dispute or special political problem before it, the Assembly has so far confined itself to granting participation in its proceedings to States, authorities or organizations likely to assist it; to creating special commissions with authority to investigate the facts; and to making use of the Interim Committee.

99. So, the United Nations Special Committee on Palestine was

---

* *Report of the Interim Committee of the General Assembly,* 3rd Session: June 16– September 18, 1950, General Assembly: Official Records, 5th Session, Supplement no. 14 (A/1388), pp. 26–27.

instructed to "conduct investigations in Palestine and wherever it may deem useful" as a basis for proposals on the future of Palestine; . . .

Measures of Settlement

100. Measures for the settlement of disputes and special political problems by the General Assembly have included direct recommendations to States, or authorities concerned; the use of the methods indicated in Article 33; the creation of special subsidiary organs with political, administrative or other functions; and the reference of the matter to other principal organs of the United Nations. The General Assembly has also taken steps to ensure continued control of the matter by the United Nations. Further, the Assembly has sometimes found it necessary to reaffirm earlier recommendations and resolutions. . . .

X Sanctions

A<small>LEXANDER</small> H<small>AMILTON</small> <small>SAID IN</small> *The Federalist,* "<small>IT IS ES-</small>
sential to the idea of law that it be attended with a sanction; or in
other words a penalty or punishment for disobedience."[1] This doctrine has been given expression by national governments in the form
of machinery and processes whereby alleged violators of the law
may be tried, and, if found guilty, punished. Although most people
would no doubt obey the law anyway for the sake of public order
and personal reputation, or out of a sense of fairness and decency,
in the last analysis, if the authority of the state is to stand, its laws
must be enforceable against those individuals who are deficient in
the traits of character that lead to obedience. Otherwise, quoting
Hamilton again, "laws will, in fact, amount to nothing more than
advice or recommendation."

In international organization there is a similar problem, but here
organized society must deal with recalcitrant states rather than anti-
social individuals. Most of the states like the advantage of a good
reputation and are law-abiding, at least most of the time; some few
take the law less seriously and violate it more flagrantly. Inevitably,
infractions become the subject of international disputes, with the
aggrieved party asserting its rights and making claims for damages;
this, for instance, was true in the Corfu Channel case, already discussed, where the United Kingdom contended that Albania had violated the law by placing mines in that waterway, and after some
controversy the matter was referred to the International Court of
Justice for judgment. The decision of the Court was accepted, but

---

[1] *The Federalist,* Ford ed. no. 15, pp. 90–94.

had either party flouted it, the problem of enforcing the law would have come up in a different form.

In its broadest sense, the problem of sanctions in international organization is one of finding effective coercive measures that can be applied against states for infractions of any part of the law. As the problem has been treated, however, it has been with the more limited purpose of devising means of coercion against states illegally resorting to force, thereby committing aggression and jeopardizing the peace; compelling obedience to the law in every particular, desirable as it might be, has been looked upon as of secondary importance in comparison with the enforcement of peace.

The prevention of aggression and war is universally conceded to be the main objective of international organization. However well its organs may facilitate and promote coöperation between states in matters of health, social welfare, and economic activities—and such coöperation must itself be looked upon as contributing to international peace and order—unless it can prevent the lawless use of force, it does not command respect and in all probability will be discarded, first or last. The Charter recognizes over and again the primary purpose of the United Nations to be the prevention of war. The very first sentence of its Preamble begins, "We the peoples of the United Nations, determined to save succeeding generations from the scourge of war, which twice in our lifetime has brought untold sorrow to mankind. . . ." The first purpose of the United Nations stated in Article 1 is "To maintain international peace and security. . . ." To accomplish this task of maintaining peace, the United Nations endeavors (1) to promote coöperation, (2) to settle disputes that arise between nations, and (3) to prevent resort to force and aggression. All three are vital activities, but in the long run the United Nations is likely to stand or fall on its ability to prevent aggression.

The prevention of aggression and resort to force is as difficult a task as it is laudable. Even within states physical violence is not entirely prevented, nor is it always punished. And when it comes to the international sphere, setting up controls about the state in the way of sanctions is immeasurably more complicated than handling the individual within the state. Within the state it is a case of one person against an organized community of several million people, with the odds heavily in favor of the community; but in the world at large it is usually one state against seventy-five or eighty others which to date do not have the advantage of a highly integrated community. It is conceivable that one state against seventy-five would have a good chance of getting its way if that one should be a great power like the United States or Russia. In this event, were the seventy-five members of the international community to take action against the one recalcitrant state, the resulting hostilities would be the equivalent of a world war.

Prior to World War I, no system of sanctions existed and none was possible for the reason that there was no permanent international organization to administer them. There had been concerted efforts to restrain individual states from violence or to compel them to meet their obligations, but they were rare and without the benefit of any established procedures or methods. For instance, in 1900 several states of the West, including the United States, combined forces to put down the Boxer Uprising in China. Again in 1902, a number of European states blockaded Venzuela to bring pressure on that state for the payment of debts. While resembling sanctions in some particulars, such action was too irregular and too limited to be considered on a par with the sanction system of the League of Nations or that of the United Nations.

The League System

The proponents of a league of nations during World War I stressed the desirability of giving the new organization the strength that it would need to prevent aggression. A plan sponsored by a private American group known as the League to Enforce Peace publicized the need for placing coercive power in the hands of the world organization then in contemplation. The point was emphasized that the preservation of peace would require a system of such effectiveness that a nation like Germany, the assumed aggressor in 1914, would never be able to embroil the nations in war again.

Article 10 of the Covenant came to grips with the problem head-on in its assertion that "The Members of the League undertake to respect and preserve as against external aggression, the territorial integrity and existing political independence of all Members of the League." Additional coercive strength was to be derived from Article 16, which stated that "Should any Member of the League resort to war, in disregard of its covenants under Articles 12, 13 or 15, it shall *ipso facto* be deemed to have committed an act of war against all other Members of the League. . . ." Together, these articles appeared to mean that if any state should attack another, the community of nations, acting through the League, would undertake to protect the victim of aggression. The system was therefore one of "collective security." Such a system in a world of sovereign states can be only an assemblage of machinery and procedures for the prevention of war and aggression; its operation would depend upon the willingness of the member states to set it in motion when faced with an international crisis.

The first evidence that the League System would not be workable in a crisis appeared in the form of interpretations given to Articles 10 and 16. In 1921 the second Assembly of the League of Nations interpreted Article 16 in such a way that (1) each member would be free to decide for itself whether or not an actual breach of the Covenant had occurred in a given situation; (2) if the Council should decide that there were a breach and convey its opinion to the members, that opinion would not be binding; and (3) "resort to war" would not automatically create a state of war with all of the members of the League.[2] It was decided at the same time that the principle of the progressive application of sanctions be substituted for that of the immediate application as appeared to be the sense of Article 16. A complete breach of diplomatic relations, it was decided, need not occur immediately, but instead the heads of

---

[2] A portion of the interpretive resolution was as follows:

Paragraph 3—The unilateral action of the defaulting State cannot create a state of war; it merely entitles the other Members of the League to resort to acts of war or to declare themselves in a state of war with the Covenant-breaking State; but it is in accordance with the spirit of the Covenant that the League of Nations should attempt, at least at the outset, to avoid war, and to restore peace by economic pressure.

Paragraph 4—It is the duty of each Member of the League to decide for itself whether a breach of the Covenant has been committed. The fulfilment of their duties under Article 16 is required from Members of the League by the express terms of the Covenant, and they cannot neglect them without breach of their Treaty obligations.

missions might be recalled while consular relations were maintained. Depriving a civilian population of food was to be regarded as "an extremely drastic measure," to be applied when other measures were clearly inadequate.

In 1924, amendments were proposed to Article 16 of the Covenant, but they never received the required number of ratifications to put them into effect. The text of the original article (paragraphs 1 and 2) is given in one column below and the proposed amendments in the other.

ORIGINAL ARTICLE 16

1. Should any Member of the League resort to war in disregard of its covenants under Articles 12, 13 or 15, it shall *ipso facto* be deemed to have committed an act of war against all other Members of the League, which hereby undertake immediately to subject it to the severance of all trade or financial relations, the prohibition of all intercourse between their nationals and the nationals of the covenant-breaking State, and the prevention of all financial, commercial or personal intercourse between the nationals of the covenant-breaking State and the nationals of any other State, whether a Member of the League or not.

PROPOSED AMENDMENTS
(September 27, 1924)

1. Should any Member of the League resort to war in disregard of its covenants under Articles 12, 13 or 15, it shall *ipso facto* be deemed to have committed an act of war against all other Members of the League, which hereby undertake immediately to subject it to the severance of all trade or financial relations and *to prohibit all intercourse at least between persons resident within the territory of the covenant-breaking State, and, if they deem it expedient, also between their nationals and the nationals of the covenant-breaking State, and to prevent all financial, commercial or personal intercourse at least between persons resident within the territory of that State and persons resident within the territory of any other State, whether a Member of the League or not, and if they deem it expedient, also between the nationals of that State and the nationals of any other State whether a Member of the League or not.*

PROPOSED AMENDMENT

2. It shall be the duty of the Council in such case to recommend to the several Governments concerned what effective military, naval or air force the Members of the League shall severally contribute to the armed forces to be used to protect the covenants of the League.

2. (October 4, 1921): *It is for the Council to give an opinion whether or not a breach of the Covenant has taken place. In deliberations on this question in the Council, the votes of Members of the League alleged to have resorted to war and of Members against whom such action was directed shall not be counted.*

3. *The Council will notify to all Members of the League the date which it recommends for the application of economic pressure under this article.*

4. *Nevertheless, the Council may, in the case of particular Members, postpone the coming into force of any of these measures for a specified period where it is satisfied that such a postponement will facilitate the attainment of the object of measures referred to in the preceding paragraph, or that it is necessary in order to minimize the loss and inconvenience which will be caused to such members.*

(Sept. 21, 1925): *The words "in such case" in the second paragraph of the original text of Article 16 of the Covenant shall be deleted.*

In 1923, an intepretation was offered in the Assembly to the effect that in the application of Article 10, each member would be free to decide for itself the extent to which it would be bound to comply with any request on the part of the Council for action in giving force to that article. This interpretive resolution was supported by twenty-nine states, with one state (Persia) in the opposition and many states abstaining from voting. The resolution, therefore, did not constitute, in the proper sense, a legal interpretation; but in view of the fact that it had such wide support, its significance was nevertheless considerable.

The first crisis to develop when the League sanctions might have been applied was in 1931–1933, when Japan invaded Manchuria, territory then belonging to China. The affair was handled as a dispute under Articles 11 and 15 of the Covenant; China did not call for an application of the sanctions under Article 16, probably because the great powers had indicated that they would not relish the inconvenience to which they would be put as the ones on whom the burden of applying sanctions would fall. Although there was no specific provision in the Covenant for diplomatic sanctions, the Assembly decided in 1933 to recommend, in accordance with the Stimson Doctrine of the United States, that members of the League should not recognize the new State of Manchukuo which had been set up by the Japanese Army. Only a few members of the League ignored this recommendation, and consequently Manchukuo was left quite isolated diplomatically. The effect of this action was disappointing; Manchukuo, as a Japanese puppet, got along well enough without the benefit of recognition. Moreover, the states which refused to establish diplomatic relations with Manchukuo found themselves embarrassed because they were without the usual means of protecting their rights and interests. What was worse, the failure to act under Article 10 or 16 tended to discredit the League's sanction system and opened the way for the later defiance of the League.

When the dispute between Paraguay and Bolivia over the Gran Chaco burst into open war in 1932, the League of Nations worked with persistence to bring about a peaceful settlement, but without success. After a report under Article 15 of the Covenant was accepted by Bolivia but not by Paraguay, the Assembly (1934) recommended an embargo on arms against Paraguay as a measure of coercion. Soon thereafter, Paraguay gave notice of her intention to withdraw from the League. Here again an improvised sanction did not appear to have had any effect upon the policy of the offending state.

The only effort to apply the sanctions of Article 16 was made in 1935, when Italy was in the process of conquering Ethiopia. After efforts at peaceful settlement had failed, a decision was taken by the Council that Italy had in fact gone to war in violation of the Covenant. The Assembly then created a Coördination Committee to make suggestions for the coördination of economic and financial sanctions. Four principal proposals were presented, as follows:

Proposal 1—to lift any embargo on arms then in effect against Ethiopia and to apply an embargo on arms to Italy.

Proposal 2—to place a ban on all loans, share issues, banking credits, and advances for or on behalf of Italy or any person in Italy.

Proposal 3—to place an embargo on imports from Italy for all goods except gold or silver coin or bullion.

Proposal 4—to add to the embargo list applied to Italian imports certain essential materials such as rubber, iron ore, scrap iron, nickel, and tin.

These proposals were accepted by from fifty to fifty-two members of the League and were put into force by from forty-seven to fifty of them.

These economic sanctions against Italy were harmful to her, but they did not prevent the conquest and annexation of Ethiopia. One reason was that in preparing for the aggression Italy had accumulated large supplies of essential materials. More important was the fact that the League members would not agree to embargo the sale of oil to Italy, and therefore the most crippling of all the economic measures that could have been taken was not employed. It is possible, too, that, had the League acted with greater promptness in the situation, better results might have been obtained.

In brief, the League of Nations system of security, when tested, was found wanting. After Japan defied the League in 1931–1933 with impunity, it became clear that the sanctions of the League were not to be relied upon. The machinery and processes were there, but the members were loath to use them.

An effort was made in 1923 to strengthen the League of Nations system of collective security through what was known as the Geneva Protocol. It was the purpose of that document to plug the holes of the Covenant in its provisions relating to the settlement of disputes and the prevention of aggression. Had it gone into effect, the result would no doubt have been constructive, but when the British Government failed to ratify the Protocol, other governments followed suit and it remained a dead letter. As a result of this failure, the quest for security was placed on a regional basis when in 1925 the Locarno Pact was concluded, with the object of stabilizing the boundary between Germany on the one hand and France, Belgium, and The Netherlands on the other.

The Charter on Sanctions

The shortcomings of the League of Nations system led to a firm resolve that the new world organization would be adequately equipped with coercive power. Wartime projects for a new organization, both public and private, stressed sanctions of one sort or another. The Culbertson Plan of 1943 attracted an unusual amount of attention with its scheme for a "World Police Force." This plan combined "national contingents" to be taken from individual countries at a time of crisis with a "mobile corps" recruited from smaller member states and at all times under the management of the world government. The plan was carefully worked out so that the quotas of the various "national contingents" would in no instance exceed 20 percent of the total forces, whereas the "mobile corps" of the world government would constitute 22 percent. This distribution was intended to bring about such a condition that no "national contingent" alone would equal the world government's own army, while the total force of the national contingents and the mobile corps added together would be strong enough to meet any emergency. Ingenious as it was, the plan did not appeal to the formulators of the Charter.

In its completed form as constructed at San Francisco, the sanction system of the United Nations was placed under the control of the Security Council. Serious consideration had been given to a project for associating the General Assembly with the Security Council on the theory that all the members of the United Nations are represented in the former whereas they are not in the latter. In the end it was decided that the Security Council offered two special advantages: (1) it was smaller and could convene more quickly; and (2) it was dominated by the large powers who would be responsible in the last analysis for the maintenance of peace. This decision conformed to the wishes of the four sponsoring governments—the United States, Great Britain, Russia, and France—whose permanent membership in the Security Council, together with the veto, would give them the position of advantage which they wanted.

Three types of sanctions are specifically mentioned in the Charter—diplomatic, economic, and military. The expectation was that normally the diplomatic and economic would first be attempted; then, if the Security Council should decide that those methods were inadequate, it could "take such action by air, sea, or land forces as may be necessary to maintain or restore international peace and security." If the Council should decide at the outset that diplomatic and economic measures would not be likely to suffice, it might employ military sanctions immediately.

In order to place the members of the United Nations under a definite obligation with regard to sanctions and thus to make the system tighter than that of the League of Nations, the Charter requires them to make special agreements with the Security Council defining what their respective contributions will be in case a crisis arises. Those agreements are to deal with such matters as "the number and types of forces, their degree of readiness and general location, and the nature of the facilities and assistance to be provided." They are to be made on the initiative of the Security Council and are subject to ratification by the individual states in accordance with their respective constitutional requirements. To date, however, those agreements have not been concluded for the reason that the Military Staff Committee of the United Nations has not been able to agree upon the general principles to be incorporated into them. Consequently, there are no military forces upon which the Security Council is entitled to call in case the peace of the world is threatened.

Another supposed advantage of the United Nations sanctions over the system of the League of Nations was embodied in the requirement of Article 45 that "in order to enable the United Nations to take urgent military measures, Members shall hold immediately available national air force contingents for combined international enforcement action." These contingents were expected to provide the Security Council with a ready means of action, although until an emergency should arise they were to remain under national control. Up to the present time they have not been made available.

To assist the Security Council in the employment of military sanctions, a Military Staff Committee has been set up. This Committee is made up of the Chiefs of Staff of the permanent members of the Security Council, or their representatives. It is authorized "to advise and assist" the Security Council on all matters relating to military sanctions and armaments, and in the event that resort is taken to military sanctions, it is to take over the strategic direction of the armed forces placed at the disposal of the Security Council.

These provisions of the Charter appear on paper to constitute an improvement over the League of Nations system. As yet, however, they have turned out to be quite lifeless. The first major step toward placing the military sanctions on a workable basis was to be taken by the Military Staff Committee, which was given the job of defining the basic principles to be embodied in the formal agreements to be made by member states with the Security Council. When the Military Staff Committee got to work on these problems, they found themselves in disagreement on a number of basic points. The most serious difference of opinion had to do with the contributions which members were to make; it was the Russian point of view that contributions should be equal, whereas the United States argued that they should be based on ability to contribute. The Committee reported on April 30, 1947, after a prolonged period of debate. The report dealt with the following aspects of the problem: the purpose, composition, and overall strength of the armed forces; the contribution of armed forces by members; the employment of armed forces and their degree of readiness; the provision of assistance and facilities for them, including right of passage; the logistic support of armed forces; their general location and their strategic direction and command. Differences of opinion on the part of the five members of the Committee—the United States, Russia, the United Kingdom, France, and China—were noted. The Russian insistence on equality of contributions was well brought out by Russia's reservation to Article 11, which was as follows: "Permanent Members of the Security Council shall make available armed forces (land, sea, and air) on the Principle of Equality regarding the over-all strength and the composition of these forces. In individual instances, deviations from this principle are permitted by special decisions of the Security Council, if such a desire is expressed by a Permanent Member of the Security Council."

On June 25, 1947, the Security Council asked the Military Staff Committee to submit an estimate of the overall strength of the armed forces to be made available in which would be indicated (1) the strength and composition of the land, sea, and air components, and (2) the proportion of this strength to be made available by the permanent members of the Council. The estimates submitted by the members of the Committee were greatly at variance. The report of the Committee gave the separate proposals of France, the United Kingdom, the United States, and Russia in view of the fact that no consensus of opinion was possible; China, supported the estimates of the United Kingdom. The estimates are on page 356. With the Military Staff Committee so hopelessly at odds on a number of basic points, the military-sanction system of the United Nations was placed on the shelf, to be left there until a more propitious time in the indefinite future.

Several times, Article 39 of the Charter has been invoked with the allegation that a certain action or situation constituted a "threat to the peace, a breach of the peace or act of aggression." For instance, when the Spanish question was before the Security Council in 1946, Poland maintained that the situation in Spain was of such character. The subcommittee, examining the allegation, came to the conclusion that the Franco regime in Spain was not of a nature to justify the Polish allegation. In its opinion there was a "potential" but not an existing menace to peace in Spain. A resolution recommending that members of the United Nations apply the diplomatic sanction by breaking off relations with the Franco Government was

	France	U.K.	U.S.	USSR
Air Forces				
Bombers	775	600	1250 (Includes only	600
Strategic		(225)	strategic and	
Medium		(150)	tactical bombers)	
Light		(400)		
Fighters	300	400	2250 (Includes fighter	300
			bombers)	
Reconnaissance	200	—	—	—
Miscellaneous	—	200	300	300
Total	1275	1200	3800 (Does not include	1200
			air transport	
			requirements)	
Ground Forces				
Divisions	16	8–12	20	12
Armored		(3)		
Airborne		(3)		
Motorized or				
mountain		(10)		
Naval Forces				
Battleships	3	2	3	—
Carriers	6	4	6	—
Cruisers	9	6	15	5–6
Destroyers	18–24	24	84	24
Escort vessels	30	48	—	24
Minesweepers	30	24	—	24
Submarines	12	12	90	12
Assault shipping and				
craft for number of				
divisions shown	1	Two-thirds	6	—
		(2 regimental		
		combat		
		teams or		
		brigade		
		groups)		

defeated by a veto on the part of Russia, disgruntled that the Spanish situation was not labeled an existing menace to peace. In December, 1946, the General Assembly applied a modified diplomatic sanction by recommending to members of the United Nations that they recall their respective ambassadors and ministers from Madrid while leaving there the remainder of their diplomatic missions. Widespread compliance with this recommendation was given, but without any observable effect upon the Franco regime. At the 1950–1951 session of the Assembly a decision was taken to allow states to restore full diplomatic representation at Madrid.

A charge was made in 1946 by Greece that the frontier incidents along her border, inspired, so she said, by her communist neighbors, constituted an act of aggression. Several resolutions in support of the Greek allegations were offered in the Security Council, but none could be adopted in the face of the Soviet veto.

Enforcement Action in Korea

After the defeat of Japan in 1945, Korea was divided at the thirty-eighth parallel for the purpose of accepting the surrender of the Japanese army, with Russian troops taking over the northern part of the country and Americans occupying territory to the south. To assist in the establishment of a Provisional Korean Democratic Government as provided in the Moscow agreement of December, 1945, a Joint Commission of the occupying powers was created, but this Commission became deadlocked. On November 14, 1947, the General Assembly set up a Temporary Commission on Korea to arrange an election in the country, with a view to national unity and ultimate independence. This Commission was not permitted to operate in North Korea, but it went ahead and arranged elections in South Korea. The result was that the Republic of Korea was established as an independent nation in August, 1948; its authority, however, was limited to the area south of the thirty-eighth parallel. In December, 1948, Russia announced the withdrawal of her troops from North Korea and the creation of a new communist regime there, known as the Peoples Democratic Republic of Korea. In spite of these untoward developments, the United Nations continued its efforts to establish a freely elected government for all of Korea; a United Nations Commission of seven nations—Australia, China, El Salvador, France, India, the Philippines, and Turkey—was sent to Korea for this purpose.

On Sunday, June 25, 1950, at 4:00 A.M. Korean time, the Russian-trained troops of North Korea crossed the thirty-eighth parallel and attacked the Republic of Korea. The United States Government immediately brought the matter to the attention of the Security Council. At a meeting held on the same day in New York City, the Security Council, Russia absent, passed a resolution calling for the immediate cessation of hostilities and the withdrawal of the invading troops to the thirty-eighth parallel; furthermore, the resolution requested members of the United Nations to refrain from giving aid to the aggressors and "to render every assistance to the United Nations in the execution of this resolution." Soon thereafter President Truman, taking note of the fact that North Korean troops had not withdrawn, announced that he had ordered United States air and sea forces "to give the Korean Government troops cover and support."

When on June 27 the hostilities were continuing on an even greater scale, the Security Council adopted another resolution recommending that members of the United Nations "furnish such assistance to the Republic of Korea as may be necessary to repel the armed attack and to restore international peace and security in the area." In a third resolution, adopted on July 7, the Council recommended that members make whatever assistance they might furnish to the Republic of Korea available to a unified command under the United States, authorized the United States to designate a commander of United Nations forces, authorized the use of the United Nations flag in operations against North Korean forces, and requested the United States to report to the Security Council on "the course of action taken under the unified command."

Under the authority of these resolutions, a United Nations army of more than 350,000 men was assembled from fifteen countries and South Korea; they were placed under the command of General Douglas MacArthur.[3] Approximately 200,000 were Americans, some 100,000 were South Koreans, about 20,000 were British, 5000 Greek, 5000 Turkish, and smaller numbers were from the other coöperating nations. In addition to ground troops, there were contributions of air and naval forces, and of medical units. The collective effort gained sufficient momentum that by the end of October, United Nations forces were well into North Korea and the enemy appeared

[3] When General MacArthur was relieved of his command in April, 1951, President Truman appointed General Matthew Ridgway to be in charge of United Nations troops.

crushed. At this time, however, Chinese communist troops began to appear on the fighting front in support of the remaining forces of North Korea; these troops were referred to as "volunteers" by the spokesmen of Russia and Communist China. By mid-December there were several hundred thousand Chinese soldiers in Korea, pushing the United Nations Forces relentlessly southward. Thousands of American and South Korean troops, trapped in North Korea, were evacuated by sea to South Korea, where they were sent back into battle against the advancing hordes of communists. The complete defeat of the United Nations army appeared inevitable for a while, but the army rallied. By the summer of 1951 the opposing armies appeared hopelessly deadlocked. At the suggestion of Mr. Jacob Malik truce negotiations were opened on July 8 at Kaesong, Korea.

Throughout this venture the Soviet Union offered every possible obstacle to the action of the United Nations. In August, 1950, she ended her boycott of the Security Council begun several months before in protest against the refusal of the United Nations to give the Chinese communists the seat in the organization to which China was entitled. Mr. Jacob Malik was sent in to take over the chairmanship which under the plan of rotation became a Russian privilege for that month. Mr. Malik then proceeded to block every effort of the Council to implement United Nations policy in Korea. The decision of the United Nations to stop the aggression of North Korea had been possible only because Russia's absence in June and July precluded her use of the veto. Trying to regain this lost ground, Mr. Malik argued that the decisions of the Council taken in Russia's absence were illegal.

In support of his bitter announcement that the doings of the Security Council during Russia's absence were illegal, Mr. Malik quoted Article 27 of the Charter to the effect that "Decisions of the Security Council on all other matters [other than procedural] shall be made by an affirmative vote of seven members including the concurring vote of the permanent members." He reasoned that the decisions of the Council in support of South Korea did not have the concurring vote of all permanent members and therefore were invalid. Ambassador Jessup gave the American answer to the Russian contention, as follows:[4]

It is necessary to recall that article 24 of the Charter says that members of the United Nations confer on the Security Council "primary responsibility for the maintenance of international peace and security." In the next place article 28 of the Charter says that—

The Security Council shall be so organized as to be able to function continuously. Each member of the Security Council shall for this purpose be represented at all times at the seat of the Organization.

This is the language of the Charter. It is perfectly clear that a state which is a member of the Security Council is obligated to be in a position at all times to take part in its work. This provision would have no meaning if in spite of having a representative at the seat of the organization the representative should have a right to refuse to attend the meetings. The Soviet Union has thus violated its obligations under the Charter by resorting to the tactics of "walking out.". . .

One of the practices in the Security Council which has developed over the years is the practice of abstaining from voting on questions which are put to the vote. The Soviet Union, beginning in April 1948, abstained in four instances on Security Council resolutions dealing with Palestine. Beginning in January 1948, the Soviet Union abstained on four resolutions dealing with the Kashmir case. Beginning in December 1948, the Soviet Union abstained on two resolutions in the Indonesian case. In none of these ten cases has the Soviet Union challenged the legality of the action taken by the Security Council. Furthermore, the Soviet Union has never questioned the legality of action taken by the Security Council in which it voted with the majority but on which other permanent members of the Council abstained. This has occurred in at least three instances. We thus already have over a dozen cases in which it has been established that the meaning of article 27 of the Charter is that, while the negative vote of a permanent member can defeat the substantive resolution, the failure of a permanent member to vote for a resolution does not defeat it.

Clearly it can make no difference in terms of the application of the Charter on this point whether the representative of a permanent member sits at the table and abstains or whether he fails to come at all. The essential difference relates to the question of a member's sense of responsibility and willingness to discharge its obligations under the Charter. The

---

[4] P. C. Jessup, "The United Nations and Korea," *Department of State Bulletin,* 1950, vol. 23, no. 576, pp. 85–86.

Soviet Union had the legal power to attend the meeting of the Security Council and, by taking the responsibility before the world, to cast a veto to block Security Council action. The U.S.S.R. did not have the power to block action by staying away from the meeting in violation of its obligations under article 28. . . .

A United Nations Guard

Several times Secretary-General Lie has urged the establishment of a guard force. In a report to the General Assembly he explained the need for such a force, its legal basis, and the manner in which it should be organized and managed. In the past a small number of guards have been employed, chiefly at Lake Success, and it would therefore seem clearly within the power of the United Nations to create a larger force and to expand the protective duties which have been performed. Mr. Lie's project looked forward to a force of about eight hundred men who would be available to accompany the United Nations missions abroad and when necessary to protect the persons and property of the missions, to assist them by furnishing transportation, communications, and supplies, to guard areas neutralized under cease-fire orders or truce, and to help in the conduct of plebiscites. The need for such a force was shown when United Nations mediator Count Bernadotte was assassinated in Palestine.

The type of guard proposed would be strictly nonmilitary in character. Small in size, it would, in some situations at least, derive its strength from its symbolic nature; any nation that defied or attacked the force would be challenging the United Nations. Clearly it would not fit into the role of an international army to stand as a defense against aggression. But even though it could not serve as a substitute for the military sanction system of the United Nations, it might be expected to add to the authority of the Security Council and the General Assembly in dealing with disputes and in handling delicate international situations. To date, a large guard force has not been created, but on November 22, 1949, the Assembly provided for a Field Service to be composed of one hundred men at first but to be increased later on to a maximum of three hundred.

The announcement was made in July, 1950, that the Field Service for duty with United Nations missions had come to include one hundred and twenty-five men selected from twenty-six countries. Its members were serving in India, Pakistan, Korea, Israel, Lebanon, Eritrea, Libya, former Italian Somaliland, the Balkans, Afghanistan, and Japan. In addition there were another one hundred and twenty-five members stationed at the headquarters of the United Nations. It was expected that by 1952 the Service would reach the limit of three hundred. Before assignment to duty, the new recruits go through a period of training at headquarters and at Toledo, Ohio, where they are given training in jeep driving and maintenance. Their preparatory training also includes courses in typing, shorthand, first aid, security duties, the Morse code, and technical training in communication equipment.

National vs. Collective Security

The inability of the members of the United Nations to set up and operate the system of sanctions called for by the Charter caused nations to fall back on Article 51 of that document, which stipulates that "nothing in the present Charter shall impair the inherent right of individual or collective self-defense if an armed attack occurs against a Member of the United Nations, until the Security Council has taken the measures necessary to maintain international peace and security." Article 51 was adopted at San Francisco principally as a means of harmonizing regionalism with the United Nations system of universalism. The article was also a safeguard to the right of self-defense, usually looked upon as an inherent right of nations as of individuals.

The North Atlantic Pact has been justified in part as a measure of collective self-defense. The Mutual Defense Treaty of the Organization of American States (1947) is also regarded as an effort at collective self-defense, as well as an expression of regionalism. Similarly, the Brussels Pact of 1948, concluded between the Benelux countries, France, and Great Britain, along with a number of other alliances, is believed to have the blessing of Article 51. Whether these alignments are founded upon a fair interpretation of Article 51 is debatable. The principal issue is whether there must be an actual attack before resort is taken to collective self-defense, or

whether it is enough that there be danger of an attack. In the case
of the North Atlantic Pact, Russia argued that the parties had
stretched the meaning of Article 51 by applying it where no attack
had occurred, or was even imminent. Certainly it was not expected
that such an arrangement as the North Atlantic Pact would be necessary under the United Nations system; the fact that such alliances
have been made is evidence that the nations will try to provide
their own means of security when they feel unable to rely on a system of collective security.

Sanctions Under the General Assembly

In his opening address to the General Assembly in 1950, Secretary of State Acheson proposed to give that organ a vital role in the
United Nations system of sanctions. He began his address by point-
ing to the success with which the aggression in Korea had been met
by United Nations forces up to that time. He referred to the pre-
carious "margin of safety" then existing and to the fact that the venture might not have been as successful as it then promised to be
had it not been for (1) the absence of Russia from the Security
Council in June, 1950, (2) the information provided by the United
Nations Commission in Korea, (3) the presence of American troops
in Japan that could be made quickly available for service in Korea,
and (4) "a series of accidents which, from the standpoint of the aggressor amounted to extraordinarily bad luck." By his plan Mr.
Acheson believed it possible to make sure that "the accidental,
which served so well in Korea, will hereafter become dependable."

The point was stressed in the proposal that the power to be
granted to the General Assembly would not in any way diminish
that of the Security Council in the maintenance of peace. The resolution embodying the project reaffirmed "the importance of the exercise by the Security Council of its primary responsibility for the
maintenance of international peace and security. . . ." It reaffirmed
the duty of the Council to take the initiative in negotiating agreements with member states for the provision of armed forces, and
stated that the purpose of the project was to provide the United
Nations with strength "pending the conclusion of such agreements."

The project was referred to the Assembly's Committee I (Political Committee). There it encountered the opposition of the Soviet bloc, but it was nevertheless reported favorably by the Committee to the General Assembly. The debate was continued in the Assembly itself, but on November 3, 1950, it was adopted in a series of resolutions by decisive majorities.[5] It is now, therefore, a part of the United Nations system of preventing aggression and maintaining the peace.

The powers of the Assembly in the sanction system do not become available unless and until the Security Council, unable to get the great-power unanimity required by the Charter, "fails to exercise its primary responsibility for the maintenance of international peace and security." In the event that such a contingency should arise, the General Assembly may recommend to members of the United Nations collective measures, including the use of armed force, to maintain or restore peace. Should the Assembly not be in session at the time, it may be called into session on twenty-four hours' notice at the request of any seven members of the Security Council. Clearly this arrangement makes possible the employment of sanctions when the permanent members of the Security Council are not in agreement as to the need or wisdom of doing so. In view of the fact that the General Assembly decides such matters by a two-thirds vote, the sanctions could be used over the opposition of Russia; for that matter, they could be invoked over the opposition of all the permanent members of the Security Council if perchance the Assembly should already be in session and therefore would not need to be called together by seven members of the Council.

A second feature of the system is a recommendation to the members of the United Nations that they maintain within their respective armed forces elements trained and ready for prompt service if and when the Assembly should require them. To facilitate this process, the Secretary-General keeps on file a panel of military experts to give advice and assistance on request to states desiring their aid

---

[5] The votes on the resolutions were 53 to 5, 52 to 5, 57 to 0, and 45 to 5, with some abstentions in all except the first vote.

in preparing elements of their armed forces for use by the United Nations.

A third aspect of the arrangement is a peace observation commission to observe and report on conditions in any area where there is international tension. This commission could be sent to a territory with the consent of the state or states concerned in the event that "the Security Council is not exercising the functions assigned to it by the Charter with respect to the matter in question." In substance, the agency would be in the nature of a roving commission of inquiry made available for emergencies. The usefulness of the Commission for Korea during the Korean crisis of 1950 in keeping the United Nations informed on conditions and events seemed to indicate that a permanently available agency of this kind could be a helpful adjunct to the equipment of the Assembly for handling such problems.

The essential virtue claimed for this Assembly system of sanctions is that it makes action by the United Nations possible when the Security Council has been paralyzed by a veto. Obviously, it does not make action certain. In addition to the fact that the Assembly might not be able to produce a two-thirds vote for coercion, there is the even more important consideration that it can only recommend collective enforcement measures to members; no right exists to demand or requisition the mobilization of armed forces in a joint enterprise. The armed forces are portions of the army, navy, and air services of the members, and they remain under the control of the members until they are voluntarily turned over to the United Nations for international duty.

By the communist bloc of members of the United Nations, the system has been called a violation of the Charter. Arguing against it, Mr. Vishinsky said: "The Charter remains, and suddenly it is not there. The Security Council is there, and suddenly it is not there. That is what you call eating your cake and having it too, and everything is well and good, and everybody is happy." Elsewhere Mr. Vishinsky quipped that the United Action for Peace, as the arrangement is called, "would explode and crush the Charter." To this remark Mr. Dulles, American spokesman in the Assembly, replied, "I say that Mr. Vishinsky's view 'would explode and crush' the peace." That the system does find a way around the veto is undeniable and was freely admitted by its proponents. That it violates the Charter, as Russia has contended, would be difficult to prove, for the provisions of that document defining the General Assembly's powers and methods are very broad. Able to amend its own rules of procedure under Article 21 of the Charter, the Assembly would seem to be in a position to provide for emergency special sessions. Authorized by Article 14 to make recommendations "for the peaceful adjustment of any situation . . ." and by Article 10 to discuss any matters within the scope of the Charter and to make recommendations thereon to members, the Assembly seems to be adequately equipped to discuss and recommend military action.

Problems

The experience of the League of Nations and the United Nations raises a serious question as to whether a reliable system of international sanctions can be constructed. There are features about the whole concept of collective security which do not square with the facts of international relations. It will be admitted that the tensions of the postwar era between Russia and the western nations have placed on the United Nations an inordinate load of problems which have weighed it down in all of its activities. In a slightly more normal atmosphere, however, the League of Nations system of sanctions proved to be equally impracticable. If it were requisite to a proper functioning of a system of sanctions that problems and tensions be eliminated, then that system would hardly be worth having. Indeed, it is only because there are problems and tensions which culminate in crises that international organization needs sanctions at all.

An obstacle almost invariably in the way of the successful application of sanctions is the clashing interests of nations. Rare is the aggression toward which every nation takes an identical attitude. Nations have friends and enemies; the friends wink at the aggression just as unhesitatingly as the enemies condemn it. When Italy went into Ethiopia in 1935, Great Britain with her African interests was strongly opposed, but France, anxious to have the support of Italy in the event of war with Germany, was indifferent; the United States, far from the scene, remained neutral, placing an embargo on arms and munitions to both belligerents. At the present time it would be difficult to imagine an aggression regarding which all members of the Security Council would be in agreement in calling for the application of sanctions, unless, as in the case of Korea, the Russian delegates were not in attendance.

A problem inherent in the use of military sanctions is that the forces to be used are to be left under national authority until a crisis arises, when they would be transferred to international control. This means that in the last analysis nations are free to turn over such forces to the international authority or not, as they choose. The method of raising an army for international use is somewhat like that of raising money under the old Articles of Confederation of the United States, when the Congress could ask the states for contributions but had no way of exacting them. The only remedy for this condition would be the transfer of control over troops even in peace to an international authority. This, in effect, would amount to the establishment of an international police. Sound as this may be, such a system is difficult to imagine in a world of sovereign states.

Another problem in the establishment of an effective system of international sanctions is that of defining aggression. Presumably it would be something of a catastrophe to name a state as an aggressor unless, in fact, such were the case. If sanctions are looked upon as punitive in nature, then it would be a miscarriage of justice to punish an innocent state. If they are regarded as measures for averting war, it would be a grave mistake to apply sanctions against a state engaged in the justifiable operation of defending itself. While it is possible that economic and diplomatic sanctions could be applied against both of the parties to a controversy, it is inconceivable that military action should be taken against both parties.

The Covenant of the League of Nations contained no definition of aggression; it was left to the individual states to decide for themselves whether a nation had committed an act of war or acted in violation of Article 10. For this reason, the Geneva Protocol of 1923 attempted to provide a definition. According to the Protocol, aggression was to be presumed where a nation had refused peaceful settlement, had failed to comply with a judicial sentence, had defied a unanimous recommendation of the Council, or had violated provisional measures enjoined by the Council. Apart from such cases, if the Council could not agree in naming an aggressor, it might impose an armistice upon the belligerents and any belligerent refusing to accept or violating that armistice would be deemed an aggressor. Because the Geneva Protocol was never ratified, this process of determining an aggressor was never put in practice.

Many nonaggression treaties were made in the 1920's and 1930's but most of them did not define aggression. Among them, however, was one concluded by Roumania, Russia, Czechoslovakia, Turkey, and Yugoslavia (1933), by which an aggressor was defined as that state first to commit any of the following acts: (1) a declaration of war; (2) an invasion with or without a declaration of war of the territory of another state; (3) an attack by land, naval, or air on the territory, vessels, or aircraft of another state; (4) a naval blockade of the coasts or ports of another state; (5) support to armed bands within its territory guilty of invading the territory of another.

The Charter of the United Nations does not define aggression. The whole subject of sanctions is under the control of the Security Council, which may decide for itself when there is a "threat to the peace, breach of the peace or act of aggression." No doubt this flexible treatment was wise, for no definition of aggression could be completely adequate. If it is an evasion of an issue, then the issue is one for which no answer has yet been made available.

The limitations of the diplomatic and economic sanctions have been noted in discussions of the occasions on which they have been applied. Diplomatic ostracism of Manchukuo after 1933 and of Franco's Spain after 1946 did virtually nothing in either case to undo what had been done. It is, to be sure, an expression of disapproval, but as a means of coercion it is a mere slap on the wrist.

Were it possible, contrary to the experience with economic sanctions against Italy, to get a world-wide economic blockade, complete in every detail, the effect could be well-nigh disastrous to an aggressor highly dependent upon trade. If, however, the aggressor were a nation with a well-balanced economy like Russia or the United States, the economic sanction would do relatively little harm. Even a nation dependent upon trade such as Germany or Great Britain might be able to insulate itself against economic sanctions, to a degree at least, by stock-piling essential materials. In cases where an aggressor could be harmed by having its trade cut off, the nations applying the sanctions must also expect to suffer, for they would stop their own trade as well as that of the aggressor. Finally, there is the objection to economic sanctions that, if effective, they lead to malnutrition, illness, and starvation; they kill gradually instead of instantly like the bullet or the bomb. Any belief that they are humanitarian is a delusion.

The point of view that any effective sanction, economic or military, improves little if any upon war is not an uncommon one. No doubt those who hold this view would point out that the collective action against North Korea was to all intents and purposes war, as much so as though it had been undertaken by the United States alone instead of by the United Nations. Members of religious sects, such as the Society of Friends, which oppose resort to violence denounce both war and military sanctions.

Advocates of military sanctions as preferable to war will say that, once proved to be effective, they would not need to be used, for no nation would dare to take the law into its own hands and run the risk of the consequences. The sanctions, according to this optimistic view, would come to be worth more for their potential effect than for their active use. Only an extended experience with effective sanctions could prove or disprove this doctrine.

By their nature, sanctions require a great deal in the way of co-operation between states, perhaps more than can be expected of sovereign states within a system of international organization. It may be that internationalism will have to give way to a stronger form of world organization before aggressive military action can be made impossible.

▲

APPENDIX TO CHAPTER X

I

*United Nations Sanctions in Korea. Resolution of June 27, 1950**

The Security Council,

HAVING DETERMINED that the armed attack upon the Republic of Korea by forces from North Korea constitutes a breach of the peace,

HAVING CALLED for an immediate cessation of hostilities, and

HAVING CALLED upon the authorities of North Korea to withdraw forthwith their armed forces to the 38th Parallel, and

HAVING NOTED from the report of the United Nations Commission for Korea that the authorities in North Korea have neither ceased hostilities nor withdrawn their armed forces to the 38th Parallel, and that urgent military measures are required to restore international peace and security, and

HAVING NOTED the appeal from the Republic of Korea to the United Nations for immediate and effective steps to secure peace and security,

Recommends that the Members of the United Nations furnish such assistance to the Republic of Korea as may be necessary to repel the armed attack and to restore international peace and security in the area.

II

Uniting for Peace†

Resolution A

Uniting for Peace

THE GENERAL ASSEMBLY, *Recognizing* that the first two stated purposes of the United Nations are:

---

* *Department of State Bulletin*, XXIII, no. 574, July 3, 1950, p. 7.

† *Department of State Bulletin*, 1950, XXIII, no. 20, pp. 823–825. At this same time resolutions were adopted permitting the General Assembly to meet on short notice

"To maintain international peace and security, and to that end: To take effective collective measures for the prevention and removal of threats to the peace, and for the suppression of acts of aggression or other breaches of the peace, and to bring about by peaceful means, and in conformity with the principles of justice and international law, adjustment or settlement of international disputes or situations which might lead to a breach of the peace," and

"To develop friendly relations among nations based on respect for the principle of equal rights and self-determination of peoples, and to take other appropriate measures to strengthen universal peace,"

Reaffirming that it remains the primary duty of all members of the United Nations, when involved in an international dispute, to seek settlement of such a dispute by peaceful means through the procedures laid down in Chapter VI of the Charter, and *Recalling* the successful achievements of the United Nations in this regard on a number of previous occasions,

Finding that international tension exists on a dangerous scale,

Recalling its resolution 290 (IV) entitled "Essentials of Peace," which states that disregard of the principles of the Charter of the United Nations is primarily responsible for the continuance of international tension, and *Desiring* to contribute further to the objectives of that resolution,

Reaffirming the importance of the exercise by the Security Council of its primary responsibility for the maintenance of international peace and security, and the duty of the permanent members to seek unanimity and to exercise restraint in the use of the veto,

Reaffirming that the initiative in negotiating the agreements for armed forces provided for in Article 43 of the Charter belongs to the Security Council and *desiring* to ensure that, pending the conclusion of such agreements, the United Nations has at its disposal means for maintaining international peace and security,

Conscious that failure of the Security Council to discharge its responsibilities on behalf of all the member states, particularly

---

(change in Assembly rules), and asking the permanent members of the Security Council to meet and discuss their differences.

those referred to in the two preceding paragraphs, does not relieve member states of their obligations or the United Nations of its responsibility under the Charter to maintain international peace and security,

Recognizing, in particular, that such failure does not deprive the General Assembly of its rights or relieve it of its responsibilities under the Charter in regard to the maintenance of international peace and security,

Recognizing that discharge by the General Assembly of its responsibilities in these respects calls for possibilities of observation which would ascertain the facts and expose aggressors; for the existence of armed forces which could be used collectively; and for the possibility of timely recommendation by the General Assembly to members of the United Nations for collective action which, to be effective, should be prompt;

(*Adopted,* 53 *to* 5, *with no abstentions*).

A

1. RESOLVES that if the Security Council, because of lack of unanimity of the permanent members, fails to exercise its primary responsibility for the maintenance of international peace and security in any case where there appears to be a threat to the peace, breach of the peace, or act of aggression, the General Assembly shall consider the matter immediately with a view to making appropriate recommendations to members for collective measures, including in the case of a breach of the peace or act of aggression the use of armed force when necessary, to maintain or restore international peace and security. If not in session at the time, the General Assembly may meet in emergency special session within twenty-four hours of the request therefor. Such emergency special session shall be called if requested by the Security Council on the vote of any seven members, or by a majority of the members of the United Nations;

2. ADOPTS for this purpose the revisions in its rules of procedure set forth in the annex to this resolution;

(*Adopted,* 52 *to* 5, *with one abstention*).

B

3. ESTABLISHES a Peace Observation Commission, which for the calendar years 1951 and 1952 shall be composed of fourteen members, namely: China, Colombia, Czechoslovakia, France, India, Iraq, Israel, New Zealand, Pakistan, Sweden, the Union of Soviet Socialist Republics, the United Kingdom, the United States of America and Uruguay, and which could observe and report on the situation in any area where there exists international tension the continuance of which is likely to endanger the maintenance of international peace and security. Upon the invitation or with the consent of the state into whose territory the Commission would go, the General Assembly, or the Interim Committee when the Assembly is not in session, may utilize the Commission if the Security Council is not exercising the functions assigned to it by the Charter with respect to the matter in question. Decisions to utilize the Commission shall be made upon the affirmative vote of two-thirds of the members present and voting. The Security Council may also utilize the Commission in accordance with its authority under the Charter;

4. The Commission shall have authority in its discretion to appoint subcommissions and to utilize the services of observers to assist it in the performance of its functions;

5. RECOMMENDS to all Governments and authorities that they coöperate with the Commission and assist it in the performance of its functions;

6. REQUESTS the Secretary General to provide the necessary staff and facilities, utilizing where directed by the Commission the United Nations panel of field observers envisaged in resolution 297 B (IV);

(*Adopted, 57 to 0, with two abstentions*).

C

7. INVITES each member of the United Nations to survey its resources in order to determine the nature and scope of the assistance it may be in a position to render in support of any recommendations of the Security Council or the General Assembly for the restoration of international peace and security;

8. RECOMMENDS to the members of the United Nations that each member maintain within its national armed forces elements so trained, organized and equipped that they could promptly be made available, in accordance with their respective constitutional processes, for service as a United Nations unit or units, upon recommendation by the Security Council or General Assembly, without prejudice to the use of such elements in exercise of the right of individual or collective self-defense recognized in Article 51 of the Charter;

9. INVITES the members of the United Nations to inform the Collective Measures Committee as soon as possible of the measures taken in implementation of the preceding paragraph;

10. REQUESTS the Secretary General to appoint, with the approval of the committee provided for in Paragraph 11, a panel of military experts who could be made available upon request of member states which wish to obtain technical advice regarding the organization, training, and equipment for prompt service as United Nations units of the elements referred to in Paragraph 8;

(*Adopted, 45 to 5, with seven abstentions.*)

D

11. ESTABLISHES a Collective Measures Committee consisting of fourteen members, namely: Australia, Belgium, Brazil, Burma, Canada, Egypt, France, Mexico, Philippines, Turkey, the United Kingdom, the United States of America, Venezuela and Yugoslavia, and directs the Committee, in consultation with the Secretary General and with member states as the Committee finds appropriate, to study and make a report to the Security Council and the General Assembly, not later than 1 September 1951, on methods, including those of part C of this resolution, which might be used to maintain and strengthen international peace and security in accordance with the purposes and principles of the Charter, taking account of collective self-defence and regional arrangements (Articles 51 and 52 of the Charter);

12. RECOMMENDS to all member states that they coöperate with the Committee and assist it in the performance of its functions;

13. REQUESTS the Secretary General to furnish the staff and facilities necessary for the effective accomplishment of the purposes set forth in parts C and D of this resolution;

(*Adopted*, 49 *to* 5, *with three abstentions*).

E

14. THE GENERAL ASSEMBLY, in adopting the proposals set forth above, is fully conscious that enduring peace will not be secured solely by collective security arrangements against breaches of international peace and acts of aggression, but that a genuine and lasting peace depends also upon the observance of all the principles and purposes established in the Charter of the United Nations, upon the implementation of the resolutions of the Security Council, the General Assembly and other principal organs of the United Nations intended to achieve the maintenance of international peace and security, and especially upon respect for and observance of human rights and fundamental freedoms for all, and on the establishment and maintenance of conditions of economic and social well-being in all countries; and accordingly

15. URGES member states to respect fully, and to intensify, joint action, in coöperation with the United Nations, to develop and stimulate universal respect for and observance of human rights and fundamental freedoms, and to intensify individual and collective efforts to achieve conditions of economic stability and social progress, particularly through the development of under-developed countries and areas.

(*Adopted*, 54 *to* 0, *with one abstention*).

13. *Requests* the Security Council to furnish the stillful *both* the necessary . . . the objective accomplishment of the purposes set forth in paragraphs 1 and 1.3 of this resolution;

Part Four: Diplomacy, Conference, and Consultation

XI Diplomacy

AN OVERALL PICTURE OF CONTEMPORARY DIPLOMACY would show every nation in constant contact with every other nation that it recognizes. For the most part, the machinery through which this intercourse is carried on belongs to and is a part of the separate governmental systems of the participating states. Ordinary bilateral diplomacy is conducted entirely by means of nationally provided procedures and officials, although there are rules of international law and long-established practices relating to such matters as the ranks, privileges, immunities, and duties of diplomats. Multilateral diplomacy is undertaken in conferences and in the organs of the United Nations and other permanent organizations; here the machinery and processes used are not the possession of any one nation, although, as in bilateral diplomacy, the individual diplomats who take part are national officials. If therefore one could get a bird's-eye view of the vast network of diplomacy, he would see the diplomatic officials of every nation at work all over the world, some at capital cities where they are permanently accredited, some at the conference tables of special gatherings, and others at meetings of the United Nations.

Shifting the spotlight from a world-wide perspective to give a picture of diplomacy from the national point of view, there will appear at the center of every nation's organization a foreign office, or Department of State as it is called in the United States. This office is the "nerve center" of the nation's system of diplomacy. It dispatches diplomatic officials to the capital cities of the nations, instructs those officials as to policies to be pursued, and in turn receives from them reports which will be helpful in further policy-making at home. At the same time that it is working through its own officials abroad, the foreign office receives the diplomats of other nations and works with them for the promotion of national policies and interests. The office also is in general charge of those diplomatic officials who are taking part in international conferences and in the meetings of the United Nations.

Complicating the picture still further are the consular missions sent by every government to the important cities of other nations, whose principal duty is to deal with matters of trade. These, too, are sent and received by the foreign offices of nations.

The Foreign Office

It is of course a purely constitutional matter as to how a nation shall organize and maintain its foreign office. The United States Department of State is constantly undergoing organizational changes, and occasionally a thorough overhauling of the Department takes place. Generally, there are several types of duties to be performed, and the organization of any foreign office must provide for their performance. Changes in organization made from time to time in every country are in the interests of efficiency or they are occasioned by a desire to give greater or less stress to some particular type of work.

Most important among the duties undertaken within a foreign office is that of policy-making. In this field it by no means has a monopoly; on the contrary, its role is often a subordinate one. In almost every constitutional system, the chief executive, president or prime minister, bears the major load of the responsibility for policy-making, using the foreign office as he may see fit to help him. Within democratic countries, legislative bodies, too, are vested with power in foreign policy. The Congress of the United States is unusually strong in the field, in keeping with the well-known American system of the separation of powers; the Congress appropriates money for foreign affairs and enacts laws relating to the subject, such as neutrality and immigration laws, and the Senate consents to treaties and approves appointments to diplomatic posts. The prominent position of Congress in foreign affairs requires the American Department of State to equip itself with offices and personnel through which it can maintain contacts with Congressional committees and leaders.

The Department of State of the United States is an arm of presidential authority. The President appoints the Secretary of State and is able to remove him from office. In the realm of policy-making this means that if he wishes to do so, the President may himself make decisions on policies after such consultations with the top men of the Department as he may desire; or he may go to the other extreme and let the Secretary of State assume full charge. It is largely a matter of personal relationship. President McKinley had the reputation of rarely showing up at the Department offices; but his successor, President Theodore Roosevelt, vitally interested in foreign affairs and eager to exert direct personal control, was on hand constantly. While the flexible nature of the relationship between the Chief Executive and the Department of State is a widely recognized feature of the American system, something similar to it may be found in many countries; the relation between Hitler and the German Foreign Office, for instance, was not rigidly fixed and in practice was a matter for personal adjustment.

In every country the decisions on relatively unimportant matters are taken within the foreign office. Universally, too, foreign offices contribute to policy-making in major issues by keeping readily available for use by top executive officials facts and information relating to foreign affairs, some supplied to it by the reports of diplomatic officials and some produced by research within the office. Furthermore, even when decisions are taken by top executive or legislative officials, the opinions and advice of foreign-office officials are usually sought and often followed; the practice on the part of American Congressional committees dealing with foreign affairs of calling in officials of the Department of State to give opinions and answer questions is a well-known case in point. In one way or another, therefore, the foreign office maintained within national constitutional systems participates conspicuously in the process of defining foreign policy.

The business of negotiating treaties and agreements is undertaken by foreign-office officials, sometimes by diplomats, and sometimes by other members of the office, including the foreign minister himself. Secretary of State Byrnes, for instance, was in attendance at the Potsdam Conference in 1945 with President Roosevelt, and he attended several meetings of foreign ministers to formulate peace settlements after World War II. Secretary Stettinius was a member of the delegation of the United States in attendance at the San Francisco Conference of 1945 to draw up a Charter for the United Nations. Nowadays, foreign-office heads are frequently present in missions for the negotiation of solutions to international problems.

A typical foreign office is organized for the performance of several commonly assumed functions other than policy-making and negotiating. In this day and age, when international problems are diverse and complex, it must employ research experts to keep itself informed in an accurate and detailed manner on events and movements relating to world affairs. The office must have experts in international law to advise it in regard to the legal problems which so often present themselves in the conduct of diplomacy. One of the most striking developments of our times in foreign-office work and organization has been the effort through publications and radio broadcasting to reach public opinion and to win support at home and good will abroad. Other types of public contacts are those relating to passports, educational exchange, and press releases. A great variety of internal administrative duties must be undertaken, such as the preparation of the departmental budget and the training and management of the foreign service. Because there are proper and improper ways of doing things in the field of diplomacy, there must be a protocol staff of officials who specialize in the fine points of etiquette and social procedure relating to the reception of foreign diplomats and distinguished alien visitors, White House ceremonies, and so on. In addition to its frequent contacts with the legislative body (at least in democracies), the foreign office must be able to maintain contacts with other government departments and with the United Nations. Finally, the office must maintain telegraphic, mail, airgram, teletype, and courier services, it must provide interpreters and translators whenever and wherever needed, and it must carry on clerical and stenographic operations on a large-scale basis.

The Russian Foreign Office, or "Minindel" as it is called, embodies most of these functions in its organizational set-up. It is headed by a foreign minister, Mr. Andrei Vishinsky in recent years, and immediately under him is a deputy foreign minister. The part played by those officials in the formulation of policy is small and at best advisory, particularly in matters of major importance; the omnipotent Politburo is the state organ that makes vital decisions both in foreign and in domestic affairs. The foreign minister has, however, acted in the role of negotiator on many occasions. Within the Minindel are several sections in charge of diplomatic activities for designated areas, as follows:

1. Great Britain, France, the Iberian countries, Belgium, and The Netherlands.
2. Central and Southeastern European countries.
3. The United States, Central and South America.
4. Scandinavia.
5. Germany and Austria.
6. The Near East, Turkey, Iran, and Afghanistan.
7. China, Australia, New Zealand, and Japan.

Such a division of the world into geographic areas from which diplomatic reports are received and through which contacts are maintained is characteristic of foreign offices generally, although the exact areas covered by the separate divisions differ widely. The principal administrative divisions of the Russian Foreign Office are (1) administrative, (2) personnel, (3) finance, and (4) training. In addition there are "functional services" relating to (1) legal questions, (2) airways, (3) consular activities, (4) protocol, (5) economic services, and (6) press and informational, not to mention the usual interpreters, translators, and clerks.

Diplomatic Functions

A diplomatic mission sent abroad includes, in addition to the ambassador or minister at its head, secretaries, counselors, attachés, clerks, and special employees. Among the duties which it must perform is that of reporting back to the home state conditions which it has been able to observe relating to political, economic, and social developments. As some one has put it, a diplomat is the "eyes and ears" of his country abroad. It is also the duty of a diplomat, when so instructed, to negotiate with the representatives of other nations. There is, too, the somewhat nebulous task of developing friendly relations between his country and the one to which he has been sent; in performing this task, the diplomat is expected to explain his own country, its problems, policies, and aspirations. This clearly is an undertaking which must be pursued with tact and dignity or it will become offensive and result in injury to the diplomat's home government. During the cold war the activities of diplomatic missions have often been regarded as objectionable, and indeed charges of espionage have been made. For that reason, governments have often imposed on each other the obligation to reduce the size of diplomatic missions and to close designated consulates.

Diplomatic Personnel

The ranks of the heads of diplomatic missions were fixed by the Congress of Vienna in 1815.[1] Prior to that time there had been a great deal of controversy about matters of precedence, the order in which the representatives of states should be listed. At one time the Pope had assumed the right to decide the order, and it was not surprising that he placed himself first, with the Emperor second, his heir-apparent third, and then the kings of France, Spain, Aragon and Portugal, and Great Britain. Even the Pope's classification was a subject of controversy, for no king or diplomat liked to be listed in an unimpressive way. One of the points most frequently debated was the manner in which treaties should be signed, each nation coveting the honor of having its name first. The order of seating at conference tables, as well as at social events, was also looked upon as a matter of great moment.

By the rules of the Congress of Vienna it was determined that the diplomatic representatives at a given capital city should take rank according to the date of their arrival. At about the same time, the method of signing treaties by the "alternat" method was adopted; according to this arrangement, each party to a treaty

[1] See text of the agreement of 1815–1818 in Appendix ɪ of this chapter.

would take back to his country a copy of the treaty with his own name appearing first, and those of the other signatories following in alphabetical order. The ranks of diplomats, as fixed in 1815, were (1) ambassador and papal nuncio, (2) envoy extraordinary and minister plenipotentiary, (3) minister resident, (4) chargé d'affaires; these ranks are still in general acceptance today.

In theory, the ambassador was regarded as the personal representative of his sovereign monarch. For the reason that the United States was a republic and consequently could not fit itself into this theory, it refrained for a long time from using this rank. Always in an inferior position abroad, American diplomats registered complaints with the result that in 1893 the United States began using the rank of ambassador. At the present time the great majority of the American heads of missions are ambassadors.

The envoy extraordinary and minister plenipotentiary is a title which originated many years ago when special envoys with full powers were the custom; now the title is something of a misfit, for few are special and their full powers extend only to the signing of agreements. Minister resident is a title which is rarely used at the present time; generally there are not more than one or two in the diplomatic service of the United States at one time. The chargé d'affaires takes over a mission when the ambassador or minister is on leave; he is normally the next senior officer of the staff, either the first secretary or the counselor.

It has been explained that the heads of diplomatic missions, until the middle of the seventeenth century, usually held office for only short periods of time. Since then, the tendency has become prevalent to make diplomacy a lifelong vocation or career. At first the practice was common of employing aristocrats with plenty of time on their hands, and even yet that practice has not been completely given up, although the industrial aristocracy has tended to supplant the old titled group.

More recently, the diplomatic service has developed into a "career" in a different sense. The common practice of nations at the present time is to select the personnel of their foreign services, excepting heads of missions, by competitive examinations or by promotion from the lower grades. Often it is possible, although it is not necessary, to choose heads of missions by promotion from the permanent service. To make the career attractive and thus to retain in the service men of ability and experience, elaborate provisions are made for promotions, leaves, retirement, and other benefits to members of the foreign service.

Foreign Service of the United States

During recent years, the American foreign service—the diplomatic and consular personnel, together with clerks and alien employees—has comprised some 11,000 persons. Only about sixty-five of them are heads of diplomatic missions. Of the heads of missions, from 60 to 70 percent have been taken from the permanent career, the remainder being political appointees. The "core of the service," as Mr. Elmer Plischke calls it, is the career officer, now numbering slightly over 1000.[2] In addition there are approximately 100 reserve officers, 3200 staff officers, 20 consular agents, and 5500 alien employees.

By a long series of executive orders and Congressional enactments, the quality of the American foreign service has been greatly improved during recent decades. First among the series was the executive order issued by President Theodore Roosevelt in 1906 bringing the consular service within the merit system. This was followed by an order of 1909 over the signature of President Taft by which diplomatic officials, excepting heads of missions, were similarly treated. Congress carried the reform further, first by the law of 1915 placing the merit system for the foreign service on a statutory basis and making some changes in the grades and compensation of officers, and then in 1924 by a general overhauling of the system which united the diplomatic and consular branches into the "foreign service" of the United States, arranged leaves of absence and retirement allowances, and in other ways gave the work greater appeal as a career. Later statutes and orders have followed, most important of which is the law of 1946, which introduced many new features.

---

[2] E. Plischke, *Conduct of American Diplomacy*, p. 175.

Now the career officers of the service are all selected and promoted on the basis of merit. Under the Act of 1946 there are seven classes of such officers, all on an improved salary basis which ranges up to $13,500 at the top. The rules with respect to the assignment, transfer, promotion, and retirement of these officers are generally quite adequate. The Act of 1946 improved the salaries of chiefs of mission, the ambassadors and ministers (the first increase in many years), and it permits a man from the career service to become the head of mission without losing the advantages which he has earned. The Act also created two new types of employees: (1) reserve officers who have "outstanding qualifications of a specialized character," and (2) staff officers such as clerks, accountants, stenographers, guards, translators, and so on.

Language of Diplomacy

For many centuries the language of diplomacy was Latin, reflecting the fact that Latin was the language of erudition, commonly used in the Church and in published books such as Hugo Grotius' volume on *The Law of War and Peace*. Diplomatic conversations, notes, and treaties were all in the accepted language of the time. The treaties of Westphalia (1648) and the Anglo-Dutch Treaty of 1674, for instance, were written in Latin. With the emergence of the nation state and its greater stress upon its own tongue, the use of Latin became less universal; gradually French rose in prominence, so that by the eighteenth century that language was in general vogue in diplomacy. The rising power of France as a nation no doubt had much to do with this development. The precision of the French language commended itself to diplomats, for precision is always an essential quality of successful diplomacy; many are the tributes that have been paid to the accuracy of the French language by diplomats of the old school. The primacy of the language was not questioned until the Paris Peace Conference met in 1919. At the Congress of Vienna (1815), the Paris Congress (1856), and the Congress of Berlin (1878), proceedings were entirely in French. There were but few exceptions to the use of French diplomacy throughout the nineteenth century: the Catholic Church continued to show preference for Latin; German was employed by the German states; and English was found to be practicable in Anglo-American negotiations.

At the Paris Peace Conference of 1919, English moved into a position of equality with French. Prime Minister Lloyd George and President Wilson could not speak French, whereas Prime Minister Clemenceau of France was able to speak English; moreover, with two of the great powers from the English-speaking world, the case for their language was strong enough to merit the recognition which it got. When English and French were given equal status by the Covenant of the League of Nations, it was clear that the French monopoly had been forever broken.

At the San Francisco Conference of 1945, English and French were obliged to make way for other languages, although not altogether on a basis of equality. Spanish, Russian, and Chinese, along with the French and English, were all designated official languages of the conference, but French and English were made the working languages for the conference in order that translating and documentation might be kept at a minimum. The Charter produced by the conference was made "equally authentic" in all five languages. Finally, therefore, it is recognized that no one language shall have a monopoly.

In the International Court of Justice, as in the old Permanent Court of International Justice, English and French are the official languages; the Court may, however, authorize the use of language other than French or English. The Charter of the Organization of American States makes English, Spanish, French, and Portuguese all equally authentic.

According equal place to several languages is a convenient method of disposing of the problem presented by several competing tongues, but it does raise problems of meaning. Various words exist in every language for which there is no exact equivalent in others, or for some other reason the phrases employed by two or more languages in the same place will carry different connotations. When this occurs, we find two or more inconsistent, but authentic, meanings to an article or passage within a document. There were discrepancies in the English and French versions of Article 21 of the Covenant of the League of Nations, the former stronger in its recognition of the Monroe Doctrine than the latter. In the Mavrommatis case, decided by the Permanent Court of International Justice in 1923, the ruling was given that, where there are two or more language texts of an instrument and they are not identical in meaning, the most restricted interpretation, the one which can be regarded as most consistent with the others, shall be given recognition.

One of the most ingenious devices now in use for the solution of the problem of language in international organization is that of simultaneous translations provided in the United Nations. It is arranged that every delegate shall have on his desk a set of headphones by means of which speeches are relayed to him in his own tongue as they are being made. Expert interpreters, enclosed in soundproof booths, change the speeches from one language to another as those speeches are given, and so effective is their work that the listeners are able to have the advantage of the speakers' gestures and facial expressions.

Present Tendencies in Diplomacy

"The old diplomacy" and "the new diplomacy" are familiar terms, and they are commonly used to signify that there has been a definite break with the past in diplomatic practice. As Mr. Harold Nicolson has put it, "the implication is that somewhere about the year 1918, diplomacy saw a great white light, was converted, found salvation, and thereafter and thence forward became an entirely different woman."[3] This idea of a "new diplomacy" may, however, be exaggerated. While there are differences between present-day and earlier practices, they are by no means revolutionary in character. M. Jules Cambon, one of the ablest French diplomatists of this century, brought this out when he said that "to talk about new and old diplomacy is to make a distinction without a difference."

One of the changes which has come into diplomacy relates to matters of form. As diplomacy developed centuries ago, it gave great emphasis to the proprieties; there was a right way and a

---

[3] H. Nicolson, *Diplomacy*, 2nd ed., New York, 1950, pp. 56–57.

wrong way to do everything and any least departure from the strictly correct was reprehensible. For instance, the reception of a new ambassador or minister was the occasion of elaborately prescribed ceremony; court dress, too, was expected to meet rigid specifications. The United States, more than any nation, has contributed to the release of diplomacy from many of these forms. Benjamin Franklin at Paris, as a representative of a republic, insisted on dressing as he pleased and felt no obligation to offer any apology.

A similar change has come into the style of diplomatic communications. Formerly, diplomacy was always polite and proper; any aspersion cast by one nation on another would be by innuendo rather than in a forthright way. This polish and restraint would be used during controversy and even in crises, until diplomacy was ended and the guns began to boom. For instance, the Monroe Doctrine of 1823, although very direct and to the point, used the term "unfriendly disposition" to refer to a possible aggression of European powers in this hemisphere. Even yet, treaties between nations refer deferentially to the signatories as the "high contracting parties," no matter how much those nations may detest each other.

In recent years there has been a noticeable change in the manner in which nations address one another. Instead of the formality and polish of the past, there is today a frankness, even a brusqueness, which at times deteriorates into name-calling. An illustration of this is the warmongering accusations made by Soviet diplomats against American political leaders in the Assembly of the United Nations. Another illustration may be found in a communication from Ambassador Smith to the Russian Government in 1947, which opened with this statement: "During the year and a half that I have resided in the Soviet Union, I have been obliged, with the deepest regret, to witness in the Soviet press, an increasing flood of half-truths, distortions of truths, and utter falsehoods about my country and my government." In Russia, the Soviet press is virtually a part of the government and a remark of this character, however true it might have been, would never have been made a century, or even a few decades, ago. It is doubtful whether the change from indirection to bluntness has in any way been helpful. While in general there may be virtue in frankness, in diplomacy it is otherwise, for public utterances of high officials reach the people of the insulted government, who may be influenced to the point that the conduct of affairs becomes still more hazardous.

For a long time, diplomacy has had a bad reputation with regard to its ethical standards. There has seemed to be one standard for the individual in his relations with other individuals, and another standard for states and their spokesmen. The French author Calliéres, writing in 1716, expressed admiration for the diplomat who might be able, by his cunning, to stir up dissension within the country to which he was sent. Sir Henry Wotton wrote sardonically several centuries ago that "an ambassador is a person who is sent abroad to lie for the good of his country." The term "Machiavellian" is often applied to diplomacy in its more devious form, perhaps with some injustice to Machiavelli, whose ethical standards were after all on a par with those of his day.

While it would be too much to say that diplomacy has turned over a new leaf and is now circumspect, at least its standards of ethics have changed, if not improved. Today, diplomatic intrigue is without the conniving of the royal courts which at one time were at the center of diplomacy. Also, today, the ever-present foreign reporter whose business it is to ferret out all news and especially any with a bad odor acts as a kind of detective service that puts the diplomat on his guard, since he is more likely to be exposed than formerly. It is sometimes said that diplomacy is better today because it is more democratic. This statement requires elucidation, for even today diplomacy is far removed from the people. It is true that at one time diplomacy was carried on between absolute monarchs and that now, in the democracies at least, diplomats are responsible to public officials who, in turn, are responsible to the people; even yet, however, popular participation in the making of foreign policy is slight, and in the administration of that policy it is almost entirely lacking. There is now more popular interest by far in foreign affairs and more of a tendency to watch and criticize; this attention to diplomacy, whether or not it be regarded as a form of democratization, is wholesome. Implying an improvement in present-day methods of diplomacy over those of the past, someone has said that "a first-class diplomatist never lies, second-rate diplomatists do."

As diplomacy developed in early modern Europe, it was an affair of great secrecy. There were secret treaties, secret articles in treaties, and secret agents to spy out facts and information, while the diplomats themselves in whatever they were doing were far removed from the public view. This was the accepted thing. Mr. John Bright brought this out in his statement made in 1858 that "When you come to our foreign policy, you are no longer an Englishman —you are recommended not to inquire. If you do you are told you cannot understand it; you are snubbed, you are hustled aside. There is too great a mystery about it. We have what is called diplomacy." Lord Rosebery said in 1912 that "By far the greater portion is what takes place behind the scenes, and as we ordinary mortals are not admitted behind the scenes, our knowledge of foreign policy must be based mainly on speculation."

During World War I, for the first time, secret diplomacy came under severe criticism. It was referred to as the "evil spirit" of international politics. No one was more articulate in expressing this point of view than President Woodrow Wilson who, in the Fourteen Points of January 8, 1918, advocated that there should be "open covenants of peace, openly arrived at, after which there shall be no private international understandings of any kind."

There was a special reason why this antagonism to secret diplomacy should have reached a peak at this time, for during World War I there were a number of secret treaties made by the allied nations at war with Germany, dealing with the peace settlement that was to come. Those treaties turned out at the Paris Peace Conference to be a serious obstacle to the negotiation of a satisfactory settlement.

No doubt a good case can be made for open diplomacy. It may be pointed out that the people are closely affected by what diplomats do and for that reason have a right to know. It may be argued further that a fair conception of democracy implies, or should imply, that the people be taken into the confidence of the men responsible for foreign policies. These contentions present only one side of the case, however.

In discussions of the problem of open diplomacy a distinction should be made between treaties and agreements once they have been concluded and made binding, and the procedures by which those agreements are formed. It is one thing to say that the people should know, or be able to know, what has in fact happened, and it is another thing to require that diplomats work in glass houses. The fact of the matter is that diplomacy requires a great deal in the way of give-and-take compromises, without which stalemate would be inevitable. To demand that the public know what is going on when diplomats are negotiating could be catastrophic, for in open view they cannot bargain and compromise without being misunderstood and criticized. The public would consider a diplomat weak and incapable were it to hear him outline six points as the just claims of his government and then see him settle for three, and then only after he had given in to several demands laid down by the government with which he was dealing.

Because it is reasonable that the accomplishments of diplomacy be made public, the Covenant of the League of Nations required that members should send copies of every treaty and agreement which they made to the Secretariat for registration and publication. This requirement is now made of members of the United Nations in accordance with Article 102 of the Charter, which stipulates that "every treaty and international agreement entered into by any member of the United Nations after the present charter comes into force shall, as soon as possible, be registered with the Secretariat and published by it."[4] The Article goes on to assert that no party to an international agreement or treaty which has not been so registered may invoke that treaty or agreement before any of the organizations of the United Nations. As a result of the thirty-odd years of registering and publishing treaties, many volumes have been made available to the public.

During recent years there has been something of a tendency to

---

[4] See Appendix II to this chapter for regulations regarding the registration of treaties.

open to the public the processes of diplomacy as well as the results. This has been noticeable in general meetings and conferences rather than in bilateral diplomacy. The Security Council, although it is able to close its doors if it chooses, has, as a matter of practice, been open to the public almost all of the time, even when highly controversial problems have been under discussion; the results have not always been auspicious, and it may not be too much to say that more and better understandings on international problems might have been reached had the Council been removed from the public view. Moreover, the openness has enabled communist delegates in the Council to engage in propaganda on a large scale.

The Paris Peace Conference of 1946 was unusually open in its proceedings. When General Jan Christian Smuts, delegate from the Union of South Africa, criticized this openness in a speech given at Aberdeen, Scotland, soon after the conference, he referred to the "extreme publicity" at Paris as one of the greatest difficulties with which the conference had to contend. "Real business," he said, is "never done with open diplomacy." Continuing, he pointed out that "you shrewd business men in Aberdeen do not conduct your business with open diplomacy."

The lesson to be learned, so it would seem, from recent experiences with openness in the processes of diplomacy is that it acts as a serious deterrent to the achievement among nations of maximum coöperation. After all, it is the accomplishments which are of concern to the people. It is, as someone has said, like a dinner, in that the intricate preliminary processes in the kitchen do not need to be explained to the guests who eat the food, since they are concerned only with the products of the cooking that are placed upon the table. President Wilson's admonition that covenants be openly arrived at was not and could not be carried out in the Peace Conference of 1919; its sessions, except for daily communiqués and the plenary sessions, were closed.

Another tendency of recent diplomacy has been for heads of states to take over somewhat more than in the past. It has always been true that heads of states have been a position to deal directly with each other and in special cases they have done so. For instance, at the Congress of Vienna in 1815, there were prime ministers and kings in attendance, and at the Paris Peace Conference of 1919, there were prime ministers and presidents. The practice was carried further during World War II, when President Roosevelt and Prime Minister Churchill were in direct communication by telephone or in person on many occasions. The Big Three which added Generalissimo Stalin or Generalissimo Chiang enlarged upon the practice. Clearly, this kind of diplomacy must be regarded as a supplement to rather than a substitute for ordinary diplomacy. Diplomacy by heads of states is useful for emergency decisions of major importance, and it is an effective method of getting the attention of the public. It is not well fitted to deal with the run-of-the-mill problems constantly under treatment in the regular diplomatic channels.

A change of great importance that has been long under way in the processes of diplomacy is the development and improvement of multilateral procedures. Behind this tendency has been the constantly widening interests of nations which now have reached the point where almost every subject of international action is of concern to many countries instead of two. This multilateral diplomacy appeared first in the form of international conferences. During recent decades it has been greatly extended by the activities of permanent international organizations, especially the League of Nations and the United Nations.

In spite of all these changes in diplomacy, it remains, as always, a process whereby sovereign states negotiate and reach agreement. It is, as ever, carried out by the appointees of governments. When the agreements reached are in the form of treaties, they must now, as was true centuries ago, be properly ratified before they become operative.

APPENDIX TO CHAPTER XI

I

Agreement on Diplomatic Ranks (1815–1818)*

In order to prevent in the future the inconveniences which have frequently occurred, and which may still occur, from the claims of Precedence among the different Diplomatic characters, the Plenipotentiaries of the Powers who signed the Treaty of Paris have agreed in the following articles, and think it their duty to invite those of other Crowned Heads to adopt the same regulations:

ARTICLE 1

Diplomatic characters are divided into three classes:

That of Ambassadors, Legates, or Nuncios.

That of Envoys, Ministers, or other persons accredited to Sovereigns.

That of Chargés d'Affaires to Ministers for Foreign Affairs.

ARTICLE 2

Ambassadors, Legates, or Nuncios only shall have the representative character.

ARTICLE 3

Diplomatic characters charged with any special mission shall not, on that account, assume any superiority of rank.

ARTICLE 4

Diplomatic characters shall rank in their respective classes according to the date of the official notification of their arrival.

The present regulation shall not occasion any change respecting the Representative of the Pope.

ARTICLE 5

There shall be a regular form adopted by each State for the reception of Diplomatic characters of every class.

---

* Regulations of Vienna, 1815, and of Aix-la-Chapelle, 1818, concerning Diplomatic Rank, *United States Diplomatic Instructions*, 1897, paragraph 18.

ARTICLE 6

Ties of consanguinity or family alliance between Courts confer no rank on their Diplomatic Agents. The same rule applies to political alliances.

ARTICLE 7

In Acts or Treaties between several Powers that admit alternity, the order which is to be observed in the signatures of Ministers shall be decided by lot.

ARTICLE 8

It is agreed between the Five Courts that Ministers Resident accredited to them shall form, with respect to their Precedence, an intermediate class between Ministers of the Second Class and Chargé d'Affaires.

II

Registration of Treaties and Agreements by the United Nations Secretariat*

1. Registration

ARTICLE 1

1. Every treaty or international agreement whatever its form and descriptive name entered into by one or more Members of the United Nations after 24 October 1945, the date of the coming into force of the Charter, shall as soon as possible be registered with the Secretariat in accordance with these regulations.

2. Registration shall not take place until the treaty or international agreement has come into force between two or more of the parties thereto.

3. Such registration may be effected by any party or in accordance with Article 4 of these regulations.

---

* *General Assembly, First Session, Text of Debates,* January 15, 1947, Journal no. 75; Supplement A-64. Add. 1. pp. 946–9.

4. The Secretariat shall record the treaties and international agreements so registered in a Register established for that purpose.

ARTICLE 2

1. When a treaty or international agreement has been registered with the Secretariat, a certified statement regarding any subsequent action which effects a change in the parties thereto, or the terms, scope or application thereof, shall also be registered with the Secretariat.

2. The Secretariat shall record the certified statement so registered in the Register established under Article 1 of these regulations.

ARTICLE 3

1. Registration by a party, in accordance with Article 1 of these regulations, relieves all other parties of the obligation to register.

2. Registration effected in accordance with Article 4 of these regulations relieves all parties of the obligation to register.

ARTICLE 4

1. Every treaty or international agreement subject to Article 1 of these regulations shall be registered *ex officio* by the United Nations in the following cases:

   a. Where the United Nations is a party to the treaty or agreement;

   b. Where the United Nations has been authorized by the treaty or agreement to effect registration.

2. A treaty or international agreement subject to Article 1 of these regulations may be registered with the Secretariat by a specialized agency in the following cases:

   a. Where the constituent instrument of the specialized agency provides for such registration;

   b. Where the treaty or agreement has been registered with the specialized agency pursuant to the terms of its constituent instrument;

c. Where the specialized agency has been authorized by the treaty or agreement to effect registration.

ARTICLE 5

A party or specialized agency, registering a treaty or international agreement under Article 1 or 4 of these regulations, shall certify that the text is a true and complete copy thereof and includes all reservations made by parties thereto.

The certified copy shall reproduce the text in all the languages in which the treaty or agreement was concluded and shall be accompanied by two additional copies and by a statement setting forth, in respect of each party:

a. the date on which the treaty or agreement has come into force;
b. the method whereby it has come into force (for example: by signature, by ratification or acceptance, by accession, et cetera).

ARTICLE 6

The date of receipt by the Secretariat of the United Nations of the treaty or international agreement registered shall be deemed to be the date of registration, provided that the date of registration of a treaty or agreement registered *ex officio* by the United Nations shall be the date on which the treaty or agreement first came into force between two or more of the parties thereto.

ARTICLE 7

A certificate of registration signed by the Secretary-General or his representative shall be issued to the registering party or agency and also to all signatories and parties to the treaty or international agreement registered.

ARTICLE 8

1. The Register shall be kept in the five official languages of the United Nations. The Register shall comprise, in respect of each treaty or international agreement, a record of:

a. the serial number given in the order of registration;
b. the title given to the instrument by the parties;
c. the names of the parties between whom it was concluded;
d. the dates of signature, ratification or acceptance, exchange or ratifications, accession, and entry into force;
e. the duration;
f. the language or languages in which it was drawn up;
g. the name of the party or specialized agency which registers the instrument and the date of such registration;
h. particulars of publication in the treaty series of the United Nations.

2. Such information shall also be included in the Register in regard to the statements registered under Article 2 of these regulations.

3. The texts registered shall be marked 'ne varietur' by the Secretary-General or his representative, and shall remain in the custody of the Secretariat.

2. Filing and Recording
ARTICLE 10

The Secretariat shall file and record treaties and international agreements, other than those subject to registration under Article 1 of these regulations, if they fall in the following categories:

a. Treaties or international agreements entered into by the United Nations or by one or more of the specialized agencies;
b. Treaties or international agreements transmitted by a Member of the United Nations which were entered into before the coming into force of the Charter, but which were not included in the treaty series of the League of Nations;
c. Treaties or international agreements transmitted by a party not a Member of the United Nations which were entered into before or after the coming into force of the Charter which were not included in the treaty series of the League of Nations, provided, however, that this paragraph shall be applied with full regard to the provisions of the resolution of the General As-

sembly of 10 February 1946 set forth in the Annex of these regulations.

ARTICLE 11

The provisions of Articles 2, 5, and 8 of these regulations shall apply, *mutatis mutandis,* to all treaties and international agreements filed and recorded under Article 10 of these regulations.

3. Publication
ARTICLE 12

1. The Secretariat shall publish as soon as possible in a single series every treaty or international agreement which is registered, or filed and recorded, in the original language or languages, followed by a translation in English and in French. The certified statements referred to in Article 2 of these regulations shall be published in the same manner. . . .

XII Independent Conferences

IN THE LITERAL SENSE OF THE TERM, THERE IS AN "INTERnational conference" when the representatives of two or more states sit together discussing a common problem. The usual practice, however, is not to refer to a meeting of the regular diplomats of only two states as a "conference," but to look upon it rather as ordinary bilateral diplomacy. On the other hand, meetings of the heads of state or of special envoys of two nations, as distinguished from regular diplomats, have often been labeled "conferences"; the Churchill-Roosevelt Conference out on the Atlantic Ocean (August, 1941) and the Attlee-Truman Conference in Washington (December, 1950) are instances in point.[1] The term has often been used for three-power meetings, such as the Yalta Conference and the Potsdam Conference, both held in 1945. The "international" part of the term seems more significant when, as is often the case, there are thirty, forty, or even more nations in attendance, as at the San Francisco Conference of 1945, where fifty nations took part in the drafting of the United Nations Charter.

Widely varying types of gatherings are commonly designated international conferences. The term is used to refer to purely private meetings of an international character, such as those of church groups, labor unions, and associations of educators. There are also

---

[1] Other two-power meetings usually called "conferences" include: United States–Canadian Joint Defense Conference, August, 1940; United States–Canadian Conference on Coördinating War Production, April, 1941; United States–United Kingdom Conference at Casablanca on unconditional surrender, January, 1943; United States–United Kingdom Military Conference, Quebec, September, 1944.

semipublic gatherings, in which governments take part along with private groups, by helping to organize the meetings, paying some or all of the expenses, or sending government delegates. The Pan-American Scientific Congresses of the past have been supported by government funds and attended by government delegates sitting alongside unofficial delegates. A meeting of the International Association to Combat Unemployment which was held several decades ago included "eight governments, seventeen national official bodies, two federations of towns, fifty-nine towns, eight provinces, twelve *fonds de chômage,* three international associations, fifteen scientific societies, six national federations of employers, three professional federations, four local federations, thirty labor federations, and individuals belonging to twenty-three different countries."[2] It is the public conference with which international organization is primarily concerned—conferences called by governments, attended entirely by official delegates, financed by governments, and set to work upon a project of interest to governments.

Looking back into the past, we note that some international gatherings have been referred to as "congresses" (Congress of Westphalia, 1648; Congress of Vienna, 1815; and the Congress of Berlin, 1878), while others have been designated "conferences" (Conference on Affairs of The Netherlands, 1830; the Hague Conference, 1899; and the Paris Peace Conference, 1919). The distinction long maintained between "congress" and "conference" was that the former was attended by national sovereigns or their principal ministers, whereas the latter was made up of officials of lesser rank. That distinction, however, is no longer regarded as worth preserving, and today the practice is general of labeling all gatherings "conferences," regardless of the rank or importance of the delegates. For instance, the Paris Peace Conference of 1919 was attended by one president and by the prime ministers of many states.

Types of Conferences

Several classifications of public international influences are possible. A distinction may be made between the peace conference at the end

---

[2] L. S. Wolff, *International Government,* New York, 1916, p. 170.

of a war to write the terms of a peace settlement (e.g., Paris Peace Conference, 1919) and the conference held in time of peace to deal with a matter of common interest (e.g., the London Naval Conference of 1935). The report of the Committee of Experts appointed by the League of Nations for the progressive codification of international law distinguished between "political and non-political conferences (administrative, economic, social, etc.)";[3] this classification, based on subject matter, is a natural one but not particularly helpful when it comes to questions of conference organization; and besides, whatever line may be drawn between political and nonpolitical subjects is bound to be somewhat hazy, even more so in international matters than in national. Another distinction was made by the Report between "legislative" and "bargaining" conferences, or, as the Report states it, between "conferences on international conventional law (codification conferences) and special conferences (conferences settling particular relations between the contracting states)." A third classification of the Report was that of "diplomatic" versus "technical" conferences, the former attended by diplomatic officials and the latter by technical experts.

A primary purpose of the League Committee of Experts in classifying conferences was to find some clues to the proper methods of organizing various types of meetings. Clearly, legislative and bargaining conferences would have to be put together along very different lines. Peace conferences and conferences in time of peace have always been quite unlike in organization and procedure. The Committee did not attempt to proceed from their classifications to the formulation of a law of conference procedure; several governments commenting upon the Report indicated their opposition to an effort to codify the law of conference organization and procedure.

It is possible, too, to differentiate between conferences which produce formal treaties, conventions, and recommendations and those which are consultative in nature. The latter are not always labeled "conference" for the reason that they are designed only to provide

[3] The report may be found in Supplement to the *American Journal of International Law*, vol. 20 (1926).

an opportunity for an exchange of information or points of view, and whatever action may be taken is in the nature of advice or informal agreement. They are, however, like conferences of the traditional type in that they are deliberative and are composed of the delegates of the participating states. This consultative function is carried on in permanent as well as *ad hoc* agencies. Much of the work of such bodies as the Security Council and the General Assembly is consultative in nature. There are also bodies which are entirely consultative in their purpose.

One of the most useful classifications of conferences is that of the independent conference as against that which is initiated, arranged, and managed by a permanent international organization. Up until a few decades ago, nearly every conference was independent of any permanent organization and was therefore the handiwork of some one or more states which considered a meeting desirable and took the initiative in its calling and management. Peace conferences have always been of this type, and in fact they were the first independent gatherings; later, as has been pointed out elsewhere, independent peacetime conferences became common.

With the establishment of permanent international organs—public unions, the Organization of American States, the League of Nations, and the United Nations—frequent meetings of all kinds within their structure became the rule. These conferences within permanent organizations have been called and organized in a manner quite different from that used for independent conferences. For that reason, the remainder of this chapter will deal primarily with the older type, the independent conference; the next two chapters will take up conferences which are related to permanent organizations.

Conferences and Conferences

Lists of international conferences that have been compiled all tell the same story, that the conference method has been given more and more application in diplomacy; for many years now it has been widely recognized as a means of multilateral action. A record drawn up by Mr. Simeon E. Baldwin for the period from 1826 to 1907 contained more than three hundred conferences, including private as well as public gatherings.[4] Best known among the public conferences from 1815 to 1913 are the following:

> Vienna, 1814–1815, to finish the terms of the peace settlement after the defeat of Napoleon
> Panama, 1826, American States, first meeting
> London, 1827–1832, Greek affairs
> London, 1830–1833, Belgian affairs
> Paris, 1856, Peace at the end of Crimean War
> Geneva, 1864, International law regarding sick and wounded soldiers
> Petersburg, 1868, Explosive bullets in war
> Geneva, 1868, International law, sick and wounded soldiers
> Berlin, 1878, Balkan affairs
> Berlin, 1884–1885, African problems
> The Hague, 1889, International law and peace
> Geneva, 1906, Revise Convention of 1864
> Algeciras, 1906, Morocco
> The Hague, 1907, International law and peace
> London, 1910, Naval affairs
> London, 1913, Balkan affairs

Clearly the treaties and conventions concluded at those conferences did much to determine the course of history, fixing boundaries, defining international law, and settling disputes of major proportions.

A strong boost was given the conference method during World War I when the Allies against Germany discovered the advantages to be gained in fighting a common enemy from getting together frequently around a table and talking over the problems that might arise. Starting with meetings of prime ministers or their alternates, this method of collaboration finally produced the Supreme War Council, which made decisions concerning munitions, food, raw materials, transportation, and military and naval strategy. In 1920, Sir Maurice Hankey, who had attended several hundred meetings himself in behalf of the British Government, prophesied that "diplomacy by conference has come to stay."

---

[4] S. E. Baldwin, "International Congresses and Conferences of the Last Century as Forces Working Toward the Solidarity of the World," *American Journal of International Law*, 1907, vol. I, Appendix, pp. 808–829.

The Paris Peace Conference of 1919 was itself one of the great landmarks in the development of diplomacy by conference, dealing with international problems on a world-wide basis and drafting the Covenant of the League of Nations and the Constitution of the International Labor Organization. Soon after it terminated its work, the self-constituted Council of Ambassadors came into being to cope with pressing postwar problems; between 1920 and 1925 this organization alone had approximately three hundred meetings.[5] Between 1920 and 1935 five disarmament conferences were held: Washington, 1921–1922; Geneva, 1927; London, 1930; Geneva, 1932–1935; and London, 1935. A large number of conferences were called to handle economic problems, including the Brussels Conference (1920), the Economic Conference at Riga (1921), the Belgrade Conference (1922), the Genoa Conference (1922), the Geneva Conference (1927), the London Conference (1933). In the 1920's and 1930's more conferences were held, by far, than during the entire preceding century. There were Inter-American conferences, League of Nations conferences, conferences of the International Labor Organization, and many independent conferences. They dealt with passports, health, security, international law, opium, emigration, air transport, double taxation, refugees, trade restrictions, statistics, arbitration, conciliation, reparations, and scores of other problems. By this time the conference method had been taken over by permanent international organizations—the League of Nations, in particular—and the majority of gatherings were called and managed by those organizations.

During World War II, the Allies against the Axis, following the practice established during World War I, met often. Shortly after Pearl Harbor, Mr. Churchill, Mr. Litvinov, Mr. Soong, and Mr. Roosevelt met in Washington and issued the famous United Nations Declaration, signed on January 1, 1942. From that time on, there were occasional meetings of the heads of state or their foreign ministers: Casablanca (January, 1943); Quebec (August, 1943); Moscow (October, 1943); Cairo and Teheran (November, 1943); Quebec (September, 1944); Yalta (February, 1945); and Potsdam

---

[5] E. Plischke, *Conduct of American Diplomacy,* New York, 1950, p. 352.

(July–August, 1945). In addition, several boards and agencies were set up, such as the Combined Civil Affairs Committee and the Munitions Assignment Board, which held frequent meetings. During the war several large-scale United Nations conferences convened, looking forward to postwar coöperation: the Food Conference at Hot Springs, Virginia (1943); the Relief Conference at Atlantic City (1943); the Bretton Woods Conference (1944); and the Civil Aviation Conference at Chicago (1944).

Since the war, the conference method has continued to be employed both in and out of permanent international organizations, but with the organization conference tending to cover a wider range of activities and the independent gathering a constantly shrinking area. The general and special meetings of UNESCO, ICAO, and the other specialized agencies have taken over fields which were once the domain of the independent conference. Among independent conferences of the past few years the following have been preëminent: the San Francisco Conference (1945), the Paris Peace Conference (1946), and the many meetings of the foreign ministers of the great powers to work out peace treaties.

Organization and Procedure

For the most part, conferences unrelated to permanent organizations have been a law unto themselves, free to organize and work very much as they or their sponsors please. Their principal limitation is mere tradition; certain ways of doing things, which in general have been found useful and acceptable, have been followed for so long that departures from them are difficult to make. An example of this is the custom that the presiding officer shall be the chief delegate of the host state. Some of the traditions have no other basis than long-continued practice, but others are founded upon the nature of the state and its participation in international relations, particularly on its claim to a sovereign status. From this fact derives the rule that a state cannot be bound by the majority against its will, and therefore, in the absence of an agreement to the contrary, the rule of unanimity prevails; agreements to the contrary, however, are not uncommon. The purpose of a conference, too, will have something to do with its methods. A peace conference of major proportions will inevitably involve a large measure of control by the victors, with the vanquished either absent or relegated to an ignominious position; and usually the more powerful states among the victors will dominate to an even greater extent than the smaller nations. A lawmaking conference, as distinguished from a bargaining conference, requires wider representation and will be more open in its proceedings.

The most characteristic feature of the organization and procedure of conferences unrelated to permanent organizations is the prominent role played by the sponsoring state or states. This shows up at the very beginning, for the state or states which conceive the idea of holding a conference take the initiative in making the preliminary arrangements for the meeting. It is probable that the initiating state or states will have a special interest in the problems which will be up for discussion; the project for a meeting at Berlin in 1884–1885 for the discussion of African problems, for example, quite naturally developed in the diplomatic correspondence of France and Germany, two of the nations most involved. There are times, however, when a disinterested nation is best fitted to put the machinery of conference into gear, and this is particularly true when the subject to be taken up has caused such a degree of rivalry that the most interested parties would be disposed to suspect each other, as in the case of a peace conference to end a war between two or more nations. President Theodore Roosevelt successfully proposed the conference which met at Algeciras in 1906 to deal with Franco-German rivalry in Morocco, and it was he who one year later got Russia and Japan to send their representatives to Portsmouth, thus bringing to an end the Russo-Japanese War of 1904–1905. There have been times, too, when a nation without any special motive of self-interest and without an advantageous neutral position has proposed a conference to advance international coöperation on a wide basis for the benefit of the world at large; Russia, under Czar Alexander II, was responsible in large measure for the conference at St. Petersburg in 1868 to humanize war, and also for the Brussels Conference of 1874 to deal with the law of land warfare. His successor, Nicholas II, was the inspiring genius behind the calling of the First Hague Conference of 1899, which adopted several conventions on the international law of war and one of great importance on the pacific settlement of disputes.

The sponsoring state or states normally begin their work of calling a conference by feeling out the attitude of other states, inquiring through ordinary diplomatic channels whether there is sufficient interest in the project to go ahead with it. If a sponsoring state finds sufficient interest, it will no doubt proceed to make the necessary preliminary arrangements. There are at least four important tasks to be performed. First, a decision must be taken as to the city in which the meeting shall be held, and once that is settled, arrangemus be made for a meeting place and for housing facilities. Commonly in the past a conference has met in a city of the sponsoring nation, or if there are several sponsors, in a city of some one of them. The disarmament conference proposed by the United States soon after World War I quite properly met in Washington, D.C. in 1921–1922, and has become popularly known as the Washington Disarmament Conference. The conference which wrote the Charter of the United Nations was sponsored by four nations—the United States, Russia, Great Britain, and China—and it convened in San Francisco. Exceptions to the rule have not been infrequent, however, for the Russian-initiated conference of 1899, already referred to, met at The Hague, and the conference of the high representatives of Russia, the United States, Great Britain, and China in 1943 met at Teheran, Iran.

The second task of the sponsoring power or powers is to decide what nations shall be invited to participate and to issue invitations to those whose presence is desired. This is a delicate undertaking for the reason that uninvited states may be offended, and the absence of an interested power can reduce the accomplishments of a conference to small significance. Viewed in the large, conferences of recent decades have been more inclusive in membership than those of the nineteenth century. The First Hague Conference of 1899, with twenty-six delegations in attendance, was the largest body of its type up to that time, and the Second Hague Conference of

1907, with forty-five delegations, set a new record. Fifty-nine states attended the International Emigration Conference at Rome in 1924, and twenty-eight were at the Genoa Conference of 1922; it has already been pointed out that the San Francisco Conference of 1945 included delegates from fifty states. These figures indicate the distinctly multilateral character which diplomacy by conference can attain. This fact would be all the more striking were conferences held under the auspices of the League of Nations and the United Nations taken into account, for they have often contained fifty or more delegations.

A third task to be performed in preparation for an independent conference is the formulation of the agenda, at least provisionally. This, too, is an undertaking requiring the exercise of caution, for nations want to know what is to be discussed before they agree to participate. As the Duke of Argyll wrote many years ago, "It is reasonable too, as it must always be, not to go into congress without some previous understanding with the powers to be assembled there." The importance of an agreement as to the subjects to be discussed was brought out at the Conference on Central American Affairs, held in Washington in 1923. When an attempt was made there to bring up a subject which had not been agreed upon in the agenda, Secretary of State Charles Evans Hughes, chairman, made the following explanatory remark: "It is usual when a conference is called to interchange some views as to what is to be discussed, because no power desires,—and I am not now speaking of the Central American powers especially—no power wishes to be put in a position where it will be compelled to discuss something that it does not want to discuss." Secretary Hughes ruled on that occasion that no new subject could be brought before the gathering without the unanimous consent of all participating states; contrary to the suggestion of one delegate, it was not allowed that the United States, which had formulated the original program and included it in the invitations, might arbitrarily add to the list of subjects to be discussed.

No set rule has been established as to the procedure by which the agenda shall be agreed upon. In some instances the questions to be taken up are stated in the invitations, while in others they have been made the subject of diplomatic negotiation before the conference. The form of the agenda, too, is not a matter of fixed rule, ranging all the way from a formal document with itemized topics and subtopics to a brief statement of purposes contained in the invitations or in the diplomatic exchanges which have preceded the meeting.

A fourth task to be accomplished in advance of a conference is the preparation of preliminary drafts and studies which will be helpful to the conferees. For independent conferences which have no relation to the United Nations or any other permanent organization, the bulk of this work is done separately by the participating governments. For instance, a number of the delegates in attendance at the Paris Peace Conference of 1919 took with them drafts of a covenant for a league of nations which had been worked out by one or more persons holding responsible governmental positions. Some independent conferences have, however, found ways of setting an international group of experts to work on preliminary drafts and studies. Before the Locarno Conference of 1925 opened its meetings, the participating states of western Europe had a body of jurists get together in London to examine the problems to come before the conference from a technical point of view and to prepare draft texts.

All of these preliminary operations are vital and their proper performance is a necessary condition to the successful functioning of a conference. Many a conference has been doomed to failure by inadequate preparation—by including on the agenda subjects which more careful exploratory exchanges of views would have shown to be beyond agreement, by excluding states whose presence would be essential to success, or by neglecting to make adequate preliminary studies and drafts.

The extent of the organization of a conference depends primarily on its size; small meetings of only three or four countries, such as the Yalta and Teheran conferences, do not need so much in the way of formal organization and rules as do large meetings with a hundred or more delegates, alternates, and experts. In any case, the initiative in the organization of a gathering is the prerogative of the state on whose territory it is to take place. An unwritten rule exists that the first session shall be opened by a high official of the country on whose soil the conference has met, usually by the minister of foreign affairs; in sizable meetings it is customary for this official to deliver a speech attempting to keynote the conference.

The usual method of organizing a conference is through the adoption of a code of rules; as President Nelidow of the Second Hague Conference of 1907 pointed out, it is the most efficacious plan when a meeting includes a considerable number of delegates. Even small conferences have sometimes made use of this system. The sponsoring state is expected to have prepared a draft of rules ready to submit for approval soon after the conference opens. Generally, the rules of a gathering are not complex or lengthy, but they must cover such items as the presidency, the committees, methods of publicity, records, official languages, the secretariat, the definition of a quorum, and the credentials of delegates.

One of the first items of business under the rules of the usual independent conference is the election of a permanent chairman. Tradition dictates that the chairman of the delegation of the host state be selected; as Lord Balfour once stated, "There is a well-understood rule, practiced so far as I know universally, that the nation which invites the conference should also provide it with its chairman and presiding genius."

The work of a conference is done officially in plenary sessions and in committees, although it is inevitable that much will be accomplished informally in the lounges and the dining rooms during the course of casual conversations. The plenary sessions, in addition to providing a showy spectacle, are the means of giving formal approval to projects which have been formulated elsewhere—to the conference rules of organization and to the decisions which have been taken in committees. Nowadays they are commonly open to the public.

The actual negotiating—the diplomatic discussions with the customary give-and-take that usually precedes agreements—goes on in the committees, subcommittees, and the private discussions of the delegates. In a typical conference, wide use is made of committees, the most conspicuous being the agenda committees among whom the items on the agenda are divided for consideration; subcommittees of these agenda committees are not uncommon. Other types of committees—steering committees, executive committees, drafting committees, etc.—are often set up by conferences. A chart of a typical conference at which the United States is the host nation will be found in the Appendix to this chapter.

There are many matters of routine in a conference which would absorb the time of the delegates unduly were it not for a coterie of officials who give these details their full time. Most of these officials are members of the conference secretariat, generally provided for in the rules. Chief among them is the secretary-general, and here again is a point at which the inviting state figures conspicuously, for the custom is to select for this post a national of that state, often after informal consultations with the heads of the various delegations in which approval of the nominee has been given.

The Work of a Conference

The nature of the action taken by a conference will necessarily depend upon its purposes. If its job is to prepare a preliminary draft of a document to be taken under consideration at a later meeting, then the results of its deliberation will quite naturally be in the nature of a tentative draft; the Dumbarton Oaks Conference of 1944 worked out tentative proposals to be made public and then to become the basis for the meeting at San Francisco in 1945.

When a conference has been given the task of formulating the constitution of an international organization, it gives the document which it negotiates the status of a treaty. The Covenant of the League of Nations, negotiated at the Paris Peace Conference of 1919, was Part I of the Treaty of Versailles, and of the other peace treaties. The Charter of the United Nations is in the nature of a treaty, and as such required ratification by the original members. The constitutions of the specialized agencies of the United Nations are the equivalent of treaties and were negotiated at international conferences; the constitutions of the International Bank and the International Fund, for instance, are in the form of treaties negotiated at the Bretton Woods Conference (1944).

Conferences on international law also put out their work in the form of treaties, although they may be designated technically as "declarations" or "conventions." The London Naval Conference of 1908–1909 produced the Declaration of London on the law of war at sea; the Hague Conferences of 1899 and 1907 produced several conventions relating to the conduct of war and neutrality.

The two forms most commonly given to the work of international conferences are treaties and resolutions. The former, upon ratification, become binding in law upon the signatories. The latter may be mere expressions of opinion or they may be recommendations to the participating states for action of some kind, usually the enactment of statutes. Basic to both of those forms of conference action is the principle that a sovereign state may not become obligated against its will.

The practice is common for a conference to compile the various treaties and recommendations adopted into one complete document known as the Final Act, *Acte Général,* or *Protocole Finale.* In it is a summary of the accomplishments of the conference, and to it is appended each of the separate acts.

When a meeting is essentially consultative in nature, its results are bound to be quite informal. Perhaps they will consist of informal agreements to do certain things or to coördinate policies along stated lines. The Potsdam Agreement of 1945, looking forward to a new peace settlement, was an executive agreement. The United Nations Declaration of January 1, 1942, made after a four-power meeting in Washington, was also an executive agreement, pledging the parties to employ their respective resources against the enemy and not to make peace separately. A consultative meeting may adopt resolutions expressing points of view or suggesting a certain action to an organization or to governments; the Caribbean Commission functions in this manner. Conceivably, the consultation may have been for the purpose of exchanging views and information, so that nothing in the way of a positive program will come out of the meeting. On occasions, too, consultation has led to an investigation or a study presumed to be of value to the participating governments.

National Delegations

In most respects the nations participating in a conference are free to use their own discretion in selecting and organizing their respective delegations. Occasionally, the number of official delegates that a nation may send is fixed beforehand, as at the Paris Peace Conference (1919), where the great powers were allowed five each, whereas the smaller nations were, by the rules, allowed from one to three. When no assigned number of delegates is made, there is much variation in the size of national delegations. The delegations at San Francisco, for instance, varied from one to fourteen. Regardless of the number of delegates, the general rule is one vote for each delegation. The chief advantage to be derived from a large delegation is that a nation will have available more men for committee appointments.

There is a chairman for each delegation, who in important conferences is likely to be the foreign minister. On several occasions a president or prime minister has assumed the role, as at the Paris Peace Conference of 1919. In addition to the regular delegates, alternates are sometimes appointed. The delegation will inevitably include nowadays a long list of experts and advisers, besides officials to deal with the press, a secretary-general, and a staff to be in charge of documents, transportation, housing, equipment, and so on. Translators, interpreters, stenographers, and clerks are also needed. All in all, a national delegation to a conference is a sizable and highly organized unit.

The Peace Conference

There have been more than a score of important peace conferences since the famous Congress of Westphalia (1648) ushered in our modern era of international relations, besides many scores of minor ones. Although these meetings have provided the world community with a great deal of experience in peacemaking, experimentation with new methods continues. Even yet, the admission must be made that the task of procuring satisfactory peace settlements after wars is an unsolved problem. Whether the problem can be solved by any procedural device is doubtful, for the difficulties arise out of the nature of war, especially the destructive wars of our day in which total conflict and wholesale destruction inflame the millions of participating people to the point that the peace is written less by in-

telligence than by passions and prejudices. As the Italian Professor
Ferrero expressed it some years ago, "The war of exhaustion is a
false and illegitimate form of war because it makes peace impossible
or difficult to attain.[6] Certainly it would be asking a great deal of
organization and procedure to make a quick transition from the
anarchy of modern war to the stability and confidence of an enduring peace.

Peacemaking after a major war is almost certain to proceed
slowly. The diplomats who met at Münster and Osnabrück after the
Thirty Years War took about three years to write the Treaty of
Westphalia (1648). So much time was consumed debating problems
of precedence that, although it was scheduled to open in 1642, the
conference did not start to work until 1645; even then, to placate
the sensitive feelings of both France and Sweden, it was found necessary to hold the conference in two cities, with the French delegates given precedence in one place and the Swedish in the other.
It took the conferences at Paris and Vienna (1814–1815) about a
year and a half to undo the work of Napoleon. At the end of World
War I, the Paris Peace Conference assembled on January 18, 1919,
and adjourned on December 9, but the heaviest part of the work
was done in less than six months. Six years after the cessation of
hostilities treaties of peace following World War II had not yet been
made with Germany or Austria. In September, 1951, a peace treaty
with Japan was formulated and signed, over the strong opposition of
Russia.

So far as organization and procedure are concerned, peace conferences since 1648 have undergone great changes, at least some of
which would seem to the casual observer to represent progress. The
Congress of Westphalia held no sessions of any kind; it employed
no committees and did no voting. In those days, negotiating was
considered incomplete unless in written form, and therefore notes
were dispatched back and forth by the diplomats at Münster,
through the mediatory efforts of the Pope and the Republic of Venice. As Mr. David Jayne Hill has described the conference at Mün-
and Osnabrück, "There was nothing in its mode of discussing the

---

[6] Guglielmo Ferrero, *Peace and War*, London, 1933, tr. by Bertha Pritchard, p. 112.

questions before it to distinguish its business from ordinary diplomatic negotiations except the proximity of the negotiators, their occupation of a neutralized area, and at Münster the presence of mediators."[7]

The Congress of Vienna (1815) was probably the first great peace conference to arouse much in the way of popular interest. An Austrian delegate wrote about the "universal expectation" and the hopes for the "return of the golden age" which preceded the Congress. When it met, the Congress turned out to be a gala affair; said Prince de Ligne, "This Congress does not march, it dances," and indeed he was right, for the kings, princes, and ministers, with their ladies, spent most of their time attending banquets and balls. Prince de Ligne complained that he wore out his hat tipping it so often to the famous ladies present.

As Professor F. S. Dunn has brought out, one of the most significant developments at the Congress of Vienna insofar as organization and procedure is concerned was the debate over the nature of the gathering, some holding that it "was something more than a collection of negotiators," that in fact is was a "kind of universal assembly acting in behalf of Europe as a single community."[8] The issue was decided in favor of the view that it was only a collection of negotiators, but quoting Professor Dunn again, the fact that the question could have been seriously discussed "marked a serious departure from the traditional conception of the conduct of international relations."

In its organization and methods the Congress of Vienna moved several steps ahead of the Congress of Westphalia. Although there were no full sessions, direct personal discussions did occur and several committees were employed. From beginning to end, the gathering was dominated by the great powers, with unofficial meetings of the "four" (Prussia, Russia, Austria, and England), the "five" (adding France), and the "eight" (adding Portugal, Sweden, and Spain). The committees were committees of the "four," "five," or

---

[7] David Jayne Hill, *History of European Diplomacy*, New York, 1905–1914, vol. 2, p. 597.

[8] F. S. Dunn, *The Practice and Procedure of International Conferences*, Baltimore, 1949, p. 55.

"eight," and the three unofficial groups met frequently to take up the problems confronting them. The presence and participation of France, the defeated enemy, along with the other great powers, was a noteworthy fact in contrast to peacemaking after World War I and World War II, when the enemy was excluded from negotiations.

The Paris Peace Conference of 1919 was less gay than the Vienna Congress and there were no kings in attendance, but there was one president, along with several eminent prime ministers, foreign ministers, and high-ranking diplomats. More than any preceding peace conference, the Paris assemblage had on hand a vast supply of data on problems under discussion, and it used experts to an unprecedented extent. The principles of settlement relied upon in 1919— self-determination, economic welfare, and historical background— required a great deal of ready information. Most of it was furnished by the participating delegations, but some was supplied by conference agencies. Literally tons of information were made available.

Although plenary sessions were used at Paris in 1919, they were devoted primarily to the formalities, and much of the work was done in committee. There were committees to deal with territorial claims, with the formulation of the Covenant of the League of Nations, with labor, with the disarmament of Germany and a multitude of other problems. Important decisions, however, always came back to the great powers which dominated the conference throughout—the United States, Great Britain, France, Italy, and Japan; at times, with the delegates of Japan or Italy, or both, absent, the big three were all powerful.

At the end of World War II, something new in the way of peacemaking machinery was attempted, at least insofar as form was concerned. The procedure was worked out at the Potsdam meeting in August, 1945, and therefore was in its origin a great-power project of which Generalissimo Stalin, President Truman, and Prime Minister Attlee were the architects. In substance, the plan was that a Council of Foreign Ministers of the great powers should work out the first drafts of the peace treaties, then should submit those drafts to a general conference of the nations that had been at war with the

Axis nations for discussion and for recommended changes. Thereupon the Council of Foreign Ministers would again go to work, this time for the purpose of considering the recommendations emanating from the general conference and adopting those among them which appeared to have merit.

This procedure of peacemaking produced heated controversy at the very outset. Meeting in October, 1945, at Paris to work on peace treaties with Italy, Finland, Hungary, Roumania, and Bulgaria, the Council of Foreign Ministers was disconcerted by an objection on the part of the Russian Foreign Minister to participation by China in the Council's deliberations and also by France (except on the treaty with Italy). After prolonged debate, the decision was reached that the Council of Foreign Ministers should have the following composition: for the Italian treaty, the United States, Great Britain, Russia, and France; for the Roumanian, Bulgarian, and Hungarian treaties, the United States, Russia, and Great Britain; and for the Finnish treaty, Great Britain and Russia. With this problem solved, the Council got to work on the "satellite" treaties and produced in the due course of time draft treaties. To discuss these drafts, twenty-one states were invited to a conference at Paris in 1946; the recommendations of this "Paris Peace Conference" were submitted to the Council of Foreign Ministers, which put the treaty drafts in final form.

Applying the procedure to peacemaking with Germany and Austria, the great powers ran into difficulties arising out of the clashing objectives of Russia and the Western nations. Because these obstacles could not be removed, no drafts of peace treaties emerged from the Council of Ministers. To blame this impasse on the new procedure would not be at all fair, for the differences between Russia and the West have perhaps been so deep-seated as to defy settlement by any means. There are, however, at least two defects of the procedure which are not present in the old-style peace conference. First, the plan of taking up settlements with the ex-enemy states separately and at different times rather than in one conference narrowed the area within which compromises—the only means of reconciling divergent national policies—are possible; the method of approaching the settlements with the different countries simultaneously would offer a better chance to make concessions and bargains. Second, the absence of the smaller states from the discussions in which the treaties were drafted eliminated one of the most fruitful sources of solutions to diplomatic tangles, for experience has shown that when the great powers are deadlocked, the suggestions of small states with their more detached points of view often lead to acceptable and workable agreements.

The San Francisco Conference

No doubt the most important independent conference of recent years was the San Francisco Conference of 1945. It was sponsored by four nations—the United States, Russia, the United Kingdom, and China. These four nations on March 5 issued invitations to forty-two governments, those which had declared war on Germany or Japan by March 1, 1945, and had signed the United Nations Declaration; because the sponsoring governments could not agree on which of the two Polish governments should be invited, Poland was left out, even though she was a signatory of the Declaration. The conference opened its session on April 25, with delegations in attendance from all forty-six sponsoring and invited governments. Soon after the opening of the gathering, it was decided to invite Argentina, Denmark, Byelorussia, and Ukrainia, so that the total number of participants was raised to fifty.

The agenda, as indicated in the invitations, made it clear that the discussion would be directed toward the formulation of a United Nations Charter and that the Dumbarton Oaks Proposals would be the basis from which the Conference would proceed. Two days after the Conference was opened, the heads of delegations met and formally adopted an agenda in which the Dumbarton Oaks Proposals "as supplemented at the Crimea Conference and by the Chinese proposals agreed to by the Sponsoring Governments, and the comments thereon submitted by the participating countries" were made the official order of business.

The permanent organization of the Conference was outlined in its rules introduced by the *rapporteur* of the Steering Committee and was adopted by the Conference. According to these rules, the chairmanship of the plenary sessions was on a rotating basis among the heads of the delegations of the four sponsoring powers; this was done at the insistence of the Russian delegation, which strongly opposed the original proposal that the head of the delegation of the United States, the host state, act as permanent chairman. Placed on a rotating basis, the chairmanship was shared by Mr. Edward Stettinius of the United States, Mr. T. V. Soong of China, Mr. V. M. Molotov of the USSR, and Mr. Anthony Eden of Great Britain. More in conformity with the usual practice, the secretary-general of the Conference was a national of the host state, Mr. Alger Hiss, at that time an officer in the Department of State.

Although the Conference held several plenary sessions, the great bulk of the work was done in committee. There were four general committees whose duties related primarily to Conference organization and procedure, as follows:

Steering Committee, composed of the heads of all the delegations, to deal with policy and procedural questions submitted to it by the cochairmen of the Conference or by the chairman of any delegation. Mr. Stettinius was its chairman.

Executive Committee, composed of the chairmen of the delegations of the four sponsoring governments and of the chairmen of the delegations of ten other states—Australia, Brazil, Canada, Chile, Czechoslovakia, France, Iran, Mexico, The Netherlands, Yugoslavia. This committee was to make recommendations to the Steering Committee and to assist the Steering Committee as requested. The chairman of this committee was Mr. Stettinius.

Coördination Committee, composed of fourteen members, one representing each member of the Executive Committee. Under the rules this Committee was to "assist the Executive Committee in the performance of the latter's functions."

Credentials Committee, composed of six members appointed by the chairmen of the delegations from Ecuador, Luxembourg, Nicaragua, Saudi Arabia, Syria, and Yugoslavia. The duty of this committee was to "verify the delegates' credentials," as the rules put it. The member representing Luxembourg was the chairman.

The formulation of the provisions of the Charter was entrusted to four commissions, as follows:

Commission I—general provisions (preamble, purposes, principles, membership, and the Secretariat).

Commission II—the General Assembly.

Commission III—the Security Council.

Commission IV—judicial organization.

Each of the four commissions had a president and a *rapporteur*, both of whom were nominated by the Steering Committee and approved by the Conference in plenary session. In each commission was an assistant secretary-general selected in the same manner. It was the duty of each commission to draft articles of the Charter within the area assigned to it. To do so, it began by formulating general principles. Then "technical committees" and "subcommittees" within each commission were given the task of formulating detailed articles, which were referred back to the main commission for amendment and approval. The four commissions maintained the following technical committees:

Commission I—Technical Committee 1—on preamble, principles, and purposes.

—Technical Committee 2—membership, amendment, and Secretariat.

Commission II—Technical Committee 1—structure and procedures.

—Technical Committee 2—political and security functions.

—Technical Committee 3—economic and social coöperation.

—Technical Committee 4—trusteeship system.

Commission III—Technical Committee 1—structure and procedure.

—Technical Committee 2—peaceful settlement.

—Technical Committee 3—enforcement arrangements.

—Technical Committee 4—regional arrangements.

Commission IV—Technical Committee 1—International Court of Justice.

—Technical Committee 2—legal problems.

The draft of each of the four commissions for that portion of the Charter assigned to it was sent to the Coördination Committee, which went over it for textual improvements.

The deliberations of the technical committees covered a period of approximately a month and a half, but there were intervals when some of them were deadlocked and consequently were relatively inactive. That much of the work of the Conference was done by them is apparent from the total number of meetings held; Technical Committee 2 of Commission I, for instance, had twenty-nine meetings, and Technical Committee 2 of Commission II had twenty-five.

The decisions of the Conference were taken by a two-thirds vote, on the basis of equality in voting. These provisions would seem to have placed all nations, great and small, on a par, but as a matter of fact this was not the case. As in any assembly of nations, the great and powerful wielded an influence far beyond that of the small and weak. Feeling that the presence of all the great powers in the United Nations as members was imperative, the nations at San Francisco were inclined to give in to them. The adoption of any proposal over the opposition of either the United States, Russia, Great Britain, France, or China would run the risk of driving that nation out of the organization. There was strong resistance, as a matter of fact, to the proposal to give each of the permanent members of the Security Council a veto, but it carried for the reason that the Big Five wanted it; during the voting on the proposal, adoption was made possible only because fifteen opposing states abstained from voting, so that, with the help of other small nations which preferred to vote with the great powers, a two-thirds vote was attained.

A large measure of great-power harmony was achieved by informal meetings of the Big Five at the penthouse used by Secretary Stettinius. Once the large nations reached agreement on a proposal, it was a foregone conclusion that they would have their way.

Problems and Limitations

As Sir Maurice Hankey prophesied in 1920, diplomacy by conference has come to stay; at any rate, it seems likely to stay as long as there are independent states which get along with each other chiefly by coöperation. What Sir Maurice apparently did not foresee was that the independent conference which had had the field up until that time would become less common as the conferences of permanent organizations became more so. The League of Nations had just opened its doors for business in 1920 and no one could tell at that time the extent to which the League would organize conferences.

That the independent conference has given way in a very considerable degree to the organization conference suggests that the former is less well fitted than the latter to do the business of nations. Chief among the limitations of the independent conference is its domination by the state or states responsible for its calling. By issuing invitations and thus deciding what governments shall be included or excluded, by taking the initiative in formulating the agenda, by organizing the conference and providing it with a presiding officer and a secretariat, and by fixing the time and place for its assemblage, the host state is rather firmly in control. Since the conference meets almost invariably on the soil of the host state, the newspapers, radio, and public pressures of that state are bound to exert much more influence on proceedings than those of any of the guest nations. Because the host state is so dominant, it is understandable that invited states have not always enthusiastically accepted invitations and that their first reaction has often been one of suspicion. Nations resent being placed at a disadvantage in diplomacy and for that reason they have been wary about accepting invitations to conferences. Perhaps one of the best examples of this caution was displayed by Japan when in 1921 she was invited by the United States to the Washington Disarmament Conference. She was particularly suspicious of the agenda and fearful lest she would be embarrassed by discussions of subjects inimical to her interests; many exchanges of notes were necessary to satisfy her government.

A second fault of the independent conference is that it is likely to be deficient in preparations. As a rule, the only preparations made are those of the individual participating states, each endeavoring to prepare only for the best possible presentation of its case; there is no international machinery of preparation to equip the conference as a unit for success. No comment has been more commonly made by diplomats with extensive conference experience than that one of the most important causes of conference failures is the lack of adequate preparations. Mr. Hugh Gibson, an experienced American diplomat, once said of conferences that "their success is usually in direct proportion to the amount of confidential and expert spadework which has been done in advance and to the measure of agreement that was already reached before they were convened."[9]

Finally, the independent conference is without machinery to follow up and check on the implementation of its decisions by the participants after the meeting has come to an end. It has no way of discovering whether the participants ratify the treaties they have signed or whether, once ratified, the treaties are put into effect by the necessary legislative enactments or by other appropriate measures. When an independent conference disbands, its machinery is completely liquidated and there is no office or authority that can be notified of subsequent developments. Consequently, it becomes easy for a nation whose delegates have signed a treaty to pigeonhole it somewhere along the line and forget the matter of ratification and enforcement.

▲

APPENDIX TO CHAPTER XII

I

List of Official International Conferences and Meetings, July 1, 1946 to June 30, 1947, in Which the U.S. Participated*

Date	Conference	Place
June 28–July 2, 1946	Third Session of the Executive Commitee of the Food and Agriculture Organization of the United Nations.	Washington
July 1, 1946–June 30, 1947 (continuous)	Meetings of the Far Eastern Commission	Washington
July 2, 1946	Meeting of the Inter-American Coffee Board	Washington

[9] H. Gibson, *The Road to Foreign Policy*, New York, 1944, p. 81.

* *Participation of the United States Government in International Conference, July 1, 1946—June 30, 1947*, Department of State Bulletin 3031, released June, 1948.

Date	Conference	Place
July 5–12, 1946	Meeting of the Preparatory Commission of the United Nations Educational, Scientific and Cultural Organization	London
July 8–9, 1946	Sixteenth General Assembly of the International Institute of Agriculture	Rome
July 8–15, 1946	Meeting of Special Representatives of the Member Governments of the Caribbean Commission	Washington
July 8–15, 1946	Second Meeting of the Caribbean Commission	Washington
July 9–13, 1946	Meeting of the First, Third and Fourth Commissions of the International Technical Committee of Aerial Legal Experts	Paris
July 15, 1946	Meeting of the International Sugar Council	London
July 15, 1946	Twelfth Session of the International Wheat Council	Washington
July 15–27, 1946	Conference on German-owned Patents	London
July 17, 1946	Special Meeting of the Governing Board of the Pan American Union	Washington
July 18, 1946	Meeting of the Inter-American Economic and Social Council	Washington
July 19–23, 1946	First Session of the Interim Commission of the World Health Organization	New York
July 22–24, 1946	General Assembly of the International Council of Scientific Unions	London
July 29–August 2, 1946	Extraordinary General Assembly of the International Union of Geodesy and Geophysics	Cambridge
July 29–October 15, 1946	Paris Conference	Paris
August 1, 1946	Meeting of the Inter-American Economic and Social Council	Washington
August 5–16, 1946	Fifth Session of the Council of the United Nations Relief and Rehabilitation Administration	Geneva
August 15, 1946	Meeting of the Inter-American Economic and Social Council	Washington
August 16, 1946	Meeting of the International Coffee Board	Washington
August 19, 1946	Thirteenth Session of the International Wheat Council	Washington
August 22–September 1, 1946	Third Pan-American Consultation on Caribbean	Caracas
August 25–September 1, 1946	Fourth General Assembly of the Pan-American Institute of Geography and History	Caracas
August 26–31, 1946	First Session of the Permanent Committee on Migration of the International Labor Organization	Montreal
August 26–31, 1946	Meeting of the International Penal and Penitentiary Commission	Bern
August 26–September 13, 1946	Caribbean Regional Air Navigation Meeting of the Provisional International Civil Aviation Organization	Washington

Date	Conference	Place
August 28–30, 1946	Fourth Session of the Executive Committee of the Food and Agriculture Organization of the United Nations	Copenhagen
August 29–30, 1946	Fifth Session of the Council of the European Central Inland Transport Organization	Paris
September 2–13, 1946	Second Session of the Conference of the Food and Agriculture Organization of the United Nations	Copenhagen
September 2–25	Fifth Congress of the Postal Union of the Americas and Spain	Rio de Janeiro
September 3, 1946	Negotiations Concerning the Disposition of German Assets in Portugal	Lisbon
September 4–November 18, 1946	Sixth Session of the Interim Council of the Provisional International Civil Aviation Organization	Montreal
September 5, 1946	Meeting of the Inter-American Economic and Social Council	Washington
September 7–15, 1946	First Inter-American Medical Congress	Rio de Janeiro
September 9–30, 1946	Demonstrations of Radio Aids to Air Navigation (United Kingdom)	London
September 14, 1946	Fifth Session of the Executive Committee of the Food and Agriculture Organization of the United Nations	Copenhagen
September 16, 17 and 27, 1946	Ninety-ninth Session of the Governing Body of the International Labor Office	Montreal
September 17–26, 1946	Conference on North Atlantic Ocean Weather Stations	London
September 19, 1946	Meeting of the Inter-American Economic and Social Council	Washington
September 19–October 9, 1946	Twenty-Ninth Session of the International Labor Conference	Montreal
September 26–October 2, 1946	Second Inter-American Regional Conference of Sanitary Engineering	Caracas
September 27–October 3, 1946	First Annual Meeting of the Boards of Governors of the International Monetary Fund and the International Bank for Reconstruction and Development	Washington
September 28–October 21, 1946	Preliminary Five Power Telecommunications Conference	Moscow
October 1, 1946	Meeting of the Inter-American Coffee Board	Washington
October 1–4, 1946	International Conference of National Travel Organizations	London
October 1–5, 1946	Second Pan-American Congress of Mining Engineering and Geology	Petropolis
October 1–15, 1946	Second Pan-American Congress of Physical Education	Mexico City
October 1–18, 1946	Middle East Regional Air Navigation Meeting of the Provisional International Civil Aviation Organization	Cairo
October 3, 1946	Meeting of the Inter-American Economic and Social Council	Washington

Date	Conference	Place
October 7–8, 1946	One Hundredth Session of the Governing Body of the International Labor Office	Montreal
October 7–12, 1946	Eighteenth International Congress for Housing and Town Planning	Hastings
October 7–26, 1946	Demonstrations of Radio Aids to Air Navigation (United States)	New York and Indianapolis
October 8–11, 1946	International Tin Conference	London
October 8–15, 1946	Intergovernmental Conference on the Adoption of a Travel Document for Refugees	London
October 14 and 23, 1946	Second Meeting of the International Emergency Food Council	Washington
October 15–November 26, 1946	First Session of the Preparatory Committee of the United Nations Conference on Trade and Employment	London
October 17, 1946	Meeting of the Inter-American Economic and Social Council	Washington
October 19–27, 1946	Second Pan-American Conference on Leprosy	Rio de Janeiro
October 23–31, 1946	Meeting of the Permanent Committee of the International Office of Public Health	Paris
October 23–December 16, 1946	Second Part of the First Session of the General Assembly of the United Nations	New York
October 24–30, 1946	Second Session of the United Nations Consultative Council	Washington
October 28–29, 1946	Demonstrations of Radio Aids to Air Navigation (Australia)	Montreal and Ottawa
October 28–30, 1946	Informal Four Power International Broadcasting Conference	Paris
October 28, 1946, January 24, 1947	Preparatory Commission on World Food Proposals of the Food and Agriculture Organization of the United Nations	Washington
November 4–13, 1946	Second Session of the Interim Commission of the World Health Organization	Geneva
November 4–December 11, 1946	Third Session of the Council of Foreign Ministers	New York
November 6, 1946	Regular Meeting of the Governing Board of the Pan American Union	Washington
November 6–17, 1946	Fifteenth Plenary Session of the International Technical Committee of Aerial Legal Experts and Meetings of the First, Second, and Fourth Commissions	Cairo
November 7, 1946	Meeting of the Inter-American Coffee Board	Washington
November 7, 1946	Meeting of the Inter-American Economic and Social Council	Washington
November 11–15, 1946	International Wool Talks	London
November 12, 1946	Negotiations Concerning the Disposition of German Assets in Spain	Madrid
November 14–15, 1946	Meeting of the Preparatory Commission of the United Nations Educational, Scientific and Cultural Organization	Paris

Date	Conference	Place
November 14–22, 1946	Meeting of the Textiles Committee of the International Labor Organization	Brussels
November 17–22, 1946	Second Inter-American Congress of Radiology	Havana
November 19–December 10, 1946	First Session of the General Conference of the United Nations Educational, Scientific and Cultural Organization	Paris
November 20, December 2, 1946	International Whaling Conference	Washington
November 21, 1946	Meeting of the Inter-American Economic and Social Council	Washington
November 25–28, 1946	Third Meeting of the Rubber Study Group	The Hague
November 25–December 3, 1946	Meeting of the Building, Civil Engineering and Public Works Committee of the International Labor Organization	Brussels
November 26–December 10, 1946	First Meeting of the Executive Board of the United Nations Educational Scientific and Cultural Organization	Paris
December 2–12, 1946	Fifth Assembly of the Inter-American Commission of Women	Washington
December 4, 1946	Regular Meeting of the Governing Board of the Pan American Union	Washington
December 6, 1946	Special Meeting of the Governing Board of the Pan American Union	Washington
December 10–13, 1946	Sixth Session of the Council of the United Nations Relief and Rehabilitation Administration	Washington
December 10–14, 1946	Third Meeting of the Caribbean Commission	Willemstad, Curaçao, N.W.I.
December 11, 1946	Fourteenth Session of the International Wheat Council	Washington
December 16–18, 1946	Sixth Session of the Executive Committee of the Food and Agriculture Organization of the United Nations	Washington
December 16–20, 1946	Sixth Plenary Session of the Intergovernmental Committee on Refugees	London
December 17, 1946	Meeting of the Inter-American Economic and Social Council	Washington
December 18, 1946	Special Meeting of the Governing Board of the Pan American Union	Washington
December 18–19, 1946	Sixth Session of the Council of the European Central Inland Transport Organization	Paris
December 26, 1946	Meeting of the Inter-American Economic and Social Council	Washington
January 6–11, 1947	Meeting of the Medical and Statistical Commissions of the Inter-American Committee on Social Security	Washington
January 7, 1947	Meeting of the Inter-American Coffee Board	Washington
January 7, 1947	Special Meeting of the Governing Board of the Pan American Union	Washington

Date	Conference	Place
January 7–April 2, 1947	Seventh Session of the Interim Council of the Provisional International Civil Aviation Organization	Montreal
January 8, 1947	Regular Meeting of the Governing Board of the Pan American Union	Washington
January 12–24, 1947	Twelfth Pan-American Sanitary Conference	Caracas
January 15, 1947	Special Meeting of the Governing Board of the Pan American Union	Washington
January 15–28, 1947	Fifteenth Session of the International Wheat Council	Washington
January 16, 1947	Meeting of the Inter-American Economic and Social Council	Washington
January 17–22, 1947	Second Pan-American Conference on Health Education	Caracas
January 22, 1947	Special Meeting of the Governing Board of the Pan American Union	Washington
January 28–February 6, 1947	South Seas Conference	Canberra
January 30, 1947	Meeting of the Inter-American Economic and Social Council	Washington
January 30–31, 1947	Third Meeting of the International Emergency Food Council	Washington
February 3–12, 1947	Meeting of the Petroleum Industry Committee of the International Labor Organization	Los Angeles
February 4–22, 1947	South Pacific Regional Air Navigation Meeting of the Provisional International Civil Aviation Organization	Melbourne
February 11–14, 1947	First Conference on Forestry Statistics of the Food and Agriculture Organizations of the United Nations	Washington
February 11–21, 1947	First Session of the Preparatory Commission for the International Refugee Organization (First Part)	Geneva
February 12, 1947	Regular Meeting of the Governing Board of the Pan American Union	Washington
February 15, 1947	Special Meeting of the Governing Board of the Pan American Union	Washington
February 18, 1947	Meeting of the International Sugar Council	London
February 27, 1947	Meeting of the Inter-American Economic and Social Council	Washington
March 3–8, 1947	Seventh Session of the Executive Committee of the Food and Agriculture Organization of the United Nations	Rome
March 5, 1947	Regular Meeting of the Governing Board of the Pan American Union	Washington
March 5–10, 1947	One Hundred and First Session of the Governing Body of the International Labor Office	Geneva
March 10, April 24, 1947	Fourth Session of the Council of Foreign Ministers	Moscow
March 12, 1947	Special Meeting of the Governing Board of the Pan American Union	Washington

Date	Conference	Place
March 14, 1947	Meeting of the Inter-American Economic and Social Council	Washington
March 17–22, 1947	Seventh Pan-American Conference on Tuberculosis	Lima
March 18–April 3, 1947; April 14–23, 1947	International Wheat Conference	London
March 27, 1947	Meeting of the Inter-American Economic and Social Council	Washington
March 30–April 12, 1947	Third Session of the Interim Commission of the World Health Organization	Geneva
March 31–April 3, 1947	First Meeting of the International Wool Study Group	London
April 1, 1947	Meeting of the Inter-American Coffee Board	Washington
April 7–12, 1947	Thirty-Sixth Conference of the Inter-parliamentary Union	Cairo
April 10, 1947	Meeting of the Inter-American Economic and Social Council	Washington
April 10–15, 1947	Second Meeting of the Executive Board of the United Nations Educational, Scientific and Cultural Organization	Paris
April 10–October 30, 1947	Second Session of the Preparatory Committee of the United Nations Conference on Trade and Employment	Geneva
April 14, 1947	Special Meeting of the Governing Board of the Pan American Union	Washington
April 14–25, 1947	Meeting of Experts to Prepare for a World Conference on Passports and Frontier Formalities	Geneva
April 14–26, 1947	Conference of Government Experts for the Study of Conventions for the Protection of War Victims	Geneva
April 14–16; June 17–19, 1947	Seventh Session of the Council of the European Central Inland Transport Organization	Paris
April 15–18, 1947	First Meeting of the International Tin Study Group	Brussels
April 22–May 5, 1947	Fifth International Hydrographic Conference	Monte Carlo
April 23, May 14 and June 18, 1947	Annual Meeting of the Governing Board of the Inter-American Indian Institute	Mexico City
April 24, 1947	Meeting of the Inter-American Economic and Social Council	Washington
April 24–May 3, 1947	Second Session of the Coal Mining Committee of the International Labor Organization	Geneva
April 25, 1947	Annual Meeting of the Council of the American International Institute for the Protection of Childhood	Montevideo
April 28–May 9, 1947	International Meeting on Marine Radio Aids to Navigation	New York
April 28–May 10, 1947	International Timber Conference	Marianske-Lazne

Date	Conference	Place
April 28–May 15, 1947	First Special Session of the General Assembly of the United Nations (Palestine)	New York
April 29–May 7, 1947	Eighth Session of the Interim Council of the Provisional International Civil Aviation Organization	Montreal
April 30, 1947	Special Meeting of the Governing Board of the Pan American Union	Washington
May 1, 1947	Meeting of the Inter-American Economic and Social Council	Washington
May 1–21, 1947	First Session of the Preparatory Commission for the International Refugee Organization (Second Part)	Lausanne
May 6–27, 1947	First Assembly of the International Civil Aviation Organization	Montreal
May 7–July 5, 1947	Twelfth Congress of the Universal Postal Union	Paris
May 7, 1947	Regular Meeting of the Governing Board of the Pan American Union	Washington
May 7–16, 1947	Second Session of the Inland Transport Committee of the International Labor Organization	Geneva
May 10–22, 1947	Sixteenth Plenary Session of the International Technical Committee of Aerial Legal Experts	Montreal
May 12–October 11, 1947	Austrian Treaty Commission	Vienna
May 15, 1947	Meeting of the Inter-American Economic and Social Council	Washington
May 16–October 2, 1947	International Radio Conference	Atlantic City
May 16–19, 1947	First Session of the Provisional Maritime Consultative Council	Paris
May 16–June 6, 1947	Meeting of the Rice Study Group of the Food and Agriculture Organization of the United Nations	Trivandrum, Travancore, India
May 26–28, 1947	Fourth Meeting of the International Emergency Food Council	Washington
May 28–July 1, 1947	First Session of the Council of the International Civil Aviation Organization	Montreal
May 30–June 3, 1947	Seventh Plenary Session of the Intergovernmental Committee on Refugees	London
June 2–6, 1947	Eighth Session of the Executive Committee of the Food and Agriculture Organization of the United Nations	Washington
June 2–6, 1947	Health Congress of the Royal Sanitary Institute	Torquay
June 2–7, 1947	Eleventh International Congress of Military Medicine and Pharmacy	Basel
June 4, 1947	Special Meeting of the Governing Board of the Pan American Union	Washington
June 4–5, 1947	Regular Meeting of the Governing Board of the Pan American Union	Washington
June 6, 1947	Meeting of the Inter-American Economic and Social Council	Washington

Date	Conference	Place
June 9–11, 1947	Sixth Meeting of the International Cotton Advisory Committee	Washington
June 13–July 10, 1947	One Hundred and Second Session of the Governing Body of the International Labor Office	Geneva
June 14, 1947	Special Meeting of the Governing Board of the Pan American Union	Washington
June 17, July 7, 1947	South American Regional Air Navigation Meeting of the International Civil Aviation Organization	Lima
June 19–July 11, 1947	Thirtieth Session of the International Labor Conference	Geneva
June 21–25, 1947	Twenty-first session of the Journées Médicales de Bruxelles	Brussels
June 23, 1947	Sixteenth Session of the International Wheat Council	Washington
June 23–28, 1947	Fourth Meeting of the Caribbean Commission	Ocho Rios, Jamaica, B.W.I.
June 24, 1947	Meeting of the International Sugar Council	London
June 26–28, 1947	International Congress on River Transportation	Paris
June 27, 1947	Special Meeting of the Governing Board of the Pan American Union	Washington

Chart of U.S. Participation in Conferences, 1936–1948

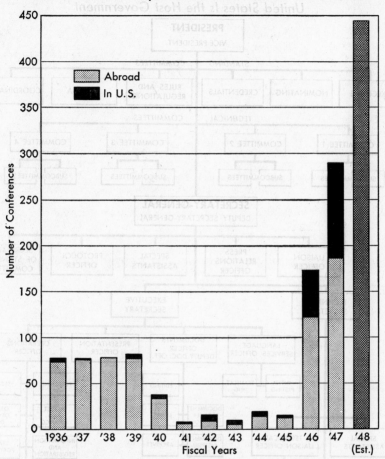

Includes principal meetings of the organs of the United Nations and the Committee meeting of International Organizations, in addition to the conferences and meetings summarized in the annual issues of the conference volume. (From *Participation of the United States in International Conferences, July 1, 1946–June 30, 1947*, Department of State Publication 3031, June, 1948.)

Organization Chart for an International Conference Where the United States Is the Host Government

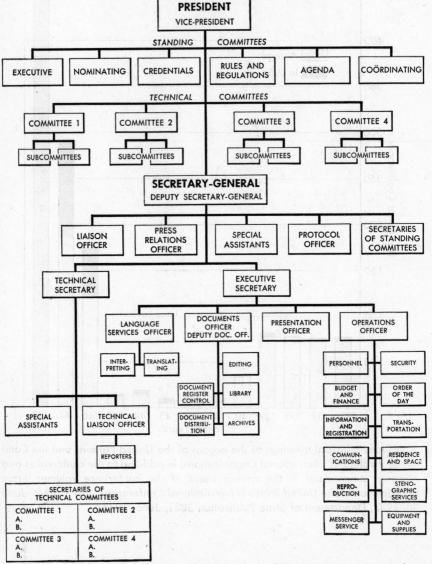

Depending on the size of the conference, a member may serve in more than one capacity on the chart. (From *Participation of the United States in International Conferences, July 1, 1946 to June 30, 1947*, Department of State Publication 3031, June, 1948, p. 19.)

XIII Organization Conferences and Meetings

THE INTERNATIONAL CONFERENCE ORIGINATED AND AT-
tained a measure of utility at a time when there was no permanent
international organization, regional or universal, in existence. It was
necessarily independent in those days, for there was nothing to
which it could be attached. Moreover, it was always an *ad hoc*
body, set up to do an assigned task, after which it disbanded once
and for all.

With the establishment of permanent international organizations,
a bright future with new possibilities was opened to the conference
method. Since a major purpose of permanent international organizations is to enable nations to get more closely in touch with each
other and to confer readily on common problems, it is not surprising
that they took over the conference method, modifying it and adapt-
ing it to their needs. Organization conferences are therefore parts of
a whole; they are not independent or unrelated agencies. A system
to which they belong is a highly developed, smooth-running instrumentality of several organs, all of which combine to give nations
every opportunity to come together, discuss their common problems, and, if they wish, negotiate toward solutions.

Conference Systems

Best known among the permanent organizations that have taken
over the conference and developed it into an instrumentality of
greater usefulness are the Organization of American States, the
League of Nations, and the United Nations, although others of a

minor nature have also utilized it. Organization conferences of several types have been set to work by these permanent bodies, all assisted by other organs and particularly by the one which serves as a secretariat. These frequent meetings keep nations in close diplomatic relationship with each other. Taken together—the conferences which are held and the operations of other organs to assist in their preparation and conduct—they have been appropriately referred to as "conference systems."

Generally speaking, there are three types of meetings held under the auspices of existing permanent organizations: (1) the sessions of the constituted organs, such as the General Assembly, the Security Council, and the various committees and commissions of the United Nations; (2) general conferences of members, typified by the Inter-American Conference, also constitutionally required by some international organizations; and (3) special conferences arranged from time to time to take up assigned problems, of which the World Disarmament Conference (1932–1935) of the League of Nations would be a fair example. Although all three of these types of meetings are "conferences" in the literal sense of the word, they are quite dissimilar. Those belonging to class (1) are sufficiently different from those of classes (2) and (3) as to require separate discussion, and for that reason they are treated in other chapters of this volume.[1] Although the General Assembly and the Security Council meet and deliberate, as do all conferences, they are unlike the general and special conferences of classes (2) and (3) in that they are more or less permanently organized and their structures, functions, and methods are fixed; they do not have to be organized from the ground up every time they meet. Even more important in the way of a distinction is the fact that such organs as the General Assembly and the Security Council of the United Nations do not negotiate treaties and conventions as do general and special conferences; it is possible that the Assembly may possess the right to formulate treaties, not expressly given by the Charter but implied from other

[1] See Chapter V on the General Assembly and Security Council of the United Nations.

rights, but so far none has been drafted. These two United Nations organs deal with many international problems but in other ways than by treaty-making; if they believe that a convention should be drafted, they ordinarily suggest it to other agencies or arrange to have a special conference set up.[2] Much of the work of the General Assembly and the Security Council could be called consultative in nature, either in relation to international problems or with regard to the functioning of the various organs and agencies of the United Nations.

One of the principal features of conference systems of permanent organizations is that general and special conferences (classes 2 and 3) are initiated, prepared, and managed by international agencies, not by one host state or by a group of sponsoring states, as in the case of independent conferences. General conferences like those of the International Labor Organization and those of the Organization of American States are on a recurring basis. Special conferences ordinarily originate within agencies or organs whose activities have disclosed some specific need for concerted action. Organized and managed by designated international bodies with knowledge and experience, both general and special conferences are provided with chairmen, secretariats, and meeting places; no one nation can assume a monopoly in such matters, as may occur in independent conferences.

With those conferences that are internationally initiated, organized, and managed, there is opportunity for a type and degree of preparation quite impossible to independent conferences. The preparatory commission or authority may send questionnaires to the participating states to ascertain their points of view; it may gather together pertinent documents, data, and books; it may draft tentative texts of treaties and recommendations to be used as bases of conference deliberation; it may provide the material comforts and conveniences that contribute to a coöperative enterprise; indeed, it

---

[2] In 1946, however, the General Assembly instructed the Economic and Social Council to draft a Convention on Genocide. With the assistance of the Secretariat, three experts, and the Committee on the Progressive Development of International Law, this was done. The Assembly approved the draft which was submitted to it.

may undertake whatever preliminary work it sees fit in order to save the time of the conference itself and to promote successful negotiations.

Another aspect of a conference system is the availability of machinery and processes by which the accomplishments of a conference can be followed up. The treaties signed must be ratified in order to become operative, and the recommendations adopted are dependent upon subsequent national action if they are to be given force. The secretariat of the international organization under whose auspices a conference is held is equipped to keep in touch with the participating nations and find out what they have done or intend to do. This check upon the nations not only makes it clear and certain as to where obligations have been created, but in addition provides a constant and necessary reminder to nations to take the appropriate action by which conference commitments can be made effective.

Taken together, a conference system within a permanent international organization displays a wholesome flexibility. There are both permanent and *ad hoc* organs wherein nations gather together to do business. *Ad hoc* organs may meet periodically, on a recurring basis without periodicity, or whenever needed. The preparations for the various meetings may be made by an existing committee or by an especially constituted committee, and in either case experienced assistance will be provided by the secretariat. These and other variations give diplomatic methods within permanent organizations an adjustability and resourcefulness unknown to the independent conference.

Early Conference Systems

The first conference systems were those of some of the public international unions set up during the closing decades of the nineteenth century. With each of them working in some one field of interest rather than with international problems broadly, as in the case of the United Nations, the organization of these unions was relatively simple. Generally, each union was made up of (1) a deliberative body known variously as a "conference," "congress," or "general assembly," (2) an administrative "bureau" or "office" to perform assigned tasks, and (3) a supervisory commission to direct the work of the bureau.

The first important public union was the International Telegraphic Union, founded in 1865;[3] in 1906 the Union was given duties relating to wireless communication, and in 1931, when its work in connection with the radio was expanded, it became known as the Telecommunications Union (now a specialized agency of the United Nations). A characteristic feature of the conference of the Telegraphic Union from the very beginning was that it was attended by both diplomatic officials and technical representatives. The former dealt with the convention of the Union, which provided the organization's constitution, defined the obligations of members, and set forth the basic principles of operation. The latter were responsible for the negotiation of the *règlement*, which contained the detailed administrative regulations of the Union. Both types of conferences—the diplomatic and the technical—were on a periodic basis, and both were assisted in some measure by the bureau of the union.

Many such public unions later came into existence, including the Universal Postal Union (1875),[4] the Bureau of Weights and Measures (1875), the Union of Railway Freight Transportation (1878), the Union for the Protection of Patents and Trade-Marks (1883), the Union for the Publication of Customs Tariffs (1890), the International Institute of Agriculture (1905), the International Office of Public Health (1907), the Union for the Establishment of Electrical Units (1908), and the International Commission for the Map of the World (1909). All but one or two of these unions maintained something in the nature of a conference system, quite rudimentary, it is true, in comparison with a highly developed system like that of the United Nations.

Generally speaking, the conference systems of the unions have followed about the same pattern. As in the Telegraphic Union, there have been periodic conferences which have met, as a rule, every few years. The use of both diplomatic and technical conferences has

---

[3] The bureau of the union was not set up until 1868.
[4] Now a specialized agency of the United Nations.

been a common practice, the former being concerned with the general convention and the latter with technical problems. In the Universal Postal Union the diplomatic conference has been called a "congress," whereas the one handling administrative problems has been known as a "conference." The congress is convened on the initiative of the host state, as designated by the preceding congress, or on the request of two-thirds of the members; the conference is called by request of two-thirds of the members.

The line between diplomatic and administrative activities within the unions has always been difficult to draw with precision. This is not surprising nor unprecedented in the realm of government, for even in national constitutional systems the legislative and administrative functions often merge to the point that an area is blocked out in which the work undertaken may very well be referred to under either heading; the Interstate Commerce Commission of the United States, for instance, is a rule-making body with regard to rates and other matters of railway practice, and therefore, although the agency is commonly labeled administrative, it possesses a form of legislative power. Within the public unions the conferences have been able to make or modify one or more of three types of documents: (1) the convention which acts as a constitution for the union; (2) other conventions prescribing general policies (as in the Postal Union); and (3) technical regulations. When they are making or changing (1) or (2), they are unquestionably acting in a diplomatic capacity. When, however, they are dealing with the "administrative regulations," as they are often called, are they acting in a diplomatic or an administrative capacity? Perhaps the question is hardly worth an argument, since it is primarily a matter of semantics. That there is a blending of functions is apparent. To recognize this fact and to understand the nature of the work are more important than trying to make arbitrary classifications where none can be convincing.

Representation in the conferences of the unions has involved some experimentation. In the Universal Postal Union, where colonial dependencies have been members in their own name, there is colonial representation. Several organizations have been more daring in their violations of the doctrine of state equality, dividing the members into classes or groups and allotting a specified number of votes to the individual states of each class. For instance, the members of the International Institute of Agriculture were divided into five categories, with an assignment of from one to five votes to each state according to its classification.

In several of the unions, the operations of the conferences are assisted by the permanent offices or bureaus. The Bureau of the Universal Postal Union, between meetings, receives proposals from member states for the agenda of conferences and congresses. In some cases the supervisory committees over the bureaus are given duties along the line of conference preparations. Referring again to the International Institute of Agriculture, we note that the "permanent committee" prepared proposals for submission to the organization's conference or "General Assembly."

Considered as a group, these unions were pioneers in developing conference systems. Although they have differed from each other in matters of detail, most of them have embodied some one or more of the following features of a conference system: (1) periodic conferences; (2) assistance in conference preparation by a permanent bureau; and (3) assistance in one form or another by a permanent supervisory committee. Where conferences have not met at regular intervals of time, a common practice has been for each conference to fix the time and place for the next meeting. The assistance provided in conference preparation by bureaus or committees has related primarily to the agenda; in making other arrangements, the host state has been expected to take the initiative.

The features of the conference system introduced by the public unions may seem elementary in comparison with a modern system such as that of the United Nations. It was only a beginning; the League of Nations and the Organization of American States carried the conference-system idea much further. More recently, the United Nations has represented a full elaboration of the method.

Present-Day Public Unions

Some of the earlier public unions have gone out of existence. The International Institute of Agriculture gave way to the Food and Agriculture Organization of the United Nations, and in 1948 transferred to the new body its assets and functions. Similarly, in 1946 the International Office of Public Health was taken over by the World Health Organization. The Universal Postal Union in 1947 became a specialized agency of the United Nations. Mention has already been made of the conversion of the Telegraphic Union into the International Telecommunications Union (1931) and its new status, attained in 1949, as a specialized agency of the United Nations.

At the present time there are several unions in existence which are independent of the United Nations. Following are those in which the United States participates:[5]

International Union for the Protection of Industrial Property
International Union for the Publication of Customs Tariffs
Central Bureau of the International Map of the World
Bureau of Weights and Measures
International Hydrographic Bureau
International Meteorological Organization
International Union of Official Travel Organizations

Most of these unions have conferences as an integral part of their permanent organization; but the Union for the Publication of Customs Tariffs functions not by means of conferences but only through an administrative bureau. Following the usual structure of public unions, those with conferences ordinarily maintain miniature conference systems. Some, but not all, hold periodic meetings. The conferences of the Union for the Protection of Industrial Property meet from time to time but not according to any fixed plan. The General Conference on Weights and Measures meets every six years to promote and perfect the metric system; delegates to it are the diplomatic representatives of the members accredited to the French Government in Paris. Following the general custom already described, the conferences of these unions are often given the assistance of supervisory committees or bureaus in matters of preparation. The bureaus also perform duties of an administrative nature which will be discussed in a later chapter.[6]

---

[5] From *International Organization in which the United States Participates*, Department of State Publication 3655, 1950. The list given does not include several relating to Inter-American affairs.

[6] See Chapter XV.

The Organization of American States

The purpose and place of the conference method in the Americas was well brought out by Secretary of State Acheson at Bogotá in 1948 when he said, "The inter-American conferences and meetings are the instruments through which the inter-American system formulates policy and reaches decisions on questions of major importance."[7] It was to the Ninth International Conference of American States, meeting in Bogotá, that Secretary Acheson was speaking, and at this same conference that the Charter of the Organization of American States was drafted defining the present structure of the Organization (already described in Chapter IV). Without the benefit of a formal constitution, prior to 1948 the Organization was carried on by means of conference resolutions. The permanent office of the Organization, the Pan American Union, had been set up and was maintained by resolutions of the general conference, and the practice had become firmly entrenched of providing by resolution for the time and place of succeeding conferences. Special conferences, too, were commonly authorized by resolutions of the regular conferences, or they were called by the Governing Board of the Pan American Union; those held to deal with problems of security, however, were exceptions, for in every instance they were initiated by some one of the member states. The rules of procedure of the regular and special conferences were, as a matter of practice, formulated by the Governing Board.

The lack of a formal constitution for the Organization of American States was widely deplored, not only because of the impermanent and haphazard status on which its organs were obliged to operate, but also because there were a number of independent inter-American agencies such as the Pan American Postal Union, each autonomous and therefore able to schedule its own meetings and make its own plans freely. There was a need for integration as well as for definition which the Bogotá Convention met.

Several types of conferences take place within the Organization of American States. First, there are the meetings of the permanent consultative organs, the Meeting of Consultation of the Ministers of

---

[7] "Ninth International Conference of American States," *Department of State Bulletin*, 1948, vol. 18, no. 458, p. 469.

Foreign Affairs and of the Council, neither of which negotiates treaties as do the regular and special conferences of the Organization. The meetings of the foreign ministers, designed primarily for emergency situations, may be called at the request of any member state. In case of an armed attack within one of the twenty-one republics, the foreign ministers are expected to meet without delay and to decide how to cope with it. An Advisory Defense Committee advises the Organ of Consultation on problems of military coöperation that arise when measures of collective security are to be undertaken.

The meetings of the Council, whose composition and duties were described in Chapter IV, are also of a specialized character and do not constitute conferences in the sense that they are able to negotiate treaties. Among the Council's duties, however, are several which have to do with the preparation and organization of the regular and special conferences. It is, therefore, a vital part of the conference system of the Organization—even more for its auxiliary work in connection with the regular and special conferences than for its own meetings. Subsidiary to the Council are (1) the Economic and Social Council, (2) the Council of Jurists, and (3) the Cultural Council, each with its separate meetings.

At a meeting held in February, 1949, the Council adopted its "Regulations," in which are set forth the rules defining its own structure and methods. Three types of Council meetings are provided for: regular meetings, special meetings, and protocolary meetings. Although most of its meetings are public, the Council may go into executive session by a majority vote of its members. The Council selects its own chairman and vice-chairman, and may set up permanent or temporary committees "as it deems necessary for the performance of its functions." The secretary for the Council is an Assistant Secretary-General of the Organization.

The second type of meeting in the Organization is the regular conference, or "Inter-American Conference" as it is officially called. It is the heart of the Organization's conference system. In that it contains delegations from all member states and each delegation is entitled to one vote, the regular conference bears a striking resemblance to the General Assembly of the United Nations. Its right to take action relating to the "structure and functions of organs of the

Organization" is even more than matched by the extensive supervisory duties of the Assembly in relation to other United Nations organs. Where the Inter-American Conference differs most from the General Assembly is in the fact that it negotiates treaties. Its meetings, too, are on a different basis from those of the Assembly, occurring normally once in five years rather than annually; both the Inter-American Conference and the Assembly of the United Nations may hold special meetings when desired. Following is a list of the regular conferences of the Organization of American States:

Washington, 1st Conference of American States, 1889
Mexico City, 2nd Conference of American States, 1901
Rio de Janeiro, 3rd Conference of American States, 1906
Buenos Aires, 4th Conference of American States, 1910
Santiago, 5th Conference of American States, 1923
Havana, 6th Conference of American States, 1928
Montevideo, 7th Conference of American States, 1933
Lima, 8th Conference of American States, 1938
Bogotá, 9th Conference of American States, 1948

The contributions of these conferences to the welfare of the Americans have reached further than would be indicated in the subject matter of the conventions and resolutions which they have drafted. Like the General Assembly of the United Nations, they have provided a forum for the free discussion of international problems of all kinds and for the exchange of opinions and attitudes. At one time the United States was a frequent target of attack in the conferences for the tendency which our government had shown to intervene in the affairs of the Latin-American nations. When at the Montevideo Conference of 1933 Secretary of State Hull cordially supported a proposed treaty providing, "No state has the right to intervene in the internal or external affairs of another," thus giving effect to the so-called Good Neighbor policy of the United States, the tide turned and subsequent conferences have met in a more friendly atmosphere. The embodiment of this doctrine of nonintervention in Chapter 3 (Fundamental Rights and Duties of States) of the Charter of American States in 1948 provided the assurance of its permanence.

The third type of meetings in the Organization of American

States is the "specialized conference" designed, as the Charter of
1948 says, "to deal with special technical matters or to develop specific aspects of inter-American coöperation." The Inter-American
Defense Conference held at Rio de Janeiro in 1947 was a specialized rather than a regular conference. For many years it has been
the practice in the Organization to hold such meetings; following
are a few of the better-known specialized conferences, all on the
subject of war and peace:

Inter-American Conference on Conciliation and Arbitration, Washing-
ton, 1929
Inter-American Conference for the Maintenance of Peace, Buenos
Aires, 1936
Inter-American Conference on Problems of War and Peace, Mexico
City, 1945
Conference to Implement the Act of Chapultepec, Rio de Janeiro,
1947

The specialized conferences also include the sanitary conferences,
conferences on agriculture, and such meetings as the Pan-American
Child Congress and the Inter-American Radio Conference.

The "specialized organizations" within the Organization, which
are permanent agencies to deal with "technical matters of common
interest to the American States," also hold conferences, a fourth type
of meetings within the Organization of American States. At the
present time the specialized organizations are these:

Inter-American Institute of Agricultural Sciences
American Institute for the Protection of Childhood
Pan-American Institute of Geography and History

Other organizations are expected to be brought within this category. The Council concludes agreements with these organizations
defining their relation to the main Organization.

In addition to the wide variety of meetings held and the arrangement of recurring meetings, the Organization of American States
stresses that close working relationship between the various organs
in the preparation and conduct of conferences that is so characteristic of well-developed conference systems. So extensive are the operations of the Council and the Pan American Union in the super-

vision and management of the various conferences and meetings that the system as a whole is one of the most highly developed to date, much more so than those of the earlier public unions, from which it borrowed freely in its earlier history.

The Council's first duty in the preparation of the regular conference, the Inter-American Conference, is to fix the date for its convocation after consultation with the government of the country where it will be held. Each regular conference is obliged to decide upon the place of meeting for the next one (in accordance with long-established practice), but the precise date is not fixed at that time; the Charter merely specifies that the conference shall convene every five years, without stipulating exact dates. If for any reason a scheduled conference cannot meet at the place designated by the preceding conference, the Council has the job of deciding upon another meeting place. The next function of the Council is to prepare the agenda and the regulations of the conference; these are submitted in advance to the member states. Obviously, this is a responsibility of far-reaching consequence to the work of the conference. Furthermore, for the regular conferences the Council may draft recommendations to coördinate the activities of the conferences with those of other American agencies. Finally, subordinate agencies of the Council—the Council of Jurists and the Cultural Council, in particular—may be assigned specific duties by the conference, such as the preparation of draft proposals and the study of assigned subjects.

The Council also has a part in the preparation of specialized conferences. The proposal for such a conference may come from the Economic and Social Council, a subsidiary of the Council itself. The Council drafts recommendations for the coördination of the activities of specialized conferences and organizations with those of other agencies; to discharge its coördinating duties, the Council has established a set of standards and a recommended procedure.

The Pan American Union, which is referred to in Article 78 of the Charter as "the central and permanent organ of the Organization of American States and the General Secretariat of the Organization," also performs a number of important duties relating to the confer-

ence systems of the Organization of American States. The Secretary-General, who directs the Pan American Union, takes part, but
without vote, in the deliberations of the regular Inter-American conferences, the meetings of the Ministers of Foreign Affairs, the specialized conferences, and the Council, and he provides the necessary secretarial services to facilitate those deliberations. The Pan
American Union is also expected to advise the Council in the preparation of the programs and regulations of the various conferences
and meetings; and it must make available to the government of the
country where a conference is to be held technical aid and personnel when requested, insofar as it may be able to do so. There are
also several more or less perfunctory duties for the Union: notifying
states of meetings, acting as custodian of conference documents and
records, serving as depository of instruments of ratification of Inter-
American agreements, and performing other "functions entrusted
to it" by a conference.

This continuing system of conferences maintained by the twenty-
one republics of this hemisphere has produced a long list of agreements and recommendations, which together add up to coöperation
on a scale rarely understood by the layman. For well over six decades these agreements and recommendations have been piling up,
as the Organization of American States has developed into a more
and more complex and effective mechanism. To be sure, many of
the conventions signed at conferences have not had sufficient ratifications to become operative, and many of the recommendations
submitted to participating governments have gone unheeded.

Fields of interest remain where much work needs to be done. Despite all that has been accomplished in the field of cultural relations,
a statement made a few years ago by Mr. Daniel Ortega of Chile
still is essentially true, "When a Latin American wants to buy a
book printed in a neighboring country he has to spend as much effort as if he were building a house";[8] he went on to explain the red
tape involved: finding out whom to address; inducing a bank to sell
him a minute draft; getting an import license from the gold-con-

---

[8] D. S. Ortega, "Cultural Relations Among the American States," in W. H. C.
Laves (ed.), Inter-American Solidarity, New York, 1942, p. 189.

troller officers; paying the customs, stamp taxes, and so on. With all its shortcomings, the successful accomplishments of the Organization of American States are, however, impressive. Coöperation in the treatment of political, economic, and social problems of all kinds has been advanced to a point not yet reached by any other regional organization of states.

The annual report of Secretary-General Alberto Lleras for the fiscal year which ended on June 30, 1948, noted that two specialized conferences had been held during the preceding twelve months: the Inter-American Conference on the Conservation of Natural Resources, and the meeting of the American Committee on Dependent Territories. The former adopted one declaration of principles and four resolutions, some of which embodied recommendations for action. In his reference to the latter meeting, the Secretary-General made the following statement, which illustrates a type of function often performed by the Pan American Union for conferences of all types: "Prior to the meeting of the Committee, the Pan American Union prepared for the use of the members an informative manual which contains all the background on the subject. . . ."

Some idea of the extent of the interests and activities of the Organization of American States may be gained from a summary of the work of the Ninth International Conference of American States, held at Bogotá in 1948. In session from March 30 until May 2, the conference negotiated five treaties and its usual Final Act, in which were included forty-six recommendations and resolutions. The five treaties were as follows: the Charter of the Organization of American States; the Treaty on Pacific Settlement, commonly known as the "Pact of Bogotá"; the Economic Agreement of Bogotá; the Convention on the Grant of Political Rights to Women; and the Convention on the Grant of Civil Rights to Women. The forty-six recommendations and resolutions dealt *inter alia* with the Inter-American Statistical Institute, tourist travel, the elimination of passports, transcontinental railways, the creation of an Inter-American bank, development and improvement of social service, health, coöperatives, social justice, the Red Cross, the rights and duties of man, and the preservation and defense of democracy in

America. This imposing array of accomplishments was not at all un-usual for a regular Inter-American Conference. It provides ample evidence that the conference system of the Americas is thriving and that, while it is performing no miracles, its accomplishments con-tribute materially toward the harmony and welfare of the twenty-one republics which operate it.

The League of Nations

The conference system of the League of Nations was the first that made any pretense at universality in membership, while at the same time aspiring to deal with all sorts of international problems. The system of the Organization of American States has also dealt with a wide range of problems, though restricted, of course, to a regional basis. Both must be looked upon merely as organizations and proce-dures by which nations have been able to work together on com-mon programs of action; neither has had any usefulness or vitality except as it has been put to work by member nations. As a pamphlet on the *Aims, Methods, and Activity of the League of Nations,* pub-lished by the League Secretariat in 1938, explained, "The League is essentially a medium of consultation and coordination." And again, "Its progress and success depend primarily upon how far Govern-ments really desire to make use of its machinery. . . ." Both of those observations are equally applicable to all conference systems, including that of the United Nations, which is patterned to some extent upon that of the League.

All of the main organs of the League of Nations played some part in its conference system. The point has already been made that such meetings as those of the Council and Assembly are to be regarded in a certain sense as "conferences," being primarily consultative rather than negotiating bodies (although the Assembly of the League did on a few occasions negotiate conventions); furthermore, those two organs played important roles in the convocation of nego-tiating conferences. The Secretariat, too, contributed its share to-ward the smoothly operating system that was developed. The most essential and vital role, however, was played by a number of auxil-iary bodies of the League set up to deal with assigned problems.

These various agencies were established for the twofold purpose of furnishing the Assembly or Council with expert advice and of helping members to fulfill their duties of coöperation.

There were four types of auxiliary bodies operating within the League of Nations: (1) the technical organizations; (2) standing advisory committees or commissions; (3) institutes authorized to work within designated fields; and (4) special committees. Each of the technical organizations—the Economic Organization, the Financial Organization, the Communication and Transit Organization, the Health Organization, and the Intellectual Coöperation Organization—was devoted to a single but significant field of endeavor. Although they varied somewhat in structure, all followed a similar general pattern, with each having an advisory or technical committee of experts and a conference of members to consider draft conventions, and each served by a section of the Secretariat. The conferences of the technical organizations were generally convened on the advice of the committees of the respective organizations and at the instigation of the Assembly or Council. The initiative behind a conference was therefore taken by the experts working within a field, who, from their vantage point, would become aware of the need for a meeting and see the possibility of reaching agreement on a common program.

The permanent advisory committees were less complicated in structure, but, like the technical organizations, each operated in a certain assigned field. The Advisory Committee on Traffic in Opium and Other Dangerous Drugs was set up by the Council in 1921 and was made up of representatives of the twenty-five states chiefly concerned in the production, manufacture, or consumption of dangerous drugs. Under an Assembly resolution of 1932, the Advisory Committee of Experts on Slavery was created to assist in the operation of the Slavery Convention of 1926. These and several other advisory committees were able to recommend special conferences to deal with subjects which appeared to them to require international deliberation and action.

The affiliated institutes, mentioned above as auxiliary bodies related to the League's conference system, were agencies essentially distinct from the League but brought into relationship with it by special arrangement. There were four such institutes: the International Institute of Intellectual Coöperation, with its center in Paris; the International Institute for the Unification of Private Law, located in Rome; the International Educational Cinematographic Institute, also located in Rome; and the International Center for Leprosy Research, operating from Rio de Janeiro, Brazil. These institutes were in a position to offer technical assistance in the initiation and procedure of conferences relating to their respective fields of action.

The most important special committees used in the calling of conferences were the preparatory committees to facilitate the scheduled meetings. They were set up and their duties defined by action of the Assembly or Council. Among the duties commonly assigned to a committee of this nature was the preparation of a draft convention to be used as a basis of discussion at a forthcoming conference.

Although consultation was constantly going on in the Assembly, Council, technical committees, affiliated institutes, and special committees, the apex of the League's conference system was the special conference to negotiate for the solution of some outstanding problem. In fact, many special conferences were held and out of them there resulted a long list of conventions. Some of the more publicized of those conferences were: the Conference of 1923 on Customs Formalities; the Opium Conference (1925); the Economic Conference (1927); the Conference of Press Experts (1927); the four conferences on communication and transit (1921, 1923, 1927, and 1931); the Disarmament Conference (1932); the Monetary and Economic Conference (1933); and the European Conference on Rural Life (1939).

An illustration of the operation of the League's machinery in the convocation of special conferences to negotiate treaties or to formulate recommendations is afforded by the Conference on the Circulation of Educational Films, which met in 1933. In 1930 the International Educational Cinematographic Institute, then a technical adviser of the League's Committee of Intellectual Coöperation, conducted a number of inquiries which indicated that it might be possible to induce governments to agree on methods of facilitating the circulation of educational films. With this finding at hand, the Committee on Intellectual Coöperation recommended to the Assembly that further investigations be undertaken to discover the possibilities of action and that the groundwork be laid for a conference, whereupon the Assembly instructed the Institute to begin preparations. The Institute first sent out questionnaires to the interested governments with a view to learning their attitudes and thus being better able to know what kind of agreement they would be willing to make. After the answers were in, the Institute went ahead and framed a draft convention, which was submitted to the conference when it met. The deliberations of the conference resulted in a convention which was opened for signature on October 11, 1933. The convention was ratified and went into effect on January 15, 1935.

The Disarmament Conference of 1932 was prepared by a special preparatory committee set up by the Council in 1925. The committee held many sessions, submitted questionnaires, and finally produced a draft convention which was placed before the Conference in 1932. Although the Conference deliberated for more than two years, it failed to agree on a final convention.

While there was no absolute uniformity in the procedures by which proposals for special conferences were initiated, passed upon, and prepared, there was a striking similarity, at least, in the major steps taken. A model procedure for calling League conferences existed, but it was not obligatory and exceptions were possible when other procedures had been established or were regarded by the Assembly or Council as more appropriate. The original suggestion for a conference might and did come from a number of sources—the Council, the Assembly, a technical organization, an advisory committee, one of the institutes, or even some earlier conference. When the suggestion originated in one of the subordinate organs of the League, it was customary for that organ to submit to the Council a memorandum in support of the proposals. From this point on, questionnaires were sent out seeking the viewpoints of governments, and draft conventions were formulated. As a rule, the Assembly gave its opinion as to whether the subject was suited to conference action before the Council finally decided to launch this project. It was a common, but not a universal, practice to give over the major responsibility for conference preparations to a special preparatory commission.

In all of the special conferences held under the auspices of the League of Nations, the organization and procedure of the gatherings as well as their preparation were under international control. The rules of conference procedure were generally provided by the Secretariat, which in the due course of time formulated model forms for use; occasionally they were drawn up by the preparatory committee. The Secretariat of the League furnished the secretarial staff for the conferences, and the presiding officer was named by the Council.

It cannot be said that the League of Nations system of consultation and conference solved all of the international problems of the day, nor that all of those problems were even tackled. The period of its functioning was a trying one, in which new problems appeared faster than old ones were brought up for discussion. With all the limitations inherent in consultation and conference as methods of coöperation—and not least among them is the possibility of deadlock and inaction—the experience of the League is testimony to their usefulness among states whose sovereignty precludes the adoption of more vigorous and more powerful methods. The makers of the Charter of the United Nations, convinced of their high utility, embodied them in the new organization which they created.

Permanent Consultative Bodies

The point has already been brought out that consultation is carried on by deliberative bodies of many kinds in international organization. Attention is now called to the fact that there are a number of international organs, called by various names—councils, commissions, and sometimes conferences—whose activities are exclusively or essentially consultative.

It will be recalled that one of the organs of the Organization of American States is the Meeting of Consultation of the Ministers of Foreign Affairs. As the Bogotá Charter expresses it, this Meeting considers "problems of an urgent nature and of common interest to the American States." Out of its discussions no formal treaty or recommendation for legislative action would be likely to emerge, but the consultations might very possibly lead to informal agreements as to how a crisis should be met.

In 1939, at a conference held in Washington, D.C., an International Cotton Advisory Committee was created. At first the Committee was composed primarily of cotton-exporting countries—Brazil, France, India, Mexico, Peru, Turkey, the USSR, the United Kingdom, and the United States; later a number of other nations interested in cotton as producers or importers joined, to make a total of twenty-seven members. The Committee has met annually. Its principal duty is to keep in touch with developments in the world cotton market and to suggest to member governments any measures which it believes suited to better international collaboration in the production and sale of cotton.

The Rubber Study Group established in 1944 by the governments of The Netherlands, the United Kingdom, and the United States is somewhat similar. Under its terms of reference, it is authorized to make studies relating to rubber as a commodity of trade, to consider measures designed to expand the world market, to take up difficulties that arise in the international trade in rubber, and to submit reports and recommendations to the participating governments. The Study Group has met annually. At its third meeting, held at The Hague in 1946, the discussion related to the difficulties experienced in the natural-rubber-production areas, the range of uses for both natural and synthetic rubber, and the disequilibrium between the world's productive capacity and its demands for consumption; the governments involved were, as usual, informed of the substance of the discussions of the Group.

One of the most interesting consultative bodies of all is the Caribbean Commission, created in 1942 by the United Kingdom and the United States, and reorganized in 1946 with France and The Netherlands admitted. As Article 3 of the 1946 convention stipulates, "The Commission shall be a consultative and advisory body and shall have such legal capacity as may be necessary for the exercise of its functions and the fulfillment of its purposes." Article 4 defines the functions of the Commission as follows:

1. To concern itself with economic and social matters of common interest to the Caribbean area, particularly agriculture, communications, education, fisheries, health, housing, industry, labour, social welfare and trade.

2. To study, formulate and recommend on its own initiative, or as may be proposed by any of the Member or Territorial Governments, by the Research Council or the Conference, measures, programs, and policies with respect to social and economic problems designed to contribute to the well-being of the Caribbean area. It shall advise the Member and Territorial Governments on all such matters, and make recommendations for the carrying into effect of all action necessary or desirable in this connection.

3. To assist in co-ordinating local projects which have regional significance and to provide technical guidance from a wide field not otherwise available.

4. To direct and review the activities of the Research Council and to formulate its rules of procedure.

5. To provide for the convening of the sessions of the Conference, to formulate its rules of procedure, and to report to the Member Governments on Conference resolutions and recommendations.

The Commission convenes conferences of the members and of the Caribbean territories at least biennially; these conferences are also consultative in nature. As Article 12 of the 1946 treaty stipulates, "The sessions of the Conference shall provide a regular means of consultation with and between the delegates from the territories on matters of common interest. . . ."

By an agreement concluded on February 6, 1947, a South Pacific Commission was created by the governments of Australia, France, The Netherlands, New Zealand, the United Kingdom, and the United States. It is referred to in the agreement as a "consultative and advisory body to the participating governments in matters affecting the economic and social development of the non-self-governing territories within the scope of the Commission. . . ." Its duties are quite similar to those of the Caribbean Commission, and, like that agency, it has associated with it a conference of participating states.[9]

---

[9] For further information on consultative agencies, see *International Organizations in Which the United States Participates*, Department of State Publication 3655 (1950). See also the issues of *International Organization* which contain accounts of the activities of many of these agencies.

XIV Conference and Consultation Within the United Nations

EXPLAINING THE ROLE WHICH THE UNITED NATIONS HAS played in the conduct of international relations, Mr. John Foster Dulles once said, "First, the United Nations is a meeting place for international discussion." The same idea was expressed by M. Paul-Henri Spaak, when, commending the General Assembly, he said that that body "makes it possible for the statesmen of the whole world to meet each other." Consultation and conference are surely key words in any description of the methods of the United Nations. After stating the purposes of the United Nations to be those of maintaining peace, developing friendly relations among nations, and achieving coöperation in the solution of international problems, Article 1 of the Charter goes on to name the fourth purpose of the United Nations: "To be a center for harmonizing the actions of nations in the attainment of these common ends." The activity of the organization as a system of consultation and conference may be seen in the fact that within a year's time approximately five thousand meetings occur within its framework to deal with international problems.

Many of the meetings held within the United Nations are those of its permanent organs—its many commissions and committees, the Security Council, the General Assembly, and the Economic and Social Council. The point has already been made that for the most part they are on quite a different basis from the conferences that are set up from time to time, that they are more consultative in character, that they sometimes exercise supervision over other organs and activities of the United Nations, and that—except for the Economic and Social Council, and possibly the General Assembly—they are not themselves in a position to negotiate international instruments. At the San Francisco Conference (1945), the question was taken up as to whether the General Assembly should be expressly given the authority to initiate international conventions, but it was decided to omit any such provision. To date, the Assembly has not attempted to draft conventions, although there are those who believe that, without specific authorization, it may do so.[1]

The right of the Economic and Social Council to prepare draft conventions is derived from paragraph 3 of Article 62 of the Charter, which states that "it [the Council] may prepare draft conventions for submission to the General Assembly, with respect to matters falling within its competence." Notice should be taken of the fact that draft conventions prepared by the Economic and Social Council are not immediately opened for signature and ratification, but must first go to the Assembly, which must adopt them before they can be signed and ratified. In practice the power of the Economic and Social Council in this connection has been found to be useful. In 1946, a committee of the Council prepared a draft Constitution for the International Refugee Organization, and in the same year another committee drafted proposed changes in existing treaties relating to narcotic drugs; both were submitted to the Assembly, where they were adopted.

Nature of the United Nations System

Like the League of Nations system, that of the United Nations is large and pretentious, involving in one way or another several of its principal organs as well as subsidiary and auxiliary bodies. The General Assembly, the Security Council, and the Secretariat may play a part in the convocation of conferences, as did corresponding

---

[1] L. M. Goodrich and E. Hambro, *Charter of the United Nations, Commentary and Documents,* rev. ed., Boston, 1949, p. 375. These authors assert the view that the power to initiate conventions is "implicit in other powers given that organ."

organs in the League. The most obvious difference, at least from the point of view of structure, between the systems of the League and the United Nations is the presence within the latter of the Economic and Social Council and the commissions and specialized agencies attached to it. This extensive equipment for the promotion of co-operation in economic and social matters by means of consultation and conference is somewhat more than the League could boast; the status of the Economic and Social Council as one of the six "principal organs" of the United Nations underlines the aspirations of the makers of the Charter to do their utmost to bring nations together in common programs of action.

Looked at in the large, three different types of special conferences may be arranged by the organs of the United Nations, using the word "conference" in the sense of a body set up to negotiate international instruments. First, there are those of most of the specialized agencies. Second, there are the conferences arranged by the Economic and Social Council under the power granted by Article 62 of the Charter to "call, in accordance with the rules prescribed by the United Nations, international conferences on matters falling within its competence." Third, it is possible for the United Nations to arrange special conferences on matters which do not fall within the purview of the specialized agencies or of the Economic and Social Council. All three types are internationally arranged and managed, but not always by the same agencies.

Conferences Within the Specialized Agencies

Reference has been made in several other connections to the specialized agencies. Those presently functioning, or provided for but not yet in operation, are as follows:

1. International Labor Organization (ILO)

Established in 1919 as an autonomous organization associated with the League of Nations, the ILO became in 1946 one of the specialized agencies. Its Constitution has been amended since World War II to bring it into harmony with the United Nations and to effect minor changes in its structure designed to improve its functioning. Because ". . . universal and lasting peace can be established only if it is based upon social justice," as the preamble of the ILO Constitution declares, it is the duty of the organization to try to improve the conditions of labor the world over. Since labor is an important item in the cost of production, it is the assumption of the ILO that nations will be more likely to act simultaneously in accordance with an international agreement, or even recommendation, to impose upon their producers heavier obligations toward labor than they would if left to act separately. The principal organs of the ILO are (1) a General Conference, (2) the Governing Body, and (3) the International Labor Office, headed by a director. A long list of conventions and recommendations dealing with hours of work, the conditions of agricultural workers, social insurance, statistics, industrial safety, labor inspection, and allied subjects has been adopted by the general conference and turned over to the members for action.

2. Food and Agriculture Organization (FAO)

The purpose of this specialized agency is to improve nutritional standards in large sections of the world habitually undernourished. It collects and disseminates information relating to nutrition, agriculture, forestry, and fisheries. It promotes national and international action for educational projects within its field, better marketing, the conservation of natural resources, agricultural credit, and international agricultural commodity arrangements. The organization provides technical help to governments: It has dispatched missions to a number of countries to study and report on agricultural production, and it has held statistical training schools to help governments set up sound statistical services. The main organs of the FAO are the Conference, the Council, and the Secretariat, headed by a Director-General.

3. The United Nations Educational, Scientific and Cultural Organization (UNESCO)

As its constitution states, the purposes of UNESCO is to contribute to peace and security by promoting international coöperation in matters of education, science, and culture. To accomplish this purpose, it is expected under its constitution to advance "the mutual knowledge and understanding of peoples," to give "fresh impulse to popular education and to the spread of culture," and to "maintain, increase, and diffuse knowledge." The programs and projects of UNESCO fall within several broad groups: raising educational standards; mass communications; educational help to war-ravaged countries; cultural activities; human and social relations of peoples; and natural sciences. Its organization includes a Conference, an Executive Board, a Secretariat in charge of a Director-General, and the national commissions.

4. International Civil Aviation Organization (ICAO)

The aims and objectives of ICAO, according to the Convention on International Civil Aviation, are "to develop the principles and techniques of international air navigation and to foster the planning and development of international air transport" so as to ensure "the safe and orderly growth of international civil aviation throughout the world," to encourage aircraft design and operation for peaceful purposes, to encourage air navigation facilities, to meet the need for passenger service, to prevent the waste of unreasonable competition, to avoid discrimination between states, and to promote safety of flight. A great variety of activities are conducted with these objectives in view, such as the securing of simpler government regulations relating to customs and immigration, holding regional meetings on selected subjects, studying current problems and publishing their findings, and encouraging agreements between members. The organs of ICAO are an Assembly, a Council, and a Secretariat with a Secretary-General.

5. The International Bank

The Bank has as its main objectives the extension of assistance to nations for reconstruction and development purposes by facilitating the investment of capital, the encouragement of private investments abroad, and the promotion of the long-range balanced growth of international trade, with the maintenance of equilibrium in balances of payments. It is able to lend funds directly, to guarantee loans made by others, and to participate with others in loans. The practice is to earmark loans for definite productive purposes. No loan is authorized, however, until the Bank has satisfied itself that the project is in every way sound. The Bank's stock on April 1, 1948, amounted to $8,263,000,000, subscribed to in stated proportions by member states. Its organization comprises a Board of Governors, Executive Directors, a President, and a permanent staff.

6. The International Fund

The Fund was created principally for the purpose of promoting monetary exchange stability among members, thereby to facilitate the orderly expansion and growth of international trade. Also numbered among its purposes in its Articles of Agreement are the "establishment of a multilateral system of payments in respect of current transactions . . . ," and "to shorten the duration and to lessen the degree of disequilibrium in the international balances of payments of members." The Fund offers the machinery for consultation and collaboration on international monetary problems. The member states have agreed not to engage in competitive foreign exchange practices, and the Articles of Agreement contain specific provisions toward that end. A pool of more than eight billion dollars has been made available by members, to be used for the purpose of making each other's currencies more available. The organization of the International Fund includes a Board of Governors, the Executive Directors, the Managing Director, and the permanent staff.

7. The Universal Postal Union (UPU)

As stated in the International Postal Convention, which first came into force in 1875, the aim of the UPU is to ensure the organization and perfection of the various postal services and to promote international coöperation within the field of postal communication. The Convention unites the members into a single postal territory for the reciprocal exchange of correspondence.

Regulations are in force for letters, single and reply-paid post cards, commercial papers, printed matter, raised print for the blind, samples of merchandise, small packets, and phonopost articles; the Convention fixes the weight limits, the dimensions, and rates for these items of correspondence. There are special agreements annexed to the Convention, binding only upon those member states which so indicate, relating to insured letters and boxes, parcel post, money orders, postal checks, collection orders, subscriptions to newspapers and periodicals, and cash on delivery. So vital are these services to the peoples of the world that years ago, before the League of Nations was created, the UPU was often referred to as the most important agency for the promotion of international understanding then in existence. The organs of the UPU are the Congress, a Conference, a permanent Executive and Liaison Committee, and a Bureau.

8. The World Health Organization (WHO)

According to the preamble of the Constitution of the WHO, "the enjoyment of the highest attainable standard of health is one of the fundamental rights of every human being without distinction of race, religion, political belief, economic or social condition." It goes on to say, 'The health of all peoples is fundamental to the attainment of peace and security . . ." and "unequal development in different countries in the promotion of health and control of disease, especially communicable disease, is a common danger." The organization attempts to coördinate international health activities, to assist governments in strengthening their health services, to promote housing and recreational facilities, to improve mental health, and to develop an informed public opinion on health measures. The principal organs of the WHO are the Assembly, the Executive Board, and the Secretariat.

9. The International Telecommunication Union (ITU)

In order to improve international telecommunication facilities, the ITU effects allocation of the radio frequency spectrum; it fosters collaboration for the purpose of keeping rates at a low level;

it works for the promotion of safety of life through the coöperation of national services; and it conducts research and publishes
information useful to members. The organization prepares and
adopts regulations dealing with the operation of international
radio as well as telegraphic and telephonic services; and it revises
them when necessary to meet changing conditions. The main organs of the ITU are the Conference, the Administrative Council,
the Administrative Conferences, and the General Secretariat.

10. The Inter-Governmental Maritime Consultative Organization (IMCO)

The main purposes of the IMCO, as defined by its Convention,
are to effect an exchange of information, to revise old maritime
conventions and draft new ones, to encourage the highest standards of maritime safety and efficiency of navigation, to promote
the availability of shipping services to commerce without discrimination, and to deal with problems relating to shipping referred
to it by any organ or specialized agency of the United Nations.
Its main organs are an Assembly, a Council, the Maritime Safety
Committee, and a Secretariat.

11. The International Trade Organization (ITO)

As provided in the Havana Charter, the objectives of the ITO
are to increase the production and exchange of goods, to promote
the economic development of the nations and particularly of
those now lacking in industry, to encourage the reduction of tariffs and other trade barriers, and to facilitate the solution of problems relating to trade in the fields of employment, economic development, commercial policy, and business practices. The more
routine aspects of the work of the ITO will relate to interpreting
and administering the provisions of the Charter, which covers the
whole field of economic relationship: tariffs, quotes, export sub-
sidies, exchange problems, customs formalities, cartels, commodity agreements, state trading, foreign investment, employment,
and economic development. According to the Charter, the organization of the ITO will include a Conference, an Executive

Board, and a staff headed by a Director-General. To date, the ITO has not been set up.

12. The World Meteorological Organization

The WMO is the successor to the International Meteorological Organization, founded in 1878. As defined by the Convention of 1947, the WMO is to promote world-wide coöperation in setting up networks of stations for the making of meteorological observations, to promote the establishment of systems for the rapid exchange of weather information, to encourage the standardization of meteorological observations, to further the application of meteorological information to aviation, shipping, and agriculture, and to stimulate research in meteorology. The main organs of the IMO are a Conference of Directors, the International Meteorological Committee, and a Secretariat.

13. International Refugee Organization (IRO—disbanded in 1951)

This organization grew out of the need for extending assistance to refugees and displaced persons. Immediately after World War II, the United Nations Relief and Rehabilitation Administration (UNRRA) was in charge of this work and accomplished a great deal. In 1948, the IRO took over, and it was understood that in 1951 the organization would go out of existence. The main duties of the IRO in regard to refugees and displaced persons have been repatriation, identification and classification, care and assistance, legal and political protection, transport, and resettlement. Included in its structure have been a General Council, an Executive Committee, and a Secretariat.

The similarity in the organization of these specialized agencies is quite apparent. Structurally, the usual arrangement is (1) a deliberative body, (2) an executive board or committee, and (3) a permanent secretariat or office. The precise names and duties of these agencies vary somewhat, but viewed collectively they follow much the same pattern.

Functionally, the specialized agencies are more diverse than structurally. Some of them have highly developed and active conference systems, whereas others have little or nothing to offer along this line. All have deliberative bodies, known variously as an "assembly," a "conference," a "congress," a "board of governors," a "board of executive directors," or a "general council." These bodies meet, some annually, as the General Conference of UNESCO and the conference of ILO; some as arranged by a preceding conference, such as the Congress of the UPU; some after intervals not to exceed a fixed number of years, as the Conference of Directors of WMO; and others according to prescribed plans of their own. All, however, have recurring meetings, and in this respect all embody one of the elements common to conference systems. It is in the functions, the kind of work they do, that the deliberative organs of the specialized agencies vary most, and the variation is so great that in certain cases the "conferences" have very little diplomatic significance.

In many of the specialized agencies the conferences are authorized to negotiate conventions and to submit recommendations to member states. The Conference of the ILO, for instance, negotiates and adopts by a two-thirds vote both recommendations to member states and conventions requiring ratification. In the General Conference of UNESCO, conventions are adopted by a two-thirds vote, whereas recommendations require only a simple majority. The conferences of the following organizations are authorized by their constitutions to adopt conventions or recommendations or both:

The International Labor Organization
The United Nations Educational, Scientific and Cultural Organization
The Food and Agriculture Organization
The World Health Organization
The Universal Postal Union
Intergovernmental Maritime Consultative Organization
International Trade Organization

These organizations therefore maintain well-developed conference systems.

In some instances the conference is limited in its negotiating function to the revision of the organization's convention (its constitution), to the revision of the regulations of the agency, or to both. Where this is the case, the conference systems are consequently less elaborate than those of the agencies which adopt new conventions and recommendations. The conferences of the following agencies come within this category:

The International Telecommunications Union
The International Civil Aviation Organization
International Refugee Organization
World Meteorological Organization

Combined with the diplomatic function of negotiating conventions and regulations, or making modifications in them, are usually some purely consultative duties. The General Conference of UNESCO, for instance, determines "policies and the main lines of work of the organization," and it receives and considers reports submitted periodically to the organization by member states. In several of the specialized agencies this consultative function outweighs the diplomatic, and vice versa.

In two of the specialized agencies the conference body has duties that belong to the field of international administration rather than to that of diplomacy—the International Bank and the International Fund. The functions of the Board of Governors of the Bank explicitly include "all the powers of the Bank," as the convention setting up the Bank states; its duties are therefore primarily those of management.

In most instances, the delegates to the conferences of the agencies are technical experts. In the WMO it is required that the delegates be the directors of the meteorological services of the ninety-two member states and colonies. In the ILO there is a unique system of representation in the conference whereby each member state has four delegates, of whom two represent the government, one employers, and one employees. The representatives to the plenipotentiary conferences of the ITU are diplomats, while those sent to the administrative conferences are experts.

It has already been pointed out that the organization of the specialized agencies includes a permanent office or secretariat and an executive board, or its equivalent under another name; these organs, too, play important roles in the conference systems to which they are attached. In many of the specialized agencies, the conference agenda is fixed by the executive board, as, for example, in the WHO, where the Executive Board performs this duty for the Assembly, and in the ILO, where the Governing Body (as the executive board is known) does so for the Conference. The permanent offices or secretariats invariably provide the secretarial staffs of the conferences. In addition, those offices make other contributions to conference activities, as prescribed by the constitutions of the respective specialized agencies; for instance, the International Labor Office prepares documents relating to items on the agenda for conference use.

Methods of "follow up" have been embodied in the conference systems of some of the specialized agencies, in order to check upon the member states and find out whether they have ratified conventions negotiated at the conference or put into force the recommendations made. In the WHO, the members agree that within eighteen months after the adoption of a convention by the Assembly, they "will take action relative to the acceptance of such convention or agreement." Each member must notify the Director-General of any action taken, and if it has not ratified a convention within the eighteen months allowed, it must give its reasons; after it has ratified a convention, the member must furnish an annual report to the Director-General of its progress in making the convention effective. The ILO maintains an elaborate system of this nature which applies both to conventions and to recommendations: the members are obliged to take action on the former within eighteen months and on the latter within a year and to notify the Director of acceptance; on request of the Governing Body, members must keep the Director informed as to conditions within their respective countries relating to the subjects dealt with in conventions and recommendations. UNESCO requires a member state to "submit recommendations or conventions to its competent authorities within a period of one year from the close of the session of the General Assembly at which they were adopted." Also, each member must report annually upon the action taken by it on recommendations and conventions.

Another feature of the conference systems of the specialized agencies is the authority to convoke special conferences to deal with designated subjects. The Constitution of FAO stipulates that "the Conference may convene general, technical, regional, or other special conferences . . . ," and in fact a number of special gatherings have been called, such as the Conference on Forestry Statistics (Washington, 1947), the International Timber Conference (Marianski-Lazne, Czechosolvakia, 1947), and Rice Study Group (Travancore, India, 1947). Several of the other specialized agencies are able to sponsor special conferences and have done so.

Conferences Arranged by the Economic and Social Council

At the San Francisco Conference of 1945, the initial proposal that the Economic and Social Council be empowered to call conferences was made by Australia and would have limited the Council to conferences for the purpose of safeguarding the economic and social functions of the organization in the event of an emergency. This proposal was later broadened to allow the Council to call a conference on any matter within its competence, limited only by the requirement that the power be exercised in accordance with rules prescribed by the General Assembly. As a matter of practice, several conferences have been brought together by the Council, though not a large number, for the reason that the specialized agencies, taken together, cover most of the economic and social field.

No permanent rules governing the calling of conferences by the Economic and Social Council were adopted by the General Assembly until 1949. During the first part of the first session of the Assembly in 1946, the following rule, known as Supplementary Rule T of the Provisional Rules of Procedure, was adopted as a temporary expedient:

Pending the adoption under Paragraph 4 of Article 62 of the Charter of definitive rules for the calling of international conferences, the Economic and Social Council may, after due consultation with Members of the United Nations, call international conferences in conformity with the spirit of Article 62 on any matter within the competence of the Council, including the following matters: international trade and employment; the equitable adjustment of prices on the international market; and health.

During this interval before the adoption in 1949 of permanent rules, the Economic and Social Council called conferences both on its own initiative and on request of the General Assembly. On its own initiative it called the International Health Conference of 1946 to write the Constitution of the World Health Organization, and on the suggestion of the General Assembly it called the Conference on Freedom of Information of 1948.

Because of the inadequacy of Supplementary Rule T, the General Assembly set the Secretary-General to work, in consultation with the Economic and Social Council, preparing more definitive regulations on the calling of conferences. The draft prepared was adopted by both the Council and the General Assembly in 1949 and has since been in effect. Under its terms the Economic and Social Council may at any time call a conference on any matter within its competence if, "after consultation with the Secretary-General and the appropriate specialized agency it is satisfied that the work to be done by the conference cannot be done satisfactorily by any organ of the United Nations or by any specialized agency." The rules are quite specific as to the methods of preparing and organizing a forthcoming conference, making available to the Council for this purpose the services of the Secretary-General of the United Nations in certain particulars, and permitting the employment, where desirable, of special preparatory committees.[2] The Council is authorized to invite not only member states of the United Nations to conferences, but also nonmembers, political communities not fully self-governing, the specialized agencies, and "non-governmental organizations having consultative status with the Council."

To a considerable extent, the rules adopted in 1949 for the calling of conferences were in harmony with the practice of the preceding years. Nonmembers had been invited to conferences, as in the Con-

---

[2] For the text of the Rules for the Calling of International Conferences of States, see Appendix II to this chapter.

ference on Freedom of Information (1948), where thirteen states not members of the United Nations were present, including states which had been rejected for membership. Representatives of specialized agencies, intergovernmental organizations, and nongovernmental organizations had also been present at conferences; all were in attendance at the United Nations Conference on Trade and Employment (1947–1948) and at the Maritime Conference (1948). The Economic and Social Council divides the nongovernmental organizations into these categories: organizations in category A are those having a basic interest in most of the activities of the Council; those in category B are concerned only with a few of the activities; and those in category C are primarily concerned with the development of public opinion.[3] The representatives of the specialized agencies, intergovernmental, and nongovernmental organizations at conferences possess only a consultative status and are without the right to vote.[4]

When, in December, 1949, the Sixth Committee of the General Assembly was discussing the present rules on the calling of international conferences by the Economic and Social Council, two questions came up and were debated.[5] One was in the form of a proposed amendment offered by the delegation of the USSR to the effect that conferences of states might be called by the Council only "after due consultation with the Members of the United Nations." The Soviet delegate argued that, because conferences impose a sacrifice of time and money on the part of the states which attend, they ought not to be called unless a substantial number of states had acquiesced. He maintained that the provision in Article 62 (4) of the Charter to the effect that the Council could call conferences only "in accordance with the rules prescribed by the United Nations" indicated a clear intention not to give the Council full discretion in the matter. He was not specific as to how many members of

---

[3] See Appendix IV to this chapter for further descriptions and lists of the nongovernmental organizations.

[4] By action taken on February 27, 1950, the nongovernmental organizations were given an even greater importance as consultative bodies in the Economic and Social Council than they had previously had.

[5] See Yuen-li Liang, "What is an International Conference?" *American Journal of International Law*, 1950, vol. 44, no. 2, pp. 333–341.

the United Nations should be consulted by the Council. This proposed amendment to the rules was opposed by several delegations, including those of the United States, Brazil, Colombia, and Cuba; they pointed to the advantage to be gained from giving the Economic and Social Council greater freedom of action. By a vote of twenty-five to fifteen, with fifteen abstentions, the Sixth Committee rejected the Russian proposal.

The second subject which was debated within the Sixth Committee on this occasion was a proposed resolution to permit the Economic and Social Council to call nongovernmental conferences. It was clear that Article 62 (4) of the Charter, giving the Council the right to call "international conferences on matters falling within its competence," permitted the calling of conferences of states, but did it authorize nongovernmental conferences? The Russian delegation contended in the negative, arguing that the purpose of Article 62 (4) was to provide a means of preparing draft conventions for nations to sign and ratify, a function which could not be performed by conferences of private groups. Other representatives in the Sixth Committee, including the American, took the opposite point of view, stressing the advantages of a more liberal interpretation of the Charter. The debate hinged on the meaning to be given to "international conferences" as those words were found in Article 62 (4), whether they should be understood as including both conferences of states and conferences of nongovernmental bodies, or only the former. In the end it was decided, at the suggestion of Argentina, to have the Secretary-General, in consultation with the Economic and Social Council, draft rules for the calling of nongovernmental conferences, to be placed before the General Assembly at a later date for examination.

The various permanent commissions attached to the Economic and Social Council may very possibly have some part to play in conferences called by the Council. At the present time there are twelve of these commissions, as follows:

Economic Commission for Europe
Economic Commission for Asia and the Far East

Economic Commission for Latin America
Economic and Employment
Fiscal
Statistical
Transport and Communications
Human Rights
Status of Women
Social
Population
Narcotic Drugs

These commissions are composed of from twelve to eighteen members.[6] Some of them maintain subcommittees; the Human Rights Commission, for instance, has a Subcommittee on Freedom of Information and of the Press. Three of the commissions (the first three listed above) are regional in character, while the others are functional. All have been created and their duties defined by the Economic and Social Council. So far there have been frequent meetings of the commissions in an effort to carry forward the work entrusted to them.

The original suggestion for a conference may emanate from some one of the commissions, and then be promoted by the Economic and Social Council. They have been requested to prepare basic conference documents, including the agenda; the Sub-Committee on Freedom of Information and of the Press, for instance, was asked to prepare the agenda of the Conference on Freedom of Information (1948).

Other United Nations Conferences

There are subjects of international concern which do not appear to come within the competence of the Economic and Social Council or of the specialized agencies, and regarding which action may be deemed necessary. They fall primarily within the political and legal fields of international relations. The League of Nations usually dealt with such problems through the medium of a special conference, like the World Disarmament Conference of 1932–1935.

---

[6] See Appendix III to this chapter for the Commission on Narcotic Drugs.

To date, the United Nations has set up no special conference to deal with a problem beyond the competence of the specialized agencies and the Economic and Social Council. No doubt, however, it would be altogether possible to do so were the need to present itself. Under Article 11, the General Assembly "may consider the general principles of coöperation in the maintenance of peace and security, including the principles governing disarmament and the regulation of armaments, and may make recommendations with regard to such principles to the Members or to the Security Council or both." Discussion of the subject has taken place in the Assembly, and a resolution was adopted in 1946 on the principles governing the regulation and reduction of armaments, after which the Security Council set up a Commission on Conventional Armaments; no specific program of armaments control has, however, been undertaken. Were such a program to become an immediate objective, it is likely that a general disarmament conference would have to be called to formulate its terms, a conference comparable to the League of Nations Disarmament Conference of 1932.

According to Article 13 of the Charter, the General Assembly may make recommendations for the purpose of promoting coöperation in the field of international law. Under this provision, an International Law Commission has been established to promote the progressive development of international law and its codification. One way of discussing and reaching final agreement on any draft code which this commission might formulate would be by special conference. Again looking back to the experience of the League of Nations, we observe that when in 1930 that organization was ready to act on the subject of nationality in international law, a conference was held at The Hague for the purpose.

Were a special conference to be called by the United Nations to deal with armament, international law, or any subject which the specialized agencies and the Economic and Social Council have no authority to treat, it is probable that the work of calling and preparing such a meeting would be divided between the Security Council, the General Assembly, the Secretariat, and a special preparatory committee. While the precise division of authority might be difficult to predict, no doubt it would duplicate in its general outlines that formerly in use within the League of Nations.

The System at Work

The accomplishments of the United Nations conference systems (exclusive of the meetings of the permanent organs of the United Nations) are legion, particularly if consultative activities be added to the purely diplomatic. To recount them would be much too ponderous a task for a volume of this nature. Most of the accomplishments have come out of the conferences of the specialized agencies, for the majority of conferences held have been within those bodies. Some idea of what these conferences have done may be gained by citing a few facts and giving a few illustrations.

The thirteenth session of the Conference of the International Labor Organization met at Geneva, Switzerland, from June 19 to July 11, 1947, and was attended by the delegates of forty-eight states. Four international agencies were also represented at the meeting: the United Nations, UNESCO, the International Fund, and the WHO. One of the notable accomplishments of the Conference was the preparation of a report on freedom of association, a problem referred to it by the Economic and Social Council. Five conventions were adopted and referred to members for ratification, all relating to social policy and labor standards for nonmetropolitan territories (colonial possessions): (1) standards of social policy; (2) application to such territories of standards contained in existing conventions; (3) right of association; (4) settlement of labor disputes; and (5) maximum length of contracts for indigenous workers. One convention and several recommendations were formulated for consideration at the next conference. Finally, a resolution was adopted codifying ILO actions on standards for women workers. Together these achievements were a substantial contribution to the improvement of the conditions of labor in the world.

The Conferences of UNESCO are less likely to result in conventions or recommendations than those of the ILO, since they are usually consultative in nature and their decisions are often in the form of instructions to the Director-General; recommendations to member states are, however, not uncommon. Listed below are some, but by no means all, of the decisions taken at the Conference held at Mexico City in 1948:

1. That the Director-General furnish information requested as to the educational needs in war-devasted countries.
2. That a recommendation be made to member states to arrange for duty-free entrance of contributed educational material in war-devasted areas.
3. That the Director-General purchase and distribute in war-devas-tated areas within the limits of allocated funds, books and scientific materials.
4. That member states be requested for information concerning the activities of governmental and nongovernmental agencies on the exchange of persons for educational purposes.
5. That the Director-General continue and expand his inquiry begun in 1947 on technical needs in mass communications.
6. That the Director-General promote the development of an interna-tional series of films on the special achievements of a number of nations in the fields of education, science, and culture.
7. That the Director-General negotiate with a library school to con-duct a summer session for librarians in coöperation with the Inter-national Federation of Library Associations.
8. That the Director-General explore all possible means of encour-aging the inexpensive production of books, periodicals, and teaching materials in the fields of UNESCO's interests.
9. That the Director-General encourage member states to fulfil the obligation of establishing a minimum fundamental education for all their people in conformity with UNESCO's Constitution.
10. That the Director-General arrange for the conduct of at least three seminars in education in 1948.
11. That the Director-General continue to support by technical advice the creation of an International Theater Institute.
12. That the Director-General promote inquiries into the distinctive character of the various national cultures, ideals, and legal systems.

On December 14, 1946, the General Assembly adopted a resolu-tion asking the Economic and Social Council to call a conference to deal with freedom of information. The Council proceeded to do so, arranging among other things that the Subcommission on Freedom of Information and the Press prepare a draft documented agenda for the conference. The Council fixed a date for the conference and decided what states, intergovernmental and nongovernmental organizations should be invited. The Secretary-General of the United Nations was asked to prepare documentation for the gathering. The Conference assembled on March 23, 1948, and lasted until April 21, 1948. It adopted three conventions, dealing with (1) the gathering and transmittal of news; (2) the institution of an international right of correction; and (3) freedom of information.

Government by Conference

The highly organized conference systems of today contrast sharply with the rudimentary style of conference diplomacy practiced at the Congress of Westphalia (1648). The mechanism of conference has been gradually improved until it has reached the point that, well-prepared and organized, it offers to nations which are in a mood to agree every reasonable opportunity to do so and to work out programs of common action. Kept in good repair, well-lubricated, and operated by states seriously seeking concord, this mechanism can manufacture many of the elements of a peaceful world, and indeed it has done so in the past. It is equipped to turn out its products faster and on a larger scale by far than simultaneous bilateral diplomacy in writing between a group of nations could ever hope to approach. As Secretary of State Hughes remarked, an hour of direct negotiations between the representatives of states may be worth months of written communications. Without doubt, the conference has proved its worth; constant resort to it indicates that it rates high in the esteem of nations.

That the conference method sometimes fails to meet the fine expectations held for it by the public may often be explained by the fact that it has not been operated properly; a meeting may have been poorly prepared, it may have been held in an unfriendly city, the delegates may have been inept, too much openness to the public may have been allowed, or a dozen and one other mistakes of a like nature committed. Moreover, a *sine qua non* of every successful conference is a genuine desire on the part of the participating nations to find an agreement and a resulting willingness to make reasonable concessions to that end. In this regard, conferences are only reflections of the international situation as it exists, whether there is amity or enmity among the participants. Professor James Burnham has stated this fundamental fact succinctly, "A conference can come to a productive agreement only when the real basis of agreement exists independently of, and prior to the conference itself."[7] This puts the conference, and for that matter all international organization, in its true light as a means to a desired end, rather than as an end in itself or even as a means to an end which is not desired.

One of the principal reasons for the failure of many conferences since World War II has been the lack of a basis of agreement. The wide split between Russia and the West has wrecked many a conference, including the meetings of the Council of Foreign Ministers whose duty it was to write treaties of peace, the meetings of the Atomic Energy Commission, and those of conspicuous United Nations agencies. It may be no exaggeration to say that Russia has not desired that agreements should come out of those meetings, that, unless her own points of view were to be accepted in their entirety, she preferred the disruptive effects of inaction. In any case, it is clear that the Russian conception of diplomacy, both bilateral and multilateral, gives a prominent place to propaganda enterprises. Propaganda activities in diplomacy are highly obstructive to agreement, for they arouse animosities and create an atmosphere of suspicion and fear that precludes any possibility of the calm give-and-take necessary to productive negotiations. Successful diplomacy requires an atmosphere of confidence, respect, and trust.

That a conference fails to produce an agreement is not always conclusive proof that it has been a failure. A clarification of issues can in itself indicate progress, particularly if the participating nations have not left the conference table in a huff. With a better understanding of each other's attitudes, the states may, after an interval of time, find themselves in a position to make a lasting agreement.

Sir Maurice Hankey commented on what he believed to be an advantage of frequent conferences between nations, "Real intimacy

---

[7] J. Burnham, *The Coming Defeat of Communism*, New York, 1949, pp. 36–37.

and friendship [of diplomats] materially contribute to the success of diplomacy by conference by rendering possible absolute frankness of discussion." On this point Mr. Harold Nicolson, another British diplomat long schooled in the art of conference diplomacy, takes issue in the following statement:

. . . it is possible that, in place of friendship, antipathy may result from such frequent contacts. The personal relations between Lord Curzon, for instance, and M. Poincaré did not assist negotiation. Even friendship may lead (as at the Thoiry luncheon party between Briand and Stresemann) to some impulsive settlement which has thereafter to be repudiated. The dangers of imprecision, misunderstanding, leakage and indiscretion are much increased. And rapidity of discussion is not, in times of peace, invariably an advantage.[8]

Certainly by this time it has become clear that, with all its advantages—and it has many—the conference is no cure-all. Back in the 1920's there was a general tendency on the part of the public to assume that once a conference was called to handle a problem, that problem would be solved forthwith. After numerous disappointments, the people have learned that conferences have their limitations, whether they be independent or United Nations gatherings, and that they have been known, indeed, to accentuate, instead of allay, international misunderstanding. Viewed in the large, however, the constructive work of conferences has no doubt outweighed their destructive results, many times over.

▲

APPENDIX TO CHAPTER XIV

I

Constitution of the Food and Agriculture Organization

Preamble

The Nations accepting this Constitution, being determined to promote the common welfare by furthering separate and collective action on their part for the purposes of:

---

[8] H. Nicolson, op. cit., pp. 157–158.

raising levels of nutrition and standards of living of the peoples
under their respective jurisdictions,

securing improvements in the efficiency of the production and
distribution of all food and agricultural products,

bettering the condition of rural populations, and thus contributing toward an expanding world economy,

hereby establish the Food and Agriculture Organization of the
United Nations, hereinafter referred to as the "Organization,"
through which the Members will report to one another on the measures taken and the progress achieved in the fields of action set forth
above.

ARTICLE 1—FUNCTIONS OF THE ORGANIZATION

1. The Organization shall collect, analyze, interpret, and dissemi-
nate information relating to nutrition, food and agriculture.

2. The Organization shall promote and, where appropriate, shall
recommend national and international action with respect to

a. scientific, technological, social, and economic research relating
to nutrition, food and agriculture;

b. the improvement of education and administration relating to
nutrition, food and agriculture, and the spread of public knowledge
of nutritional and agricultural science and practice;

c. the conservation of natural resources and the adoption of improved methods of agricultural production;

d. the improvement of the processing, marketing, and distribution of food and agricultural products;

e. the adoption of policies for the provision of adequate agricultural credit, national and international;

f. the adoption of international policies with respect to agricultural commodity arrangements.

3. It shall also be the function of the Organization

a. to furnish such technical assistance as governments may request;

b. to organize, in coöperation with the governments concerned,
such missions may be needed to assist them to fulfill the obligations

arising from their acceptance of the recommendations of the United Nations Conference on Food and Agriculture; and

c. generally to take all necessary and appropriate action to implement the purposes of the Organization as set forth in the Preamble.

ARTICLE 2—MEMBERSHIP

1. The original Members of the Organization shall be such of the nations specified in Annex I as accept this Constitution in accordance with the provisions of Article 21.

2. Additional Members may be admitted to the Organization by a vote concurred in by a two-thirds majority of all the members of the Conference and upon acceptance of this constitution as in force at the time of admission.

ARTICLE 3—THE CONFERENCE

1. There shall be a Conference of the Organization in which each Member nation shall be represented by one member.

2. Each Member nation may appoint an alternate, associates, and advisers to its member of the Conference. The Conference may make rules concerning the participation of alternates, associates, and advisers in its proceedings, but any such participation shall be without the right to vote except in the case of an alternate or associate participating in the place of a member.

3. No member of the Conference may represent more than one Member nation.

4. Each Member nation shall have only one vote.

5. The Conference may invite any public international organization which has responsibilities related to those of the Organization to appoint a representative who shall participate in its meetings on the conditions prescribed by the Conference. No such representative shall have the right to vote.

6. The Conference shall elect its own officers, regulate its own procedure, and make rules governing the convocation of sessions and the determination of agenda.

7. Except as otherwise expressly provided in this Constitution or

by rules made by the Conference, all matters shall be decided by the Conference by a simple majority of the votes cast.

ARTICLE 4—FUNCTIONS OF THE CONFERENCE

1. The Conference shall determine the policy and approve the budget of the Organization and shall exercise the other powers conferred upon it by this Constitution.

2. The Conference may by a two-thirds majority of the votes cast make recommendations concerning questions relating to food and agriculture to be submitted to Member nations for consideration with a view to implementation by national action.

3. The Conference may by a two-thirds majority of the votes cast submit conventions concerning questions relating to food and agriculture to Member nations for consideration with a view to their acceptance by the appropriate constitutional procedure.

4. The Conference shall make rules laying down the procedure to be followed to secure:

a. proper consultation with governments and adequate technical preparation prior to consideration by the Conference of proposed recommendations and conventions; and

b. proper consultation with governments in regard to relations between the Organization and national institutions or private persons.

5. The Conference may make recommendations to any public international organization regarding any matter pertaining to the purpose of the Organization.

6. The Conference may by a two-thirds majority of the votes cast agree to discharge any other functions consistent with the purposes of the Organization which may be assigned to it by governments or provided for by any arrangement between the Organization and any other public international organization.

ARTICLE 5—THE EXECUTIVE COMMITTEE

1. The Conference shall appoint an Executive Committee consisting of not less than nine or more than fifteen members or alternate or associate members of the Conference or their advisers who are

qualified by administrative experience or other special qualifications to contribute to the attainment of the purpose of the Organization. There shall be not more than one member from any Member nation. The tenure and other conditions of office of the members of the Executive Committee shall be subject to rules to be made by the Conference.

2. Subject to the provisions of paragraph 1 of this Article, the Conference shall have regard in appointing the Executive Committee to the desirability that its membership should reflect as varied as possible an experience of different types of economy in relation to food and agriculture.

3. The Conference may delegate to the Executive Committee such powers as it may determine, with the exception of the powers set forth in paragraph 2 of Article 2, Article 4, paragraph 1 of Article 7, Article 13, and Article 20, of this Constitution.

4. The members of the Executive Committee shall exercise the powers delegated to them by the Conference on behalf of the whole Conference and not as representatives of their respective governments.

5. The Executive Committee shall appoint its own officers and, subject to any decisions of the Conference, shall regulate its own procedure.

Article 6—Other Committees and Conferences

1. The Conference may establish technical and regional standing committees and may appoint committees to study and report on any matter pertaining to the purpose of the Organization.

2. The Conference may convene general, technical, regional, or other special conferences ánd may provide for the representation at such conferences, in such manner as it may determine, of national and international bodies concerned with nutrition, food and agriculture.

Article 7—The Director-General

1. There shall be a Director-General of the Organization who shall be appointed by the Conference by such procedure and on such terms as it may determine.

2. Subject to the general supervision of the Conference and its Executive Committee, the Director-General shall have full power and authority to direct the work of the Organization.

3. The Director-General or a representative designated by him shall participate, without the right to vote, in all meetings of the Conference and of its Executive Committee and shall formulate for consideration by the Conference and the Executive Committee proposals for appropriate action in regard to matters coming before them.

ARTICLE 8—STAFF

1. The staff of the Organization shall be appointed by the Director-General in accordance with such procedure as may be determined by rules made by the Conference. . . .

ARTICLE 19—WITHDRAWAL

Any Member nation may give notice of withdrawal from the Organization at any time after the expiration of four years from the date of its acceptance of this Constitution. Such notice shall take effect one year after the date of its communication to the Director-General of the Organization subject to the Member nation's having at that time paid its annual contribution for each year of its membership including the financial year following the date of such notice.

ARTICLE 20—AMENDMENT OF CONSTITUTION

1. Amendments to this Constitution involving new obligations for Member nations shall require the approval of the Conference by a vote concurred in by a two-thirds majority of all the members of the Conference and shall take effect on acceptance by two-thirds of the Member nations for each Member nation accepting the amendment and thereafter for each remaining Member nation on acceptance by it.

2. Other amendments shall take effect on adoption by the Conference by a vote concurred in by a two-thirds majority of all the members of the Conference. . . .

II

*Rules for the Calling of International Conferences of States**

RULE 1

The Economic and Social Council may at any time decide to call an international conference of States on any matter within its competence, provided that, after consultation with the Secretary-General and the appropriate specialized agencies, it is satisfied that the work to be done by the conference cannot be done satisfactorily by any other organ of the United Nations or by any specialized agency.

RULE 2

When the Council has decided to call an international conference, it shall prescribe the terms of reference and prepare the provisional agenda of the conference.

RULE 3

The Council shall decide what States shall be invited to the conference.

The Secretary-General shall send out as soon as possible the invitations, accompanied by copies of the provisional agenda, and shall give notice, accompanied by copies of the provisional agenda, to every member of the United Nations not invited. Such Member may send observers to the conference.

Nonmember States whose interests are directly affected by the matters to be considered at the conference may be invited to it and shall have full rights as members thereof.

RULE 4

With the approval of the responsible State, the Council may decide to invite to a conference of States a territory which is self-governing in the fields covered by the terms of reference of the conference but which is not responsible for the conduct of its foreign

---

* Adopted by the General Assembly, December 3, 1949. General Assembly Resolution 366 (IV). General Assembly, 4th Session. Official Records, Resolutions, 1944, U.N. Document A/1251, pp. 64–65.

relations. The Council shall decide the extent of the participation in the conference of any territory so invited.

RULE 5

The Council shall, after consultation with the Secretary-General, fix the date and place of the conference or request the Secretary-General to do so.

RULE 6

The Council shall make arrangements for financing the conference, except that any arrangements involving the expenditure of funds of the United Nations shall be subject to the applicable regulations, rules and resolutions of the General Assembly.

RULE 7

The Council:

a. Shall prepare, or request the Secretary-General to prepare, provisional rules of procedure for the conference;

b. May establish a preparatory committee to carry out such functions in preparation for the conference as the Council shall indicate;

c. May request the Secretary-General to perform such functions in preparation for the conference as the Council shall indicate.

RULE 8

The Council may invite specialized agencies in relationship with the United Nations and non-governmental organizations having consultative stature with the Council to take part in conferences called under these rules. The representatives of such agencies or organizations shall be entitled to the same rights and privileges as at sessions of the Council itself, unless the Council decides otherwise.

RULE 9

Subject to any decisions and directions of the Council the Secretary-General shall appoint the executive secretary for the conference, provide the secretariat and services required and make such other administrative arrangements as may be necessary.

III

The Commission on Narcotic Drugs (Created February 18, 1946)*

1. The Economic and Social Council, in order to provide machinery whereby full effect may be given to the international conventions relating to narcotic drugs, and to provide for continuous review of and progress in the international control of such drugs, establishes a Commission on Narcotic Drugs.

2. The Commission shall:

a. assist the Council in exercising such powers of supervision over the application of international conventions and agreements dealing with narcotic drugs as may be assumed by or conferred on the Council;

b. carry out such functions entrusted to the League of Nations Advisory Committee on Traffic in Opium and other Dangerous Drugs by the international conventions on narcotic drugs as the Council may find necessary to assume and continue;

c. advise the Council on all matters pertaining to the control of narcotic drugs, and prepare such draft international conventions as may be necessary;

d. consider what changes may be required in the existing machinery for the international control of narcotic drugs and submit proposals thereon to the Council;

e. perform such other functions relating to narcotic drugs as the Council may direct.

3. The Commission may make recommendations to the Council concerning any subcommission which it considers should be established.

4. The Commission shall be composed of fifteen Members of the United Nations, which are important producing or manufacturing countries or countries in which illicit traffic in narcotic drugs constitutes a serious social problem. The term of office of members is three years. They are eligible for reappointment.

---

* G. A. Morlock, "International Control of Dangerous Drugs," *Department of State Bulletin*, 1946, vol. xv, no. 385, p. 886.

5. The Commission is authorized by the Council to appoint in a consultative capacity, and without the right to vote, representatives of bodies created under the terms of international conventions on narcotic drugs.

6. The Council requests the following Governments to designate one representative each to constitute the Commission: Canada, China, Egypt, France, India, Iran, Mexico, Netherlands, Peru, Poland, Turkey, United Kingdom, United States of America, Union of Soviet Socialist Republics, and Yugoslavia.

IV

Nongovernmental Organizations with Consultative Status to the Economic and Social Council*

Nongovernmental Organizations Granted Consultative Status with the Economic and Social Council

With the exception of four organizations which are followed by the name of a country, all of the nongovernmental organizations granted consultative status, as listed below, are international.

Category (a): Organizations which have a basic interest in most of the activities of the Council and are closely linked with the economic or social life of the areas which they represent:

World Federation of Trade Unions (WFTU)
International Co-operative Alliance (ICA)
American Federation of Labor (AF of L)
International Chamber of Commerce (ICC)
International Federation of Agricultural Producers (IFAP)
International Federation of Christian Trade Unions (IFCTU)
Inter-Parliamentary Union (IPU)
International Organization of Employers (IOE)
World Federation of United Nations Associations (WFUNA)

---

* *Handbook of the United Nations and Specialized Agencies,* Department of Public Information of the U.N., pp. 47–50.

Category (*b*): Organizations which have a special competence but are concerned specifically with only a few of the fields of activity covered by the Council:

Agudas Israel World Organization

All-India Women's Conference (India)

Associated Country Women of the World (ACWW)

Boy Scouts International Bureau

Carnegie Endowment for International Peace (United States)

Catholic International Union for Social Service

Commission of the Churches on International Affairs (CCIA)

Consultative Council of Jewish Organizations

Co-ordinating Board of Jewish Organizations for Consultation
    with the Economic and Social Council of the United Nations

Econometric Society, The

Friends World Committee for Consultation

Howard League for Penal Reform (United Kingdom)

Inter-American Council of Commerce and Production

International Abolitionist Federation

International African Institute

International Alliance of Women—Equal Rights, Equal Respon-
    sibilities

International Association of Democratic Lawyers

International Association of Penal Law

International Automobile Federation (IAF)

International Touring Alliance (ITA, to be jointly represented)

International Bureau for the Suppression of Traffic in Women and
    Children

International Bureau for the Unification of Penal Law

International Carriage and Van Union—R.I.C., and the Interna-
    tional Wagon Union—R.I.V., to be jointly represented

International Committee of the Red Cross

International Committee of Schools of Social Work

International Co-operative Women's Guild

International Council of Women (ICW)

International Criminal Police Commission

International Federation of Business and Professional Women
International Federation of Friends of Young Women
International Federation for Housing and Town Planning
International Federation of University Women
International Fiscal Association (IFA)
International Institute of Administrative Sciences
International Institute of Public Finance
International Institute of Public Law
International Law Association, The (ILA)
International League for the Rights of Man, The
International Organization of Journalists (IOJ)
International Organization for Standardization (ISO)
International Road Transport Union (IRW)
International Social Service (SIS) (formerly International Migration Service)
International Statistical Institute (ISI)
International Student Service (ISS)
International Transport Workers' Federation (ITWF)
International Union of Architects
International Union of Catholic Women's Leagues (IUCWL)
International Union for Child Welfare
International Union of Family Organizations
International Union of Local Authorities
International Union of Official Travel Organizations
International Union of Producers and Distributors of Electric Power
Liaison Committee of Women's International Organizations
National Association of Manufacturers (NAM) (United States)
Pax Romana—International Catholic Movement for Intellectual and Cultural Affairs and *Pax Romana*—International Movement of Catholic Students, to be jointly represented
Salvation Army, The
Service Civil International (no English title)
Women's International Democratic Federation (WIDF)
Women's International League for Peace and Freedom (WILPF)
World Association of Girl Guides and Girl Scouts, The

World Federation of Democratic Youth (WFDY)

World Jewish Congress (WJC)

World Movement of Mothers

World Power Conference (WPC)

World Women's Christian Temperance Union (World WCTU)

World's Alliance of Young Men's Christian Associations (World Alliance of YMCA's)

World's Young Women's Christian Association (World's YWCA)

Category (c): Organizations which are primarily concerned with the development of public opinion and with the dissemination of information:

International Federation of Secondary Teachers

Lions International—International Association of Lions Clubs

Rotary International

World Organization of the Teaching Profession

V

United Nations Maritime Conference (1948)*

The United Nations Maritime Conference was convened by the Economic and Social Council of the United Nations by the following resolution adopted on the 28th March 1947:

"*The Economic and Social Council*

"*Requests* the Secretary-General:

"(a) To convene a conference of interested Governments to consider the establishment of an intergovernmental maritime organization. The draft convention prepared by the United Maritime Consultative Council on this matter, concerning the scope and the purpose of the proposed organization, will serve as a working paper forming the basis of the discussion for the Conference. The Conference will also consider if the scope and purposes of the Organization should include the removal or prevention of unfair restrictive practices by shipping concerns;

---

* *United Nations Maritime Conference,* Final Act and Related Documents, U.N. Publications, 1948, VIII, 2.

"(b) To circulate the above-mentioned draft convention to all the Governments invited to the Conference;

"(c) To inform the Governments which are invited to the Conference that any comments which they may wish to make on specific articles of the draft convention or amendments which they may wish to propose in advance of the Conference, should be submitted to the Secretary-General for circulation to all Governments participating in the Conference and for consideration by the Conference itself:

"(d) To draw up a provisional agenda for the Conference including the items mentioned above;

"(e) To invite all the Members of the United Nations and the following Governments to participate in the Conference: Albania, Austria, Bulgaria, Ireland, Finland, Hungary, Italy, Portugal, Roumania, Switzerland, Trans-jordania, Yemen.

"The Economic and Social Council

"Expresses the hope that the Governments invited to the Conference may give their respective delegations full powers enabling them to sign such Convention on the establishment of an intergovernmental maritime organization as may be concluded at the Conference.

"The Economic and Social Council

"Requests the Secretary-General to invite the specialized agencies, inter-governmental organizations and international organizations in this field, as may be appropriate, to send observers to the Conference. The Conference shall meet, if practicable, in the autumn of 1947, at a place to be determined by the Secretary-General after consultation with the President of the Council."

The United Nations Maritime Conference met in the City of Geneva from 19 February 1948 to 6 March 1948.

The Governments of the following States were represented at the Conference by Delegations:

Argentina	Canada
Australia	Chile
Belgium	China
Brazil	Colombia

Czechoslovakia	New Zealand
Denmark	Norway
Dominican Republic	Pakistan
Egypt	Panama
Finland	Peru
France	Poland
Greece	Portugal
India	Sweden
Ireland	Switzerland
Italy	Turkey
Lebanon	United Kingdom
Netherlands	United States of America

The Governments of the following States had observers at the Conference:

Cuba	Iran
Ecuador	Union of South Africa

The following organizations were represented by observers:

A. *Intergovernmental organizations*
International Labour Office
World Health Organization
International Civil Aviation Organization
International Telecommunication Union
International Meteorological Organization

B. *Nongovernmental organizations*
International Chamber of Commerce
International Co-operative Alliance
International Law Association
International Transport Workers' Federation

The Conference had before it and used as a basis for discussion the draft agreement for an intergovernmental maritime organization prepared by the United Maritime Consultative Council. This document was submitted as a working paper for the Conference in accordance with the resolution adopted by the Economic and Social Council on the 28th of March 1947, at its fourth session, on the recommendation of its Transport and Communications Commission.

Structure of the Economic and Social Council

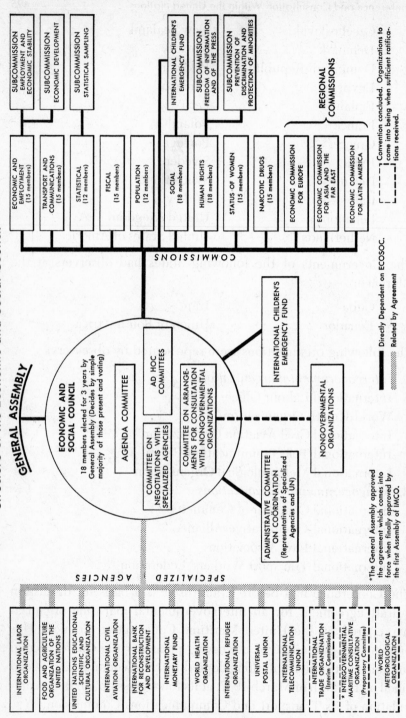

(From *United States Participation in the United Nations, Report by the President to the Congress for 1948, p. 284.*)

Part Five: International Administration

XV Methods of International Administration

To be on an international level, administration must be an effort of two or more coöperating states or of an international organization such as the United Nations. International enterprises commonly referred to as "administrative" are quite diverse in character, but considered in the large they fall into two main types: those which give the administrative agency a power of control or management over an activity or area; and those of a routine or perfunctory character, principally in the nature of services performed for the benefit of other agencies, of states, or even of individuals.

Methods of international administration may be differentiated on the basis of the role played by the participating nations. In the first place, there are administrative agencies completely free from the control of national governments, with their personnel acting in the capacity of international officials; the Secretariat of the United Nations is a case in point. Second, there are international commissions, councils, or boards whose members are representatives of the participating states, typified by the International Joint Committee for the United States and Canada. A third method of administration is the condominium, where several governments or their officials work side by side at a given task, as in the condominium for the Sudan set up in 1889, whereby Great Britain and Egypt have shared in the government of that area. Finally, in the old mandate system of the League of Nations and in the present trusteeship system of the United Nations, the administrative function has been exercised im-

499

mediately by some one nation, acting under the supervision of one or more international organs; the trusteeship system is under the Trusteeship Council and the General Assembly. Of these four methods, the first—an agency with an international personnel—is the one commonly employed when the work to be done is essentially routine or perfunctory. The commission and the condominium are usually endowed with powers of control, for the reason that when power is to be exercised, governments prefer to have it done by their own officials or representatives rather than by international agents outside the pale of their authority. In the trusteeship system, where the government of a territory and its people is undertaken, there is propriety in appointing national governments as trustees, with international agencies, the Trusteeship Council and the Assembly, possessing only the rights of investigation and recommendation.

International Secretariats and Bureaus

A permanent office with a staff of international officials was first used in the public unions which have already been described in the discussion of conference systems. It will be remembered that those unions began to appear on the scene of world affairs during the late decades of the nineteenth century, and that a number of them are still in existence, some few as specialized agencies of the United Nations, while others are independent. A public union is so organized as to include both the diplomatic or conference function and the administrative function. The conferences, committees, and bureaus which as a rule are to be found in them are closely related in all of their activities, with the bureaus serving the conferences and committees in prescribed ways, the conferences providing for and defining the work of the bureaus, and the committees having general supervision of the bureaus. These unions are therefore in the nature of miniature leagues of nations, each, however, confined to some one field of interest instead of trying to cover a wide expanse of international problems; they travel on a single track, unlike the United Nations of today, which operates over a most complex track system, with trains headed for many destinations. That some of the public unions have been made into specialized agencies of the United Nations is indicative of the multiple-track system of the international organization now located at New York City.

The functions of the bureaus of public unions, as already has been brought out, are largely ministerial and perfunctory. The duty most commonly assigned to them is that of obtaining and circulating information. The office of the old Institute of Agriculture published several yearbooks and other periodical issues, and it was estimated that at one time approximately 30 percent of the information received from abroad by the United States Department of Agriculture came from the union's office; the work once performed by the Institute is now undertaken by the Food and Agriculture Organization, one of the specialized agencies of the United Nations. A second duty performed by the bureaus is to render assistance on request to national governments, usually by means of consultation on national projects and problems. The Bureau of the Universal Postal Union was frequently asked whether proposed national postal regulations would be in contravention of the Union's rules. The office of the International Institute of Agriculture was in a position to influence national policies by suggesting to governments on its own initiative "measures for the protection of the farmers. . . ." Some of the bureaus have called to the attention of member states acts by those states in violation of the union regulations. Many of the bureaus have served as registries, as for instance the Bureau of the Union for the Protection of Industrial Property, which registers trademarks for the purpose of giving them international protection. The Bureau of the Universal Postal Union has acted as "a clearinghouse for the settlement of accounts of every description relative to the international postal service between the administrations which claim its services." These and other administrative activities of the bureaus, although lacking in any element of compulsion or authority, have been decidedly constructive. At the present time, the permanent offices or secretariats of the specialized agencies of the United Nations perform much the same type of work as that of the bureaus of the public unions, sometimes with other duties added.[1]

---

[1] In "Some Notes on the United Nations Secretariat," *International Organization*, 1950, vol. 4, no. 4, pp. 600–601, Mr. W. R. Crocker gives the following types of du-

The Secretariat of the League of Nations was constructed along the lines of the earlier bureaus, except that it was much larger and operated in many more fields of interest. Its personnel included approximately seven hundred persons, representing some fifty nationalities, all regarded as international officials and kept as free as possible from the control of their respective governments in the accomplishment of their duties. At the head of the organization was a Secretary-General, assisted by two Deputy and three Under Secretaries-General. The following list of fourteen sections within the office indicate the wide range of its activities: Central Section; Minorities Section; Mandates Section; Opium Traffic and Social Questions Section; Disarmament Section; Legal Section; Information Section; Financial Section and Economic Intelligence Service; Section of Economic Relations; Communication and Transit Sections; Health Section; International Bureaus and Intellectual Coöperation Section; Political Section; and Treasury. Added to these sections were a number of services, including the Personnel Office, the Documents Service (for editing, translating, précise-writing, etc.), Internal Services (stenographic, duplicating, etc.), the Registry and Indexing Branch, and the Secretariat of the Administrative Board of the Staff Pensions Fund. Outside of Geneva, special branch offices were maintained in London, Paris, Rome, Berlin, and The Hague.

The relation of the Secretariat to the League of Nations conference system has already been mentioned, particularly its duties in the preparation of the work of the Assembly, Council, committees and special conferences, and in providing secretarial staffs for those meetings. In addition, the organ had the following tasks to perform:

1. It was delegated to carry out the decisions of the Assembly, Council, and other League meetings
2. It kept the archives and published the records of League meetings

---

ties of international secretariats: (1) servicing international meetings; (2) running its own internal economy; and (3) carrying out "special functions which require technicians such as legal counsellors, economists, demographers and . . . negotiators who can deal with foreign governments."

3. It collected and distributed information (statistics and other data)
4. It corresponded with members and nonmembers on behalf of the League and its organs
5. It registered and published the treaties and agreements made by members and sent to it for that purpose, as required by the Covenant.

In the Organization of American States, the office known as the Pan American Union has similar duties to perform. By the Charter of Bogotá (1948), the Union is referred to in Article 78 as "the central and permanent organ of the Organization of American States and the General Secretariat of the Organization." The head of the Pan American Union is a Secretary-General who "shall be elected by the Council for a ten-year term and who may not be reelected or succeeded by a person of the same nationality." As in the case of the bureaus and secretariats of other international organizations, the Union is active in giving assistance to the various conferences and meetings within the Organization; in addition it has been assigned other duties which include the following:

1. Serving as custodian of the documents and achives of the various organs of the Organization
2. Serving as a depository for instruments of ratification of international agreements
3. Performing "special functions entrusted to it by the Inter-American Conference, and the Meeting of Consultation of Ministers of Foreign Affairs," as Article 83 of the Charter provides.

The Union is divided into departments, which are headed by "the Executive Secretaries of the Inter-American Economic and Social Council, the Council of Jurists and the Cultural Council," provided by Article 89.

The Central International Office for the Control of Liquor Traffic in Africa, established in 1919 and still at work, is similar to the bureaus that have been described, Eight nations support the Office: Belgium, France, Italy, Japan, Portugal, the United Kingdom, the United States, and Egypt. Its business is to collect and disperse information relating to the liquor traffic in Africa. The parties to the arrangement furnish the Office with annual reports on liquor importation and manufacture in African territories under their control. The Office maintains a small secretariat within the Belgian Foreign Office. Unlike the bureaus of the ordinary public union, there is no conference provided for in the convention creating the Office.

International Administrative Commissions—Their Role

The commission has been and still is a most useful instrumentality in the work of international administration. Its practicality has derived in large part from its representative character, by which states can share in the work to be done; and, as pointed out before, such participation seems highly important to states when that work involves the exercise of authority. The commission is therefore an ideal agency when administration is of such a nature as to carry with it control over matters of vital concern to nations.

Another advantage of the commission is its flexibility in composition and organization so that it can be adapted to almost any situation. It can be so small as to have only two members, if the nations prefer. The International Joint Commission of the United States and Canada is composed of the representatives of only two nations, but it includes six members, three named by each. There have been individual "commissioners" used in place of commissions. When this is the case, the incumbent is not expected to represent any particular nation; he is rather the representative of an international organization or a group of nations. The League of Nations, acting under the authority of the Treaty of Versailles, appointed a High Commissioner for the Free City of Danzig and endowed him with certain powers of control over the government of that city.

The adjustability of commissions extends, too, to the method by which they are selected and to their duration. The members of commissions are usually named by states as their representatives, but they may be appointed by such an organization as the United Nations; the Saar Basin Commission, established under the Treaty of Versailles as the agency to govern the Saar Basin for a period of fifteen years, was selected by the Council of the League of Nations. In the matter of duration, the sole consideration is convenience. In practice the majority of commissions are *ad hoc,* created to accomplish a given task with the understanding that they will go out of existence when the task is finished. Some have been set up for a specific period of years (e.g., Saar Basin Commission for fifteen years). Still others, again, are intended to be permanent (e.g., Joint Commission for the United States and Canada).

A third advantage offered by the commission as an administrative agency is its availability for a wide variety of services and problems. Two types of work relating to nationality problems have been given to commissions: to assist in the protection of minority peoples, and to administer plebiscites. A well-known example of the former was the Mixed Commission of eleven members set up under the Convention of Lausanne (1923) to take part in the exchange of Greek and Turkish populations. There had been large groups of Greeks living in Turkey, and a smaller number of Turks living in Greece. The Lausanne Convention obligated those minorities to move to the country of their respective nationalities. The job of the Mixed Commission was "to supervise and facilitate the emigration provided for in the present convention and to carry out the liquidation of movable and immovable property for which provision is made. . . ." A somewhat similar commission had been used under a pact of 1919 between Greece and Bulgaria by which a voluntary exchange of minorities was arranged.

Plebiscite commissions were employed for several areas after World War I to supervise the balloting and in some instances to be in control of the area in which the plebiscite was to be held, all with the purpose of guaranteeing a measure of fairness in the voting. The admission must be made, however, that they were not always, and probably not often, successful in preventing abuses, as evidenced by well-founded complaints. The fault was a lack of sufficient power, particularly in the policing of the areas in question. The most successful of all was the Plebiscite Commission for the

Saar Basin, which began its work some six months prior to the popular balloting on January 13, 1935; an international force of 3300 men was made available to keep order and ensure a fair ballot, and the whole procedure was conducted under the careful supervision of foreign officials, with the result that there was no evidence of irregularities.

The duties turned over to administrative commissions have included a number on social and economic problems, such as reparations, the Ottoman public debt, sanitation and health. They have dealt with waterways of international concern, ports of international concern, and in some few instances they have been delegated the power to govern in designated areas. In recent years they have been used under commodity agreements with regulatory authority over trade in the commodity in question.

An interesting example of a commission (or "board" in this case) used in a commodity agreement was the Inter-American Coffee Board set up in 1940 and brought to an end in 1948, when an auxiliary body of the Inter-American Economic and Social Council took its place. Coffee is, of course, Latin America's most important export commodity, and the trade in that product has long been an economic barometer for that part of the world. The United States, too, is deeply concerned with the condition of the coffee market, not only as a consumer, but also by reason of the fact that when Latin-American nations are unable to make dollars in a stable market, they are without funds to purchase United States goods. The provision of a stable international market for coffee is therefore a vital necessity both for the twelve Latin-American coffee-producing nations and for the United States. Conferences were held in 1936 and 1937 to deal with the problem, but they ended without any agreement. Finally, at a conference held in New York City in 1940, an agreement was reached, allocating both the United States market and the European market among the coffee-producing nations in such manner that each would know just what its share for export would be. "In order to adjust supplies to estimated requirements," the allocations could be altered, and it was to administer this phase of the arrangement that a Coffee Board was established and given the right of passing upon requests for allocation changes. It could increase or decrease a nation's quota up to 5 percent but not oftener than once every six months. The Board was authorized to appoint employees considered necessary for the performance of its work, to approve an annual budget and fix the amount to be contributed by each government, and to make annual reports; as the convention said, it was responsible for the "general administration of the present Agreement." It was composed of delegates from all of the fifteen participating states (including the United States), most of whom had one vote each, though Colombia had three, Brazil nine, and the United States twelve.

In 1934, by the Agreement of London, concluded by the governments of Great Britain, India, The Netherlands, France, and Thailand, an international regimen for rubber was set up.[2] Behind the Agreement was a wide coincidence of interest: the producers wanted to avoid a price slump; manufacturers were anxious to have a steady supply at stable prices; and several governments were concerned for the welfare of their national economies and revenues. Under the arrangement, an International Rubber Regulation Committee was established and given the job of fixing export quotas in the proportion of the basic quotas, thereby deciding the total volume of rubber exports. It also had the following duties: It could dispose of rubber delivered to it from Indo-China under her special arrangement; it could change within limits the areas for new planting; and it was responsible for the dissemination of information and for publicity. Representation and voting strength on the Committee were unequal, based on the quotas of exports assigned to the members. The arrangement was modified in minor particulars in 1938. During World II, it lapsed, and with the new conditions brought by war—synthetic rubber and the disorder within some of the rubber-producing nations—it has not been revived.

Until the period of World War II, it was customary to name the International Commission for the Danube River and the European Commission for the Danube as outstanding examples of the possi-

---

[2] See Kurt Wilk, "International Administrative Regulation: The Case of Rubber," *American Political Science Review*, 1942, vol. 36, pp. 323–337.

bilities of administrative action on an international level. Both of these commissions possessed powers of control designed to maintain and improve the navigability of the river, with the European Commission assigned that section of the river below Isatcha, and the International Commission managing the remainder of the river, known as the "internationalized river system." The authority of these agencies was extensive; the European Commission, for instance, could modify national improvement plans for the river, draw up plans of its own and submit them to the riparian states, carry out improvements which the riparian states were unable to do, authorize the riparian states to levy dues on river traffic to pay for improvements, and levy dues of its own to cover improvements.

Although this Danubian system was instituted in 1856 (amended in 1921) and operated with satisfaction until World War II, it was not renewed after the war for the reason that Russia opposed its continuance, preferring to leave the control of the river to the riparian states which had come within the Russian orbit. The question was discussed at several conferences, but the Russian delegation would make no concessions to the American point of view that the river should be kept open in the future as in the past to the shipping of all nations, and that states other than the riparian states should be allowed representation on the new control commission to be set up. The delegations of the United States, Great Britain, and France, in a conference at Belgrade on August 18, 1948, submitted twenty-eight amendments to the Soviet draft, but all were rejected. In 1949, Russia announced the creation of a new Danubian Commission based upon its earlier draft. Under the system set up by the plan, only riparian states are on the Commission and only they have a right to the navigation of the river. On November 15, 1949, the United States protested against the new regime as follows:

The Convention signed by seven delegates over the objections of the Governments of France, the United States, Austria, and the United Kingdom and, in contravention of the well-established rights of Belgium, Greece and Italy, violates the concept of international waterways which has been recognized in Europe for more than 130 years. It fails to provide an adequate basis for freedom of navigation on the Danube. In this failure it negates the provision of the peace traties with Bulgaria, Hungary, and Rumania, and also fails to crry out the decision of the Council of Foreign Ministers of December 6, 1946. Moreover, the Convention omits any provision for nonriparian representation in a Danube Commission. It seeks to deprive the United Kingdom, France, Italy, Belgium, and Greece, without their consent, of treaty rights established by international agreement in 1921 and disregards the legitimate interests of nonriparian states. The rejection by the majority at the Belgrade Conference of any relationship between the Danube Commission and the United Nations indicates an intention to seal off the Danubian area from normal intercourse with the rest of the world to the area's own direct disadvantage.

Although the Convention professes to devise a regime of navigation in the interest of all riparian states, Austria is at present denied representation on the so-called Danube Commission and no provision whatsoever is made with respect to German participation.

The Belgrade Convention, when coupled with the device of Soviet-controlled joint companies which acquired long-term exclusive control of facilities essential to the conduct of Danube commerce, is clearly designed to enable the Soviet Union to maintain a monopoly of Danubian commerce.[3]

Prominent Administrative Commissions of Today

The Central Rhine Commission, the first administrative agency of any importance to be created, is still in existence. The commission was first set up in 1804, and later was modified on several occasions; the Convention of Mannheim (1868) still supplies the basic principles in the system of today, although there have been minor changes since that time. With the defeat of Germany in World War II, it became necessary to effect some modifications, and therefore in December, 1945, the regime was reorganized on a provisional basis; this provisional system is expected to be continued until a treaty of peace with Germany is concluded.

There are now six governments represented on the Central Rhine Commission, all on an equal basis: Belgium, France, The Netherlands, Switzerland, the United States (for the first time), and the United Kingdom. The three nations in occupation of Germany—France, the United States, and the United Kingdom—are expected

---

[3] *A Decade of American Foreign Policy, Basic Documents*, 1941–1949, 81st Congress, 1st Session, Senate Document no. 123, pp. 807–808.

to speak for the interests of Germany. The Commission has a president and a secretary-general, and it employs a small number of technicians. All six member nations are represented at the four meetings held by the Commission during the year at Strasbourg. Decisions are taken by a majority vote.

The duties of the Central Rhine Commission are to ensure that the river and its mouth shall be open to the vessels of all nations for commercial purposes and to maintain the technical conditions necessary for its full navigability. It can recommend the construction of works necessary for the improvement of navigation, and it has the power of review over projects of the riparian states that may affect the navigability of the river. It furnishes regulations for the navigation of the stream and it serves as a high court of appeal for litigation in which the navigation of the Rhine is involved.

Another commission with a fairly long history behind it is the International Joint Commission for the United States and Canada, established by the convention of 1909 for the purpose of dealing with the boundary waters of the two countries. The administrative duties of the Commission have to do with the use and diversion of the water from the lakes and rivers between the two countries.[4] It may pass upon new projects for any use or diversion of the waters which will affect their natural level, and upon projects for dams and other obstructions which will raise the level. It is also authorized to direct the measurement and apportionment of water from the St. Mary and Milk rivers to be used for irrigation purposes. A list of principles is given in the convention for the guidance of the Commission in issuing permits to petitioners for the use of the water. The procedure of the Commission in its hearings on petitions is semijudicial. Prior to 1909, problems of the kind now handled by the Commission had to be treated by the diplomatic representatives of the United States and Canada, obviously a slower and more cumbersome method of dealing with them.

At the end of World War II, several international administrative

---

[4] In addition to its administrative duties the Commission is an organ of conciliation for disputes "involving the rights, obligations, and interests of either in relation to the other or to the inhabitants of the other along the common frontier. . . ."

authorities were created, presumably of a temporary nature, to deal with occupation and reparations problems. The Potsdam Agreement of 1945 laid down the conditions of occupation for Germany, under which four zones were set up—the Russian, American, British, and French. Even before that time, in 1944, an agreement had been made to establish an Allied Control Council for Germany. As constituted, the Council contains the representatives of the four occupying powers. Its duties are to coördinate policy in the four zones and to determine policy for Germany as a whole. It was looked upon as the repository of supreme authority in the country, and its powers were such as to enable it to issue the laws, decrees, and directives necessary to carry out its duties. Almost from the beginning, the work of the Council was paralyzed by the clashing interests and policies of Russia and the Western states. On March 20, 1948, the Soviet delegate walked out of the organization; since that time no meetings of the Council have been held. On June 28, 1949, the occupation authorities of the four nations, however, resumed discussions of matters of common interest.

Somewhat different organizations were set up for Austria and Japan. The Allied Commission for Austria, composed of the same nations that were on the German Control Council, at the beginning had complete control over the administration of Austria, but after the creation of a freely elected Austrian Government in 1946, its authority was restricted to such matters as demilitarization, security, and disposition of former German assets. The Allied Council for Japan has no genuine administrative power and is more in the nature of a consultative body to advise the commander in the Far East.

By the Potsdam Agreement it was decided that the reparations taken from Germany would be chiefly in the form of industrial equipment, with minor amounts from German foreign assets. The Control Council was designated as the agency to earmark the industrial equipment to be taken. An Inter-Allied Reparation Agency (IARA) was set up at Brussels, Belgium, as the mechanism for the division of German reparation assets among the eighteen governments which were to receive goods. Each of the governments was represented on the Agency by a delegate and his staff. The delegations collectively were known as the Assembly. A Secretariat, international in character and serving the Agency rather than the individual governments. was an important part of the structure.

Among the older administrative agencies still active is the International Commission of the Cape Spartel Light, set up in 1865 under a treaty concluded by eleven states. There has been some shift in the list of states supporting the arrangement, but at the present time the following are included: Morocco, Belgium, France, Great Britain, Italy, The Netherlands, Portugal, Sweden, the United States, and Norway. The duty of the Commission is to maintain, manage, and ensure the neutrality of the Cape Spartel Light in order to provide safety to ships passing through the Straits of Gibraltar. It is composed of the diplomatic representatives of the participating powers stationed at Tangier. The president of the Commission—the presidency is a rotating office—is responsible for the execution of decisions taken and may call meetings at his pleasure. The light is of course operated by a keeper under the Commission who is subject to the regulations supplied by that body.

The Condominium

The presence of the officials of several governments who share in some way the control of an area is usually in the nature of a compromise arrangement resulting from inconclusive diplomatic competition in which each party has sought exclusive control. This was true in the case of the city of Tangier in Northwest Africa, where several of the European nations—Germany, France, Spain, Italy, and Great Britain—vied with each other. As early as 1887, the suggestion was made by an American citizen that the city be placed under an international commission, but it was not until 1904 that a special status was given the area by the Franco-Spanish Treaty. About a year later, the police force of the city was placed under the joint management of Spanish and French officials for a period of fifteen years. The famous Treaty of Algeciras of 1906 altered the status of Tangier only in minor respects: an International Sanitary Council was created, and the State Bank of Morocco was placed under the supervision of four censors selected by the banking institutions of Germany, France, Spain, and Great Britain, respectively. In 1912, negotiations were undertaken for the first time to create a general system of international administration there, but World War I blocked its application. In 1923, a system was devised and put into operation, but the opposition to it from Mussolini's Italy, which by that time was important enough to gain a hearing in the European councils, led in 1928 to the conclusion of a new convention.

The Government of Tangier under the 1928 convention was a hodgepodge if ever there was one. The legislative functions of the zone were delegated to a group of twenty-seven persons in accordance with Article 34, which read as follows:

In consideration of the number of nationals, the volume of commerce, the property interests and importance of local trade at Tangier of the several Powers signatory to the Act of Algeciras, the International Legislative Assembly shall be composed of

4 French members,
4 Spanish members,
3 British members,
3 Italian members,
1 American member,
1 Belgian member,
1 Dutch member,
1 Portuguese member,

nominated by their respective consulates, and in addition

6 Mussulman subjects of the Sultan nominated by the Mendoub and
3 Jewish subjects nominated by the Mendoub and chosen from a list of nine names submitted by the Jewish Community.

The administrative branch of the city government, expected to enforce the terms of the convention and the acts of the Legislative Assembly, also distributed authority in accordance with the principles of condominium. The chief administrator for the first six years was French, while his three assistants, acting as directors of health, finance, and justice, were Spanish, British, and Italian, respectively. After the first six years, the Assembly selected new administrators in such a manner that no two were nationals of the same state. The native police force, maintained at the expense of France, Spain, and the city of Tangier itself, was placed under a Spanish officer, with a French assistant. A Committee of Control consisting of "the consuls *de carriere* of the Powers signatory of the Act of Algeciras or of their substitutes *de carriere*" was assigned the task of seeing to it that "the regime of economic equality and the provisions of the statute of Tangier" were observed. On the judicial side a Mixed Court with judges of Belgian, British, Spanish, French, and Italian nationality held forth.

During World War II, Franco's Spain, in violation of the convention of 1928, took over the Zone of Tangier. In 1945, at the end of the war, condominium was revived and placed in operation under a slightly modified system. The United States and Russia were admitted as partners to the new regime. Each was given three members of their respective nationalities in the city's Legislative Assembly, while the number of Italian participants was reduced from three to one. The Committee of Control was retained, with American and Russian membership provided. The chief administrator now must be a person of Belgian, Netherlands, Portuguese, or Swedish nationality, and he is selected by the Committee of Control. He is aided by an assistant administrator of French nationality selected by the French Government (who is the adviser for Moroccan affairs), and by an assistant administrator selected by the Committee of Control as a person of Belgian, Netherlands, Portuguese, or Swedish nationality (to be in charge of finances). The police force is recruited in the main from native inhabitants, and it is under a commandant appointed by the native head on the recommendation of the Committee of Control.

To put an end to the rivalry between France and Great Britain over the New Hebrides Islands in the southwestern Pacific, the islands were placed under a condominium in 1906. Revised in 1922, this agreement authorized government by the official appointees of France and Great Britain. A Joint Court of three judges, one appointed by France, one by Great Britain, and a third by Spain, was set up. Legislative power was lodged jointly in the two High Commissioners representing France and Great Britain, respectively. The administrative branch of the government was placed under these same two High Commissioners. The local police force has been organized in two divisions, each of which operates under one of the commissioners. The following public services are undertaken by joint action: posts and telegraphs, public works, ports and harbors, buoys and lighthouses, public health, and finance.

At the end of the conquest of the Sudan by the joint effort of Great Britain and Egypt, that territory was placed under a condominium by the Anglo-Egyptian agreement of January 19, 1899. By that agreement "the supreme military and civil command in the Sudan shall be vested in one office, termed the Governor-General of the Sudan." He is appointed by Khedival decree on the recommendation of the British Government, and his powers include lawmaking as well as those of chief executive. The civil service includes British, Egyptian, and Sudanese officers, all of whom are chosen by the Governor-General. The higher administrative officials, including the heads of departments, the provincial governors, and inspectors, have been British, while the police officers have been both Egyptian and British.

During recent years, Egyptian leaders have agitated strongly for an end to the condominium and for full control by their country over the Sudan. They have argued that the geographic unity of the Nile Basin requires annexation by Egypt and that the Sudan can serve as an outlet for Egypt's agricultural population. As a result of this agitation, a new Anglo-Egyptian Treaty was concluded in 1936. This agreement did not alter the major outlines of the condominium but specifically provided "that the administration of the Sudan shall continue to be that resulting from the said agreements" (1899). The principal innovations had to do with nongovernmental matters, allowing both British and Egyptian troops to be kept at the disposal of the Governor-General, permitting Egyptian immigration into the Sudan, and prohibiting discrimination between British subjects and Egyptian nationals "in matters of commerce, immigration, or the possession of property." Recently Egypt has endeavored to effect a termination of the treaty of 1936 but without success.

Viewed from the standpoint of effective government, condominium leaves much to be desired; it is only as a diplomatic device for the reconciliation of conflicting national ambitions that the system can be justified. It almost inevitably invites suspicion and friction

between the governing powers and therefore leads either to inaction
or to action based on compromise rather than to comprehensive programs designed to promote native welfare. In 1894, President Cleve-
land remarked about a condominium which operated in the Samoa
Islands from 1889 to 1899 that "The present government has failed
to correct, if indeed it has not aggravated, the very evils it was intended to prevent." Referring to the condominium for Egypt exercised by France and Great Britain from 1879 to 1882, Lord Cromer
made the following observations: "The result cannot be said to be
encouraging to those who believe in the efficacy of international action in administrative matters. What has been proved is that international institutions possess admirable negative qualities. They are
formidable checks to all action, and the reason why they are so is
that, when any action is proposed, objections of one sort or another
generally occur to some member of the international body."[5]

The League of Nations and the United Nations

New techniques in administration were made available by the creation of large-scale international organization of the nature of the
League of Nations and the United Nations. The permanent agencies
of those organizations—the Council and Assembly of the League,
and the Security Council, General Assembly, and Economic and Social Council of the United Nations—were available for the planning
and arrangement of administrative enterprises, and for the selection, remuneration, supervision, and direction of the personnel of
administration. It is not surprising, therefore, that the League and
the United Nations have pushed forward the work of administration, borrowing here from the practice of the past as in other fields
of activity, and adding to it new methods where possible. The mandate system of the League and the Trusteeship system of the United
Nations rank high among the contributions of the two world organizations, and there have been many others. The next chapter will
deal with the activities of the two organizations, with emphasis
upon those of the United Nations.

---

[5] Quoted in G. L. Beer, *African Questions at the Paris Peace Conference,* New
York, 1923, p. 423.

XVI The United Nations in Administration

BROADLY SPEAKING, THE ADMINISTRATIVE WORK OF THE
United Nations falls within the following categories: (1) activities
carried on during World War II (particularly the United Nations
Relief and Rehabilitation Administration—the UNRRA); (2) those
of the Secretariat; (3) those of the specialized agencies, notably the
Bank and the Fund; (4) those especially assigned to it or to its organs; and (5) those of the trusteeship system. The operations carried on within those categories are most diverse. Some of the services rendered are to states, some to individuals, and some to organs
within the United Nations. They may be purely ministerial, or they
may involve powers of control. Where there is an element of control, it is supervisory in certain instances but quite direct in others.

UNRRA

The purpose of UNRRA, in the words of Director-General Lehman,
was "to assist each of those countries which have suffered from the
attack of the common enemy to relieve and rehabilitate their people
and their lands." In the areas liberated from German and Japanese
occupation, food supplies had been destroyed or wasted, innumer-
able homes and factories had been left in ruins, roads and railroads
had been damaged, and many men and women had been removed
from their homelands to work as slaves in the factories of the enemy.
It was imperative to make life tolerable to the peoples of those lands
by placing in their possession the basic necessities of life and the
equipment by which they would be enabled to renew productive

activities on a self-sustaining basis. They needed food, seeds, clothing, medicine, tools, and countless other things which could be made available from the United States and other countries that had come out of the war still strong and productive.

UNRRA was organized in the East Room of the White House on November 9, 1943, when the representatives of forty-four nations signed an agreement to collaborate in assisting the many countries —Greece, Czechoslovakia, Poland, Yugoslavia, Ethiopia, China, and others—that lay prostrate after the forces of the conqueror had been routed from their lands. They agreed to contribute jointly in the financing of the organization, as nearly as possible on the basis of their ability to pay.

The policy-forming body in UNRRA was the Council; it performed such tasks as recommending the standards for money raising, and appropriating funds for administrative purposes, thus filling the role of a board of directors. Because the Council met only twice a year, a Central Committee, composed of representatives of the United States, the United Kingdom, Russia, and China, was organized to meet between Council sessions and to act on any problems that presented themselves. Besides the Council and the Central Committee, a network of special committees was set up to deal with designated geographical areas, such as Europe or the Far East, or to work in a special field of operation, such as public health or industrial rehabilitation. The administrative work of the organization was under a Director-General and a large staff of assistants. By early 1945, this staff included some two thousand individuals of more than thirty nationalities, and later on it grew to even larger proportions. These men and women were located in many parts of the world negotiating with governments when necessary and bringing assistance on the spot to needy people. They were looked upon as international officials, and to secure from them the utmost in unprejudiced and devoted service, UNRRA required them to sign a declaration by which they agreed to work loyally and "not to seek or receive from any government or authority external to the Administration any instructions. . . ." UNRRA closed its doors at the end of 1946, after part of its work was completed; its remaining duties were taken over by other agencies.

Although the work of UNRRA was widely criticized, in the main it justified the expenditure of time, effort, and money which it represented. The tons of supplies which it made available to needy nations made the difference between life and death to millions of people. There were, to be sure, blunders and wastes, but these will always accompany any human endeavor in greater or less degree, and when the organization in question is serving an emergency need, they are bound to be considerable. Director-General Lehman often pointed out the administrative problem of getting an efficient coördination of effort from so many employees scattered so widely over the world, employees of diverse languages and backgrounds. Mr. Lehman once illustrated this difficulty by quoting a question asked by one of the non-American members of his staff who was puzzled by the word "nonpartisan" as used within one of the nations: "Does a 'nonpartisan government' mean one in which the Partisan party shall have no participation?" Differences in language, political background, and cultural concepts are always obstacles in the way of international coöperation of all kinds, even in the field of administration.

The Secretariat

The structure and duties of the Secretariat were described in Chapter V of this volume; the nature of its activities as an administrative body may be made clearer by a few illustrations. Like secretariats in general, that of the United Nations has no control over states, confining itself to the performance of services, countless services, in behalf of other organs and enterprises.

Not least among the activities of the Secretariat are those relating to its vast publishing program. Four main types of publications are put out: the official records of the proceedings of the various organs; special surveys and reports designed principally for the use of experts and persons with a special interest in the subjects treated; semipopular publications describing current programs, giving reference material, etc.; and pamphlets making factual data easily available for speakers, teachers, librarians, and other engaged in spreading information concerning the United Nations. A special effort has been made recently to increase the number of languages in which United Nations publications are issued. At the present time, the languages of more than twenty member states are represented in publications of the Secretariat, and they are sold through forty-six sales agents in forty-four countries.

In the field of the radio, the work of the United Nations and its agencies provides a large amount of material for programs of all kinds in many of the member states. In 1949, there were thirty-six nations relaying daily news programs prepared by the United Nations Radio; in addition, many other member states make use of programs on a less regular basis. Secretary Lie has recently stated, "The United Nations Radio has emerged from the experimental phase and is now firmly established on a solid footing, professionally recognized by the broadcasting agencies of the world."[1]

Another illustration of the activity of the Secretariat is in the field of statistical services. The Statistical Office is concerned with the development and promotion of an adequate system of comparable statistics on a world-wide scale, and with the collection and dissemination of statistical information. Assisting the Statistical Commission, the Statistical Office of the Secretariat in 1949 prepared studies on statistics relating to capital formations, consumers' expenditure, and other subjects. The Office has recently developed uniform methods for measuring national income at constant prices. Material needed for a study of price indexes for external trade and price indexes for expressing national income has been assembled by the Office.

These examples of the activities of the Secretariat could be multiplied many times over. A United Nations mission to another country, such as the dispatch of a mediator to Palestine in 1948, invariably includes a sizable group of Secretariat officials. Nearly every

---

[1] See *Annual Report of the Secretary-General on the Work of the Organization,* July 1, 1948—June 30, 1949. General Assembly *Official Records,* 4th session, Supplement no. 1, (A/930), p. 143.

United Nations program imposes a responsibility on one or more officials of the Secretariat. In his annual report of 1950, Secretary Lie said that the tendency to place more and more responsibility upon the Secretariat to make studies and reports was imposing such heavy duties upon the staff that he was finding it difficult to finance them within budgetary limits.

The Specialized Agencies

Like the United Nations itself, the specialized agencies maintain permanent offices in the nature of secretariats to perform the multitude of day-to-day tasks that need to be done.[2] As a rule, there is a "secretary-general" or a "director' 'in charge of those offices and a staff appointed according to directives furnished by the conference of the agency. By way of illustration, the General Secretariat of the International Telecommunications Union has been assigned the following duties:

1. To carry on secretarial work preparatory to, and following conferences of the union.
2. To provide the secretariat of the conference and other meetings within the union.
3. To publish the recommendations and reports of the permanent organs of the union.
4. To publish international and regional telecommunications agreements sent to it by the parties, and to keep records of those agreements.
5. To "prepare, publish, and keep up to date" a record of the composition and structure of the union, general statistics, and documents.
6. To collect and publish data, both national and international, regarding telecommunications throughout the world.
7. To collect and publish information helpful to member states with a view to assisting them in the achievement of an efficient operation of their telecommunications services.

---

[2] See Appendix to this chapter for the duties of the Bureau of the Universal Postal Union.

8. To publish a journal of general information and documentation concerning telecommunications.
9. To prepare an annual budget.

In addition to the activities of their secretariats, the unions are engaged in administrative work of quite a different type. Two of the agencies—the International Bank and the International Fund—are engaged to an unusual extent in the work of administration. Among the activities of the World Health Organization are some of an administrative nature designed to help and improve national health services. As a rule, they are undertaken by a group of employees, perhaps experts, and in substance they put into operation policies and programs which have been decided upon by the methods of conference and consultation. The WHO has, on request, provided advisory services to governments, and it has assisted them in meeting emergencies, as it did a few years ago during the cholera epidemic in Egypt, when vaccines and supplies were distributed in that country. It has, on request, sent demonstration teams to countries for the purpose of explaining the techniques available in the treatment of disease. Another aspect of the work of WHO is the supervision of the execution of international sanitary conventions, thus helping to prevent the spread of disease. Medical missions have been dispatched to several countries, including Austria, China, Ethiopia, Greece, Italy, and Poland, in which are ordinarily included medical teachers and technicians. As many as thirty-two of the staff members of WHO have served in China at one time. In Italy the organization has assisted health authorities in programs of maternal and child care and in planning for the construction of a penicillin plant. Two laboratories are maintained by WHO—the State Serum Institute at Copenhagen and the Medical Research Council's Laboratory in London—for the preparation and distribution of samples of biologicals such as vitamin E, for which standards have been set by the Expert Committee on Biological Standardization.

The Food and Agriculture Organization engages in similar activities which, as in the WHO, put into operation policies adopted by processes of conference and consultation. It has sent special missions to Greece and to Poland for the purpose of studying the agricultural systems of those countries and recommending projects for improvement. Prior to the taking of the 1950 World Census on Agriculture, special training schools for statisticians were held. In January, 1948, eight agricultural scientists were sent to Siam to advise that nation on such matters as rice-growing, the development of water supplies, marketing and distribution of farm products, and forestry. A livestock artificial-insemination school was held in Italy in 1947. Demonstration teams have been sent to a number of countries to show the best methods of food preservation.

The administrative operations of the International Bank are in the hands of a Board of Governors, the Executive Directors, a President, and a staff of subordinate officials. Its purposes, as stated in Article 1 of its Articles of Agreement, are these:

1. To assist in the reconstruction and development of territories of members by facilitating the investment of capital for productive purposes, including the restoration of economies destroyed or disrupted by war, the reconversion of productive facilities to peacetime needs and the encouragement of the development of productive facilities and resources in less developed countries.

2. To promote private foreign investment by means of guarantees or participations in loans and other investments made by private investors; and when private capital is not available on reasonable terms, to supplement private investment by providing, on suitable conditions, finance for productive purposes out of its own capital, funds raised by it, and its other resources.

3. To promote the long-range balanced growth of international trade and the maintenance of equilibrium in balances of payments by encouraging international investment for the development of the productive resources of members, thereby assisting in raising productivity, the standard of living and conditions of labor in their territories.

4. To arrange the loans made or guaranteed by it in relation to international loans through other channels so that the more useful and urgent projects, large and small alike, will be dealt with first.

5. To conduct its operations with due regard to the effect of international investment on business conditions in the territories of members and, in the immediate post-war years, to assist in bringing about a smooth transition from a wartime to a peacetime economy.

The President is responsible for the conduct of the business of the Bank, and it is he who appoints and dismisses the staff. The President, on the basis of information provided by the staff, recommends loans; the Executive Directors make the final decisions on the basis of those recommendations. This administrative authority possessed by the President and the Executive Directors, involving as it does control over the resources of the Bank and the right to extend or refuse financial assistance to governments and to private business enterprises, is quite unusual in character and its exercise could have far-reaching consequences to nations. The policy of the officials of the Bank in making loans has in practice been highly cautious, and loans have not been extended unless they have appeared thoroughly safe and sound. Those nations which have been in need of funds and have been unable to meet the Bank's conditions have been prone to criticize the Bank's policy and have urged the adoption of a more liberal loan policy.

Although the Bank is authorized to have $10,000,000,000 of capital stock, the total subscribed capital at the present time is $8,263,-000,000. Only 20 percent of this capital may be called up by the Bank to serve as a working fund; the remaining 80 percent of the subscription of each member is subject to call only when needed to meet the obligations of the Bank for funds borrowed or for loans guaranteed. On July 15, 1947, the Bank, using its right to borrow, sold $250,000,000 of bond issues to private investors in the United States, thus making more money available for loaning purposes. The Bank has made a number of loans, among which are the following:

1. On May 9, 1947, a sum of $250,000,000 was loaned to France, through the Credit National, a semipublic company, to make possible the importation of equipment needed to modernize industry.

2. On August 28, 1947, an amount of $12,000,000 was loaned to Luxembourg to finance the expansion of the steel industry and the improvement of railroads.

3. On March 25, 1948, a loan of $2,500,000 was made to a semipublic Chilean corporation to finance the purchase of agricultural machinery from the United States.

Operations of this nature continue to be carried on by the Bank. While they do not solve all, or even many, of the world's economic problems, they have been sufficiently helpful to evoke a general admission that the Bank has won for itself a firm place in the machinery of international administration.

The officers of the International Fund, like those of the Bank, possess administrative powers of control over designated international financial transactions. The Fund is governed by a Board of Governors (one from each member state), a Board of Executive Directors (five appointed by the countries with the largest quotas, and nine elected by the other member nations), and a Managing Director. The purposes of the Fund, as stated in Article 1 of its Articles of Agreement, are these:

1. To promote international monetary cooperation through a permanent institution which provides the machinery for consultation and collaboration on international monetary problems.

2. To facilitate the expansion and balanced growth of international trade, and to contribute thereby to the promotion and maintenance of high levels of employment and real income and to the development of the productive resources of all members as primary objectives of economic policy.

3. To promote exchange stability, to maintain orderly exchange arrangements among members, and to avoid competitive exchange depreciation.

4. To assist in the establishment of a multilateral system of payments in respect of current transactions between members and in the elimination of foreign exchange restrictions which hamper the growth of world trade.

5. To give confidence to members by making the Fund's resources available to them under adequate safeguards, thus providing them with opportunity to correct maladjustments in their balance of payments without resorting to measures destructive of national or international prosperity.

6. In accordance with the above, to shorten the duration and lessen the degree of disequilibrium in the international balances of payments of members.

To accomplish these purposes, the Fund maintains through its Board of Directors a sort of continuous consultation on monetary matters, it furnishes to states upon request technicians to assist in the solution of monetary problems, and it makes available to members its foreign-exchange resources to meet short-term payment difficulties. By April, 1948, when the Fund had been in operation for about two years, its officials had concluded more than thirty such transactions with ten of its members. In those transactions some $600,000,000 (U.S.) and £1,500,000 had been made available to requesting nations, of which the largest were as follows: to the United Kingdom, $300,000,000; to The Netherlands, $62,500,000 and £1,500,000; to France, $125,000,000; to Belgium, $33,000,000; to India, $28,000,000. These transactions and others like them made since 1948 by the officials of the Fund have affected only a small percentage of the world's trade, it is true, but that they have made a real contribution to stability in the economic sphere is unquestionable.

Special Administrative Activities

The League of Nations, during its brief career, engaged in a number of special administrative activities, thus setting a precedent for the United Nations. Among the first undertaken by the League were those in Austria (1922) and Hungary (1924). Because of the helpless economic position of Austria resulting from World War I and the disintegration of the Austro-Hungarian Empire, the League was asked to take up the problem of reconstruction. In accordance with the recommendations made by a special group sent to study the situation, several reforms were inaugurated, a loan of 650,000,000 gold crowns was arranged, a Bank of Issue was established, and a program to cover the deficit during the period of transition was adopted. To achieve the best possible progress, the League was given control over some of the internal affairs of Austria; the control was exercised by the Commissioner-General, appointed by the Council. This official, with his subordinate staff, was empowered to "ensure that the program of reforms is carried out and to supervise its execution." The Commissioner-General possessed the right of giving or withholding his consent to many policies and actions of the Austrian Government; his consent was required to spend any amount of money from the special loan, and he controlled the revenues assigned for the service of the loan. None of his powers was more far-reaching than that of vetoing any project which in his opinion was likely to diminish the value of the Austrian assets earmarked as security for the loan. Clearly this arrangement, and a similar one made for Hungary two years later, gave the Council of the League, acting through its appointed officials, administrative power of considerable substance.

Among the special involvements of the League of Nations in the administrative field was its work in the Free City of Danzig. At the end of World War I, Poland laid claim to the city, but because of the German population there, the Peace Conference at Paris refused the Polish claim, even though the city could not be left under German control. The final decision was to make it an autonomous city, subject to certain limitations and controls. Because of the importance of the city's port facilities, they were placed under an agency jointly managed by the Free City and Poland, known as the Danzig Port and Waterways Board. A High Commissioner was appointed by the League of Nations and assigned the following duties: helping the Free City draft its Constitution; dealing in the first instance with disputes between the City and Poland; vetoing "any treaty or international agreement, in so far as it applies to the Free City of Danzig, which in the opinion of the Council of the League of Nations is inconsistent with the provisions of the present treaty or with the status of the Free City"; and approving loans made by the city if Poland should raise any objection to them. This system was brought to an end by World War II, and the city of Danzig became a part of Poland.

Reference has already been made to the governmental system set up for the Saar Basin by the Treaty of Versailles to last for a period of fifteen years; a plebiscite was held in 1935, and the territory became a part of Germany. During that interval of fifteen years, the Saar Basin was governed by "a commission representing the League of Nations," as the Treaty put it. The Council appointed the five members of the commission, received and examined quarterly reports from it, and received and examined petitions emanating from the natives of the Basin. The powers of the commission extended to the whole realm of government. The system was the butt of frequent criticism, but, with all its shortcomings, it is only fair to point out that the job given to the commission and the League was one of unusual difficulty because of the strong nationalistic leanings of the German people of the Basin and the rival claims and ambitions of Germany and France.

Like the League, the United Nations has provided useful machinery and processes for special administrative enterprises which have been put to work in a number of situations. One such instance is the regime set up for the city of Trieste after World War II. In the Council of Foreign Ministers, whose job it was to decide the future of the city, Yugoslavia, supported by Russia, claimed the city on the ground of its economic importance as a port to the Slav hinterland, while Italy, aided and abetted by the Anglo-American bloc, argued that she should hold it because the people of the city were predominantly Italian and because since World War I it had been an Italian possession. In the end, an agreement was concluded making Trieste a Free Territory whose independence and integrity would be ensured by the United Nations. The city's head was to be a governor, with the Security Council of the United Nations empowered to name the man to fill the post. Continued disagreement between Russia and the Anglo-American group left the Council in a state of deadlock over the person to be appointed as governor, and the office remained unfilled.

The United Nations has assumed a highly active role in the work of narcotic control. The problem is an old one and has long been recognized to be international in scope, beyond the ability of individual nations to solve when acting alone. Since 1912, it has been treated on an international level by multilateral action. The League of Nations made notable contributions to the solution of the problem, particularly by assisting in the conclusion of several conventions to regulate the trade in opium, made in 1925, 1931, and 1936. The United Nations took up where the League left off, not only by maintaining under the Economic and Social Council a Commission on Narcotics Control, but also by working with the Permanent Central Board and the Drug Supervisory Body, both older organizations active for some time in the field.

The Permanent Central Board consists of eight members appointed by the Economic and Social Council. It receives from governments party to the Geneva Convention of 1925 statistical returns on the production, manufacture, consumption, import and export of raw materials of narcotic drugs covered by the convention. It is, therefore, in a position to discover whether any country is piling up an unneeded supply and is in danger of becoming a center of illicit traffic. The Board is authorized to ask for explanations and to report its findings to the Economic and Social Council and to other parties to the convention, with recommendations for action.

The Supervisory Body examines the estimates submitted by the participating nations each year as to their respective medical and scientific needs. It may amend those estimates only with the consent of the governments concerned. Once definite amounts are fixed, they become maximum figures for manufacture. The Supervisory Body has four members, one appointed by the United Nations Commission on Narcotic Drugs, one by the Permanent Central Board, and two by the World Health Organization. The Secretary-General of the United Nations furnishes the Supervisory Body with a secretarial force. Both the Permanent Central Board and the Drug Supervisory Body are on the budget of the United Nations.

The Trusteeship System

The trusteeship system is an outgrowth and an adaptation of the mandate system of the League of Nations. From an administrative point of view, the two have presented very similar organizational principles and methods, although in matters of detail many differences may be pointed out. In both, certain undeveloped parts of the world have been under international control, exercised by advanced nations serving as trustees for the international community, represented by the League of Nations in the one case and by the United Nations in the other.

The essence of the mandate or trusteeship principle was well stated in Article 22 of the Covenant of the League of Nations, as follows:

1. To those colonies and territories which as a consequence of the late war have ceased to be under the sovereignty of the States which formerly governed them and which are inhabited by peoples not yet able to stand by themselves under the strenuous conditions of the modern world, there should be applied the principle that the well-being and development of such peoples form a sacred trust of civilization and that securities for the performance of this trust should be embodied in this Covenant.

2. The best method of giving practical effect to this principle is that the tutelage of such peoples should be intrusted to advanced nations who by reason of their resources, their experience or their geographical position can best undertake this responsibility, and who are willing to accept it, and that this tutelage should be exercised by them as Mandatories on behalf of the League.

3. The character of the mandate must differ according to the stage of the development of the people, the geographical situation of the territory, its economic conditions and other similar circumstances.

Although imperialist nations have often asserted, and at times with some sincerity, that their colonial possessions were regarded by them as "sacred trusts," exploitation and abuses of all sorts have always been practiced to a greater or less degree in every empire. As one of the publications of the League of Nations pointed out, "At the beginning of the period of modern colonisation (in the 16th and 17th centuries) colonisers concerned themselves almost solely with the exploitation of the conquered areas for their own benefit and that of the mother-country."[3] Gradually, humanitarian, political, or economic considerations led to a reaction from this concept of colonialism. By the end of the eighteenth century, and to a greater extent in the nineteenth century, religious leaders and politicians of a liberal brand began to talk and write against such abuses as slavery and the slave trade, and bent their efforts toward the awakening of the masses to the need for a more generous treatment of the so-called backward peoples. By the time the intensive competition of the great powers began for the acquisition of possessions in Africa

---

[3] *The Mandate System,* Geneva, 1945, League of Nations Publications, VI, A, p. 7.

(about 1880), humanitarianism within colonies was a widely publicized ideal. The General Act of the Conference of Berlin (1885) stated among the objectives of the European nations in taking over colonies in Africa the furthering of "the moral and material well-being of the native populations." However sincere or insincere the European nations subscribing to this doctrine may have been, and much insincerity no doubt was present, the fact that they felt obliged to make such a statement was a tribute to the humanitarian tenets of the day.

Even the idea of a mandate in colonial management made some headway during the nineteenth century. In 1815, Great Britain took over the Ionian Islands under a kind of mandate conferred upon her by Russia, Prussia, and Austria. In 1860, France was given a mandate by the great powers to intervene in Lebanon for the purpose of protecting the Christian people there.

The mandate system written into the Covenant of the League of Nations in 1919 was an elaboration and a combination of the ideals of humanitarianism and mandatory action with which the world had already become fairly familiar. It was made possible by the organization of the League as a body representative of the international community, from whom advanced nations might take mandates for "backward" areas and to whom they would be responsible for their actions within those areas.

The immediate problem whose solution gave rise to the mandate system in 1919 was that of disposing of the colonies taken from Germany and the territory detached from Turkey in the peace settlements following World War I. Annexation of those colonies and territories by the nations that had defeated Germany was politically impossible, for during the war those nations had preached self-determination so loudly that they could not hope to get away with a program so obviously contrary to their preachments. On the other hand, independence to those areas would surely have been inexpedient, for they were too backward and weak to maintain themselves in the rigorous conditions of world politics. General Smuts of South Africa, the eminent statesman who for more than a generation contributed ably to the progress of international action, was the author of the plan for a mandate system which was considered at the Paris Peace Conference and, with some modifications, was adopted and inserted in the Covenant as Article 22.

The San Francisco Conference of 1945 decided that the principles of the mandate system should be carried over in the new era which would be inaugurated by World War II. The change in name from the "mandate system" to the "trusteeship system" was not a matter of any significance. By Article 75 of the Charter, it was provided that "The United Nations shall establish under its authority an international trusteeship system for the administration and supervision of such territories as may be placed thereunder. . . ." The basic objectives of the system, according to the following Article, are: (1) to "further international peace and security"; (2) to promote the well-being of the inhabitants of the trust areas toward self-government of independence; (3) to encourage "respect for human rights and for fundamental freedoms" and a "recognition of the interdependence of the peoples of the world"; and (4) to "ensure equal treatment in social, economic and commercial matters for all Members of the United Nations and their nationals. . . ."

Neither the mandate system nor the trusteeship system made any pretense of putting an end to imperialism the world over. The nations with colonies—Great Britain, France, The Netherlands, Belgium, the United States, and the rest—might keep them unhampered, except that under Article 73 of the Charter those nations agreed to "recognize the principle that the interests of the inhabitants of these territories are paramount; and accept as a sacred trust the obligation to promote to the utmost, within the system of international peace and security established by the present Charter, the well-being of the inhabitants of these territories. . . ." The Article contained detailed objectives which the nations with colonies agreed to adopt in furtherance of the principle stated, and it imposed upon those nations an obligation to "transmit regularly to the Secretary-General for information purposes . . . statistical and other information of a technical nature relating to economic, social, and educational conditions in the territories. . . ." It was possible for a nation to place its colonies under the trusteeship system but not obligatory; needless to say, this kind of invitation has not induced, nor could it be expected to induce, nations to disband their empires.

Under the Charter, three categories of territories were specified as eligible for status as trust areas, all with the stipulation that they "may be placed thereunder," not that they *must* be. Those three were: (1) territories then under mandates; (2) territories which might be "detached from enemy states as a result of the Second World War"; and (3) "territories voluntarily placed under the system" by the possessing nations. To date, all of the territories once under the mandate system either have become independent or have been placed under the trusteeship system, except Southwest Africa. Prior to World War I, Southwest Africa was a German colony, and after that war it was made a mandate exercised by the Union of South Africa, a dominion within the British Commonwealth of Nations. Maintaining that Southwest Africa was sparsely populated and unable to support itself, the Union undertook after World War II to incorporate its former mandate into its own territory. Reporting to the General Assembly on the matter, the Union asserted that the people of Southwest Africa had been consulted and that a majority of the inhabitants desired to be a part of the Union of South Africa. Despite the persistent efforts of the General Assembly to get the Union to reverse its policy and turn Southwest Africa over to the trusteeship system, the territory has remained a part of the Union of South Africa. From a strictly legal point of view, the Union's action appears to be sound, for the Charter merely provides that the old mandates "may" be turned into trust areas, not that they must be. This interpretation of the Charter was given by the International Court of Justice in an advisory opinion of 1950, already referred to in an earlier chapter of this book.[4] The Court said explicitly, "The provisions of Chapter XII of the Charter do not impose on the Union of South Africa a legal obligation to place the territory under the Trusteeship System"; it went on to assert that the Union of South Africa continued to have the obligations toward Southwest

---

[4] See Chapter VII on the International Court of Justice. See also the text of the Court's opinion in *American Journal of International Law*, 1950, vol. 44, no. 4, p. 770.

Africa which were assumed under the mandate system, and that the Union alone could not modify the status of the territory. From a broader point of view, however, the policy of the Union of South Africa is difficult to support, and must be regarded as a blow to the prestige of the trusteeship system.

Each area placed under trusteeship is the subject of a special trusteeship agreement, which defines the terms under which the territory will be administered and designates the administering authority. In the making of this agreement there is much leeway for the adjustment of authority to local conditions. The possible range of provisions for inclusion in the trust agreements is somewhat greater than that of the old mandate agreements, by reason of the fact that in the latter the areas were classified into three groups—A, B, and C—by the Covenant with the requirement that stated conditions should obtain in each. Class A were the "communities formerly belonging to the Turkish Empire," and since they were relatively advanced, the mandatory was to give them "administrative advice and assistance" until they could "stand alone." Class B were the Central African areas, where the mandatory was to be "responsible for the administration of the territory under conditions which will guarantee freedom of conscience and religion, subject only to the maintenance of public order and morals, the prohibition of such abuses as the slave trade. . . ." Class C territories were defined as those where "sparseness of their population or their small size, or their remoteness from the centers of civilization, or their geographical contiguity to the mandatory . . ." made their administration as integral parts of the territory of the mandatory logical; they included Southwest Africa and the old German islands in the far Pacific. The division of the mandated areas into these groups precluded a wide variation in the provisions of the mandate agreements. It is doubtful, however, that this difference between the trusteeship system and the mandate system is highly significant, for the League classification did not impose restrictions which were in any way unreasonable or out of tune with local conditions.

The agreements concluded and approved by the General Assembly are as follows:

New Guinea, under Australia.

Ruanda-Urundi, under Belgium.

Part of Togoland, under France.

Part of Togoland, under Great Britain.

Part of the Cameroons, under France.

Part of the Cameroons, under Great Britain.

Western Samoa, under New Zealand.

Tanganyika, under Great Britain.

Marshall, Mariana, and Caroline Islands, under the United States.

Italian Somaliland under Italy for ten years.

The American trusteeship for the Marshall, Mariana, and Caroline Islands, under an agreement of February 17, 1947, is a "strategic area" as defined by the Charter. As required, this agreement was approved by the Security Council rather than the General Assembly. Its terms are for the most part identical with those of the nonstrategic areas; the main differences are that the United States may for security reasons designate certain places in the islands as closed, and that the subject of air-traffic rights is reserved for special treatment at a later date. This status of a strategic area was given to the American trust areas at the insistence of the United States Government, which wanted to possess the military powers implied, and wanted them so much that it made clear its intention to annex the islands outright if necessary in order to get those powers. This action, like that of the Union of South Africa in Southwest Africa, tended to discredit the trusteeship system.

The connecting link between the administering authorities and the United Nations is the Trusteeship Council. Although one of the "principal organs" of the United Nations under the Charter, the Trusteeship Council acts under the authority of the General Assembly. This arrangement differs from the mandate system of the League in two particulars: (1) the Mandate Commission was not one of the main organs of the League; and (2) the Council of the League, not the Assembly, was the ultimate authority in control of the system. By giving the Trusteeship Council the status of a principal organ, the framers of the Charter expected that the prestige of the agency would be enhanced; and by naming the General Assem-

bly instead of the Security Council as the ultimate authority, they
intended to give small and disinterested nations a stronger position.

The Trusteeship Council is composed of the representatives of
three groups: (1) nations acting as administering authorities; (2)
permanent members of the Security Council not administering trust
territories; and (3) as many other nations elected for three-year
terms by the General Assembly as may be necessary in order that
the Council be equally divided between nations which administer
territories and nations which do not. This brings the membership at
the present time up to fourteen members. Seven of the fourteen administer trust territories: Australia, Belgium, France, New Zealand,
Great Britain, Italy and the United States. There are two permanent
members of the Security Council not administering territories:
China and Russia. The elective members are five in number, and because of the temporary nature of their tenure, they are constantly
changing.

The personnel of the Trusteeship Council are selected as representatives of nations; the American member, for instance, Mr. Fran-
cis Sayre, has acted as a representative of the United States Government. This is a departure from the practice followed in the League
of Nations Mandates Commission, where the members were selected as individuals free from governmental control. In practice it
must be conceded that both agencies have been well manned. There
has, however, been a more rapid turnover in the individual membership of the Trusteeship Council than in the Mandates Commission, and considered generally, there have been fewer colonial experts in the Trusteeship Council, no doubt for the reason that there
are more nations without colonial possessions on the present agency
than on the old League Commission.

The Trusteeship Council has several procedures at hand by which
it can keep itself informed on the policies and activities of the administering authorities in the trust territories. Most important in this
respect are the annual reports submitted by the administering authorities to the Council in which those policies are explained and
the conditions within the territories are described. In order to assure
itself that the points omitted from the reports will not be more sig-

nificant than those included, the Trusteeship Council formulates questionnaires with from two to three hundred specific queries on the political, economic, social, and educational advancement of the natives, which the administering authorities are expected to use as bases for the subjects reported upon. The annual reports are examined with great care by the Trusteeship Council, and out of their examination may come recommendations for policy adjustments or requests for further information.

A second procedure by which the Trusteeship Council is kept in touch with the policies of the administering authorities is the dispatch by native peoples of petitions alleging grievances and asking for adjustments. After accepting these petitions, the Trusteeship Council examines them in consultation with the administering authorities concerned, trying thereby to ascertain the facts and to determine what, if any, recommendation it should make. During its first two sessions (there are two sessions a year), the Trusteeship Council received several petitions from Germans and Italians living in the British trust area of Tanganyika in Africa, asking for United Nations intervention to prevent their repatriation to Germany and Italy, respectively. The Council discussed these petitions in the presence of a British spokesman who assured it that the policy of his government was to be selective in returning individuals to their homeland. The Council expressed its approval of British policy. Petitions on other subjects have been handled in much the same manner.

A procedural advantage possessed by the Trusteeship Council over the Mandates Commission is its right to send missions to the trust territories "at times agreed upon with the administering authority" to examine and report on conditions. Several visiting missions have in fact been dispatched. They have, for instance, been sent to Tanganyika and Ruanda-Urundi in Africa and have returned with reports on conditions as they found them.

That these methods furnished by the trusteeship system of checking on the nations in charge of undeveloped territories is an advance over outright imperialism is indisputable. There is injected an interest, a right of investigation, and a right of recommendation on the part of the international community as a whole that makes for openness, publicity, and humanitarianism. That the system is imperfect cannot be denied. The substitution of the right of demanding in place of recommending on the part of the international community —the United Nations—would have the approval of observers who at many points become impatient with the practice of handling sovereign powers with kid gloves. The extension of the trusteeship system to all colonial possessions, those of Great Britain, the United States, France, Belgium, and others, is also an aspiration which, regardless of its merits, must be looked upon as hopeless idealism in this world of sovereign states. To justify the system for the former possessions of Germany, Turkey, Japan, and Italy on the ground that those nations were defeated in war, or even on the ground that they are incapable of governing colonies, while opposing the regime for the colonial possessions of other nations is discriminatory and unconvincing; it is power politics.

An International Civil Service

Added together, the permanent staffs of existing international organizations make up a "civil service" which is astonishingly large. Mr. Walter Crocker estimates that the international secretariats of today employ "well over 10,000 officials," most of them in the Secretariat of the United Nations or in the permanent offices of the specialized agencies. The Secretariat of the United Nations alone has between 3000 and 4000 employees, and the Secretariat of UNESCO has more than 700 officials on its staff. Outside of the United Nations, the Office of European Economic Coöperation under the Marshall Plan has more than 800 employees.

Mention has already been made of the fact that the permanent employees of the United Nations and its specialized agencies are hired and governed in accordance with rules set up by the General Assembly. In 1949, the Assembly established an Administrative Tribunal "to hear and pass judgment upon applications alleging nonobservance of contracts of employment of staff members of the Secretariat of the United Nations or of the terms of appointment of such staff members."[5] The competence of the Tribunal extends to the secretariats of the specialized agencies "brought into relationship with the United Nations in accordance with the provisions of Articles 57 and 63 of the Charter upon the terms established by a special agreement to be made with each such agency by the Secretary-General of the United Nations." The Tribunal handed down its first judgment on June 30, 1950.[6]

To improve the quality of international administration, the Economic and Social Council on February 24, 1928, asked the Secretary-General of the United Nations to undertake an examination into the possibility of providing facilities for the study of administration; the Council hoped that means might be found for offering adequate training for an increasing number of candidates recruited widely from countries the world over. To date, no such facilities have been made available.

Clearly, international administration has made great strides during recent years, and today its activities are a boon to mankind. That it will expand into new fields and become more efficient in the future is a foregone conclusion.

---

[5] See Appendix v of this chapter for the text of the Statute of the Administrative Tribunal.

[6] See *Annual Report of the Secretary-General* for the period July 1, 1949, to June 30, 1950.

The United Nations Secretariat

SECRETARY-GENERAL

Chief Administrative Officer of the UN; supervision of Departments of secretariat; provision of secretariat services to the General Assembly, Councils, and their subsidiary bodies; administrative implementation of decisions of principal organs by

a. Carrying out assigned tasks and
   Advising members of their obligations;
   notification to Security Council of threats to maintenance of peace and security; maintenance of liaison between UN and

a. Members
b. Specialized Agencies and other international organizations and
c. Private individuals and organizations

DEPARTMENT OF SOCIAL AFFAIRS

Human Rights, Health, Narcotic Drugs, and other social welfare, cultural and educational matters; secretariat assistance to the Third Committee of the General Assembly, the Economic and Social Council, the Social Commission and the Commissions on Human Rights, Status of Women, Population and Narcotic Drugs.

1. Division of Population
2. Division of Narcotic Drugs
3. Division of Human Rights
4. Division of Social Activities

DEPARTMENT OF TRUSTEESHIP AND INFORMATION FROM NON-SELF-GOVERNING TERRITORIES

Trust territories, Non-Self-Governing Territories, Non-Security Aspects of Strategic Areas; secretariat assistance to the Fourth Committee of the General Assembly and the Trusteeship Council.

1. Division of Trusteeship
2. Division of Non-Self-Governing Territories

DEPARTMENT OF PUBLIC INFORMATION

Advice to Secretary-General on all matters of information policy; execution of the information program of the UN; development of facilities and services for the press, radio, films and other information media.

1. Press and Publications Bureau
2. Radio Division
3. Films and Visual Information Division
4. Special Services
5. External Services
6. Library Services

DEPARTMENT OF ECONOMIC AFFAIRS

General economic, financial, transport and communications problems; statistics; secretarial assistance to the Second Committee of the General Assembly; the Economic and Social Council and its economic commissions.

1. Division of Economics, Stability, and Development
2. Fiscal Division
3. Transport and Communications Division
4. Statistical Office
5. Joint Division of Coördination and Liaison

DEPARTMENT OF SECURITY COUNCIL AFFAIRS

Political and security matters; general administrative and secretarial services to the Security Council and its subsidiary organs and to the First Committee of the General Assembly.

1. General Political Division
2. Armaments and Enforcement Measures Sections
3. Atomic Energy Commission Group
4. Administrative and General Division

ADMINISTRATIVE AND FINANCIAL SERVICES

Planning and execution of the budgetary, personnel and fiscal program of the UN; provision of staff assistance in administrative and organizational planning.

1. Inspection Service
2. Bureau of Finance
3. Bureau of Personnel

CONFERENCE AND GENERAL SERVICES

Arrangements for meetings of the General Assembly, the Councils, the Commissions, Committees and special conferences held under the auspices of the UN; provision of general management services for the UN.

1. Bureau of Documents
2. Documents Control Staff
3. Bureau of General Services

DEPARTMENT OF LEGAL AFFAIRS

Advice to the Secretariat and other organs of the UN on legal and constitutional questions; encouragement of the progressive development of international law and its codification; maintenance of liaison with the International Court of Justice; Registration of Treaties.

1. General Legal Division
2. Division for Development and Codification of International Law
3. Division of Privileges and Immunities and of Registration of Treaties

II

Bureau of the Universal Postal Union*

ARTICLE 26—GENERAL FUNCTIONS

1. A central Office, operating at Bern under the name of International Bureau of the Universal Postal Union, and placed under the supervision of the Swiss Postal Administration, serves as an organ of liaison, information and consultation for the countries of the Union.

2. That Bureau is charged, in particular, with assembling, coordinating, publishing and distributing information of all kinds concerning the international postal service; with giving, at the request of the interested parties, an opinion on questions in dispute; with making known requests for modification of the Acts of the Congress; with giving notice of the changes adopted; and, in general, with undertaking such studies and work in connection with editing and arranging material as the Convention, the Agreements and their Regulations may assign to it, or which may be entrusted to it in the interests of the Union.

3. It acts as a clearing-house for the settlement of accounts of all kinds relative to the international postal service, between Administrations requesting such intervention.

ARTICLE 27—EXPENSES OF THE INTERNATIONAL BUREAU

1. Each Congress fixes the maximum figure for the ordinary annual expenses of the International Bureau. Those expenses, as well as the extraordinary expenses arising from the meeting of a Congress, a Conference or a Committee, and the expenses incurred in connection with special work entrusted to that Bureau, are shared by all the countries of the Union.

2. The latter are divided, for that purpose, into 7 classes, each of which contributes to the payment of the expenses in the following proportion:

---

* Convention on the Universal Postal Union, Revision of July 5, 1947.

1st Class, 25 units	5th Class, 5 units
2d Class, 20 units	6th Class, 3 units
3d Class, 15 units	7th Class, 1 unit
4th Class, 10 units	

III

Text of the Agreement for United States Trusteeship for the Pacific Islands

(*Background Summary,* Non-Self Governing Territories and the Trusteeship System, Office of Public Affairs, Department of State, 11 February 1947.)

PREAMBLE

WHEREAS Article 75 of the Charter of the United Nations provides for the establishment of an international trusteeship system for the administration and supervision of such territories as may be placed thereunder by subsequent agreements; and

WHEREAS under Article 77 of the said Charter the trusteeship system may be applied to territories now held under mandate; and

WHEREAS on December 17, 1920, the Council of the League of Nations confirmed a mandate for the former German islands north of the equator to Japan, to be administered in accordance with Article 22 of the Covenant of the League of Nations; and

WHEREAS Japan, as a result of the Second World War, has ceased to exercise any authority in these islands;

Now, THEREFORE, the Security Council of the United Nations, having satisfied itself that the relevant articles of the Charter have been complied with, hereby resolves to approve the following terms of trusteeship for the Pacific Islands formerly under mandate to Japan.

ARTICLE 1

The Territory of the Pacific Islands, consisting of the islands formerly held by Japan under mandate in accordance with Article 22 of the Covenant of the League of Nations, is hereby designated as a strategic area and placed under the trusteeship system established in the Charter of the United Nations. The Territory of the Pacific Islands is hereinafter referred to as the trust territory.

ARTICLE 2

The United States of America is designated as the administering authority of the trust territory.

ARTICLE 3

The administering authority shall have full powers of administration, legislation, and jurisdiction over the territory subject to the provisions of this agreement as an integral part of the United States, and may apply to the trust territory, subject to any modifications which the administering authority may consider desirable, such of the laws of the United States as it may deem appropriate to local conditions and requirements.

ARTICLE 4

The administering authority, in discharging the obligations of trusteeship in the trust territory, shall act in accordance with the Charter of the United Nations, and the provisions of this agreement, and shall, as specified in Article 83 (2) of the Charter, apply the objectives of the international trusteeship system, as set forth in Article 76 of the Charter, to the people of the trust territory.

ARTICLE 5

In discharging its obligations under Article 76 (a) and Article 84, of the Charter, the administering authority shall ensure that the trust territory shall play its part, in accordance with the Charter of the United Nations, in the maintenance of international peace and security. To this end the administering authority shall be entitled:

1. To establish naval, military and air bases and to erect fortifications in the trust territory;

2. To station and employ armed forces in the territory; and

3. To make use of volunteer forces, facilities and assistance from

the trust territory in carrying out the obligations towards the Security Council undertaken in this regard by the administering authority, as well as for the local defense and the maintenance of law and order within the trust territory.

ARTICLE 6

In discharging its obligations under Article 76 (b) of the Charter, the administering authority shall:

1. Foster the development of such political institutions as are suited to the trust territory and shall promote the development of the inhabitants of the trust territory toward self-government, and to this end shall give to the inhabitants of the trust territory a progressively increasing share in the administrative services in the territory; shall develop their participation in local government; shall give due recognition to the customs of the inhabitants in providing a system of law for the territory; and shall take other appropriate measures toward these ends;

2. Promote the economic advancement and self-sufficiency of the inhabitants and to this end shall regulate the use of natural resources; encourage the development of fisheries, agriculture, and industries; protect the inhabitants against the loss of their lands and resources; and improve the means of transportation and communication;

3. Promote the social advancement of the inhabitants, and to this end shall protect the rights and fundamental freedoms of all elements of the population without discrimination; protect the health of the inhabitants; control the traffic in arms and ammunition, opium and other dangerous drugs, and alcohol and other spiritous beverages; and institute such other regulations as may be necessary to protect the inhabitants against social abuses; and

4. Promote the educational advancement of the inhabitants, and to this end shall take steps toward the establishment of a general system of elementary education; facilitate the vocational and cultural advancement of the population; and shall encourage qualified students to pursue higher education, including training on the professional level.

ARTICLE 7

In discharging its obligations under Article 76 (c), of the Charter, the administering authority, subject only to the requirements of public order and security, shall guarantee to the inhabitants of the trust territory freedom of speech, of the press, and of assembly; freedom of conscience, of worship, and of religious teaching; and freedom of migration and movement.

ARTICLE 8

1. In discharging its obligations under Article 76 (d) of the Charter, as defined by Article 83 (2) of the Charter, the administering authority, subject to the requirements of security, and the obligation to promote the advancement of the inhabitants, shall accord to nationals of each Member of the United Nations and to companies and associations organized in conformity with the laws of such Member, treatment in the trust territory no less favorable than that accorded therein to nationals, companies and associations of any other United Nations, except the administering authority.

2. The administering authority shall ensure equal treatment to the Members of the United Nations and their nationals in the administration of justice.

3. Nothing in this Article shall be so construed as to accord traffic rights to aircraft flying into and out of the trust territory. Such rights shall be subject to agreement between the administering authority and the state whose nationality such aircraft possesses.

4. The administering authority may negotiate and conclude commercial and other treaties and agreements with Members of the United Nations and other states, designed to attain for the inhabitants of the trust territory treatment by the Members of the United Nations and other states no less favorable than that granted by them to the nationals of other states. The Security Council may recommend, or invite other organs of the United Nations to consider and recommend, what rights the inhabitants of the trust territory should acquire in consideration of the rights obtained by Members of the United Nations in the trust territory. . . .

Structure and Functions of the International Trusteeship System

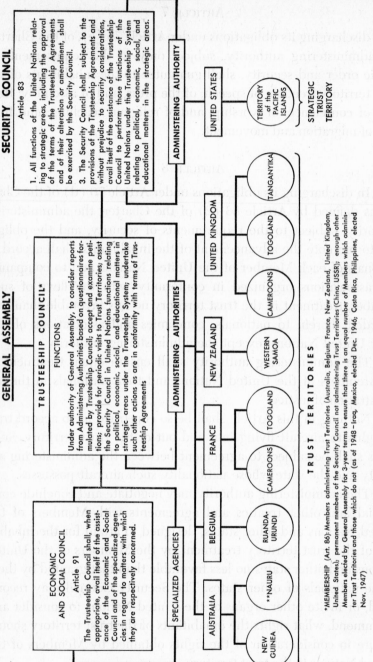

GENERAL ASSEMBLY

SECURITY COUNCIL

Article 83

1. All functions of the United Nations relating to strategic areas, including the approval of the terms of the Trusteeship Agreements and of their alteration or amendment, shall be exercised by the Security Council.

3. The Security Council shall, subject to the provisions of the Trusteeship Agreements and without prejudice to security considerations, avail itself of the assistance of the Trusteeship Council to perform those functions of the United Nations under the Trusteeship System relating to political, economic, social, and educational matters in the strategic areas.

ECONOMIC AND SOCIAL COUNCIL

Article 91

The Trusteeship Council shall, when appropriate, avail itself of the assistance of the Economic and Social Council and of the specialized agencies in regard to matters with which they are respectively concerned.

TRUSTEESHIP COUNCIL*

FUNCTIONS

Under authority of General Assembly, to consider reports from Administering Authorities based on questionnaires formulated by Trusteeship Council; accept and examine petitions; provide for periodic visits to Trust Territories; assist the Security Council in United Nations functions relating to political, economic, social, and educational matters in strategic areas under the Trusteeship System; undertake such other actions as are in conformity with terms of Trusteeship Agreements

ADMINISTERING AUTHORITY

UNITED STATES

TERRITORY of the PACIFIC ISLANDS

STRATEGIC TRUST TERRITORY

ADMINISTERING AUTHORITIES

| AUSTRALIA | BELGIUM | FRANCE | NEW ZEALAND | UNITED KINGDOM |

| NEW GUINEA | **NAURU | RUANDA-URUNDI | CAMEROONS | TOGOLAND | WESTERN SAMOA | CAMEROONS | TOGOLAND | TANGANYIKA |

TRUST TERRITORIES

SPECIALIZED AGENCIES

*MEMBERSHIP (Art. 86): Members administering Trust Territories (Australia, Belgium, France, New Zealand, United Kingdom, United States); permanent members of the Security Council not administering Trust Territories (China, USSR); enough other Members elected by General Assembly for 3-year terms to ensure that there is an equal number of Members which administer Trust Territories and those which do not (as of 1948 – Iraq, Mexico, elected Dec. 1946; Costa Rica, Philippines, elected Nov. 1947)

**Administered by Australia, on behalf of Australia, New Zealand, and the United Kingdom as joint Administering Authorities

(From *United States Participation in the United Nations, Report by the President to the Congress for 1948*, p. 285.)

V

Statute of the Administrative Tribunal of the United Nations*

Adopted by the General Assembly on 24 November 1949
(Resolution 351 [IV])

ARTICLE 1

A Tribunal is established by the present Statute to be known as the United Nations Administrative Tribunal.

ARTICLE 2

1. The Tribunal shall be competent to hear and pass judgment upon applications alleging non-observance of contracts of employment of staff members of the Secretariat of the United Nations or of the terms of appointment of such staff members. The words "contracts" and "terms of appointment" include all pertinent regulations and rules in force at the time of alleged non-observance, including the staff pension regulations.

2. The Tribunal shall be open:

    a. To any staff member of the Secretariat of the United Nations even after his employment has ceased, and to any person who has succeeded to the staff member's rights on his death;

    b. To any other person who can show that he is entitled to rights under any contract or terms of appointment, including the provisions of staff regulations and rules upon which the staff member could have relied.

3. In the event of a dispute as to whether the Tribunal has competence, the matter shall be settled by the decision of the Tribunal.

4. The Tribunal shall not be competent, however, to deal with any applications where the cause of complaint arose prior to 1 January 1950.

---

* *Administrative Tribunal, Statute and Rule,* Lake Success, 1950.

Article 3

1. The Tribunal shall be composed of seven members, no two of whom may be nationals of the same State. Only three shall sit in any particular case.

2. The members shall be appointed by the General Assembly for three years, and they may be re-appointed; provided, however, that of the members initially appointed, the terms of two members shall expire at the end of one year and the terms of two members shall expire at the end of two years. A member appointed to replace a member whose term of office has not expired shall hold office for the remainder of his predecessor's term.

3. The Tribunal shall elect its President and its two Vice-Presidents from among its members.

4. The Secretary-General shall provide the Tribunal with an Executive Secretary and such other staff as may be considered necessary.

5. No member of the Tribunal can be dismissed by the General Assembly unless the other members are of the unanimous opinion that he is unsuited for further service.

6. In case of a resignation of a member of the Tribunal, the resignation shall be addressed to the President of the Tribunal for transmission to the Secretary-General. This last notification makes the place vacant.

Article 4

The Tribunal shall hold ordinary sessions at dates to be fixed by its rules, subject to there being cases on its list which, in the opinion of the President, justify holding the session. Extraordinary sessions may be convoked by the President when required by the cases on the list.

Article 5

1. The Secretary-General of the United Nations shall make the administrative arrangements necessary for the functioning of the Tribunal.

2. The expenses of the Tribunal shall be borne by the United Nations.

ARTICLE 6

1. Subject to the provisions of the present Statute, the Tribunal shall establish its rules.

2. The rules shall include provisions concerning:
   a. Election of the President and Vice-Presidents;
   b. Composition of the Tribunal for its sessions;
   c. Presentation of applications and the procedure to be followed in respect to them;
   d. Intervention by persons to whom the Tribunal is open under paragraph 2 of Article 2, whose rights may be affected by the judgment;
   e. Hearing, for purposes of information, of persons to whom the Tribunal is open under paragraph 2 of Article 2, even though they are not parties to the case; and generally
   f. Other matters relating to the functioning of the Tribunal.

ARTICLE 7

1. An application shall not be receivable unless the person concerned has previously submitted the dispute to the joint appeals body provided for in the staff regulations and the latter has communicated its opinion to the Secretary-General, except where the Secretary-General and the applicant have agreed to submit the application directly to the Administrative Tribunal.

2. In the event of the joint body's recommendations being favourable to the application submitted to it, and in so far as this is the case, an application to the Tribunal shall be receivable if the Secretary-General has:
   a. Rejected the recommendations;
   b. Failed to take any action within the thirty days following the communication of the opinion; or
   c. Failed to carry out the recommendations within the thirty days following the communication of the opinion.

3. In the event that the recommendations made by the joint body

and accepted by the Secretary-General are unfavourable to the applicant, and in so far as this is the case, the application shall be receivable, unless the joint body unanimously considers that it is frivolous.

4. An application shall not be receivable unless it is filed within ninety days reckoned from the respective dates and periods referred to in paragraph 2 above, or within ninety days reckoned from the date of the communication of the joint body's opinion containing recommendations unfavourable to the applicant. If the circumstance rendering the application receivable by the Tribunal, pursuant to paragraphs 2 and 3 above, is anterior to the date of announcement of the first session of the Tribunal, the time-limit of ninety days shall begin to run from that date. Nevertheless, the said time-limit on his behalf shall be extended to one year if the heirs of a deceased staff member or the trustee of a staff member who is not in a position to manage his own affairs, file the application in the name of the said staff member.

5. In any particular case the Tribunal may decide to suspend the provisions regarding time-limits.

6. The filing of an application shall not have the effect of suspending the execution of the decision contested.

7. Applications may be filed in any of the five official languages of the United Nations.

ARTICLE 8

The oral proceedings of the Tribunal shall be held in public unless the Tribunal decides that exceptional circumstances require that they be held in private.

ARTICLE 9

If the Tribunal finds that the application is well founded, it shall order the rescinding of the decision contested or the specific performance of the obligation invoked; but if, in exceptional circumstances, such rescinding or specific performance is, in the opinion of the Secretary-General, impossible or inadvisable, the Tribunal shall within a period of not more than sixty days order the payment to the applicant of compensation for the injury sustained. The applicant shall be entitled to claim compensation in lieu of rescinding of the contested decision or specific performance. In any case involving compensation, the amount awarded shall be fixed by the Tribunal and paid by the United Nations or, as appropriate, by the specialized agency participating under Article 12.

ARTICLE 10

1. The Tribunal shall take all decisions by a majority vote.

2. The judgments shall be final and without appeal.

3. The judgments shall state the reasons on which they are based.

4. The judgments shall be drawn up, in any of the five official languages of the United Nations, in two originals which shall be deposited in the archives of the Secretariat of the United Nations.

5. A copy of the judgment shall be communicated to each of the parties in the case. Copies shall also be made available on request to interested persons.

ARTICLE 11

The present Statute may be amended by decisions of the General Assembly.

ARTICLE 12

The competence of the Tribunal may be extended to any specialized agency brought into relationship with the United Nations in accordance with the provisions of Articles 57 and 63 of the Charter upon the terms established by a special agreement to be made with each such agency by the Secretary-General of the United Nations. Each such special agreement shall provide that the agency concerned shall be bound by the judgments of the Tribunal and be responsible for the payment of any compensation awarded by the Tribunal in respect of a staff member of that agency and shall include, *inter alia,* provisions concerning the agency's participation in the administrative arrangements for the functioning of the Tribunal and concerning its sharing the expenses of the Tribunal.

Part Six: The Future

XVII Revision of the United Nations

T HE UNITED NATIONS IN ITS PRESENT FORM IS NOT THE ultimate in world organization. That it will be superseded by something else in due course of time is as inevitable as the process of change everywhere. Conceivably, it may be the victim of war, as was the League of Nations, after which something new will be tried; throughout the lifetime of the United Nations a third world war has seemed imminent. Even without a general war, the solidification of the breach between the communist nations and the rest of the world might very likely require permanent alterations in the structure of world society. A more pleasing turn of events, if less probable, would be a healing of the breach and a stabilization of international relations so as to permit a normal development in the future to the institutions of internationalism, a gradual improvement based upon successful practice, perhaps in the direction of federation but certainly toward a stronger world organization. Least pleasing of all the possibilities would be a reorganization of the world or a large part of it by the communists, who by present indications would bring back imperialism, in new attire, to be sure, but as hideous as ever.

If by some lucky chance the world should have an opportunity to develop without the interference of war or revolution, its point of departure in matters of government would be international organization in its present form, as described in the preceding chapters of this book. There is no escaping the past in the field of government; this has been noticeable in successions of institutions within states,

as in France and Germany during modern times, where new constitutions invariably preserve much of the old. Even were present international organization to be ended by violence, the wager would
be safe that whatever took its place would draw heavily upon the
past experience which men and nations have had in providing peace
and prosperity to the diverse peoples of the world.

Criticism of the United Nations

As Mr. A. M. Rosenthal, New York *Times* reporter at the United
Nations, has pointed out, "The pastime of 'let's take a crack at the
U.N.' has devoted fans in all . . . member countries."[1] He goes on
to say, "It's been blamed for what it hasn't done, blamed for what it
has. It's been blamed for spending too much money, and it's been
blamed for being penny-wise and stingy. It's been accused of taking
too much authority on itself; it's been accused of doing nothing
while the world slid into another war. It's been denounced as a sort
of home base for Communist spies; it's been scolded for not having
the full quota of Russians on its staff." Certainly the United Nations
has been the butt of harsh and hostile criticism. Few are they who
have professed to be entirely satisfied with it. Compliments have
been paid the organization sparingly, and those that have been
given have often seemed labored.

To some extent the derogatory remarks which have been so frequently hurled at the United Nations must be regarded as expressions of the tendency of people toward extreme views on matters
political, fastening on the United Nations the same all-black or all-
white labels which they attach to the Truman Fair Deal or to the
Republican Party. The League of Nations suffered in the public
esteem from a similar method of evaluation, for throughout its lifetime it had its supporters who would say nothing against it and its
opponents who could find nothing good in it; only very rarely would
a critic occupy a moderate position and point out both its strength
and its weaknesses. As a rule, the more moderate position, even
though it is the least common, is the most convincing of any, for rare

---

[1] A. M. Rosenthal, "U.N. is Doing a Job," *Colliers,* July 9, 1949.

is the human institution that is completely devoid of virtue or entirely free of faults.

Strength of the United Nations

Those who apply to the United Nations such slurs as "All they do is talk" and "We would be just as well off without all that nonsense" are disappointed at the organization's limitations in dealing with critical international controversies and preventing them from degenerating into open resort to arms. They naturally deplore the fighting that has taken place in Palestine, Indonesia, India, and Korea. Focusing their eyes on what the United Nations has not done, they are inclined to overlook what it has done, and the fault is not altogether theirs, for it is the organization's failures rather than its successes that get in the news. As Mr. John Foster Dulles has said, "One veto in the Security Council captures more public interest than an entire session of the Economic and Social Council."

A proper evaluation of the United Nations will take into account its purposes. As stated in Article 1 of the Charter, the purposes are these: (1) "to maintain international peace and security . . ."; (2) "to develop friendly relations among nations based on respect for the principle of equal rights and self-determination of peoples and to take other appropriate measures to strengthen universal peace"; (3) to promote "cooperation in solving international problems of an economic, social, cultural, or humanitarian character . . ."; and (4) "to be a center for harmonizing the actions of nations in the attainment of their common ends." More tersely stated, the United Nations is expected to work for the pacific settlement of disputes, for collective security against war, and for the prosperity and welfare of mankind. These purposes have not been accomplished to an equal degree, and it must be admitted that little or nothing substantial has been done in the way of creating a reliable system of collective security.

The conference method of international action, which the United Nations embodies, has unquestionably been most succssful in dealing with problems of an economic, social, cultural, or humanitarian character, and although it could scarcely be said that the accomplishments in those fields have gone so far as to eliminate the causes of war, they have undoubtedly tied the nations together more closely and brought many advantages both to nations and to individuals. No one can estimate how much was done to promote the welfare of China by the FAO mission, which went to that country and inoculated 500,000 head of cattle and buffalo against the black plague. The $200,000,000 worth of supplies—books, microscopes, typewriters, pencils, etc.—distributed by UNESCO no doubt made a contribution to the solution of the world problem of education, even though it would be impossible to pin down the results to definite figures. The loans of the International Bank, the operations of the International Fund, the work of the IRO in providing assistance to refugees, and a score of similar activities may not have made the headlines, but their far-reaching effect in developing a world community among the seventy-five or eighty sovereign states and a greater sense of unity among them cannot be denied—all in addition to the benefits conferred in individual cases.

Even within these fields of action it would be a mistake to picture the United Nations as an unqualified success. Looking back on the first two years of United Nations activities, Mr. Hector McNeil said in 1948, "The economic and social side of the United Nations is not in any sense free from its teething troubles." Even yet, this side of the work of the United Nations is in the experimental stage, and there are those who share the view expressed by Mr. McNeil on the same occasion—that the organization is trying to do too much.

Perhaps the most severe criticism that could be made of the work of the United Nations within the economic sphere is that it has not succeeded in eliminating those conditions which are commonly referred to as causes of war, in particular the widespread trade barriers that prevail the world over. That it has endeavored to do so is evident in the Charter of the ITO, which enumerates many eloquent principles and envisages drastic action in the matter but to date has not been given life. That the United Nations has not completely failed in its effort is proved by the Geneva Agreement on trade made in 1947, by which tariffs were lowered on a reciprocal basis by the twenty-three governments concerned; this work was carried further by a similar agreement made at Annecy, France, in 1949. The admission must be made, however, that these accomplishments are little more than a dent in the armor of the trade restrictions which have long hampered the commercial intercourse of nations.

If less has been done to remove trade barriers than might be wished, the cause is not so much the lack of machinery and processes within the United Nations for so doing as it is the fact that there has existed among the nations no basis for such action. Trade barriers are an essential part of the system of economic nationalism, by which nations strengthen themselves for war, diversifying their industry through protective measures and thus insulating themselves against the rigors of blockade and making available industrial products of a strategic nature to be used for fighting purposes. As long as war and the threat of war remain, there will be little willingness on the part of nations to relinquish their means to economic power.

Handicaps to United Nations Success

Two conditions in the world have been insuperable obstacles to a better functioning of the United Nations. One has been the lack of peace treaties with all of the nations involved on the losing side in World War II. This fact was brought out by Secretary-General Trygve Lie in his annual report made public on August 5, 1950, when he said that "Throughout its existence the Organization has been gravely hampered by the conflicts among the victorious Powers over the peace settlements of the second World War." Under the Potsdam Agreement of 1945, it became the duty, not of the United Nations but of the Council of Foreign Ministers, aided in some degree by the smaller nations which had been at war against the various Axis powers, to draft the peace treaties. Although treaties of peace were negotiated for Italy, Bulgaria, Hungary, Roumania, and Finland, none has been concluded for Germany or Austria; only recently a treaty with Japan was signed. There are therefore gaping holes in the political geography of large and important areas of the world. Expanding further on the effect of this condition upon the work of the United Nations, Mr. Lie said in his report of 1950:

Without the basic settlements required to establish a foundation of reasonable stability and order in the world, the great and inevitable changes that are taking place will condemn mankind to chaos. It is the failure to make such settlements that, for five years, has prevented the United Nations from creating the system of collective security provided for in the Charter. . . .

It should be clear by now that the creation of a United Nations system of collective security as it is envisaged in the Charter can be expected only as it results from a settlement of the conflicts for power and position resulting from the defeat of Germany and Japan.

The second condition of world affairs which has hamstrung the United Nations is closely related to the first one mentioned—the deadlock between the "East" and "West." No international organization could be expected to produce results of the highest order with its leading members so implacably opposed. The settlement of this impasse is far more than a matter of machinery, for it goes deeply into the very structure of the world society. If the world is divided into two camps, no amount of organization can hide that fact. No organization, either by its fiat or by some sleight-of-hand trick, can make its members get along when they take adamant and irreconcilable positions on issues, particularly when those members are sovereign states with all the rights and appurtenances belonging thereto. This split has been expressed in the form of vetoes by Russia, the refusal of Russia to join nearly all of the specialized agencies, the willful absence of Russia from most of the meetings of the United Nations for more than seven months because of the refusal of members to seat Communist China in place of the Nationalist delegates, and the protracted and futile debate in the Security Council in August, 1950, on the Korean question, to mention only a few. This East-West split was neither caused nor perpetuated by the weaknesses of the United Nations; on the contrary, that split has been a primary cause of those weaknesses.

Some Limitations of the UN

The frustrations which the United Nations has faced go a long way toward explaining the "failures" with which it is charged, although, as has been pointed out before, its failures are less those of its organization than of its members. Only in one sense is it possible to criticize international organization *per se*, or for that matter any governmental system, apart from the nations or individuals that make the wheels go around, and that is on the basis of its ability to do what it is expected to do. A satisfactory organization or govern-ment is one that works, attaining the objectives set for it. Govern-ment ought ideally to be adapted to those people who live under it and make it function; an alert, intelligent people with high stand-ards of human conduct probably ought to have a democracy, whereas an illiterate, indifferent people require some form of dic-tatorship to get along. World organization or government is no more of an abstraction than is national government and cannot be sepa-rated from the community that it serves. The fact is that the mem-bers of the world community are egocentric states, each concerned first and foremost with its own welfare; they are not docile, amica-ble entities, nor do they go about looking for every opportunity to coöperate. Testing the United Nations on the basis of its objectives —the peace and welfare of the world—and keeping in mind the character of its member states, is it adequate? Can it, run by sover-eign states as it must be, produce what is expected of it—peace and prosperity?

One of the most serious faults of the United Nations, and one which reflects political immaturity in matters of world government, is that its procedures allow so many "entrances" to deadlock and so few "exits" from them. This is largely the result of the voting meth-ods used, which, with all their limitations, are somewhat less ob-structive than those of the League of Nations. The veto is, of course, the principal cause of deadlocks; its excessive use in the treatment of disputes and in the admission of new members to the United Na-tions has been particularly annoying. The action by the General Assembly in 1950, creating for itself a procedure for recommending concerted action against an aggressor when the Security Council is prevented by a veto from doing so, was at least an ingenious effort to find an exit from deadlocks, but its practical utility has yet to be proved. Aside from the veto, requirements that decisions in the Se-curity Council must be supported by at least seven members, and that those of the General Assembly must have at least two-thirds of the members behind them, are more rigid than those ordinarily obtaining in national governmental agencies.

There is, of course, nothing in the United Nations comparable to a national legislature. When it comes to action in the nature of law-making, the United Nations must arrange for a period of negotiating (ordinarily in a conference), and, in accordance with the principle that has held for centuries, no nation can be bound by a new rule of law unless it gives its acquiescence. Here no majority, however large, can impose its will on any minority, however small. If a state acquiesces in a new rule, it ratifies the convention in which the rule is embodied; if it opposes, it does not ratify.

Considered with respect to its objectives and to the nature of the state, the United Nations is open to the further criticism that it does not have sufficient law-enforcing authority against its members. This means ultimately that it cannot be counted upon to keep the peace and to maintain order in the world with anything like the certainty that the executive authority of a state can be relied upon within that state's territory. The inadequacy of the sanctions of the United Nations either in the hands of the Security Council or of the General Assembly has been brought out in an earlier chapter.

The system used by the United Nations for dealing with disputes between nations, as shown before, is not as tight as that commonly found within states. There is a limited area of compulsory court jurisdiction, but beyond that, disputes can be allowed to go unsettled at the whim of either party. This is not to deny that the United Nations has handled many disputes with satisfaction, but only to point out that it cannot be counted upon to do so with the high degree of efficiency ordinarily characteristic of national governments.

Summing up the situation, it becomes clear that the United Nations is not equipped with the organization and procedures that it needs to reach the objectives set for it. It lacks the authority and power, without which its objectives are made to appear as hopeless ideals. With the limited means at its disposal it has worked valiantly, and indeed it can show much in the way of constructive accomplishment—a surprising amount—but it has not produced security. Perhaps the job is too big for any world organization that is now within our grasp.

The Amendment of the Charter

In order to improve the United Nations, observers often suggest that use be made of the amendment process, either to modify the veto or to effect more far-reaching changes. In 1948, the problem of strengthening the organization was discussed in the House of Representatives of the United States, and its Committee on Foreign Affairs conducted hearings on the subject, at which Secretary of State Marshall and Ambassador Austin, among others, aired their views, both expressing themselves as doubtful whether much could be accomplished by formal amendment of the Charter.

From the very nature of the amendment process, it is easy to see why Secretary Marshall and Ambassador Austin were not optimistic about the project of improving the United Nations by that method. As it would ordinarily operate, the amendment process has two steps: (1) the adoption of a proposal by two-thirds of the members of the General Assembly, and (2) its ratification by two-thirds of the members of the United Nations, including all of the permanent members of the Security Council. It may be noted that in step one, two-thirds of the *members* of the Assembly, not two-thirds of those present and voting, are required.

The Dumbarton Oaks project would have required a two-thirds vote in the Assembly and ratification by all of the permanent members of the Security Council plus a majority of the other members. At the San Francisco Conference of 1945, some of the delegates expressed preference for this rule; others advocated that the initial Assembly approval of proposed amendments require a three-fourths instead of a two-thirds vote. The subject was not one of those which the Conference debated at great length, however, and agreement on the present formula was not difficult to get.

A significant fact in the amendment process is that there is the equivalent of a veto exercisable by the nations with permanent seats on the Security Council. In the strict sense, it is not a veto because the Security Council does not act on amendments and the veto occurs only in that organ. In the process of ratifying amendments, the requirement is that all of the five nations with permanent seats on the Security Council must ratify if a proposal is to be adopted. The existence of this rule is the main reason why improvement of the United Nations by amendment—in particular, the elimination of the veto in the Security Council—would be most difficult, if not impossible, to attain.

An alternative method of amending the Charter is provided in Article 109. This was inserted because so many of the nations participating in the San Francisco Conference were disappointed at the results of their labors and insisted upon a later chance to reconsider what had been done. According to the Article, a general conference "for the purpose of reviewing the present Charter" may be held at a date and place decided upon by two-thirds of the Assembly and any seven members of the Security Council; such a conference may recommend amendments, but as always, those proposals cannot become effective until ratified by "two-thirds of the Members of the United Nations including all the permanent members of the Security Council." If no general conference has been held at an earlier date, the proposal to call one must be placed on the agenda of the General Assembly at its tenth regular session.

At the request of Ambassador Austin, the five permanent members of the Security Council met on January 19, 1948, to discuss the project of amending the Charter with respect to the use of the veto in the treatment of international disputes and in votes on the admission of new members of the United Nations. Only one of the five nations represented—the United States—was willing to support such a project. Sometime later, Ambassador Austin stated that in his opinion "at least four of the permanent members will exert their influence to prevent a convention being called under Article 109 for reviewing the present Charter with a view of amending it." While it is true that four of the permanent members of the Security Council could not in law keep a convention from being called, the influence of their opinions as great powers could go far toward preventing its calling; in any case, whatever proposals for amending the Charter might emerge from such a convention would fail if any one of the five were to withhold ratification.

Change Without Amendment

Students of government are well aware of the fact that constitutional forms and processes may be extensively altered without formal amendment. This is because every constitutional document possesses some degree of flexibility as to the manner in which it shall be applied; its loopholes leave room for development by custom or by legislation, and its wording can never be so definitive as to preclude interpretations with expansive implications. It is a well-known fact that the present governmental system of the United States bears so slight a resemblance to that originally set up in 1789 that it is difficult to believe that both had their origins in the same formal Constitution. Although that document has been amended twenty-two times, those amendments do not account for the great bulk of the changes made: the introduction of the party system and the cabinet, the civil-service examination system, the Interstate Commerce Commission, and countless others. These innovations are the product of custom and Congressional enactment.

The United Nations is only a few years old, but already its organization has been considerably changed by informal processes. No better example of this could be given than the establishment in 1947 of an Interim Committee or "Little Assembly" by the General Assembly, and the assignment to that organization of specific functions, including the treatment of disputes referred to it and the recommendation of a special session of the General Assembly. While it is probably true that the Interim Committee has been less important than was expected, the creation of the body is illustrative of a method by which the United Nations may be and has been developed. In this connection it will be recalled that "subsidiary organs" may be set up when found necessary. Whether the Interim Committee is a subsidiary organ or not has been the subject of debate between the USSR and the United States; to regard it as such is in any case to interpret the Charter liberally.[2] The development of the organization by the creation of the Interim Committee and by setting up such subsidiary organs as the Social Commission and the

---

[2] On this subject see Yuen-li Liang, "Notes on Legal Questions Concerning the United Nations," *American Journal of International Law*, 1948, vol. 42, no. 2.

Statistical Commission is broadly analogous to the establishment by act of Congress of the Interstate Commerce Commission and the Federal Trade Commission.

Another conspicuous development of the United Nations that has been accomplished by informal methods is the United Action for Peace, adopted in 1950 in the midst of the Korean crisis. The system of sanctions which it set up has been explained in Chapter X. That it shifts the center of gravity in the matter of sanctions is apparent. Instead of being entirely under the control of the Security Council, as in the past, the sanctions are now in that body only in the first instance; when a deadlock is produced by a veto in the Security Council, the General Assembly may take over and recommend coercion against an aggressor. This is indeed a fundamental change in the manner in which the United Nations operates, and yet it has been done without formal amendment. Had the proposal contravened a provision of the Charter, a formal amendment would have been requisite, but such was not understood by the General Assembly to be the case; the arrangement, so the Assembly assumed, could be adopted without amendment because it entailed no change in the text of the Charter. It must be regarded as an expansion of the Charter rather than as a revision.

In some respects, the manner in which the veto in the Security Council has come to be used may be looked upon as developing the United Nations by custom, this time chiefly by pressure of the USSR in the direction of her assumed interests, rather than by and for the Western powers. There is nothing in the Charter bearing on the question of the applicability of the veto in a vote to determine whether a question before the Council is substantive or procedural, but the practice has developed of so using it. The resolutions of the General Assembly urging moderation on the part of the permanent members of the Council in the use of the veto were futile efforts to guide the development of practice along different lines.

There are, of course, changes in the United Nations considered desirable by some people which could not be effected without formal amendment of the Charter. There would no doubt be a difference of opinion as to where that limit is; the point has been brought out that Russia considered the Interim Committee and the United Action for Peace to be such important changes as to require amendment. Certainly it would be impossible to make the use of the veto illegal in the treatment of disputes and in the admission of new members except by revising the Charter. If the conversion of the United Nations into an effective instrument of peace and world prosperity be the objective, the program of change entailed would be so far-reaching that the job could not be done either by amendment or by practice unless and until greater harmony be attained among the member states.

The Hoover Proposal

Speaking to the American Newspaper Publishers Association on April 27, 1950, ex-President Herbert Hoover stirred up public discussion throughout the world by his proposal "that the United Nations be reorganized to exclude the Communist nations." He supported his proposal by the statement that he was not seeking the "extension of a military alliance or any color of it" but that he wanted "to redeem the concept of the United Nations to the high purpose for which it was created." Further, Mr. Hoover alleged that Russia has violated in spirit or in letter "about a dozen provisions" of the Charter, and that "The Kremlin has reduced the United Nations to a propaganda forum for the smearing of free peoples."

Taking up the cudgel against the Hoover proposal, General Romulo, President of the General Assembly in 1949, argued that the remedy to the conflict between the great powers "is not to harden the cleavage by splitting the United Nations." He contended that the United Nations is "the only workable bridge that we have today between the two hostile camps on either side of the chasm."

There is truth on both sides of the argument. Russia has been, at least from our point of view, an obstructionist and a propagandist in the United Nations. As we see it, she is less interested in the organization as an instrument of peace than as a vehicle for the world revolution. On the other hand, to oust the USSR and its satellites is to change the entire concept of the United Nations from a world organization into one devoted to the welfare of the anticommunist nations. The choice between one world organization split into two hostile camps and separate organizations representing two hostile camps may not after all be too significant. The significant fact is that the split exists and that it has defied all remedies.

Proposals and Hearings in the U.S. Senate[3]

In the Senate of the United States, as well as in the House of Representatives, the subject of strengthening the United Nations has come under discussion. Late in the session of 1949, the Foreign Relations Committee of the Senate established a subcommittee under the chairmanship of Senator Elbert Thomas of Utah to consider a variety of proposals, some of which dealt with the revision of the Charter of the United Nations while others envisaged federation in some form (to be taken up in the next chapter).

When Senator Thomas opened the hearings on February 2, 1950, he regretted the fact that "the United Nations has not functioned as satisfactorily as we had hoped," mentioning specifically "the excessive use of the veto and the general unwillingness of the Soviet Union to coöperate except on its own terms. . . ." The subcommittee invited the sponsors of the resolutions, representatives of the Department of State, and individuals from many walks of life—farmers, lawyers, students, housewives, among others—to express their views.

Among the resolutions taken up was Senate Concurrent Resolution 52 (The Thomas-Douglas Resolution), which, as explained by Senator Douglas, would "pledge the Congress to support a supplementary convention which the United States may propose to the other members of the United Nations under which the signatories agree to use force against any nation which is adjudged to be an aggressor by a two-thirds vote of the General Assembly of the United Nations, including three of the so-called Big Five powers." By the terms of the special agreement which was advocated, each nation could specify the forces which it would maintain "for immediate use of the United Nations." If the Security Council should

---

[3] See *Hearings before a Subcommittee of the Committee on Foreign Relations of the U.S. Senate*, Revision of the United Nations Charter, 1950.

become deadlocked by a veto and unable to act against an aggressor, one of the parties to the agreement that was also a member of the Security Council must take action to remove the problem from the agenda of that body, whereupon the General Assembly would be ready to take it up. The main objection raised to the project was that it could place signatory nations in such a position that they would be obligated, in law at least, to use their armed forces where they preferred not to do so. Senator Douglas maintained that his project would in no way be contrary to the provisions of the Charter, that in fact it would have the full authorization of Article 51, which stipulates that "nothing in the present Charter shall impair the inherent right of self-defense if an armed attack occurs against a member of the United Nations, . . ."

It is apparent that the plan of Concurrent Resolution 52 is essentially that of the United Action for Peace, adopted in 1950. The plan was not incorporated into a treaty, as suggested by Senator Douglas, but was adopted in the form of a resolution by the General Assembly.

Another proposal considered was Senate Resolution 133, otherwise known as the Sparkman Resolution or the A.B.C. Plan. This project called for certain amendments to the Charter: (1) to eliminate the veto in matters relating to aggression, (2) to avert atomic catastrophe, and (3) to create "a tyranny-proof international police force . . ." under a "workable Security Council and World Court." If any permanent member of the Security Council should defeat any of these proposed amendments by failing to ratify them, then other members of the United Nations would enter into an agreement exclusive of those states that would not accept the changes. The resolution also called for implementation of the North Atlantic Pact by the creation of an emergency defense force, to be called the Atlantic International Contingent. At the time of the resolution was offered, the North Atlantic Pact had not been ratified, and the defense organization which it would produce was not foreseen; defense arrangements are now in effect among members of the Pact, but they do not follow the somewhat complicated proposals of the Sparkman Resolution.

One of the most detailed proposals was Senate Concurrent Resolution 72 (Ferguson Resolution) urging the strengthening of the United Nations principally by the interpretation of the Charter, by the development of new usages, and by supplementary agreements among nations. The specific suggestions made were as follows:

1. Voluntary agreement not to use the veto in matters relating to the settlement of disputes and the admission of new members
2. An effort "to achieve immediate membership of all states qualified for membership under Article 4 of the Charter to the end of making the United Nations universal"
3. Elimination of the reservations inserted by the United States to its acceptance of the optional clause of the International Court of Justice, and acceptance by all nations of the optional clause without reservations
4. The creation of a United Nations guard force
5. Renewed efforts to secure the contribution of armed forces under Article 43 of the Charter
6. Suitable measures of collective self-defense under Article 51 of the Charter
7. Direct administration by the United Nations of disputed areas
8. Independent sources of revenue for the United Nations in addition to the contributions of members
9. Support for the "principles of the United Nations Charter respecting fundamental freedoms"
10. Preparation of an international criminal code and the establishment of an international criminal court
11. Technical assistance to undeveloped areas

Generally, the Ferguson Resolution would develop the United Nations by evolutionary processes, its purpose being to speed up processes that normally are slow. It was the most comprehensive of all the proposals to strengthen the United Nations, but the proposals embodied contained little that was new.

The Department of State manifested faint enthusiasm for the various reform proposals, particularly those requiring Charter amendments. Its spokesmen displayed more interest in Resolution 72 (the Ferguson Resolution) than the others, apparently because it stressed strengthening the United Nations by strengthening the world community itself. Assistant Secretary of State Rusk made the following assertion:

. . . the problem is not solved by putting up a new form of organization. If we could set up the elements of a solution we could solve problems which are urgent under existing machinery. It may be that some important changes in the Charter of the United Nations will be required or will be desirable, but I think we would reverse the connection if we considered that you change the form of organization and that that change then solves the problem. We won't be able to get basic changes in the organization unless there are basic changes in the situation with which the organization is dealing. Our big problem in the United Nations is the Soviet Union. Well now, it already is unwilling to accept the Charter as written. The Charter is already too much for the Soviet Union. . . .

Assistant Secretary Hickerson of the Department spoke against radical change in the United Nations and more particularly against projects for a new world organization of a stronger nature (to be taken up in the next chapter), asserting that "We cannot afford to risk jeopardizing or losing what we have without real assurance that we are getting something better in its place."

After the hearings of the subcommittee were concluded, the Committee on Foreign Relations considered the testimonies that had been submitted and came to the conclusion that they should not "at this time" recommend to the Senate any of the proposals that had been offered. The committee pointed out that some of the proposals would require amendments to the Constitution of the United States (especially those proposing federations of states). It also expressed the view that none of the projects would offer much toward a solution of the main world problem, namely, the East-West controversy. Although none of the projects—those outlined in this chapter or those looking toward a new and stronger union— was adopted, it is pertinent to point out again that Resolution 52 (Thomas-Douglas Resolution) was heavily drawn upon in the United Action for Peace.

XVIII Federation

IN THEIR SIMPLEST FORM (AS SHOWN IN THE PRECEDING chapter), plans for a new world order call for a strengthening of the United Nations by the development of new practices and without formal revision. Slightly more complicated are those projects which look to formal revision or amendment of the Charter. Involving a truly drastic change are the schemes which would scrap the United Nations completely, and move on to a new basis of world organization predicated upon states which are no longer sovereign, but which, like the forty-eight states of the United States, are reduced to the position of members of a federation. For some years now, there has been a rather widespread discussion of the pro's and con's of federation, so that within limited circles in the United States and a few other countries its implications are fairly well understood.

Meaning of "Federation"

While the definitions of federalism given by political scientists are not always in complete agreement, there are certain principles of organization that are commonly associated with it. First, it is understood that a federation divides the powers of government between the central government and the states, the former to deal with interests and problems common to the whole, while the latter is authorized to manager affairs of a more local nature. In the second place, powers are so allocated that neither the central government nor the states are constitutionally unable to annihilate or to weaken substantially the position of one another. Finally, it is characteristic of federation that both the central government and the states are able to deal directly with the individual within their respective fields of action. These principles are all brought out in Professor J. W. Garner's assertion that the distinguishing marks of a federal union are "first, the existence of a number of political communities (states, cantons, provinces, territories) possessing of right their own constitutions and forms of government, and being supreme within a more or less extensive sphere; and second, a common constitution and government for the direct administration of certain general concerns." Within these principles there is room for a wide latitude of variation in the details of government.

A system of federation may be looked upon as a half-way station between the present international structure of the world and a centralized or unitary world government in which the individual states have gradually vanished. While world government might conceivably be highly centralized or unitary in form, with the sovereign states of today completely discarded, it is generally conceded that a project for a union of this type would have little serious consideration. Certainly with so much separatism and nationalism in the air today, a voluntary union into a unitary world state is unthinkable. Only by force could this kind of world state be forged. The product of such an effort would be world empire or world communism. The model for the former was set by the Roman Empire, a model which all of the great conquerors—Genghis Khan, Napoleon, and Hitler—have hoped to duplicate by achieving domination over most or all of the civilized world. However great the need for world unity may be, this method of attaining it is bound to be objectionable to all but the conqueror. No union could be expected to endure in the face of the opposition of hundreds of millions of subject peoples. The disintegrating forces now at large in the British, French, and Dutch empires are evidence that, over long periods of time, peace and order do not thrive under the heel of imperialist conquerors.

The world unity sought by the communist is open to the same objection. Brought about by revolution, it, too, would mean oppression. In its essence, a universal state achieved by communist methods would be little different from the old-style imperialism which the communists go to great length to denounce. To dress up imperialism with a new name and a new ideology will not change its spots.

Because a centralized world state, freely entered into, has no chance at this time, and because the opposition to a forced union is so general, a voluntary union of a weaker type and in the nature of federation has been urged. This, it is reasoned, will provide unity where it is most needed and separatism where it is required by the fact of nationalism. Federalism would, therefore, be a compromise between complete unity and present-day internationalism.

The Federal Idea as Applied to World Organization

It is the success with which the principles of federation have been applied nationally that has led to the suggestion that they be tried on a wider basis. Writing in 1863, Professor E. A. Freeman gave it as his opinion that the four most famous federal unions of the past were the Achaean League from 281 B.C. to 146 B.C., Switzerland from 1291 to the present, the United Provinces of The Netherlands from 1579 to 1595, and the United States of America since 1789. The first and last of the four he believed to be the "most perfect development of the federal principle that the world has ever seen." Since Professor Freeman's day, other federal unions have been established, such as Canada since 1867, Germany under the Hohenzollerns from 1871 to 1918 and under the Weimar Constitution from 1919 to 1933, Brazil since 1891, Australia since 1900, and Austria from 1920 to 1938. Among the experiments in federal union, certainly none is alluded to more frequently by world federalists than the United States of America.

While the idea of organizing the world, or some substantial portion of it, on a federal basis is an old one, it has been only since World War I that speculation on the subject has attracted any considerable interest. In 1922, Count Coudenhove-Kalergi founded an association to promote a European Union, supported by a number of active politicans, including M. Herriot, one-time Prime Minister of France. The association assisted M. Briand when, in 1929, he laid his plan for a United States of Europe before the League of Nations. After M. Briand's plan was dropped a few years later, the idea of federal union fell into decline until the late 1930's, when the weaknesses of the League of Nations became apparent and the need for something stronger was felt. Just prior to and during World War II, several plans for federal union were published, all of them inspired by the common desire to create a system of security strong enough to make war impossible. Following World War II, agitation reached a new high as thoughtful people became convinced that the atomic bomb had made internationalism, including the United Nations, even more antiquated than ever.

Aside from M. Briand's plan of 1929, projects for federation have originated in nongovernmental circles, usually in the mind of some individual sponsor. The two plans published just before World War II which attracted the most attention were those of Mr. Lionel Curtis and Mr. Clarence Streit. Mr. Curtis had had a great deal of practical experience within the organization of the British Commonwealth of Nations which he brought to bear in his *Civitas Dei*, published in 1938. *Union Now*, written by Mr. Streit and published in 1939, gave expression to the author's convictions gained in large part from his work at Geneva in the capacity of a newspaper correspondent. Later, Mr. Streit published a second plan, *Union Now with Britain* (1941), advocating a union of only two countries, the United States and Great Britain.

During World War II, the discussion of federation continued to follow the lines set by Mr. Streit and Mr. Curtis, but many new projects and points of view were advanced. The last chapter of Mr. Harold Nicholson's *Why Britain Is at War* (1939) provided the outlines of a plan, the substance of which was presented in the columns of *The New Republic* on February 20, 1940. Mr. W. Ivor Jennings in *A Federation for Western Europe* (1940), Mr. R. W. G. MacKay in *Federal Europe* (1940), M. Georges Scelle in an article on "Le Probléme du Fédéralisme" published in 1940 in *Politique Etrangére*, and Mr. Wm. Rappard in "Fédéralisme International" published by *L'Esprit International* (1940) contributed interesting ideas to the discussion of the subject during the early part of the war. Later, Mr. Ely Culbertson (1943) published a widely read project for federation in which the provision of an international police force was emphasized. In 1944, a federal constitution for the United Nations was proposed by Mr. H. O. Eaton, working in collaboration with other scholars. The Commission to Study the Organization of Peace, in its preliminary report (November, 1940), advocated a world organization essentially federal in character. Throughout the war, other groups, such as the World Citizenship Association, a conference of international law experts under the chairmanship of Judge Manley Hudson, and the Inter-American Juridicial Committee, continued to bring the problem of world organization to the attention of the general public, always recommending a stronger system of peace than the League of Nations had provided, and sometimes advocating ideas that would lead first or last to federalism.

Meanwhile, as the war was still in progress, a number of public officials voiced their approval of federalism, usually on a regional basis. Mr. Hubert Ripka, Czechoslovak Minister of State, in 1944 advocated a grouping of small states into different federations. Foreign Minister Padilla of Mexico, speaking to the American Bar Association in 1944, argued, "First there should be a limitation of the sovereignty of all nations, then federation, and finally a unification of all the peoples of the world." Dr. Edward Beneš of Czechoslovakia on several occasions proposed two new federations after the war —one for Central Europe and one for the Balkans. Other statesmen committed themselves in one way or another to the principle of federalism, but as a rule they were from small countries, and usually they limited their proposals to selected regional areas.

Methods and Problems of Federation

In the many projects and statements that were published before and during World War II, there was necessarily a great variety of detail. All of them brought out problems of organization, and it is not surprising that these problems were met in different ways, depending upon the background and points of view of the men behind the plans. While it is obviously impossible to analyze here the details of all the projects, it will be pertinent to select from some of the more prominent among them the major points of agreement and disagreement in meeting the problems of organization that are inevitably raised when federation is suggested.

First it may be noted that a number of the more elaborate projects

borrowed heavily from the constitutional system of the United
States. Some of the authors cite the formation of the American Constitution in 1787 after the failure of the Articles of Confederation
as evidence that sovereign states with different interests can be
brought together, and then they go on to complete the analogy by
asserting that world federation would be the same forward move
from the League of Nations or the United Nations that the American Constitution was from the Articles of Confederation. Mr. Streit
emphasized this point and, after comparing the obstacles in the way
of the American Union and those opposing his own project, concluded that "Union is easier now than then." In the second issue of
the new journal *Common Cause* (August, 1947), published by the
Committee to Frame a World Constitution, Mr. Richard J. Hooker
goes into some detail in his analysis of "community and conflict in
the thirteen states" prior to the adoption of the American Constitution. He explains the national background of the population of the
thirteen states, their religious diversity, their difficulties of transportation and communication, economic differences, and other conditions of that time. Although Mr. Hooker drew no conclusion as to
the relative strength of the forces opposing the American Union in
1787 and those which block world federation today, a foreword by
one of the editors states that the article may "serve those who are
wary of contrary opinions and conflicting ideas on the route to world
federal union." Analogies of this sort are, of course, always difficult
to make convincing, and no doubt those who draw them would admit as much; they are interesting, however, and stimulating to the
general reader, who is the target of such discourses.

Mr. Streit in his illustrative constitution took over the general
form and many of the details of the American Constitution. He incorporated a preamble which begins "We the people of the Union
. . . ," a bill of rights, an enumeration of the powers of the union, a
"full faith and credit" clause, and many other familiar principles and
statements. Professor H. O. Eaton's project, too, sounds in many
places like the American Constitution, although it borrows less than
does the Streit plan from the document of 1787.

One of the most frequent subjects of disagreement in projects for federation is the matter of membership in the' union. The idea of regional federations is a common one, and the region most often mentioned is Europe or some part of it. Reference has already been made to Dr. Beneš' plan for a Central European and a Balkan federation, the Briand project of 1929 for a United States of Europe; and Count Coudenhove-Kalergi's efforts for a European union. Behind these regional projects was the belief that the many small states of Europe would be unable to stand alone either in economic matters or in their efforts to defend themselves, as well as the conviction that an organized peace in Europe would do much to establish world peace.

Mr. Culbertson proposed nine regional federations and two "autonomous regional federations" which, taken together, would cover the earth's surface; these regional groups would be brought together into one world federation. While much less explicit, the Commission to Study the Organization of Peace admitted the desirability of "regional variations in any practical plan for world society"; Europe, it believed, would need to sacrifice "a greater degree of the sovereignty of its states than would be possible or desirable in other continents."

Another problem of membership, and one which has engaged the attention of British writers particularly, is whether the British dominions should be brought into a projected union, especially if organized on a European basis. Sir William Beveridge in his article on *Peace by Federation* took the position that it is desirable, but not essential, that the dominions be admitted. In his *Federation for Western Europe*, Mr. W. Ivor Jennings pointed out that if admitted to a European union, the dominions should be given a special status, relieving them of some of the obligations of the other members.

Few of the plans have advocated immediate universal participation, but many of them look forward to ultimate universality. In a number of them, as illustrated by Mr. Eaton's project and by "A Design for a Charter of the General International Organization" (providing for a union which would be something less than federation), the constitution would come into effect when ratified by a specified number of nations. The Commission to Study the Organization of Peace sought immediate universality in some sort of organization, tempered, however, by regionalism.

The Streit plan provided that the democracies furnish the nucleus for a federal union. This was justified on the ground that to organize "world government soundly we must turn to the people most advanced and most experienced politically"; Mr. Streit reasoned that people who accept dictatorships must be regarded as "politically, among the immature, or retarded, or inexperienced, high as they may rank otherwise." The fifteen democracies which he regarded as qualified for immediate membership were those of western Europe, the United States of America, and the British dominions; other states might later be admitted as their qualifications were recognized. It was because of the conquest or encirclement of many of the fifteen by Germany that Mr. Streit later modified his proposal to the effect that the original members be the United States, Great Britain, and her dominions. Mr. Lionel Curtis in his *Civitas Dei* suggested an even smaller nucleus of membership: Great Britain, Australia, and New Zealand, three states whose language, institutions, and experience, he believed, would furnish a strong basis for organization. He suggested that, later on, states along the route connecting Great Britain and Australia, such as Egypt and India, might join; still later, The Netherlands, Belgium, the Scandinavian countries, and others might be admitted.

Although all of the projects for federation agreed that the central government must have substantial power, there was disagreement as to the precise distribution of power between the component states and the central authority. A number of the plans advocated what has sometimes been called an "imperfect federal union." This type of federation retains some of the remnants of the confederation, so that the central government is not impressive in its strength; the German Empire (1871–1919), in which the states retained diplomatic and military powers and had the duty of enforcing national laws, was a good illustration of this type of organization. Generally, plans for a federal union have agreed, in principle at least, that certain attributes of the sovereignty of the nation state must be curtailed. The Commission to Study the Organization of Peace would take from the state five powers commonly associated with sovereignty; (1) the right to be the final judge in controversies to which it is a party; (2) the right to use force, except for self-defense; (3) the right to maintain aggressive armament; (4) the right to treat minorities in any way it pleases; and (5) the right to pursue an economic policy to the detriment of other peoples.

Since the main objective of all projects for federal union is world peace, it is generally agreed that the central government should have a predominant military position. Mr. Culbertson's plan was concerned almost entirely with military power, proposing as it did an international police force, a part of which would be in the nature of "national contingents" from member states, and the remainder a "mobile corps" recruited from the smaller members. Many of the projects, however, have left member states free to have their own military forces.

Other plans contemplated stronger unions, "perfect federal unions," as they are often called. Such a union has none of the elements of confederation, the central government having a position of supremacy in external affairs and in specified internal affairs of general concern. The Streit and Eaton proposals went about as far as any in conferring power on the central government. The former would grant to the central government the right to regulate commerce among member states and with foreign states, the right to coin money, to provide uniform bankruptcy laws, to issue copyrights and patents, to grant citizenship, to tax, and to regulate private rights and interests in other ways. The details of the Eaton plan are quite similar, although on the whole they grant even more authority to the union government.

Federalists have not been in agreement as to the precise framework of government which they would set up. Usually they propose legislative, judicial, and executive branches of government, but from that point on opinions diverge. Mr. Culbertson described the organization of the federal union which he proposed as follows: "LIKE OUR OWN, the Constitution of the World Federation provides for three branches—executive, legislative and judiciary. The World President is chosen from each Regional Federation in turn, beginning with the American Federation, for a single term of six years. From each of the 11 Regional Federations is selected one World Trustee. A World Supreme Court of 11 members interprets the Federation's Constitution; a World Court of Equity deals with all economic or territorial disputes between nations."

The Commission to Study the Organization of Peace suggested (1) "an international court with jurisdiction adequate to deal with all international disputes on the basis of law," (2) "international legislative bodies to remedy abuses in existing law and to make new law . . . ," (3) "adequate police forces . . . ," (4) "international machinery with authority to regulate international communication and transportation and to deal with such problems as international commerce, finance, health, . . ." and (5) "appropriate authorities to administer backward areas. . . ." The Eaton and Streit plans were quite elaborate in their provisions for the three branches of government, following in many respects the example set by the American constitutional system. For instance, the latter would have a legislature consisting of two houses—a Senate and a House of Deputies—an Executive Board of five members, and a High Court.

Not many projects struggled with the details of representation in the legislative body. Again, the Streit and Eaton plans, following their characteristic preoccupation with details, were the exceptions. The latter proposed a lower house or Assembly chosen by popular vote, each state having one representative for each two million votes cast, and an upper house or Council in which each state would have one representative for each fifty million inhabitants, except that no state could have more than three representatives.

It is generally admitted in proposals for federal union that provision must be made for future change. The usual method provided has been formal amendment, as constitutions are commonly modified. This idea of future modifications has been given a significant application by certain proponents of federalism who believe that it is necessary to begin with a weak union but that by the adoption of amendments later on and by practice there will be a gradual evolution to something much stronger. Professor Georges Scelle in his article, previously cited, regarded gradual federation as the inescapable method of progress. Opposed to this is the view of Mr. T. K. Finletter, who wrote in the *Atlantic Monthly* (March, 1946) that "gradualism is just another way of avoiding the issue."

A Recently Proposed Constitution for World Federation (1947)

Since World War II, the cause of world federation has been given fresh impetus from several quarters. Mr. Clarence Streit has continued to press for a union of the mature democracies under a plan now called Federal Union. The Citizen's Committee for United Nations Reform, headed by Mr. Ely Culbertson, has sponsored a United Nations so completely done over as to embody the "quota force" plan which the bridge expert first brought to the attention of the public in 1942. The United World Federalists, under the leadership of Mr. Cord Meyer, have rallied thousands of Americans behind their principles. Added together, these efforts and others have given wide publicity in the United States to the federal plan of world organization.

A different type of contribution to world federalism was in the form of a draft constitution prepared under the leadership of Chancellor Hutchins of the University of Chicago by a group known as the Committee to Frame a World Constitution. The stimulus for the enterprise was the atomic bombing of Hiroshima on August 6, 1945. Six days later, on a University of Chicago Round Table broadcast, Chancellor Hutchins stated, "The only hope . . . of abolishing war is through the monopoly of atomic force by a world organization." Soon thereafter, the Committee to Frame a World Government was constituted and in November, 1945, it set to work.[1] Thirteen meetings were held between that date and July, 1947, and 146 preparatory documents were framed. The Committee studied the American Federalist Papers and the constitutions of a large number of federations. The Committee did not think of itself as writing *the* world constitution; the "ambition or hope," as expressed by the members themselves, was "to do their part in taking down to earth or, so to speak, spelling out the general movement for world government that

---

[1] The following were members of the Committee: R. M. Hutchins, G. A. Borgese, M. J. Adler, S. Barr, A. Guérard, H. A. Innis, E. Kahler, W. G. Katz, C. H. McIlwain, R. Redfield, R. G. Tugwell.

has been growing not always in definite shapes, during these years." Early in 1947, the Committee's project was published.[2]

The proposed constitution opens with a preamble in which the "Federal Republic of the World" is used to designate the organization to be created. The Declaration of the Rights and Duties of Man which follows contains a list of abstractions as to the proper roles of government and the individual. It claims release for the individual "from the bondage of poverty and from the servitude and exploitation of labor, with rewards and security according to merit and needs," "freedom of peaceful assembly and association," "protection . . . against subjugation and tyrannical rule," and "any such other freedoms as are inherent in man's inalienable claims to life, liberty, and the dignity of the human person." The four elements of life— earth, water, air, energy—are declared to be the "common property of the human race"; the management and use of these resources, whether under private, corporate, national, or regional ownership, must be subordinated "to the interest of the common good."

Following the constitutional system of the United States, this project for global federation makes the central government one of enumerated powers. A long list of powers is assigned to the central government, including several which have to do with peace and the relations of the states to each other, as well as the right to tax, to regulate commerce affected with a federal interest, to issue passports, and so on. Powers "not delegated to the World Government . . . , and not prohibited by it to the several members of the Federal World Republic" are reserved to the member states.

The machinery of government which the plan would set up include the following:

1. The Federal Convention.
2. The President.
3. The Council and the Special Bodies.
4. The Grand Tribunal, the Supreme Court, and the Tribune of the People.
5. The Chamber of Guardians.

----

[2] The text is given in the Appendix to this chapter.

The first of these, the Federal Convention, would be elected directly by the people of all the member states. Its meetings would occur every third year, and its principal task would be electoral—selecting a president and a World Council of ninety-nine members; important roles are played in these elections by nine regional "electoral colleges" in order to ensure that all parts of the world would have a fair share in the selections made.

The World Council would be esentially a legislative body. The three Special Bodies to be set up by it are a House of Nationalities (concerned with minorities), a syndical or functional Senate (concerned with labor interests), and an Institute of Science, Education, and Culture.

The executive power would be vested in a president, selected for a six-year term, who would have the right of initiating legislation. The president would appoint a chancellor to represent him in the Council, and the chancellor, in turn, would select a cabinet. The chancellor and the cabinet members could be interrogated by the Council, and they would be obliged to resign when the Council voted a lack of confidence. At this point, the plan obviously borrows heavily from the so-called cabinet system of government.

On the judicial side there would be a Grand Tribunal and a Supreme Court. The former, composed of sixty judges, would be divided into five "Benches," to each of which is assigned a field of jurisdiction. The Supreme Court, made up of seven members, would distribute cases among the five Benches and would be able to review the decisions of the Benches. The Tribune of the People, selected by the Federal Convention, would serve as a spokesman for minority groups.

The Chamber of Guardians, the last of the agencies listed, would take over the responsibility for controlling and using the armed forces of the Federal Republic in the interests of peace. Presumably, this function would be reduced to a minimum, for the states themselves would possess no armed forces.

Viewed as a whole, the governmental system which the constitution described would be highly complicated. The many and varied duties assigned to the world government, the obvious effort of the constitution-makers to avoid too much concentration of authority, and the need for providing a balanced participation of all member states in the work of the government, all combine to produce this complexity. While the constitution borrows from the American system of government, from the British and others, most of it would appear to any given nation living under it as quite novel. For the world to adapt itself to an intricate system of this nature with its unfamiliar methods would, indeed, be a herculean undertaking.

Official Consideration of Federation

In the United States, the idea of solving the problem of peace by federation has been under consideration both in the Senate and in a number of state legislatures. Twenty-one of the states had by 1950 passed resolutions favorable to world federation of one type or another.[3] In some states there have been referenda on the subject, revealing a considerable popular support for the project.

Among the resolutions proposed in the Senate was Concurrent Resolution No. 56, introduced by Senator Tobey, as follows:

Resolved by the Senate (and the House of Representatives concurring), That it is the sense of the Congress that it should be a fundamental objective of the foreign policy of the United States to support and strengthen the United Nations and to seek its development into a world federation open to all nations with defined and limited powers adequate to preserve peace and prevent aggression through the enactment, interpretation, and enforcement of world law.[4]

Explaining the resolution in the subcommittee of the Senate Committee on Foreign Affairs early in 1950, Senator Tobey asserted, "Our goal may seem distant and its realization difficult, but we will never achieve our hope of a lasting peace, unless we at least start to move in the right direction now." The resolution was intentionally lacking in concrete measures of implementation in order that appropriate measures might be taken when they were found to be possible, without the handicap of a specific program.

---

[3] Alabama, Arkansas, California, Colorado, Connecticut, Florida, Louisiana, Maine, Maryland, Massachusetts, Missouri, New Hampshire, New Jersey, North Carolina, Oklahoma, Oregon, Rhode Island, Tennessee, Utah, Virginia, and Washington.

[4] *Hearings before a Subcommittee on the Committee on Foreign Relations of the Senate,* Revision of the U.N. Charter, p. 73.

A second proposal taken up in the subcommittee was Concurrent Resolution 57, popularly known as the Atlantic Union Resolution. It reads as follows:

Resolved by the Senate (*the House of Representatives concurring*), That the President is requested to invite the democracies which sponsored the North Atlantic Treaty to name delegates, representing their principal political parties, to meet this year with delegates of the United States in a Federal Convention to explore how far their peoples, and the peoples of such other democracies as the convention may invite to send delegates, can apply among them, within the framework of the United Nations, the principles of free federal union.[5]

The supporters of the resolution, led by Senator Kefauver, have indicated that the nations which sponsored the North Atlantic Pact —Canada, the United Kingdom, France, The Netherlands, Belgium, Luxembourg, and the United States—would be the original members and that other democracies might be invited to join at a later date. The constitution envisaged by this plan would include a bill of rights, an executive capable of enforcing law against citizens, and a judiciary able to deal with disputes between citizens. Mr. Justice Roberts, who testified in behalf of the resolution, explained that powers under such a constitution might be divided in three ways: (1) those reserved to the people; (2) those reserved to the states; and (3) those delegated to the union. Clearly, the project looked forward to a strong central government. Like the other plans for federation, it was inspired in large part by the fear of Russian aggression.

Concurrent Resolution No. 12 (the Fulbright-Thomas Resolution) was to the effect "that the Congress favors the political federation of Europe."[6] The resolution was first proposed when the Marshall Plan was under consideration. It expressed the view, as Senator Thomas said, that it "was necessary for European countries to move along political lines in connection with any movement along economic lines or social lines, in bringing about that unity."

---

[5] *Ibid.*, p. 228.
[6] *Ibid.*, p. 344.

Finally, the subcommittee considered Concurrent Resolution No. 66 (the World Constitution Resolution). It read as follows:

Resolved by the Senate (the House of Representatives concurring), That it is the sense of Congress that the President of the United States should immediately take the initiative in requesting a general conference of the United Nations pursuant to article 109 for the purpose of establishing a true world government through adoption of such a constitution; and if such a general conference is not called within one year after the adoption of this resolution, the President of the United States should then call a world constitutional convention of delegates elected directly by the people for the purpose of adopting a world government constitution.[7]

Senator Taylor, who introduced the resolution, said that his plan called for such a revision of the United Nations Charter as "to provide a true world government constitution . . . preferably one such as that drafted by the Committee to Draft a World Constitution."[8] He explained that the world government which he advocated would be one able to tax and to raise sufficient armed forces to keep the peace, and that it would require its members "to sacrifice considerable sovereignty."

Reference has already been made to the State Department's lack of enthusiasm for the proposals for federation, and to its feeling that the expedient course of action would be to go on with the United Nations, trying to improve it, chiefly by practice, with the passing of time. Assistant Secretary of State Hickerson made the following remarks, expressive not only of the attitude of the Department but also of the views held by many individuals who have not supported plans for federation:

Any proposal, Mr. Chairman, for world federation must deal with certain stubborn and inescapable facts.

Among the predominant characteristics of the world today are still hunger and ignorance. Two-thirds of the world's peoples live on less than adequate diet, one-half are illiterate, and only a minority live under truly democratic governments. How would a world federation based on democratic principles prosper in such a setting? We should recall from our own

---

[7] *Ibid.,* p. 318.
[8] This refers to the committee headed by Chancellor Hutchins.

history that it takes more than a constitution, more than a framework, to construct a federation. We must also keep in mind that there exist profound traditional differences among nations based on history, differing political institutions, economies, and geographical conditions.

If we proposed to go into a world federation, some compromise, at least some adjustment, would be necessary. Just how far are we willing to go in compromising our way of life and our institutions? It would be most dangerous to assume that other nations will agree that the American way of life is the best, and that for them to go into a world federation would mean to join our concept of a federal union.

There must be obviously some common basis between the majority and minority to make a workable concern of any international organization, and in particular so close an organization as a federation. There must be some agreement on fundamental laws and institutions. We have known from our own national experience that law is effective only when it does represent common ground among the people. There must be some assurance that the majority will not take advantage of the minority and that the minority will not suspect the majority of injustice. A police force in order not to be a menace to its community must have an accepted body of law to enforce. It must be an arm of the government which has the respect and confidence of the people. What law and what institutions would govern the world federation?

The agencies of the proposed world federation would presumably enact, interpret, and enforce world law. This means a federal legislature in which the United States would be only one of the area represented. Are the American people willing to abide by laws enacted not necessarily with their concurrence? It also assumes a federation judiciary to interpret those laws. Are the American people willing to subject themselves to the decision of the courts of the world federation? It further assumes a federation enforcement arm. This conceivably could be an enforcement arm against the will of the American people. Then there is a question of financing the federation. Are the American people prepared to agree to be taxed in support of the federation? Since we are wealthier than any other country our share would be proportionately higher.[9]

The Senate Committee on Foreign Relations did not adopt any of the plans examined by its subcommittee, either those proposing federation or those asking for revision of the United Nations. It pointed out that most of the proposals would require amendment of the

---

[9] *Hearings before a Subcommittee of the Committee on Foreign Relations of the U.S. Senate*, Revision of the Charter, 1950, p. 428.

Constitution of the United States, and it expressed an unwillingness to take a position on propositions of such a fundamental nature "until the issues have been debated, discussed, and understood the length and breadth of this land."

The Future of Federalism

Can federalism be lifted from the plane of projects and agitation into the realm of reality? Are the planners and agitators merely idealists with ideas too visionary for the practical world of affairs? In one respect at least, it must be admitted that their feet are firmly planted on solid ground, and that is in their contention that the world needs federal union; in this particular, their case is sound and convincing.

In support of their position, proponents of federation point to the many interests which nations have in common and to the problems that need to be handled on a world-wide basis; they point to the shortcomings of the nation state and assert that the coöperative processes which it uses are not equal to the demands put upon them. World organization, we are told, has not kept abreast of the actual changes brought about by modern technological developments in the way men and nations live and get a living. In short, our present international structure is a relic of the horse-and-buggy days, trying to make its way in a fast-moving world of atomic energy.

There was a time when the processes of internationalism provided a fairly satisfactory method of getting things done. True, they had never solved the problem of war, but before the advent of modern technology, war was not such an urgent problem. Although peacetime affairs which did not relate closely to national security were handled with reasonable success, when it came to the radio, the airplane, and atomic energy, the methods of international organization proved to be inadequate, as has been shown.[10] The free trade demanded by modern technology appears today as unattainable as ever.

Most imposing of all is the argument that federation will be a means of outlawing war. As technology has made war more terrible,

[10] See Chapter I.

its devastation has impressed thoughtful people with the need for a secure system of peace. Recently, atomic bombs and bacteriological warfare have made the question of peace or war crucial. No doubt many converts to federalism have been won by the uncontrollable terror of modern warfare.

The benefits to be derived from federalism are many, and the federalists are performing a useful service in bringing them to our attention, even though they are frequently presented in an oversimplified form. Specific plans for world federation are useful, too, and most of them are highly logical in their approach to the problem of world organization. But in the realm of government, logical projects are rarely treated with the respect that is their due. Irrational factors are often more powerful than the rational. It is a relatively easy task to prove the logic of federalism and to draft a convincing world constitution. The difficult part of any reform movement is to lift the dead weight of public thinking to a new level. No doubt it is a common mistake of federalists to figure more in terms of organization and less in terms of public thinking than they should. They are likely to overemphasize the virtues of organization, and to neglect the human element in the achievement of a stable community. They overlook the profound wisdom stated in the preamble of the constitution of UNESCO that "wars begin in the minds of men."

Generally, political organization and methods tend to reflect rather than to form political ideas. When there is a general demand for democracy, that is what is adopted, and when people believe that dictatorship will be their salvation, that is what they get. Similarly, in the world at large, we have internationalism because public thinking is not yet geared to anything better. To adopt the organization of federalism and then expect to reform our thinking is placing the cart before the horse. No doubt political organization can proceed a little in advance of public thinking without dire consequences; just how much in advance is debatable. Perhaps the American Constitution of 1787 was close to the limit in this regard. In any case, one fact is clear: there is nothing magic in political organization, whether it be national or world-wide in its application. Organization has its place; without it, order would be impossible, but standing alone, without popular understanding and support, organization will be well-nigh futile. Given an alert and informed public, organization becomes easy, almost automatic, and what is more, it will work.

Fundamentally, the ideological difficulty in the way of world federalism is the present-day strength of the nation state. No federation is possible without completely overhauling the modern state, and no doubt it ought to be overhauled, but to do so would be a major operation. Never before has the state occupied so prominent a place in human affairs. It is omnipresent both in the regulation of the activities of the individual at home, and in the promotion and protection of his interests abroad. This position of the state has been strengthened by socialism in many parts of the world.

The state has dominated political thought and action for centuries. As it has changed, its hold has been strengthened. Not only has it enlarged its range of activities, but in many quarters it has come to have a certain mystic quality, to be looked upon as "the march of God on earth" in the Hegelian manner. The wide prevalence of this attitude, even in democratic states, is evident in the appeals which politicians make to the people. The statement was made by Mr. James Farley to the effect that "We must realize that the United States is greater than each of us and greater than all of us" is typical. It is cited not because it represents inferior thought but rather because it is the usual thought in a country which regards itself as well-educated politically. Obviously, with the state at the peak of its strength, its sudden reform on a large scale appears outside the range of possibilities. No doubt, however, it is because the state is so strong today and the consequences to world order so disastrous that the need for reform has become urgent.

The mystic quality attributed to the modern state and the place it has come to occupy in popular thinking are strengthened by nationalism. Peoples everywhere have developed a strong group consciousness, and they have written much of their political history on this basis. Nationalism is of more recent origin in China, India, and among the Arabs than it is in the western world, but everywhere it has been growing stronger. Attacks upon it to date are largely intellectual in nature. Even in Russia, where the prevailing doctrine of communism does not accept nationalism, it flourishes, even more, in fact, than before the communists came into power.

The essential reform to which modern states must submit in order to fit into a federal union is the destruction of their sovereign character, deflating them to the level of the forty-eight states of the United States in rights and powers. This point is frequently made by federalists. For instance, Mr. Emery Reves asserted in an article published in *World Review* (February, 1947), "Peace between sovereign-power-units can never be maintained by force, because the use of force against a sovereign state is war." A statement of this nature is quite convincing and will be accepted by most people. The objection to it is not that it is untrue but that it implies an oversimplified solution to world problems—the assumption that peace will be established when we have agreed that sovereignty is no more. But it is not so simple. As Professor Herbert Briggs has put it in an article in the *American Journal of International Law* (Jan. 1947), "If you could abolish the concept, power would remain." He goes on to explain that "Manpower, natural resources, and industrial potentials would remain in Soviet Russia or the United States even if the legal concept of 'sovereignty' could be 'renounced' or 'transferred.'" In other words, while sovereignty is only a theory, it conforms to certain facts of a sociological, economic, and political nature. Abolish the theory and you still have the facts that make national groups disagree and fight—ideological differences, ethical concepts, historical traditions, and nationalism. Again, world peace is not a matter of organization, nor is it a matter of a legal theory; it is and always will be a matter of people, their ideas, ethics, and outlook.

In short, world federation, sound as it is in principle, does not appear to be around the corner. If it comes at all, the process will be a slow one, as the attitudes of people are gradually changed. Perhaps the first step may be to alter the United Nations so as to strengthen its processes. The strong feeling that has developed against the veto reflects some advance in popular attitudes, brought, no doubt, by atomic energy; if it should eventuate in the abolition of the veto, one important step will have been taken.

There is another way that federalism might grow, starting in this instance on a regional basis and later expanding to include other areas. Federation assumes a higher degree of similarity in traditions and ideals than the world at large can provide, a similarity which may be found in certain regions. The wide diversity of political ideals in the world, with three-fourths of the masses unfamiliar with democracy—the kind of world federation which Anglo-American traditions would insist upon—is prohibitive of union. Equally obstructive to immediate world federation are the differences of economic ideology and cultural background. From a regional point of view, these differences—political, economic, and cultural—are not so profound.

At the present time, it appears that the region most likely to adopt federalism is western Europe. In addition to an essential similarity of background and ideology, the states of western Europe have the incentive to unity which a common enemy provides. A common enemy can be a powerful stimulus, as it was to the thirteen American states in 1787; now, with Russia and communism taking long strides in eastern and central Europe, the states of the west are fully aware of the danger to which they are exposed. The Council of Europe, the Organization for European Economic Coöperation, and the North Atlantic Pact all indicate the trend of western Europe toward unity. On May 5, 1950, General William J. Donovan, chairman of the American Committee on United Europe, announced that a poll of 10,000 people questioned in Norway, Holland, France, Italy, and Western Germany revealed that 64 percent of them believed European Union to be desirable.

Every effort toward federalism, whether world-wide or regional, thus far undertaken shows that the nation state is a hardy animal and does not easily succumb to the attacks made upon it. Although its demise is not likely to be sudden, for it is still vigorous and healthy, its ultimate doom is certain. The pattern of world organization is never static. As medieval feudalism gradually gave way to the nation state, so it may be expected that the nation state will sometime in the future give way to something new and probably better.

▲

APPENDIX TO CHAPTER XVIII

Preliminary Draft of a World Constitution (1947)*
(By the Committee to Frame a World Constitution)†

Preamble

The people of the earth having agreed
    that the advancement of man
in spiritual excellence and physical welfare
is the common goal of mankind;
    that universal peace is the prerequisite
for the pursuit of that goal;
    that justice in turn is the prerequisite of peace,
and peace and justice stand or fall together;
that iniquity and war inseparably spring
from the competitive anarchy of national states;
    that therefore the age of nations must end,
and the era of humanity begin;

the governments of the nations have decided
    to order their separate sovereignties
in one government of justice
to which they surrender their arms;
    and to establish, as they do establish,
this Constitution
as the covenant and fundamental law
of the Federal Republic of the World.

---

    * Taken from G. A. Borgese, *Preliminary Draft of a World Constitution,* University of Chicago Press, 1948.
    † The Committee included Chancellor Robert Hutchins, G. A. Borgese, M. J. Adler, Strongfellow Barr, Albert Guérard, H. A. Innis, E. Kahler, W. G. Katz, C. H. McIlwain, R. Redfield, R. G. Tugwell.

Declaration of Duties and Rights

A

The universal government of justice as covenanted and pledged in this Constitution is founded on the Rights of Man.

The principles underlying the Rights of Man are and shall be permanently stated in the Duty of everyone everywhere, whether a citizen sharing in the responsibilities and privileges of World Government or a ward and pupil of the World Commonwealth: to serve with word and deed, and with productive labor according to his ability, the spiritual and physical advancement of the living and of those to come, as the common cause of all generations of men; to do unto others as he would like others to do unto him; to abstain from violence, except for the repulse of violence as commanded or granted under law.

B

In the context therefore of social duty and service, and in conformity with the unwritten law which philosophies and religions alike called the Law of Nature and which the Republic of the World shall strive to see universally written and enforced by positive law, it shall be the right of everyone everywhere to claim and maintain for himself and his fellowmen: release from the bondage of poverty and from the servitude and exploitation of labor, with rewards and security according to merits and needs; freedom of peaceful assembly and of association, in any creed or party or craft, within the pluralistic unity and purpose of the World Republic; protection of individuals and groups against subjugation and tyrannical rule, racial or national, doctrinal or cultural, with safeguards for the self-determination of minorities and dissenters; and any such other freedoms and franchises as are inherent in man's inalienable claims to life, liberty and the dignity of the human person, and as the legislators and judges of the World Republic shall express and specify.

C

The four elements of life—earth, water, air, energy—are the common property of the human race. The management and use of such portions thereof as are vested in or assigned to particular ownership, private or corporate or national or regional, of definite or indefinite tenure, of individualist or collectivist economy, shall be subordinated in each and all cases to the interest of the common good.

Grant of Powers
1

The jurisdiction of the World Government as embodied in its organs of powers shall extend to:

a. the control of the observance of the Constitution in all the component communities and territories of the Federal World Republic, which shall be indivisible and one;
b. the furtherance and progressive fulfillment of the Duties and Rights of Man in the spirit of the foregoing Declaration, with their specific enactment in such fields of federal and local relations as are described hereinafter (Articles 27 through 33);
c. the maintenance of peace; and to that end the enactment and promulgation of laws which shall be binding upon communities and upon individuals as well;
d. the judgment and settlement of any conflicts among component units, with prohibition of recourse to interstate violence;
e. the supervision of and final decision on any alterations of boundaries between states or unions thereof;
f. the supervision of and final decision on the forming of new states or unions thereof;
g. the administration of such territories as may still be immature for self-government, and the declaration in due time of their eligibility therefor;
h. the intervention in intrastate violence and violation of law which affect world peace and justice;
i. the organization and disposal of the federal armed forces;
j. the limitation and control of weapons and of the domestic militias in the several component units of the World Republic;
k. the establishment, in addition to the Special Bodies listed hereinafter (Articles 8 and 9) of such other agencies as may be con-

ducive to the development of the earth's resources and to the advancement of physical and intellectual standards, with such advisory or initiating or arbitrating powers as shall be determined by law;

l. the laying and collecting of federal taxes, and the establishment of a plan and a budget for federal expenditures;

m. the administration of the World Bank and the establishment of suitable world fiscal agencies for the issue of money and the creation and control of credit;

n. the regulation of commerce affected with federal interest;

o. the establishment, regulation and, where necessary or desirable, the operation of means of transportation and communication which are of federal interest;

p. the supervision and approval of laws concerning emigration and immigration and the movements of peoples;

q. the granting of federal passports;

r. the appropriation under the right of eminent domain, of such private or public property as may be necessary for federal use, reasonable compensation being made therefor;

s. the legislation over and administration of the territory which shall be chosen as Federal District and of such other territories as may be entrusted directly to the Federal Government.

2

The powers not delegated to the World Government by this Constitution, and not prohibited by it to the several members of the Federal World Republic, shall be reserved to the several states or nations or unions thereof.

The Federal Convention, the President, the Legislature
3

The sovereignty of the Federal Republic of the World resides in the people of the World. The primary powers of the World Government shall be vested in:

a. the Federal Convention,
b. the President,

c. the Council and the Special Bodies,
d. the Grand Tribunal, the Supreme Court, and the Tribune of the People,
e. the Chamber of Guardians.

4

The Federal Convention shall consist of delegates elected directly by the people of all states and nations, one delegate for each million of population or fraction thereof above one-half million, with the proviso that the people of any extant state, recognized as sovereign in 1945, and ranging between 100,000 and 1,000,000, shall be entitled to elect one delegate, but any such state with a population below 100,000 shall be aggregated for federal electoral purposes to the electoral unit closest to its borders.

The delegates to the Federal Convention shall vote as individuals, not as members of national or otherwise collective representations (except as specified hereinafter, Article 46, paragraph 2, and Article 47).

The Convention shall meet in May of every third year, for a session of thirty days.

5

The Federal Convention shall subdivide into nine Electoral Colleges according to the nine Societies of kindred nations and cultures, or Regions, wherefrom its members derive their powers, such Regions being:

1. the continent of Europe and its islands outside the Russian area, together with the United Kingdom if the latter so decides, and with such overseas English- or French- or Cape Dutch-speaking communities of the British Commonwealth of Nations or the French Union as decide to associate (this whole area here tentatively denominated *Europa*);
2. the United States of America, with the United Kingdom if the latter so decides, and such kindred communities of British, or Franco-British, or Dutch-British, or Irish civilization and lineage as decide to associate (*Atlantis*);

3. Russia, European and Asiatic, with such East-Baltic or Slavic or Danubian nations as associate with Russia (*Eurasia*);

4. the Near and Middle East, with the states of North Africa, and Pakistan if the latter so decides (*Afrasia*);

5. *Africa,* south of the Sahara, with or without the South African Union as the latter may decide;

6. *India,* with Pakistan if the latter so decides;

7. China, Korea, Japan, with the associate archipelagoes of the North- and Mid-Pacific (*Asia Major*);

8. Indo-china and Indonesia, with Pakistan if the latter so decides, and with such other Mid- and South-Pacific lands and islands as decide to associate (*Austrasia*);

9. the Western Hemisphere south of the United States (*Columbia*).

Each Electoral College shall nominate by secret ballot, not more than three candidates, regardless of origin, for the office of President of the World Republic. The Federal Convention in plenary meeting, having selected by secret ballot of panel of three candidates from the lists submitted, shall elect by secret ballot one of the three as President, on a majority of two-thirds.

If three consecutive ballots have been indecisive, the candidate with the smallest vote shall be eliminated and between the two remaining candidates a simple majority vote shall be decisive.

6

Each Electoral College shall then nominate by secret and proportional ballot twenty-seven candidates, originating from the respective Electoral Area or Region, for the World Council; with the proviso that one-third and not more than one-third of the nominees shall not be members of the Federal Convention; and the nine lists having been presented to the Federal Convention, the Federal Convention in plenary meeting shall select by secret and proportional ballot nine Councilmen from each list, with the same proviso as above.

The Federal Convention shall also select by secret and proportional ballot, on nominations, prior to the opening of the Convention, by such organizations, of world-wide importance and lawfully active in more than three Regions, as shall be designated (for the first election by the United Nations Assembly and subsequently) by the Council, eighteen additional members, regardless of origin; and the total membership of the World Council shall thus be ninety-nine.

7

The primary power to initiate and enact legislation for the Federal Republic of the World shall be vested in the Council.

The tenure of the Council shall be three years.

The Council shall elect its Chairman, for its whole tenure of three years.

Councilors shall be re-eligible.

8

Within the first three years of World Government the Council and the President shall establish three Special Bodies, namely:

a. a House of Nationalities and States, with representatives from each, for the safeguarding of local institutions and autonomies and the protection of minorities;

b. a Syndical or functional Senate, for the representation of syndicates and unions or occupational associations and any other corporate interests of transnational significance, as well as for mediation or arbitration in non-justifiable issues among such syndicates or unions or other corporate interests;

c. an Institute of Science, Education, and Culture; each of the three bodies with such membership and tenures and consultative or preparatory powers as shall be established by law and with no prejudice to the establishment of other advisory or technical agencies in accordance with the purposes stated hereinbefore (Article 1, k).

9

Within its first year the World Government shall establish a Special Body to be named Planning Agency, of twenty-one members appointed by the President, subject to vetoes by two-thirds of the

Council, for tenures of twelve years (except that the terms for the initial membership shall be staggered by lot, with one-third of it, seven members, ceasing from office and being replaced every fourth year).

It shall be the function of the Planning Agency to envisage the income of the Federal Government and to prepare programs and budgets for expenditures, both for current needs and for long-range improvements. . . .

10

The executive power, together with initiating power in federal legislation, shall be vested in the President. His tenure shall be six years.

The President shall not have membership in the Council.

The President shall not be re-eligible. He shall not be eligible to the Tribunate of the People until nine years have elapsed since the expiration of his term.

No two successive Presidents shall originate from the same Region.

11

The President shall appoint a Chancellor. The Chancellor, with the approval of the President, shall appoint the Cabinet.

The Chancellor shall act as the President's representative before the Council in the exercise of legislative initiative. The Chancellor and the Cabinet members shall have at any time the privilege of the floor before the Council.

But no Chancellor or Cabinet member shall have a vote or shall hold membership in the Council, nor, if he was a member of the Council at the moment of his executive appointment, shall he be entitled to resume his seat therein when leaving the executive post unless he be re-elected at a subsequent Convention.

No one shall serve as Chancellor for more than six years, nor as Cabinet member for more than twelve, consecutive or not.

No three Cabinet members at any one time and no two successive Chancellors shall originate from the same Region.

The Council shall have power to interrogate the Chancellor and the Cabinet and to adopt resolutions on their policies.

The Chancellor and the Cabinet shall resign when the President so decides or when a vote of no confidence by the absolute majority of fifty or more of the Council is confirmed by a second such vote; but no second vote shall be taken and held valid if less than three months have elapsed since the first.

12

The sessions of the Council, as well as those of the Grand Tribunal and the Supreme Court, shall be continuous, except for one yearly recess of not more than ten weeks or two of such recesses of not more than five weeks each, as the body concerned may decide.

13

The budget of the World Government, upon recommendation by the Planning Agency, shall be presented every three years by the President to the Council, which shall pass it, or reject it in whole titles, by majority vote; the same procedure to apply when at other intervals the President requests additional appropriations or approval of changes.

14

Any legislation of the Council can be vetoed by the President within thirty days of its passage. But the Council can overrule the veto if its new vote, by a majority of two-thirds, finds support, within sixty days of the President's action, in the majority of the Grand Tribunal (and no such support shall be required during the tenure of the first President).

15

The President can be impeached on grounds of treason to the Constitution, or usurpation of power, or felony, or insanity, or other disease impairing permanently his mind.

The vote of impeachment shall be final when three-quarters of the Council and three-quarters of the Grand Tribunal concur and the majority of the Supreme Court validates the legality of the proceedings.

If a President is impeached or resigns or dies in the interval between the two sessions of the Federal Convention, the Chairman of the Council shall become Acting President until the new Convention elects a new President; and the Council shall elect a new Chairman.

The Grand Tribunal and the Supreme Court
16

The supreme judiciary power of the World Republic shall be vested in a Grand Tribunal of sixty Justices, with the President of the World Republic as Chief Justice and Chairman, and the Chairman of the Council as Vice-Chairman ex officio.

The President as Chief Justice shall appoint the Justices of the Grand Tribunal and fill the vacancies, subject to vetoes by the Council on majorities of two-thirds. He shall have power to overrule any such veto if he finds support in a two-thirds majority of the Justices in office (except that no such power shall be vested in the first President).

No one, except the Chairman of the Council, shall hold membership at the same time in the Council and the Tribunal; nor shall a Chancellor or Cabinet member hold membership in the Tribunal or be eligible to it until six years have elapsed from the termination of his executive office.

17

The tenure of the Chief Justice and Chairman and of the Vice-Chairman of the Grand Tribunal shall be the time of their tenure of office respectively as President of the World Republic and as Chairman of the Council. . . .

The terms of the sixty Justices shall be fifteen years (except that the terms for the initial membership shall be staggered by lot, with one-fifth of it, twelve Justices, ceasing from office and being replaced every third year). . . .

18

The sixty Justices shall be assigned twelve to each of five benches:

the First Bench to deal with constitutional issues between the primary organs and powers of the World Government as well as with all issues and cases in which the Tribune of the People shall decide to appear in his capacity of World Attorney and defender of the Rights of Man;

the Second Bench to deal with issues and conflicts between the World Government and any of its component units, whether single states or unions thereof or Regions, as well as with issues and conflicts of component units of the World Republic among themselves;

the Third Bench to deal with issues and conflicts between the World Government and individual citizens or corporations or unions or any other associations of citizens;

the Fourth Bench to deal with issues and conflicts among component units, whether single states or unions of states or Regions, and individual citizens or corporations or unions or any other associations of citizens when such issues and conflicts affect the interpretation or enactment of federal law;

the Fifth Bench to deal with issues and conflicts, when they affect the interpretation and enactment of federal law, either among individual citizens or among corporations, unions, syndicates, or any other collective organizations of citizens and interests.

Each region shall be represented in each Bench by at least one member and not more than two.

19

The Supreme Court shall be of seven members: five representing one each Bench, with the Chief Justice as their Chairman and the Chairman of the Council as their Vice-Chairman ex officio; and the active membership of the Benches shall thus remain of eleven each.

No two members of the Supreme Court shall originate from the same Region. . . .

20

The Supreme Court shall distribute the cases among the five Benches of the Grand Tribunal according to competences as specified hereinbefore (Article 18).

Cases where competences overlap or are otherwise doubtful shall be referred to such Bench or Benches jointly as the Supreme Court shall decide. . . .

22

The Grand Tribunal, with the approval of the Supreme Court, shall establish Lower Federal Courts in such number and places as conditions in the component units of the World Republic shall require, and a Federal Appellate Court in each Region. It shall also determine the rules and competence of such courts, and appoint their officials on the basis of competitive examinations. . . .

The Tribune of the People and the World Law
26

The Federal Convention, after electing the Council, shall elect by secret ballot the Tribune of the People as a spokesman for the minorities, this office to be vested in the candidate obtaining the second largest vote among the eligible candidates; ineligible to the office of Tribune being any candidate having also been nominated by any Electoral College for the office of President in the current convention, or having been a President or Acting President or Alternate, or a member of the Grand Tribunal at any time in the nine years preceding said Convention, or originating from the same Region as the President simultaneously in office.

The Tribune of the People shall not have membership in the Council.

The tenure of the Tribune of the People shall be three years. He shall have power to appoint a Deputy, subject to the same ineligibilities as above, with tenure to expire not later than his own.

He shall not be re-eligible, nor shall he be eligible to the office of President or Alternate or Justice of the Grand Tribunal, until nine years have elapsed from the expiration of his present term.

The Tribune, or his appointed Deputy, shall have the privilege of the floor before the Grand Tribunal and, under such regulations as shall be established by law, before the Supreme Court; but no vote in either; and he shall not be present when a vote is taken.

27

It shall be the office and function of the Tribune of the People to defend the natural and civil rights of individuals and groups against violation or neglect by the World Government or any of its component units; to further and demand, as a World Attorney before the World Republic, the observance of the letter and spirit of this Constitution; and to promote thereby, in the spirit of its Preamble and Declaration of Duties and Rights, the attainment of the goals set to the progress of mankind by the efforts of the ages.

28

No law shall be made or held valid in the World Republic or any of its component units:

1. inflicting or condoning discrimination against race or nation or sex or caste or creed or doctrine; or
2. barring through preferential agreements or coalitions of vested interests the access on equal terms of any state or nation to the raw materials and the sources of energies of the earth; or
3. establishing or tolerating slavery, whether overt or covert, or forced labor, except as equitable expiation endured in state or federal controlled institutions and intended for social service and the rehabilitation of the convicted criminal; or
4. permitting, whether by direction or indirection, arbitrary seizure or search, or unfair trial, or excessive penalty, or application of ex post facto laws; or
5. abridging in any manner whatsoever, except as a punishment inflicted by law for criminal transgression, the citizen's exercise of such responsibilities and privileges of citizenship as are conferred on him by law; or
6. curtailing the freedom of communication and information, of speech, of the press, and of expression by whatever means, of peaceful assembly, of travel; . . .

The Chamber of Guardians
35

The control and use of the armed forces of the Federal Republic of the World shall be assigned exclusively to a Chamber of Guardians under the chairmanship of the President, in his capacity as Protector of the Peace. The other Guardians shall be six Councilmen elected by the Council and the Grand Tribunal in Congress assembled, for terms of three years. (But the Grand Tribunal shall not participate in the first election.)

One former President shall also sit in the Chamber of Guardians, the sequence to be determined term for term, or, if he resigns or dies, for the fractional term, according to seniority in the presidential office; he shall have the privilege of the floor in the deliberations of the Chamber, but no vote in its decisions.

Officers holding professional or active rank in the armed forces of the Federal Republic, or in the domestic militia of any component unit thereof, shall not be eligible as Guardians.

36

The election of the six elective Guardians shall be by secret and proportional vote, with each Elector casting a ballot of six names or less; but no three Guardians of the seven, including the President and excluding the ex-President, shall originate from the same Region; and any presumptive electee whose election would contravene this norm shall be declared ineligible and replaced by the candidate fulfilling the norm and having obtained the next largest vote.

Regions which have not been represented among the seven Guardians referred to above, for two successive three-year terms, shall have mandatory precedence in the subsequent elections; but the Guardian or Guardians originating from a nation or Region where sedition against the World Republic is actual or, according to the majority of the Chamber, imminently expected, shall cease from office and be replaced; unless the other Guardians decide unanimously otherwise. . . .

38

Appropriations for the budget of Peace and Defense, under control of the Chamber of Guardians, as proposed by the Chamber at the beginning of each term for the whole duration thereof, shall be submitted by the President to the Council, in conformity with Article 13. But if a state of emergency is declared, in the manner and limits as specified hereinbefore (Article 28, last paragraph), the Chamber shall have power to demand and appropriate such additional funds as the emergency demands, subject to auditing and sanction by the Council when the emergency is closed; whereafter, if sanction is denied, the Guardians responsible shall be liable to impeachment and prosecution for usurpation of power with the same procedure as specified for the President and the Tribune of the People hereinbefore (Articles 15 and 34).

39

The Chamber shall have power to propose by absolute majority, subject to approval by two-thirds majority votes of the Council and of the Grand Tribunal concurrently, extraordinary powers, worldwide or local, to be conferred on the President beyond those assigned to him by this Constitution, when a state of emergency, as provided in Article 28, is proclaimed; such powers not to be granted for periods exceeding six months each and to be relinquished before the expiration of any such period as soon as the state of emergency, in conformity with Article 28, is proclaimed closed. . . .

Selected Bibliography

Basic Documentary Sources

A *Decade of American Foreign Policy, Basic Documents,* 1941–49, 81st Congress, 1st Session, Senate Document, no. 123, 1950. Contains selected documents relating to the United Nations, the specialized agencies, and the Organization of American States.

Documents of the United Nations Conference on International Organization, The United Nations Information Office, 1946.

International Court of Justice, *Reports of Judgments, Advisory Opinions and Orders.*

International Court of Justice, *Acts and Documents Concerning the Organization of the Court.*

Monthly Summary of the League of Nations.

Official Journal of the League of Nations.

Permanent Court of International Justice, Publications, Series A, B, C, D, and E.

United Nations Documents—in particular:

> *Security Council, Official Records.*
> *Official Records, General Assembly.*
> *Reports of the Interim Committee of the General Assembly.*
> *Treaty Series.*
> *Reports of International Arbitral Awards,* 3 vols.
> *Official Records of the Economic and Social Council.*
> *Resolutions of the General Assembly.*
> *Rules of Procedure of the General Assembly,* Doc. A/520, 1948.
> See also the reports of the various specialized agencies to the Economic and Social Council and the reports of the Secretary-General, annually submitted.

United Nations Conference on International Organization, San Francisco, April 25–June 26, 1945. Selected documents. Department of State publication 2490.

General References

Annual Review of United Nations Affairs, ed. by C. Eagleton, New York.

Arne, S., *United Nations Primer,* rev. ed., New York, 1948.

Bentwick, N., and Martin, A., *A Commentary on the Charter of the United Nations,* New York, 1950.

Ball, M. E., *The Problem of Inter-American Organization,* Stanford University, 1944.

Chase, E. P., *The United Nations in Action,* New York, 1950.

Davis, H. E. (ed.), *Pioneers in World Order,* New York, 1945.

Department of Public Information, United Nations Secretariat, publications on the organization and work of the United Nations. Background Papers.

Department of State, *International Organizations in Which the United States Participates,* Washington, 1949.

Dickinson, E. D., *The Equality of States in International Law,* Cambridge, 1920.

Dolivet, L., *The United Nations,* New York, 1946.

Eagleton, C., *International Government,* rev. ed., New York, 1948.

Evatt, H. V., *The United Nations,* Cambridge, 1948.

Evatt, H. V., *The Task of Nations,* New York, 1949.

Ewing, A. C., *The Individual, the State, and World Government,* New York, 1947.

Ferrero, G., *Peace and War,* London, 1933.

Finer, H., *The United Nations Economic and Social Council,* Boston, 1946.

Florio, F., *Le Organizzazioni Internazionali,* Milan, 1949.

Fox, W. T. R., *The Super-Powers,* New York, 1944.

Goodrich, L. M., and Hambro, E., *Charter of the United Nations, Commentary and Documents,* 2nd ed., Boston, 1949.

Guggenheim, P., *L'Organisation de la Société Internationale,* Neuchatel, 1944.

Harley, J. E., *Documentary Textbook on the United Nations—Humanity's March Towards Peace,* 2nd ed., Los Angeles, 1950.

Harley, J. E., *International Understanding,* Stanford University, 1931.

Hedges, R. Y., *International Organization,* London, 1935.

Hill, N. L., *International Relations, Documents and Readings,* New York, 1950.

Howard-Ellis, C., *The Origin, Structure and Working of the League of Nations,* Boston, 1928.

Hughan, J. W., *Study of International Government,* New York, 1923.

Keeton, G. W., *National Sovereignty and International Order,* London, 1939.

Kelsen, H., *Law of the United Nations,* New York, 1950.

Knudson, J. I., *History of the League of Nations,* Atlanta, 1938.

Koo, W., Jr., *Voting Procedures in International Political Organization,* New York, 1947.

Lansing, R., *Notes on Sovereignty,* Washington, 1931.

Lauterpacht, H., *The Function of Law in the International Community,* Oxford, 1933.

League of Nations Secretariat, *League of Nations, The Aims, Methods and Activity,* rev., Geneva, 1938.

League of Nations, *Handbook of International Organizations,* Geneva, 1938.

Leonard, L. L., *International Organization,* New York, 1951.

Levi, Werner, *Fundamentals of World Organization,* Minneapolis, 1950.

Mance, Sir H. O., *Frontiers, Peace Treaties, and International Organization,* New York, 1946.

Mander, L. A., *Foundations of Modern World Society,* Stanford University, 1947.

Marburg, T., *Development of the League of Nations Idea,* New York, 1932.

Miller, D. H., *Drafting the Covenant,* New York, 1928.

Myers, D. P., *Handbook of the League of Nations,* World Peace Foundation, Boston, 1935.

Morley, F., *The Society of Nations,* Washington, 1932.

Mower, E. C., *International Government,* Boston, 1931.

Potter, P. B., *Introduction to the Study of International Organization,* 5th ed., New York, 1948.

Riches, C. A., *Majority Rule in International Organization,* Baltimore, 1940.

Ross, A., *Constitution of the United Nations*, New York, 1950.

Russell, F. M., *Theories of International Relations*, New York, 1936.

Schuman, F. L., *International Politics*, New York, 1948.

Sharp, W. R., and Kirk, G., *Contemporary International Politics*, New York, 1940.

Telders Study Group, *United Nations Textbook*, The Hague, 1950.

United States and the United Nations, Annual Reports by the President to the Congress, 1946.

United Nations Department of Information, *Everyman's United Nations*, New York, 1948; rev. ed., 1951.

Vinacke, H. M., *International Organization*, New York, 1934.

Voting in International Organizations, United Nations Department of Information, Information Paper no. 2, 1947.

Weldon, T. D., *States and Morals*, London, 1946.

White, L. C., *Structure of Private International Organization*, Philadelphia, 1933.

Woolf, L. S., *International Government*, New York, 1916.

Wright, Q., *A Study of War*, 2 vols., Chicago, 1942.

Yearbook of the United Nations, annual publication.

Zimmern, Sir A. E., *The League of Nations and the Rule of Law*, London, 1939.

Treatment of Disputes and the Maintenance of Peace

Conwell-Evans, T. P., *The League Council in Action*, London, 1929.

Carlston, K. S., *The Process of International Arbitration*, New York, 1946.

Department of Public Information of the United Nations, *Korea and the United Nations*, October, 1950. United Nations Publications, 1950–1–8; also Background Paper no. 62, 1950, *The Korean Question;* Background Paper no. 58, 1950, *The Indonesian Question*.

Department of State of the United States, *United States Policy in the Korean Crisis*, 1950, Publication 3922, Far Eastern Series 34.

Feller, A. H., *The Mexican Claims Commissions, 1923–34: A Study in the Law and Procedure of International Tribunals*, New York, 1935.

Highley, A. E., *The First Sanction Experiment*, Geneva, 1938.

Hill, N. L., "International Commissions of Inquiry and Conciliation," in *International Conciliation,* no. 278, 1932.

Hudson, M. O., and others, *The International Court,* Washington, 1945.

Hudson, M. O., *International Tribunals, Past and Present,* Washington, 1944.

Hudson, M. O., *The World Court, 1921–1938,* World Peace Foundation, Boston, 1938.

Hudson, M. O., *The Permanent Court of International Justice,* New York, 1943.

Interim Committee of the General Assembly of the United Nations, *Organization and Procedure of United Nations Commissions,* I–XI Sub-Committee Reports, 1949.

Mitrany, D., *The Problem of International Sanctions,* London, 1925.

Ralston, J. H., *Law and Procedure of International Tribunals,* Stanford University, 1926.

Ralston, J. H., *International Arbitration from Athens to Locarno,* Stanford University, 1929.

Systematic Survey of Treaties for the Pacific Settlement of International Disputes, 1928–1948, United Nations Publication, October, 1948.

Vulcan, C., *Conciliation dans le Droit International Actuel,* Paris, 1932.

Wilde, P. S., *Sanctions and Treaty Enforcement,* Cambridge, 1934.

Yearbook of the International Court of Justice, annual publication.

Diplomacy and Conference

Caribbean Commission, monthly bulletin, 1948—

Chamberlain, L. H., and Snyder, R. C., *American Foreign Policy,* New York, 1948.

Department of State, *Participation of the United States Government in International Conferences,* July 1, 1941–June 30, 1945, Washington, 1947. Also later issues.

Department of Public Information of United Nations, Background Paper no. 53, 1949, *Economic and Social Council.*

Department of Public Information of the United Nations, Background Paper no. 54, 1949, *The Specialized Agencies.*

Dunn, F. S., *Practice and Procedure of International Conference*, Baltimore, 1929.

Gihl, T., *International Legislation*, New York, 1937.

Hill, M., *Immunities and Privileges of International Officials*, Washington, 1947.

Hill, N. L., *The Public International Conference*, Stanford University, 1929.

Hunt, E. E., *Conferences, Committees, Conventions*, New York, 1925.

Huxley, J., *UNESCO, Its Purpose and Its Philosophy*, Washington, 1947.

Jessup, P. C., *A Modern Law of Nations*, New York, 1948.

Mathews, J. M., *American Foreign Relations; Conduct and Policies*, 2nd ed., New York, 1938.

McCamy, J. L., *The Administration of American Foreign Affairs*, New York, 1950.

McClure, W. M., *World Prosperity as Sought Through the Economic Work of the League of Nations*, New York, 1933.

McClure, W. M., *The International Executive Agreement*, New York, 1941.

Miller, D. H., *My Diary at the Peace Conference*, New York, 1928.

Nicolson, H., *Diplomacy*, 2nd ed., New York, 1950.

Norton, H. K., *Foreign Office Organization*, Philadelphia, 1929.

Parkes, J. W., *International Conferences*, Geneva, 1933.

Pastukov, V. D., *A Guide to the Practice of International Conferences*, Washington, 1945.

Price, J., *The International Labour Movement*, New York, 1946.

Reinsch, P. S., *Secret Diplomacy*, New York, 1922.

Russell, F., *The International Government of the Saar*, Berkeley, 1926.

Satow, Sir E., *Guide to Diplomatic Practice*, 3rd ed., New York, 1923.

Satow, Sir E., *International Congresses*, London, 1920.

Scott, J. B., *The Hague Peace Conferences*, Baltimore, 1909.

Stuart, G. H., *The Department of State*, New York, 1950.

Stuart, G. H., *American Diplomatic and Consular Practice*, New York, 1936.

Temperley, H. W. V. (ed.), *A History of the Peace Conference of Paris,* London, 1924.

United States, *Treaty Series,* Washington.

International Administration

Carnegie Endowment for International Peace, *Conference on Training for International Administration,* Washington, 1944.

Chacko, C. J., *The International Joint Commission Between the United States and Canada,* New York, 1932.

Chamberlain, J. P., *The Régime of International Rivers,* New York, 1923.

Commission of Enquiry on the Organization of the Secretariat, the International Labour Office and the Registry of the Permanent Court of International Justice, Report, League of Nations, 1930 (A, 16, 1930).

Department of Public Information of the United Nations, Background Paper no. 57, 1950, *The International Trusteeship System.*

Hill, N. L., *International Administration,* New York, 1931.

Hobson, A., *The International Institute of Agriculture,* Berkeley, 1931.

Hostie, J., *The Communications and Transit Organization of the League of Nations,* Washington, 1948.

Inter-American Coffee Board, annual reports, Washington, 1942–1948.

Leonard, L. L., *International Regulation of Fisheries,* Washington, 1944.

Mance, Sir H. Osborne, and Wheeler, J. E., *International Telecommunications,* New York, 1943.

Mance, Sir H. Osborne, and Wheeler, J. E., *International River and Canal Transport,* New York, 1944.

Mance, Sir H. Osborne, and Wheeler, J. E., *International Road Transport,* New York, 1947.

Ranshofen-Wertheimer, E. F., *The International Secretariat,* New York, 1946.

Reiff, H., "The United States and International Administrative Unions," in *International Conciliation,* no. 332, 1937.

Reinsch, P. S., *Public International Unions,* Boston, 1911.

Renberg, B. A., *International Drug Control: A Study of International Organization by and through the League of Nations*, Washington, 1947.

Report of the International Bank to the Economic and Social Council, annual reports.

Rogers, W. C., *International Administration: A Bibliography*, Chicago, 1945.

Sayre, F. B., *Experiments in International Administration*, New York, 1919.

Stuart, G. H., *The International City of Tangier*, Stanford University, 1931.

Swerling, B. C., *International Control of Sugar, 1918–1941*, Stanford University, 1949.

Wedgewood, Sir R. L., and Wheeler, J. E., *International Rail Transport*, New York, 1946.

Wright, Q., *Mandates under the League of Nations*, Chicago, 1930.

Projects for World Organization

Coudenhove-Kalergi, R. N., *Crusade for Pan-Europe*, New York, 1943.

Durand, C., *Les Etats Fédéraux*, Paris, 1930.

Eaton, H. O. (ed.), *Federation*, Norman, Oklahoma, 1944.

Greaves, H. R. G., *Federal Union in Practice*, London, 1940.

Hoover, H., and Gibson, H., *Problems of Lasting Peace*, Garden City, 1942.

Jennings, W. I., *A Federation for Western Europe*, New York, 1940.

Maddox, W. P., *European Plans for World Order*, 1940.

Meyer, C., Jr., *Peace or Anarchy*, Boston, 1947.

Newfang, O., *World Government*, New York, 1942.

Revision of the Charter, Hearings before a Subcommittee of the Commitee of Foreign Relations of the U.S. Senate, Senate document.

Reves, E., *Anatomy of Peace*, New York, 1945.

Scott, J. B., *The United States of America: A Study in International Organization*, Washington, 1920.

Streit, C. K., *Union Now*, New York, 1939.

York, E., *Leagues of Nations*, London, 1919.

Journals and Periodical Issues

American Journal of International Law, published by the American Society of International Law.

Annals of the American Academy of Political and Social Sciences.

Courier, published by UNESCO.

Department of State Bulletin.

Foreign Affairs, published by the Council on Foreign Relations.

Foreign Policy Reports, published by the Foreign Policy Association.

International Conciliation, published by the Carnegie Endowment for International Peace. Pamphlet series.

International Law Quarterly, British publication.

International Organization, published by the World Peace Foundation.

United Nations News, published by the Woodrow Wilson Foundation.

United Nations Weekly Bulletin, published by the United Nations Department of Public Information.

World Affairs Interpreter, published by the Los Angeles University of International Relations.

Index

619